THE PRACTICAL BOOK OF THE
GUITAR

HOW TO PLAY ACOUSTIC AND ELECTRIC

THE PRACTICAL BOOK OF THE
GUITAR

HOW TO PLAY ACOUSTIC AND ELECTRIC

300 CHORDS • AN ILLUSTRATED HISTORY • A VISUAL DIRECTORY

JAMES WESTBROOK, TED FULLER AND TERRY BURROWS

LORENZ BOOKS

This edition is published by Lorenz Books,
an imprint of Anness Publishing Ltd,
108 Great Russell Street,
London WC1B 3NA;
info@anness.com

www.lorenzbooks.com;
www.annesspublishing.com;
twitter: @Anness_Books

If you like the images in this book and would
like to investigate using them for publishing,
promotions or advertising, please visit our website
www.practicalpictures.com for more information.

© Anness Publishing Ltd 2017

A CIP catalogue record for this book is available
from the British Library.

Publisher: Joanna Lorenz
Senior Editor: Felicity Forster
Designed and produced by Ivy Contract
Project Editors: Georgia Amson-Bradshaw,
    Jonathan Bastable, Kim Davies and
    Judith Chamberlain-Webber
Art Directors: Kevin Knight and Lisa McCormick
Photographer: Laurie Evans
Designer: JC Lanaway
Production Controller: Ben Worley

Contents

Introduction   6

THE ACOUSTIC GUITAR   12

How to play acoustic guitar   14
Buying your guitar   16
Anatomy of the guitar   18
Tuning the guitar   20
Changing strings   22
Guitar care   24
Holding the guitar   26
Basic left-hand technique   28
Strumming with three chords   30
More chords and strumming   32
Syncopated strumming   34
Seventh chords   36
Guitar notation   38
Using the fingers   40
Simple fingerpicking patterns   42
Using the thumb in fingerpicking   44
Using a capo   46
Playing tunes   48
The C major scale and first position   50
The major scales   52
Introducing the blues   54
The sixth shuffle   56
Building a blues solo   58
Advanced blues   60
Barre chords   62
More on barre chords   64
Understanding keys   66
Chord construction   68
How to find any note   70

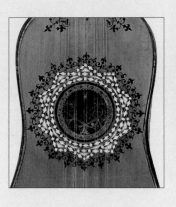

m7♭5 chords	142
Dominant seventh jazz voicings	144
Minor seventh jazz voicings	146
Major seventh jazz voicings	148
Suspended fourth	150
Half-open chords	152
Essential chords in open G	154
Essential chords in open D	156
Essential chords in DADGAD	158

History of the acoustic guitar | **160**
Early ancestors of the guitar	162
The five-course Baroque guitar	164
The transitional guitar	166
Early 19th-century guitars	168
Arcas, Torres, Tárrega and beyond	170
The flamenco guitar	172
Pioneers of the steel-string guitar	174
The guitar today	176

Directory of acoustic guitars | **178**
Early guitar-related instruments	180
16th- to 18th-century guitars	186
18th- and early 19th-century transitional guitars	190
18th- and early 19th-century six-string guitars	194
18th- and early 19th-century guitars	196
19th-century guitars	198
19th-century classical guitar makers	204
19th- and early 20th-century classical guitar makers	206
20th-century classical guitar makers	208
Mid 20th-century classical guitars	214
Late 20th- and early 21st-century classical guitars	216

How to transpose without a capo	72
Left-hand embellishments	74
Country picking	76
Advanced country guitar	78
Integrating a melody	80
Altered tunings	82
Drop D tuning	84
Open tunings	86
More open tunings	88
DADGAD tuning	90
Introducing jazz chords	92
More jazz chords	94
The 12-bar blues in jazz	96
A dozen classic blues licks	98
Double stopping	100
Half-open chords	102
Improvising with the major scale	104
Advanced left-hand techniques	106
Practice patterns	108
Party tricks	110
Slide guitar	112
Classical guitar	114
Further classical guitar techniques	116
Gypsy jazz	118
Latin jazz	120
Flamenco	122
The 12-string guitar	124

Chordfinder | **126**
Introduction	128
Major chords	130
Minor chords	132
Seventh chords	134
Minor seventh chords	136
Major seventh chords	138
Diminished seventh chords	140

20th-century flamenco guitars 220
Late 20th- and early 21st-century
  flamenco guitars 222
20th-century flat-top steel-string guitars 224
20th- and 21st-century flat-top
  steel-string guitars 232
20th-century archtop guitars 236
20th-century gypsy guitars 242
19th- and 20th-century multi-string
  harp-guitars 244
20th-century guitars 246
20th-century resonator guitars 248
20th-century acoustic bass guitars 250
20th- and 21st-century acoustic bass guitars 252

THE ELECTRIC GUITAR 254

How to play electric guitar 256
Buying an electric guitar 258
Amplifiers and other equipment 260
Popular set-ups 262
Anatomy of the electric guitar 264
From acoustic to electric 266
Introducing lead guitar 268
Lead techniques 270
Electric blues guitar 272
Rhythm guitar styles 274
Rock chord vocabulary 276
Rock 'n' roll 278
Power chords 280
Rock rhythm guitar 282
More on lead guitar 284
Grunge 286
Riffs 288
Indie rock 290
Accompaniment with fills 292

Using wah-wah and other effects 294
Funk and disco 296
Melodic jazz guitar 298
Reggae 300
Country guitar techniques 302
Electric slide guitar 304
Buying a bass guitar 306
Bass guitar: first steps 308
Constructing a bass line 310
Melodic bass playing 312
Slap bass 314
Heavy rock techniques 316
Exploring rock and metal styles 318
Metal guitar in drop D 320
Musical resources: scales 322
Musical resources: melodic arpeggios 324
Advanced scales and modes 326
Right-hand tapping 328
Jazz/rock fusion techniques 330
Unusual guitars and techniques 332

History of the electric guitar 334
The principles of sound 336
The first electric guitars 338
Experimenting with solidbodies 340
The great rivalry 342
The electric explosion 344
Altering the face of music 346
The rise and fall of guitar groups 348
The modern era 350

Directory of electric guitars 352
Electric lap steels 354
Early archtops 356
The luxury Gibsons 358
Gibson ES-175 family 360

Early Epiphone electrics 362
The solidbody pioneers 364
The Fender production line 366
Gibson Les Paul 368
The electric bass 370
Gretsch solidbody electrics 372
Gretsch hollowbodies 374
American hollowbodies 376
The new Rickenbacker 378
Danelectro 380
The Gibson Modernistic line 382
Europe in the 1950s 384
Fender: the second generation 386
Jim Burns 388
Britain in the 1960s 390
The birth of the SG 392
Gibson ES thinlines 394
Gibson Firebirds 396
Player-endorsed Gibson models 398
Bass guitars in the 1960s 400
Epiphone: after the Gibson takeover 402
Rickenbacker in the 1960s 404
Japan in the 1960s 406
Northern Europe in the 1960s 408
Double-neck guitars 410
Guitars from the Eastern Bloc 412
Rickenbacker 12-string electrics 414
Other 12-string electrics 416
Fender in the 1960s 418
Other 1960s US solidbodies 420
Italian electrics 422
Is it a guitar or a bass? 424
Curious shapes 426
Near misses 428
The new Gibson Les Pauls 430
The last Gibson originals 432

Yamaha 434
1970s American solidbodies 436
Britain in the 1970s 438
Far Eastern copies 440
The new Fender classics 442
Alternative materials 444
Curiosities 446
B. C. Rich 448
Fenders from the 1980s 450
Gibsons from the 1980s 452
Music Man and G&L 454
Ibanez 456
Beyond six strings 458
Diffusion ranges 460
Europe in the 1980s 462
Signature Stratocasters 464
Travel guitars 466
The birth of the superstrat 468
The growth of the superstrat 470
Guitar synthesizers 472
The modern bass 474
Curious Strats 476
Fender in the 1990s 478
The reissue vogue 480
Washburn and Parker 482
Les Paul special models 484
Perverse guitars 486
Boutique brands 488
Paul Reed Smith 490
The growth of PRS 492
Do-it-yourself guitars 494
Gibson Robots 496

Glossary 498
Index 506
Acknowledgements 512

Introduction

The guitar has become established as an icon of 20th-century music and continues to be the instrument of choice for many popular artists. Though its design has evolved from earlier instruments, and many of its musical advantages are mirrored by the piano, the guitar has several unique features that influence the way its music is created and heard.

History

The ancestry of the modern guitar can be traced back through many instruments and thousands of years to ancient central Asia. Guitar-like instruments appear in early carvings and statues recovered from towns in what is now Iran. There is also an ancient Hittite carving – dating back more than 3,000 years – that depicts an instrument bearing many of the same features as today's guitar. The appeal of the guitar has been so universal that virtually every society throughout history appears to have used a variation of the instrument.

In the last few hundred years, the guitar has evolved from guitar-like instruments such as the lute, the vihuela and the Baroque guitar into the acoustic guitar as we know it today. It was only in 1924 that Gibson engineer Lloyd Loar first attached an electric pickup to an instrument – a viola – translating the vibrations of the strings into an electrical signal which could be amplified. The first purpose-built electronic instrument wasn't produced for a further seven years – the Ro-Pat-In 'Frying Pan'.

Over the next decade, the amplified hollow-bodied guitar slowly grew in popularity, particularly among jazz guitarists who needed to be heard during ensemble playing. Then, in 1940, Lester William Polsfuss, or Les Paul, took the design of the electric guitar a step further, creating the first ever solidbody electric guitar: 'the Log'. By 1950, a young electronics hobbyist, Leo Fender, had designed and begun manufacturing the Fender Broadcaster, the first mass-produced solidbody guitar.

How a guitar works

A member of the family of musical instruments called chordophones, the guitar produces its sound by the plucking of a series of strings running along the instrument's body. While the strings are plucked with one hand, they are simultaneously shortened and lengthened with the other hand against frets, which are metal strips placed on the instrument's neck. The sound that is made is then amplified through a hollow resonating body.

In an acoustic guitar, sound is produced when the vibrations of the strings are amplified by air resonating in the hollow cavity of the body. In an electric guitar, the vibration of the strings is sensed by a magnetic pickup mounted on the body, and converted into an electric signal. This is passed through the guitar's circuitry to the amp, which converts the electrical signal back into vibrations, or soundwaves, at a volume that is loud enough for us to hear.

Construction of a guitar

Acoustic guitars are extremely varied in their design and construction, to a far greater extent than electric guitars. The back and sides of the guitar's body are usually built with East Indian or Brazilian rosewood. Historically, Brazilian

LEFT: *A woodcut from Luis Milan's Vihuela book* El Maestro *from 1536, showing Orpheus taming wild beasts with his vihuela.*

ABOVE: *An example of a modern-looking nylon-string classical guitar. This one is made by Hernández y Aguado from Spain.*

ABOVE: *A flamenco guitar is depicted in this 1897 painting by Pierre-Auguste Renoir entitled* Girl with a Guitar.

ABOVE: *This photograph of 1901 shows an acoustic guitar that was made by Antonio de Torres in 1888 being played by Francisco Tárrega.*

rosewood has been the choice of connoisseurs. However, in an attempt to preserve the wood's dwindling supply, the Brazilian government has placed restrictions on its export, thus raising the price, and making East Indian rosewood the current wood of choice. Mahogany is sometimes used for steel-string guitars, and maple is nearly always found in archtop guitars.

The top (or soundboard) of the guitar is traditionally constructed of Alpine spruce, although American Sitka spruce has also become popular among manufacturers in the USA. Cedar and redwood are often substituted for spruce, although these woods are soft and can be easily damaged during the construction of a guitar.

The neck, which must resist distortion by the pull of the strings and changes in temperature and humidity, is usually constructed from mahogany or cedar, and joins the body either at the 12th or the 14th frets. Ideally, the fretboard is made of ebony, but rosewood is often used as a cheaper option.

Acoustic guitar

The acoustic guitar uses only acoustic methods to project the sound produced by its strings. There are two main categories of acoustic (non-electric) guitars, which are differentiated by the material used for the strings: gut or nylon-string and steel-string.

Gut or nylon-string guitars include the classical guitar (also called the 'Spanish guitar') as well as the flamenco guitar. The classical guitar is a six-stringed instrument and was established from the designs of the 19th-century Spanish luthier Antonio de Torres. Guitar terminology can be confusing, so the term 'modern classical guitar' is sometimes used to distinguish the classical guitar from older forms of

guitar. The sound of this guitar is much more mellow and rounded than a steel-string acoustic, and tends to sound better played with the fingernails.

A steel-string acoustic guitar is a modern form of guitar descended from the classical guitar, but strung with steel strings for a brighter, louder sound. It is often referred to simply as an acoustic guitar, although strictly speaking the nylon-string classical guitar is acoustic as well.

The most common type can be called a flat-top guitar to distinguish it from the more specialized archtop guitar and other variations. Steel-string acoustic guitars are used more often in rock, country, blues and also in folk music, and generally are more suited to strumming or playing with a guitar pick than the nylon-string guitar.

ABOVE: *Learning the guitar is a gateway into a musical world of many genres, from blues and country to jazz and Latin.*

Electric guitar

The electric guitar relies on electronic amplification to make its sound audible. More than any other instrument, it defines the sound of rock music, a vastly diverse musical genre which in turn has influenced and characterized much of popular culture over the latter half of the 20th and the early 21st century. In fact, the electric guitar is arguably the single most important musical instrument of the modern age. At the forefront of much popular musical innovation since the 1940s, it has taken centre stage across genres and decades, from 1950s rock 'n' roll through to present-day pop and indie. Evoking rebellion, youth and glamour, the electric guitar's popularity shows no sign of waning.

In the 1950s, the advent of rock 'n' roll in America coincided with the rise of the 'teenager'; a new conception of adolescence as a distinct, stormy, rebellious stage of life. Rock 'n' roll, a fusion of blues, country and jazz, was fast, fun, and easy to dance to. The electric guitar, with its versatility, and its inherent melodic and rhythmic potential, was perfectly suited to this groundbreaking new musical style.

Early electronic amplification of the guitar generated unintended but pleasing sonic side effects. Being low on output, the sound produced by early amps would often distort when played at full volume, giving a pleasant, 'warm' tone. Artists began deliberately recreating the distorted sound by damaging their amplifiers. Eventually, in the early

1960s, the first purpose-built distortion effects circuits came to market. From that point on, the technology surrounding the electric guitar became increasingly important, and the effects available to players proliferated. Present-day guitarists have an astonishing level of electronically generated sonic possibility available to them, with the newest guitars featuring sophisticated onboard computer technology.

Back in the 1960s, wielding electric guitars and making use of the instrument's cutting-edge capabilities, The Beatles burst on to the international scene. The best-selling band in history, their hugely varied output paved the way for the rock-centered pop culture paradigm of the next two decades and beyond. At the centre of it all was the electric guitar.

At the same time, virtuoso guitarists such as Eric Clapton and Jimi Hendrix established a new iconography – the guitar hero. The influence of these solo players, as well as the Beatles-esque guitar groups, propelled the popularity of the guitar to pole position, with millions of aspiring players worldwide taking up the instrument.

The seminal musical styles of the early rock pioneers have generated endless mutations and variations in the decades since, through prog rock, punk, new wave, metal, grunge, Britpop, and all the derivations thereof. However, in spite of the wide array of generic innovation, the electric guitar has remained the central component of a great proportion of popular musical output, right up to the present day.

Many electric guitars aren't simply valued for their practical use as musical instruments. Perhaps because of their physical beauty, or their historic and cultural significance, many guitars are highly collectible as objects in themselves. Sales of particularly rare models, or instruments that belonged to musical icons, will sell at auction for large sums of money. In 2005, a Stratocaster was sold at auction to raise funds for victims of the 2004 Tsunami signed by Bryan Adams, Eric Clapton, Jimmy Page, Mick Jagger, Keith Richards, Ronnie Wood, Brian May, Liam and Noel Gallagher, Jeff Beck, Pete Townshend, Ray Davies, David Gilmour, Tony Iommi, Mark Knopfler, Angus and Malcolm Young, Paul McCartney and Sting. It reached an incredible $2.8 million.

Learning to play

The guitar has long been a desired choice for beginner musicians, partly because of its iconic position in popular culture, and partly because of its inherent virtues, which include portability, great versatility and the availability of reasonable instruments for comparatively little cost. The steel-string acoustic, classical guitar and electric guitar are

BELOW: *Les Paul, musician and creator of the first-ever solidbody electric guitar, and his wife Mary Ford demonstrate two Les Paul Gibson guitars in 1952.*

ABOVE: *A Custom Shop Fender Snake Head Telecaster – an exact reproduction of the prototype that Leo Fender would take around clubs for artists to try.*

all closely related (for example, the tuning is usually the same). This means that much of the knowledge that is related to one type of guitar can be of use when playing another, and can even to some extent be transferred to other fretted and stringed instruments such as the banjo or mandolin.

Many people learn to play guitar first on an acoustic instrument, due to budget considerations. As the basic tuning and the fingering on electric and acoustic guitars are the same, it doesn't matter whether you come to the electric guitar from the acoustic, or start on the electric as a complete beginner. However, certain styles of music are better suited to the electric guitar than the acoustic, and the greater sensitivity of an electric guitar, combined with the variety of sonic textures that can be created with electrical effects, means that electric guitarists can play around with a vast array of sounds.

In this book

This volume is divided into two parts covering acoustic and electric guitars. Firstly, 'How to Play Acoustic Guitar' covers the basics of looking after your guitar, playing chords and

scales, how to use the fingers and the basics of reading music and more advanced techniques used in blues and jazz. It also introduces the different genres of music played using the guitar. A 'Chordfinder' explains a guitarist's basic vocabulary and illustrates all the essential chords that you can practise and learn. A detailed description of the evolution of the guitar is featured in 'History of the Acoustic Guitar', and a 'Directory of Acoustic Guitars' explores 150 forms of acoustic guitar from the 16th century up to the modern day.

The second part of the book will guide you through all the information and techniques you need to master the electric guitar. 'How to Play Electric Guitar' explains how to get your perfect setup, refine your riffing and learn diverse playing styles, including grunge, indie and jazz fusion. 'History of the Electric Guitar' gives a detailed account of the invention and evolution of the electric guitar, and a 'Directory of Electric Guitars' showcases over 200 models, from the first-ever electric instruments to some of the more technologically cutting-edge models on the market. Finally, a glossary of musical terms is included at the back of the book.

ABOVE: *The electric guitar was so popluar during the 20th century that the available repertoire of music created for the instrument is now unimaginably vast. Aspiring players can learn music in a diverse range of genres and styles.*

ABOVE: *A large part of the appeal of the electric guitar in comparison with the acoustic guitar is the huge variety of addtional tones and musical effects that can be created, including vibrato produced by using a tremolo arm.*

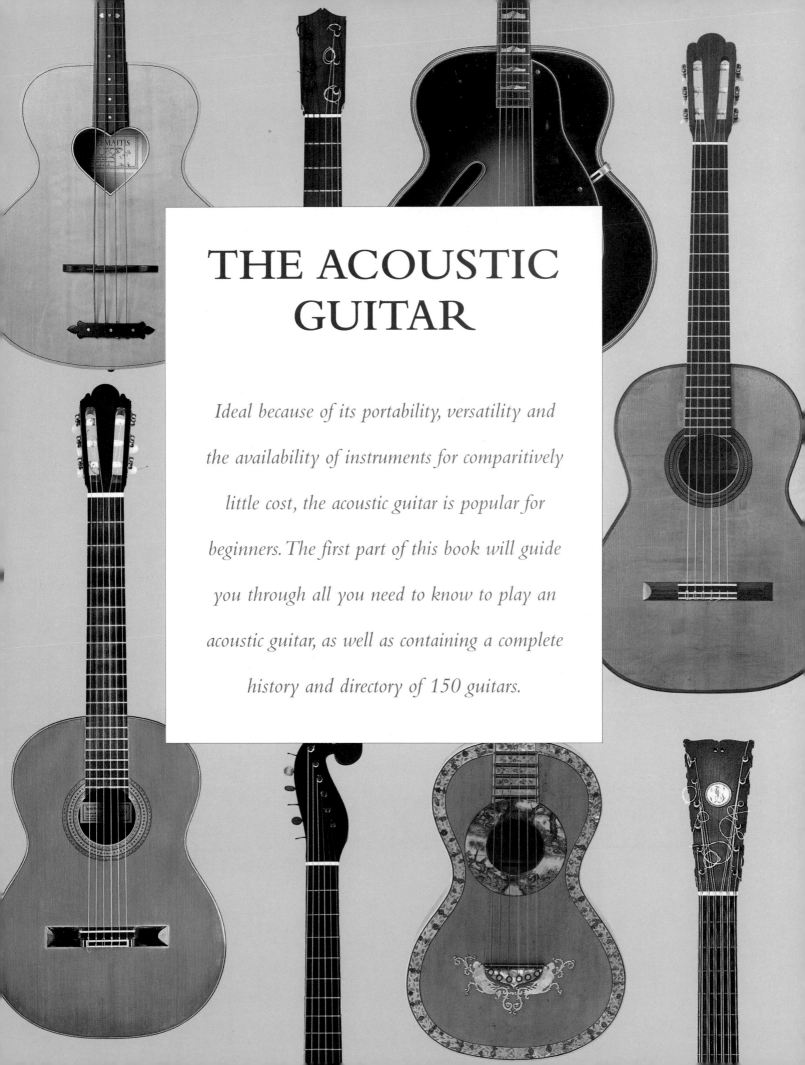

THE ACOUSTIC GUITAR

Ideal because of its portability, versatility and the availability of instruments for comparitively little cost, the acoustic guitar is popular for beginners. The first part of this book will guide you through all you need to know to play an acoustic guitar, as well as containing a complete history and directory of 150 guitars.

Guitar music spans such a wide range of styles that learning to play opens up a whole world of musical possibilities, from rock and jazz through to classical.

How to play acoustic guitar

This chapter will guide you through the basic steps and provides exercises to help you develop your skills. You will discover scales, tuning and chords to get you started in a variety of musical styles.

Buying your guitar

There are several types of acoustic guitar, and the price and quality of new instruments varies widely. Your choice will depend on the style of music you want to play, and on how much you are prepared to pay. The goal is to end up with a reasonably decent guitar that you can begin to learn on.

Choosing a guitar

Acoustic guitars can be broadly divided into two types: the classical (or Spanish) guitar, and the steel-string acoustic guitar. Naturally enough, the classical guitar is mainly associated with classical music and related styles originating from Spain or South America. The tone of a classical guitar is generally softer and gentler than that of a steel-string instrument – although a high-end classical guitar, played with correct technique, can be surprisingly loud.

Until recently, a classical guitar was widely regarded as the natural choice for a beginner, partly because the soft nylon strings are a little kinder to the left-hand fingertips than steel strings. But the idea that classical is best has lost ground. On a technical level, its wide, flat neck makes some chord shapes unnecessarily difficult for small hands (although smaller 'student' models are available).

Generally, most people who take up guitar are more interested in modern styles such as pop and rock than classical, and for this kind of music a steel-string guitar is the natural choice. Other contemporary styles such as country, folk and blues also sound best when played on a steel-string guitar. This kind of guitar is also the best starting point if you aspire to play electric guitar, since these, too, are steel-strung. Many respectable makers produce guitars at various prices, among them Yamaha, Washburn, Ibanez, Takemine, Taylor and Martin.

On the other hand, if you already feel drawn towards classical playing or related styles such as flamenco, a classical guitar may be the best choice for you.

RIGHT: *Classical and steel-string guitars look superficially similar. However, most steel-string acoustics have a larger, squarer body as well as a protective plastic scratchplate.*

Steel-string guitar

Classical guitar

New or used?

The quality of even the lowest-priced instruments available (which are usually produced in the Far East) has improved dramatically in recent years. Although there are always good guitars available on the second-hand market, there are also some very poor ones produced in the years when cheaper guitars were often very badly made. So buying new is usually a safer bet, unless you know what you are doing, or you have a friend who does.

Most reputable guitar shops will check that a new guitar is well 'set up' (meaning that playing action and neck curvature are adjusted for both sound and playing comfort). You should ask whether this has been done or can be done, and think twice about buying from a seller who refuses. Many new instruments will also need to be adjusted after a few months of use (see 'Guitar care'), so you may wish to establish whether this service can be included in the purchase price, or for a modest extra fee.

RIGHT: *Electro-acoustic guitars often feature a cutaway body design for improved access when playing the higher frets.*

FAR RIGHT: *The pre-amp is usually placed here for easy access in the playing position. Controls may include volume, tone shaping, the ability to blend the outputs of more than one pickup, and sometimes even a tuner.*

Electro-acoustic guitars

An electro-acoustic guitar is a steel-string that comes with a built-in pickup (or microphone). This enables the guitar to be directly connected to an amplifier, PA system or recording equipment – in the same way as an electric guitar. Unlike the solid-bodied electric guitar, however, an electro-acoustic is a fully functioning acoustic instrument. It does not require amplification in order to work, and it does not sound like an electric when it is amplified. If you already envisage performing live with your first guitar, or you have access to recording equipment (which can be a valuable practice aid), this choice makes perfect sense.

Accessories

Here is a list of guitar accessories, listed in order of importance:

- Plectrums
- Tuner
- Strap
- Guitar stand
- Case
- Capo

Clip-on tuner

Plectrums

Capos

Strap

Anatomy of the guitar

Guitar making involves a complicated combination of materials, where old-fashioned woodworking techniques meet modern mechanical engineering. Each part of the guitar has a specific function; centuries of accumulated knowledge have resulted in an essentially standardized design for each component. It is useful to understand how these parts work together, in both steel-string and classical guitars.

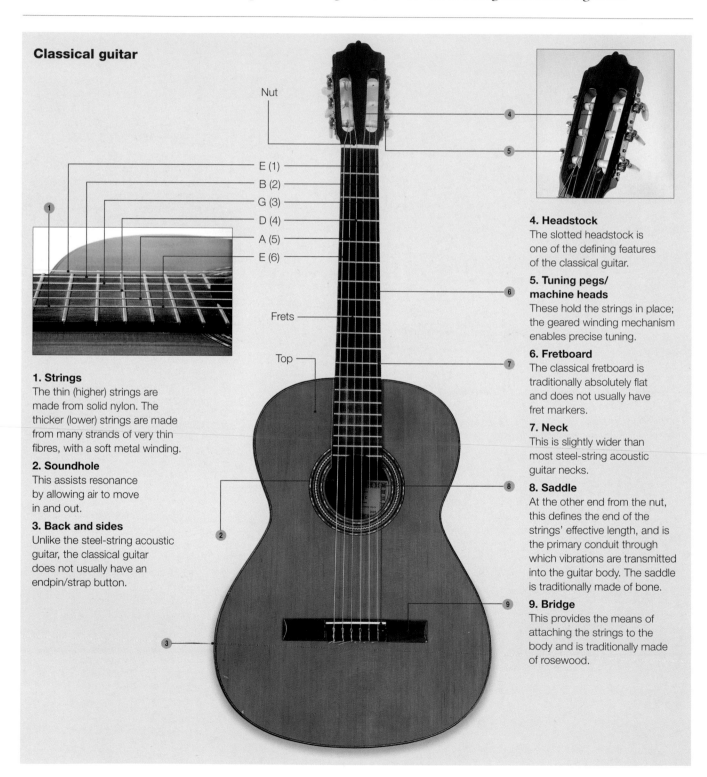

Classical guitar

Nut

E (1)
B (2)
G (3)
D (4)
A (5)
E (6)

Frets

Top

1. Strings
The thin (higher) strings are made from solid nylon. The thicker (lower) strings are made from many strands of very thin fibres, with a soft metal winding.

2. Soundhole
This assists resonance by allowing air to move in and out.

3. Back and sides
Unlike the steel-string acoustic guitar, the classical guitar does not usually have an endpin/strap button.

4. Headstock
The slotted headstock is one of the defining features of the classical guitar.

5. Tuning pegs/ machine heads
These hold the strings in place; the geared winding mechanism enables precise tuning.

6. Fretboard
The classical fretboard is traditionally absolutely flat and does not usually have fret markers.

7. Neck
This is slightly wider than most steel-string acoustic guitar necks.

8. Saddle
At the other end from the nut, this defines the end of the strings' effective length, and is the primary conduit through which vibrations are transmitted into the guitar body. The saddle is traditionally made of bone.

9. Bridge
This provides the means of attaching the strings to the body and is traditionally made of rosewood.

Steel-string acoustic guitar

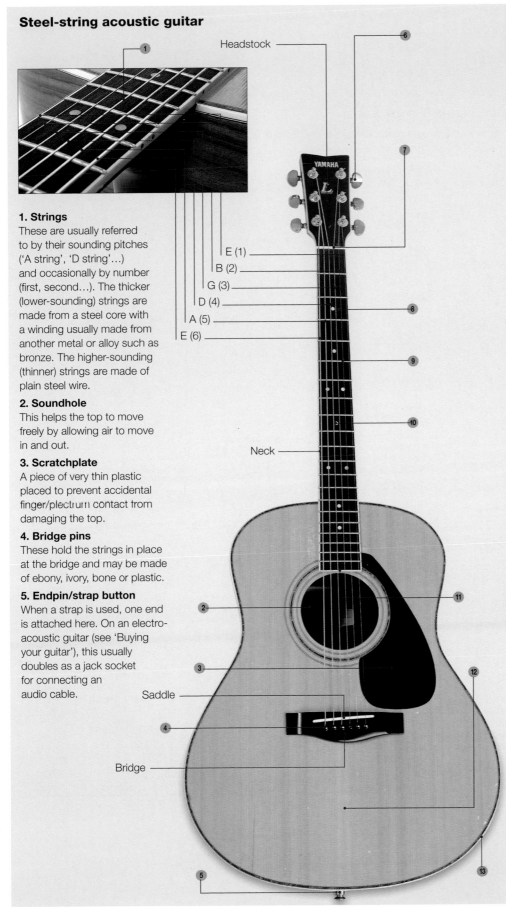

Headstock

E (1)
B (2)
G (3)
D (4)
A (5)
E (6)

Neck

Saddle

Bridge

1. Strings
These are usually referred to by their sounding pitches ('A string', 'D string'...) and occasionally by number (first, second...). The thicker (lower-sounding) strings are made from a steel core with a winding usually made from another metal or alloy such as bronze. The higher-sounding (thinner) strings are made of plain steel wire.

2. Soundhole
This helps the top to move freely by allowing air to move in and out.

3. Scratchplate
A piece of very thin plastic placed to prevent accidental finger/plectrum contact from damaging the top.

4. Bridge pins
These hold the strings in place at the bridge and may be made of ebony, ivory, bone or plastic.

5. Endpin/strap button
When a strap is used, one end is attached here. On an electro-acoustic guitar (see 'Buying your guitar'), this usually doubles as a jack socket for connecting an audio cable.

6. Tuning pegs/ machine heads
These work exactly the same way as those found on the classical guitar.

7. Nut
A narrow strip of bone or plastic with slots cut for the strings to pass through. The nut holds the strings in place and defines their vibrating length.

8. Fretboard
The neck's playing surface. This area is usually made of a separate piece of dark hardwood such as rosewood. The surface is usually flat but may also be slightly curved.

9. Frets
Thin strips of metal, placed at precisely calculated positions, which govern the pitches of notes produced when the strings are pressed down towards the fretboard and lie on the frets.

10. Fret markers
These dots, usually made of mother-of-pearl or a similar material, allow easy navigation of the fretboard while playing and reduce the risk of accidentally pressing down at the wrong fret.

11. Truss-rod access
The truss-rod is a steel bar inside the neck, which may sometimes require adjustment if the strings buzz. This should only ever be carried out by a professional guitar technician.

12. Top
This is the most important sound-shaping part of the instrument, since it is responsible for translating vibrations from the strings into vibrations in the air (sound). The top is usually made from one or two pieces of thin, tight-grained wood (almost always either spruce or cedar), and is usually reinforced by a system of braces (thin strips of wood) on the inside.

13. Back and sides
These are usually made from the same type of wood. Many different woods are used, including rosewood, mahogany and various exotic African hardwoods such as bubinga and wengé.

Tuning the guitar

For the music you make to sound right, your instrument must be in tune. Guitars go out of tune in the course of being played, and tuning can also be affected by temperature, air pressure, humidity and other external factors. No amount of flashy technique can compensate for a badly tuned instrument; conversely, the simplest ringing chord can sound pleasing if it's perfectly in tune.

What is tuning?

On a guitar, the six strings are tuned, from lowest to highest, to the notes E, A, D, G, B and E. Their pitch is determined partly by the thickness of the string, but also by the degree of tension in the string. Tuning involves adjusting the tension of each string by turning the machine head, or tuning peg, to which it is attached, until the correct pitch is reached. The auditory reference for each string may come from a note on another string, a piano or keyboard, or an electronic tuner.

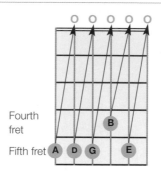

LEFT: *Relative tuning involves tuning each open string with reference to a fretted note on the next lowest string. For perfect results, the low E string still needs to be tuned to an external reference first.*

Relative tuning

To get the guitar in tune with itself, you need to use a process called relative tuning. This means that you can play alone and sing along, however, your guitar may not be in tune with someone else's instrument. Assuming that the bottom E string is in tune, or not far off, the next step is to tune the next string (A) relative to the E string. To do this, play the bottom E string but hold down the note at the fifth fret (see below).

Now play the next string – the open A string. The two notes produced should be the same pitch; the A string should be adjusted up or down until the two notes are the same. Listen for the distinct 'warbling' effect produced when two notes are very nearly, but not exactly, the same pitch. The

speed of this warbling will slow down as the notes approach the same pitch, at which point it will disappear.

Now proceed to tune the next string (D) relative to the A string, using exactly the same method. This pattern is repeated until the top E (thinnest) string is in tune, with one exception: the B (second thinnest) string is tuned to the G string's fourth fret.

You may well find that the very act of tightening the higher strings puts the lower strings out of tune. If this happens, there is nothing for it but to begin the process over again, and perhaps again after that. Using this method, eventually you will reach a point where all six strings are simultaneously in tune with each other.

RIGHT: *The low E (6) string, fretted at the fifth fret, produces the note A, which is used as a reference note for tuning the A string.*

E (6)
A (5)
D (4)
G (3)
B (2)
E (1)

Tuning a string

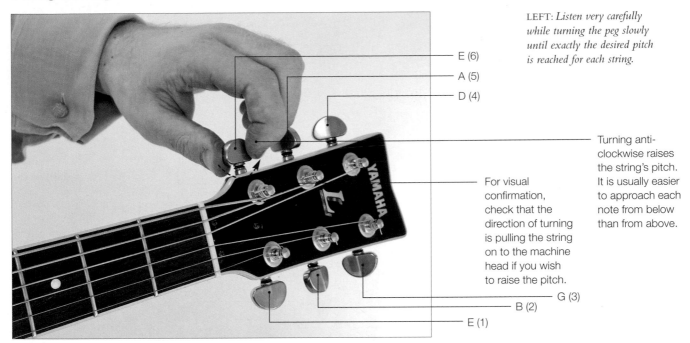

E (6)
A (5)
D (4)

LEFT: *Listen very carefully while turning the peg slowly until exactly the desired pitch is reached for each string.*

Turning anti-clockwise raises the string's pitch. It is usually easier to approach each note from below than from above.

For visual confirmation, check that the direction of turning is pulling the string on to the machine head if you wish to raise the pitch.

G (3)
B (2)
E (1)

Tuning to a piano or keyboard

If you tune your guitar to a keyboard, especially an electronic one that cannot itself go out of tune, then you are in a position to play with other musicians. As with relative tuning, you use your own ear to arrive at the correct pitch. This is not always easy, but it is good training, a form of musical calisthenics.

First locate bottom E on the keyboard (see diagram right). Play the note on the keyboard, and while it is ringing in the air, pluck your open E string and manipulate the machine head to find the same pitch. This will take several attempts. Once the E is pitched right, adjust each string very slowly, listening as you go, to avoid the possibility of tuning far too high and breaking a string.

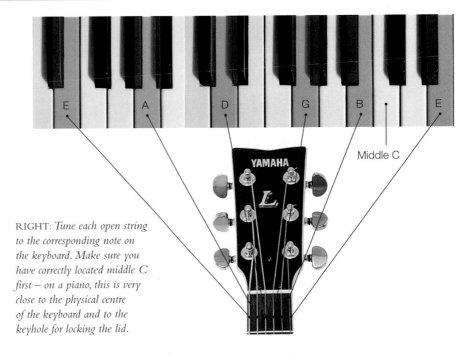

E   A   D   G   B   E

Middle C

RIGHT: *Tune each open string to the corresponding note on the keyboard. Make sure you have correctly located middle C first – on a piano, this is very close to the physical centre of the keyboard and to the keyhole for locking the lid.*

RIGHT: *This type of tuner is very popular and has an integrated microphone as well as an input socket, allowing an electro-acoustic to be connected directly. It can be very useful for tuning in noisy environments.*

Using a tuner

You can take the effort out of tuning by investing in an electronic tuner. Some guitar tuners are restricted to tuning the open strings of a six-string guitar in standard tuning. Others, known as chromatic tuners, are far more useful in that they allow tuning to any note within a large part of the musical spectrum, giving guitarists access to alternative tunings (see 'Altered tunings'). Some chromatic tuners can also be switched to 'guitar mode'.

Changing strings

Guitar strings inevitably pick up moisture from the player's hands. This has a corrosive effect on the strings, which grow dirty over time. Dirt on the strings dulls the sound of the guitar, and makes them more likely to break. So sooner or later, you will have to change a single string and eventually you will need to change the whole set. Just like guitar playing, changing strings is a skill that requires practice.

Choosing strings

You should change your strings from time to time, as soon as you notice that they have become lacklustre. It is a tedious task, but worth the effort, because new strings sound bright and zingy, and feel great under your fingers.

It is important to get the right type of strings: nylon for classical guitars, steel otherwise. Do not under any circumstances try to fit steel strings to a classical guitar: they exert far too much pressure, and are then likely to damage the neck of your guitar.

Steel strings come in different thicknesses or 'gauges'. The gauge of the strings that came with your guitar can be looked up on the manufacturer's website. But there is nothing to stop you from trying a different gauge. Medium or heavy strings have a full sound with lots of volume. Light or extra-light strings are easier to press down, and so are not so punishing for the fingertips, but they sound both quieter and thinner.

ABOVE: *A new string stretches, and so goes flat after a few minutes' playing, so you may need re-tune* *repeatedly at first. But you can speed up the stretching process by tugging the string towards you a few times.*

Changing a classical guitar string

Pass the string through the bridge from the soundhole side, then loop the string around itself at the point of entry. Now wrap the end around the string two or three times on the top side of the bridge for extra friction (some players omit this step for the wound strings). Finally, tuck the end under the looped string behind the bridge and pull tight. Pass the other end of the string through the hole in the machine head roller, again twisting the string around itself to ensure that that it does not continually slip out of tune. Remember to leave the string slack enough to allow it to be wound around the roller several times, but try to avoid leaving so much that an ugly 'ball of wool' effect is created.

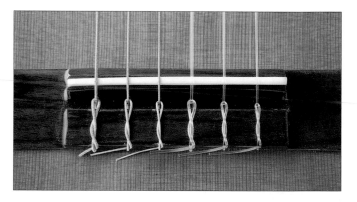

ABOVE: *Classical guitar strings secured at the bridge. There should* *be enough twists that the string is held in place by friction.*

A string winder

This useful gadget speeds up the laborious process of winding strings by hand. Most players favour a combination winder/cutter tool that can be used to trim the end of the string after it has been wound on to the machine head. The cutter also helps when removing strings.

LEFT: *This winder/cutter also has a third function: the small notch at the end of the winder is the perfect shape for removing bridge pins (right).*

Changing steel strings

Many players replace all six strings at once. This provides an excellent opportunity for you to clean and polish those parts of the guitar that are hard to reach with the strings in place.

As a beginner, you may, however, find it useful to replace one string at a time, using the old strings as a guide to help you get the new ones attached correctly.

1 The string is anchored to the bridge by means of an ivory or plastic pin. This must be removed in order to free the string. Some string trimmers incorporate a tool to do this; if not, you need to push the pin out from inside the guitar using a hard object such as a coin.

2 Fasten the new string to the bridge using the same bridge pin. One end of each string is attached to a steel ring, known as a ball end. Feed this end into the hole in the bridge, insert the pin and pull on the string until you feel that the ball end is anchored firmly.

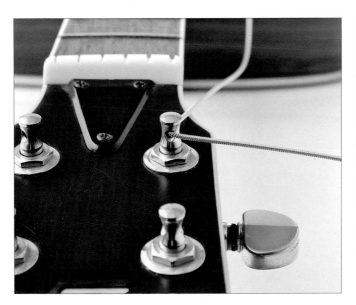

3 Feed the other end through the hole in the machine head. Make a kink in the string on the far side of the hole, leaving enough slack to enable the string to be wound four or five times around the machine head before it is tight. This can be hard to estimate; if in doubt, leave more slack rather than less. Slowly wind the string anti-clockwise until it is tight enough to sound a note.

4 Trim the end of the string, leaving about 10mm/⅜in protruding from the headstock. Tuck this downwards, but make sure the end doesn't make contact with the guitar headstock. Trimmed ends pointing upwards will tear the inside of a soft guitar case to shreds, while a string that touches the headstock may gouge a groove around the machine head.

Guitar care

Your guitar is a machine for making music, and like all machines it requires careful handling as well as a certain amount of maintenance. Look after your guitar properly, and you will be helping to keep it sounding like new as well as protecting your investment. Above all, take some basic steps to make sure that it does not get damaged beyond repair. Most tasks are fairly easy and require no specialist equipment.

Protection

If you are planning to take your guitar anywhere, some form of case is essential. The very cheapest soft cases offer little or no protection against knocks. A padded soft case, known as a 'gig bag', is a much better option if you want to protect your guitar by a sensible minimum. Gig bags usually have backpack straps as well as carrying handles, which makes them a good way of transporting your guitar on foot over short distances. A hard case is a more cumbersome solution but it is a safer choice – particularly for car travel.

Waterproof outer

External pockets

Back strap

Accessory compartment

All-round protection

Secure clasps

Hard exterior shell

LEFT: *A padded gig bag with backpack straps and useful external pockets.*

Neck support

Soft 'velvet' lining

ABOVE/LEFT: *Hard guitar cases may be heavier and more difficult to transport, but they will ensure that your instrument is properly protected.*

Guitar stands

Most damage to guitars occurs for want of one simple accessory: a guitar stand. If you do just one thing to look after your guitar, buy a stand. Countless instruments have been spoiled as a result of falling down while propped up against a wall or a chair. It stands to reason that you should keep your guitar in the house (not the garage or the shed), and that you should not expose it to direct sunlight if possible. Keep it in a shady room, and avoid playing outdoors too much (enjoyable as that is). While a stand is useful if you wish to pick the guitar up and put it down several times a day, putting it back in its case for longer periods will prevent it from gathering too much dust or getting accidentally damaged.

RIGHT/FAR RIGHT: This guitar stand holds the neck of the guitar in place and gives some support to the body.

Cleaning

It is important to keep your guitar clean. A good time for a spring clean is when you change the strings, because this presents an excellent opportunity to clean areas that are otherwise impossible to reach.

The area between the bridge and soundhole tends to gather dust, as does the headstock. This is best removed using a soft cloth. The mysterious gunk that builds up under the strings can also clog up the fretboard. This should not be scraped off directly, as fretboard damage may result, but gently wiped instead. Most music shops carry guitar polish, which will help with general cleaning without damaging the guitar's finish.

The useful life of your guitar strings can be extended by wiping them down after playing – especially underneath each string, where dirt tends to accumulate very easily.

RIGHT: Use a soft cloth that is thin enough to pass under the strings without getting stuck.

When to get help

Some maintenance tasks should be left to professional technicians. One clear sign that you should take your guitar to the mender's is a problem called fret buzz.

If one or more note on your guitar produces a nasty buzzing sound instead of a clean note, that is a symptom of a problem that needs technical help (see box on the right for more details).

The solution will probably involve adjusting the truss-rod, which is embedded inside the neck. It is important to note that attempting this yourself could make matters worse or even possibly lead to permanent damage if it is not tackled properly.

Fixing fret buzz

If a buzzing sound is produced, one of the following procedures may be required to correct it.

Truss-rod adjustment: The neck of a steel-string acoustic guitar is reinforced with a steel rod under the fretboard. The tension in the truss rod is adjusted in order to balance the tension in the strings to result in the correct curved neck shape. This is a skilled and delicate task, and incorrect adjustment can easily make things worse. Do not attempt it at home!

Fret dress: Guitar frets can become worn with use. This can often manifest as small dips or notches in the most frequently fingered frets. The procedure, known as 'fret dressing', involves removing these dips by filing all the frets on the fretboard so that they are once again uniformly smooth, while maintaining equal height. As with fixing the truss-rod, this is no job for the amateur.

Refret: After many fret dresses, the frets may eventually have to be removed and replaced.

Holding the guitar

Classical guitarists and teachers tend to follow exact rules for posture and hand positions, but most acoustic guitarists in other styles like to be a little more relaxed. The most important thing when you sit down with your guitar is to find a comfortable playing position – but make sure that you don't fall into any bad habits that might be hard to shake off later on.

Sitting and standing positions

While many guitarists perform standing up, you will probably want to practise the guitar sitting down at first. For a right-handed player, the guitar rests comfortably on the right thigh. Your legs should not be crossed. The whole length of the neck of the guitar is then within easy reach of the left hand.

The position of the guitar when you are in a comfortable sitting position serves as a rule of thumb for strap adjustment if you wish to play standing up. When standing, the strap should be adjusted so that sitting down has little effect on the tension of the strap. If the strap goes completely slack when you move from standing to sitting, it is definitely too low. Many rock guitarists wear the guitar very low when standing. For the purposes of learning to play, this pose should be avoided since as well as being uncomfortable, it is likely to cause injury to the back and the left wrist.

RIGHT: *A comfortable seated position for a right-handed player. Using a strap, even when sitting, may help to prevent the guitar from sliding off the thigh.*

ABOVE: *This position is about right for playing while standing. The guitar is held at the correct height, avoiding injury to the back and wrist.*

ABOVE: *Here, the guitar is worn too low. This makes good technique difficult for both hands, and can also result in back strain.*

ABOVE: *Wearing the guitar too high is equally inadvisable, for similar reasons to wearing it too low, and also looks rather silly.*

The position of the hands

If you are right-handed, you finger the strings with the left hand and pick or strum with the right. If you are left-handed, the roles of the hands are reversed. The right arm of a right-handed player rests lightly on the bulge of the guitar's body, so that the hand is poised over the soundhole. The left hand holds the neck of the guitar and frets the strings (we will be looking at the position of the left hand for right-handers in detail on the following pages).

For now, we will concentrate on playing with a pick or plectrum in the right hand (we will come to finger-style technique later). The plectrum is held in the right hand, usually between the thumb and index finger. The plectrum should protrude around 5mm (¼in) beyond the end of the index finger. It should not be so exposed that it flaps around noticeably when you are strumming. How tightly it is held is a matter of personal preference and style – but you should hold it firmly enough so that it does not fly out of your hand when you play a big chord.

ABOVE: *The plectrum in position, ready to play. For optimal control, try to avoid having any more of the plectrum protruding from between the fingers than shown here.*

1 Position the thumb and index finger in a 'T' shape.

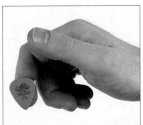

2 Place the plectrum on the finger with the point facing downwards.

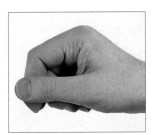

3 The angle of the plectrum depends on the shape of your hands.

Strumming

The strumming technique is the simplest of all right-hand movements. It involves playing several strings, often all six, in rapid succession using a fluid arm movement. This may come from the elbow or wrist, depending on the playing style. We will start by learning to strum from the elbow – just doing downward strokes for now.

Holding the plectrum as described above, bring the right forearm downwards across the strings in a fluid motion. The plectrum should make contact with all six strings in sequence. Reverse this motion, bringing the arm upwards towards its starting position but *without striking the strings*. Repeat this entire cycle – down and up – trying to keep your arm moving rhythmically and regularly.

ABOVE: *The plectrum should make contact with all six strings in rapid sequence in order to make a single sound rather than separate notes.*

ABOVE: *Reverse this motion, bringing the arm upwards towards its starting position but without striking the strings.*

Basic left-hand technique

The job of the left hand is to push the strings on to the fretboard so as to alter their pitch by shortening their active length. Generally, the thumb is anchored at the back of the guitar's neck in order to provide leverage to the pressure of the fingers at the front. These basics are fundamentally the same for all playing styles, although some styles require stricter 'rules' than others.

Thumb position

Classical guitar teachers insist that the thumb of the left hand never strays from an imaginary line down the very centre of the neck. In this, as in other matters of technique, classical players are the sticklers. As a matter of playing style, most rock and folk players allow the thumb to move upwards from the classical position, and even occasionally to wrap around in order to help form chords. The thumb should never be allowed to drift below the centre line, however, as this makes it harder to form chords, while providing no balancing pressure. Likewise, the thumb should be kept roughly perpendicular to the neck and not allowed to stray sideways.

ABOVE: *Classical thumb position – the thumb is positioned squarely at the centre of the neck, and does not stray from this position.*

ABOVE: *Rock thumb position – the thumb is allowed to move up around the back of the neck, and occasionally even over on to the fretboard.*

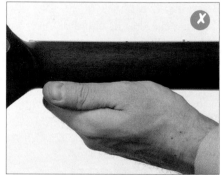

ABOVE: *Poor thumb position – the thumb position here is too low, resulting in loss of pressure and control.*

Finger position

When fretting a note, the finger presses the string down to make contact with a fret so that its vibrating length is reduced. Generally speaking, the finger should not be positioned directly above the fret, but rather just behind it. The further the finger is allowed to stray back from the active fret, the greater the finger pressure required. Sometimes there are two or even three fingers positioned on adjacent strings in the same fret, in which case one or more fingers has to be further back. Try to listen out for the buzzing of the string, which is the sound that may be produced if the finger is too far from the active fret.

ABOVE: *Good finger position – the finger is placed as close as possible to the active fret, but not actually on top of it, producing a clean note.*

ABOVE: *Poor finger position: here, the finger is too far away from the fret, which is likely to result in a buzz rather than a clean sound.*

Left-hand nails

The nails of the left hand should be cut as short as possible. This is one point on which it is unfortunately not possible to compromise: long nails will prevent you from fretting notes properly and can also damage the guitar's fretboard. Right-hand fingernails can be allowed to grow, however. Finger-style players and classical guitarists pay considerable attention to their right-hand fingernails.

Chords and chord boxes

When two or more notes are played together on the guitar (or any other instrument), the result is called a chord. Many songbooks use chord symbols (G, C, F7, C♯13…) on the assumption that you will know how to play each named chord. Guitar books often provide additional help in the form of a chord box (or fret box) that tells you exactly where to place your fingers. This takes the form of a grid where six vertical lines represent the guitar's six strings; horizontal lines represent the frets. Dots represent the fingers. In this book and other beginners' books, the dots are numbered to tell you which finger to use: 1 is the index finger, 2 the middle finger, and so on. An 'X' placed above a string means this string is not played; 'O' tells us that the open string is played.

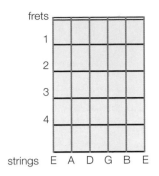

ABOVE: *This empty chord box is labelled to show the names of the strings along the bottom and the fret numbers up the left-hand side of the box, for reference.*

ABOVE: *On this chord box, the finger dots are added, which tell you exactly where to place the left-hand fingers. Finger numbering starts from the index finger.*

Forming the D major chord

Our first chord is the chord of D major, usually known simply as 'D'.

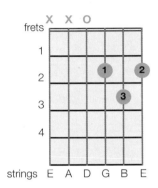

1 Study the chord box. All the information enabling you to form this chord is contained here.

2 Use the first finger (1) to fret the G string at the second fret.

3 Use the second finger (2) to fret the top E string at the second fret.

4 Use the third finger (3) to fret the B string at the third fret.

EXERCISE D CHORD

Try strumming the D chord, lifting the fingers and strumming the open strings, then making the D shape again as you continue to strum. The more frequently you have to form a chord shape, the more quickly and easily you will be able to do it. Later, you can add other chords while still maintaining this approach.

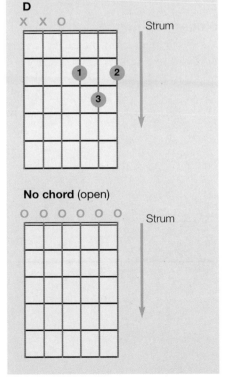

Strumming with three chords

One of your first tasks as an aspiring guitarist is to build up a vocabulary of chords. The more chords you know, the more songs you will be able to play in various moods and keys. At the same time, a surprising number of pop, folk and country songs can be played with a repertoire of just three related chords, universally known as the 'three-chord trick'. These three shapes are easier in some musical keys than others.

Tackling the C, D and G chords

You already know D; the two chords that you are about to tackle are G and C. These three chords occur together in the key of G. Once you can play these three chords fluently, you will be in a position to unlock a vast treasure house of

popular music – songs as diverse as "Twist and Shout", "Breakfast at Tiffany's", "This Land is Your Land", "Mr Tambourine Man", "Peggy Sue" and "Wild Thing" – and the addition of just a few more chords will give you access to an even greater variety.

C

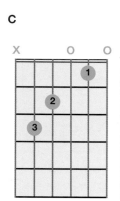

The C chord requires the use of three fingers, each at a different fret. This is a relatively easy shape, because the fingers are not crowded together. Remember, 'X' indicates that the low E string does not sound – in simple playing styles, this is achieved by starting each strum from the next string.

G

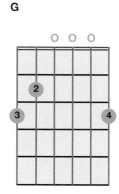

The G chord involves the full width of the fretboard: you have to fret both the top and the bottom string at once. This will probably present a challenge at first. If you find yourself really struggling to get your fingers into this shape, there is an easier version using just one finger (see Easy G below).

Easy G

As with the D chord, the bottom two strings are not played here. If you fall back on this shape at first, resist the temptation to use a different finger (the fourth finger does at least help towards the goal of perfecting the full shape), and do remember to practise the full G shape, as the easy version, while fine for strumming, will be less useful for more advanced playing styles.

Changing between chords

Almost all 'real' songs involve frequent chord changes, which you have to perform while maintaining a strict tempo. This will seem like an impossible feat at first, but the key is to start slowly. One way of getting used to making chord changes at speed is to practise moving between them in as many combinations as possible:

G	→	C	→	D
G	→	D	→	C
C	→	D	→	G
D	→	C	→	G

This will seem hard to start with, but don't worry if it takes a while before it becomes anywhere near fluent. The key is to do it very slowly at first and build up the tempo as you get faster at the changes. Aim for minimal movement of the fingers, for example, when moving the first and second fingers between the G and C shapes.

EXERCISE FIRST THREE-CHORD PIECE

Now you can attempt chord changes at a real-life tempo, in time with your strumming. The diagram below is a simple strumming instruction. The downward arrows indicate downward strums (there are other symbols that we will come to later). The vertical lines indicate the beginning and end of a bar. In this piece, as in a large proportion of Western music, there are four beats in each bar, as indicated by the $\frac{4}{4}$ symbol (this is called the time signature).

Set your metronome to 60 beats per minute. Strum down with each beat, trying to change to the chords as shown above the line as you strum. If you find yourself struggling to change chords cleanly or in time, try playing just one strum per bar: let the chord ring for as long as possible while counting through the bar. The most important thing is that whatever you do choose to play, however busy or sparse, it should be played in time.

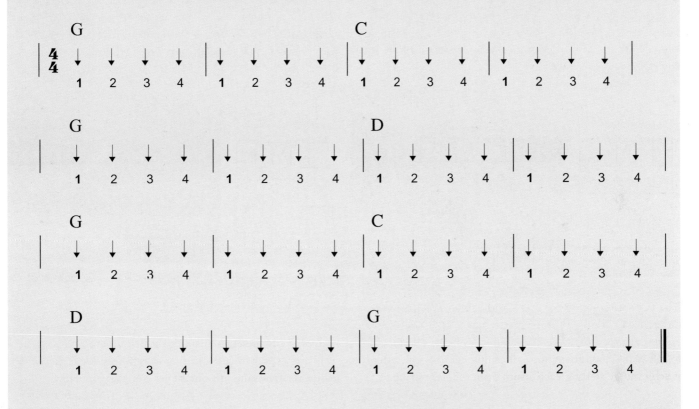

Bob Dylan

A much better guitarist and all-round musician than he is usually given credit for, Bob Dylan is a master of the craft of simple songwriting, often using only three or four chords to underpin some of the most memorable songs of the 20th century. Dylan's guitar playing and early songwriting were both heavily influenced by his hero Woody Guthrie, whose spirit can be felt in the lyrical themes, vocal mannerisms and guitar style of early albums such as *The Freewheelin' Bob Dylan* and *The Times They Are A-Changin'*. Seen as the leading figure of the American folk music revival of the early '60s, Bob Dylan triggered a surge in the popularity of the acoustic guitar across the world. The Beatles, Rolling Stones and other major acts of the time were all drawn to incorporate 'folky' elements into their records as a direct result of Dylan's success.

ABOVE: *Bob Dylan with a Dreadnought acoustic guitar in the early 1960s.*

More chords and strumming

You will greatly expand the number of songs you can play in G by adding two chords to your repertoire: E minor and A minor, usually abbreviated as Em and Am. Notice that these chords have a different character from the first three, which were all major chords. Minor chords are often said to sound 'sad', but they are actually much more expressive than is suggested by that simple description.

E minor and A minor

These chord diagrams and photographs show how to make E minor and A minor. They are both fairly easy shapes to make. What is more, it is not difficult to move between the two.

When changing from Em to Am, fingers 2 and 3 move across one string together. As they arrive at strings 3 and 4, the first finger will naturally be poised to come into play on the second string, first fret.

Am

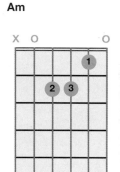 

ABOVE: *The Am chord has two fretted notes in common with the C chord; when changing between the two, only the third finger need move.*

Em

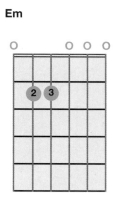 

ABOVE: *The Em chord is a relatively simple shape as it requires only two fingers – usually the second and third as shown here.*

Four-chord sequence

The exercises on these pages will help you get used to playing these new chords in combination with the ones you have already learnt, but first try this progression, which involves C, G, D and Em.

| G | Em | C | D |

Like the three-chord trick, this four-chord sequence (here in the key of G) has been used in hundreds of songs. It is known as the '50s sequence' or "Stand by Me", after one of the many songs which use it. Others include "Every Breath You Take", "Earth Angel", "Up on the Roof" and "I've Just Seen a Face". Once you have looked at the strumming exercises, come back and try singing along to some of those songs while you play.

EXERCISE 1

In this exercise you will be applying the simplest downstroke-upstroke strumming pattern to the E minor chord you learnt earlier.

Make sure that you are strumming downwards on the beat (1, 2, 3, 4) and upwards on the offbeat (each 'and'), not the other way round.

Em

1 & 2 & 3 & 4 &   1 & 2 & 3 & 4 &   1 & 2 & 3 & 4 &   1 & 2 & 3 & 4 &

Strumming upwards

One way to use these new chords in more musically interesting ways is to expand the strumming technique at your disposal. So far we have used down strums only. Deliberately missing the strings on the way up again actually requires extra effort, so adding up strums in between should come fairly naturally. In most strumming styles, down strums are used on the beat, while up strums are used in between beats, otherwise known as the offbeat. In other words, staying with our metronome click of 60 beats per minute, we would play down strums in time with the click, and up strums exactly halfway between clicks. By convention, this is counted as follows: '1 and 2 and 3 and 4 and 1 and 2 and 3 and 4 and…'. Practise the exercise shown here until you feel intuitively comfortable with it.

1 Strum downwards across all of the strings that need to be used in the chord shape.

2 Now strum upwards. Up strums between down strums are usually a little lighter/softer than the down strums. Repeat steps 1 and 2.

EXERCISE 2

Offbeats with missed up strums are shown in brackets below the arrows. Don't play the upstrokes shown in grey type: they are there just to show you which direction your hand should be going at that point. The important thing is that the right hand should always move downwards on the beat, and upwards on the offbeat, whether strumming or not. It may help to tap your foot on the beat and imagine that your right hand and foot are connected by an invisible string.

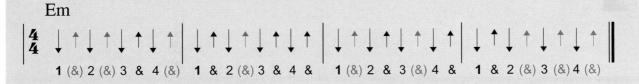

EXERCISE 3

The following piece makes use of all five chords encountered so far, and incorporates various combinations of the above strumming patterns.

We have dispensed with the grey arrows: you should now know instinctively which way your strumming hand should be moving.

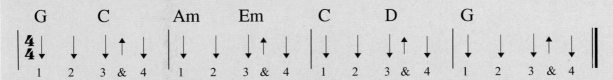

Syncopated strumming

All your strumming so far has involved playing downstrokes on the beat, plus upstrokes on one or more offbeats. But it is also possible to create different patterns where the downstrokes are missed out, and the offbeat is accented. This effect is known as syncopation; it is common in many styles of music from classical to dance music, and it is subtly present in most pop rhythm playing.

Using syncopation

To understand syncopation, start by counting quavers (half beats) in $\frac{4}{4}$ time: '1 and 2 and 3 and 4 and…'. Now modify this so that the offbeats ('and') are louder, while the beats are barely muttered: '(1) AND (2) AND (3) AND (4) AND…'. This accent on the offbeat is so prevalent in most jazz melodies and solos, for example, that removing it would make them sound strangely wooden.

Other styles characterized by heavy syncopation include jive and ska, which simply would not work without it. Many familiar pop songs are driven by less obvious syncopation: the 'recommended listening' examples listed in the box opposite are all memorable mainly because of syncopated strumming

patterns which manage to bring to life otherwise very ordinary-sounding chord sequences. In some styles, the presence of bass and drums means that the guitar can play offbeats only, but this does not really work when the guitar is played on its own.

Recommended listening:

- George Harrison: "My Sweet Lord"
- Oasis: "Wonderwall"
- Paul Simon: "Me and Julio Down by the Schoolyard", "Kodachrome"

Two new chords

Before you practise some simple syncopated strumming, take this opportunity to enlarge your chord vocabulary with two new chords: E major and A major.

These, together with the chords learnt already, make several new keys available on the guitar. Any three-chord song can be played in the key of A using the chords A, D and E.

E

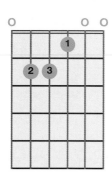

A

You will notice that the E major chord is the same shape as the A minor chord, but played on different strings. This is convenient, since a change from E to Am and then back again is a very common progression.

When changing between them, try not to break up the shape of your hand as it moves across the strings; instead, aim to lift the whole shape smoothly off the strings and then place in the new position. This chord may also be viewed as the same shape as Em, but with the index finger added to turn it into a major chord. Try alternating between the two to highlight the difference between major and minor qualities.

The A major chord is slightly unusual in that three fingers are placed at the same fret. If you have large hands, it can be difficult to squeeze the fingers together for this shape. Although the chord box represents all three fingers in a straight line, this is physically impossible; in reality, the three fingers form a diagonal back from the second fret, with the index finger furthest away.

If you do have large hands, you may continue to find this shape difficult. Later, you may wish to try another way to fret these three notes, using just one finger (see 'Barre chords'). For now, some perseverance may be necessary.

Syncopated strumming patterns

As with all the downstroke–upstroke patterns that you have already encountered thus far, it is crucial that the right hand should move down on the beat and up on the offbeat, whether striking the strings or not. If you find yourself playing upstrokes on the beat, or downstrokes on the offbeat, it may help to tap your foot on the beat and imagine that your right hand and foot are connected by an invisible string.

EXERCISE 1

This exercise explores some possible syncopated patterns. Ghosted (missed) strokes are greyed out, and shown in brackets on the counting line.

Remember, it essential to maintain consistent down/up motion, whether striking or missing the strings – anything else will prevent the development of fluid strumming.

EXERCISE 2

This sequence uses a one-bar syncopated pattern created by missing the downstrokes on beats two and four. This works well when playing with a drummer, as the snare drum is usually played on these beats.

For an even more syncopated effect, the down strum on beat 3 may also be ghosted; in this case, the down strum on beat 1 should be made louder so that the ear can still identify a clear downbeat in the rhythm.

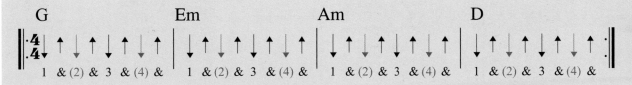

EXERCISE 3

The first beat of the second bar is the only missing downstroke in this two-bar pattern. Set your metronome to a comfortable speed and concentrate on maintaining the rhythm of each piece in time with the click; gradually increase this speed.

Try working up from 60 to 90 beats per minute with these exercises. For added colour, try changing the Em chord to E major the second time through. Coming after Am, this would lend the sequence a slightly Spanish flavour.

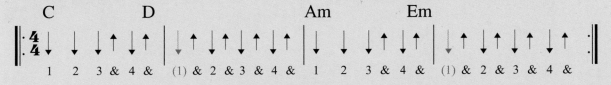

Seventh chords

Major and minor chords are the main building blocks of most Western music, but there is another essential type of chord, the dominant seventh (usually known simply as the seventh, written as E7, for example). It is formed by adding a fourth note to the basic three. This additional note is most easily found by playing the note a whole tone below the root note of the chord.

The importance of seventh chords

Dominant seventh chords have a darker, richer sound than ordinary major or minor chords; this is because they contain four unique notes rather than three. In classical music, the dominant seventh is only carefully used in certain contexts, but in all these styles it is almost ubiquitous, and our ears have become very used to it.

To form the seventh of G, you add an F to the G, B and D – because F is one tone below G. To play F7, you add an E♭ (meaning 'E flat') to F, A and C, because E♭ is one tone below F. The simple addition of one note can totally alter the character of the harmony. Play any dominant seventh, and

you will hear that the ear (and the heart) yearns for it to go somewhere else: there is a tension built into the sound that needs to be resolved by its going 'home' to another chord.

For this reason, the dominant seventh chord is crucial to all Western harmony, particularly to the sound of the blues and all styles derived from it, including jazz and rock 'n' roll. Its unresolved nature means that it often functions as a pivot chord when changing keys. And it is no secret where sevenths want to go. They resolve as shown below.

E7 ⟶ A (or Am)

A7 ⟶ D (or Dm)

D7 ⟶ G (or Gm)

G7 ⟶ C (or Cm)

BELOW: *First-position seventh chords are all easy to learn, because their shapes are closely related to the major chord shapes. Here are four of the most common sevenths. Learn the shapes, and try them out in various combinations with the chords that you already know.*

E⁷
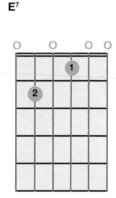

A⁷
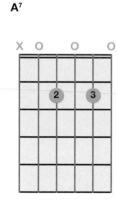

D⁷
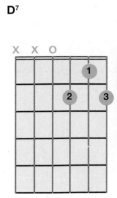

G⁷
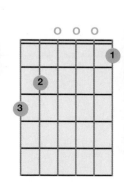

The least movement principle

Sevenths are a good illustration of the 'least movement principle'. In order to move from one chord to the next as cleanly and efficiently as possible, it is important not to make the fingers of the left hand do more work than necessary. For example, the second and third fingers need not move at all when changing from G to G7. And when changing from E to E7, the third finger is simply lifted while the first and second fingers stay in place. For many other chord changes, one or more fingers may slide between frets on the same string while the other fingers move around. For an example not involving sevenths, try moving from A to D. The first finger stays on the B string but slides from the second fret to the third fret: no need to lift it. But finger pressure should be relaxed when doing this so that the slide is not audible (and so as to avoid hurting your fingertips).

James Taylor

This artist would figure near the top of any list of influential singer/songwriters; he was at the height of his success in the early '70s. His successful *Greatest Hits* album sold more than 11 million copies and burned deeply personal yet instantly memorable songs such as "Fire and Rain" and "Carolina in My Mind" into the hearts of a generation, along with definitive versions of other writers' songs, including Carole King's "You've Got a Friend". Many of Taylor's best-known songs are written around his own highly accomplished fingerstyle guitar playing, which combines elements of jazz harmony with country/folk roots.

RIGHT: *Most critics agree that James Taylor is one of the finest acoustic guitarists in the world.*

EXERCISE

This exercise uses syncopated strumming patterns, and also mixes seventh chords with some of the major and minor shapes learnt previously. All of the seventh chords here either resolve to a major/minor chord or form part of a sequence that eventually resolves. They are a good way to become acquainted with the eloquent effect that can be achieved with just a few standard chords. The exercise also use a new key signature: $\frac{3}{4}$ i.e. 3 beats in the bar.

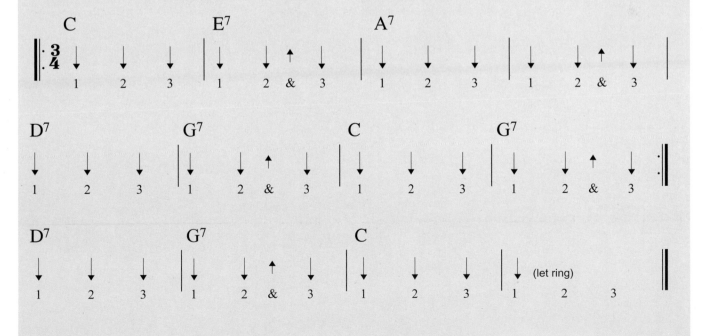

Guitar notation

Guitar music can be written down in a number of different ways. One is the strumming system that we have already looked at – but those arrowed diagrams can only express whole chords. They are not suited for putting melodies down on paper, or even for complex rhythms. For these tasks, there is standard music notation and also a specifically guitar-based notational system called tablature.

Standard music notation

The best way of understanding standard notation is to think of it as a kind of musical alphabet. It is a way of writing down any note of any length, any combination of notes (chords), as well as the gaps between them. It also includes ways of indicating the manner in which the notes should be played – loudly, softly, slurred together or crisply distinct.

Standard notation uses a system of five horizontal lines, called the stave (or staff), to represent musical pitch (how high or low each note is). In most cases, the lines – and the spaces between them – represent steps of one tone up or down. The adjacent pairs B-C and E-F span only a semitone (half a tone).

Most guitar music, in common with most melodic music, is written in the so-called treble clef – also known as the G clef. This is simply a way of indicating which note corresponds to which line. In the G clef, the second line from the bottom represents the note G, and is indicated by an elaborate stylized

G anchored on that line, thus: ⨎. All the other notes can then be worked out from that one: the bottom line must be E, the space above F, and so on.

The other component of standard notation is rhythm. The appearance of each note tells us its rhythmic value – how long it is in terms of beats or parts of a beat. A crotchet is usually used to denote one beat; a minim is two beats long; a quaver half a beat long. (Different terms are used in American English – see the chart below.) A corresponding set of symbols is used to indicate rests – gaps or silences – of specified lengths. All of the note values in any bar must add up to the total defined by the time signature. The chart below gives all the basic symbols with their values in $\frac{4}{4}$ time (four beats in a bar).

BELOW: *Note values in British and American English. The majority of Western music can be notated using very little else.*

Music notation: the basics

Single note	Group	Note name (UK)	Note name (US)	Duration in $\frac{4}{4}$	Rest
o	-	semibreve	whole note	4 beats	▬
♩	-	minim	half note	2 beats	▬
♩	-	crotchet	quarter note	1 beat	𝄽
♪	♫	quaver	eighth note	½ beat	𝄾
♬	♬	semiquaver	sixteenth note	¼ beat	𝄿

Finding the notes

The beauty of standard notation is that it is universal; the music written for one instrument can usually be played on any other. A violinist or pianist who can read music can play a piece written for the guitar, and vice versa.

One thing this system doesn't tell you on its own is where to find these notes on the guitar. Many instruments, such as keyboards and wind instruments, have just one place to find

each note. On the guitar, any given note can often be found in two, three or four places on the fretboard. As a result, playing from standard musical notation is harder for guitarists than for some other instrumentalists, because they have to work out for themselves where to put their fingers.

This is often used as a lazy excuse for not learning to read music at all, but getting to understand musical notation is something that all guitarists will benefit from doing.

David Gray

Few musicians have successfully crossed over from the British folk scene to international chart success, and none have done this as spectacularly as David Gray. More important than this transition, however, is Gray's success in combining many of the hallmarks of the acoustic folk sound with elements of contemporary pop production: layers of guitars, often using open tunings and making prominent use of the capo (raising the guitar's pitch for sonic effect), combined with drum loops and synth washes in a musical blend. Gray succeeded in achieving prominence in the late '90s music scene, which was dominated by electric Britpop and bleeping electronica.

ABOVE: *David Gray has played a leading role in returning acoustic sounds to the pop mainstream.*

ABOVE: *Most beginners start playing the guitar simply by strumming – but guitar music, like any form of music, can be read and played from the page.*

Tablature

There is a notational system designed specifically for the guitar, which is known as tablature, often abbreviated to TAB. It does the very thing that standard notation cannot: it tells you exactly where to place your fingers in order to play each note. Tablature looks superficially like standard notation in that it is written on a stave-like set of horizontal lines. However, the six lines of the tablature stave represent not pitch, but the strings of the guitar. A number placed on a given line indicates that the string in question should be played at the specified fret.

As with standard notation, you scan left to right – playing the notes in the order in which they occur. In the example below, three notes are played on the bottom E string: on the third fret, the second fret and finally the open string indicated by a zero (0). Chords are shown vertically, as notes on several strings are played simultaneously.

The weakness of tablature is that it gives little indication of rhythm. This omission may be solved in several ways. Some publications add tails and stems to the notes on the TAB stave in order to convey rhythms corresponding to those found in standard notation. In recent years, however, most publishers and guitar magazines have opted to combine standard notation and tablature. The TAB stave is placed underneath the music stave, in effect acting as a companion to the otherwise complete top stave. Chord symbols or boxes are usually placed above the top stave.

This combined system has many advantages for the guitarist: confident sight-readers can follow the top stave and ignore the TAB; learners can follow the TAB but glean crucial rhythm information from the top stave. Each system of notation compensates for the disadvantages of the other, creating a solution that is greater than the sum of its parts.

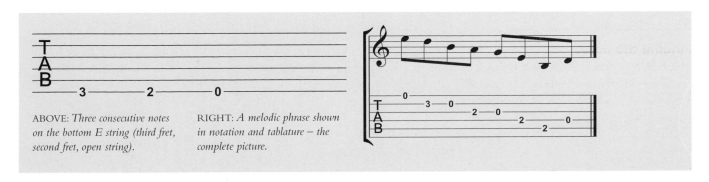

ABOVE: *Three consecutive notes on the bottom E string (third fret, second fret, open string).*

RIGHT: *A melodic phrase shown in notation and tablature – the complete picture.*

Using the fingers

The guitar is an incredibly versatile instrument, capable of strummed chords, fast melodic playing and anything in between. Fingerstyle technique, while still mainly based on chord shapes and primarily focused on accompaniment, may be seen as a first step away from pure strumming towards melodic playing. The simplest fingerstyle technique involves picking bass notes with the thumb and strumming with the fingers.

Bass/strum style

The technique of bass/strum playing is particularly popular in country and folk music. As its name suggests, the bass/strum style involves alternating between bass notes (played with the thumb) and strums (which are usually played with the first, second and third fingers together).

Bass/strum style also requires you to strum without the use of the plectrum, although we will be coming back to it later. The plectrum can in fact be used to play many 'fingerpicking' ideas, but it is useful to be able to use the fingers of the right hand independently. If you can play with your fingers a wider range of techniques are open to you; the musical effect can sound rather different from notes played with a plectrum.

Fingerpicking involves using the nails of the right hand to pluck the strings. Serious fingerstyle players devote considerable attention to shaping their fingernails to this end. Don't worry if your right-hand nails are too short for fingerpicking, since you can initially get by using the fleshy part of the fingertips. The fingernails don't have to be long or well shaped for strumming, anyway; it matters more when you come to play single picked notes (see 'Simple fingerpicking patterns').

You may also wish to investigate an alternative to using your own fingernails: a set of fingerpicks. These are attached to the individual fingers and thumb of the right hand and act as nail extensions. For maximum control, it is important to find a set that fits your fingers snugly, without protruding too far.

LEFT: *Fingerpicks are often favoured by country players, and provide an alternative which cuts out the need for nail care. Some players also prefer the resulting angle of the thumb.*

Recommended listening:

- The Beatles: "Rocky Raccoon"
- Bob Dylan: "North Country Blues"
- Johnny Cash: "Ring of Fire"
- Paul McCartney & Wings: "Mull of Kintyre"

Johnny Cash

One of the towering figures of country music, Johnny Cash became known for the distinctive 'boom-chick-a-boom' style of his rhythm section. Cash forged a path that combined a deep respect for the traditions of country music with a range of other influences, from blues to gospel. The common thread in much of his output is simplicity: simple chord sequences and a simple guitar-accompaniment style geared to serving his songs, which often deal with the themes beloved of country music without falling prey to its most obvious clichés. As one of the major artists in the Sun Records stable (along with Elvis Presley, Carl Perkins and Jerry Lee Lewis), he was almost automatically propelled to legendary status; this association, as well as doing his own standing no harm at all, helped keep simple guitar-driven country music central to American culture when it might otherwise have been completely dominated by rock'n'roll.

RIGHT: *Johnny Cash epitomized one of country music's favourite sayings: "All you need to write country music is three chords and the truth."*

Practising the bass/strum

There is more than one way to do the bass/strum – or at least the strumming part of it. Many players bring the fingers into the palm of the hand and then 'flick' them outwards to strum; others maintain a looser hand position and strum from the wrist.

As with many issues of guitar technique, the general rule is: if it feels relaxed, it's probably alright. If it feels awkward, it's probably not going to result in fluid playing. Either way, it is going to feel odd at first if you are used to playing with a plectrum. Try the exercises below and persevere: the technique will start to feel natural with practice. Remember, if a chord box has an 'X' on any string, this string should not be used as a bass note.

RIGHT: *This breakdown of a basic bass/strum pattern uses the D chord. Practise this for a while, then attempt the exercise below, which also begins with D.*

1 The left hand forms the D major chord. The right hand plays the open D (fourth) string (beat 1).

2 The first, second and third fingers of the right hand strum the top three strings (beat 2).

3 Pick the D string again (beat 3). For variety, try the A string instead.

4 Strum again (beat 4). You will need to practise this until it feels natural.

EXERCISE

This bass/strum exercise involves chord changes, and also asks you to pluck the bass on different strings. Follow the tablature: notes stacked on top of each other should be played simultaneously – as a strum, in other words.

Tip

For musical variety, you may want to vary this pattern by repeating the bass note on beat 3 (instead of strumming), as shown in the step-by-step sequence above.

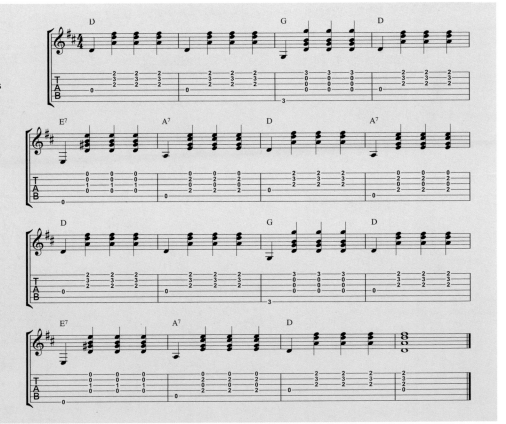

Simple fingerpicking patterns

The next step in fingerpicking is learning to use the right-hand fingers and thumb independently. You will still be making chord shapes with your left hand, but you will be playing them in a succession of rising and falling notes. The effect can be beautiful, almost magical, as if you were weaving melodic tapestries on the air. This style works well if a less dense texture is required.

Arpeggios and fingerpicking styles

Many fingerpicking styles are built on arpeggio patterns. The term 'arpeggio' is from the Italian word *arpeggiare*, which translates as 'to play on a harp'. It means that the individual notes of a chord are played in sequence. In guitar circles, arpeggios are sometimes known by the less technical term 'spread chords'. Stringed instruments, by their nature, lend themselves to arpeggios, because a number of notes are always simultaneously available to the player: four to the violinist, six to the guitarist, dozens to the harpist.

Arpeggios played on a guitar can be very simple – say, the top three strings played one after the other in a repeating cycle – or they can take the form of complex patterns. Guitar arpeggios are usually produced by the thumb and first three fingers of the strumming hand (the little finger is rarely used). As a general rule, the thumb moves between the bass strings as necessary, while each finger covers just one of the top strings. The labelling system is shown below.

Each note of an arpeggio pattern should be allowed to ring for as long as possible – generally until the same string is played again. This effect is not always directly reflected in written note durations, as it would be visually messy. But it is taken for granted wherever fingerpicked arpeggios are shown, and sometimes reinforced by the indication 'let ring'.

Now try the fingerpicking exercises opposite. Notice that both of these exercises are in the 3/4 time signature. This seems to lend itself particularly well to arpeggio-style guitar accompaniments, since there are six quavers (notes of half a beat), which is exactly enough for the ascending/descending motion described above.

You may also wish to try these patterns using a plectrum. At slow tempos, this can be achieved using downstrokes only, but for greater fluency (and usually a more musical result), alternating down/upstrokes are recommended, following the general rule established for strumming 'downstrokes on the beat, upstrokes on the offbeat'.

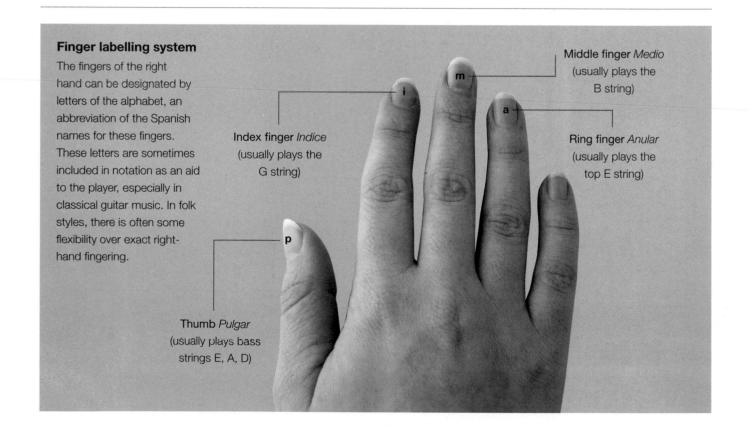

Finger labelling system

The fingers of the right hand can be designated by letters of the alphabet, an abbreviation of the Spanish names for these fingers. These letters are sometimes included in notation as an aid to the player, especially in classical guitar music. In folk styles, there is often some flexibility over exact right-hand fingering.

Index finger *Indice*
(usually plays the G string)

Middle finger *Medio*
(usually plays the B string)

Ring finger *Anular*
(usually plays the top E string)

Thumb *Pulgar*
(usually plays bass strings E, A, D)

EXERCISE 1

While the left hand frets the C major chord, the right hand arpeggiates the notes of the chord: first ascending, then descending. This exact right-hand pattern will also work for any other chord that has the root on the A string, including C major and A major. Other chords may have the bass note on the D string or low E string, as seen in Exercise 2 (below). For these chords, the right-hand fingers may also move down by one string (to the D, G and B strings).

Recommended listening:
● Garth Brooks: "If Tomorrow Never Comes"
● Eva Cassidy: "Songbird"
● Simon and Garfunkel: "Scarborough Fair"
● James Taylor: "Sweet Baby James"

EXERCISE 2

The arpeggio picking piece here uses the same right-hand picking pattern throughout – the fingers do exactly the same thing in each bar; the only elements that change are the chords and strings picked by the thumb. Remember to let each note ring for as long as possible; this is particularly important in the case of the bass notes: their sound underpins each chord and so helps to create an effective bass line.

Using the thumb in fingerpicking

The right thumb fulfils the same role in fingerpicking as the bassist does in a band: it plays the low notes that add depth to the sound. But this job need not be pedestrian or dull. The guitarist's thumb (like a creative bass player) can put notes together in a variety of ways to produce a satisfying melodic bass line. At its best, this can sound like a second melodic strand accompanying the voice or melody instrument.

Additional notes

Simply introducing an additional note to the bass line is enough to create a much more interesting effect when playing arpeggios. This might mean no more than using the thumb to pluck two of the lower strings in turn, while keeping the same chord shape. Some pairs of bass notes sound better than others, but one combination that nearly always sounds good is the root (the note on which the chord or scale begins) together with the fifth note of the scale.

Root and fifth

For details of how to construct chords, see 'Chord construction'. For present purposes, you need only know where to find the root note and fifth of each chord of the chords you have learnt so far. Almost all of them naturally contain the fifth on one of the bass strings, so the left hand does not need to move for the thumb to alternate between them.

Look at the chord diagrams below. Available root notes are shown in red, and fifth bass notes in blue. Sometimes they are on open strings, in which case the **O** at the top of the diagram is coloured. Notice that playing a C chord with the fifth in the bass requires you to move the third finger to the bottom E string. None of the other chords here require movement of the left hand to achieve this. Only the major chords learnt so far are shown. As for the minor and seventh chords learnt so far, they are all variations on these major shapes, and both the root and fifth are to be found in the same places. Practise finding the root and fifth with your thumb, then try Exercise 1, opposite.

Passing notes

Another way to create interesting bass lines is to introduce passing notes – bass notes that bridge the gap between chords. These are notes that do not belong to the chord, but are (usually) part of the scale or key of the piece. When combined with chord notes, passing notes make it possible to construct bass lines that add melodic interest.

One easy approach is to find notes that lie between the root notes of consecutive chords and see if they sound good. For example, many songs use the sequence C–Am. The root notes of these chords are found on the A string, third fret and open A string respectively. Therefore, either one or both of the notes in between (A string, first and second fret) could in theory be used as passing notes; which one sounds best will depend on the key of the piece.

As a rule, passing notes between chords should be fretted using whichever left-hand finger is most easily available. The aim is to cause the least disruption to the chord shape, and to allow other sounding notes to continue.

RIGHT: *The use of a thumb pick can add a brighter, crisper quality to bass notes, but can take some time to get used to.*

root and fifth of D	root and fifth of C	root and fifth of A	root and fifth of G	root and fifth of E

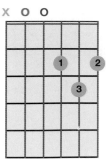

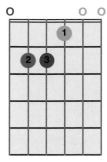

EXERCISE 1

This exercise applies the concept of moving between root and fifth to a simple arpeggiated pattern using first-position chords. To get even more value out of this exercise, try re-ordering the notes on the G, B and top E strings in each chord pattern (for example, try P a m i or P m i a).

EXERCISE 2

This exercise uses root notes, fifths and passing notes to create a simple 'joined up' bass line. The time signature of this piece is $\frac{6}{8}$. This means that there are six quavers (eighth notes) in each bar. Although the number of quavers is the same as in $\frac{3}{4}$, they are accented as two groups of three: ONE two three, FOUR five six. This time signature also lends itself particularly well to arpeggiated accompaniment, and is often encountered in ballads.

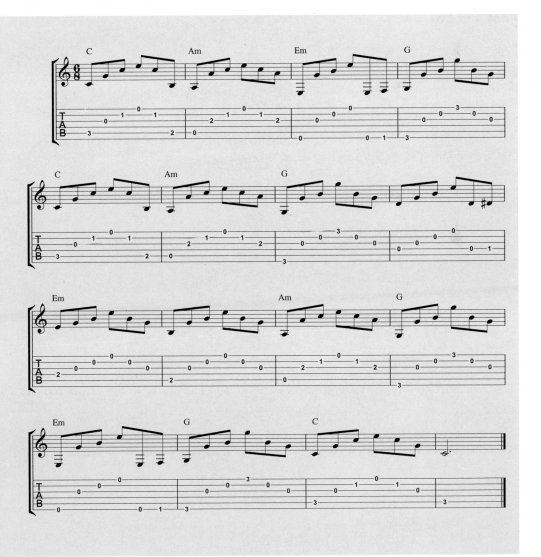

Using a capo

The capo is a device that raises the pitch of the guitar by placing a 'clamp' over all the strings at a given fret. This makes it possible to change the key of a song to suit a singer's vocal range and style, while retaining the sound and shape of chords being played. In folk styles, in particular, many players use a capo almost all the time so the song falls comfortably within their vocal range.

How to change key

Transposing a song into a different key is a tricky business on some instruments – a piano or a clarinet, for example – because all the fingering has to change. But it is easy on a guitar if you use a capo: you play all the same chords, but higher up the neck. All that has changed, in effect, is the position of the nut. If you are transposing with a capo to suit your own voice, you may not need to know the names of the sounding chords. Just find a capo position that works for you.

If you are playing with other musicians or singers, however, you may need to agree on a key. The basic unit of pitch on

Western instruments is the semitone. On the guitar, two notes that are one fret apart on the same string are also one semitone apart. Most other musicians will understand if you tell them how many semitones you have transposed. For details of transposition, see the chart opposite.

The capo can also be used on the higher reaches of the fretboard to make the guitar sound more like a mandolin (which has a shorter neck).

In the Beatles' "Here Comes the Sun", for example, the bright, zingy tone of the guitar part is achieved by playing with a capo way up at the seventh fret.

Types of capo

It is essential that your capo is the right shape for your guitar. Some are designed to be used on guitars that have a completely flat fretboard (as almost all classical guitars do); while others are shaped for a curved fretboard (as is the case with most steel-string acoustics). There are many different types of capo are available, and each has its own advantages. The mechanism is usually designed either to enable fast application or removal, or to prioritize tuning accuracy and clean-sounding notes. Only the best types of capos manage to achieve both. The most common varieties of capo are shown below.

ABOVE: *The clamp capo offers the most precise adjustment. However, the disadvantage of it is that it cannot be moved quickly between frets. The reason for this is because the clamp tension has to be adjusted for each position.*

ABOVE: *The quick-release capo cannot be adjusted as accurately as a clamp capo, but is very easy to move between frets. This is the best type for most guitars, and is the one to use if you are performing on stage.*

ABOVE: *The advantages of the wrap-around capo are that it is inexpensive, and can be moved quickly around the neck. However, the downside is that the tension of the elastic cannot usually be adjusted precisely.*

Paul McCartney

Every pop band needs a bass player, and when the Beatles' original bassist left the band, the role naturally fell to Paul McCartney, who inhabited the position superbly, bringing a fresh approach to the instrument. McCartney has never stopped playing the guitar, and many of his best-known songs feature his acoustic guitar playing and often incorporate highly original techniques and ideas, ranging from hybrid fingerpicking/strumming for his lyrical "Blackbird", to tuning the guitar down a tone (the reverse of using a capo) for "Yesterday". By doing this, he managed to transpose the song into a comfortable key, while keeping the rich sound of first-position chords.

FAR RIGHT: *Though his main instrumental role in the Beatles was to play the bass, Paul McCartney has played both the acoustic and electric guitar throughout his long career..*

BELOW: *This chart shows the actual sounding notes achieved by six familiar major chords at capo positions up to the seventh fret.*

Transposition guide

No capo	E	A	D	G	B	E
1st fret	F	Bb (A#)	E♭ (D#)	A♭ (G#)	C	F
2nd fret	F#	B	E	A	C# (D♭)	F#
3rd fret	G	C	F	B♭ (A#)	D	G
4th fret	G# (A♭)	C# (D♭)	F# (G♭)	B	D# (E♭)	G# (A♭)
5th fret	A	D	G	C	E	A
6th fret	B♭ (A#)	E♭ (D#)	A♭ (G#)	D♭ (C#)	F	B♭ (A#)
7th fret	B	E	A	D	F# (G♭)	B

Tuning with a capo

In theory, one should be able to apply the capo at any given fret and, so long as the guitar is already in tune, it will remain in tune with the capo in place. In fact, the capo exerts a lot of pressure on the strings, and this is enough to affect their tuning. So it may be necessary to adjust the tuning once you have put the capo on. A small amount of relative tuning should be sufficient.

If you use an electronic tuner that needs to be set manually, you will need to know the pitch of all six strings at the fret where you are fitting the capo. The chart above shows the pitches of the 'open' strings (with capo) up to the seventh fret. Notes in parentheses are alternative names for the same note. Your tuner may describe these as sharps (#), flats (♭) or both.

ABOVE: *As with fretting fingers, the capo should generally be placed as close as possible to the active fret to avoid buzz. However, make sure the strings aren't pushed out of alignment (see above).*

Playing tunes

So far we have been dealing mainly with ways of playing chords. However, the guitar is not just for rhythmic accompaniment; it is also an instrument on which you can play tunes. If you can get to grips with the guitar's melodic potential, a whole new world of musical possibilities will open up to you – from improvised blues to gypsy jazz. In fact, just about any conceivable melody can be played on the guitar.

The musical vocabulary

When strumming on the guitar, you can get by without really knowing much about the components and musical construction of the chords. But to play a tune, you really need to have some familiarity with the notes. You probably already know that there are 12 notes in the musical vocabulary: on a piano, these correspond to the seven white keys plus the five black ones that occur before the pattern of keys repeats itself. On a guitar, they are the 12 frets that you have to climb before you get to the note where you started – but an octave higher.

Few tunes use all these notes – and many fine melodies can be played using five notes or fewer. The first five notes that you are going to learn are C, D, E, F and G. They are shown below in ascending order in standard musical notation and in 'TAB'. The fretted notes here should be played with the

finger number corresponding to the fret number: so the second fret is played with the second finger and the third fret with the third finger. This approach, known as *position playing*, is the most efficient way of achieving this since it involves the least finger movement.

When playing an ascending figure on one string, such as the three notes played here on the D string, fingers may stay in place on lower frets as higher notes are played: after playing the note E (second finger, second fret), there is no need to remove this finger before playing the next note (F: third finger, third fret). However, when moving from one string to another, care should be taken that notes sounding on the first string played should not ring on over notes on the next string. For example, in playing the ascending figure here, the third finger should be lifted after playing the first note (C) and again after playing the note F.

C   D   E   F   G

LEFT: *The first five notes of the C major scale, in first position. Remember to play the fretted notes using one finger per fret, as described above.*

Pat Metheny

Although his records are usually filed under 'jazz', Pat Metheny's output spans a far broader range of styles: folk, rock, Latin and classical influences are often prominent, to name a few. Equally at home on both electric and acoustic guitars of various types, Metheny has been stretching boundaries ever since he came to prominence in the mid-'70s, while remaining one of the few players with such a distinctive 'voice'.

The right hand

Strumming with the plectrum often involves the whole right forearm, but melodic playing requires greater precision, and so demands a lighter touch from the right hand – a delicate rocking of the wrist at most. The right hand may rest lightly on the bridge when playing single notes, but it should also be poised so that it can be lifted at any time in order to go into strumming mode.

RIGHT: *The right hand in picking position.*

LEFT: *Pat Metheny is widely recognized as one of the most fluent melodic guitarists of his generation. He has accomplished this through both his own work as well as collaborations with Steve Reich, Joni Mitchell and many other musicians.*

FIVE-NOTE MELODIES "WHEN THE SAINTS GO MARCHING IN"

Many well-known tunes can be played using just the five notes that you now know – from simple pieces, such as "When the Saints Go Marching in", to magnificent uplifting melodies, such as Beethoven's "Ode to Joy".

Be sure to take account of the rests when playing this piece – including the one that is the first beat of the first bar.

FIVE-NOTE MELODIES "ODE TO JOY"

Beethoven's famous piece is not ideally suited to the guitar, but it is still excellent practice. The beat is very regular throughout, but watch out for those two pairs of quavers in the third line.

Now see if you can work out some tunes for yourself. This is one of the best possible ear-training exercises. Try your hand at the following melodies to start with:

"Jingle Bells"
(hint: the first note is E)

"Hot Cross Buns"

"Au Clair de la Lune"
(first part)

The C major scale and first position

You already know the first five notes in the scale of C major; now you will learn the rest of it. The whole scale can be played in 'first position', meaning that the four fingers of the left hand never leave their base on the first four frets. Once you know the whole scale, you can play tunes in the key of C major. All other major scales can be found in first position, although some are easier to play than others.

Positions

In first position, notes at the first fret are played by the first finger, notes at the second fret by the second finger – and so on. In second position, the first finger is at the second fret, and the other fingers take up their posts at the third, fourth and fifth frets. This is the most economical way of getting to the note you want to play, and it is a principle that you should aim to absorb: one finger to a fret, wherever musically possible.

RIGHT: *The left hand in first position – each finger covers one fret. In first position, open strings also form part of many scales, whereas higher positions usually use fretted notes only.*

Playing the scale of C major

Below is the scale of C major, beginning on the lowest C note that a guitar can play. The musical notation shows you the scale rising and falling one step at a time; the TAB shows you how far you can go while keeping the fingers in the first position (as far as G on the third fret of the top string – an octave plus a fifth).

The scale is written out in quavers. As we have seen, these occupy half a beat each. As with quaver-strumming patterns in $\frac{4}{4}$ time, this means that every other note here is on the beat, while those in between are on the offbeat.

While it is possible to play every note here using only downstrokes, greater speed and fluency can be achieved by alternating downstrokes on the beat with upstrokes on the offbeat. Here, the direction of the picking action is marked on the score:

ABOVE: *The right hand playing a downstroke. This is usually used on the beat.*

ABOVE: *An upstroke, usually used on offbeats (between beats).*

The symbol ⊓ indicates a downstroke, and ∨ indicates an upstroke.

The tunes opposite both use the major scale in first position and only the note/rest values we have used so far. Try recording yourself strumming the chords, and then play the melody along with this, or get a friend to play the chords while you play the melody. Or various software programs will allow you to generate a complete backing track by simply typing in the chords.

BELOW: *The C major scale in first position, using upstrokes and downstrokes. The picking pattern in the first bar is repeated throughout.*

Dots, ties and upbeats

The exercises below introduce a few new symbols and conventions. Neither of the two pieces of music begins on beat 1. Sometimes a piece can begin with an incomplete bar, also known as a pickup bar or *anacrusis*. This usually means that the final bar of the piece is also incomplete (especially if there is a repeat marked), so that the two add up to a full bar, enabling the piece to be repeated seamlessly.

EXERCISE "CAMPTOWN RACES"

A dot placed immediately after a note indicates that its duration is half as much again as its undotted value.

So, a dotted minim 𝅗𝅥. is read as three beats (2+1), and a dotted crotchet ♩. is one and a half beats.

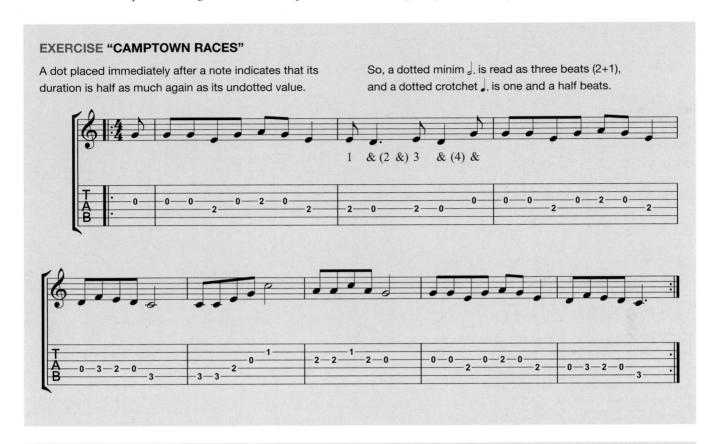

EXERCISE "ON TOP OF OLD SMOKEY"

The curved horizontal line seen between notes is called a tie. This symbol is used to join the durations of notes together, even across bar lines, so they become one long note. In this piece there are two points where two dotted minims are joined across a bar line, meaning that the note lasts for two whole bars of $\frac{3}{4}$, or six beats.

The major scales

Learning scales is a useful discipline in many ways. Committing scales to memory expands your musical vocabulary, and strengthens your command of the instrument. If you practise your scales regularly (as all serious players do), you will become better acquainted with your guitar, undertake a good practical workout and at the same time expand your theoretical knowledge of music.

What is a scale?

A scale consists of all the notes in a particular key. When we play a tune in C, we expect that most or all of the notes will be drawn from the scale of C. The scale is an inventory of structural elements of a tune, a map of the melodic landscape. When you know your scales, you are less likely to be caught out by the direction that a tune takes.

Daily practice

Starting to play the guitar can be physically wearing, particularly for the fingertips of the left hand. Calluses (pads of hardened skin) will develop but, in the meantime, don't overdo things, and stop practising if your fingertips become painful.

Understanding scales

An excursion into music theory may be helpful at this point. A Western musical scale can be seen as an arrangement of tones and semitones. Notes that are one fret apart on the same string of a guitar are one semitone apart; a tone is equal to two semitones, and is two frets apart.

The piano keyboard provides a useful way of visualizing how scales work. On the piano, adjacent keys are one semitone apart, whether they are black or white. The scale/key of C major is defined as having no sharps or flats. On the piano, this means that if you start on C and play the white notes in succession, you will hear a perfect major scale.

Most adjacent white notes are one tone apart, but the adjacent pairs B-C and E-F have no black note between them, and so are only one semitone apart. It follows that the third and fourth notes of the major scale are a semitone apart, as are the seventh and eighth.

It further follows that a scale starting from any note other than C will not have the same internal configuration of tones and semitones if only the white notes are used. One note or more will have to be adjusted (raised or lowered) in order to preserve the intervals of the major scale/key. This is where sharps and flats are introduced. If you start a scale on G, to get the semitone gaps to fall in the right place you will have to play one black note, F♯; that is the note a semitone above F. It can be said that the scale of G is defined by the fact that it contains one sharp. In fact, every key is defined by the number of sharps (or flats) that it contains.

BELOW: *Two octaves from G–G on the piano. Notice that there are no black notes (sharps/flats) between E–F or B–C.*

Middle C

Some new scales

Try playing the three major scales that are shown here. They are all in first position and use open strings where possible. Each scale starts on the lowest available root note, ascends to the highest note available in first position, descends to the lowest note in first position, and finally returns to the root – so this version of the C major is a little more extensive and challenging than the one you have already tried. Remember to stay in first position: one finger per fret.

Tip

Short daily practice sessions are far more beneficial than longer, infrequent ones, even if the total time spent is the same overall.

EXERCISE C MAJOR SCALE

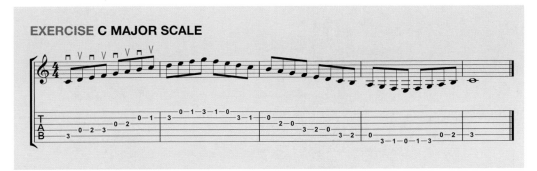

EXERCISE G MAJOR SCALE

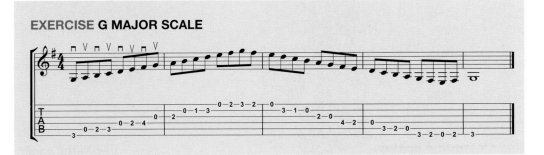

EXERCISE D MAJOR SCALE

EXERCISE CHROMATIC SCALE

This exercise is not a major scale but the chromatic scale – which simply means that it involves playing every available note. This makes it an excellent practice tool, since every fret in the first position is covered. You will notice in the musical notation that the scale contains sharps on the way up, and flats on the way down. These are the piano's black notes. A sharp or flat symbol remains in force for the rest of the bar in which it is written, unless cancelled by a 'natural' sign (symbol).

Since a sharp is a semitone above a given note, and a flat a semitone below, there are some notes that can be described either in terms of the note above or the note below: the note between A and B could be called A# or B♭. It is a convention of chromatic scales that notes are given as sharps in the ascending form, and as flats in the descending form.

Introducing the blues

It is hard to overestimate the importance of the blues to modern popular music. Without the blues, there would be no Elvis, no Beatles, no Rolling Stones, no jazz... Blues guitar can be a lifetime's study in itself, but there are two important starting points when studying the blues: the blues scale (for melodic playing and solo construction) and the twelve-bar blues chord sequence.

The blues scale

Most blues-based music gets its distinctive sound from certain notes being flattened (that is, lowered by one semitone) in relation to the major key. If you take the most important notes in the major key and add to them the flattened notes, the result is a set of notes usually known as the blues scale. Like any scale, the blues scale can generate an infinite variety of melodic effects, but the basic formula is straightforward, and it is easy to get to grips with on the guitar.

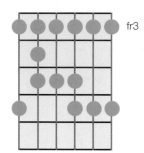

fr3

LEFT: *The notes of the blues scale form this pattern on the fretboard of the guitar. The pattern is the same whatever the key you play in (that is, wherever you start on the neck). Stick to these notes when you jam, and the result is bound to sound right.*

The 12-bar blues sequence

Many blues and rock songs are based on a simple progression of three chords – the first, fourth and fifth in the scale – played in a sequence of 12 bars. For the purposes of learning the basics, we are sticking to the key of G in all the examples and exercises on this and the opposite page.

G7	G7	G7	G7
C7	C7	G7	G7
D7	C7	G7	D7

Play this chord sequence with a simple pattern of four strums per bar at first, to get used to the sound. Singing any 12-bar blues song will further help to internalize the structure of the sequence. Try "Sweet Home Chicago", "Johnny B. Goode" or "Shake, Rattle and Roll". Better still, use the blues scale to improvise a solo of your own on top of these chords. To play the blues in G, place your fingers in the third position (that is, with the first finger based on the third fret).

Recommended listening
- B. B. King: *Live at the Regal*
- John Mayall: *Bluesbreakers with Eric Clapton*
- Stevie Ray Vaughan and Double Trouble: *Texas Flood*
- Taj Mahal: *Taj Mahal*

Charlie Patton

Often called 'The Father of the Delta Blues' as so many styles have evolved from the blues, Charlie Patton must rank as one of the most important figures in the history of popular music. Patton grew up in Mississippi around the turn of the 20th century, and developed a diverse and adaptable guitar style. Many of the best-known Delta blues musicians hailed from Patton's corner of Mississippi, and he is thought to have influenced most of them, from Robert Johnson to Howlin' Wolf and John Lee Hooker.

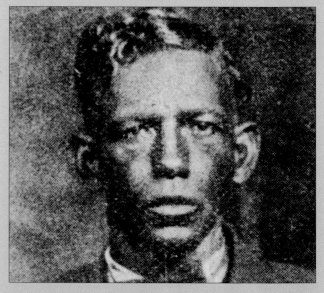

ABOVE: *Charlie Patton's voice and guitar, through the medium of scratchy and faint recordings such as "Pony Blues", provide a compelling insight into the birth of the blues.*

EXERCISE G BLUES SCALE

Play this blues scale in third position by placing your first finger at the third fret, your second at the fourth, and the third and fourth fingers at fifth and sixth frets. Notice the flattened fifth notes in each octave.

EXERCISE SIX BLUES LICKS

One of the great things about blues styles is that more or less any melodic idea constructed using the blues scale will work over any part of the chord sequence. Here are six classic blues 'licks' to get you started with this process.

EXERCISE "BEGINNER'S BLUES"

This piece combines a simple melody using the G blues scale with the 12-bar chord sequence. The best way to hear this to full effect is to record yourself playing the chord sequence (or programme the sequence using accompaniment software such as Band In A Box) and play the melody over the top.

The sixth shuffle

The sixth shuffle is a simple guitar trick, widely used in acoustic blues and electric rock 'n' roll. It is a variant of the 12-bar sequence that combines the root note with a pattern that alternates between the fifth and sixth note of the prevailing chord. That is the technical explanation; the reason the sixth shuffle is so popular is that it sounds great and really adds momentum to a song.

Using the sixth shuffle

The sixth shuffle creates a kind of driving bass rhythm that works well in any kind of bluesy jam session. Only three notes are involved, but the motion between the fifth and sixth is such a strong musical figure that the chord sequence is implied – even though the full chords do not sound in the most basic version of the idea.

Recommended listening:
- Chuck Berry: "Johnny B. Goode"
- Gary Moore: "Movin' on Down the Road"
- Tommy Tucker: "Hi-Heel Sneakers"

The basic moves

The key of A is the simplest key in which to learn the blues shuffle pattern as the root note of each chord can be found on an open string. The left hand stays in second position throughout: fretted notes are played by the first finger at the second fret and the third finger at the fourth fret. The key of A is unique in that all three chord roots of the 12-bar blues (I, IV and V) can be found on open strings. In order to transpose the sixth shuffle into other keys, the right hand forms a movable shape, with the root and fifth on the bottom two strings; the little finger stretches to play the sixth. This is simply shifted up the neck for chords IV and V. For example, C is found at the eighth fret while D is found at the tenth.

sixth shuffle

LEFT: *The left hand in position for the sixth shuffle. The first finger stays at the second fret, while the third finger 'rocks' on and off the string at the fourth fret.*

Adding the seventh

The basic sixth shuffle pattern can be elaborated in a number of ways. In the key of A, the left hand may stay in second position but proceed up to the seventh of each chord; this extra note is played by the little finger at the fifth fret. Adding the seventh in other keys requires that the movable shape explored above (G) be turned into a G7 barre chord (see 'Barre chords').

sixth shuffle G chord

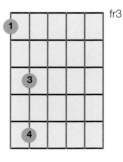

fr3

ABOVE: *The sixth shuffle G chord. The first and third fingers play the root and fifth; the little finger stretches to play the sixth.*

Swing/shuffle feel

The shuffle pattern here is written in quavers (eighth notes), or half-beat notes in $\frac{4}{4}$, but the indication 'swing' or 'shuffle' tells us something important about how these quavers should be played. In the absence of such an indication, offbeats should be played exactly halfway between beats: '1 and 2 and 3 and 4 and...' This is also known as a straight feel. Swing feel changes this by making the offbeat arrive late: '1 and2 and3 and4 and...'

The exact timing of swing offbeat depends on the tempo of the music and also varies between players and styles. It is important to be familiar enough with the swing/shuffle feel to be able to play it naturally, since it forms the rhythmic basis of most blues and jazz. To this end, all of the listening recommendations given below demonstrate the shuffle feel. However, very many classic rock'n'roll songs use a straight feel, so you need to be able to do both.

EXERCISE BASIC SHUFFLE

This exercise uses the basic shuffle pattern to play the twelve-bar blues sequence. The pattern remains the same except that it is transferred up to the D and G strings (for the D chord) and down to the low E and A strings (E).

Tip

Some blues songs simplify the structure by staying on the tonic chord in the last bar. In this example, this would mean staying on the A pattern for the last bar rather than changing to E.

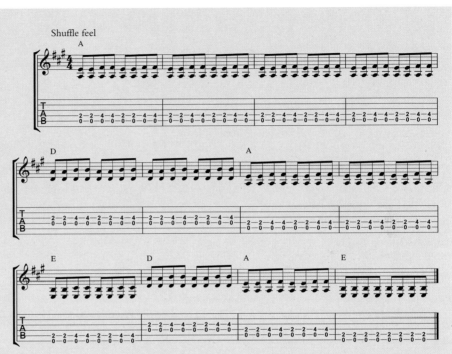

EXERCISE ADDING THE SEVENTH

This exercise adds sevenths to the blues shuffle sequence – the fourth finger is added to play the seventh at the fifth fret for each chord.

Tip

A different effect can be achieved by alternating between the two strings used for each chord rather than playing them simultaneously, somewhat in the manner of the classic "James Bond Theme" guitar line.

Building a blues solo

The blues scale is the blues guitarist's road map, but to improvise well on the guitar, you need to know your way around the fretboard instinctively. Learn licks and make up your own, but beware of trotting out the same figures every time. Instead, explore the blues scale: one route to finding new and even better solos is shown on the page opposite, but this is by no means the only way.

Tension and release

The blues scale works by creating and releasing tension in relation to the chord sequence. Some notes are consonant (they belong together) against certain chords, while others are dissonant (they clash) against others.

Arguably, the defining note of the blues scale is the flattened third (the note Bb in the key of G). When played over chord I (G7), this creates the dissonance that is characteristic of all blues-related music. However, when played later in the sequence over chord IV (C7), this note actually belongs to the chord and therefore does not sound dissonant. It is therefore possible to play a phrase over chord I in the first line, which creates tension; this is released when the same phrase is played over chord IV in the second line. In any case, repetition usually works well in a blues context.

This 'tension and release' approach is found in many blues themes and improvised solos. Although it is possible to extend this effect into the third line of the blues, another popular soloing ploy involves modifying the melodic material used in the first two lines to create an 'answer'.

This call-and-response style has been central to the development of the blues, and is reflected in the lyrics of many blues songs. The first line of the verse is an opening statement or question, the second line repeats this (usually exactly), and the third line 'rounds off' the verse in the form of an answer or explanation.

Blues classics such as "Dust My Broom" (Robert Johnson), "Stormy Monday" (T-Bone Walker) and "Before You Accuse Me" (Bo Diddley) all contain this idea. Exercise 1 (opposite) is a blues solo using this pattern.

Outside the blues

The blues scale is such a powerful vehicle for improvisation that it often works well even when the chords are not strictly a blues sequence. When used in the minor key, the flattened third is no longer dissonant, because it belongs to the key. The scale still has a bluesy flavour, however, especially if you lean heavily on the flattened fifth. This possibility is explored in Exercise 2 on the opposite page.

When using the blues scale over any chord sequence, the important thing is to identify the key correctly. Using a blues scale in the wrong key will generally result in some strange dissonances that do not contribute to a blues feel. The key may be identified from a music theory perspective, but it is also important to be able to hear where the key centre lies: listen for the chord that sounds like 'home', the point in the music where the harmony feels as though it has come to rest. For this reason, the tonic chord (chord I) is often found as both the first and last chord of many chord sequences.

Recommended listening:

- Buddy Guy & Junior Wells: *Alone & Acoustic*
- Eric Bibb: *Natural Light*
- Eric Clapton: *Unplugged*

RIGHT: *Brownie McGhee's name is often omitted from the 'front rank' of 20th-century blues guitarists, perhaps because he focused so well on accompanying Sonny Terry's harmonica.*

Brownie McGhee

Best known as one half of a duo with the harmonica player and singer Sonny Terry, Brownie McGhee bestrode the worlds of blues and folk, creating subtle but powerful accompaniments to Terry's wailing, honking, pleading harmonica lines. One of the 'classic' Southern bluesmen born in the second generation of the 20th century, McGhee's career included fruitful collaborations with some of the biggest names in blues, from Champion Jack Dupree to Big Bill Broonzy. Brownie McGhee's style is often sensitively minimal, but he was not afraid to embark on gutsy solo ideas, even with no supporting musicians.

EXERCISE 1

A new rhythm value is introduced in this solo: the quaver triplet. A group of three quavers with a '3' above indicates that the beat here is divided into three (rather than two, as with an ordinary pair of quavers).

Tip

The triplet is arguably the basis of the swing feel, at least at slow/medium tempos: the swing offbeat is in time with what would be the third note of a quaver triplet.

EXERCISE 2

This exercise overlays the G blues scale on a G minor chord sequence. For maximum benefit, either record yourself playing the chords or get a friend to play them while you play the solo.

Tip

Automatic accompaniment software can also be very useful for the purpose of this exercise, and may even inject some blues 'feel' for added inspiration.

Advanced blues

The blues scale, powerful as it is, is not the sum total of the melodic possibilities that are available to blues players. For increased melodic potential when improvising in a blues style – or in any other style – you can also make full use of all the notes that make up the chords in the progression, paying attention to which of these chords you are playing over at any one time.

Using notes with chords

Almost every note in the octave can be used in a blues context. Fluid improvisation is about knowing which notes can be used over which chords. The table below represents an analysis of each note in relation to the three chords of the 12-bar sequence. For this exercise, we are using the key of G: I7 (G7), IV7 (C7) and V7 (D7). Bear in mind that the *relationships* of the notes to the chords will be the same in any other key. So, for example, the note that is a semitone above the tonic (A♭ in this instance) is always to be avoided.

BELOW: *All the notes shown here in the notation and in the tablature relate to the blues scale in third position.*

	Note	Part of chords	Comments		Note	Part of chords	Comments
	G	G7 C7	The tonic (key) note		C#/D♭	-	Dissonant/bluesy against all chords in the sequence; resolves down to C or up to D
	A♭	-	AVOID		D	G7 D7	Usable anywhere
	A	D7	Not used much, but part of the dominant (D7) and used as a passing note		E♭	-	AVOID
	B♭	C7	The flattened third – THE blue note in relation to the key, also part of the C7 chord		E	C7	The third of C7; also used as a passing note
	B	G7	The third of G7; the flattened third resolves to this note; to be avoided over C7		F	G7	The seventh of G7 and a blue note in relation to both the key and the D7 chord
	C	C7 D7	Usable anywhere		F#	D7	The third of D7; avoid this note over G7

The blues sequence

This is much the same as saying that the blues scale itself can be used over any part of the blues sequence. Notes that are not present in the blues scale may be used either as chord tones or as passing notes against other chords.

Recommended listening:

● Big Bill Broonzy: *Big Bill Broonzy Sings Country Blues*
● Lightnin' Hopkins, Sonny Terry & Brownie McGhee: *Blues Hoot*
● Jimmy Reed: *Jimmy Reed at Carnegie Hall*

ABOVE: *Brownie McGhee and blues singer/harmonica player Sonny Terry. Their on-and-off blues partnership lasted for several decades (1958–80).*

RIGHT: *Hopkins usually played alone, owing much to Blind Lemon Jefferson's fingerpicking style, maintaining a full accompaniment of bass and chords under his vocal line.*

Lightnin' Hopkins

Sam 'Lightnin' Hopkins was one of the handful of bluesmen with a direct link to the blues tradition through the early musicians who were active into the late 20th century (he died in 1982). Hopkins grew up in the heart of Texas and learnt both from family members who were steeped in the blues, and also from the legendary Blind Lemon Jefferson, one of the first singers to record the blues. Jefferson's influence is one of many that can be heard in Hopkins' guitar work, as well as in his singing style. Although his contemporaries John Lee Hooker and Muddy Waters achieved greater fame, Hopkins continued the 'lone bluesman' tradition of Jefferson; his influence can be heard in the next generation's acoustic and electric players alike.

EXERCISE ADVANCED BLUES

This blues solo here uses both chord notes and passing notes. Note the hammer-ons (slurring to produce a smooth sequence) between B♭ and B natural (and later between F and F♯): the first note is written as a cue note (small) with a line through it, often called a grace note, indicating that it should be played as quickly as possible just before the main note. Every note here can be found in third position; any notes outside the blues scale do not require moving the left hand out of position.

The 12-bar sequence is also modified slightly here, by introducing chord IV7 (C7) in bar 2.

Barre chords

In all the chords that you have learnt so far, the fingers of the left hand have fretted one note each. But in order to make some chords, especially the more unusual ones, it may sometimes be necessary for one finger to act like a movable capo that frets some or all six strings at once. The chords that are formed in this manner are called barre chords, and form an essential part of most players' chord repertoire.

Making barre chords

Barre chords (sometimes called 'movable chords') make it possible to move the standard chord shapes up and down the neck, and so to access the full range of chords. Making the barre involves flattening a finger – usually the first finger – across all the strings (or most of them). This will feel difficult and unnatural at first – but you will get used to it. It is worth the effort, because you will be limited in what you play if you can only manage the first-position chords.

Since your first finger is occupied in making the barre, you have only three fingers available to make the rest of the shape – and not the three fingers that you are used to using. For example, the F major chord here uses fingers 2, 3 and 4 to form the fretted notes of the E shape.

Fretting the F chord

1 Form the barre with the first finger at the first fret. For the F chord, the barre should span all six strings.

2 Consulting the chord box, form the E shape with the second, third and fourth fingers relative to the barre (one fret higher than the standard E shape).

3 Check that the chord sounds clearly, paying particular attention to fret buzz, which may occur if the barre is too far away from the fret.

Moving the barre

An alternative way of forming a G major chord can be achieved by moving the barred shape up to the third fret. Sometimes this is the most economical way to move from F to G or vice versa.

The barre is shown in chord-box format as a curved line linking notes at the same fret. For visual simplicity, only the sounding notes are shown, even though the barre is in place behind the other fretted notes.

ABOVE: *F and G major barre chords based on the E shape. Exactly the same shape is used for both chords.*

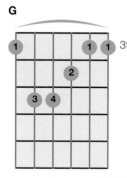 

ABOVE: *The symbol '3fr' indicates that the G chord box starts at the third fret.*

Other shapes

In principle, almost any three-finger chord can be moved up the neck using a barre. In practice, some shapes are much more convenient than others. The E major shape is essential; E minor and A minor are also extremely useful shapes from which to make barre chords, and quite easy to do. The C shape also works well, but is harder to hold down, because it stretches over four frets, making it more susceptible to accidental buzzing and muffled sounds.

B♭m

Fm

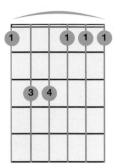

D♭

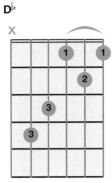

Chord slash notation

The chord sequences below are shown in a form of notation generally known as chord slashes. Each bar contains four diagonal slashes, corresponding to four beats in the time signature, but these are not necessarily intended to dictate four strict strums per bar. Rather, the exact strumming (or even picking) pattern is left to the player's own taste. Where there are exact rhythms that are required in the piece, these are integrated by adding stems and tails (as in the final bar of Exercise 2 here); the note-heads remain in the 'slash' style to indicate that only rhythm (rather than pitch) is being conveyed. Even here, there is some freedom in the exact technique that is used to deliver the rhythm.

EXERCISE 1

If you form barres from E, Am and C at the first fret, these three shapes result in Fm, B♭m and D♭ chords respectively. These are all useful chords. This exercise combines Fm and B♭m with open chords to produce an interesting sequence.

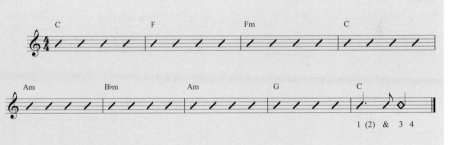

EXERCISE 2

Barre chords can be hard work, even a little painful at first. The easiest way to bring them into use is to employ them in combination with open chords to allow the fingers some rest. This exercise uses the E-shaped F chord within a chord sequence in the key of C major.

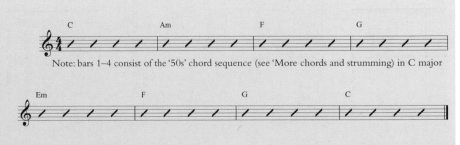

Note: bars 1–4 consist of the '50s' chord sequence (see 'More chords and strumming') in C major

More on barre chords

The beauty of barre chords is that they make hundreds more chords available to you as a guitarist and are therefore widely used in many styles of music. You don't have to learn every chord separately: instead, you deploy a few shapes – most of which you already know – combined with some barre technique and a little theoretical knowledge. The E shape and the A shape alone will take you a long way.

The two magic shapes

If you knew just one barre chord shape for each chord type, you would theoretically be able to use this shape anywhere on the neck, and so open up the full range of musical keys. But this would still require a lot of movement, and would sometimes take you into the difficult upper areas of the neck.

But if you knew two shapes in different parts of the scale, you would always have an option. You could barre any chord in a sensible, economical way. This route is in fact open to you. Once you know all the important chord types associated with the E shape and the A shape (that is: major, minor, seventh and minor seventh), then you will have a way of playing the vast bulk of rock, pop, blues and folk songs – and a fair amount of jazz, too.

RIGHT: *The A-shaped barre. On the first fret, this makes B♭, which is an important chord when you are playing in the key of F.*

Some players find the A shape hard to use in barre chord form, as it involves all four fingers in a rather awkward stretch: the first finger barres all six strings; the other three must crowd into one fret that is quite a stretch away.

Chords for the shapes

Here are all the chord types for both the E shape and the A shape. None of them are as difficult to master as the A major shape that you have just learnt, and there is in any case an alternative way of playing that shape – that is, by using the first finger on the fifth string and a short barre across the second third and fourth (the top E string is usually not played).

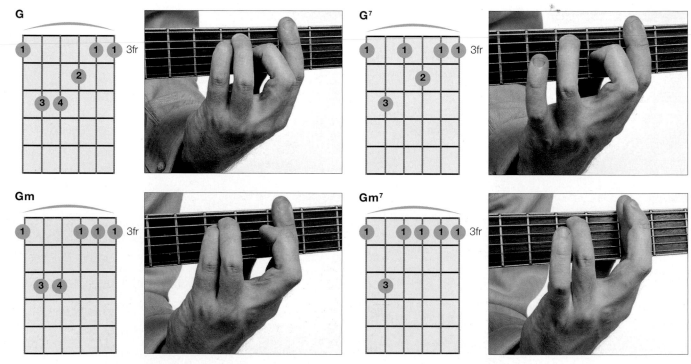

ABOVE: *Barre chords – root E string. All of these chords are based on first position chords (E, E7, Em, Em7).*

Third-fret barre chords

For comparison, barre chords are shown here at the third fret. As this corresponds to the note G on the E string and the note C on the A string, this produces 'G' chords and 'C' chords respectively. This fact demonstrates the benefit of knowing two shapes for each type: you can go from, say, Gm7 to Cm7 while staying at the third fret (a very common chord change). With only one shape in your repertoire, a shift up the neck of five or seven frets would be required.

C

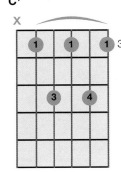

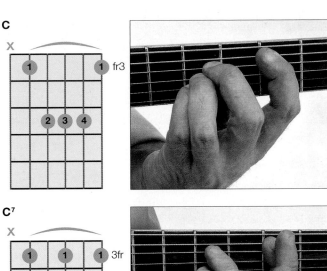

C Alternative shape

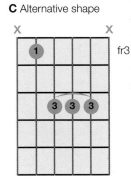

C⁷

Cm

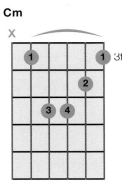

Cm⁷

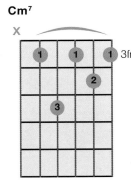

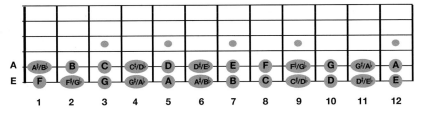

Finding the root

To get the maximum potential out of these shapes, you need to know where to find the root of any given chord. With practice this becomes second nature; until then, the fretboard chart to the right shows every note on the bottom two strings.

	1	2	3	4	5	6	7	8	9	10	11	12
A	A♯/B♭	B	C	C♯/D♭	D	D♯/E♭	E	F	F♯/G♭	G	G♯/A♭	A
E	F	F♯/G♭	G	G♯/A♭	A	A♯/B♭	B	C	C♯/D♭	D	D♯/E♭	E

EXERCISE

The best way to memorize the note locations on the fretboard chart is to have to find them yourself. To this end, any chord sequence can be used as two separate exercises; choosing an 'E'-based shape for the first chord will result in one set of shapes, while an 'A' shape will result in another. In this exercise the first two chords may be played in two ways: Fm7 (1st fret) followed by B♭m7 (1st fret) or Fm7 (8th fret) followed by B♭m7 (6th fret).

Fm⁷ B♭m⁷ A♭ D♭

Gm⁷ C⁷ Fm⁷ Fm⁷

(let ring)

Understanding keys

Getting to grips with how key signatures work makes it possible to play melodies and construct chord sequences in any key. It also opens up the entire fretboard for practice and for musical exploration. The relationships between the major keys are built on a few simple principles, which are explained here. Each major key is also closely related to a minor key – equally important in many styles.

THE CIRCLE OF FIFTHS

As we have seen, the key of C major is unique in that it has no sharps or flats (which are the 'black' notes on the piano). It is constructed entirely using 'white' notes, also known as naturals. All other keys contain sharps and flats. These occur in a logical arrangement that can be described with a device called the circle of fifths.

In the circle of fifths, each key has one more sharp (going clockwise) or flat (going anti-clockwise) than the preceding one. And each key is one fifth above the one that comes before it. For example, D major is a fifth above G major, and has two sharps in the key signature where G major has only 1.

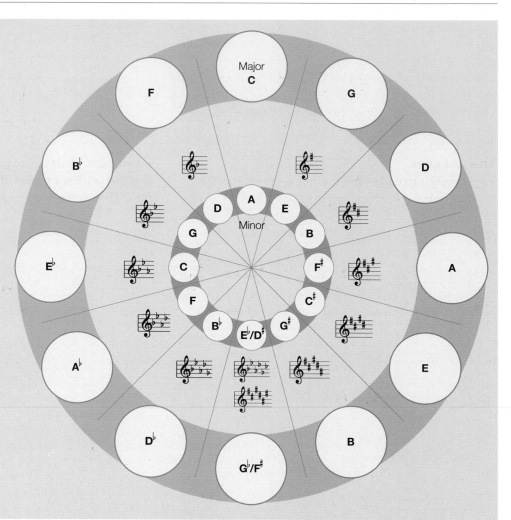

Davey Graham

Among the most influential of British folk guitarists, Davey Graham was one of the first musicians to expand the bounds of 'folk' music to flavours from beyond the UK or even Europe. His compositions incorporated elements of Indian and Arab music, and borrowed blues ideas for use in a Celtic folk context. His most famous composition, "Anji", has become one of the classic guitar instrumentals, with recorded versions by Simon and Garfunkel, Gordon Giltrap and John Renbourn, among others. The early date of this composition (1962) makes a strong case for him as the inventor of the modern folk instrumental.

LEFT: *As well as pioneering DADGAD tuning (see 'DADGAD tuning'), which was later widely adopted among folk players, Davey Graham is sometimes credited as the father of World Music for using elements of folk music from other cultures.*

The major keys: sharps

The scale of G major is a perfect fifth above C. It contains one sharp (F#), and so is the first key in the cycle of 'sharp' keys. Each new key in the circle is a perfect fifth above the last, and introduces a new sharp that is also a perfect fifth above the last and the leading note of the new key.

Ascending in fifths gives us the keys C – G – D – A – E – B – F#. The 'new' sharpened notes in each key are F# – C# – G# – D# – A#. New sharps appear in the key signature at the start of each line in this order.

Although we have defined sharps and flats as 'black notes' on the piano keyboard, there are actually only five black keys in each octave, and we have still only defined eight keys in this way. In fact, the last sharp in this sequence, E#, is not even a black note, but the same physical note as F. Likewise, the note Cb (physically B natural) is found in the key of Gb major.

The relative minor

Each major key shares its key signature with another key: its relative minor. For each key signature, the relative minor is found a minor third below the major (or the sixth step of the scale). For example, the key signature with no sharps or flats is shared by C major and A minor; one flat indicates F major or D minor. Because the key centre is different, the internal arrangement of notes in the scale is different, resulting in a different mood from the major key (just as minor chords sound different from major chords). The natural minor scale uses the same set of notes as its relative major; other types of minor scale are constructed by modifying it in various ways, for example by raising the seventh note by one semi-tone, resulting in the harmonic minor scale (see 'Gypsy jazz').

The flat keys

It is important to understand that just as the notes of the C major scale can be sharpened (or raised), they can also be lowered, or in other words, flattened. In the same way as F becomes F# to give us the first sharp key, the note B is lowered to Bb (B flat) to give us the key of F major, the first 'flat' key. F is a perfect fifth *below* C. The flat key side of the circle is constructed by proceeding downwards in fifths, which gives guitar players each new key, as well as giving them each new flat note.

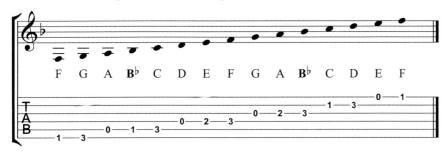

F G A B♭ C D E F G A B♭ C D E F

LEFT: *The F major scale in first position. Every note is a natural except for B♭, which defines the key signature.*

EXERCISE FINDING NEW KEYS ON THE FRETBOARD

All of these new keys can be located easily in first position on the guitar. The fretboard chart here shows the name of every note on the first four frets. To play any major scale, proceed as follows:

1 Find the lowest available root note (for example, for an F major scale, find the lowest F: bottom E string, first fret).

2 Using the circle diagram, check which notes of the scale will be sharps or flats (in F, the note B is lowered to B♭).

3 Play all the available note names in first position, from the lowest root note to the highest available root note, remembering that all notes will be natural except those specifically modified by the key signature (e.g. F major: F, G, A, B♭, C, D, E).

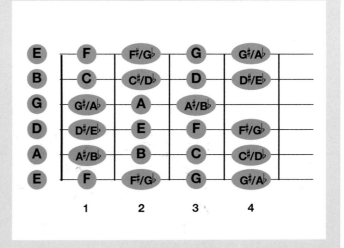

Chord construction

Some combinations of notes sound pleasing, while others sound dissonant – but why should this be? Fundamentally, the effect of a combination of notes derives from the intervals between them. The space between any two notes represents a harmonic relationship to which we instinctively have an emotional reaction. A minor third is inexplicably melancholy; a major third, universally upbeat.

Understanding intervals

The interval between two notes simply describes how far apart they are. The interval is defined by the number of steps up the scale from the lower note to the higher one. For example, the interval C–E is a third, because we can count three steps (C, D, E), whereas A–E is a fifth because it represents five steps (A, B, C, D, E).

These simple terms do not give the whole picture, however. Consider the two intervals C–E and D–F. Both are thirds, yet they sound different. Closer inspection reveals that the interval

C–E spans two tones, whereas D–F is only one tone and a semitone. The former, being the larger interval, is called a major third, and the latter a minor third. All other intervals are also broadly defined by the number of scale steps, and precisely defined by the number of semitones.

A few intervals are particularly important if you want to understand basic chord construction. The best way to view them is in relation to a fixed lower note. Using the note C on the A string (third fret), we can find all the important intervals in first position and listen to them for comparison (see below).

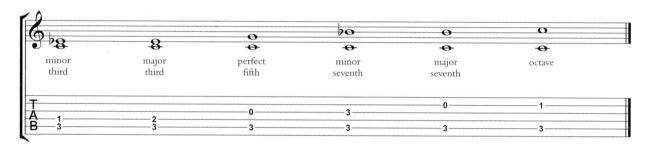

What makes a chord?

Any simultaneous sounding of two or more notes may be considered a chord. Western classical harmony uses mainly three-note chords (also known as triads), but jazz, pop and rock often use more complex chords with four notes or more (for example, dominant seventh and minor seventh chords

contain four notes). It is important not to confuse the number of different notes in a chord with the number of strings played in a guitar chord shape. Open guitar chords such as E and G use all six strings but many notes are doubled in different octaves (for example, the familiar E shape contains three E notes), so there are still only three unique notes.

C triad (C major triad)

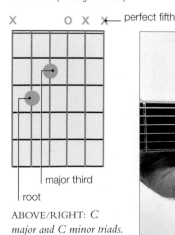

ABOVE/RIGHT: *C major and C minor triads.*

Cm triad (C minor triad)

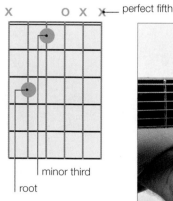

Thirds

Chords are usually constructed as a stack of thirds. Starting with the root note of the chord, we add a note a third above, and then another note a third above that.

To minimize confusion, both of these are usually defined in terms of their relationship to the root note, and therefore known as the third and fifth of the chord. The third and fifth are defined independently in relation to the root. For example, a major chord is said to contain a major third and a perfect fifth; a minor chord contains a minor third and perfect fifth. From the intervals chart shown on the opposite page, we can simultaneously play the root (C), perfect fifth (G), and either the major or minor third (E or E♭). These combinations will result in the major and minor triads respectively.

More complex chords

Chord construction may be continued in this way, becoming progressively more complex as we add more thirds: after the third and fifth various sevenths, ninths, elevenths and thirteenths may be added (although these notes are not often used all together to avoid internal clashes, and for the simple reason that the guitar has only six strings).

Seventh chords are commonplace in most popular music styles; more complex chords, originating in jazz, have also found their way into many pop styles, perhaps the most notable of these is soul music. We have encountered two types of third interval and two types of seventh. When combined with the root and perfect fifth, this results in four types of seventh chord. These are shown below as extensions of the C major and minor triads that are illustrated on the opposite page.

Normally in C the fifth would be played on the open G string. In some of the chords below, we use the G string to play the minor seventh – a B♭ on the third fret. This means that there is no fifth in the chord as it is played, but this does not matter as seventh chords sound strong even when the fifth is omitted, and in fact this is often the case in jazz, where seventh chords are very often outlined using just the root, third and seventh.

Cmaj7 (C major seven)

major seventh

major third

root

Cm(maj7) (C minor, major 7)

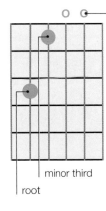
major seventh

minor third

root

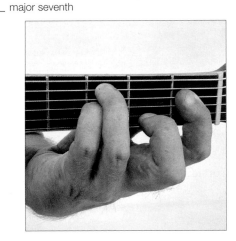

C7 (C seven)

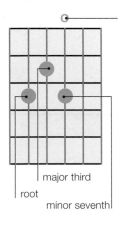
perfect fifth

major third

root

minor seventh

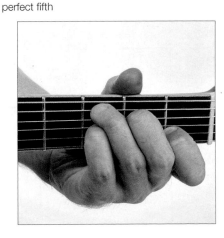

Cm7 (C minor seven)

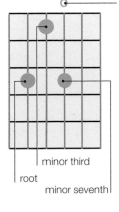
perfect fifth

minor third

root

minor seventh

How to find any note

Acquiring total knowledge of the guitar fretboard is a gradual process. Being able to name any note on the fretboard instantly (or, in reverse, to be able to find any named note on a given string) is the first step towards this. If you have the right theory knowledge, you can then start to construct chords yourself from first principles, rather than looking them up each time.

Knowing the notes

There are several ways to become familiar with all the available notes on the fretboard. You could simply learn the names of all the notes on all the strings by memorizing them individually, but this is time-consuming and dull, and it is hard to make use of the knowledge in a practical playing situation. There are other, more helpful ways to get to know your way around the neck, and to learn the names of all the places your fingers might want to stop. One approach involves thinking about the relationships between known and unknown notes.

Octave relationships

It makes sense to prioritize memorizing the notes on the two bottom strings (E and A). This is because the root notes of movable chord shapes are usually found on one of these strings. Playing as much material as possible using movable shapes (while also excellent practice in itself) will help these names to sink in. The chart of barre chords (see 'Barre chords') is a useful reference.

Once you know the names of the notes on the bottom strings, you can quickly find other notes by 'referring back' to those strings, using the octave interval and its shape on the fretboard. Two notes an octave apart (with the same letter name) will have a fixed physical relationship on the guitar fretboard: they are separated by a certain distance of strings and frets. Thus, a note on the upper strings may be named by quickly finding the note one or two octaves below. The shapes represented by these octave relationships are also important in themselves to many playing styles.

BELOW: *Octave intervals span two strings in all cases and two frets if the lower note is on the bottom E or A string, or three frets if the lower note is on the D or G string.*

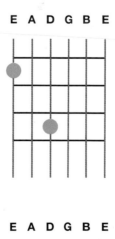

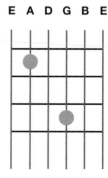

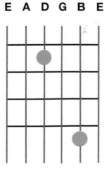

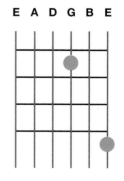

Identifying notes

The process for this is as follows:

• To identify an unknown note on the D or G string, find the note an octave below by jumping two strings down and two frets back.

• To identify an unknown note on the B string, find the note an octave below by jumping two strings down and three frets back. If this note is also unknown, repeat the process for finding an unknown note on the D string.

• The low and high E strings are two octaves apart and thus share the same note names at any given fret, making it unnecessary to learn the notes on the top E string separately.

ABOVE: *To find the note name of the D string, on the sixth fret, relate back to the E string on the fourth fret (G#/Ab).*

ABOVE: *To find the note name of the G string, on the seventh fret, relate back to the A string on the fifth fret (D).*

Horizontal relationships

The octave relationship is complemented by a horizontal relationship: the fixed interval of one semitone between frets. Therefore, an unknown note can be related to a known note on the same string by counting the frets between and proceeding up or down the chromatic scale, remembering that there is no sharp/flat between the notes B and C, or between E and F.

Any notes at or above the 12th fret can also be related back to the lower frets: the 12th fret is an octave above the open string. Therefore, the 13th fret is an octave above the first fret; the 14th fret corresponds to the second, and so on.

ABOVE: *Because there are 12 frets to a complete octave, note names start again above the 12th fret. Therefore, the top E string at the 13th fret produces an F (an octave above the first fret).*

EXERCISE 1

Place one left-hand finger anywhere on the fretboard, without looking. Then, using the methods outlined above, work out the name of the note.

EXERCISE 2

In reverse: choose a string and a note name at random. Then find it, either working up the string one fret at a time or by relating to a known note.

How to transpose without a capo

As we have seen, the capo is extremely useful in that it enables quick transposition without any knowledge of music theory. Sometimes we need to transpose a song without using the capo. The chords in the new key will have different shapes, and in some cases will only be playable as barre chords. Finding the chords in the new key can require a little more knowledge.

Interval analysis

There are several ways to transpose a chord sequence into a new key, but they all require a good working knowledge of both intervals and keys.

The most direct approach simply involves analyzing the relationship between the two keys and applying that relationship to each chord in the sequence. For instance, if we wish to move a song from the key of C major to D major, as C and D are a major second (one tone) apart, each chord in the sequence will have to be transposed upwards by this interval. It is important to note that the chord type is always unaffected by transposition: only the chord root changes. In this example, C major becomes D major, Dm becomes Em, G7 becomes A7, and so on.

The safest way to analyze any interval relationship is in terms of semitones: on the guitar this is equivalent to a number of frets on the same string: count the number of semitones between the original key and the desired new key, and apply this to each chord in the sequence. It is also important to realize that the absolute direction of transposition is unimportant: there are ten semitones between G to F when counted upwards, but only two (or a whole tone) when counted downwards, and this is a far easier interval to deal with. In this way, you will never have to deal with any interval greater than a fifth.

Picking the key

If you have any freedom to choose (for example, when playing with a singer who simply needs a song a little higher rather than being restricted to a certain key), it is usually a good idea to bear in mind the relative difficulty of the chord shapes you will encounter in the new key. For example, a chord sequence in G major may be entirely composed of easy first-position shapes, but will require barre chords (or other movable shapes) throughout if transposed up one semitone to A♭ major. The key of A major (another semitone up) would usually be a better choice, as the main chords in this key can also be played in first position.

When deciding on a new key for a song, you may wish to consult the table below. This shows the main chords in the six most guitar-friendly keys; the really important chords (the major chords or three-chord trick) are shown in bold. Each row shows the main chords in one key; simply locate the original chord in that key, and then find the new chord in the appropriate row of the same column. For example, when transposing from the key of A to D (one row down), the D chord becomes a G chord.

The majority of songs can be transposed in this way, and of course any chord types not found here can still be transposed in the same way – only the root note or 'letter' name of the chord is important in determining the transposed chord.

Transposition table

	I	II	III	IV	V	VI
E major	**E**	F#m	G#m	**A**	**B**	C#m
A major	**A**	Bm	C#m	**D**	**E**	F#m
D major	**D**	Em	F#m	**G**	**A**	Bm
G major	**G**	Am	Bm	**C**	**D**	Em
C major	**C**	Dm	Em	**F**	**G**	Am

1950s chord sequence

This chord sequence (see 'Syncopated strumming') can be transposed easily. Let's go from the key of G to the key of E.

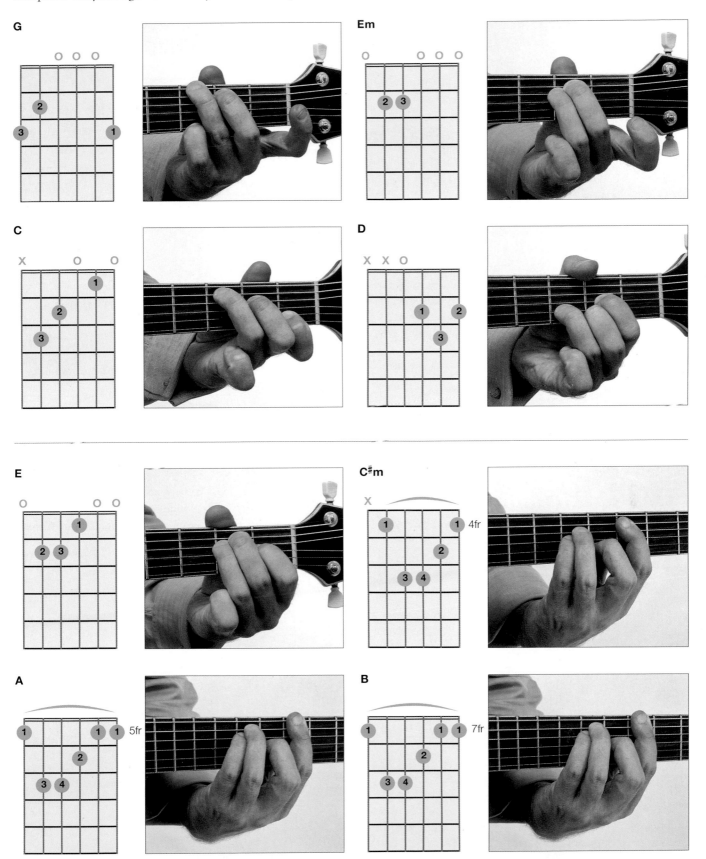

G

Em

C

D

E

C#m

A

B

Left-hand embellishments

The left hand can do more than fret the strings while the right hand plays the notes. It can fret the strings when they are already sounding, so as to elicit two notes from each right-hand stroke. You can add a finger at a higher fret to raise the pitch of a ringing string (a hammer-on), or remove a finger to lower it (a pull-off). Some styles incorporate both techniques liberally.

Slurring

Hammer-ons and pull-offs are fundamental techniques that can add a great deal of texture to your playing. They are both forms of 'slurring', which is a musical term that means deliberately altering the pitch without separately enunciating the change. Hammer-ons and pull-offs are often used sequentially in order to produce a smooth sequence of three or more notes – a kind of extended slur.

Hammer-on

In its simplest form, this technique involves a sequence of two sounding notes, but only the first is played by the right hand. As the name suggests, the second note is produced by 'hammering' a left-hand finger on to a string which is already ringing. The first note may be either an open string or a lower fretted note. This technique can be integrated into fingerpicking, on either bass or treble strings and in either bass/strum or arpeggio styles. Hammer-ons are also often used in melodic playing; a two-note phrase played in this way can sound more fluid than two individually picked notes. The hammer-on is usually shown in both standard notation and tablature using a slur (curved line) joining two ascending notes on the same string, sometimes with the letters 'H' or 'HO'.

1 Hammer-on from open string: play the open D string, then hammer on to the second fret (E).

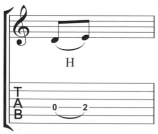

2 Hammer-on between fretted notes: play the second fret (E), then hammer on to the third fret (F).

Slur symbol

Pull-offs are also shown using a slur symbol, and may be accompanied by the indication 'PO'. The 'H' and 'PO' symbols are not always used, though, because the context differentiates them: if the slur is ascending, it is accomplished by hammering-on; if it is descending, then it must be a pull-off. Slurs should not be confused with ties (see 'The C major scale and first position').

Pull-off

The pull-off creates a descending figure that is, in effect, the opposite of a hammer-on. After playing the first note conventionally, the fretting finger is pulled away from the string to allow a second note to sound. Again, this can either be an open string or a lower fretted note.

Most pull-offs involve some downward motion of the finger. This has the effect of setting the second note ringing; in effect the left-hand finger is lightly plucking the string.

This is done because pulling-off, in its basic form, can have the effect of deadening the string, so the volume would be reduced if it were not given a little extra boost.

This type of pull-off is particularly effective on the top E string, since there is no adjacent string in the way, and is often used in folk guitar styles as an embellishment when finger-picking the chord of D major. Although not his unique invention, this is one of James Taylor's stock-in-trade ideas (see 'Using the fingers').

1 Pull-off to open string: play the second fret (E), then pull off to the open string (D).

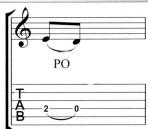

2 Pull-off between fretted notes: play the third fret (F), then pull off to the second fret (E).

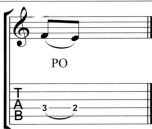

EXERCISES 1 and 2

The major scale can be adapted into an excellent exercise, which manages to incorporate these techniques. The two examples here use hammer-ons in the ascending G major scale and pull-offs on the way down. Exercise 1 uses hammer-ons and pull-offs involving open strings, while Exercise 2 places the two of them between fretted notes.

Country picking

The acoustic guitar is central to the sound of country music. But country-style guitar is defined more by the technique than the instrument itself. The terms *banjo style*, *clawhammer* and *chicken pickin'* are often used to describe country guitar-playing. These involve busy thumb movement in the right hand, combined with fluid chordal figures and percussive rhythmic stabs played on the treble strings.

Elements of the style

In country-picking style, the thumb maintains a constant 'rocking' motion, alternating between bass notes on every beat of the bar. The root and fifth (see 'Chord construction') work well for this purpose with most chord shapes, although the driving rhythm is actually more important than the exact choice of bass notes. Merle Travis, regarded as the founder of this style, often struck several bass strings together for added power. The bass notes should be combined with the fingers in such a way as to give the impression of independent parts, rather as a pianist may maintain a bass line with the left hand while playing chords or a melody with the right hand. While arpeggio-based fingerstyle work uses the index, middle and ring fingers separately, country picking often uses two or three of them together to pluck chords on the treble strings.

The B7 chord

The B7 chord, another dominant seventh in first position, works well in the key of E major – a popular key in country, blues and rock'n'roll. Particular care should be taken not to let the open bottom E string sound when playing this chord.

Pick 'n' fingers

As we have seen, conventional fingerstyle players use the nails of the right hand, which may be supported by a thumbpick and one or more fingerpicks. Many players also use a plectrum for strumming or melodic playing, but it can be awkward to have to pick up and put down the plectrum when shifting from one manner of playing to the other.

A solution to this technical problem, one favoured mainly by country players, involves playing the bass line with a plectrum held between the thumb and index finger, while the other three fingers do the picking on the top three strings. Since the rarely used index finger is occupied holding the plectrum, the rarely used little finger is then brought into play to cover the top string.

Some players find it hard to get the fourth finger to work independently of the third, so it is worth focusing on this aspect by practising arpeggio figures with this combined plectrum/fingerpicking technique.

Recommended listening
- Chet Atkins: "Travelin'"
- Elizabeth Cotton: "Freight Train"
- Dolly Parton: "Jolene"
- Elvis Presley (Scotty Moore): "Mystery Train"
- James Taylor: "Oh Susannah"

LEFT: *The right hand here is using a hybrid pick/fingers technique. Some work may be necessary to achieve independence between the third and fourth fingers.*

Merle Travis

Born in 1917, Merle Travis belonged to the generation that laid the foundations of modern country music before World War II. Although he contributed a clutch of songs that have earned a place in the American songbook (Tennessee Ernie Ford, a recording artist and TV presenter, had a huge radio hit with Travis's classic "Sixteen Tons"), Travis will probably be remembered even more for his style of guitar playing. As one of the first players to adopt and popularize the thumbpick, Travis developed the combination of constant bass motion and syncopated chords or melodic ideas that is today so instantly identifiable as 'country picking', but is in fact a rich mix of stylistic influences, including jazz, blues and ragtime (which was strongly represented in Travis's instrumental recordings). His influence can be heard on many country records, not least via Chet Atkins, who adopted and refined Travis's picking technique.

ABOVE: *Merle Travis is one of the few who can justifiably be said to have invented a whole style of guitar playing.*

EXERCISE 1

This exercise shows a bass line in the Merle Travis style. It should be played with the thumb only, and needs to be fluent before you can add the treble strings. Don't worry if the moving thumb sometimes cuts notes off: this staccato effect is often a key part of the style.

EXERCISE 2

Here, chord notes are added separately and together. Unlike the bass movement, these chord notes should be allowed to ring on for as long as possible, even when shown as quavers (half beats). You can use the staccato effect here, too, for a contrasting result. The notes on the top string, if accented and allowed to ring on, will function as a melodic strand.

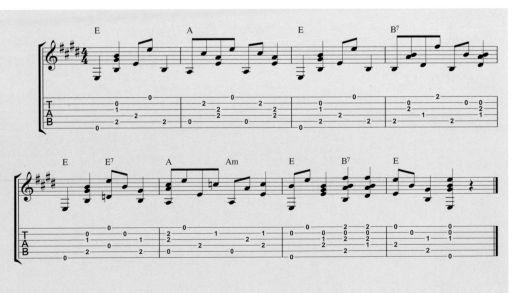

Advanced country guitar

Country guitar often combines left- and right-hand techniques such as arpeggiated chords and the fluid use of hammer-ons and pull-offs. First-position chord shapes are favoured since they require little movement in the left hand. These chords also make for an effective sound: all the notes can ring freely, and melodic ideas can be integrated into the accompaniment.

Adding melody

The next step in developing banjo-style fingerpicking is to embellish a chordal accompaniment by adding fragments of melody. The easiest approach, particularly for fast playing, is to start with a familiar chord sequence so that the bass (thumb) motion will remain secure. Hammer-ons and pull-offs form an important part of this style, as they allow rapid melodic motion between beats. These slurs help to create a melodic

line, and at the same time they sound much more fluid than the same notes picked individually.

Country ballads are often supported by sparse instrumental accompaniment dominated by the acoustic guitar. As the vocal line is often delivered using long, slow notes, the guitar maintains a sense of motion using continuous arpeggio patterns. This is sometimes known as 'ballad style', and is explored in Exercise 2, opposite.

Two new chords

You will encounter the E7 chord in Exercise 1, below. Here, the seventh is added on the B string (third fret) instead of the open D string. This is useful here, as it allows the top notes of the chords in bars 5 and 6 to form a descending melody.

Exercise 2 features the B minor barre chord. This is formed by barring the A minor shape at the second fret. The B string hammer-on used in the exercise (from the barre to the third fret) is a stock-in-trade folk/country guitar figure. Another popular move, as used in Dolly Parton's classic "Jolene", involves a simultaneous hammer-on by the second, third and fourth fingers: strum or pick the notes formed by the barre alone, then hammer the rest of the fingers into place.

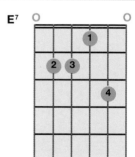

ABOVE: *This is an alternative E7 shape with the seventh on the B string.*

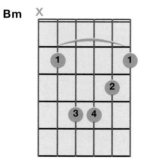

ABOVE: *The chord of B minor (the Am shape barred at the second fret).*

EXERCISE 1

This exercise builds on the country-picking exercise (see 'Country picking'): the chords and bass/thumb motion are the same. The E chord is often embellished here by using a hammer-on from the open G string to the first fret (G#). This gives a bluesy effect, as the note G is the flattened third of the chord (see 'Introducing the Blues').

Chet Atkins

One of the towering figures of commercial country music, Chet Atkins was influential as both a guitarist and a record producer, and played both roles on scores of hit records by the biggest names in country music (as well as being a key figure in the development of Elvis Presley's career). Chet's famous 'Atkins style' right-hand technique, itself a development of Merle Travis's style, has been widely imitated, although his use of two fingers per string to pick melodies while maintaining bass motion is actually very difficult to master. In a career spanning five decades, Atkins collaborated with other guitarists of a similar stature, including Les Paul, Mark Knopfler and Tommy Emmanuel. Jazz influences abound in Atkins's own work; these, together with his apparent debt to classical right-hand technique, may have played a part in his migration from the Gretsch electric guitar to the Gibson nylon-strung acoustic model that bore his name.

RIGHT: *Chet Atkins may have won countless Grammy awards as a record producer, and is remembered as the father of 'The Nashville Sound', but his contributions to guitar playing are arguably even greater.*

A new chord sequence

The eight-bar chord sequence used for Exercise 1 is one of the standard chord sequences found in many styles of popular music, from ragtime and jazz to rock 'n' roll, and the second half of the progression turns up as an ending in many other songs. As with other stock chord sequences such as the '50s sequence and the 12-bar blues, it is well worth learning this progression in as many keys as possible.

I	IV	I	V7
I I7	IV IVm	I V7	I

ABOVE: *The eight-bar chord sequence in Exercise 1 is easy if you apply the harmonic analysis method (see 'Chord construction'). This sequence can be analyzed as above.*

EXERCISE 2

This exercise shows a typical example of a country/folk ballad accompaniment. The hammer-ons and pull-offs are illustrated using slurs. Each note here should be allowed to ring on for as long as possible. It is important to take particular care not to cut off ringing notes when performing hammer-ons and pull-offs.

Integrating a melody

We have seen how to make musical patterns by fingerpicking, and we have also learnt how to embellish those figures by using passing notes and other techniques. From here, it is a short step to playing melody and chords simultaneously on the guitar. This may take many different forms, but as a rule, you pick out a tune on the top strings, while plucking the lower strings to provide a bass accompaniment.

Rhythm and melody

Generally speaking, melodies are made up either of chord notes or the passing notes found between them. That is to say, when you make a chord in first position, some of the notes you need to pick out a tune are already there, at your fingertips. The other notes are unlikely to be far away – you might only have to move one finger to find them. The difficult part is keeping the accompaniment going in a rhythmic way – maintaining the arpeggios on the lower strings – while you play the tune.

Ringing strings

The left-hand fingers have to do a little extra work to play the melody, and it is the job of the thumb to compensate and provide the arpeggio motion. The right-hand fingers may also have to shift around the strings to some extent. That is to say, you may have to depart from the beginner's principle whereby the first three fingers are anchored to the top three strings. For example, it is often better to deploy two fingers when playing consecutive notes on the same string (one finger naturally has to move off its 'home' string to do this). The result is likely to be more fluent than when one finger-plucks the same string twice in a row.

First-position chords using two or three left-hand fingers lend themselves to melodic embellishment, because the fourth finger can be used to fret the passing notes without disrupting the shape of the chord. Other notes not in the chord can be found on open strings by lifting fingers.

Occasionally, however, the chord shape will have to be disrupted in order to fret a passing note. For example, the notes B–G are available on the top two strings when playing the C chord: C and E are part of the chord; the open B string is revealed by lifting the first finger; D and G can be added using the fourth finger.

Sometimes you will have to be inventive to find the note you want. Say your melody contains an F over the C chord. It can be found on the top string's first fret, which means that your first finger is close by – on the right fret, one string away. You might move that finger to make the F if you can do without it for a moment, or you might flatten it into a partial barre covering both strings. As long as there are notes sounding from the lower part of the shape (and the open B string does not sound), this need not disrupt the sense of harmony. This is exactly what happens in the first bar of Exercise 2 (opposite).

Tommy Emmanuel

Few players have caused as much excitement in the acoustic guitar world in recent years as the Australian Tommy Emmanuel. Emmanuel's style owes much to the lineage of Merle Travis and Chet Atkins, the latter of whom was one of Tommy's childhood heroes (and later a musical collaborator: their duo album was Atkins's last recording). Although often overtly country-based, Tommy Emmanuel's dazzling solo acoustic work draws on a far wider spectrum of styles and musical resources, including folk, jazz and classical guitar. An Emmanuel performance epitomizes the solo guitarist's dream of juggling multiple strands so skilfully that they meld into one.

RIGHT: *In a Tommy Emmanuel performance, the bass line, chords and melody seem to pour forth simultaneously, belying the fact that there really is just one man playing.*

EXERCISE 1

This exercise explores the melodic possibilities that can be found on the top E and B strings, while maintaining an arpeggio accompaniment using the chords of C, Am and G.

EXERCISE 2

This exercise is a melodic study using the main chords in G major. The melody consists of both chord notes and passing notes. All right-hand fingerings are shown on the stave to help you. In the first bar, you will have to use the partial barre, as described above.

EXERCISE 3

This is the traditional melody "Greensleeves", with a harmony constructed from first-position chords.

Tip

Sometimes you will have to interrupt the flow of bass and chords to fit in a melodic idea. Try to do this with confidence and without interrupting the basic pulse.

Altered tunings

The guitar's standard tuning, E A D G B E, is just one of many possibilities. There are other ways to tune a guitar, and these alternatives can make the instrument sound and feel very different. This can be a refreshing experience, but also a confusing one. However, different tunings are an experiment worth trying, because they might open up new avenues for you as a guitarist.

Non-standard tunings

There are many approaches to changing the guitar's tuning. Broadly speaking, the non-standard tunings can be divided into two groups: altered tunings, where the starting point is standard tuning but one or more strings are tuned differently; and open tunings, where the open strings are tuned to the notes of a chord. We will be looking at open tunings later. For now, let's take a look at a couple of altered tunings.

Described on the right are two tunings that require you to alter the pitch of just one string. This means that standard chord shapes will now sound different. Depending on the shape and context, the result may be either musically interesting or alternatively very dissonant.

E A D G B D# – the top E string is lowered by one semitone. To achieve this quickly with relative tuning, tune the guitar as normal and then tune the top E string to the B string, fourth fret. This has an interesting effect on many familiar shapes: E and G become maj7 chords and the simple A shape turns into a very complex-sounding 'add#11' chord. (This is a major chord and added note which is an augmented fourth above the root note.)

E A D G A E – the B string is lowered by one tone. (After tuning to standard tuning, the B string should be tuned to the G string, second fret.) This has an equally complex effect on basic shapes such as E, A and G.

Retune with care

Acoustic guitar strings are designed to produce optimal sound at fairly high tension. The string gauges in a standard set are designed with standard tuning in mind, so that string tension will be even across all the strings. So, tuning a string higher than its standard intended pitch can result in breakage. A semitone, or even a tone, is usually safe, but going beyond this is generally unwise. It is no coincidence that altered tunings tend to involve lowering strings more often than raising them.

LEFT: *Be prepared for string breakages if you turn the strings too far above their normal range. Tuning down is safer.*

Joni Mitchell

Without exaggeration, Joni Mitchell can be described as one of the most influential musicians of the late 20th century. Although she emerged from a folk background, playing clubs and coffee bars in late 1960s New York, within her first few albums Mitchell had staked out a musical territory encompassing folk, rock, modern jazz and avant-garde sonic experimentation. As a guitarist, Mitchell has probably explored the world of altered tunings more deeply than any other major singer/songwriter: many of her musical ideas stem from the harmonic possibilities of a unique tuning; she has claimed that she originally did not know there was such a thing as standard tuning.

RIGHT: *Joni Mitchell often works with some of the world's finest jazz musicians, but her folk roots and her own highly innovative guitar style are ingredients that are vital to most of her well-known songs.*

USING DIFFERENT STRINGS

String breakage, at least at home, is only a big problem when you run out of strings, so you should keep spares if you intend to experiment with tunings. Having spare strings around the house also allows you even more room for experimentation. If, for example, you would like to try raising the D string by a fourth to G, replace it with a standard G string, since this is the pitch it is designed for.

Recommended listening:
- Coldplay: "Yellow"
- Crosby, Stills, Nash & Young: "Guinevere"
- David Gray: "My Oh My"
- Joni Mitchell: "A Case of You"

EXERCISE TUNING: E A D G B D#

This exercise uses the first of the two non-standard tunings described opposite. For comparison, many shapes are the same in both pieces, although they sound different and have different names. Where a shape corresponds to a familiar chord's standard tuning, this is given in brackets. All the chord shapes are shown; some of them, you will notice, are new and unfamiliar, but in fact they are all essentially just simple shapes.

Tuning: E A D G B D#

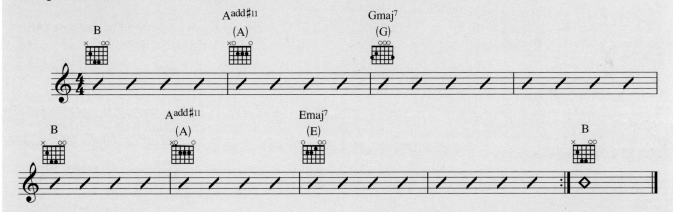

EXERCISE TUNING: E A D G A E

Dropping the B string down to A creates some interesting tensions, particularly against shapes with the third on the G string, such as E and Em.

Tip

In some instances, familiar shapes from standard tuning can result in really dissonant chords in other tunings, but usually only a slight modification will produce something usable and often interesting.

Tuning: E A D G A E

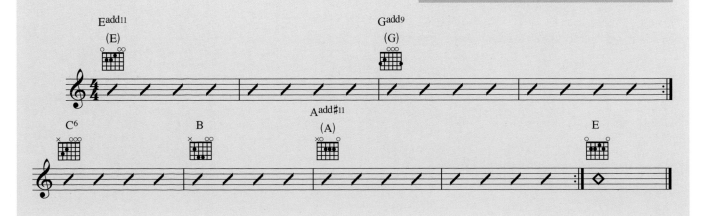

Drop D tuning

Perhaps the most useful of the altered tunings, drop D is very popular with guitarists. As with the tunings we have already looked at, drop D involves adjusting just one string: the bottom E, which is tuned down a tone to D. This extends the range of the guitar and adds a resonant bass thrum to the sound – this is especially effective when you are playing in the key of D or D minor.

The bass D note

In standard tuning, a bass D note is not really available. The lowest D you can have is to be found on the open fourth string. So, tuning the bottom string down to D slightly extends the range of the guitar and has a surprisingly profound effect on the character of the chords you play. Songs to listen to include "Fat Bottomed Girls" (Queen), "Stuck in the Middle" (Stealer's Wheel) and "Polly" (Nirvana Unplugged).

Detuning the bottom string

To retune to drop D, pick the bottom E string together with the D string while dropping the pitch of the E string. It should be very obvious when the two notes are exactly an octave apart, as the slight rhythmic 'beating' effect, caused by two notes that are almost but not quite in tune, will disappear.

One advantage of drop D tuning is that open D chords (major and minor) can now be supported with a truly deep bass note. The disadvantage is that familiar chords with the root on the E string need to be modified to work in drop D. The principle is easy to learn: since it has been detuned by one tone, the bottom string must be fretted two frets higher than in standard tuning to play the same note. This is easier to achieve with some shapes than others.

As with most non-standard tunings, most players tend to utilize the strengths of drop D and avoid using shapes that do not lend themselves to smooth execution.

LEFT TOP, CENTRE AND BOTTOM: *Some important chords modified for use in drop D. Notice the muted A string in the G chord for strumming; this should be muted with the side of the third finger.*

BELOW: *The D minor chord is especially sonorous with the deep low D bass available in drop D tuning. (As with the D major chord, the bottom E string would not be played in standard tuning.)*

E

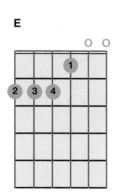

Em

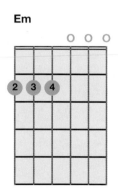

G

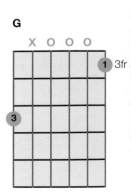

Dm

Barre chords in drop D

Although the open E chord is easy to modify to drop D, barre chords based on the E shape cannot be used in this tuning (at least, not with the bottom string sounding). However, the rich sound of the three lowest open strings can easily be moved around using a partial barre: the first section of the index finger (usually) plays the three lowest strings simultaneously at the same fret. This produces a movable chord consisting of the root, perfect fifth and octave. As there is no third, this chord is neither major nor minor, and is usually known as a '5' chord (A5, C5 etc) or a 'power chord'. '5' chords are playable in standard tuning too (simply play the bottom three strings of an E-derived barre chord), but there is something especially gutsy about the sound of a '5' chord in drop D tuning.

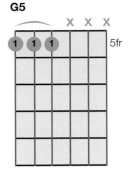

G5

RIGHT: *The G5 chord in drop D, played with a partial barre.*

EXERCISE 1

This exercise is an introduction to the sound of drop D: a simple arpeggio accompaniment in D major, using the D major chord (the standard shape, but including a low open D), as well as modified G and Em shapes (see opposite). The Am shape is unchanged, as the bottom string is not used.

EXERCISE 2

This exercise uses the full ringing open Dm chord along with the movable one-finger power chord (F5 and G5). This type of riff works well in many settings, from folk-rock to grunge.

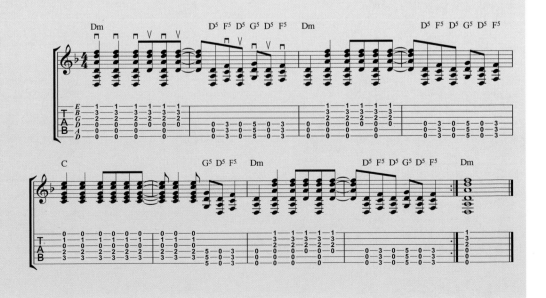

Open tunings

In open tunings, all six strings are tuned to the notes of a particular chord, meaning that the open strings ring pleasingly together. This euphony serves as a kind of platform on which complex harmonies can be built, often using simple movable shapes. So open tunings can lead to unexpected musical results, and for that reason they are popular among singer/songwriters.

Tuning for songwriting

Many great songs have been written around open tunings. Some very fine players – Nick Drake, John Martyn, Richard Thompson, for example – have used open tuning in preference to standard tuning most of the time.

In theory, any chord of any type can be used as the basis of open tuning. If you wanted to, you could tune your guitar to a minor chord, a seventh, or something more complex. In practice, however, straightforward major chords work best – and only a few of the major chords at that. The most widely used open tunings are D, C and G. We will deal with open D and C overleaf. Here, by way of introduction to the possibilities of open tuning, we will look at open G, sometimes known as 'Spanish' tuning.

Open G

To tune to open G, start in standard tuning and drop both the E strings and the A string down by one tone. The open strings are now tuned to D G D G B D (the notes of a G major triad are G, B and D). Just as for drop D tuning, this can be easily achieved by comparing octaves: the new string pitches should be tuned to the existing D and G strings.

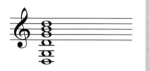

ABOVE: *The pitches of the open strings in open G.*

Recommended listening:

- Stefan Grossman: "Just a Closer Walk with Thee"
- Joni Mitchell: "Little Green"
- Dire Straits: "Romeo and Juliet"

EXERCISE OPEN G TUNING: D G D G B D

This exercise introduces some partly familiar shapes on the G, B and D strings, ringing against open strings.

Strum the shapes shown in the given rhythm below, changing the chords where indicated, playing all the strings shown as open or fretted. Be careful not to play the bottom string where marked with an 'X'.

After this, feel free to try a sparser approach, picking individual strings or strumming only some of them. Don't worry too much about the names above the chord boxes: when playing an open tuning, simple shapes can result in complex harmony, but most players using open tunings tend to think in terms of shapes rather than theory.

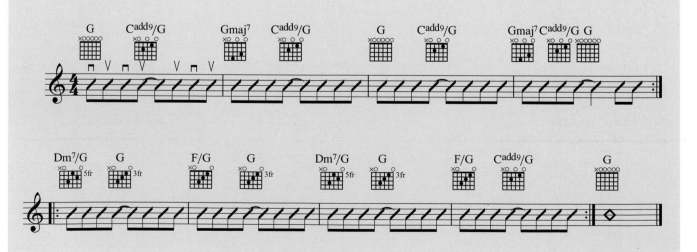

G, B and D

You will notice that three adjacent strings – G, B and D – are tuned the same way as in standard tuning. In other words, half the notes you might potentially want to play are in the places you are used to finding them. This is one of the things that makes G a popular open tuning, as well as the best introduction to the device. The familiar harmonic relationships here can be exploited, either on their own or against one or more open strings.

Of course, entirely new chord shapes are also possible and sometimes necessary, as you will see when you come to do the exercises. Open tunings lend themselves well to barre chords, because the simplest way to play any major chord is simply to make a full barre on the appropriate fret.

ABOVE: *A very simple chord shape – in open tunings, major chords can be found by barring across all six strings. In open G tuning, this full barre at the fifth fret produces a C major chord.*

EXERCISE OPEN G TUNING: D G D G B D

Many ideas in open tunings are constructed from very simple melodic movement using fretted notes against open strings. This piece is played entirely in quavers (half-beat notes) and will sound great if you allow all the notes, whether open or fretted, to ring until another note is played on the same string. This instruction is not reflected in the note values shown here, since it would look extremely messy. Note also that changing the tuning changes the normal correspondence between the top stave (with the musical notation) and the tab stave. If in doubt, follow the tab. This dreamy piece may be played using either fingerstyle or picking technique. Note the use of double hammer-ons (see 'Left-hand embellishments') to play an ascending melody. This is a popular folk guitar move.

More open tunings

In all open tunings, the open strings contain the notes of the tonic chord, while full barres at frets 5 and 7 are a way of making chords IV and V very easy to play. However, open tunings are much more than merely convenient. Their value also lies in the interesting effects that can be achieved when single fretted notes, or very simple shapes, sound against the open strings.

Open D

Sometimes called 'Sebastopol' tuning after a famous tune of the same name, open D is probably the most widely used open tuning after open G. It was popular with many of the

LEFT: *The strings in open D: D A D F♯ A D.*

early acoustic blues guitarists, and it has also been favoured by more contemporary players, such as Ry Cooder and Joni Mitchell. Open tunings tend to have a set of shapes or 'moves' that bring out the essence of the tuning. In the case of open D, particularly in a folky context, double-stopped sixths on the bottom A and the F♯ (G) strings have this effect. Each shape outlines a chord in the harmonized D major scale. The remaining open strings (all either D or A, the tonic and fifth of the key), either 'agree' with the fretted notes or create interestingly tense chords.

LEFT: *Double-stopped sixths in open D tuning.*

Open C

Any tuning with a low C on the bottom string is bound to have a rich, dark sound. This pitch is about as low as you can go with a standard string, and you get some 'rattle' from the string because it is so much slacker than usual. Some players consider this effect part of the charm of such tunings; if you don't agree, then change the bottom string for a heavier one. The beauty of open C tuning is that the upper strings are in their usual range, so there is plenty of 'zing' that contrasts intriguingly with the murkiness of the bottom string.

LEFT: *The strings in open C: C G C G C E.*

There are open tunings for other keys, too. Many of them are actually the same tunings as some of the ones already described, but at different pitches. The most popular open A tuning, for example, is open G transposed up a tone. Likewise, the most popular open E tuning is the open D given above, but raised by a tone across all the strings.

If you want to play in open E, bear in mind that it will necessitate raising the pitch of three of the strings above the pitches that they have in standard tuning, so both the neck and strings are placed under greater strain. A safer way to achieve open E is to tune to open D and place a capo at the second fret. Apart from effectively reducing access to the very top of the fretboard, there is no musical difference.

Phil Keaggy

During the course of a career spanning more than 50 albums, Phil Keaggy's eclectic style has crossed musical barriers with breathtaking ease, all the way from folk-rock to contemporary jazz; his technical virtuosity is always in evidence and yet it never gets in the way of his musical vision. Keaggy often explores a far wider range of sonic possibilities than most players: unusual tunings, two-handed tapping, drumming on the body and strings, and even managing to simultaneously play the shaker with his picking hand. His live solo performances frequently make use of electronic delays to create loops, enabling him to build up complex harmonies, textures and rhythms.

RIGHT: *Phil Keaggy lost most of his right-hand middle finger in an accident at the age of four, yet he has often been voted one of the greatest fingerstyle guitar players in the world.*

EXERCISE OPEN D

All of the chords here contain just two fretted notes, which sound against open strings. To avoid congestion on the stave, each chord is spelt out in full initially; rhythms using slash notation mean 'keep playing this chord in the rhythm shown.'

Tip

Although the shapes here use all six strings, it can also be appropriate to vary the number of strings used to create musical accents.

EXERCISE OPEN C

This piece looks much harder than it really is. The F and G bars are played using a full barre at the fifth and seventh frets respectively – no other left-hand finger movement is required here. C bars require a little more attention: take care not to cut off ringing open strings as you play the fretted notes. The final chord at the 12th fret may also be played as harmonics (see 'Advanced left-hand techniques').

DADGAD tuning

DADGAD occupies a special niche because it is neither an open tuning nor an altered tuning. It is so called because those are the notes the strings are tuned to. It is especially dear to acoustic folk guitarists, and it has an instantly identifiable, unmistakably Celtic flavour, but is also found in rock music. There are dedicated DADGAD players who have made a lifetime's study of the tuning.

How to achieve DADGAD tuning

DADGAD tuning can be reached by using standard tuning as a reference. First, drop the low and high E strings to D (using the octave interval to get them in tune with the D string), then drop the B string to A (an octave above the open A string). DADGAD can be seen as a close relative of the open D tuning that you have already encountered. The difference is that in DADGAD, the third string is tuned to G rather than F♯.

ABOVE: *This shows the pitches of the open strings when using DADGAD tuning.*

The nature of DADGAD

DADGAD is an unusual type of guitar tuning. Most guitar tunings are built on combinations of thirds, fourths and fifths between adjacent strings. In DADGAD, two of the strings (G and A) are tuned just a major second (one whole tone) apart. This 'crunch' interval plays a large part in the unworldly sound of DADGAD. If the open strings can be said to make a chord at all, it is not a major or minor chord, but a 'suspended' chord (Dsus4 or Gsus2, depending on which note is considered the root), and most simple fretted shapes in this tuning can be given similarly complex names. The suspended open chord can be turned into a D5 power chord using just one finger: the G string, second fret. Try executing a rapid hammer-on from the open string to this note while you are strumming all six strings. This high-impact sound can be achieved only in DADGAD tuning.

Muting strings

Some of the chords in Exercise 2 opposite contain unplayed muted strings. As we have seen, these can often be muted 'as if by accident' with the side of a fretting finger. However, it is not possible to mute the bottom string in this way, and the energetic strumming style required here makes it difficult to control which strings are struck with the right hand. The solution is to wrap the left-hand thumb around the neck to mute the bottom string, a technique that would incur disapproval from most classical guitar teachers.

RIGHT: *The left-hand thumb muting the bottom string. The thumb should touch the string with enough pressure to mute it but not enough to produce a note.*

An ear for open tunings

If you have a good ear, you may be tempted to approach retuning by making approximate adjustments and then fine-tuning until strumming all six strings simply sounds 'right'. This approach has pitfalls in open tunings especially, as the guitar's frets are spaced according to equal temperament, a compromise system in which all the intervals sound equally good, although none is quite perfect. Tuning the open strings by ear (even in standard tuning, but especially in open tunings and DADGAD) will give an uneven result, where some chords are built on the intervals that sound really good, while others will sound really bad. In open tunings, use the strings that are an octave apart as the basis of your tuning by ear, because the octave interval is constant regardless of temperament. This rule may be relaxed when using open tunings for slide playing (see 'Advanced left-hand techniques').

EXERCISE 1

This is a classic DADGAD folk accompaniment. As with open tunings, some of the chord names here get rather complex, but the basic ideas are simple. This piece is strummed in semiquavers; this means doubling the usual rate of down/upstroke motion, as shown in the first bar. To reduce visual congestion, each chord change is reflected in the TAB stave, but after this slashes in the top stave only are used until the next chord change.

Tip

Fast strumming does not always have to be extremely loud: playing slightly softer most of the time leaves some room to create accents when you need them.

Tuning: D A D G A D

EXERCISE 2

This exercise is written in a similar strumming style. The indication 'cont. sim.' means 'carry on like this'. While continuing to play in a similar way, there is also some freedom to vary the strumming pattern while staying true to the style established in the previous measure. Feel free to use hammer-ons and pull-offs with both the D5 chord (as in Exercise 1) and the A7sus4 chord. Placing the pull-off on beat 4 (so that the last three semiquavers are played on open strings) allows plenty of time for changing chord. Don't worry too much about this, however: occasional muffled notes just before a chord change let the ear know that the player is human rather than a machine!

Tip

Try playing this exercise with a metronome, slowly at first, making sure that strums on the beat (the first of each group of four) occur exactly on the beat.

Tuning: D A D G A D

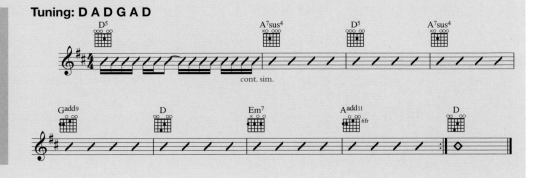

Introducing jazz chords

To play jazz chord sequences, you have to take a slightly different approach to chord construction. Instead of using first-position open chords or movable barre shapes, you will have to adopt a minimalist approach where only the essential notes are played. This pared-back method is the essence of jazz guitar and, when done right, it makes for a highly sophisticated sound.

Voice leading

There are two main reasons why jazz harmony requires a different approach. The first is the principle known as voice leading. Ideally, each note except the root should move to the nearest available note within the next chord, rather than leaping randomly around the neck, as can often happen with barre chords.

So, voice leading means thinking 'horizontally' about the melodic sequence that each note in the chord is making. This is far removed from the bar-by-bar block of sound that ordinary strumming produces. And if some notes are doubled on several strings, as is the case with ordinary chord-making, then voice leading becomes practically impossible.

The other reason for the fact that jazz chords take a sparse form is that jazz, by its nature, uses many notes beyond the root, third, fifth and seventh.

If these extensions are added to the full chord, the result is likely to sound messy or to contain internal clashes. In any case, the guitar has only six strings, so an economical approach to basic chords is very useful.

Three essential notes

The simplest jazz chord shapes contain just three notes, but these are rarely the standard root, third and fifth of the scale. Seventh chords form the basis of jazz harmony, but normally, a seventh chord contains four notes: root, third, fifth and seventh. To achieve a jazzy three-note voicing, the fifth is omitted. The third is what tells you whether a chord is major or minor, and is therefore essential. The seventh note has to be there to make the chord a seventh. The fifth does not define the chord, and so is dispensable.

We now come to the key question of where to find the three required notes. Placing the root on either the low E string or the A string results in two sets of chord shapes with the third and seventh on the D and G strings in both cases. The conventions of jazz harmony mean that most chord sequences can be played by alternating between these two types, thus enabling the thirds and sevenths to move in steps rather than by leaps. It is only the bass note that needs to move in larger leaps.

There are three basic types of seventh chord: dominant seventh (7), major seventh (maj7) and minor seventh (m7). These are shown below, based on root notes at the third fret. This gives us a set of G chords (root: E string) and a set of C chords (root: A string).

These shapes (often used without the bass note when playing with a band) form a useful basis for more advanced harmony using extensions such as ninths and 13ths (see 'More jazz chords').

Recommended listening:
- Count Basie Quartet (Freddy Green): "I Don't Know"
- James Taylor: "Gorilla"
- Joe Venuti & Eddie Lang: "Wild Cat"
- Jim Hall: "Bossa Antigua"

BELOW: *The three basic seventh chords in G and C, with the root on the E string and A string at the third fret. These six shapes form the basis for a lifetime's worth of exploration.*

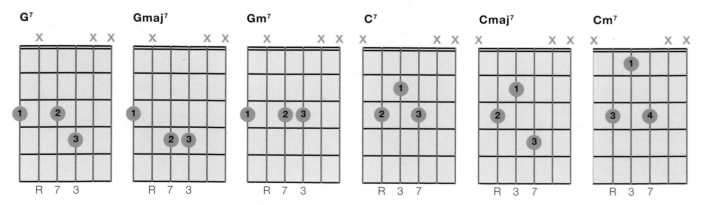

Muting

A chord shape with three sounding notes inevitably has three unplayed strings. It is of course possible to pick only the three fretted notes with the thumb and first two fingers. However, many jazz accompaniment styles are based on rhythmic strums. In order to be able to strum with some rhythmic drive, it is not feasible to use only the right hand to control which strings will sound. Instead, the left hand should mute the unplayed strings.

The fretting fingers therefore do two jobs: the fingertips fret the notes of the chords while the sides of the fingers mute the unwanted strings. Experimentation is the best way to arrive at your own version of this technique. By way of an example, here is a G7 shape. Note that the fretting fingers fall across the unplayed strings to mute them.

ABOVE: *The G7 chord at the third fret.*

EXERCISE 1

This exercise strings together dominant seventh chords. Alternating between shapes with the roots on the E and A strings allows for elegant voice leading: the thirds and sevenths move largely in semitones.

EXERCISE 2

This exercise uses a series of moves called the II-V-I progression. It consists of the harmonized seventh chords on steps II, V and I of any key, and is such a strong progression in its own right that it effectively establishes a temporary key centre each time it is transposed. This effect is exactly what happens in this exercise.

More jazz chords

Jazz harmony is based on seventh chords, but has gradually evolved in complexity. Dominant seventh-type chords, in particular, are often spiced up further by the addition of various other notes. The theory behind these additional notes can get a little complicated, but fortunately it is possible to take a guitar-based approach that avoids most of the theoretical complexity.

Building a jazz chord vocabulary

Our two basic three-note dominant seventh shapes (see 'Introducing jazz chords') provide an excellent basis for adding extensions without tying our fingers in knots. The simplest approach is to look at all the notes that can be added on the B string. With the root either on the E string or the A string, all notes at nearby frets on the B string can be added to produce usable extended jazz chords.

Our basic three-note shapes all use the first three fingers of the left hand. Most available notes on the B string can be added easily with the fourth finger, but this does not work for all permutations: for some shapes, the fingers need to be swapped around. These chords are again shown with the root at the third fret (G7 and C7 chords).

The ninth chord shown here can also be played using a partial barre with the third finger for the G and B strings.

Natural and altered tension

Extended dominant seventh chords are used almost constantly in modern jazz. If you play through the six chords shown below, you will notice that the '9' and '13' shapes (C9 and G13) have a simpler, less dissonant sound than the rest. The ninth and 13th chords are known as natural tension chords, whereas the rest are altered tension chords. These are usually easy to spot, because the chord symbols are longer and more complicated.

The two natural tension shapes can be used in any part of a chord sequence in place of a dominant seventh (7) chord. Altered tension chords should be used with a little more care, generally only in place of a dominant seventh chord that is resolving up a fourth (or down a fifth – see 'Seventh chords'). For example, if a G7 chord is followed by a C chord (whether major or minor), an altered tension chord may be used. If it is followed by anything else, it is usually safer to stick to a natural tension chord (9 or 13).

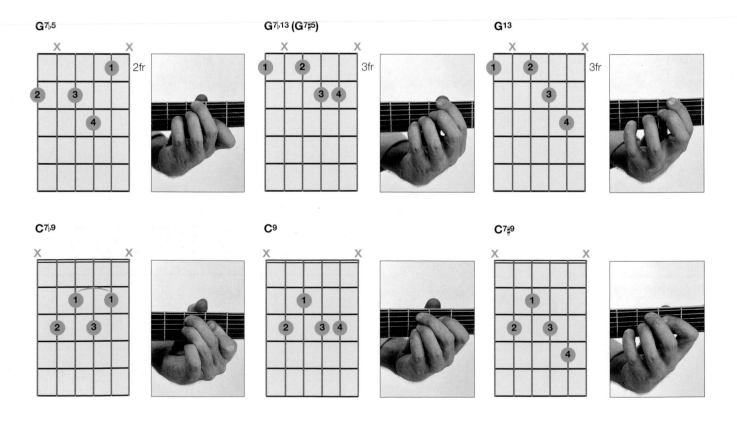

EXERCISE 1

This exercise is based on the cycle of fifths (see 'Understanding keys') – a sequence in which each chord resolves up a fourth. The sequence could therefore use altered tension chords throughout, but in fact it alternates between natural and altered tension for ease of fingering; each 'voice' (string) moves musically nonetheless.

EXERCISE 2

This exercise is based on the same sequence as the exercise above, but it reverses the tensions. Doing this results in a slightly richer sound. This is because the 7#9 chord has a particularly 'spiky' dissonant quality, which makes it a popular choice not only when playing jazz but in blues and rock, too.

EXERCISE 3

As before, the chords here may be strummed with the plectrum, but you may also wish to try picking the notes of each chord simultaneously, either using the thumb and first three fingers, or the plectrum and fingers in hybrid right-hand technique (see 'Country picking'). This immediately lends the piece a Latin jazz flavour; feel free to experiment.

The 12-bar blues in jazz

The basic three-chord blues can be modified in a great many ways. It is almost infinitely adaptable, and it crops up in musical genres that, on the face of it, appear to have little to do with the blues. The 12-bar sequence runs like a thread through jazz (which is related to the blues), but the chords and their uses are altered in some quite intriguing ways; the possibilities explored here are just the beginning.

Blues with a jazzy accent

In a jazz context, almost every chord in the 12-bar sequence can be substituted by a different chord. Such is the strength of the underlying blues structure that the result is always recognizable as a 12-bar blues.

As we have seen, the II–V progression is central to modern jazz. There are many places in the blues sequence where a II–V progression can be added. One way is to change the last line so that the chords V–IV (D7–C7 in the key of G) become II–V (Am7–D7).

This simple move is the most important in turning the sequence into a jazz blues. The same II–V progression can also be added in the final bar. Exercise 1 (opposite, top) puts these two changes into effect, along with the use of chord IV (C7) in the second bar.

The dominant seventh chord always 'wants' to resolve to a major or minor chord a perfect fourth above. So it can be said that almost any chord has its own related V chord. For

example, the dominant seventh chord in G major is D7. The chromatic chord of A7 can be used in the key of G major, even though it does not strictly belong to the key. The A7 chord resolves to D7, which makes it 'chord V of chord V', or the secondary dominant. Secondary dominants can be used freely in the jazz blues.

In the same way, any dominant seventh-type chord can be preceded by a m7 (minor seventh) chord a fourth below to give a II–V progression. In our example, the blues in G, the II–V (Am7–D7) can be preceded by its own secondary II–V (Bm7–E7). Exercise 2 (opposite, below) adds some secondary II–V progressions to the sequence.

The last two bars of the structure now take the form of a jazz turnaround: as the name suggests, this is a short chord sequence which rounds off a chord structure and leads us back to the first chord. These four chords can be analyzed in terms of the key as follows: I7 – VI7 – IIm7 – V7. This is a very useful sequence to learn in as many keys as possible.

Pulling off the turnaround

The turnaround can also be modified by means of tritone substitution to G7 – B♭7 – A7 – A♭7 – another stock-in-trade jazz progression. The tritone is an interval of a diminished fifth or augmented fourth, so called because it spans three tones. This interval sounds rather dissonant on its own, especially in the context of simple harmony. Banned in church and known by the term *diabolo in musica* ('the devil in music'), it was rarely found in classical music until the 19th century.

However, the tritone is crucial to the sound of modern jazz, because it is at the heart of the dominant seventh chord. The fact that every tritone interval is actually present in two seemingly unrelated chords makes it possible to substitute one for the other.

In the jazz turnaround described above, the chord B♭7 can be substituted for E7, because they have a tritone in common. (D7 becomes A♭7 in the same way, C7 becomes G♭7 and so on.)

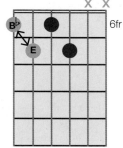

B♭7 & E7

6fr

LEFT: *E7 and B♭7 chords – note the common tritone (shown in red).*

FAR LEFT: *The tritone interval – two notes that exemplify the sound of jazz. Many 'spiky'-sounding jazz compositions have been written around this sound.*

EXERCISE **BASIC JAZZ BLUES**

This sequence uses three-note jazz voicings (see 'Introducing jazz chords') rather than full/open chords.

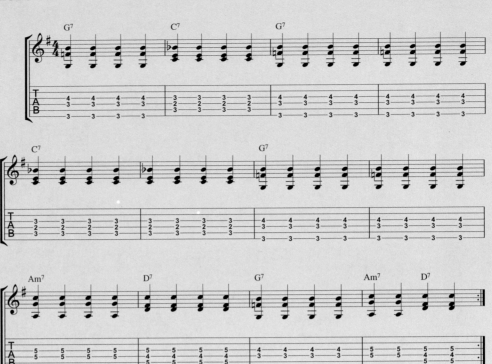

Tip

This sequence may be transposed into any key by simply moving it up the fretboard. Beyond approximately the eighth fret, however, the bass notes will sound rather high, so it would usually be better to start with a shape that has the root on the fifth string.

EXERCISE **JAZZ BLUES NO. 2**

This exercise expands the blues sequence further by adding relative II–V progressions and a jazz turnaround at the end.

Tip

The turnaround here can be modified using tritone substitutions in any number of ways; all of them will resolve to G7 for the next repeat of the sequence.

A dozen classic blues licks

Every musical style has an associated vocabulary of melodic and harmonic devices. In the blues, certain guitar 'licks' (short phrases) are so widespread that they have become the common currency of every player. It is worth learning these licks off by heart, so that you can deploy them at will while jamming, or use them as a starting point for your own improvisations.

Building your blues vocabulary

Some of the riffs on the opposite page go right back to the roots of the blues. Nobody can claim to have written them – any more than a composer or songwriter can claim to have invented the basic chord sequences.

As with chord sequences, what matters with these riffs is how you play them, and how you imbue them with your own individual style. If you do nothing but wheel out these tried and trusted set phrases, your playing will sound clichéd. But if you use them in combination with your own musical ideas, they will add instant authenticity to your playing.

Many of these licks can also be treated as starting points for explorations of your own. The trick here is to identify the core concept, and then do something else with it: transpose it to a different part of the scale, move it up or down an octave, change the rhythm…

Some sort of accompaniment is highly recommended, to help you try these in context once you have got them under your fingers – either a recording of yourself or an automatically generated accompaniment using a keyboard or computer software, or both together (automatic accompaniment plus rhythm guitar for a full sound with some natural 'feel').

Seasick Steve

In an age dominated by youth and the cult of celebrity, Seasick Steve's story is refreshingly different. Steve Wold first achieved widespread public recognition and commercial success in his 60s. He is one of the few current blues musicians who can claim real experience of lifestyles such as sleeping rough, jumping freight trains and working as a farmhand, having spent nearly 20 years of his life living like this in the American South. Steve also worked as a session musician and sound engineer for many years, but was as surprised as anyone when his performing career took off, initially in the UK. His guitar style is deeply rooted in the blues tradition, but has also been shaped by necessity and his own resourcefulness. As well as his more conventional guitars, many of Steve's instruments are highly individual creations, including a one-stringed slide guitar and one made largely from the hubcaps of a Morris Minor.

ABOVE: *There is not a shred of revivalism in this version of the blues. Seasick Steve's blues represent a rare commodity sometimes called 'the real deal'.*

LEFT: *Seasick Steve is well known for his range of customized electric and acoustic guitars.*

EXERCISE 12 RIFFS

The licks given here are classified harmonically: some work best over chord I, some over chord IV and some over chord V. In addition to these, you will find a couple of stock blues endings, which act as a kind of flourish when used in the last two bars of the structure. All the licks are shown in the key of G, and work best using a shuffle rhythm (see 'The sixth shuffle'). The chord symbols show which part of the sequence each lick works best with, but many can be used elsewhere.

Chord I

* Slide: see 'Advanced left-hand techniques'

Chord IV

Chord V

Endings

A DOZEN CLASSIC BLUES LICKS 99

Double stopping

So far we have looked at chord-based playing and single-note melodic work. However, there is an extremely effective technique, double stopping, that falls somewhere between the two. Double stopping simply means playing two notes at once. It makes for a very expressive sound which can be seen as a sequence of incomplete chords, but could also be described as two melodies running in tandem.

Movable two-note shapes

Double stopping, in its usual form, involves two notes moving melodically in parallel. The interval between the two notes can be anything, but the most widely used intervals for double stopping are thirds and sixths. This is no accident: thirds always harmonize in a pleasing way (to take an example from the world of pop music, think of the two voices in Abba's "Fernando": they are moving side by side in strictly parallel major and minor thirds). As for sixths, they are no more or less than inverted thirds: that is, the lower note of the third has been transposed up an octave.

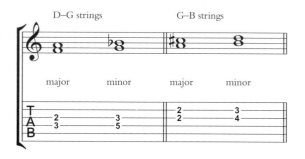

ABOVE/BELOW: *Major and minor third shapes.*

Fingering double-stopped shapes

To double stop effectively on the guitar you need a working knowledge of the guitar fretboard and the key signatures. For example, if you want to play double stops in the key of G major, you really have to know where the notes of G major (including the F#) are to be found on the fretboard.

You also have to know what your chosen interval looks like on the fretboard. Thirds are usually played on two adjacent strings. On most adjacent pairs, the higher note is found one fret back from the lower note on all the strings.

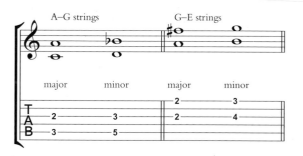

ABOVE/BELOW: *Major and minor sixth shapes.*

G and B

The exception is the G and B pair. Here, the interval between the open strings is already a major third (on all the others it is a perfect fourth), so to form a major third anywhere on the neck, you play the same fret on these two strings.

The minor third interval is one semitone narrower than the major third, so to make a minor interval you fret two frets back on the higher string on all pairs except G and B, where you fret one fret back. Sixths can be played in several shapes. The easiest shapes are found using two strings separated by one unplayed string. If you know where the notes of a given scale are to be found, all you need to do to be able to play it in thirds is to find pairs of notes a third apart which belong to the scale. This is complicated by the fact that open strings cannot usually be used to play the lower note, as there is no room for the upper note on the string above (see Exercise 2 for an example of this).

ABOVE: *Van Morrison devised possibly the most famous double-stopped guitar theme ever for the introduction to his song "Brown-Eyed Girl".*

EXERCISE 1

This is a simple melody in G major harmonized in thirds. All the shapes used can be found on the harmonized major scale.

EXERCISE 2

This exercise is derived from the G major scale in first position. Instead of being harmonized in thirds, it is harmonized in sixths (the upper line is transposed down an octave).

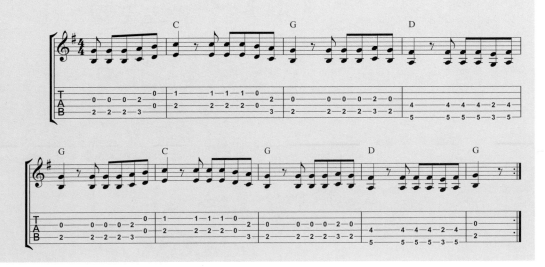

Half-open chords

These types of chords are shapes that can be moved around like barre chords, but include some open strings. Using this technique allows you to make complex-sounding chords with simple shapes, moved up and down the neck. The ringing open strings, top or bottom, provide a sense of harmonic continuity. This very fruitful manoeuvre is popular in many genres, especially pop and folk.

Lazy barres

The most common form of half-open chord is sometimes known as a 'lazy barre', because it is like a barre-chord shape but features some open strings (which makes it easier to play than a full barre).

The E shape works well as a half-open chord or lazy barre. Instead of making a full barre behind the E shape, you use the index finger to fret the low E string only, leaving the B and top E strings open. When the shape is moved up the neck, the E and B notes sound against the rest of the chord.

In some positions, the half-open E-shape delivers some complex-sounding (but usable) chords as well as some rather dissonant (and generally unusable) ones. The most usable positions for this shape are: first fret (this gives Fmaj7#11 – a rather dark sound with a flamenco flavour); second fret (F#7add11); third fret (G6), fifth fret (Aadd9); seventh fret (Badd11), eighth fret (Cmaj7); and tenth fret (D6/9). In fact, only three positions are too dissonant to be of much use.

If your guitar allows access, try the shape at the 12th fret, which results in a richly sonorous E major).

Aadd9

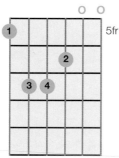 

ABOVE: *The 'lazy barre' E shape at the fifth fret. The chord produced is Aadd9.*

Dmadd9

ABOVE/BELOW RIGHT: *Two easy movable shapes at the fifth fret: Dmadd9 and Am9.*

Am-based shape

The Am-based barre shape sounds great in many positions with the top E string left open, as does the Em7 shape with the root on the E string with open top E and B strings. The best way to familiarize yourself with the possibilities here is to experiment to see what sounds good. Don't worry about the exact names of the complex resulting chords: it is more important to know what works here. At the ninth fret, the open strings duplicate the fretted notes on the G and B strings, producing a rich 'chiming' C#m7.

Am9

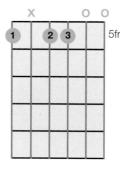 

Bass notes in open chords

Good effects can be achieved by making fretted shapes on the higher strings and moving them in relation to an open bass string. Try playing a standard first-position D chord, then moving the fretted notes up first by two frets (E/D) and then one more (F/D). This slightly mysterious effect has always been popular in folk-rock and related styles. Note the use of the slash in these chord symbols: E/D ('E over D') signifies an E chord with a D in the bass. Chord symbols like this are also very common in contemporary jazz.

EXERCISE 1

This exercise uses the E shape in a typical indie-pop sequence. To achieve the maximum effect, you should aim to keep both the B and top E strings ringing throughout the whole sequence.

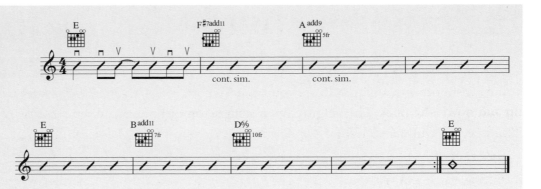

EXERCISE 2

This exercise uses just two half-open shapes to achieve some rather complex sounds, which become increasingly dissonant towards the end of the sequence. The tension is ultimately released with the simple Em chord ending.

EXERCISE 3

This exercise introduces a folk/rock cliché – moving the C chord shape up two frets (D^add9/11). Unlike the other shapes that are shown here, the C shape doesn't work very well anywhere else.

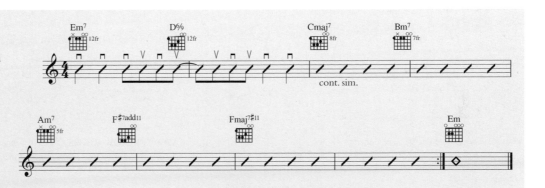

Paul Simon

Although it took a back seat for most of his later solo career, Paul Simon's deft acoustic-guitar work powered a string of hits for Simon & Garfunkel in the 1960s, on both steel-string and classical guitars. His relaxed, rolling fingerpicking style, influenced by British folk players such as Bert Jansch and John Renbourn, often incorporates melodic elements that weave a third strand in counterpoint with the duo's vocal harmonies; songs such as "Homeward Bound", "I Am a Rock" and "The Boxer" are memorable as much for their distinctive guitar figures as for their lyrics or melodies. Paul Simon's influence can in turn be heard in both the songwriting and guitar styles of many singer/songwriters from later decades, including Suzanne Vega and Edie Brickell.

ABOVE: *Paul Simon's early work with Art Garfunkel epitomizes the tradition of a folk duo with a single accompanying instrument.*

Improvising with the major scale

For the past 500 years, almost all Western music has been based on the major–minor key system. The ability to improvise using the major scale is an important part of learning to play *ad lib* solos in any style, including jazz. The major scale, familiar to millions as 'do, re, mi, fa, so, la, te, do', is the musical foundation on which most other melodic building blocks stand.

The importance of listening

Improvisation is at least as much about listening as it is about playing. At any given moment, the note you are playing produces a certain sound, or flavour, in relation to the underlying chord sequence.

This can only be properly appreciated if that chord is actually sounding, so it is far more useful to practise improvising with a friend playing chords (or you could try a recording of yourself playing chords) than if the chords are only present in your head.

Constructing an *ad lib* melody

Having played your first note over the underlying chord, the next step is to listen and react musically. Knowing which notes of the scale are present in each chord is essential: these notes, which agree with the harmony, will sound 'sweet' or stable. But if no other notes are used, the result may be rather bland. When we were exploring the blues scale, we looked at the mechanism of 'tension and release'. The same mechanism applies in relation to improvisation in the major scale: a note that does not belong to the underlying chord results in dissonance, or tension, but this tension can be released by resolving to a note belonging to the chord. Try playing up and down the parent scale of the chord sequence (for example, the scale of G major over the chord sequence used for the exercises opposite), and try to hear whether each note is or is not present in the chord.

All melodies essentially consist of a combination of chord notes and other notes (known as neighbour notes or passing notes). For example, if you start a solo using the note A over a G major chord, moving to either G or B will resolve the tension generated, as these notes are both found in the chord.

The next step to improvising an effective melodic line is simply to mix things up a little. Try combining arpeggio notes with step-wise motion, vary the rhythm (this immediately produces a more 'natural' result than a constant stream of crotchets or quavers), add interest with hammer-ons, pull-offs or other embellishments – and dare to leave a few rests.

Another ingredient of successful melodic improvisation is structure. Having played a musical idea (even just two or three notes) that seemed to work, try repeating them. Using the same melodic idea in different parts of the chord sequence will automatically create an element of structure.

Eddie Lang

This talented guitarist can justifiably be called the father of jazz guitar. Born at the dawn of the 20th century, Lang was working professionally by the end of the World War I, and was one of the first players to make the transition from the banjo (ubiquitous in 'Dixieland' – the very earliest recorded jazz and its various revivals) to the guitar. Such changes in instrumentation were an important part of the evolution of swing jazz in the 1920s and '30s. Eddie Lang worked in ensembles both large and small, appearing with many of the big names of the day including Paul Whiteman, Bing Crosby and Bix Beiderbecke. It is chiefly for his collaboration with violinist Joe Venuti that he is remembered today, however. The duo context liberated Lang's guitar from the 'padding' role usually required in big bands, allowing his unamplified acoustic guitar to be heard loud and clear.

ABOVE: *Eddie Lang playing an archtop acoustic guitar typical of the era.*

EXERCISE 1

This exercise is a chord sequence using four chords in the key of G major: G, Am7, C and D7. The melody line consists entirely of notes belonging to these chords, or arpeggios, all drawn from the major scale in second position (see 'Practice patterns').

EXERCISE 2

This exercise uses the same chord sequence as Exercise 1, but here each arpeggio note is preceded by a neighbour note, which creates a temporary dissonance before it is resolved.

EXERCISE 3

Still using the same chord sequence, this exercise combines arpeggio notes with step-wise motion, using varied technique and rhythm.

Advanced left-hand techniques

The standard interplay of the left and right hands, where the right hand picks each note and the left hand changes the pitch of the notes in question by fretting the strings, is only a small part of the range of available guitar techniques. There are two other techniques involving the interplay of both hands which are useful to get to know: harmonics and slides.

Harmonics

These are notes with a pure, bell-like sound produced by touching the string lightly rather than pushing it down on to the fretboard. Unlike ordinary notes, harmonics can only be produced at certain points along the string. These points are mathematically defined, and correspond to exact fractions of the string's length. The easiest harmonics to produce are found at the 12th, seventh and fifth frets (a half, one third and one quarter of the string's length, respectively).

To produce a harmonic, touch the string lightly with any left-hand finger and pluck the string with the right hand. The left-hand finger should make contact with the string without moving it. It may help to concentrate on using only the very tip of the finger; if you have very large hands, you may find that the little finger works best at first. The exact position is critical: for 12th, seventh and fifth fret harmonics, the note is found exactly above the fret, rather than in the area between frets, as for ordinary notes.

If you stray from this position even very slightly, the result will be a 'dead' or muted percussive sound rather than a pitched note. Higher harmonics can be found between the fifth fret and the nut, but these are both harder to find (the position of each will not be exactly above a fret) and harder to produce clearly.

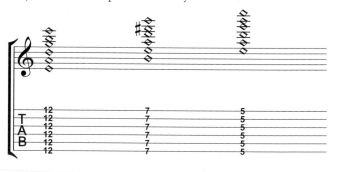

ABOVE: *The twelfth fret harmonic on the top E string.*

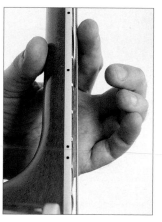

LEFT: *Multiple harmonics can be produced at the same fret, using the side of the finger.*

ABOVE: *This shows harmonics across all six strings at the 12th, seventh and fifth frets.*

EXERCISE HARMONIC CHORDS

This exercise uses harmonics as chords (sometimes supported by fretted bass notes). In each case, as several ringing harmonics are to be played at the same fret, use the side of the left-hand finger, as shown. Harmonics are shown as diamond-shaped note heads.

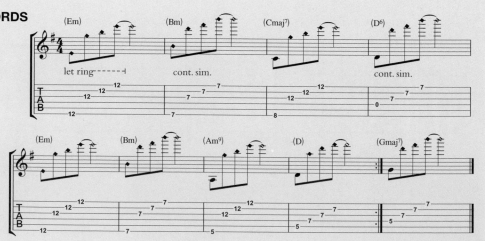

Slides

The slide technique (also known as *glissando* or *gliss*) is both simple and effective: the left hand slides between notes on the same string. To play a slide between two notes, pick the first note, then slide the fretting finger along the string while maintaining finger pressure until you reach the second note. It is important to maintain enough pressure so that the sound does not die off before the second note is reached; however,

be careful not to apply too much pressure either, as it is quite possible to cut your finger tip on the guitar string, especially if you have not yet developed calluses.

Slides are shown using straight diagonal lines between notes. Each of these is usually accompanied by a slur (curved line). To produce a grace note slide (shown using a small note preceding the main note), use the same technique, but make the first note as short as possible, emphasizing the second note.

Sliding from C to E on the G string

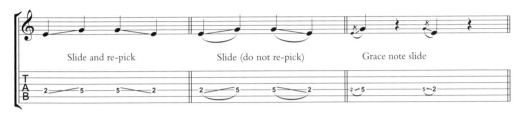

Slide and re-pick   Slide (do not re-pick)   Grace note slide

LEFT: *Three major scales in second position. Remember to maintain alternate picking throughout, as shown in the first bar.*

1 Begin by playing the note C (G string, fifth fret).

2 Maintain finger pressure and slide the finger to the ninth fret (E).

3 Allow the note E to sound once your finger is in position.

EXERCISE SLIDES AND HARMONICS

This exercise is a simple melody constructed using both slides and harmonics. The piece moves around the neck considerably; therefore recommended left-hand fingerings are shown using small numbers above the notes where necessary.

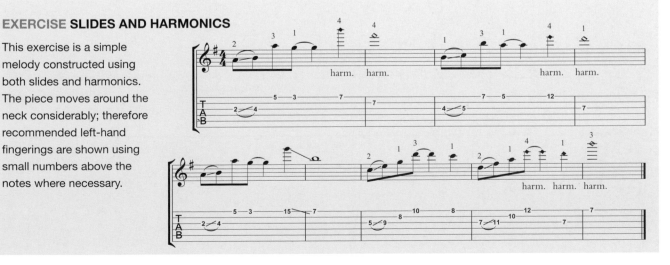

Practice patterns

The major scale contains enormous potential for generating practice material that will expand your knowledge of the fretboard. While there is nothing wrong with the traditional approach of simply playing up and down each scale, this represents only one possibility. The number of ways in which a scale can be arranged is limited only by the imagination, and borders on the realm of musical composition.

Scales and positions

The first-position scales we have encountered so far have all included open strings. Like first-position open chords, these cannot be transposed. The first requirement for a movable scale shape is that it should contain no open strings. Learning just one movable major-scale shape enables us, to some extent, to play any major scale, by moving this shape up the neck.

However, the ultimate aim for much more elegant results is to know all scales in all positions. There are a number of scale shapes to learn, as a first step towards this goal. Here, we will concentrate on three shapes. In second position, these shapes give us the scales of C, G and D major. We have seen these scales before, but in second position they have no open strings

and are therefore movable. The G and D major scales shown below are both in strict second position: that is to say, the first finger always plays the second fret, the second finger plays the third fret and so on. Because of the guitar's tuning, this strict approach sometimes has to be relaxed in order to make some notes accessible. The C major scale in second position can only be played by incorporating two stretches – the index finger stretches out of position by one fret, in this case to play the note F on both the high and low E string.

BELOW: *Three major scales in second position. Remember to maintain alternate picking throughout, as shown in the first bar.*

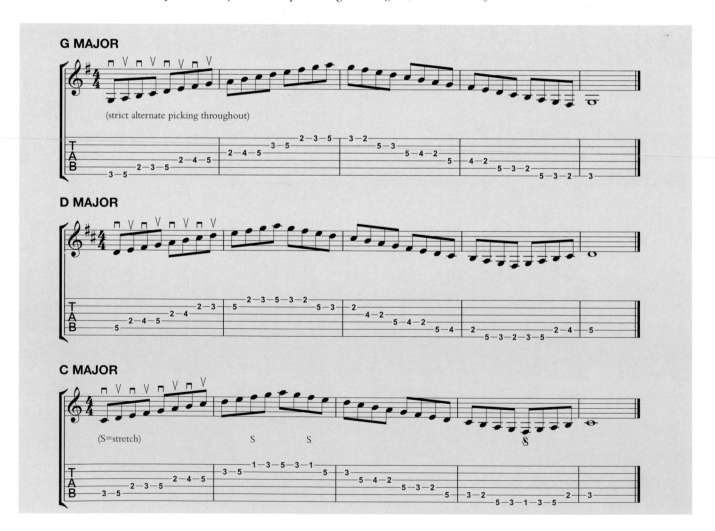

Generating patterns

The G major scale 'workout' below introduces some of the possibilities for practice material generated from the major scale. These ideas are all consistently realized: a simple interval or melodic idea is generated from the tonic note (G).

This idea is then transposed to begin on the second note (A), and so on all the way up and then down the scale, taking in every available note in the given position. The first idea in

the workout is a simple ascending third interval (G–B), which is transposed to begin on every note in the ascending scale. This becomes a descending third on the way down the scale (although maintaining the ascending third would be equally valid; try both versions for variety).

The patterns contained in this workout may also be applied to the D and C major scale, or to any other scale in any other position – the combinations are almost infinite.

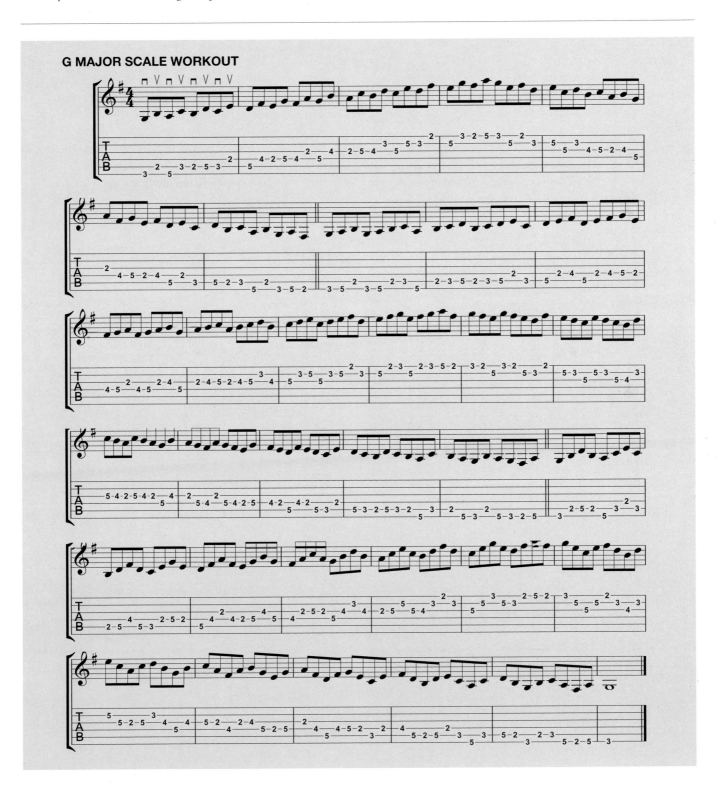

G MAJOR SCALE WORKOUT

Party tricks

We are now going to look at some novel ways of getting sounds out of your guitar. Artificial harmonics allow you to produce any harmonic you like, and thumb chords make new chord shapes possible high up the neck. Or you can try right-hand tapping, which is an unusual way to fret notes and produce a note in places other than where the left hand happens to be.

Artificial harmonics

As we have seen, to produce a natural harmonic on an open string, you lightly touch the string at a certain point with the left hand, and pick with the right. But the open strings can produce only a limited range of natural harmonics. To access a wider range of harmonic notes, it is first necessary to change the basic pitch of the string by fretting a note in the normal way. For example, if the left hand frets the first fret, the octave harmonic is now located at the thirteenth fret rather than the twelfth, and the next harmonic is at the eighth fret rather than the seventh. To sound the note, the fingers of the right hand

must be deployed both to touch the string at the correct point, and to pick the note. Harmonics produced in this way are generally known as artificial harmonics, and they are trickier to pull off than they sound. There is more than one way to produce them – see below. All these methods take practice, because it is hard to keep the finger that is touching the string quite still while also moving other fingers to sound the string.

In practice, most players only ever use harmonics an octave (12 frets) above the fretted note. This is usually shown in notation using diamond-shaped note heads, as for natural harmonics, but with the additional indication 'AH'.

ABOVE: *Fingerstyle technique: the thumb picks the string while the index finger produces the harmonic.*

ABOVE: *Plectrum technique: the plectrum is used between the thumb and middle finger, and the index finger reaches over to produce the harmonic.*

ABOVE: *Pinch harmonic: the string is played holding the plectrum conventionally, but the thumb simultaneously 'digs' into the string at exactly the right point to produce a harmonic.*

Tapped harmonics

An alternative technique may be used to produce a harmonic one octave above the fretted note. This involves a sharp but light tap with a left-hand fingertip. The string is tapped directly above the active fret; as for artificial harmonics, this is 12 frets above the note fretted by the left hand. The idea is to push the string down so that it makes momentary contact with the fret; the tap should have enough energy to set the string in motion, but should not remain in contact for long enough to have a muting effect. Like the other techniques here, some practice is required to master tapped harmonics, but the effort is worthwhile as no other technique produces quite this sound.

Thumb chords

In normal play, the left-hand thumb stays behind the neck most of the time. However, as we have seen, it may also be used to mute the bass strings. Many players take this technique one step further, and use the thumb to fret the low E string. Some guitarists use this technique as an alternative to barre chords: the index finger covers only the top E and B strings, while the thumb covers the bottom E string. This technique enables otherwise impossible shapes, such as the descending suspension/release sequence used by Pete Townshend in the verse pattern of The Who's "Pinball Wizard": as an alternative to barre chords based on the E shape, Townshend uses his thumb to fret the root of each chord on the bottom E string and mute the A string at the same time. This frees the fourth finger to add the suspended fourth on the G string without moving the rest of the fingers.

Right-hand tapping

There are many ways to produce a note without using both hands simultaneously. Hammer-ons and pull-offs fall into this category. The right-hand fingers can also be used directly on the fretboard – a technique known as 'tapping'. Practitioners of the most advanced version of this technique use the two hands to tap on the fretboard independently, enabling an almost piano-like independence of lines and chords.

Most players limit themselves to occasionally using a single right-hand finger to tap an otherwise impossible note. This is often encountered as a 'party piece' ending: the left hand plays a high chord on the upper strings; while the chord is ringing, the right hand 'crosses over' the left hand to tap a low bass note and finish the piece. This crowd-pleasing manoeuvre is actually much easier than it looks, and is definitely worth trying to master.

ABOVE: *This thumb chord is a popular alternative to the F major barre chord.*

ABOVE: *The right hand crossing behind the left hand to tap a bass note.*

EXERCISE

This exercise uses artificial harmonics and adds a right hand-tapped ending. Note that the fret numbers given for artificial harmonics apply to the left-hand fingering; the harmonic is produced by the right hand 12 frets higher, unless otherwise noted.

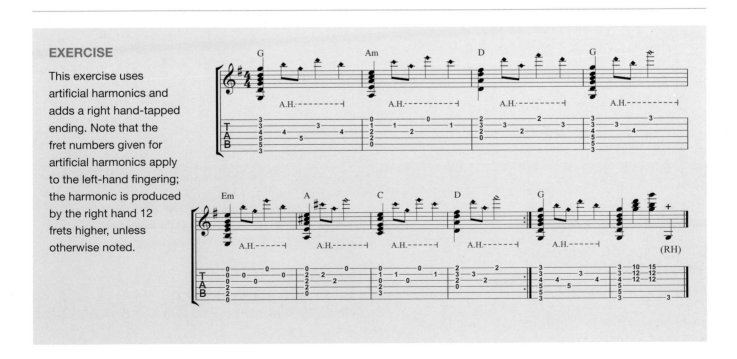

Slide guitar

The sounding lengths of the strings can be changed by using a technique known as slide guitar, whereby a metal or glass tube is used as the primary means of sliding. This produces a very different sound from regular left-hand work. It makes for a kind of plangent twang that works well in a blues or folk context, but it is also a distinctive ingredient of country music.

Basic bottleneck

The slide is often called a 'bottleneck', because the neck of a bottle can serve as a rough-and-ready slide. It is far preferable, however, to invest in a slide designed specifically for the task. These hollow cylinders – usually made of brass, steel or glass – come in various sizes to suit different players. The slide is usually worn on the little finger; the other fingers are used to damp the strings behind the slide to control the sound.

Some slide players employ conventional fretting technique using the other fingers. It is also common practice among players to use the right hand to pick one note at a time to play melodically, or several strings simultaneously to produce chords. The most effective slide ideas tend to use a combination of both of these approaches.

ABOVE: *Glass and metal slides come in a range of sizes.*

Using the slide

Slide guitar (like the steel-string acoustic guitar itself) is a quintessentially American invention, and it lends itself to American styles of music. As its name suggests, slide playing often involves sliding between notes or chords. Although this is a crucial part of the slide style, it can also be over-done – hence the need for damping by the other fingers. It should also be noted that for most purposes the slide needs to be positioned exactly above the corresponding fret, otherwise the notes will sound out of tune. When playing blues, however, the in-between positions of notes and chords have considerable expressive possibilities.

When you are sounding notes with the right hand, you must keep the slide parallel with the frets (perpendicular to the neck) in order for the result to be in tune. Since all the notes that you can play at any given moment are on the same fret, it makes a great deal of sense to use open tunings when using the slide. That way, you will always have a major chord at your disposal. Melodic slide playing is perfectly possible, however, and not unusual in standard tuning.

One of the first things you will notice if you try using a slide with an ordinary acoustic guitar is that it can be rather difficult to produce a clean sound without also making unwanted noises as the slide strikes the fretboard and frets. There is a fine line between exerting enough pressure to produce a clean note, and pressing so hard that the string makes contact with the fret.

ABOVE: *The slide in use – it should be exactly parallel to the frets.*

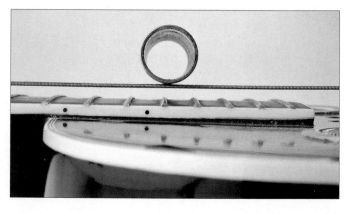

ABOVE: *An acoustic guitar set up for slide. Note the high action.*

Slide set-up

In fact, it is quite hard to play slide satisfactorily on a guitar set up for ordinary duties. Slide guitar generally requires a much higher action, which is achieved by raising the height of both the bridge and nut. It also calls for heavier strings. This is usually addressed by having a guitar specifically set up for slide playing. With this in mind, it might be worth considering investing in a second guitar if slide playing appeals to you. Inexpensive instruments often work very well for slide, as the usual considerations concerning a finely calibrated action, intonation and fret buzz do not apply, since the strings do not ordinarily come into contact with the fretboard.

EXERCISE 1

This exercise is a simple 12-bar blues melody in standard tuning. Where two notes are linked by a slur and a line, the second note should not be picked. Try to hit each note as accurately as possible; extra slides may be added according to taste. To play open strings, simply lift the slide momentarily.

Standard tuning

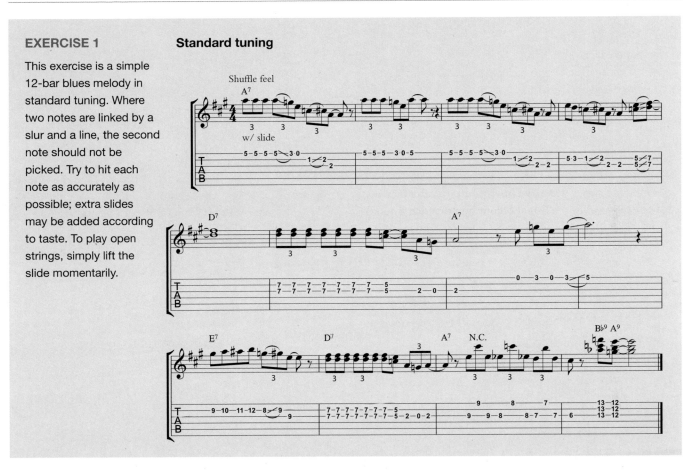

EXERCISE 2

This exercise is in open G tuning, but since only the top three strings are used, only the top string need be re-tuned (to D).

Open G tuning: D G D G B D

(★ = fret notes at eighth fret using first finger behind slide)

Classical guitar

The term 'classical guitar' describes not only a particular type of guitar, but also the range of music that is conventionally played on it. At its broadest, classical guitar music is 'serious' Western concert music played on a nylon-strung guitar. However, the instrument is Spanish in origin, and much of the standard repertoire has a correspondingly Mediterranean flavour.

A different instrument

Classical guitar is a style that really does require a specific instrument. To play it seriously, you need to have a classical guitar strung with nylon strings: a steel-string acoustic guitar will not make the right sound. That is not to say that acoustic players have nothing to learn from the classical tradition. It is still worth looking at exploring the music and techniques of the classical players, and perhaps borrowing a few ideas.

The strict rules of classical guitar

In classical guitar, the right hand always plays fingerstyle; plectrums and fingerpicks are never used by classical players. The rules governing the roles of both hands are considerably stricter than for general-purpose fingerstyle acoustic playing. The left-hand thumb is always positioned on an imaginary line running down the centre of the guitar's neck.

The strings are plucked with the fingernails of the right hand, which means that classical players have to take considerable care of their right-hand fingernails. They file and polish them to achieve the optimum shape as well as length – because even the slightest roughness can produce unwanted sounds and impede the exact control of volume and tone required from the guitar.

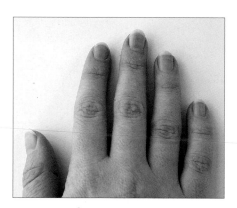

ABOVE: *The thumb- and fingernails of the right hand should be filed so that they are a consistent length and shape.*

ABOVE: *Right-hand fingernails should be just visible (1–2mm/less than ⅛in) when the hand is viewed with the palm to the front.*

Posture

Classical teachers insist on a very specific posture. The guitar sits on the left thigh, with the neck pointing upwards at a slight angle. To facilitate this while maintaining a straight back, the left foot is placed on a footstool. Any kind will do – even a pile of books can be used – but the specifically designed guitarist's footstools are slightly angled so that the position of the foot is absolutely correct.

ABOVE: *Classical guitar posture. The footstool ensures the guitar is at the correct angle to the body.*

Basic technique

The fingers of the left hand usually only fret notes that are actually played – even when, from the point of view of an acoustic guitarist, these notes might seem to belong to a familiar and easily formed chord shape. This is one respect in which the formal approach of classical players is markedly different from that of other guitarists. The aim of a classical guitarist is to achieve a high level of 'finger independence' (see 'Further classical guitar techniques'), and fretting unused notes is seen as superfluous and counterproductive.

Classical guitar music is usually written using standard notation only. It is generally up to the guitarist to work out the fingering, but both right-hand (p i m a) and left-hand (0 1 2 3 4) fingerings may sometimes be shown.

In many situations, the right hand employs a technique similar to that used for fingerstyle folk playing: the thumb covers the three bass strings (E, A, D) while the fingers cover one treble string each (G:i, B:m, E:a). However, classical guitar often breaks this mould in a number of ways: consecutive notes on the same string are often played by alternating fingers, and the fingers, rather than the thumb, are often used to play melodies on the bass strings.

Recommended listening:

- Leo Brouwer: "Berceuse"
- Manuel de Falla: "Fisherman's Song" (from *El Amor Brujo*)
- Fernando Sor: "Variations on a Theme by Mozart"

EXERCISE OP. 35 BY FERNANDO SOR (1778–1839)

Try this simple piece, which is written entirely in C major in first position. If you are unsure, all of these notes may be located by consulting the C major scale (see 'The C major scale and first position'). Both left- and right-hand fingerings are given, but omitted where a note or figure is repeated. Bass notes (E, A and D strings) are always played with the thumb, but watch out for the open G in the first bar of the last line – this is also played with the thumb.

Further classical guitar techniques

Classical guitar demands more discipline than most other styles of guitar playing. This is because you need to have strength and flexibility in your left hand. At the same time, agility plus extremely fine control of volume and tone are important for the right hand. Here, we will explore in detail some ideas which can help you build these goals into your practice from the beginning.

Finger independence

One of the main technical aims of classical guitar study is to achieve a high level of finger independence in both the left and right hands. The left-hand fingers should be able to find any conceivable shape within a space of at least four frets and to move independently of each other; all combinations of right-hand fingers should be equally usable.

In particular, any left-hand finger should be able to sustain a note on one string while the other fingers are in use on other strings. This principle can be used to generate an almost infinite variety of practice exercises. For example, choose any pair of strings, such as the B string and the D string. Keep the left hand within first position (the first four frets), and only allow each finger to play notes at its 'own' fret. Begin by playing the B string, first fret with the first finger, then the remaining three frets on the D string without cutting off the note on the B string. Next, play the B string, second fret with the second finger, letting this note ring while the remaining fingers play frets 1, 3 and 4 on the D string, and so on.

It is important to make sure that all the fingers hover directly above the fretboard when not in use. The result will not be musical, but will be very useful for developing finger strength and independence. An example pattern using this approach is shown below.

Tremolando

Classical guitar achieves various interesting textures using specific techniques. One of these is tremolando, in which alternating fingers are employed to play rapid repeated notes. With sufficient speed and smoothness, the result is perceived not as individual notes but as a homogenous musical texture. This is usually combined with a moving bass line or counter-melody played by the thumb. Tremolando technique cannot be achieved in one step, however; speed must be increased slowly while taking care that the correct right-hand fingers are used throughout and as evenly as possible.

Tremolando playing usually uses the same right-hand fingering pattern repeatedly: p a m i (thumb, ring, middle, index), in which the thumb plays a bass note which is allowed to ring and the fingers then play a note on a higher string three times in quick succession.

ABOVE: *The left hand in first position. Although only one note is being fretted, the remaining three fingers are hovering just above the fretboard.*

EXERCISE FINGER INDEPENDENCE

This exercise is shown in TAB notation for ease of reading. Make sure that all notes on the upper string of each pair are allowed to ring over the lower string. To add value for the right hand, make sure you alternate strictly between the index finger (i) and middle finger (m); starting on either is equally valid.

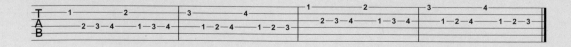

Basic tremolando technique

This basic pattern uses only open strings, so that you may concentrate entirely on the right hand. For variety, you could also find an E major scale using just the E string.

Recommended listening:

- Isaac Albéniz: *Asturias*
- Stanley Myers/John Williams: "Cavatina"
- Joaquín Rodrigo: *Concierto de Aranjuez*
- Francisco Tárrega: *Recuerdos de la Alhambra*
- Heitor Villa-Lobos: *Guitar Concerto*

1 Play the open bottom E string with the thumb (p). Let this bass note ring on underneath the next three.

2 Play the open top E string with the ring finger (a).

3 Play the open top E string with the middle finger (m).

4 Play the open top E string with the index finger (i).

EXERCISE "ALLEGRO" BY CARCASSI (EXCERPT)

This piece uses repeated notes that create the tremolando effect if played fast enough, but is also musically satisfying at a slower tempo. All the notes that are shown here can be found in first position except the very last note, which is found at the fifth fret. Follow both left- and right-hand fingerings exactly, and aim to play this piece fluently at 60 beats per minute before you start increasing the tempo of the piece.

Gypsy jazz

The gypsy-jazz style combines elements of the musette style of Parisian café entertainers with jazz-influenced compositions and improvisation. Gypsy jazz ensembles typically include a rhythm section consisting of double bass and several acoustic guitars, along with a selection of underpinning melody instruments including the violin, guitar and accordion.

Rhythm and melody styles

Drums are rarely heard in gypsy jazz, at least in its purest form. Instead, one or more guitars lay the rhythmic foundations using a forceful strumming style with a great deal of attack. As with all swing jazz, beats 2 and 4 are emphasized heavily. Chords on beats 2 and 4 should be played much louder than beats 1 and 3, and also more *staccato* (shorter). This is usually achieved by left-hand muting: play the chord, then quickly release finger pressure to stop it from ringing. Open strings should therefore be avoided.

Melodies should be played with as much attack as possible. Most serious players in this style use a particular type of acoustic guitar based on the Selmer-Macaferri model that was made famous by Django Reinhardt. However, the bright, almost nasal sound quality of this type of guitar can also be approximated by playing close to the bridge (although playing too close will result in loss of volume as well as carrying a greater risk of string breakage).

Some players deliberately vary the right-hand position between strums to help accent beats 2 and 4.

The harmonic minor scale

One of the identifying features of gypsy-jazz improvisation (and many of its original tunes) is the use of the harmonic minor scale. There are a few different types of minor scale, all of them related to the major scale. The harmonic minor scale is based on the same set of notes (starting a minor third lower, or on the sixth step of the major scale). However, the harmonic minor gains its unique flavour as a result of modifying one note: the seventh note is raised by a semitone.

For example, the A harmonic minor scale is based on the same notes as C major (no sharps or flats) but the seventh note (G) is raised to G$\sharp$. This means that one interval in the scale (from the sixth to the raised seventh, F to G$\sharp$ in A minor) is neither a tone nor a semitone, but an augmented second (three semitones). The diatonic chords of the minor key are obtained from harmonizing this scale.

ABOVE: *Moving the right hand closer to the bridge can help achieve a sharp, cutting sound for melodic playing.*

The Hot Club Quintet

Django Reinhardt and Stéphane Grappelli's seminal Hot Club Quintet recordings established a template which gypsy jazz has followed ever since. Two rhythm guitarists (including Django's brother Joseph) and double bass provided a good backdrop for Reinhardt and Grappelli's virtuosic melodies and free-wheeling improvisational interplay.

ABOVE: *The Hot Club Quintet featuring Reinhardt and Grappelli.*

Recommended listening:

- Boulou Ferré Quartet: *Relax and Enjoy*
- Django Reinhardt and Stéphane Grappelli: *Swing from Paris*
- Stochelo Rosenberg: *Ready'n Able*
- Trio Manouche: *The Nu Gypsy*

EXERCISE HARMONIC MINOR SCALE

This exercise consists of the A harmonic minor scale in second and then fifth position. Both positions require some stretches (see 'Practice patterns') performed by either the first or fourth finger, marked 'S' here. The other fingers stay in position. Once you can play this fluidly, try using it to improvise over the chord sequence in the exercise below.

EXERCISE GYPSY JAZZ MELODY

This melody mainly uses the notes of the A harmonic minor scale in both second and fifth position, as shown above. However, there are a few chromatic passing notes which occur between these scale notes. It may help to try recording yourself playing the chord sequence – use short, sharp strums on each beat, emphasizing beats 2 and 4.

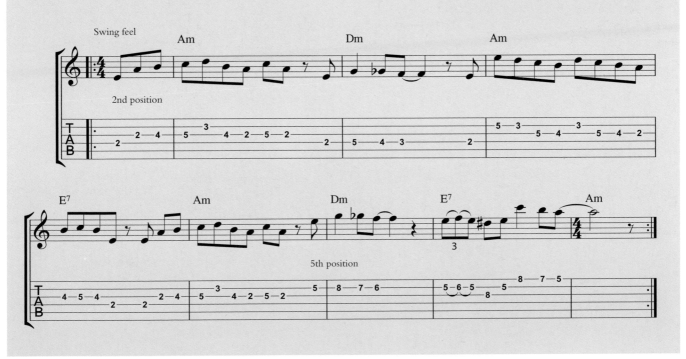

Latin jazz

The term 'Latin' in its musical sense covers a range of styles, from Cuban salsa to Argentinean tango. When jazz musicians use the term, however, they are usually concerned with the various forms of *bossa nova*. This style of jazz evolved in Brazil in the 1950s, and it can be said to consist of rich jazz harmonies fused with the dance rhythms of Brazilian samba.

Bossa nova basics

The nylon-strung acoustic guitar usually plays an accompanying (but central) role in bossa nova music. Typical guitar patterns outline the harmony, bass line and the characteristic rhythms of the style. The bass line usually alternates between the root and fifth of each chord; the harmony makes almost constant use of extended chords (mainly ninths, whether major, minor or dominant). Latin-jazz guitarists usually stick to the conventions of jazz chord voicing and movement (see 'Introducing jazz chords'). Many patterns voice the tonic chord using a shape with the root on the fifth string so that the root and fifth of the bass line can be found at the same fret. Exercise 1 applies the 'signature' bossa nova guitar pattern (bass line and chords) to a typical Latin-jazz chord sequence.

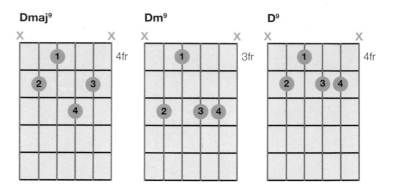

ABOVE: *Major, minor and dominant ninth chords in D. For all of these shapes, the second finger can shift to the bottom E string (at the same fret) to play the fifth in the bass.*

Antonio Carlos Jobim and João Gilberto

The bossa nova craze that swept America and the world in the early 1960s heralded the mass-market arrival of Latin jazz. Since then, the style has maintained its position at the more commercial end of the jazz spectrum. One man's legacy still looms larger than any other in this music: Brazilian composer, guitarist and pianist Antonio Carlos Jobim. Jobim wrote a staggering proportion of the songs that have become Latin standards, including "The Girl from Ipanema", "Desafinado" and "Wave". His collaboration with Stan Getz and guitarist João Gilberto on the album *Getz/Gilberto* is a milestone and one of the best-selling records in jazz history; its infectious bossa nova rhythm is largely Gilberto's personal invention. The bossa nova is one of those styles that can be identified on hearing one instrument playing two bars of music. The instrument in question is the nylon-string guitar and the birth of the archetypal guitar pattern is documented in Gilberto's introduction to "Desafinado" on this album.

LEFT: *Between them, Jobim (far left) and Gilberto (left) played an enormous part in both the creation of the bossa nova style and subsequently its huge popularity in the USA and Europe.*

Montuno

This is another type of musical figure that is very common in Latin jazz. It usually describes a repetitive syncopated figure with a descending bass line used as a basis for improvisation. This technique originated in Cuban salsa, but is also often heard in a jazz context. Each repeated two-bar section may be played many times before continuing to the next.

Repetition is a key feature of montuno; playing each figure only once or twice would detract from the feeling of continuity, which is essential to this dance-derived style. One of the defining features of Latin jazz is that the quaver (eighth note) feel is not swung, unlike most modern jazz. A pair of quavers should be played exactly as written, with the offbeat falling precisely halfway between beats.

EXERCISE **BOSSA NOVA SEQUENCE**

This exercise is written using polyphonic notation: there are two independent sets of notes in each bar. One set of notes (tails down) represents the bass line, played with the thumb, while the other set (tails up) represents the rhythmic chords. This allows independent rhythms to be written while showing the full duration of each note or chord.

Tip

For some variety, try playing this bossa nova sequence using left-hand muting, which will produce much shorter, percussive chords.

EXERCISE **MONTUNO VARIATIONS**

This exercise consists of various montuno patterns, each of which should be played repeatedly before moving on to the next. For variety, each figure is transposed into a new key (a popular montuno device). All the chord shapes here use a partial barre across the top three strings; this should be played using the first finger for the first three shapes, shifting to the second finger for the fourth (m6) shape (allowing the first finger to play the bass note).

Flamenco

As well as being a living traditional style in its own right, the Spanish folk music known as flamenco has had a considerable influence on many composers' work for classical guitar. The musical flavour of flamenco is a product of an advanced repertoire of right-hand techniques that can be difficult to learn, but are well worth it since they are highly rewarding to play.

Components of the style

An important component of flamenco is the energetic rhythmic strumming technique known as *rasgueado*. The rasgueado technique is unusual in that, unlike plectrum strumming or general-purpose fingerstyle strumming, several right-hand fingers (and sometimes the thumb) are used separately. This makes it possible to play fast and complex rhythms. Proper rasgueado technique is not easy to learn, however, and can constitute a lifetime's study in itself. The exercises opposite are intended only as an introduction to the very basics of the technique.

Rapid rhythms are achieved in rasgueado by strumming with individual fingers. The basic motion of each finger is either an outward 'flick' (known as an out-stroke) in which the finger starts by being tucked into the palm of the hand and then rapidly extends, strumming as it goes, or the reverse of this (an in-stroke) in which the finger strums upwards before curling back into the palm.

To learn rasgueado technique, you should first get used to making the individual finger strokes that will then be combined in rhythmic patterns. As rasgueado is essentially a percussive technique, try to make each finger hit (rather than strum) the strings, but in order to avoid a bottom-heavy sound, focus on the top E string even when playing all the strings.

Practise individual out-strokes and in-strokes using each right-hand finger. Each stroke should be short and sharp; maintain focus on this aspect when putting together strokes into rhythmic patterns such as Exercise 1 (opposite). For greater focus, rasgueado patterns may be practised on open strings at first – or even without the guitar (you can flick against the left wrist).

ABOVE: *Rasgueado out-stroke: the finger 'flicks' outwards until it is fully extended.*

ABOVE: *Rasgueado in-stroke: the finger curls back into the palm of the hand.*

ABOVE: *Spanish flamenco guitarist Paco de Lucia performs on stage in Madrid.*

Rest stroke technique

The second major component in learning flamenco guitar is the execution of fast – often very fast – melodic playing using the 'rest stroke' technique. Rather than pulling away from the string after plucking it, as in arpeggio patterns, the fingertip moves downwards, coming to rest on the next lowest string. This produces a different tone and enables more precise control and faster playing. Rest-stroke passages are usually played by alternating the index (i) and middle (m) fingers. This technique is also common in advanced classical guitar.

Tip

To play flamenco using a standard classical guitar, a removable transparent scratchplate, called a *golpeador*, may be worth buying.

Recommended listening:

- Juan Martín: *Classic Flamenco*
- Paco de Lucia: *Dos guitarras flamencos en stereo*
- Paco Peña: *Fabulous Flamenco!*
- Manitas de Plata: *Feria Gitane*

Rest stroke on the top E string

1 Rest the tips of both the index and middle fingers on the B string, so that drawing either finger back will result in playing the string with the nail.

2 Play the top E string using the nail of the index finger, then bring the fingertip back to rest on the B string, allowing the E string to ring.

3 Play the top E string again, this time using the nail of the middle finger. Again, bring the tip of the finger back to rest on the B string.

EXERCISE BASIC RASGUEADO PATTERN

Each strum here is assigned both a finger and a direction: the downstroke symbol ⊓ is used for the out-stroke, and the up-stroke ∨ for the in-stroke. The pattern remains the same throughout the exercise and should be practised very slowly at first, gradually building up speed while making sure you stick to the pattern exactly. Don't expect to get instant results in this style! Experienced performers interpret each strum themselves in long passages of music. While different guitarists play rasgueados with individual flair, the part of the rasgueado that is most important is the final strum.

EXERCISE SPANISH PHRYGIAN

This scale should be played using rest strokes throughout. Alternate strictly between fingers i and m (the index and middle fingers).

Don't expect to achieve instant fluency here; diligent practice at very gradually increasing tempos will ultimately give a greater reward.

The 12-string guitar

You may feel daunted by the idea of playing double the usual number of strings – but the good news is that if you can strum away on a six-string you will probably be able to get a decent sound out of a 12-string. There is no difference in the fundamental technique – the only aspect that is different is that the fingering is a little harder in some ways.

What is a 12-string guitar?

The 12 strings on a 12-string come in six pairs of two – six 'courses' to use the technical term. The pairs lie close together on the neck, so that each finger always frets both at once. This makes playing a bit more difficult than playing a single string, because rather more precision and pressure are required. Moreover, the neck of a 12-string is wider than the neck of a standard six-string acoustic – and this, too, takes some getting used to. All in all, playing a 12-string is physically more demanding than playing an ordinary guitar, but well within the reach of any competent player.

The chord shapes that you make are the same as the ones you are used to, because the tuning of a 12-string is the same as that of a six-string – in a manner of speaking. The top two pairs of strings (B and E) are tuned in unison (exactly the same note). The remaining four (E, A, D, G) are tuned an octave apart. Each pair consists of one string tuned to the same pitch as a six-string, and one string tuned an octave higher. Usually, the higher string of each pair is placed above the standard string, so that the higher string is struck first when strumming or picking downwards.

The sound

This doubling-up of the strings is reminiscent of the configuration of other guitar-like instruments, such as the mandolin. However, the 12-string guitar as we know it is a modern invention – undoubtedly American, and dating from around the turn of the 20th century. The effect of the double courses is to yield a very full, resonant sound when the guitar is strummed. This derives not only from the fact that you are playing twice as many notes at a time, but also from the chorus effect produced when two notes are very nearly, but not quite, the same pitch (or an octave apart). The tiny differences in pitch are not enough to make the guitar sound out of tune; instead they create a slow, shimmering effect that is extremely lush and pleasant to listen to.

> ### Recommended listening:
> - **Joan Armatrading:** "All the Way From America"
> - **Boston:** "More Than a Feeling"
> - **Pink Floyd:** "Wish You Were Here"
> - **The Rolling Stones:** "As Tears Go By"

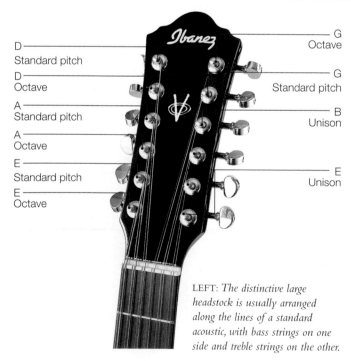

D — Standard pitch
D — Octave
A — Standard pitch
A — Octave
E — Standard pitch
E — Octave

G — Octave
G — Standard pitch
B — Unison
E — Unison

LEFT: *The distinctive large headstock is usually arranged along the lines of a standard acoustic, with bass strings on one side and treble strings on the other.*

ABOVE: *Almost all 12-string guitars have a scratchplate to protect the top of the guitar from the vigorous strumming often associated with the instrument.*

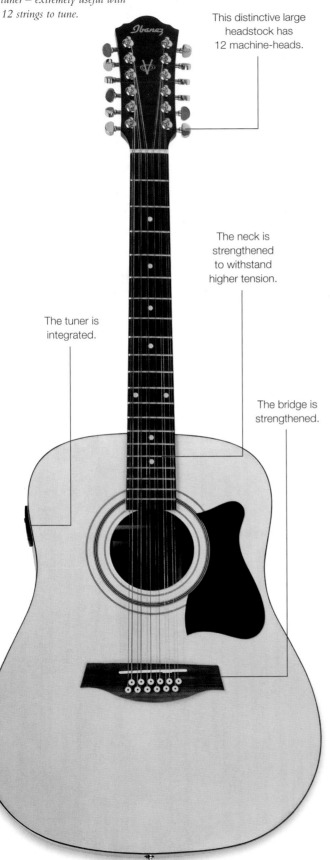

BELOW: *The 12-string shown here, although not an electro-acoustic model, has an integrated tuner – extremely useful with 12 strings to tune.*

This distinctive large headstock has 12 machine-heads.

The neck is strengthened to withstand higher tension.

The tuner is integrated.

The bridge is strengthened.

Leadbelly

Huddie Ledbetter, known as Leadbelly, described himself as 'the king of the 12-string guitar', and he undoubtedly played an important role in popularizing the instrument. Today, Leadbelly's recordings are also a vital bridge between the past and present. Born in 1888 in Louisiana, USA, Leadbelly was among the oldest of American folk musicians to make recordings in the 1930s and '40s. His originals, as well as the traditional songs he learnt as a labourer and during his many spells in prison, have found their way into the repertoire of artists as diverse as Bob Dylan, Led Zeppelin and Nirvana. Although often labelled a blues singer, Leadbelly drew on a far broader range of styles, and his best-known song "Goodnight Irene" is essentially a country ballad. In Leadbelly's original recordings, he accompanies himself on a variety of different instruments, including piano and accordion, but most often on a 12-string guitar, usually tuned a fourth below standard tuning (B E A D F♯ B), resulting in his powerful and sonorous 'roaring' signature guitar sound.

ABOVE: *Leadbelly playing the large Stella 12-string guitar with which he was most often seen.*

Tuning a 12-string guitar

The chorus effect is desirable, but this does not mean that a lazy approach can be taken to tuning: there are few sounds as grating as that of a badly tuned 12-string, and in any case, the chorus effect will be produced well within the limits of 'perfect' tuning. The usual approach is to get the lower string of each pair in tune first, and then to make sure the higher octave agrees exactly. This (along with changing strings) is a time-consuming process. However, the tuning arrangement is part of what gives this guitar its distinctive sound.

Chords are the guitarist's basic vocabulary,

the universal starting point for mastery

of the instrument's special language.

Chordfinder

To begin to play, you need to know just

a handful of chords, just as to speak another

language you need to know only a few words

at first. But to play eloquently on the guitar,

you must have a large lexicon at your disposal.

Introduction

This chordfinder is a kind of basic dictionary. It is not exhaustive, because there are many more obscure chords, and many more ways of playing the better-known chords than can be accommodated in one book or section of a book. However, if you master the chords on the following pages – or even half of them – then you will be reasonably well equipped to express yourself through your guitar.

Explore and experiment

Having access to a ready reference set of chord diagrams can be enormously useful. For example, whenever you encounter an unfamiliar chord in a songbook, it is likely you will be able to match it to a comparable chord shape in the finder. You may also wish to set off on a 'journey of discovery' to expand your knowledge of a certain chord type, key or tuning. Be aware, however, that there is a limit to the amount of new data that you can absorb in one session. The best way to learn a new chord is to find as many uses for it as you can, and experiment by combining it with other ones.

Reading the chord diagrams

Each chord is presented in three formats: as a chord diagram, in the standard musical notation that is common for all instruments, and in guitar tablature. A chord box (also known as a fret box) is a grid with six vertical lines representing the guitar's strings and horizontal lines representing the frets. Dots or circles are placed within this grid to show the position of the fingers. In this chordfinder, the finger dots are numbered (fingers 1–4) although many songbooks do not show these numbers.

There are certain graphic conventions connected with chord boxes. Where the highest horizontal line – that is, the top edge of the box – is drawn as a double line, this represents the 'nut' of the guitar. The nut is the raised ridge at the top of the neck. When the nut is not shown, the chord is fingered further up the fretboard. The number next to the chord tells you exactly where: 5fr indicates that the lowest active fret in this chord is the fifth fret. There are a few other symbols that you need to know: an O placed directly above the string indicates that the open string is part of the chord; an X shows that the string is not to be played. Two or more finger dots at the same fret may be joined by a curved line, indicating a full or partial barre – that is, the underside of the finger (usually the first finger) presses down on two or more strings at once.

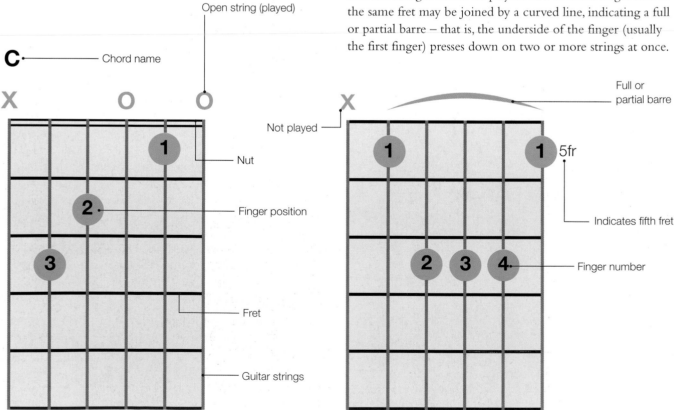

Notation and tab

Next to each chord box you will find two staves yoked together. Each of these staves represents a different way of representing the chord in question. The upper stave is standard musical notation: if you can read music, it tells you which notes are in the chord. The notation is universal in the sense that the chord shown in the notation could be played on any instrument that can play more than one note at a time (a piano, for example), or indeed on a group of instruments played by different individuals.

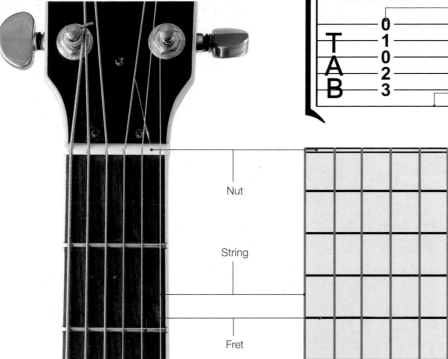

Standard musical notation and guitar tablature

Standard notation

Guitar tablature

Indicates fret to be played

Lowest string (E)

LEFT: *The chord box represents the frets and strings as seen face on: vertical lines represent the strings, while the frets are horizontal. When reading chord boxes, as with tablature, it is vital not to interpret the order of the strings in the wrong direction.*

Nut

String

Fret

The lower stave is guitar tablature ('TAB' for short). The lines, although superficially similar to the five-lined stave above, represent not the pitch of the note, but the six strings of the guitar. The bottom line stands for the lowest string, low E in standard tuning. The number on each line or string shows the fret that is to be played. Note that it does not show which finger to use, unlike the adjacent chord diagram. The numbers in TAB show which fret to play. The notes of the chord are arranged vertically, indicating that they are to be played together as a single chord.

X and O indications

In most of the first-position chords (and many other shapes further up the neck) the open-string notes must be able to sound clearly. If you concentrate only on producing the fretted notes, it is very easy to accidentally mute the 'O' notes. Try playing the strings one at a time to make sure that these are also sounding. Similarly, letting the 'X' strings sound will often result in a discordant effect.

A final note

For all the common chord families included in the following pages, at least one shape is shown per chord type for each step of the chromatic scale (the series of notes that rises and falls in semitones, or half notes).

All of the chords are in standard tuning (E, A, D, G, B and E) unless otherwise stated. However, some basic chord shapes for other tunings are also provided – and these are all clearly flagged in the introductory text on those pages. There are also some 'jazz voicings' that you can experiment with once you have mastered the basic shapes of the chords, as well as understand what their effect is.

Here and there, 'Try this' boxes are also included, which contain interesting and useful information about the construction of certain chord types. They also explain each type's sound and character, or their relationship to other members of the wide family of chords. Some suggestions for possible musical uses are detailed along with examples of songs that have used those chord types.

Major chords

The major chords consist of the root note plus the third and fifth notes of the major scale. In C, for example, those notes would be the root note C, plus E and G. In this section, you will find at least one way of playing the simple major chord for every step in the chromatic scale. Note that some notes can be expressed more than one way: D♭ is the same note as C♯, and B♭ is the same note as as A♯. The names used here are those most likely to be encountered. In Western music, major chords are often described as sounding 'happy'.

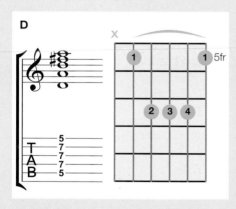

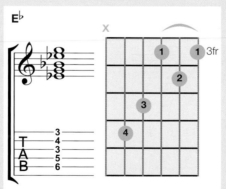

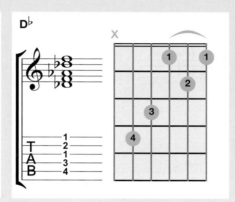

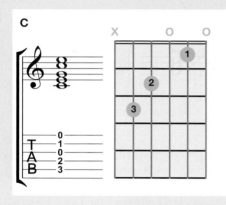

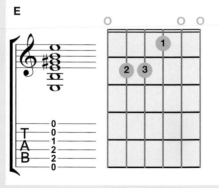

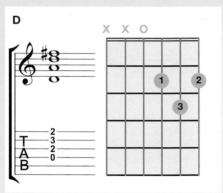

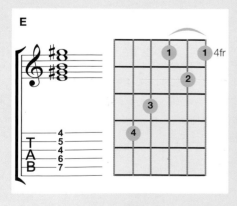

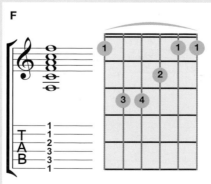

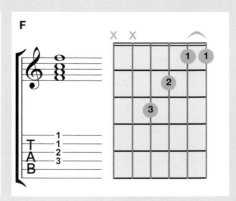

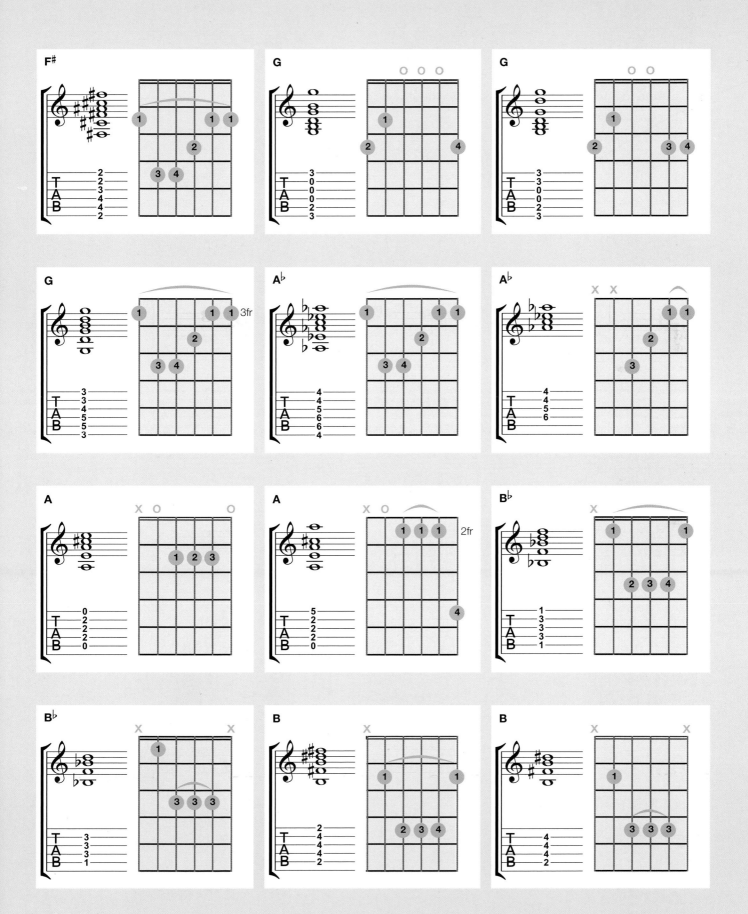

Minor chords

The minor chords consist of the first, third and fifth notes of the minor scale. The third note is flattened (lowered) in comparison with the major chord; it is a semitone lower. For the guitar player this means that many chord shapes can be changed from major to minor by changing one fretted note, or moving one finger. For example, E major becomes E minor by lifting the first finger from the first fret of the G string, thereby changing the major E-G♯-B to the minor E-G-B. In Western music, minor chords are often characterized as having a sad sound.

Key
X = don't play
O = play open string

Cm
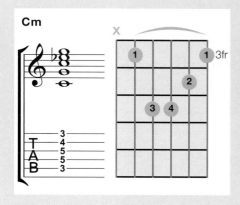

C♯m
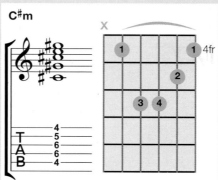

Dm
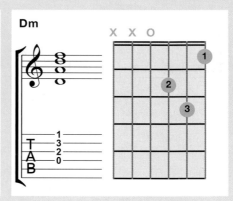

E♭m
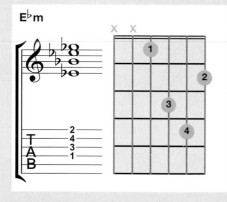

E♭m
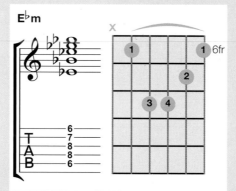

Em
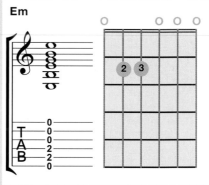

Fm
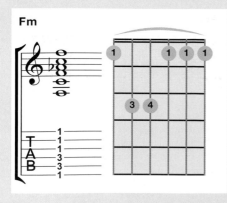

Fm
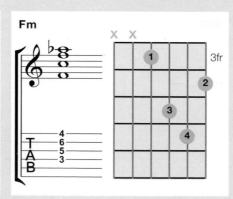

F♯m
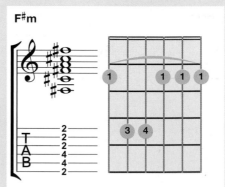

F#m

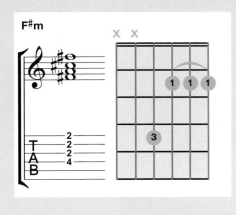

Gm

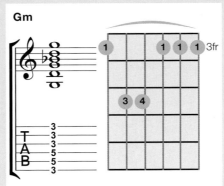

Gm

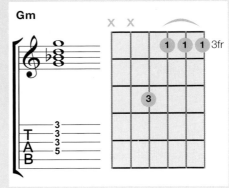

G#m

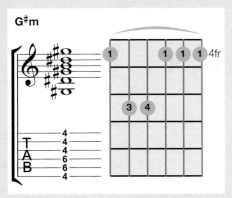

G#m

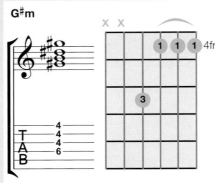

Am

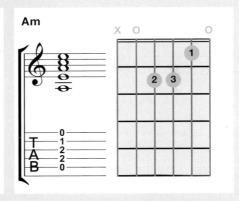

Am

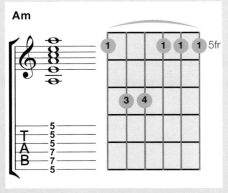

Am

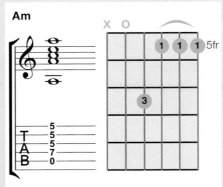

B♭m

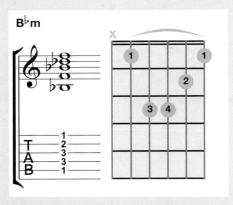

B♭m

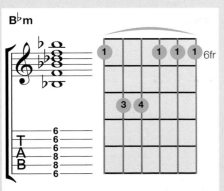

Bm

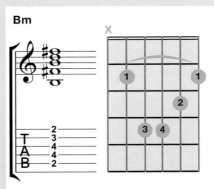

Bm

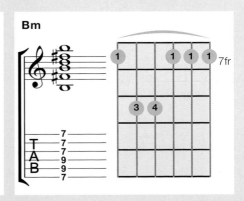

Seventh chords

The seventh, also known as the dominant seventh, is denoted by a number 7 after the root name. The chord consists of four notes: the root note, the major third, the perfect fifth, and the flattened seventh (a semitone below the seventh of the major scale, or one tone below the root note). The dominant seventh has an unresolved feel that makes it 'want' to resolve to a chord a perfect fourth above – an essential element of any guitarist's box of tricks, particularly when playing blues or derived styles including jazz and rock 'n' roll.

Key
X = don't play
O = play open string

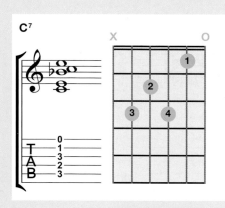

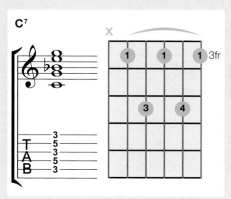

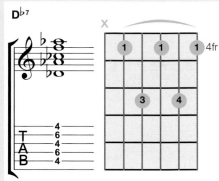

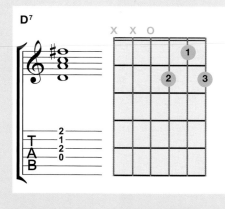

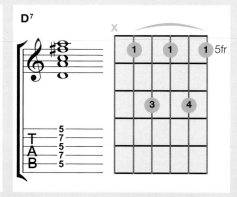

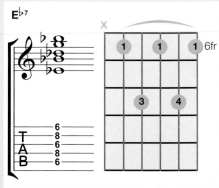

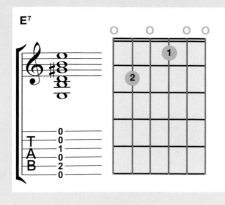

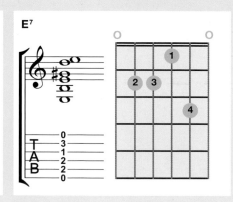

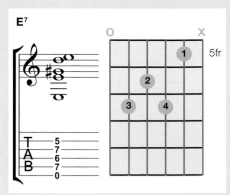

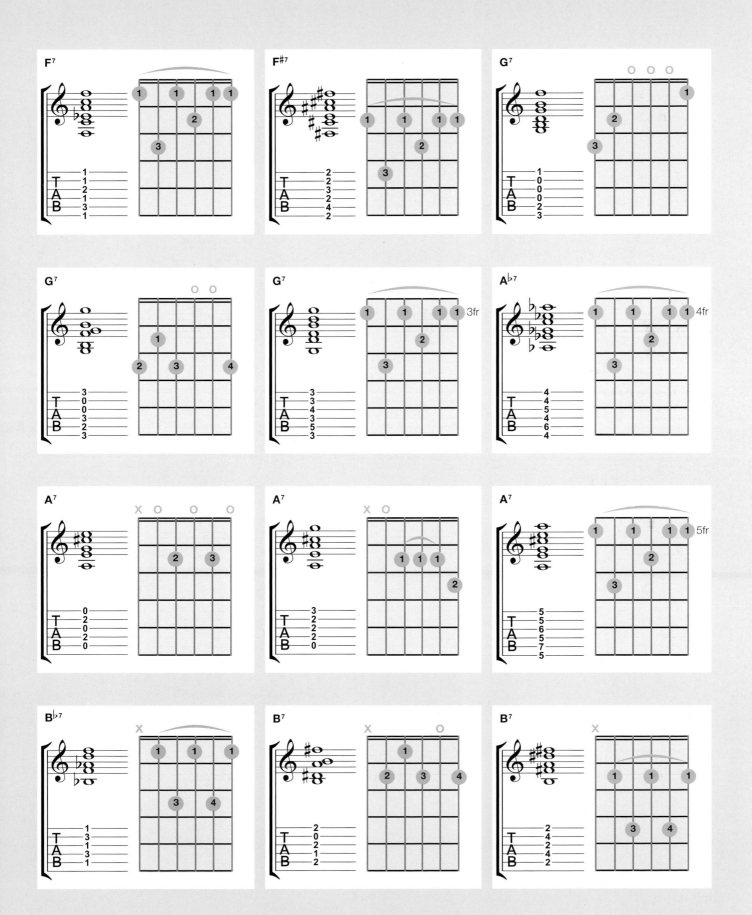

Minor seventh chords

The minor seventh chord is constructed by adding a fourth note to the minor triad – a minor seventh interval from, or a tone below, the root. This is the same note as the seventh in a dominant seventh chord. Minor seventh chords are denoted by m7, min7 or -7 after the root note. Like the dominant seventh, minor seventh chords often seem to 'want' to move to another chord: in their case, a dominant seventh chord a fourth above. This chord relationship is known as a II-V progression, and is crucial to modern jazz and many related styles, particularly Latin jazz.

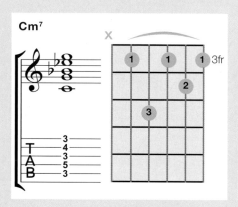

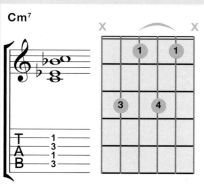

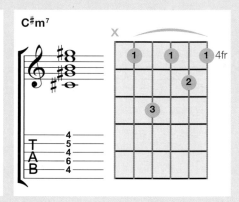

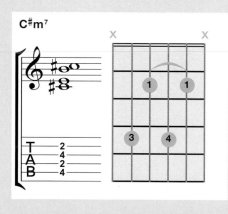

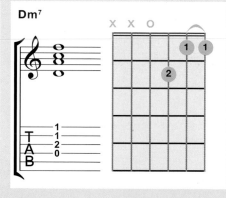

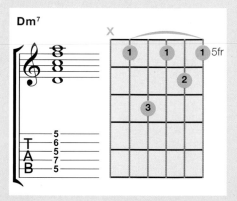

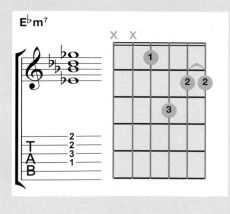

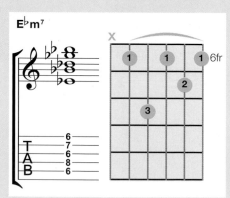

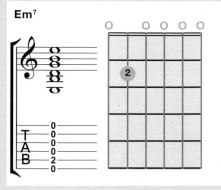

Em⁷
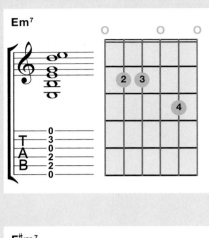

Fm⁷
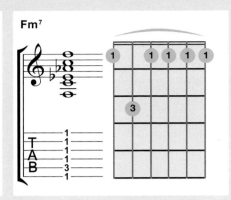

Fm⁷
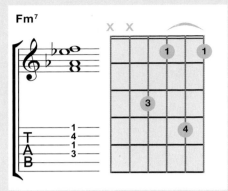

F♯m⁷
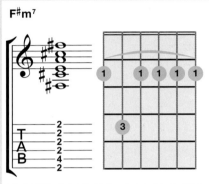

F♯m⁷
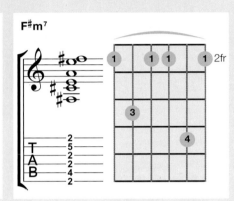

Gm⁷
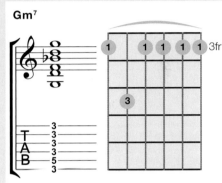

Gm⁷
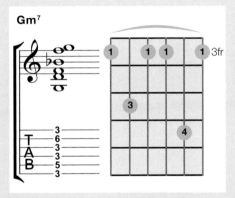

Am⁷
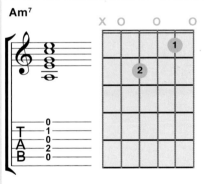

Am⁷
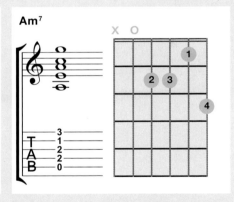

B♭m⁷
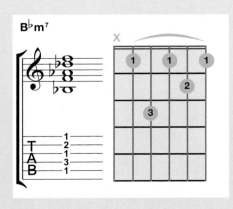

Bm⁷
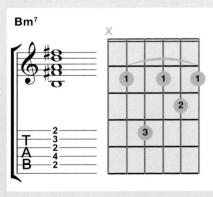

Bm⁷
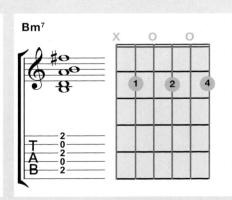

Major seventh chords

The major seventh is the archetypal sweet-sounding jazzy chord, and is constructed from four notes: the root, the major third, the perfect fifth, and the seventh note of the major scale (or to put it another way, a semitone below the root). The major seventh is usually denoted as maj7, but is occasionally indicated with a triangle thus: △ or △7. The major seventh chord can often be used as chord I or chord IV in the major key (if a jazzy sound is desired), but beware of using it in any style where a bluesy effect is required.

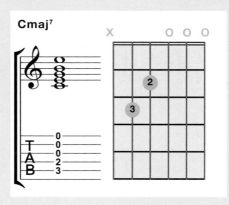

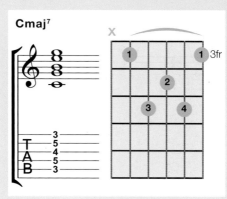

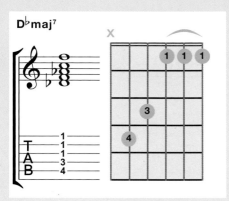

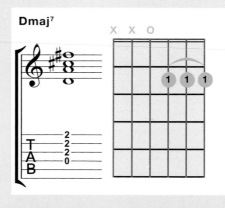

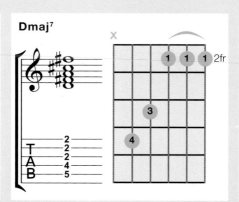

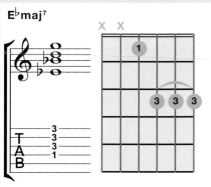

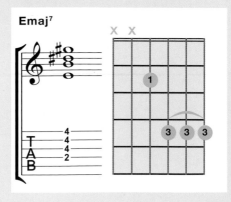

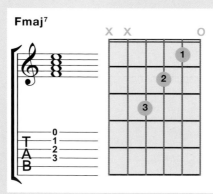

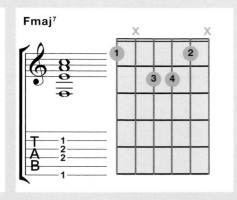

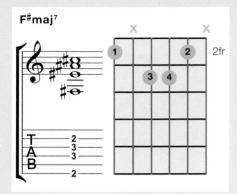

F#maj7 2fr

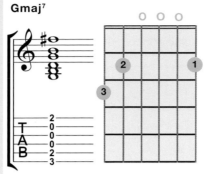

Gmaj7

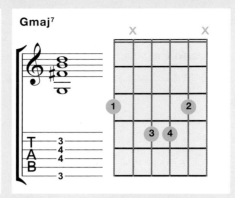

Gmaj7

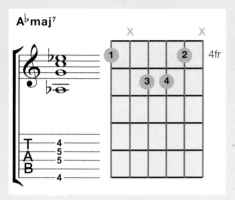

A♭maj7 4fr

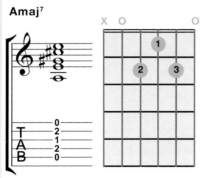

Amaj7

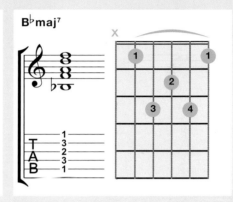

B♭maj7

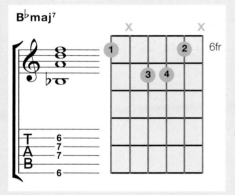

B♭maj7 6fr

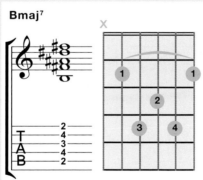

Bmaj7

Bmaj7 7fr

Try this

The major seventh is found on steps I and IV in the major key. That is to say, if you play the first, third, fifth and seventh notes of the scale, or the fourth, sixth, eighth and tenth (going into the next octave), then the result is a major seventh. This means that the major seventh can often be played instead of the simple major chord at the fourth or fifth step. So in C, for example, try playing Cmaj7 or Fmaj7 instead of plain C or F. It won't always work (in particular, there may be some tension created if the melody contains the root note of the chord), but sometimes it will give an interestingly sophisticated sound.

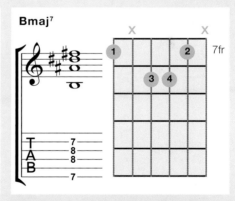

ABOVE: *Listen to Wings' "Band on the Run".*

Diminished seventh chords

The diminished seventh is constructed from four minor thirds stacked on top of each other. This makes for a chord that can be described as spooky or jangly. For simplicity, some notes in diminished seventh chords may be re-spelled in notation. The top note of C diminished seventh, for example, is B♭♭ (B double flat) but it is often written as A, which is physically the same note. The symmetrical construction means that two diminished seventh chords a minor third apart (for example A and C) contain exactly the same notes, so can be freely substituted for each other.

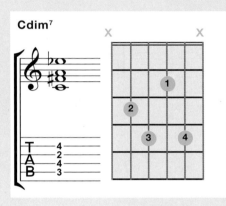

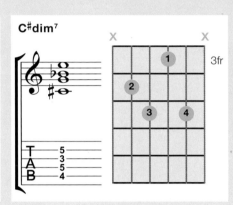

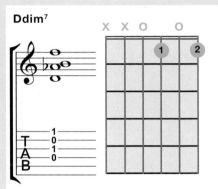

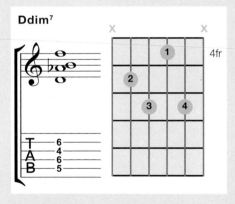

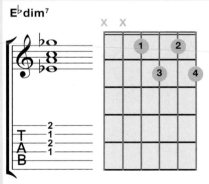

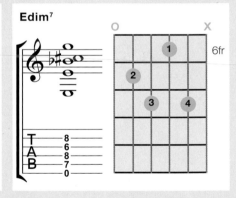

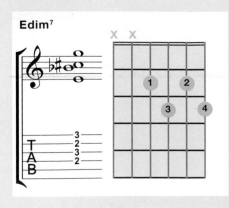

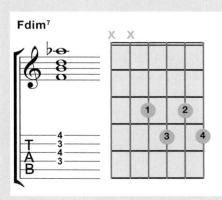

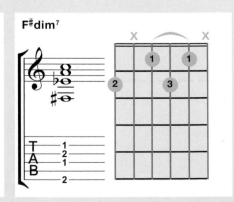

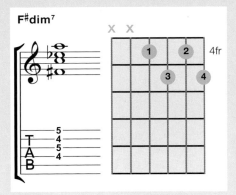
F#dim7

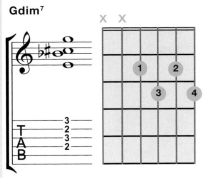
Gdim7

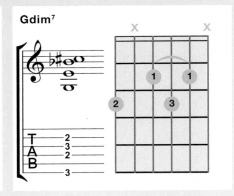
Gdim7

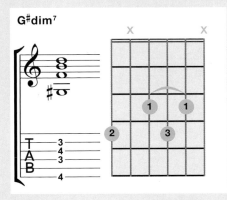
G#dim7

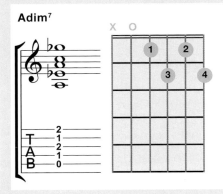
Adim7

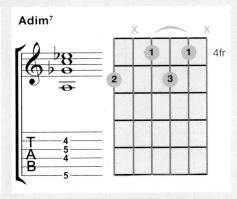
Adim7

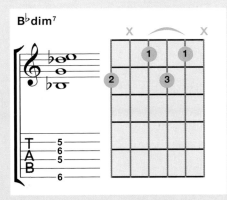
Bbdim7

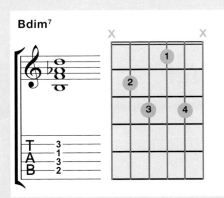
Bdim7

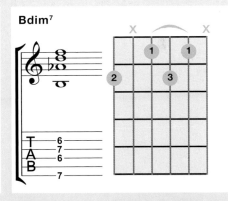
Bdim7

Try this

Diminished chords can be moved around the fretboard against a ringing open bass string. The open low E, A and D strings between them provide bass notes that will work against any diminished chord here. Try moving any shape up or down the fretboard in intervals of three frets at a time, perhaps arpeggiating the fretted notes with the right-hand fingers, while the open-string bass note (played by the thumb) is allowed to ring. This is one of those 'guitaristic' moves that is well worth incorporating as a stock-in-trade idea, though beware of over-using it as it can sound a little too much like horror-film music for some styles.

ABOVE: *Listen to James Taylor's "Don't Let Me Be Lonely Tonight"*.

m7♭5 chords

The m7♭5 chord consists of the root note, the minor third, the diminished fifth and the minor seventh. It is also known as 'half-diminished' because of its similarity to the diminished seventh. The only difference is that in m7♭5, the seventh note is a semitone higher. Although the half-diminished chord is found in the major key (chord VII), it is not encountered very often, and is most often used by players as a substitute for a dominant ninth chord a major third below – for example, Em7♭5 may be played when C9 is written.

Cm7♭5

Cm7♭5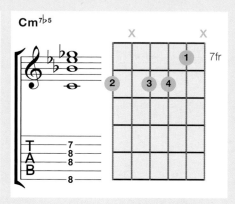

C#m7♭5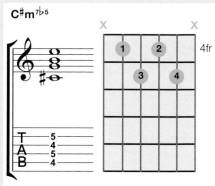

C#m7♭5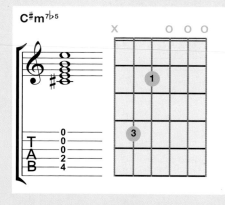

Dm7♭5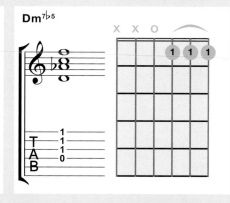

Dm7♭5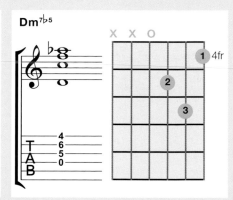

D#m7♭5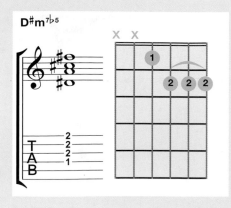

Em7♭5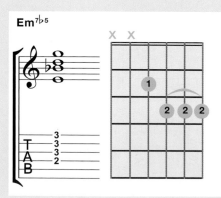

Em7♭5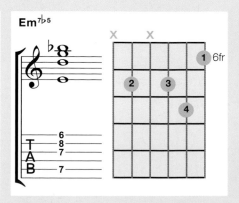

Fm^{7♭5}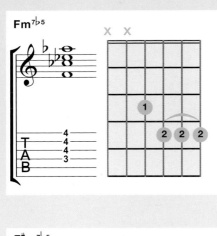

Fm^{7♭5}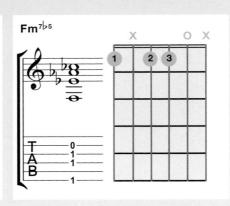

F#m^{7♭5}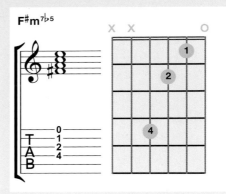

F#m^{7♭5}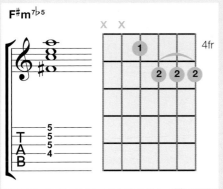

Gm^{7♭5}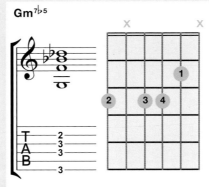

Gm^{7♭5}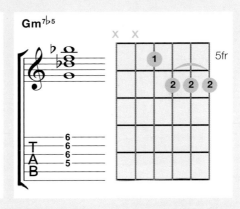

G#m^{7♭5}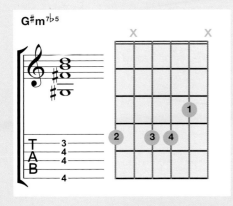

Am^{7♭5}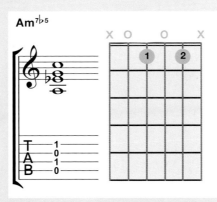

Am^{7♭5}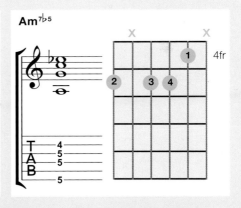

A#m^{7♭5}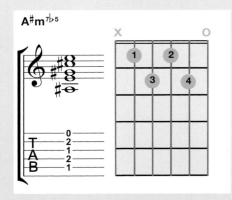

Bm^{7♭5}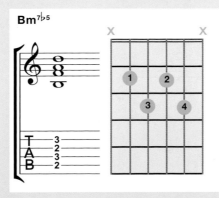

Bm^{7♭5}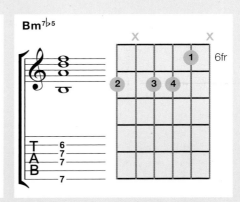

Dominant seventh jazz voicings

A voicing is an alternative way of stacking up the three or four notes that make up a chord. In these voicings of the dominant seventh, the fifth is omitted. This lends a sparse quality to the sound, and creates a kind of space which a singer's voice can explore. In the context of a band, a bass player might choose to omit the root note too – since this provides an opportunity for much greater finger movement, and also frees up fingers to add more advanced extended notes such as ninths and 13ths on the top two strings.

Key

X = don't play

O = play open string

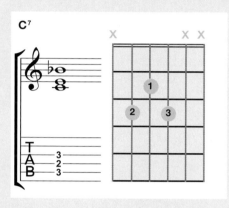

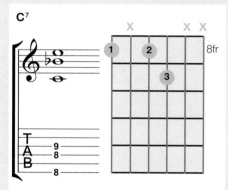

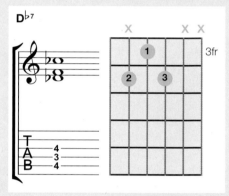

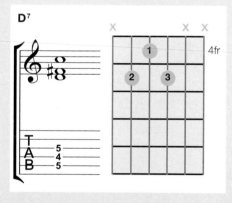

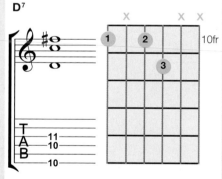

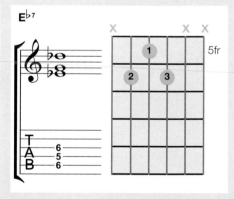

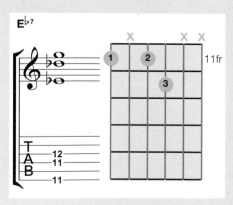

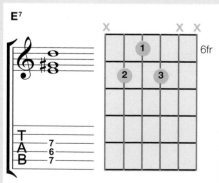

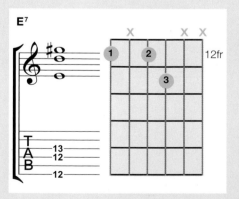

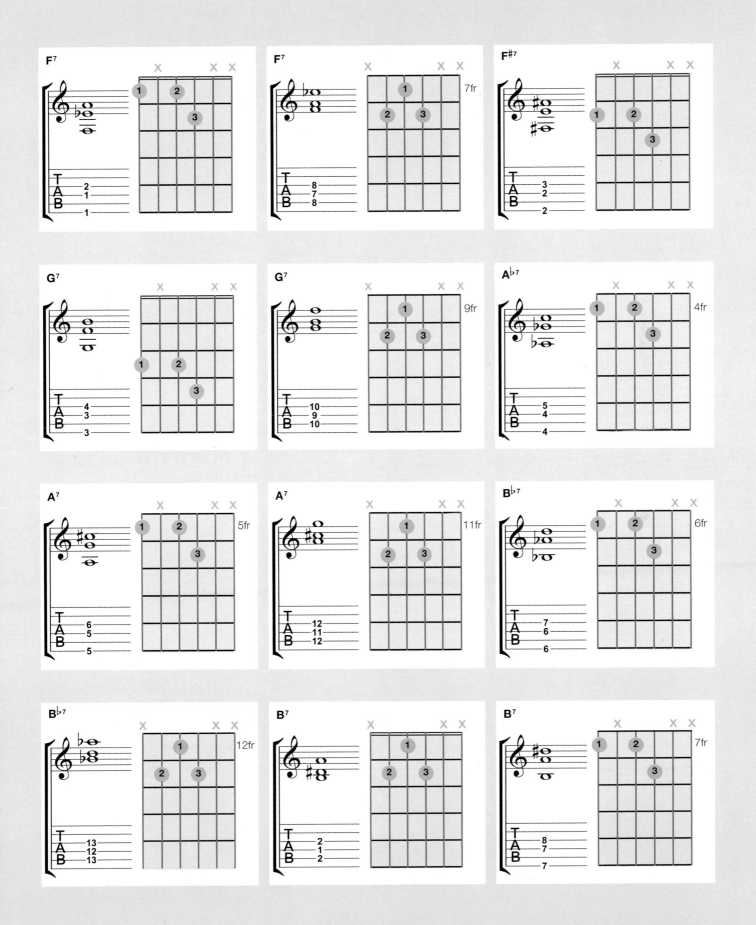

Minor seventh jazz voicings

The minor seventh jazz voicings, like the dominant seventh jazz voicings, omit the fifth. They often occur as chord II in a II–V progression. In this instance, the seventh note usually resolves downwards by a semitone to the third of the V chord. As the fifth is omitted, these shapes may also be used freely where m7♭5 is written. All the shapes here with the root on the A string can easily be turned into m9 (minor ninth) chords by re-assigning the fingers so that the fourth finger is free to play the B string at the same fret as the note on the G string - great for Latin jazz.

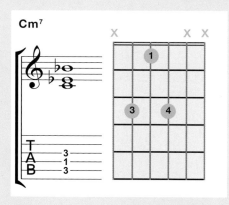

Cm⁷

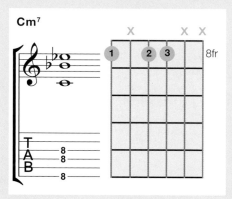

Cm⁷

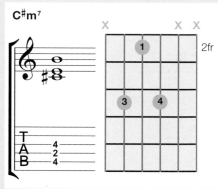

C#m⁷

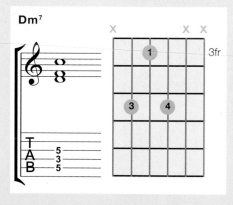

Dm⁷

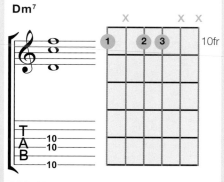

Dm⁷

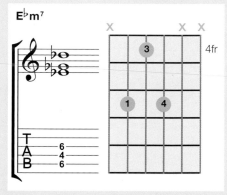

E♭m⁷

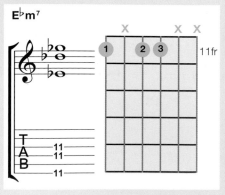

E♭m⁷

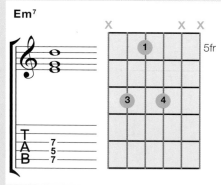

Em⁷

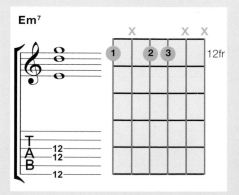

Em⁷

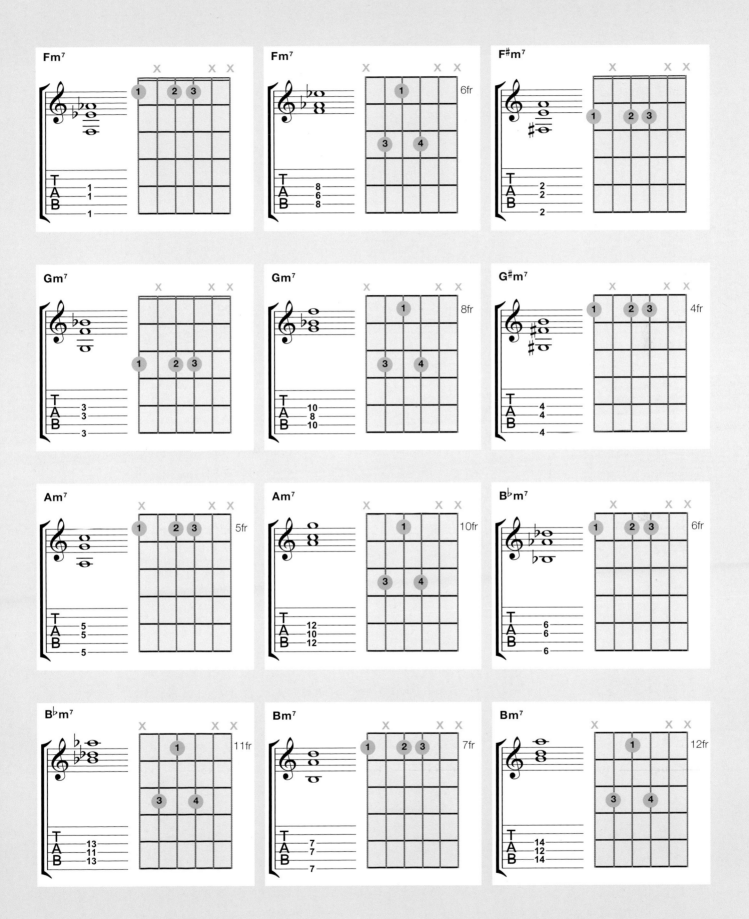

Major seventh jazz voicings

This minimal jazz voicing, like those for the dominant seventh and minor seventh, omits the fifth of the chord, and so consists of the root, the major third and the major seventh. The major seventh chord is often found as chord I after a II–V progression; all three shapes should be chosen for minimal movement. If chords I and II are voiced with the root on the bottom string, chord V will be found with the root on the A string, and vice versa. The third of chord V will remain present in chord I (as the seventh), while the seventh of chord V falls by a semitone to become the third of chord I.

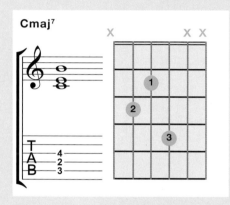

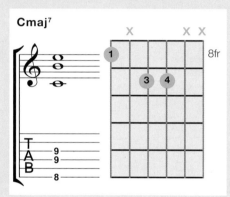

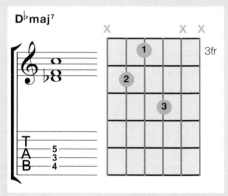

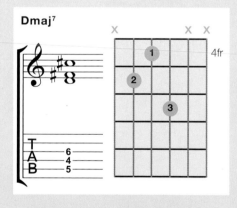

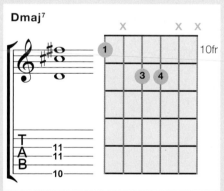

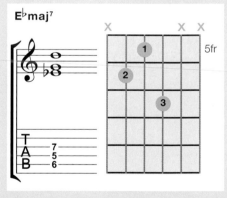

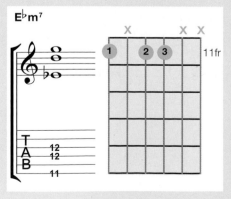

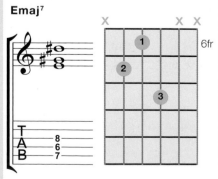

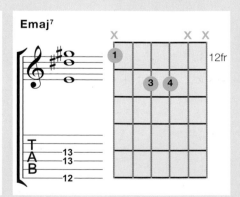

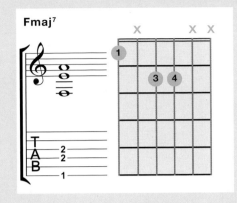

Fmaj⁷

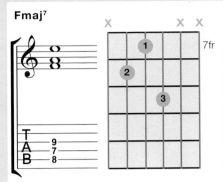

Fmaj⁷

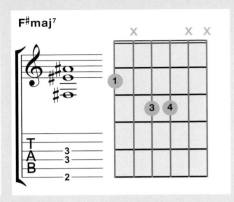

F#maj⁷

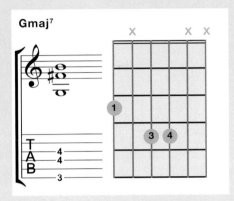

Gmaj⁷

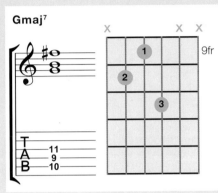

Gmaj⁷

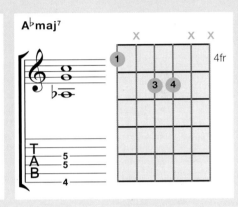

A♭maj⁷

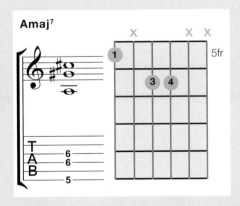

Amaj⁷

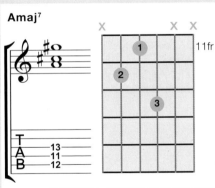

Amaj⁷

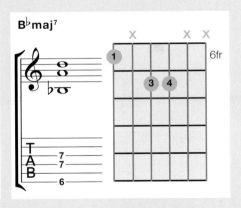

B♭maj⁷

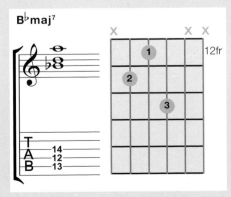

B♭maj⁷

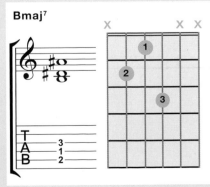

Bmaj⁷

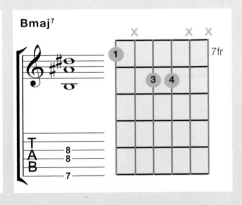

Bmaj⁷

Suspended fourth

A suspended fourth consists of the root, perfect fourth and perfect fifth of the scale. A suspension is created when one of the notes in a chord is replaced with another which sounds like it 'wants' to resolve to the note replaced. In popular music, this usually takes the form of raising the third in a major chord by one semitone. As this note is a perfect fourth above the root, the result is known as a suspended fourth chord (denoted as sus4). The same suspension works well with dominant sevenths, and is denoted as 7sus4. The Who's "Pinball Wizard" has suspensions in action.

Key
X = don't play
O = play open string

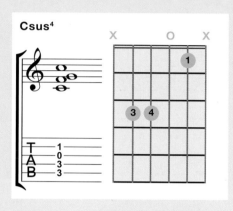

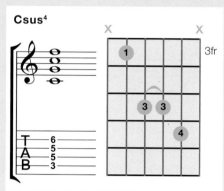

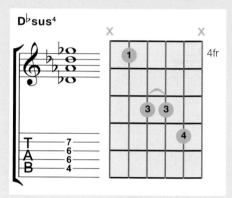

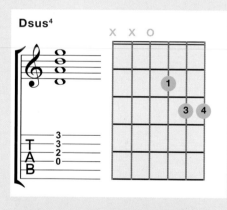

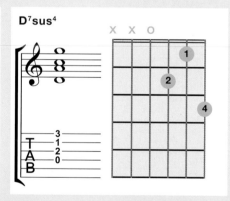

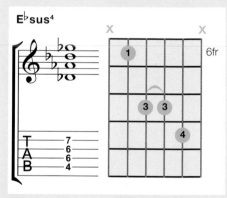

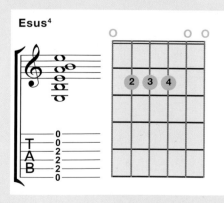

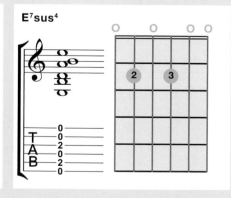

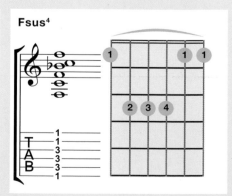

F#sus⁴

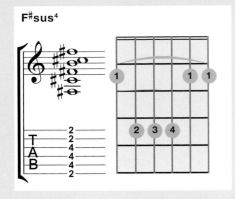

Gsus⁴

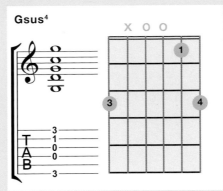

A♭sus⁴

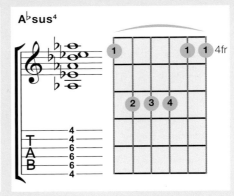

Asus⁴

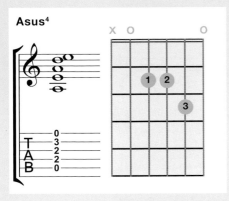

A⁷sus⁴

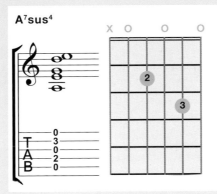

B♭sus⁴

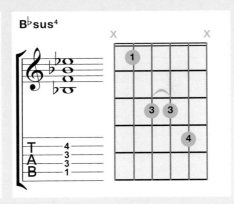

Bsus⁴

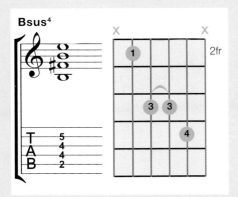

Bsus⁴

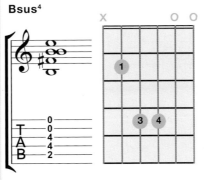

B⁷sus⁴

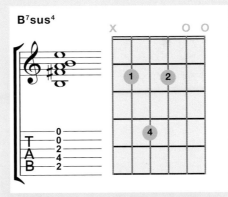

Try this

Although the suspended fourth is the most common suspension, a different one is heard in many acoustic guitar styles. This is the suspended second (sus2) chord. Here, the major third is replaced by the note one tone below (a second from the root), which also resolves to the third. Dsus2 and Asus2 are the most popular first-position sus2 chords as the suspension is created by removing a finger to leave one string open (the top E and B strings respectively in these chords). Try the sequence D – Dsus4 – D – Dsus2 – D: many famous songs have been written around this kind of figure, most famously James Taylor's "Country Road".

ABOVE: *Listen to James Taylor's "Country Road".*

Half-open chords

These chords all produce interesting sounds by moving familiar chords into unfamiliar positions, while one or more open strings remain unchanged. This creates tension, but there is a compensating 'drone' effect from the open strings. Extensive use of these chords is generally limited to keys that contain the notes of the open string or strings. This means E and B – in other words, sharp keys rather than flat keys, although this can of course also be used to created more dissonant sounds if that is the effect you want to create.

Key

X = don't play

O = play open string

Cmaj⁷
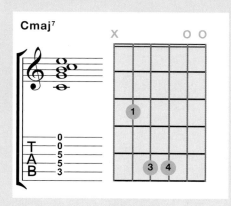

Cmaj⁷
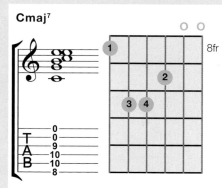

C♯m⁷
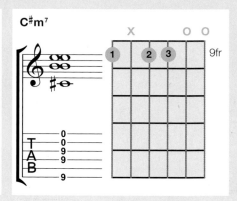

C♯m⁷
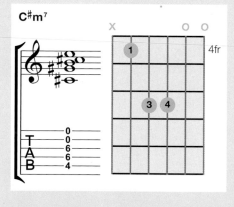

D⁽ᵃᵈᵈ ⁹/¹¹⁾
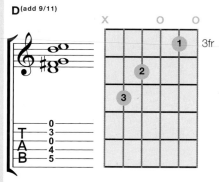

Dm⁽ᵃᵈᵈ ⁹⁾
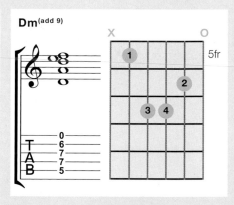

D⁶/⁹
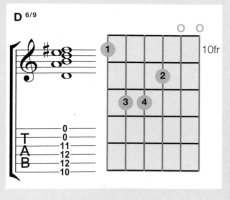

Dmaj⁹
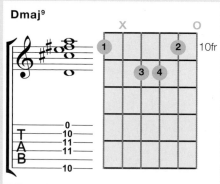

Dm⁶/⁹
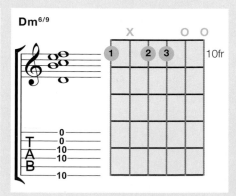

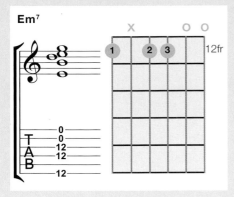

Em7

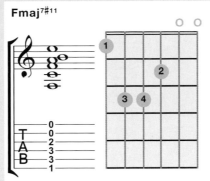

Fmaj7#11

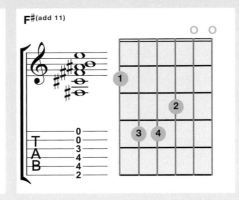

F#(add 11)

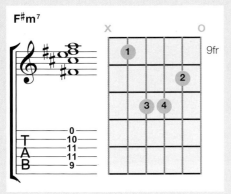

F#m7

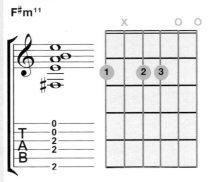

F#m11

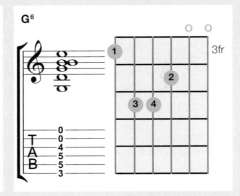

G6

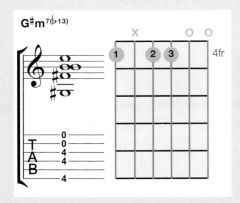

G#m7(♭13)

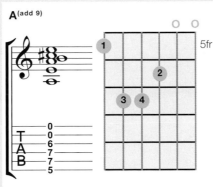

A(add 9)

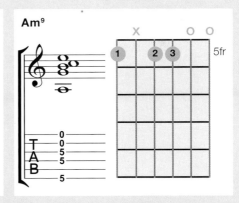

Am9

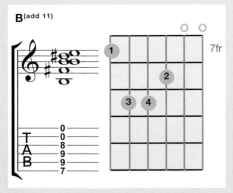

B(add 11)

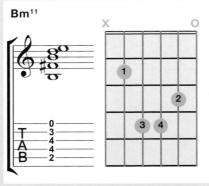

Bm11

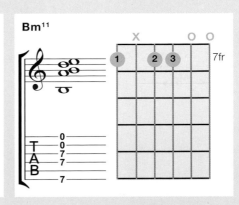

Bm11

Essential chords in open G

In open G, the strings are tuned to DGDGBD. As with any open tuning, the point of playing in open G is to explore the tensions that can be created by moving fretted notes against open strings. This usually means that the notes D and G will be ringing. This will not directly contradict the harmony as long as you stick to the keys of G or G minor, and it can give interesting results in other keys that contain these notes. Chord shapes in open G can be viewed as variations on shapes found in standard tuning, as the tuning of the second, third and fourth strings is unchanged.

Key
X = don't play
O = play open string

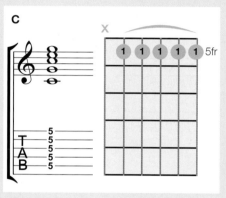

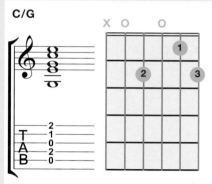

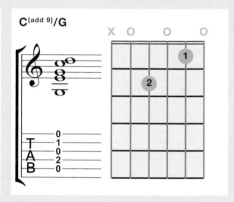

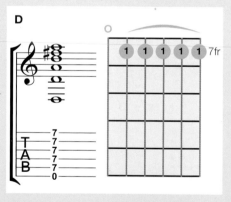

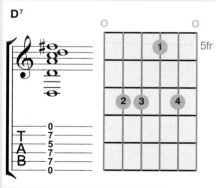

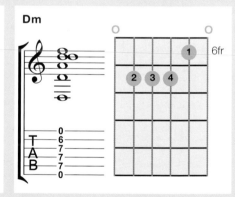

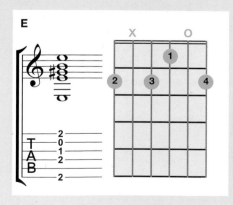

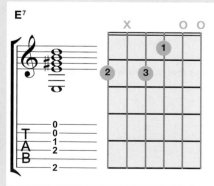

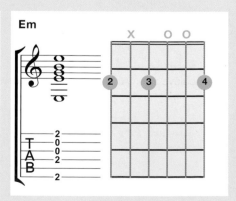

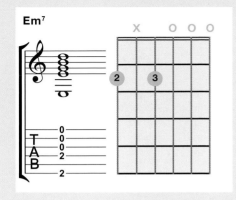

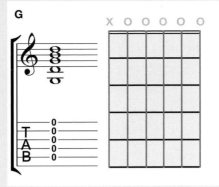

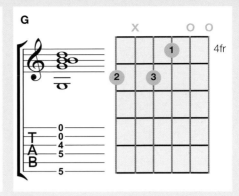

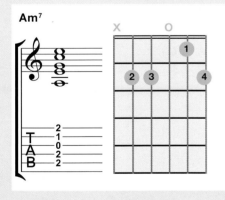

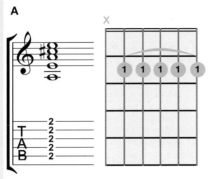

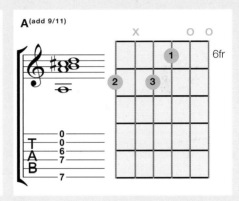

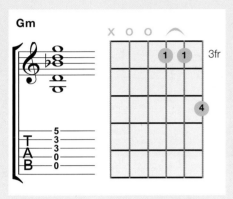

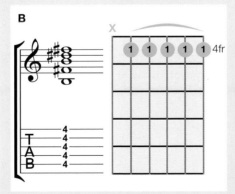

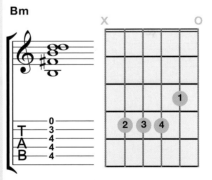

Try this

The capo is even more useful in open tunings than it is in standard tuning. For example, placing the capo at the second fret in open G is the best way to achieve open A tuning without the running the risk of breaking strings. Moreover, the sound and feel of the guitar can be changed radically by using the capo at higher frets, and many people find that this is frequently a better way to play in remote keys. The combination of using an open key along with the capo at a high fret can result in a sound that is significantly different from that created by standard tuning.

ABOVE: *Listen to Nanci Griffith's "Love at the Five and Dime".*

Essential chords in open D

In open D, the strings are tuned to DADF#AD. The character of most open tunings is defined by the string that is tuned to the third of the tonic chord. There is usually only one such string: the other five are generally tuned to the root or the fifth. Open D takes some getting used to, since the third (F#) is on the third string – not one of the top two, as is the case with many open tunings. As a result of the location of the third, some of the essential shapes in open D can be a little unwieldy, and some seemingly familiar shapes can result in very unusual sounds.

Key

X = don't play

O = play open string

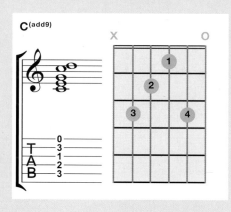

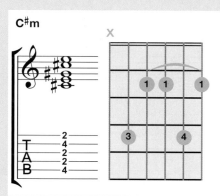

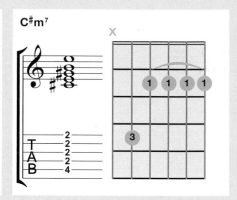

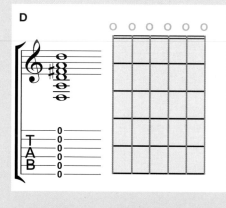

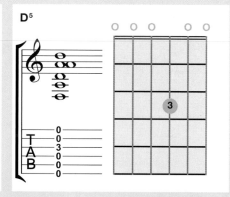

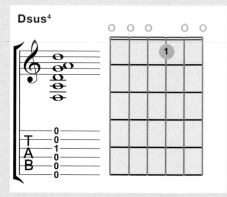

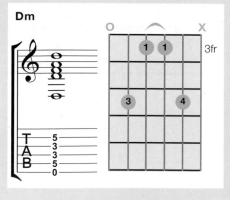

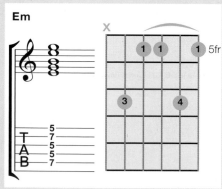

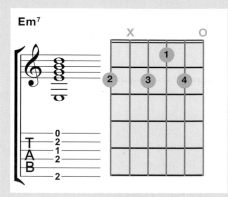

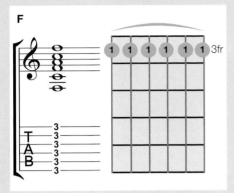

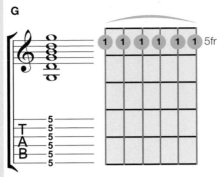

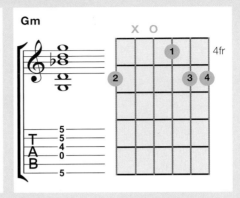

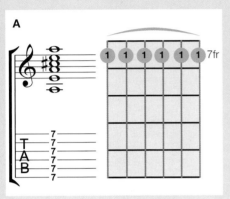

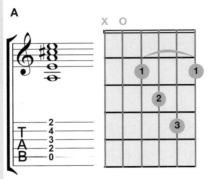

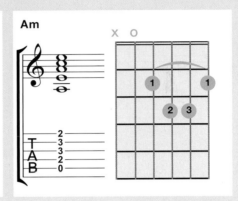

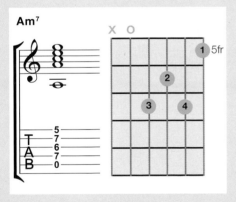

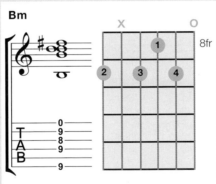

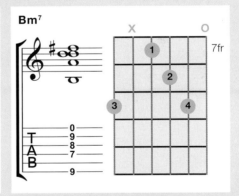

Try this

One way that you can maximize the possibilities of open D chords is to explore double-stopped sixths on the A and F# strings (that is, the second and fourth strings). The beauty of this idea is that where a shape creates tension, it can instantly be resolved by moving to an adjacent sixth shape. For some added spice, try sixths that contain notes from outside the key of D, or even moving chromatically (one fret at a time). If in doubt, lean heavily on the open bottom E string to provide a drone. This will give a sense of continuity even to shapes that are actually musically unrelated.

ABOVE: *Listen to Joni Mitchell performing "Chelsea Morning".*

Essential chords in DADGAD

DADGAD tuning is similar to open D tuning, but with a G instead of F#
on the third string, giving a Dsus4 chord on the open strings. The resulting
major second 'crunch' interval between the G and high A strings lends
DADGAD a more sophisticated sound than open tunings. But as with
many alternative tunings, interesting sounds can be obtained with minimal
finger movement. The D5 shown here is a favourite among DADGAD
players, and is often executed by first strumming or picking with the
G string open, and then adding the fretted note using a hammer-on.

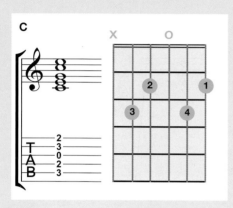

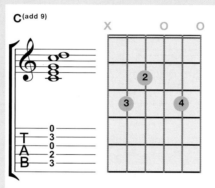

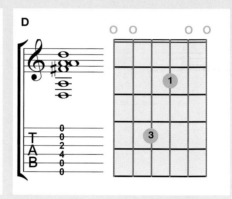

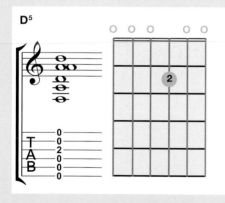

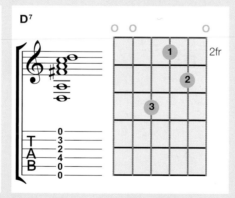

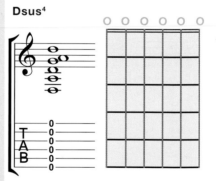

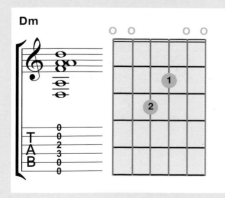

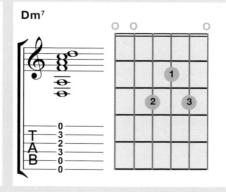

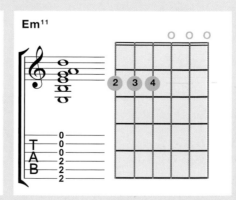

F⁶

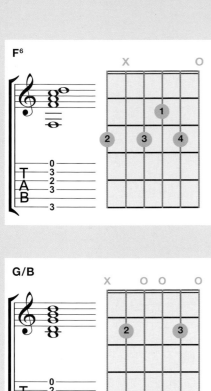

G

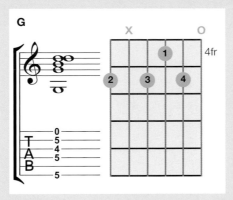
4fr

Gm

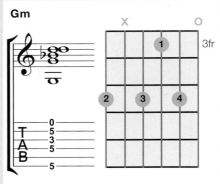
3fr

G/B

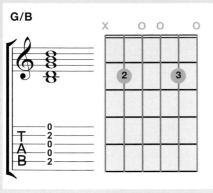

Gsus²/B

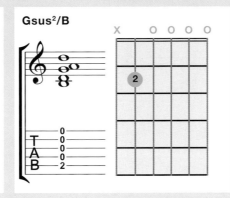

G⁽ᵃᵈᵈ ⁹⁾

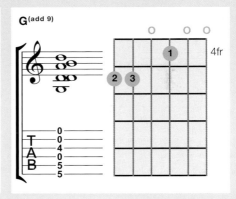
4fr

Gmaj⁹

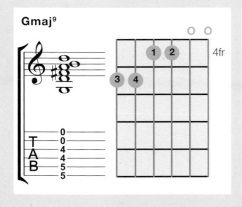
4fr

A

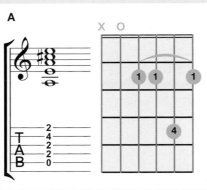

Am

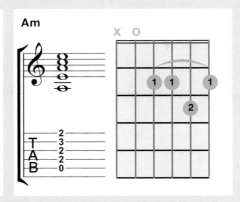

Aᵃᵈᵈ ¹¹

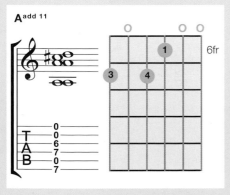
6fr

A⁷ˢᵘˢ⁴

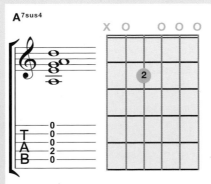

Bm⁷

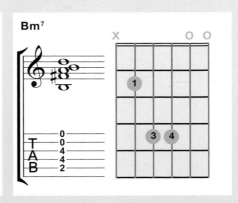

There is an extensive range of guitars available

nowadays, but they can all be traced back to

an ancestor around 3,000 years ago.

History of the acoustic guitar

This chapter follows the development of the

guitar from the first plucked strings, through the

Baroque period to the classical guitar of the early

19th century and beyond, and looks at some of

the pioneering makers who together helped to

ensure the guitar is as popular today as ever.

Early ancestors of the guitar

Some of the earliest depictions of people playing stringed instruments – and therefore the distant ancestors of the modern guitar – are to be found in Babylonian reliefs dating from *c*.1800BC. While chordophones (as stringed instruments are called) may well have existed for many centuries before this, hard evidence of their development, and therefore that of the guitar, can only be traced from more recent times.

The first plucked strings

Because of the kinds of materials used in the construction of stringed instruments – generally wood and other degradable products – they do not survive the ravages of time, and, in consequence, unravelling the history of the guitar involves a fair amount of guesswork. There are bas-reliefs from early in the second millennium BC that show us that the Hittites of Anatolia, modern Turkey, played stringed instruments that were distinctly guitar-shaped. Much later depictions also survive from medieval Europe, including a 14th-century carving in Exeter Cathedral, UK, which shows an angel

playing a guitar-like instrument. However, any research into the metamorphosis of such instruments into the lute, vihuela or Baroque guitar is speculative, and it is perhaps in looking at the origins of the instruments' names that we can find more solid evidence for their history and development.

Early relatives

As the Roman Empire expanded, guitar-like chordophones such as the *pandura* (ancestor of the Greek bouzouki) and the *fidicula* were adopted far and wide. After the decline of Rome and the growth of the Muslim sphere of influence throughout the southern and eastern Mediterranean, the Middle Eastern *oud* was introduced into Europe by the invading Moors. This was an Arabic instrument dating back to at least the eighth century and originally called the *al ʿūd*, literally meaning 'the wood'. This instrument soon became the similarly named and shaped *lut*, or in English, the lute. By the 14th century, the lute-shaped *guitarra moresca* (Moorish guitar) and the guitar-shaped *guitarra latina* (Latin guitar) had both become common instruments in Spain, and eventually the distinction between them was abandoned, leaving simply the word *guitarra*, which is still the Spanish word for 'guitar'. This name has its origins ultimately in the Greek *kithara*, 'lyre', which in its turn may have come from the Persian *setar*, meaning 'three-stringed'.

The Renaissance

By the 16th century, the lute had become one of the most widely played musical instruments throughout Europe, although in Spain and Portugal the vihuela (possibly derived from the *fidicula* of Rome) was also very popular. Like the lute, the vihuela had 'courses' (pairs of strings) rather than single strings – six in the case of the vihuela, frequently a single top string that was used to play the melody while the courses provided the accompaniment. While the *vihuela de arco* (played with a bow) and the *vihuela de peñola* (with a plectrum) both appear in medieval sources, the *vihuela de mano* (played with the fingers and later abbreviated simply to 'vihuela') seems to have existed only since the 15th century.

LEFT: *A Babylonian terracotta relief plaque from the second millennium BC, depicting a man playing an early form of guitar. These instruments are commonly referred to as the Hittite guitars.*

From the Renaissance to the Baroque

The transformation of the guitar from courses to single strings was a gradual one, and many developments often took place in parallel. The model that emerged in the 16th century of having a single high string with paired courses was an interim development that took many forms over a number of centuries. One was the four-course guitar, an instrument for which the French lutenist and guitarist Guillaume Morlaye (*c.*1520–1577) composed, and he published a collection of these compositions in 1552. However, this was a short-lived design, and it was the five-course Baroque guitar that came to dominate the field. Infinitely more versatile than its ancestors, this new instrument went on to become a star performer in an age of musical virtuosity.

LEFT: *An Angel musician c.1310, Gothic, from the Cathedral of the Virgin, Rouen, France. It clearly shows many of the components of a plucked instrument, such as the bridge, soundhole and fretboard. This gittern is being played with a plectrum (probably a quill).*

RIGHT: *A modern copy of a Renaissance lute by David Rubio. It has all the elements of an original 16th-century kind, including seven courses and tied gut frets.*

The extreme angle of the head improves the intonation and also assists iconographic identification.

The spruce soundboard is carved in a geometric design to produce the soundhole 'rose'.

Like the Renaissance lute, the vihuela was tuned mainly in fourths – actually 44344 or GCFADG (low to high) – very close to the modern guitar's standard tuning of 44434 or EADGBE, albeit higher in pitch. The vihuela came in different sizes and therefore different keys, but maintained the same intervals between the strings – the various pitches were mentioned in 1538 in *Los Seys Libros del Delphín* by the Spanish lutenist and composer Luis Narváez (*c.*1500–*c.*1560), as well being evident from various contemporary pictures.

Seven-course variants also remained popular for a long time – there are surviving examples of such instruments made around 1760 in Seville by Francisco Sanguino (*c.*1705–1771) – and they are mentioned as late as 1799 in a guitar 'method' (instruction manual) called *Principios para Tocar la Guitarra de Seis Ordenes* by the Italian composer Federico Moretti (1760–1838), who wrote extensively for the guitar.

The five-course Baroque guitar

The closing years of the 16th century saw the earliest music written for the five-course guitar. At first this involved a simple chord-strumming technique for accompanying other musicians, and its very simplicity made it hugely popular. In Spain it began to replace the traditional vihuela and, elsewhere in Europe, the lute, which had by this time become an unwieldy, oversized instrument with anything up to 14 courses.

Early guitar music

It was in the Baroque period (roughly between 1600 and 1750) that the guitar acquired its own music. The celebrated Italian guitarist and guitar teacher Francesco Corbetta (*c.*1520–1577) was one of the first to develop the early five-course guitar's repertoire by writing attractive, melodic but uncomplicated music for amateurs to play. Since these amateurs included King Carlos II of Spain and Queen Anne of Great Britain, the place of the guitar in popular music making was secured. Many guitar methods were published all over Europe during this time. One of the most popular was *Instrucción de Música sobre la Guitarra Española* (*An Instruction in Music for the Spanish Guitar*) of 1674 by the Spanish composer Gaspar Sanz (1640–1710), whose music still forms an important part of the modern instrument's repertoire.

The five-course guitar's tuning was not unlike that of today's standard EADGBE (from low to high), Sanz specifying ADGBE for the five courses, rising from low A upwards. Musicians in Italy and France used a slight modification.

While instruments were also tuned to ADGBE, the 'bottom' A was pitched a fifth above the D string next to it. This system of the bottom strings being tuned higher than the ones above them, known as 're-entrant tuning', still survives in instruments such as the ukulele and the five-string banjo. Some Baroque guitar composers were attracted to the *campanelles* (bell-like sounds) that were produced by re-entrant tuning, and made effective use of it, notably Corbetta himself as well as the French lutenist and guitarist Robert de Visée (*c.*1655–*c.*1732), who worked at the court of Louis XIV. De Visée's music also gives the bass line a prominent role in the suites he composed.

BELOW: *Sanz's music using the Alfabeto system. An important advance in the 17th century was the shift from writing music out in tablature (similar to the way fingered chords are still written in popular guitar accompaniments) to notating it on the five-line stave like all other music then and now.*

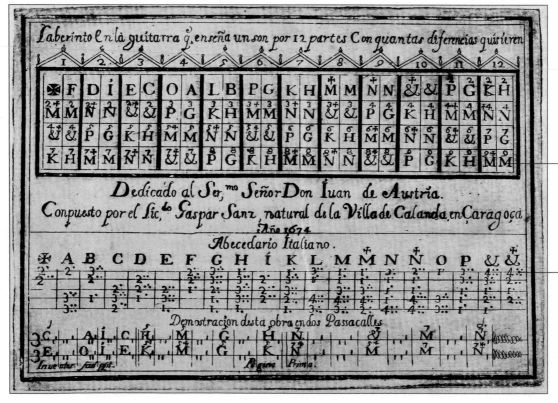

Alfabeto-tablature by Gaspar Sanz from his *Instrucción de Música sobre la Guitarra Española* (1674). With the 12 divisions of the fretboard, each square of the chord grids shows both the minor and major chord shapes.

The Alfabeto system for naming chords. The strings go from top to bottom, which differs from today's chord boxes and tablature system.

Changing tastes and decoration

Ever-changing musical tastes brought other instruments to the fore. In England in the 18th century, the Continental five-course guitar gave way to the English guitar (a cittern-shaped instrument usually with six courses tuned to CEGCEG, low to high). It also seems that the guitar-making trade was largely taken over by violin makers, especially in France. This is particularly evident in the changing range of materials used to construct the instruments, with ivory, ebony, tortoiseshell and cypress giving way to maple.

We cannot be entirely sure of the actual ratio of decorated guitars to plain ones because it is likely that the lavishly ornamented instruments stood a better chance of survival than plain models, which may have been less well looked after. The traditional decorative materials continued to be commonplace in instruments made for wealthy customers, although in many cases it is doubtful if the guitar makers themselves did the inlay work. It may be that the crafts guilds prohibited them from doing so, as there is some evidence that makers sometimes imported ready-made inlaid soundboards.

Another decorative feature that was typical of this time was the delicately carved grille covering the soundhole and known as a 'rose', which also served an acoustical purpose by lowering the bass resonances.

LEFT: *A rose in a late 18th-century five-course French guitar. Although there are ten tuning pegs, only nine are being used, the top 'course' remaining single. At the same time as this guitar was made, many other guitar makers were already constructing guitars with five single strings and without the decorative rose.*

Stradivari

One guitar maker who achieved great fame in a different field was Antonio Stradivari (1644–1737) of Cremona, probably the best-known violin maker of all time. Very few of his guitars have survived, perhaps because of their lack of decoration – his designs tended to be plain. It is intriguing to note that he designed roses that lay flush with the soundboard both inside and out, similar to those found in the soundholes of lutes, rather than the more typical roses of other makers that extended deep into the body of the instrument.

The involvement of such an inspired craftsman in guitar making was a sure sign of the instrument's increasing importance in the musical landscape, and that its continued use and development were assured.

BELOW: Two Ladies of the Lake Family *by Sir Peter Lely c.1660 features a lady playing a five-course Baroque guitar, complete with bridge moustachios and a sunken rose, both features of this period. The lady is holding the guitar in the position later favoured in the 19th century.*

RIGHT: *Stradivari made many guitars of all shapes and sizes, despite being more famous as a violin maker. Sadly only a few are known today, but from the surviving workshop templates it is known that many more were made, making him a renowned guitar maker of his time.*

The transitional guitar

As the Baroque style of music began to give way to simpler Classical forms in the mid–18th century, so the music written for the guitar was evolving into the less elaborate style of melody with accompaniment that characterizes this period. Perhaps symbolically, the delicately carved rose covering the soundhole of the guitar fell into disuse at this time, to be replaced with the plain, open soundhole so familiar today.

The different guitar forms

Towards the end of the 18th century, two dominant forms of guitar coexisted in Europe: the six-course guitar in Spain, and the five-course guitar, which was found elsewhere on the Continent. In England (and also Ireland and Scotland) in the middle of the 18th century, there was a vogue for an instrument that was called the 'guittar' or 'English guitar'. This resembled a traditional cittern but, unlike the cittern which was plucked with a plectrum, the English guitar was played with the fingers. When the 'regular', or classical, guitar was introduced to England at the beginning of the 19th century, the term 'Spanish guitar' was adopted to differentiate it from the English type.

The route to single strings

Changing the top double course, which would normally carry the tune, to a single string to make the melody ring out clearer, led eventually to the idea of using single strings throughout the guitar's range, and the five-course guitar with ten strings soon became one with five single strings. This change – perhaps as a result of the music for the instrument becoming more chord-based – appeared around 1785 in Naples, and all the surviving five-string instruments from this time are Neapolitan in origin. Contemporary examples from other parts of Europe of five-course guitars that were converted to single-string instruments do survive, although these all underwent later modification to six single strings.

ABOVE: *A portrait of Anne Ford posing with a wire-strung English guitar, by Thomas Gainsborough, 1760. Ford also played the gut-strung Spanish guitar, harp and viola da gamba (pictured in the background).*

ABOVE: Blind Man Playing the Guitar, *a painting by Francisco De Goya y Lucientes (1746–1828). Painted in 1778, it shows a five-course Spanish guitar, but many of his later sketches depict six-course guitars.*

New styles of playing and tuning

The Neapolitan five-string guitars show the instrument at its mid or transitional point. The earlier double-stringing had been abandoned. However, in Spain at the end of the 18th century, five-course guitars were still being played, although gradually being adapted for six-course playing, with the addition of extra strings.

In 1799, three works were published to teach this instrument to meet a growing public interest. Two of these guitar methods, by Fernando Ferandiere (*c*.1750–1816) and Federico Moretti (1760–1838), tell us much about the style of music written for the instrument, and how it was

RIGHT: The Lute Player, a painting by Cesare Saccaggi c.1900. A young lady is 'playing' a French or Italian lyre-guitar (not lute, as the title suggests) although the instrument was actually in vogue a century earlier.

ABOVE: Dionisio Aguado playing a guitar, painted by Etienne Laprevotte, taken from his method of 1843. His guitar is supported by his special invention, the so-called tripodium.

tuned and played. Ferandiere's *Arte de Tocar la Guitarra Española por Música* (*The Art of Playing the Spanish Guitar*) is especially significant, since it shows an unrivalled understanding of the techniques he advocated such as playing near the soundhole to produce a 'sweet and agreeable tone', and also reflects the changing musical fashions of the time, although he was still using instruments with a mixture of paired courses and single strings.

In a significant move towards modern standard tuning, Ferandiere recommended that the guitar be tuned as E (coursed, but with one string an octave higher than the bass E), ADGB (unison paired courses), and ending on a single top E. The downwards extension of the pitch to a bass E was the end of the old-fashioned re-entrant tuning where the bottom course was pitched higher than the pair next to them, and Ferandiere's prescribed range and intervals have remained in use ever since.

Six single strings

The time when the six-course guitar fell out of use in Spain is impossible to pinpoint exactly. Many surviving double-course instruments of the period were later converted to be able to accommodate six single strings, and the celebrated Spanish composer-performer Dionisio Aguado (1784–1849) expresses his own preference for single strings in his method of 1825. However, there are surviving six-course guitars built around this time – such as one from 1822 by the Cadiz maker Joséf Pagés (1762–?) – so it seems fair to conclude that in Spain at least the paired six-course guitar was still very much in vogue in the early 19th century.

Towards the early modern guitar

We can see that there were two distinct, concurrent routes to the modern stringing of the classical guitar. The first, in Spain, moved from five to six courses to six single strings between the 1750s and 1820s, while in Italy and France (but not England) the trend went from five courses to five single strings in the 1780s, and then the sixth was added later. However, this probably happened in the same decade, i.e. the 1780s. It is from these developments and on through the 19th century that we see the guitar begin to evolve steadily towards the form we recognize today.

Early 19th-century guitars

By the early 19th century, with the addition of the sixth string and the adoption of EADGBE tuning as standard, the guitar was beginning to look recognizably modern. With these advancements guitar makers could increase the range of notes available and performers could extend their playing techniques, thus enabling composers to introduce new colours and ideas into their music.

New music for a new instrument

An age of elegant simplicity followed the intricacies of the Baroque era: the Classical period, from which we derive the term 'classical guitar'. Key composers for the instrument at the time – who also published methods, studies and other material designed to teach people to play – included the Neapolitan Ferdinando Carulli (1770–1841), and the Spaniards Fernando Sor (1778–1839) and Dionisio Aguado (1784–1849), and their works helped to keep the instrument's growth in popularity on track.

An important London-based luthier was the French-born Louis Panormo (1784–1862). Possibly under the influence of Fernando Sor, who spent several years in London, Panormo started making Spanish-style instruments, and by 1823, when Sor left London, Panormo was employing the Spanish technique of 'fanbracing', that is, reinforcing the soundboard inside with thin, fan-shaped struts of wood. This was unusual outside of Spain, since at this time most craftsmen were still using the transverse bracing system developed by the likes of Lacôte and the Fabricatores.

The new makers

Two of the earliest makers of the new six single-string guitar, Giovanni Battista Fabricatore (*c.*1750–*c.*1812) and Gaetano Vinaccia (*c.*1759–after 1831), were working in Naples at the turn of the 19th century, but there is one maker whose guitars were mentioned time and time again by the leading players of the day: René Lacôte of Paris (1785–*c.*1860). Lacôte's instruments seem to have been prized above all others, and they are still in great demand among today's players of historic guitars.

Lacôte's construction techniques and principles remained largely consistent throughout his career, although he did experiment and was sensitive to the needs of individual performers. He made guitars from different woods, and preferred to veneer the necks with the same material as the back and sides, to give the instruments a visual harmony. He also made some guitars with adjustable necks, adjustable frets and even some with double soundboards and two soundholes, as well as models with more than six strings.

By the second quarter of the 19th century, most countries in Europe had their own favoured master builders of these new guitars. Italy had the Fabricatores and Guadagninis, both large families of makers and active throughout the century, while Spain boasted many makers – including Joséf Pagés (1762–?), Antonio de Lorca and José Recio (1806–?) – all emerging from the tight control of the crafts guilds and all of them vying for supremacy.

ABOVE: One of only a couple of known portraits of the Spanish composer Fernando Sor. This image is taken from a painting of 1815, the year he moved to London when he was 37 years old.

BELOW: Early fanbracing usually consisted of three splayed bars, which were increased to seven in the 1820s by Louis Panormo. This X-ray shows a typical example of Panormo's fanbracing.

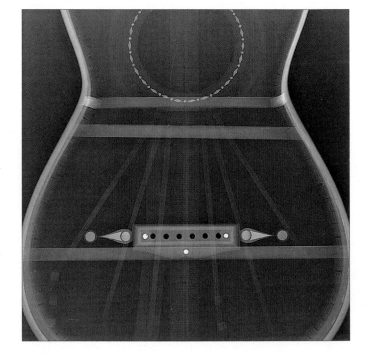

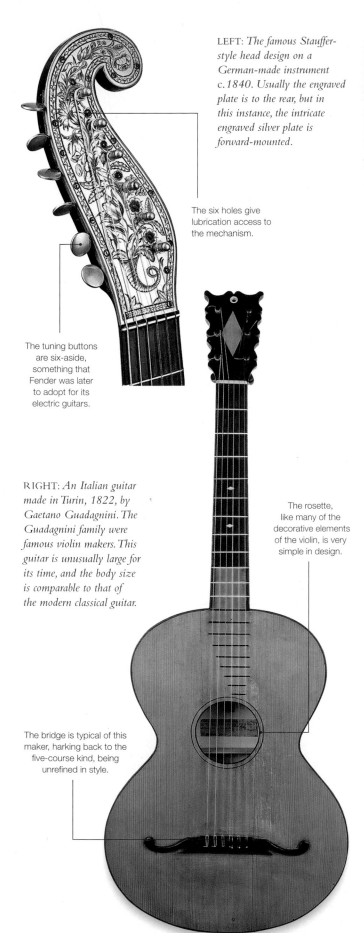

LEFT: *The famous Stauffer-style head design on a German-made instrument c.1840. Usually the engraved plate is to the rear, but in this instance, the intricate engraved silver plate is forward-mounted.*

The six holes give lubrication access to the mechanism.

The tuning buttons are six-aside, something that Fender was later to adopt for its electric guitars.

RIGHT: *An Italian guitar made in Turin, 1822, by Gaetano Guadagnini. The Guadagnini family were famous violin makers. This guitar is unusually large for its time, and the body size is comparable to that of the modern classical guitar.*

The rosette, like many of the decorative elements of the violin, is very simple in design.

The bridge is typical of this maker, harking back to the five-course kind, being unrefined in style.

ABOVE: Girl with a Guitar, *1897, by Pierre-Auguste Renoir, depicts a young female flamenco guitarist. Interestingly, another of his (French) paintings from the same year seemingly features a guitar with a split ebony/pearl fingerboard as the one above shows.*

To the New World

Another important manufacturer at the time was Johann Georg Stauffer (1778–1853), whose much sought-after instruments sometimes contained little or no bracing at all. Stauffer and his son Johann Anton were the leading makers in what had become the new musical capital of Europe, Vienna. It was here that a famous composer/maker relationship grew up between the builders in the Stauffer workshop and the celebrated virtuoso Luigi Legnani (1790–1877), giving rise to the renowned Legnani–Stauffer models, many of which featured adjustable necks and a twin-octave range in pitch.

It is thought that the influential German maker Christian Frederick Martin (1796–1873) may have been apprenticed in the Stauffer workshop. Martin eventually emigrated to the USA in 1833 and started the foundations of the seminal guitar company of C. F. Martin & Co. Martin's influential guitars were widely copied, both in the USA and in many German factories, and for nearly two centuries the firm has remained pivotal in maintaining the guitar's position, particularly with its role in the development of the steel-string guitar.

A steady decline

The second half of the 19th century saw the popularity of the instrument decline in many countries. By this time many of the top European makers, including Panormo, Stauffer and Fabricatore, had ceased their activities. The classical guitar was in danger if not of extinction, at least of being sidelined as a serious instrument. However, the flame was kept burning brightly in Spain, and developments were taking place in the USA that would bear fruit many years later.

Arcas, Torres, Tárrega and beyond

The second half of the 19th century witnessed the birth of the modern classical guitar as developed by Antonio de Torres (1817–1892). The high quality of his guitars and the influential performers who played them meant that the classical guitar, in Spain at least, continued to be celebrated rather than being forgotten, as had so many other once-popular instruments over the centuries.

Arcas, Torres and the Lioness

While the fashion for the guitar had begun to fade by the middle of the 19th century in many countries, in Spain, where guitar music was a national institution, and the USA, the instrument continued to hold its own. In Spain, interest was kept alive by the genius of some brilliant composer-performers, the first of whom was Julián Arcas (1832–1882). Early in his professional life as a travelling virtuoso he had met and befriended the instrument maker Antonio de Torres, whose own career was boosted enormously when Arcas began playing an instrument that he had lent to him in 1856 called 'La Leona' (the Lioness). Torres went on to become the maker of some of the finest guitars in the world, changing the way classical guitars have been built ever since.

Tárrega and the next generations of performers

Arcas was also a guiding influence upon another, younger composer-performer, Francisco Tárrega (1852–1909). Tárrega had played to him as a ten-year-old, and Arcas was so impressed that he invited the boy to study with him. Tárrega went on to become one of the greatest performers of his time, and he played at least three guitars made by Torres – two of maple and one of rosewood. Tárrega became a key figure in the development of the guitar's repertoire, a composer

LEFT: *A drawing by the Spanish artist Ramon Cases, 1900, of Miguel Llobet, the Catalan guitarist and student of Tarrega. Llobet's famous Torres guitar of 1859 was the inspiration behind the guitars by Hermann Hauser.*

ABOVE: *A photograph of Francisco Tárrega in 1901 playing an 1888 guitar by Antonio de Torres, which Tárrega's widow said was his favourite guitar. Most people will know at least four bars of Tárrega's music as the Nokia ringtone is taken from his* Gran Vals.

of many famous pieces for the instrument who laid the foundations of 20th-century classical-guitar playing through his own pupils, including Miguel Llobet (1878–1938) and Emilio Pujol (1886–1980). His transcriptions of works by Schumann, Chopin, Beethoven and others became hugely popular.

Equally important, though, were Tárrega's performing style and his understanding of what the guitar could do. After hearing Tárrega play transcriptions of some of his piano pieces, the great Spanish composer and pianist Isaac Albéniz (1860–1909) remarked that they were better than his originals.

LEFT: *Andrés Segovia during a performance in 1970 playing a Hauser-made guitar. Segovia's concerts were typically in three 'halves' instead of the more traditional two, and his solo repertoire consisted of orchestral and piano transcriptions as well as original guitar compositions. Despite enduring the traumas of the Spanish civil war and two world wars, his long career and the fact that he was still playing concerts late in his life meant he managed to give approximately 5,400 performances.*

Given Tárrega's influence, it is no surprise that the greatest classical guitarist of the 20th century, Andrés Segovia (1893–1987), began his professional career playing many of Tárrega's guitar transcriptions. Segovia inspired the best composers of the day to write for the guitar. He also did a great deal to encourage young instrument makers, although throughout his long career he mainly played guitars made by only four different makers: Santos Hernandez (1874-1943), Hermann Hauser (1882-1952), Ignacio Fleta (1897–1977) and José Ramírez III (1922-95). His two longstanding companions, the famous 1912 Santos Hernandez guitar (made in the workshop of Manuel Ramírez) and his 1937 Hauser I guitar, were bequeathed to the Metropolitan Museum of Art, but sadly with the proviso that no one is ever allowed to play them.

Torres' lasting influence

While experts continue to debate the specific contributions that Torres made to the design of the modern classical guitar, there is no doubt that his instruments represent a summit of achievement in guitar design, and his influence has continued into the 20th century and beyond. Even today there are makers who still follow his construction methods very closely, and no other luthier has had anything like the same influence on the refinement of the classical instrument. Just as many contemporary violin makers still base their instruments on the designs of Stradivari, since the 19th-century guitar makers have continued to follow the lead set by Antonio de Torres.

By the mid-20th century nearly every feature of the modern classical guitar was in place – its size and shape, woods used in its construction, and a host of other technical improvements. The final element was the switch from unreliable gut strings to nylon ones, pioneered by Segovia in the years after World War II, which has brought the design of the classical guitar to a state approaching perfection.

Guitar strings

Here are depicted some unused 100-year-old gut guitar strings, marketed by Viennese and English companies, but probably made in Naples. They were prone to breaking, especially when the tuning instructions were: "tuning the top string just before breaking point"; hence musicians bought them by the box. Before the 1940s, 'cat gut' (actually sheep or pig intestine) was the chosen material for Spanish guitar strings. With this material being in short supply during World War II, possibly exacerbated by its use in the stitching of wounded soldiers, it was clear that a new substance was needed. This coincided with the invention, just a decade earlier, of DuPont's nylon and, from 1947, nylon became the preferred material for classical guitar strings.

The flamenco guitar

Although the Spanish art form of flamenco today is inextricably linked with the guitar, its origins certainly pre-date the guitar as we know it. Flamenco guitar is as much a rhythm instrument as it is a melodic one, and one of its chief functions is to enhance the clapping and stamping that traditionally accompany the songs and dance, which are at the heart of flamenco.

Origins

The flamenco dance is popularly understood to be an Andalucian form, particularly associated with Romany communities, although its influences are far more diverse than this would suggest, bringing together many sources going back hundreds of years. When the guitar began to be used as an instrument to accompany flamenco is not recorded, but a flamenco-guitar rhythmic-strumming technique known as *rasgueado* began to be heard quite clearly in some Baroque guitar music from the 17th century, such as Gaspar Sanz's *Spagnolettas* and *Canarios* of the 1670s. From its outsider roots, flamenco's emergence as a serious art form owes much to the early 20th-century composer Manuel de Falla (1867–1936), who organized the first flamenco festival in Granada in 1922. It is now listed as one of UNESCO's "Masterpieces of the Oral and Intangible Heritage of Humanity".

BELOW: *Manuel de Falla, shown late in life. Although not a guitarist himself, de Falla captured the flamenco essence in his orchestral works, and also wrote the masterpiece for solo guitar,* Le Tombeau de Debussy.

ABOVE: El Jaleo *by John Singer Sargent was completed in 1882, but it is based on earlier contemporary sketches. It depicts the essence of the flamenco dance through clapping, tapping and guitar rhythms.*

Tools of the trade

Some of the earliest guitars made specifically to accompany a flamenco troupe came from the workshops of José and Manuel Ramírez, and the actual term 'flamenco guitar' appears in Manuel's workshop catalogue of *c.*1913. In an earlier Ramírez catalogue of *c.*1888, two different kinds of guitar are mentioned: *guitarras de concierto* (concert guitars) and *guitarras de sevillanas* (Sevillanas guitars). Despite the reference to the Andalucian dance, the Sevillana, and the distinction made between *guitarras de sevillanas* and concert instruments, these were not yet the flamenco guitar familiar to us today.

It may be that the first instruments specifically for flamenco resembled the '1916' model made in Manuel Ramírez's workshop by Santos Hernandez. Hernandez made flamenco guitars in both cypress (known as *blanca*, white) and rosewood (*negra*, black). These guitars have a pure, percussive sound, which makes them the ideal accompanying instrument for flamenco, since true flamenco guitars are constructed so that the sound decays quickly, unlike the sustained sonority required for a classical instrument.

The *cejilla*

Singing is a vital element of flamenco, and accompanying guitarists will need to be able to adjust their playing to the vocal ranges of each singer. To do this the guitarist sometimes is required to use a device called a *cejilla*, or capo. A fortuitous side-effect of using the *cejilla* is that it causes the instrument to sound more sharp and percussive, something that the guitar maker also strives to achieve in a flamenco instrument.

Rámon Montoya

The father of the modern solo flamenco guitar is generally considered by today's aficionados to be Rámon Montoya (1880–1949). Other famous performers, some of whom are traditionalists while others have added new elements, include Rámon's nephew Carlos Montoya (1903–1993), Niño Ricardo (1904–1972), Sabicas (1912–1990), Paco Peña (b. 1942), Paco de Lucia (b. 1947) and Juan Martín (b. 1948).

Another way to achieve the necessary 'timbre' for flamenco comes from keeping the 'action' – that is, the height of the strings above the fingerboard – somewhat lower than on a classical guitar, thus producing a more raspy sound. With the strings nearer to the frets, the guitarist can play with greater virtuosity, which reduces left-hand fatigue during lengthy performances. Finally, flamenco instruments are often equipped with a distinctive tap-plate called a *golpeador*, which is today commonly made of transparent plastic and similar to a scratchplate on a steel-string or electric guitar. The purpose of this is to protect the guitar body from the guitarist's rhythmic finger taps, called *golpes*.

Flamenco guitar style

The rhythmic structure of flamenco music is called its *compas*, and some of its musical forms have a distinctive and recognizable 12-beat pattern. One musical scale used in flamenco – for voice and guitar – is known as the 'Phrygian' mode (based on ancient Greek scales) rather than standard Western scales, giving the characteristic sound.

Guitarists make use of *falsetas*, gaps between the singing where they can demonstrate their virtuosity, and this has led over time to the flamenco guitar being developed as a solo instrument as well.

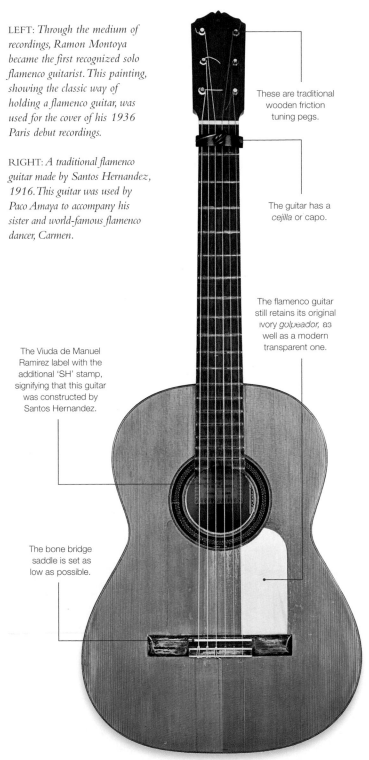

LEFT: *Through the medium of recordings, Ramon Montoya became the first recognized solo flamenco guitarist. This painting, showing the classic way of holding a flamenco guitar, was used for the cover of his 1936 Paris debut recordings.*

RIGHT: *A traditional flamenco guitar made by Santos Hernandez, 1916. This guitar was used by Paco Amaya to accompany his sister and world-famous flamenco dancer, Carmen.*

These are traditional wooden friction tuning pegs.

The guitar has a *cejilla* or capo.

The flamenco guitar still retains its original ivory *golpeador*, as well as a modern transparent one.

The Viuda de Manuel Ramirez label with the additional 'SH' stamp, signifying that this guitar was constructed by Santos Hernandez.

The bone bridge saddle is set as low as possible.

Pioneers of the steel-string guitar

Just as the classical guitar was being refined in Spain, the steel-string guitar was being developed in the USA towards the end of the 19th century. It was all about volume. Guitarists playing in traditional and folk groups needed to be able to compete with the much louder banjos, mandolins and fiddles, all of which had become metal-strung, and with the advent of jazz, a guitarist using a classical instrument would not have been able to compete in volume against the brass.

An earlier idea

The use of metal strings on musical instruments goes back to at least the Italian *battente* guitars of the 17th century. Likewise, the English 'guittar' had metal strings, and this instrument was very popular in North America between around 1760 and 1810. However, one must assume they were long forgotten before the idea of using metal strings on regular guitars was proposed, although it may not have been much later

ABOVE: *A photograph of Christian Frederick Martin, the most famous name in American guitar history.*

that the first US guitars were fitted with steel strings. Certainly by the second half of the 19th century, various references can be found – for instance, in advertisements – to suggest that the idea of equipping guitars with steel strings was in place.

C. F. Martin & Co.

The guitar-making lineage of C. F. Martin goes way back to the 1830s, when Christian Frederick Martin emigrated to New York from Germany. Although perhaps not the only

company making steel-string instruments in the early 20th century, C. F. Martin was pioneering in this regard and remains the best known of the early manufacturers. It is also very likely that today's steel-string guitars incorporate many innovations that Martin brought with him from Johann Georg Stauffer's Vienna workshop, including the pin-bridge design and the jazz guitar, with its floating fingerboard.

In 1916, Martin introduced the popular Dreadnought model, which, with its enlarged soundbox and its loud, resonant, bassy tone, has become a template for the steel-string acoustic guitar ever since. Steel-string Martin instruments are still highly prized, and early examples can now change hands at auction for huge sums of money.

Flat-tops and archtops

The Dreadnought and its ilk are what are known as 'flat-top' instruments, in that, like the classical guitar from which they derive, the front and back of the body are relatively flat and braced internally to strengthen the body. However, in 1902, Orville Gibson's (1856–1918) Gibson Mandolin-Guitar Manufacturing Co. Ltd (now the Gibson Guitar Corporation) patented an 'archtop' design for a mandolin that also covered its guitars. The front of the soundbox – mandolin or guitar – is distinguished by its carved, arched top (and often back), which meant that internal bracing could be eliminated by using a stronger body, so creating a clearer-sounding instrument without any internal structures interfering with the tone.

While Gibson was not the first to produce an archtop, following the patent, the company exploited the method in its instruments, initially using it for mandolins.

When the guitar maker Lloyd Loar (1886–1943) joined the firm in 1919, he introduced the idea of f-shaped

LEFT: *Hampton Institute, Hampton VA, c.1898. Guitar, mandolin and banjo orchestras were all the rage at the turn of the 19th century, and they were actively promoted by the major musical instrument manufacturers.*

soundholes to the archtop designs that are now so common. Gibson's first model in the new shape, the Gibson L5, was introduced in 1922 and quickly became the brand leader for use in the rhythm sections of big bands as well as for jazz and blues players, both rhythm and lead.

Gibson also introduced flat-top models, such as the smaller 00, which bears a significant resemblance to a classical instrument, and the larger Grand Auditorium, or 000, similar in style to the 00 but larger and more powerful. All these flat-tops needed a higher degree of reinforcement than a classical instrument because of the greater strain imposed upon them by the tension of the steel strings. A primitive form of bracing was used in early Martin guitars by the 1840s, and this led eventually to the development of the system that was known as 'x-bracing'.

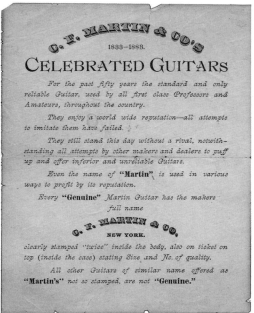

LEFT: *The 50-year anniversary (1833–83) advertisement cites Martin as being in New York, but the guitars were actually made in Pennsylvania. Others tried to copy its guitars, some even using the name of 'Martin'.*

Other makers

Martin and Gibson were by no means the only guitar makers in the USA. Others included the Chicago-based instrument manufacturer Lyon and Healy, makers of the Washburn brand from the 1880s, which they sold in vast numbers. They mostly produced budget guitars, but also made lavishly inlaid ones that won a considerable number of awards.

Another important maker was Joseph Bohmann (1848–1928), who arrived in Chicago from Europe in 1873. He was soon at the head of a highly successful company that made steel-string guitars with stronger 'double-x-bracing'. Bohmann also made mandolins and harp guitars, curious crossbreeds which featured, in addition to the standard set of six strings, a row of unfretted harp-like strings that could be individually plucked. These unusual instruments continue to find a niche market even today.

Worldwide popularity

After World War II, and particularly following the 'folk revival' and the global reach of rock 'n' roll from the 1950s onwards, the guitar in all its forms has become ubiquitous across the world. Besides the individual luthiers worldwide who produce high-quality handmade instruments, the sustained popularity of the steel-string acoustic guitar now means that relatively affordable factory-made models of all levels are now produced in many countries, notably China, Korea and Japan, and not just in the guitar manufacturing heartland of the USA. The majority of guitars produced still bear close family resemblances to those pioneering models made by Martin, Gibson and their contemporaries.

RIGHT: *This guitar by Joseph Bohmann, c. 1915, exemplifies how individual he was with respect to his design. The head, body and fingerboard shape, as well as the position markers, show little influence from other makers. Bohmann was careful to take out patents for this design, not that many other makers were likely to have copied his design.*

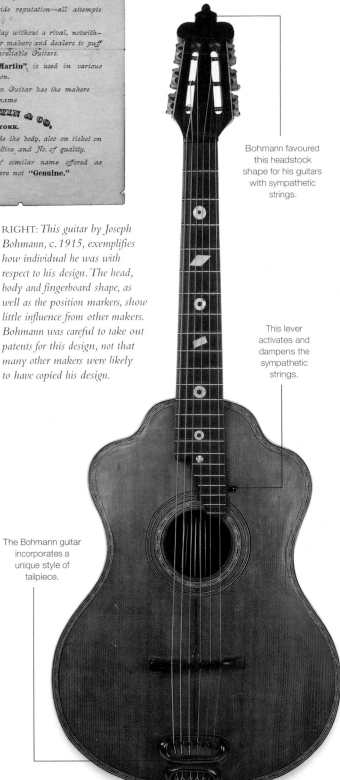

Bohmann favoured this headstock shape for his guitars with sympathetic strings.

This lever activates and dampens the sympathetic strings.

The Bohmann guitar incorporates a unique style of tailpiece.

The guitar today

The acoustic guitar market today is so large and diverse that there is room for a seemingly endless array of instruments at all price levels and with numerous different designs. Bespoke instruments, skilfully hand-crafted by luthiers, and factory-made guitars both have their place, and guitar making is an expanding industry in many countries throughout the world.

Independent specialisms

Most of the big companies make a range of instruments – classical, steel-string and all the sub-categories of these. However, today's independent acoustic-guitar makers often tend to specialize in making either nylon or steel-string instruments – after all, to build a strong reputation for making a particular style of guitar makes good business sense. Within the broader nylon or steel-string categories, each can be further subdivided – for example, nylon-strung classical, flamenco or historical guitars, or steel-strung flat-top or archtop instruments, and many additional variants, including resonator, lap-steel, harp or gypsy guitars (for more details on makers, see the Directory section).

ABOVE: *Modern luthier Martin Woodhouse is carving the braces which support and strengthen the soundboard against the pull of the strings. The resulting flexibility of the soundboard is one of the most important factors that determine the final sound of a guitar.*

RIGHT: *A modern harp-guitar by English luthier Stephen Sedgwick. It covers a staggering five-octave range, which in the hands of a professional, sounds like a miniature orchestra.*

Makers of both classical and steel-string guitars can be split into traditionalists and experimenters – although even traditionalists probably experiment at some point. This might seem like reinventing the wheel – the advice might be, 'don't mess with a successful formula' – but for luthiers it can represent a move forward or serve to justify why they build in a particular way and distinguish them from the competition.

Innovation versus tradition

As the history of guitar making shows, 19th-century craftsmen in particular were very quick to adapt to new ideas, and many of today's 'innovations' were actually first tried out at various points over the last couple of centuries – for example, London-based D. and A. Roudhloff used x-bracing in their guitars in the 1840s, and some makers in the early 19th century constructed guitars with arched tops. All these changes help to create a healthy, buoyant market as well as preventing makers from becoming stale and players becoming complacent. Whether it be Thomas Humphrey's raised fingerboards, Robert Ruck's soundports (holes drilled into the side of an instrument for increased sonority), Greg Smallman's carbon fibre-lattice soundboard bracing or Ovation's fibreglass bowl backs, these and countless other innovations in recent decades can all help to meet the demands of increasingly exacting players.

Trends and fashions come and go, and many ideas and forms disappear, only to reappear at some point in the future. For example, many players today feel that 'oversized' guitars,

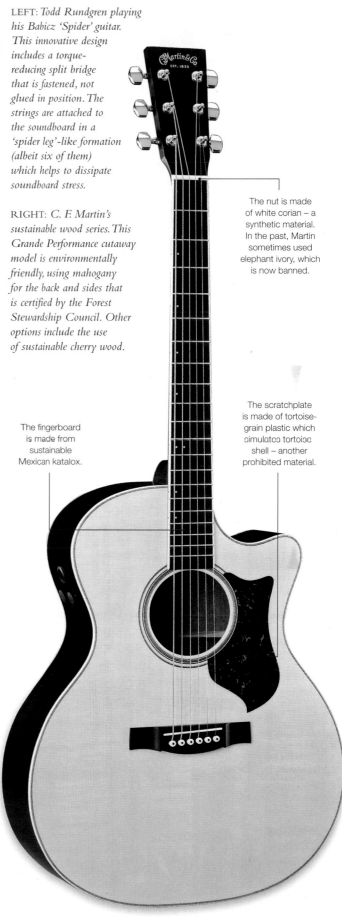

LEFT: *Todd Rundgren playing his Babicz 'Spider' guitar. This innovative design includes a torque-reducing split bridge that is fastened, not glued in position. The strings are attached to the soundboard in a 'spider leg'-like formation (albeit six of them) which helps to dissipate soundboard stress.*

RIGHT: *C. F. Martin's sustainable wood series. This Grande Performance cutaway model is environmentally friendly, using mahogany for the back and sides that is certified by the Forest Stewardship Council. Other options include the use of sustainable cherry wood.*

The nut is made of white corian – a synthetic material. In the past, Martin sometimes used elephant ivory, which is now banned.

The scratchplate is made of tortoise-grain plastic which simulates tortoise shell – another prohibited material.

The fingerboard is made from sustainable Mexican katalox.

once considered indispensable – such as the large-bodied Martin Dreadnought steel-string and the 664mm (26.1in) scale Ramírez classical guitars – are less essential today due to readily available amplification. Instead, players are returning to smaller instruments with a clearly defined sound, sometimes even to copies of Lacôte- or Panormo-style guitars. The once-popular late 19th-century small parlour guitar is also enjoying a revival, and makers respond to this by producing modern copies – although older originals are often no more expensive to buy (even if you might then need to spend a small fortune restoring an antique instrument).

The green guitar

Today, makers have to be aware of the CITES ('Convention on International Trade in Endangered Species of Wild Fauna and Flora') Act and how it affects the supply of materials traditionally used to build musical instruments. The preferred wood used to make the back and sides of a guitar has long been Brazilian rosewood; not only is it beautiful, but many believe that a guitar made from this wood sounds better as well as making their instrument a cannier investment.

Since the material comes from the tropical rainforests of Brazil, there is now a ban on exporting new guitars made of certain woods unless the instrument is accompanied by a certificate stating that the wood was logged prior to the date that is stated in the CITES Act. Fortunately, guitar makers and their customers are slowly accepting that there are plenty of perfectly good alternatives to Brazilian rosewood, such as Indian rosewood.

The future

It's been a long road from the *kithara* to the modern acoustic guitar, and many once-popular instruments have fallen by the wayside, but on current evidence it looks like the guitar – as near a perfect tool for the job in hand as you will find – is going to be around in a recognizable form for some considerable amount of time yet.

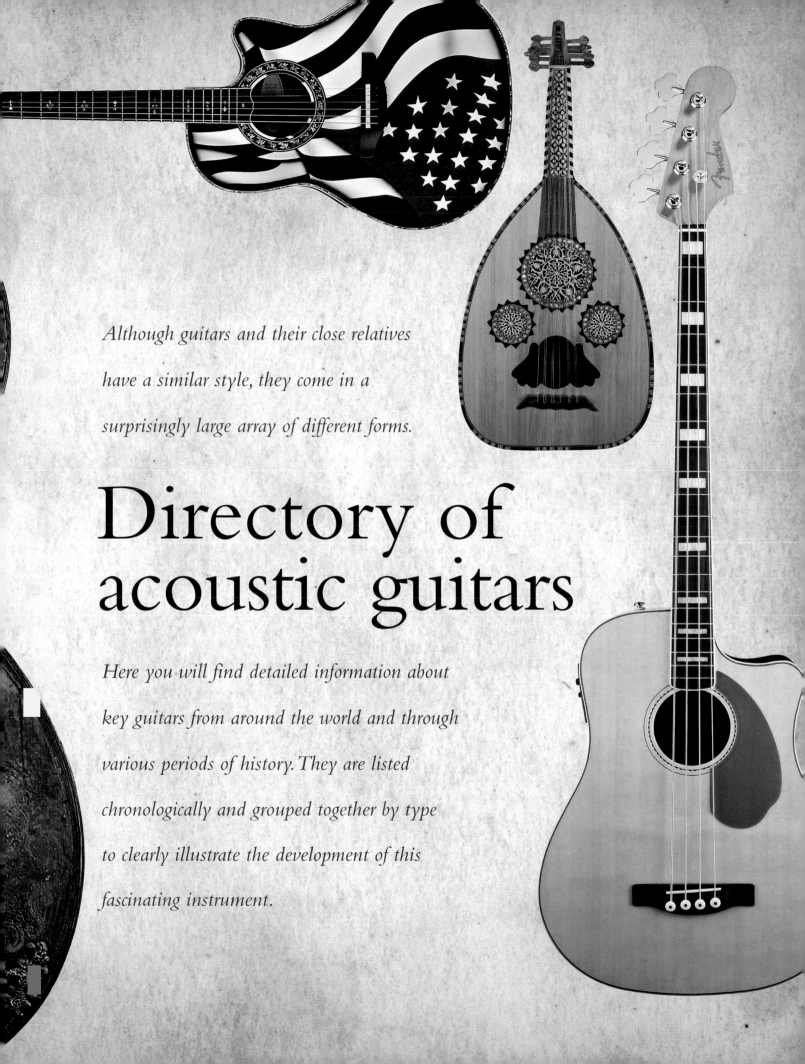

Although guitars and their close relatives
have a similar style, they come in a
surprisingly large array of different forms.

Directory of
acoustic guitars

Here you will find detailed information about
key guitars from around the world and through
various periods of history. They are listed
chronologically and grouped together by type
to clearly illustrate the development of this
fascinating instrument.

Early guitar-related instruments

The oud, which dates back to at least the eighth century, came from North Africa and the Middle East. It originally had frets, but these were dropped from the instrument by about 1300, which was quite late in the history of the oud. The European version of this instrument became known as the lute, which retained the frets.

Oud, c. 1990

This modern oud has 11 strings and, unlike its relatives seen elsewhere in this section, it is fretless. Another distinguishing feature is that the neck is much narrower than that of the lute, for example. The three rosettes of this modern copy have a Moorish design, and the body is constructed of alternating dark- and light-wood staves. The five double courses of strings and single bass string – the latter an unusual feature – terminate at a moustache-shaped tie-bridge.

Wendelio Venere: theorbo, 1600s

The German master luthier Wendelio Venere worked in Padua, Italy, between around 1570 and the 1630s. The spruce soundboard has three roses, reminiscent of an oud. The back is made of 11 ribs of maple with black-and-white stringing. This instrument has six short double courses with eight long single bases. Currently it is in chitarrone tuning. It was mainly used as an accompanying *basso continuo* instrument for opera.

The length of this instrument makes it difficult to manoeuvre and transport.

There are an odd number (11) of tuning pegs.

The fingerboard has elaborate inlays.

- **DATE** *c.*1990
- **ORIGIN** Middle East
- **WOOD**
  Front/Back & Sides
  Spruce/padouk, mahogany and rosewood
- **UNUSUAL FEATURE**
  Ouds, like the violin family, have no frets.

- **DATE** 1600s
- **ORIGIN** Italy
- **WOOD**
  Front/Back & Sides
  Spruce/maple
- **UNUSUAL FEATURE**
  Save for a pipe organ, a theorbo is the longest musical instrument.

The scratchplate is made from imitation-tortoiseshell.

The neck is wide compared with that of a guitar but still not wide enough to accommodate all of the strings.

Notice the oud-shaped body.

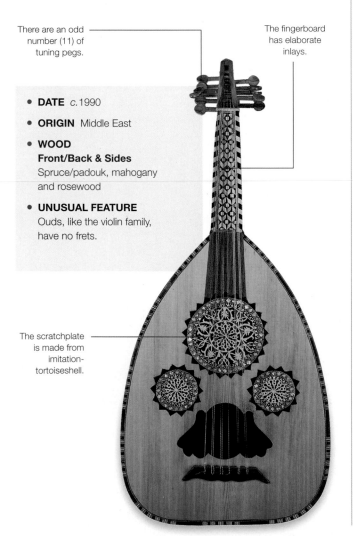

Joachim Tielke: Baroque lute, 1707

The most decorative of all Baroque string instruments came from the workshop of Joachim Tielke (1641–1719). Tielke built many guitars and lutes in Hamburg between around 1672 and 1718. Many have ivory backs and ivory inlaid decorations on ebony-veneered necks. The Baroque lute has two pegboxes, the second on a curved extension of the neck, a style sometimes referred to as a 'swan neck'. It has 12 courses, seven over the neck, which are fretted, and another five that are played open.

The curved shape here is sometimes described as a 'swan neck'.

The tuning pegs are staggered to make the access easier when turning them.

- **DATE** 1707

- **ORIGIN** Germany

- **WOOD**
  Front/Back & Sides
  Spruce/ivory and ebony

- **UNUSUAL FEATURE**
  The twin pegboxes must seem strange to today's guitarist.

Lutes rarely had any binding, which made it easier to remove the soundboard for repairs.

The glue holding the narrow bridge to the soundboard is very strong to withstand the pull of so many strings.

John Dowland and the Renaissance lute

One of England's finest composers for, and players of, the lute was John Dowland (1563–1626). It is perhaps fitting that the finest 20th-century British work written for the guitar, Benjamin Britten's *Nocturnal After John Dowland*, is a set of variations on a theme by Dowland, "Come Heavy Sleep", from his *First Booke of Songs or Ayres*. Britten composed this with Julian Bream, himself a keen lutenist, in mind. Bream had many lutes made for him, and a favoured maker was David Rubio, whom he first commissioned to make an 'Elizabethan' lute in 1965. The lute here is a 1973 Rubio Renaissance lute.

Note the steep angle of the head.

The instrument has eight courses.

ABOVE: *The frontispiece of John Dowland's* First Booke of Songs or Ayres of Foure Parts, With Tableture for the Lute. *The four volumes were published individually between 1598 and 1612, and are today a major source for the repertoire of the eight-course lute.*

RIGHT: *A traditional Renaissance lute from the workshop of David Rubio. Some of Rubio's lutes from this period are more guitar-like, with fixed wooden frets. This one has tied gut frets and the soundboard is bound with parchment, making it easier to remove when it needed replacing or re-bracing.*

Early guitar-related instruments: citterns

Although the cittern reached the height of its popularity in France, Germany and Britain during the 18th century, it can be traced back a number of centuries prior to this. The 18th-century instruments were deeper-bodied than earlier models, and, although many varieties were produced, the most common type had a pear-shaped body, a floating (not fixed) bridge and metal strings that were played with the fingers.

Petrus Rautta, 1579

This is the only known English-made cittern from the Renaissance. It is a four-course metal-string variety. The depth of the body is shallower than the later 'English guitar' and the sides taper in depth from top to bottom, opposite to the way most guitars are shaped. The pegbox is carved with a dog's-head finial. The fretting employs a temperament closely matching one-sixth-comma meantone rather than a modern equal-tempered instrument.

- **DATE** 1579
- **ORIGIN** England
- **WOOD**
  Front/Back & Sides
  Spruce/maple, plum and pear or apple
- **UNUSUAL FEATURE**
  This is the only known English cittern from the Renaissance period.

Gerard Deleplanque, 1777

The extant examples of Gerard Deleplanque's (1700s–after 1792) guitars and citterns testify that he was one of finest makers in 18th-century France. They are finely crafted and usually highly decorated, as this example shows: it is inlaid with over a thousand pieces of hand-cut mother-of-pearl. French citterns of this time typically had seven courses of strings, tuned EADEAC♯E. The four treble strings are pairs and the lower strings are single basses, making eleven strings in total.

- **DATE** 1777
- **ORIGIN** Lille, France
- **WOOD**
  Front/Back & Sides
  Spruce/maple with mother-of-pearl
- **UNUSUAL FEATURE**
  This instrument has seven courses of strings.

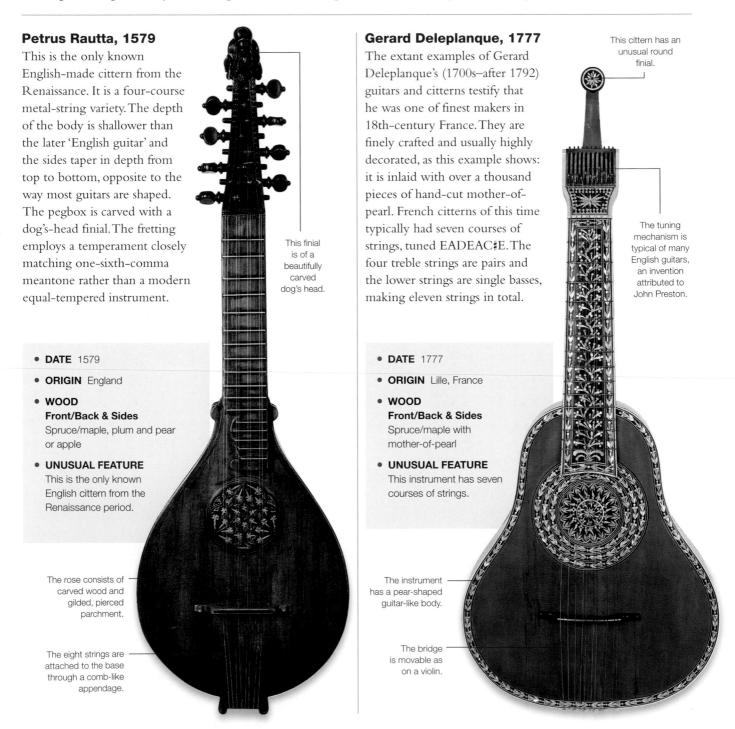

This finial is of a beautifully carved dog's head.

This cittern has an unusual round finial.

The tuning mechanism is typical of many English guitars, an invention attributed to John Preston.

The rose consists of carved wood and gilded, pierced parchment.

The eight strings are attached to the base through a comb-like appendage.

The instrument has a pear-shaped guitar-like body.

The bridge is movable as on a violin.

German cittern (anonymous), *c.*1780s

This *waldzither* was made in Saxo-Thuringia in the late 18th century; the stepped body shape was common for citterns from this part of Germany. The fretting employs a temperament closely matching one-sixth-comma meantone (similar to the fifth-comma) rather than a modern equal-tempered instrument. Many cittern tablatures for dances and songs survive from this period, and the main application was chord-based song accompaniment; many different tunings were used. The strings are attached to the base of the cittern via little pins.

The head terminates in a male angel with wings.

- **DATE** *c.*1780s

- **ORIGIN** Eastern Germany

- **WOOD**
  Front/Back & Sides
  Spruce/maple

- **UNUSUAL FEATURE**
  Frets are positioned in the fifth-comma-meantone temperament position.

Notice the irregularly spaced frets.

The rose is carved from the soundboard and not an insert.

The strings are hooked around little ivory pegs at the base of the instrument.

The body shape is typical of citterns from Saxo-Thuringia.

John Preston: keyed cittern, *c.*1790

In the 18th century, John Preston (1727–98) was the most prolific maker of English guitars. He started making English guitars around 1765 which were just known as 'guittars' at the time. There are two main kinds of citterns with added keyboards: those with an internal mechanism, such as those by Christian Claus, and those by Preston in which a removable keyboard is mounted to a regular instrument. The strings are hit rather than plucked, producing a tone similar to that of a hammer-dulcimer. The right-hand technique employed is similar to the standard guitar. Preston is attributed with inventing the watch-key tuning mechanism seen here, as an alternative to wooden tuning pegs.

The finial here is purely decorative.

The string-ends are looped and attached to a 'rider' which, when moved, tightens or loosens the string.

ABOVE: *The finial and fingerboard are inlaid with tortoiseshell, which is underlaid with a red substance producing a beautiful red and brown mottled effect. The strings are tuned with the use of a pocket-watch key. This particular example has the earlier wooden rose rather than the more commonly seen later removable metal design. It has its original and very rare wooden 'coffin' case.*

There are six ivory piano-like keys, one for each course.

Early guitar-related instruments: the mandolin family

As a plucked gut-string chordophone with frets, the Baroque mandolin was closely related to both guitar and lute, and luthiers such as Stradivari made all three instruments. Around 1800 the mandolin went its separate way, now having wire strings and being played with a plectrum rather than the fingers, and its standard tuning being the same as that of the violin: GDAE.

Stradivari: choral *mandolino*, 1680

This *mandolino* is one of only two known surviving examples thought to be by Antonio Stradivari (1644–1737). The back is made of seven maple ribs. Notice that the soundboard is not 'cant', or bent, at the bridge as in the modern form. The head was reconstructed according to Stradivari's original templates, which have survived. It has five courses of strings, and the tuning would have been the same as a modern mandolin (EADG, probably in unison pairs) with octave Bs added to the bass.

The head is a faithful reproduction of the original.

There are ten tuning pegs.

The neck has ivory binding.

- **DATE** 1680
- **ORIGIN** Italy
- **WOOD**
  Front/Back & Sides
  Spruce/maple
- **UNUSUAL FEATURE**
  There are five courses rather than the four that are found on modern mandolins.

The fifth courses are tuned an octave apart.

Some 19th-century guitar makers, for example Guadagnini, continued to shape their bridge-ends in the same manner.

Antonio Vinaccia, 1772

The Vinaccia family were famous Neapolitan instrument makers. Antonio Vinaccia (active 1750s–1790s) was the son of Gennaro Vinaccia. Other family members included Giovanni, Vincenzo, Gaetano and Pasquale (said to be the inventor of steel strings). Notice the 'cant', or bent, soundboard, which is a feature of another wire-string instrument, the *chitarra battente*. The back is made of 20 scalloped maple ribs interspersed with ebony and ivory stringing. The decoration features tortoiseshell and is lavishly inlaid with mother-of-pearl.

The head is decorated with tortoiseshell and mother-of-pearl.

- **DATE** 1772
- **ORIGIN** Italy
- **WOOD**
  Front/Back & Sides
  Spruce/maple with ebony and ivory stringing
- **UNUSUAL FEATURE**
  The instrument has fanciful f-holes.

The scratchplate is inlaid.

This instrument has a cant, or bent, soundboard.

Raffaele Calace: mando-lyre, 1913

Like Antonio Vinaccia, Raffaele Calace (1863–1934) came from a leading Neapolitan family of instrument makers. He was also a mandolinist and prolific composer for the instrument. Apart from its lyre shape, this example is no different from a regular mandolin. However, the back is more rounded than the traditional kind. The two arms are hollow, which purportedly enhances the sound. The strings are attached to the bottom of the body and are covered by an engraved metal cover.

- **DATE** 1913
- **ORIGIN** Italy
- **WOOD**
  Front/Back & Sides
  Spruce/rosewood
- **UNUSUAL FEATURE**
  The two arms give it
  a lyre-like appearance.

The arms have small ornamental finials.

A traditional oval-shaped soundhole is used.

This instrument has a metal string-guard.

Luigi Embergher: Type-B study model, 1924

The Rome workshops of Luigi Embergher (1856–1943) produced some of the finest mandolins ever made. However, their superb workmanship and exceptional quality are not their only appeal; the sound they make also ensures there is a high demand for these instruments. Embergher's mandolins were commonly made in different sizes for ensemble playing. This model was first created *c.*1907 to satisfy demand for high-quality but moderately priced models for both beginners and more experienced players.

- **DATE** 1924
- **ORIGIN** Italy
- **WOOD**
  Front/Back & Sides
  Spruce/rosewood
- **UNUSUAL FEATURE**
  This model is almost austere
  when compared with other
  mandolins.

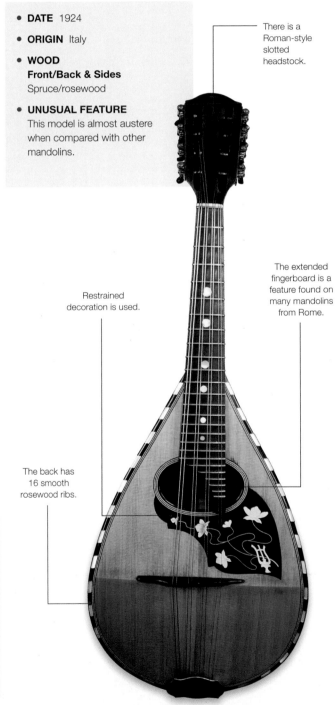

There is a Roman-style slotted headstock.

The extended fingerboard is a feature found on many mandolins from Rome.

Restrained decoration is used.

The back has 16 smooth rosewood ribs.

16th- to 18th-century guitars:
the Renaissance and the Baroque

Surviving written documentation and pictorial evidence show that the four-course guitar was popular during the Renaissance. The Baroque guitar was favoured in Spain and Italy during the early 17th century, catching on later in France. Each country generated important centres of instrument manufacture, with names such as the Sellas family in Venice, Stradivari in Cremona and Voboam in Paris becoming celebrated.

Matteo Sellas (attributed): Baroque guitar, c.1640

Matteo Sellas (c.1600–1654) established his workshop in Venice in the 1620s where his son Domenico also worked. This guitar has a vaulted back in which the strips of ebony are also fluted. The rose is unusual, being constructed of four layers of parchment, paper and leather that have been cut and pierced and then either left natural, stained red or gilded. This example still has its original string length; most instruments were altered over time as fashions changed.

'Matteo Sellas 1638' is engraved into the head.

Engraved details of rural scenes are shown on ivory plaques.

- **DATE** c.1640
- **ORIGIN** Italy
- **WOOD**
  Front/Back & Sides
  Spruce/fluted ebony with ivory stringing
- **UNUSUAL FEATURE**
  This is a rare example as it has its original string length still intact.

The rose has four tiers.

The soundboard is inlaid with ivory and ebony.

Alexandre Voboam: Baroque guitar, 1670

René, Jean, Nicolas Alexandre and Alexandre Voboam (d. c.1679) all made guitars in Paris during the 17th century. This one has ten tied gut frets and two inlaid wooden frets and is edged with ebony and ivory in a diagonal pattern. Although it is unusual for guitars to have the back and sides made of different woods (here dark ebony sides with a light juniper back) it was less uncommon in this period. It has two ivory buttons on the back and bottom to secure a strap.

The guitar is signed and dated on the head.

The instrument has ten tied gut frets and two wooden ones.

- **DATE** 1670
- **ORIGIN** France
- **WOOD**
  Front/Back & Sides
  Spruce/ebony with ivory (sides); juniper with ebony and ivory (back)
- **UNUSUAL FEATURE**
  The maker used different woods for the back and sides.

The barber-pole decoration is typical of Parisian instruments.

Antonio Stradivari: Baroque guitar, 1700

Although Antonio Stradivari (1644–1737) is probably the most famous name in the world of bowed-instrument making, fewer people know about the harps, lutes, *mandolinos* and guitars that also carry his name. There are two known extant *mandolinos* and four surviving guitars (dated 1679, 1680 [or 1688], 1681 and this one from 1700) and the remains of a neck and head (1675). Stradivari's guitars differ from others of the period in that the bodies are generally bigger and the string lengths longer.

- **DATE** 1700

- **ORIGIN** Italy

- **WOOD**
  Front/Back & Sides
  Spruce/maple

- **UNUSUAL FEATURE**
  This guitar has fixed frets rather than tied gut frets.

This guitar would originally have had tied gut frets.

The rosette around the hole is similar in design to that which Louis Panormo adopted the following century.

The instrument has a lute-like linear rose that is glued into place.

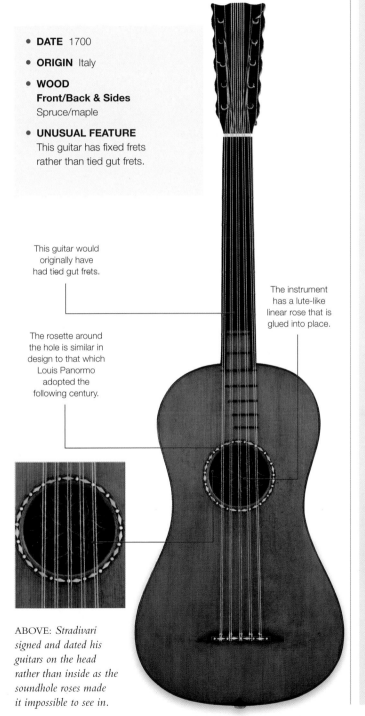

ABOVE: *Stradivari signed and dated his guitars on the head rather than inside as the soundhole roses made it impossible to see in.*

Evidence for the four-course Renaissance guitar

The four-course Renaissance guitar was small in comparison with the later five-course Baroque instrument. It was tuned in intervals of fourth–third–fourth, for example GCEA, with the fourth (bass) course tuned an octave apart. In Spain it coexisted alongside the vihuela, and Alonso Mudarra's famous *Tres Libros de Música en Cifra para Vihuela*, published in Seville in 1546, included music for both vihuela and four-course guitar. The instrument also enjoyed some popularity in Italy, England and, especially, France. A picture on the title page of Guillaume Morlaye's *Le Premier Livre*, published in Paris in 1552 – and backed up by many other contemporary illustrations – shows that this guitar was commonly strung with paired strings but with the top 'melody' string left single. This idea was later to take the five- and six-course double-strung guitar towards the single-stringed instruments (both five- and six-stringed) that ultimately led to the modern guitar.

ABOVE: *In the absence of any original surviving four-course guitars from the Renaissance period, iconographic and written evidence such as this French engraving from 1570 is vitally important to help guitar historians and organologists understand more about how these instruments worked.*

16th- to 18th-century guitars:
the vihuela and chitarra battente

There are very few existing early (that is, pre-mid-17th-century) guitar-related instruments that have survived the ravages of time or conversion (and often inappropriate reconversion) as fashions changed. In fact, only three original vihuelas still exist. Consequently, the instruments here are exceedingly rare and valuable examples of a particular period in the development of the modern guitar.

Belchior Dias (attributed): Baroque guitar, c.1590

This is an extremely important early guitar, one of the world's oldest surviving examples of a Baroque instrument. Although there is no label, it is attributed to the Portuguese maker Belchior Dias, as its decoration is similar to a 1581 example by Dias housed at the Royal College of Music, London. The instrument has a replacement soundboard.

A five-course Baroque guitar has ten tuning pegs.

The interlaced marquetry pattern is in the style of Dias.

- **DATE** c.1590
- **ORIGIN** Portugal
- **WOOD**
  Front/Back & Sides
  Spruce (originally)/rosewood
- **UNUSUAL FEATURE**
  There is no maker's identification label on the instrument.

The instrument has a flat rose.

The applied mustachios complement the inlays to the upper soundboard.

Chitarra battente conversion from a Baroque guitar, 1626

This instrument probably started out as an Italian-made five-course Baroque guitar but was converted, as many were, to a chitarra battente. This was done by shortening the neck, changing the sides to accommodate a 'cant' mandolin-like soundboard, removing five tuning pegs and altering the bridge to allow for the use of wire strings. One later transformation took place to convert it to a six-string guitar, once again in keeping with the fashion of the day.

This guitar originally had ten tuning pegs, but only six are currently being used.

- **DATE** 1626
- **ORIGIN** Italy
- **WOOD**
  Front/Back & Sides
  Spruce/ebony and ivory
- **UNUSUAL FEATURE**
  The heads of converted guitars were usually cut down – this one has survived intact.

The fingerboard and pegbox feature ivory panels showing hunting scenes and Orpheus charming the beasts.

The bridge is modified for a reduced number of strings.

Chitarra battente, c.1690

In Italian, the words 'chitarra battente' literally mean 'beating guitar'. The soundboard has a 'cant' (bend) below the bridge that gives the instrument the greater strength needed from the pull of wire strings. These instruments usually had a rounded back, as this example does. The number of strings varied and were sometimes arranged in triple rather than double courses. They were played with a plectrum and used for accompaniment. This particular instrument has typical Italian-style soundboard inlays with a layered soundhole rose.

This guitar has 14 tuning pegs, thus indicating some sort of triple stringing.

The ebony head facing is beautifully inlaid with ivory.

- **DATE** *c.*1690
- **ORIGIN** Italy
- **WOOD**
  Front/Back & Sides
  Spruce/yew
- **UNUSUAL FEATURE**
  This chitarra battente has 14 tuning pegs.

LEFT: *Like most chitarra battentes, the back is rounded and the sides are angled to accommodate the bend in the soundboard.*

The strings pass through the bridge and are anchored to the base of the guitar.

Vihuela de mano

ABOVE: *The 'Chambure' vihuela. The conservation policies of many museums mean that this instrument will likely remain with its soundboard detached. From an organological perspective, this is a priceless opportunity to study how instruments were made in the past.*

There were at least three forms of vihuela in the 16th century, the *vihuela de arco* (bowed), the *vihuela de peñola* (plucked with a plectrum) and the *vihuela de mano* (plucked with the fingers), the latter becoming simply known as the vihuela. It is thought that Spain adopted the vihuela because the other popular instrument of the day throughout Europe, the lute, was too similar to the oud, which had connotations with Moorish Spain and was thus out of favour following the Reconquista. Of the only three known surviving vihuelas, one is in the Iglesia de la Compañia de Jesús de Quito in Ecuador and the others – the 'Guadalupe' instrument and the recently rediscovered 'Chambure' vihuela – are both in Paris, at the Musée Jacquemart-Andrée and the Cité de la Musique respectively. The 'Chambure' vihuela (pictured above) has a seven-piece, deeply fluted back of jujube wood, and the head accommodates 12 tuning pegs for strings arranged in six paired courses. The outline of the bridge can be seen.

18th- and early 19th-century transitional guitars: part one

The move towards the modern guitar took in many developments. In Spain, a direct line can be drawn from the 16th-century vihuela through the six-course guitar (mid-18th to mid-19th centuries). However, other countries, notably France, adopted the six-string lyre-guitar – tuned as a modern guitar – and a great deal of music was written for this instrument, mostly simple accompaniments to songs.

Francisco Sanguino: seven-course guitar, c.1759

Francisco Sanguino (c.1705–1771) was one of the first makers to use simple fanbracing to support the soundboard against the tension of 14 strings – and thus avoid what earlier lutenists had to be prepared to do in regularly disassembling and rebracing their soundboards. The exact tuning is unknown, as is the type of music it was used for, but the Spanish composer Federico Moretti mentions in his 1799 method *Principios Para Tocar la Guitarra de Seis Orderes* that he preferred guitars with this string arrangement.

The long head accommodates 14 tuning pegs.

Although it has a short neck, it has a longer-than-average string length of 663mm (26⅛in).

- **DATE** c.1759
- **ORIGIN** Spain
- **WOOD**
  Front/Back & Sides
  Spruce/cypress
- **UNUSUAL FEATURE**
  A seven-course guitar, this has 14 strings, which are tuned in pairs.

The intricate soundboard decoration was probably inlaid by an expert rather than the instrument maker.

(Anonymous) lyre-guitar, c.1815

With Classicism in vogue, lyres in the form of a guitar started to appear in the 1780s – mainly in Paris, but examples from Italy, Germany and Spain also survive. A substantial amount of music was written for the lyre-guitar, principally by Italian composers in Paris, including Matteo Carcassi (1792–1853), Ferdinando Carulli (1770–1841) and Francois Molino (1775–1847). Unlike the harp-guitar of today, however, the lyre-guitar was played upright.

The head is reminiscent of Napoleon's hat, and the arms end in decorative brass finials.

There are six wooden tuning pegs, and the ivory studs help guide the outer strings towards the neck.

- **DATE** c.1815
- **ORIGIN** France
- **WOOD**
  Front/Back & Sides
  Spruce/maple
- **UNUSUAL FEATURE**
  The soundhole roses resemble those that are found on lutes.

Juan Pagés: six-course guitar, 1802

Surviving guitars by Juan Pagés (1741–1821), one of the foremost makers in Cadiz, are exceptional. This is a six-course instrument, tuned as a modern 12-string. The scale length is 654mm (25⅗in), similar to standard guitars today, rather than the more usual 630mm (24⅜in) of a 19th-century guitar. Many surviving six-course guitars underwent brutal modifications during the rise of the classical guitar, having their heads truncated and oversized bridges added to convert for playing with six single strings. This one was lucky.

Joseph Pagés: six-course guitar, 1822

Made by Joseph, or Joséf, Pagés (1762–?), who was the son of Juan Pagés, this guitar was brought to Gibraltar by 1822, where it ended up being owned by the Galliano banking family in Gibraltar. It is a very late example of the Spanish six-course guitar, made at a time when the rest of the guitar-playing world had switched to six single strings. With its squared-off head and minimal soundboard decoration – so much plainer than his father's 1802 example – the advent of the classical guitar seems not far off.

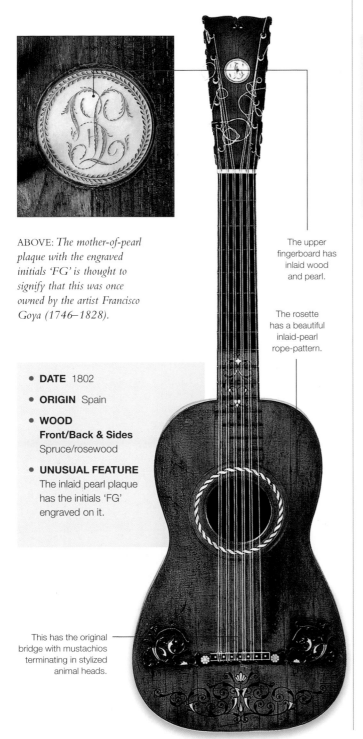

ABOVE: *The mother-of-pearl plaque with the engraved initials 'FG' is thought to signify that this was once owned by the artist Francisco Goya (1746–1828).*

- **DATE** 1802
- **ORIGIN** Spain
- **WOOD**
  Front/Back & Sides
  Spruce/rosewood
- **UNUSUAL FEATURE**
  The inlaid pearl plaque has the initials 'FG' engraved on it.

This has the original bridge with mustachios terminating in stylized animal heads.

The upper fingerboard has inlaid wood and pearl.

The rosette has a beautiful inlaid-pearl rope-pattern.

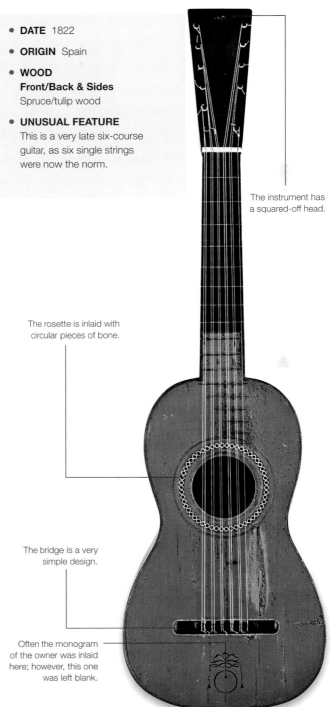

- **DATE** 1822
- **ORIGIN** Spain
- **WOOD**
  Front/Back & Sides
  Spruce/tulip wood
- **UNUSUAL FEATURE**
  This is a very late six-course guitar, as six single strings were now the norm.

The instrument has a squared-off head.

The rosette is inlaid with circular pieces of bone.

The bridge is a very simple design.

Often the monogram of the owner was inlaid here; however, this one was left blank.

18th- and early 19th-century transitional guitars: part two

By the late 18th century, the five-course guitar was moving away from its earlier Baroque style. In France, guitars were becoming plainer, and the move to six single strings had begun. These guitars exemplify this, with the sunken rose, double stringing and tied frets all on their way out. One feature that survived was the extension of the soundboard over part of the neck, but this went when raised fingerboards came in.

George Cousineau, c.1770

In Paris, George Cousineau (1733–1800) made violins and harps as well as guitars. This guitar has sloping sides, meaning that the back is much smaller than the front, which was thought to enhance sound projection. Although Cousineau was of the last generation to fit guitars with a sunken rose, compared with earlier five-course guitars this – apart from the rose itself and bridge mustachios – is very plain, which was not only the fashion but made a better sound.

LEFT: *Here we can see that the sides are not parallel. Instead, they are angled inwards, thus resulting in a much smaller back compared to the front.*

The hole in the top of the head was to tie a ribbon, either for decoration or to use as a guitar strap.

This guitar has tied gut frets.

This instrument has a rose of layered parchment.

- **DATE** *c.*1770
- **ORIGIN** France
- **WOOD**
  Front/Back & Sides
  Spruce/maple
- **UNUSUAL FEATURE**
  The sides are sloping.

Villaume and Giron, c.1790

Alexis Villaume and Claude Giron worked in Troyes, France, from *c.*1789 into the 1830s. This guitar must have been one of the last made with ten tuning pegs, and it was probably played – as it is today – with nine strings, the top course being single. It it is very similar in appearance to the Cousineau guitar, except that the Baroque feature, the sunken rose, has now gone, in this case leaving it with a rather small soundhole.

There are ten tuning pegs.

Although it has ten tuning pegs, this guitar uses only nine strings, the top course being single.

- **DATE** *c.*1790
- **ORIGIN** France
- **WOOD**
  Front/Back & Sides
  Spruce/maple
- **UNUSUAL FEATURE**
  The soundhole is very small.

There is an open soundhole instead of a sunken rose.

Many French-made guitars have alternating ebony and ivory edging.

Five-string guitar, *c.*1780

There are few surviving five-string guitars – this, of course, being the next evolutionary step towards the modern instrument. This guitar was probably made by either Giovanni Battista Fabricatore (*c.*1750–*c.*1812) or one of the Vinaccia family. Mother-of-pearl is inlaid in brown-coloured shellac and is flanked by tortoiseshell on the head. Although this guitar has much pearl decoration, it is roughly shaped and crudely placed into position. The back and sides are also of a cheap pine painted to imitate rosewood. These are all features which are lacking the finesse of Baroque instruments.

- **DATE** *c.*1780
- **ORIGIN** Italy
- **WOOD**
  Front/Back & Sides
  Spruce/pine
- **UNUSUAL FEATURE**
  The back is of cheap pine, painted
  to look like expensive rosewood.

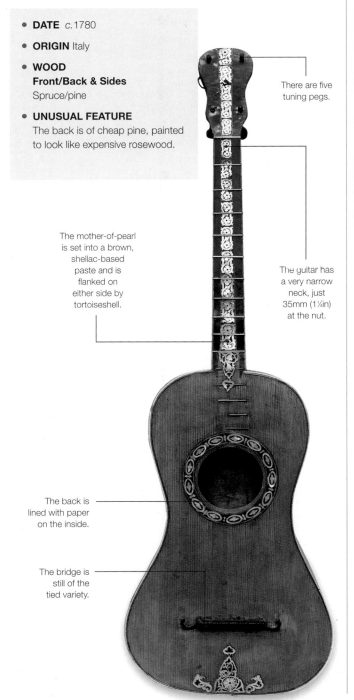

The mother-of-pearl is set into a brown, shellac-based paste and is flanked on either side by tortoiseshell.

There are five tuning pegs.

The guitar has a very narrow neck, just 35mm (1¼in) at the nut.

The back is lined with paper on the inside.

The bridge is still of the tied variety.

Converted five-course guitar, *c.*1770

This guitar was made originally as a five-course instrument, then a few years later it was converted to a five-single-string guitar. This was done by truncating the head and adding a five-pin bridge to the instrument. It does, however, still have its original nut, complete with ten grooves. It is actually a miracle that it was not converted again for six-string playing. Dendrochronology dates the soundboard to around 1757, so with time allowed for the curing of the wood, and also taking into account its stylistic features, its original date of manufacture is likely to be *c.*1770.

- **DATE** *c.*1770
- **ORIGIN** Italy or France
- **WOOD**
  Front/Back & Sides
  Spruce/maple
- **UNUSUAL FEATURE**
  This modified form of guitar would
  not have existed for very long, due
  to the making of five-stringed
  guitars and the almost immediate
  invention of the six-string guitar.

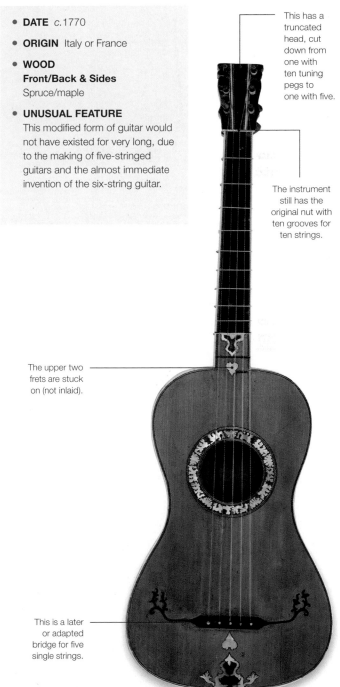

This has a truncated head, cut down from one with ten tuning pegs to one with five.

The instrument still has the original nut with ten grooves for ten strings.

The upper two frets are stuck on (not inlaid).

This is a later or adapted bridge for five single strings.

18th- and early 19th-century six-string guitars: Mediterranean

After the adoption of six single strings, the art of guitar making rose in the first half of the 19th century to a high not seen since the Baroque. The four makers whose instruments are shown here all used a similar concept for soundboard bracing, with diagonally placed bars being used to strengthen the boards against the tension of the strings, as distinct from the more usual Spanish use of fan-shaped bracing.

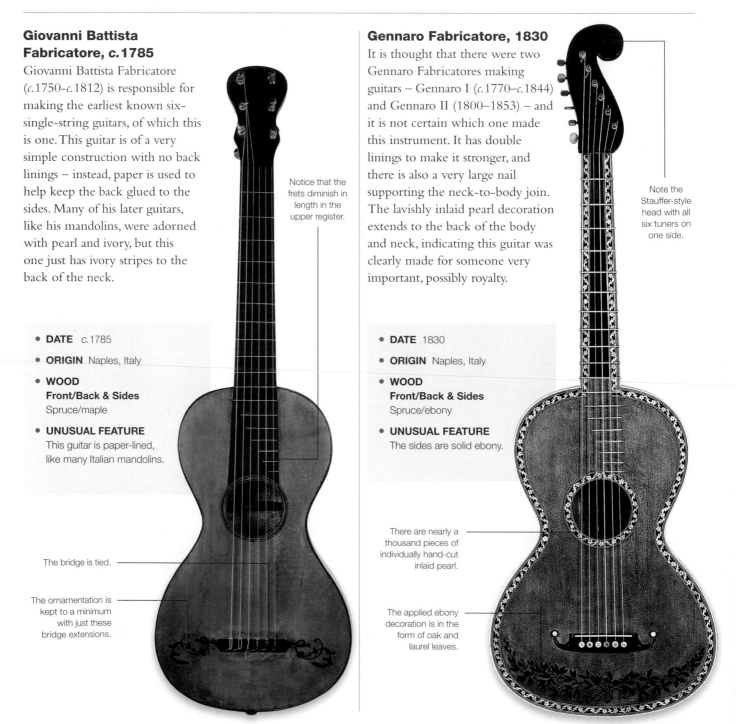

Giovanni Battista Fabricatore, c.1785

Giovanni Battista Fabricatore (c.1750–c.1812) is responsible for making the earliest known six-single-string guitars, of which this is one. This guitar is of a very simple construction with no back linings – instead, paper is used to help keep the back glued to the sides. Many of his later guitars, like his mandolins, were adorned with pearl and ivory, but this one just has ivory stripes to the back of the neck.

Notice that the frets diminish in length in the upper register.

- **DATE** c.1785
- **ORIGIN** Naples, Italy
- **WOOD**
  Front/Back & Sides
  Spruce/maple
- **UNUSUAL FEATURE**
  This guitar is paper-lined, like many Italian mandolins.

The bridge is tied.

The ornamentation is kept to a minimum with just these bridge extensions.

Gennaro Fabricatore, 1830

It is thought that there were two Gennaro Fabricatores making guitars – Gennaro I (c.1770–c.1844) and Gennaro II (1800–1853) – and it is not certain which one made this instrument. It has double linings to make it stronger, and there is also a very large nail supporting the neck-to-body join. The lavishly inlaid pearl decoration extends to the back of the body and neck, indicating this guitar was clearly made for someone very important, possibly royalty.

Note the Stauffer-style head with all six tuners on one side.

- **DATE** 1830
- **ORIGIN** Naples, Italy
- **WOOD**
  Front/Back & Sides
  Spruce/ebony
- **UNUSUAL FEATURE**
  The sides are solid ebony.

There are nearly a thousand pieces of individually hand-cut inlaid pearl.

The applied ebony decoration is in the form of oak and laurel leaves.

René Lacôte, 1830

Throughout the 'golden' period in the middle of the 19th century, René Lacôte (1785–c.1860) made guitars, which were played by Fernando Sor, Dionisio Aguado, Matteo Carrassi and Napoleon Coste, to name but a few. This one was made for Aguado, or at least one of his students, having signs that a tripodison (a type of guitar stand that Aguado endorsed) was once fitted. It must have been very much an experimental guitar, having an adjustable neck – one of only two known to have been made by Lacôte – and because it has two soundboards.

- **DATE** 1830
- **ORIGIN** Paris, France
- **WOOD**
  Front/Back & Sides
  Spruce/satinwood
- **UNUSUAL FEATURE**
  This has two soundboards with a second soundhole at the back.

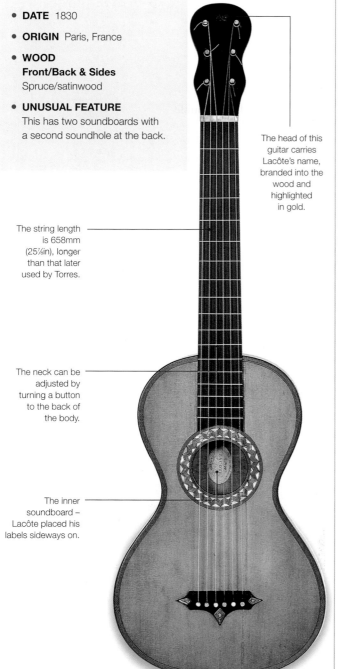

The head of this guitar carries Lacôte's name, branded into the wood and highlighted in gold.

The string length is 658mm (25⅞in), longer than that later used by Torres.

The neck can be adjusted by turning a button to the back of the body.

The inner soundboard – Lacôte placed his labels sideways on.

Agustín Altimíra, 1840s

The reason why this guitar is made in a French style remains a bit of a mystery as the maker, Agustin Altimíra (1805–82), lived and worked for his whole life in Barcelona, and died there. This example could easily pass as a French import, were it not for the fact that the head-to-neck joint, although executed in a French manner, retains a Spanish character. On closer inspection, it can be seen that the joint has a 'fake' Spanish-style carved 'dart'. An inlaid portrait on the back uses many exotic materials to give it depth and colour.

- **DATE** 1840s
- **ORIGIN** Barcelona, Spain
- **WOOD**
  Front/Back & Sides
  Spruce/burred walnut
- **UNUSUAL FEATURE**
  The elements are in a French style.

Note the enclosed French Lacôte-style tuning machines usually reserved for Lacôte's finest instruments.

The rosette features a hunting scene.

ABOVE: *The back is inlaid and painted beautifully using ivory and coloured shells depicting a scene of a Spanish soldier and the lady he loves playing the guitar.*

Two angels either side of the bridge are made from mother-of-pearl.

18th- and early 19th-century guitars: English

London was an exciting place to be in the 1800s. For the many foreign makers there it was a place to seek fame and fortune – for some it was also a refuge from political unrest. There were many forms of guitar in England, including the guittar and the many variants of harp-guitars. These all gave way to the Spanish guitar, and by the 1830s London-based makers were looking to French and Spanish makers for inspiration.

Early London-made guitar, c.1810

This was made at a time when the classical guitar was becoming popular and was one of the first six-string guitars made in London. Its overall appearance and style are that of the Baroque guitar, and it was built before the London makers had established their own style. It has ivory frets, both inlaid and painted purflings and grand mustachios radiating from the bridge. This example has no bracing below the soundhole bars.

There are six wooden tuning pegs.

There are 11 ivory frets to the neck.

- **DATE** *c.*1810

- **ORIGIN** London, England

- **WOOD**
  Front/Back & Sides
  Maple

- **UNUSUAL FEATURE**
  The painted-on decoration is found on some violins but no other guitars.

The bridge decoration is in a Spanish style.

Edward Light Dital-Harp, c.1816

The 'British harp-lute' – or 'dital-harp' – was patented by Edward Light (*c.*1727–1832) in 1816. Its selling point was its portability, compared with a regular harp, and there were many variants, some six-stringed tuned like the guittar, others, such as this, with many strings. It was taken up as an alternative to the waning English cittern and new Spanish guitar, but was short-lived, as the British people soon adopted the regular guitar.

The decoration is lavish gold-leaf and wood turning.

- **DATE** *c.*1816

- **ORIGIN** London, England

- **WOOD**
  Front/Back & Sides
  Spruce/maple

- **UNUSUAL FEATURE**
  The lower-string pitch is changed by pressing a button.

It has a fretboard for the upper register – perhaps another reason why it is classed as a harp-guitar. rather than a harp.

It has 19 strings, of which 14 can be shortened by using stops, thus increasing the range of the instrument.

Louis Panormo: Madame Pratten's guitar, 1831

Louis Panormo (1784–1862) was born in Paris and died in Auckland, New Zealand but was best known as a key figure in London. He and other family members built guitars at a time when the guitar was at its mid-Victorian height. The most famous guitarist and guitar teacher of the day was Madame Sidney Pratten (1821–95). She played many guitars throughout her long career – this example not only has her name stamped into the head, but also a red wax seal with her initials 'SP'. It is a very typical Panormo instrument, built, as the label suggests, "in the Spanish Style".

Dominic and Arnould Roudhloff, 1840s

The Roudhloff brothers came to London from Mirecourt, an area of France well known for its instrument makers, in the 1830s. They made some guitars in the French style and others, such as this example, which they called the 'melophonic guitar'. This was radically different: it was larger than the French instruments, the bridge saddle was angled and the internal soundboard used what later became known as x-bracing (something further developed by the American company C. F. Martin & Co.). The Roudhloff brothers also made many eight-string instruments.

The head follows the distinctive Panormo-style.

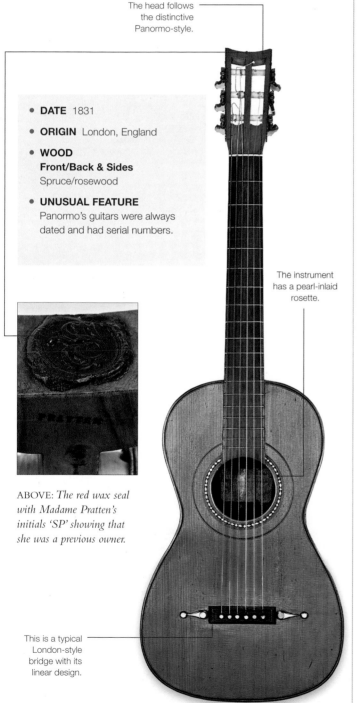

- **DATE** 1831
- **ORIGIN** London, England
- **WOOD**
  Front/Back & Sides
  Spruce/rosewood
- **UNUSUAL FEATURE**
  Panormo's guitars were always dated and had serial numbers.

The instrument has a pearl-inlaid rosette.

ABOVE: *The red wax seal with Madame Pratten's initials 'SP' showing that she was a previous owner.*

This is a typical London-style bridge with its linear design.

- **DATE** 1840s
- **ORIGIN** London, England
- **WOOD**
  Front/Back & Sides
  Spruce/rosewood on mahogany
- **UNUSUAL FEATURE**
  This is a large instrument for the period.

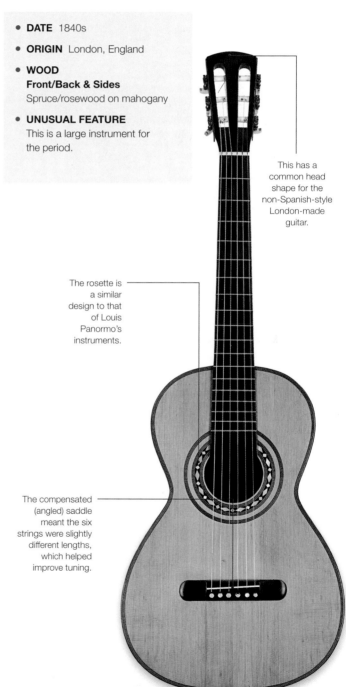

This has a common head shape for the non-Spanish-style London-made guitar.

The rosette is a similar design to that of Louis Panormo's instruments.

The compensated (angled) saddle meant the six strings were slightly different lengths, which helped improve tuning.

19th-century guitars:
Germanic and Russian

Early Viennese makers tended to follow Italian styles, later establishing their own school, which in turn influenced Germany and Russia. All three guitars here have adjustable necks – neck angle and thus string height can be altered. String lengths tended to be shorter than other European schools; this, coupled with generally narrower necks, mean players can use techniques such as fretting the bass string with the thumb.

Johann Stauffer: Legnani Terz model, c.1830

Johann Anton Stauffer (c.1805–1851) was the son of Johann Georg Stauffer (1778–1853). Stauffer guitars from this period tend to have a rounded 'figure-of-eight' shape, and many had adjustable necks with raised fingerboards and a higher compass of notes, some ranging three octaves. This guitar is tuned a minor third higher than standard, in Terz tuning.

- **DATE** c.1830
- **ORIGIN** Vienna, Austria
- **WOOD**
  Front/Back & Sides
  Spruce/maple
- **UNUSUAL FEATURE**
  The string length is very short, being only 560mm (22in).

The head shape was adopted by Leo Fender in the 1940s for his electric instruments.

The instrument has extra frets that go up to high F (in Terz tuning).

The bridge is made of liquorice wood, as were many cheaper violin fingerboards at the time.

Mortz Gläsel guitar, c.1870

A highly regarded luthier, Mortz Gläsel (1829–1917) worked in Markneukirchen, Saxony – also C. F. Martin's hometown. The unusual shape of this guitar – that of an early 17th-century viola da gamba – probably came from the fact that he was a connoisseur of ancient instruments. Many German-made guitars are unlabelled, so the makers' identities are unknown, but this one had Gläsel's label hidden in the lining of the original case.

- **DATE** c.1870
- **ORIGIN** Saxony, Germany
- **WOOD**
  Front/Back & Sides
  Spruce/burred walnut
- **UNUSUAL FEATURE**
  The body shape is that of a viola da gamba.

The neck is inlaid with ivory and abalone.

The instrument has a unique body shape similar to a viola da gamba.

The bridge is ornate and rather heavy.

Russian seven-string guitar, c.1880

Guitar music in Russia (also in Poland and Bohemia) called for seven-string instruments tuned to DGBDGBD, the open chordal tuning possibly influenced by the English guitar's CEGCEG. Like many Viennese and German guitars the neck is adjustable, although here it is to allow the musician to manipulate the neck while playing, thus raising and lowering the pitch. The label here reads: "Trading House of Musical Instruments/Founded in 1879 by Kulakov", suggesting he was a wholesaler. The German stylistic features make it clear that this was a German-made guitar that was exported to Russia.

Note the seven metal barrels.

- **DATE** c.1880

- **ORIGIN** Russia

- **WOOD**
  Front/Back & Sides
  Spruce/rosewood

- **UNUSUAL FEATURE**
  There are specially adapted tuning machines for seven strings.

ABOVE: *The octagonal-shaped rosette sits perfectly around the round sound-hole, and even the edge of the fingerboard meets the rosette with precision. This is typical of the highly gifted craftsmen (and possibly women) who operated from Saxony.*

The join is just visible between the two halves of the soundboard.

Luigi Legnani

ABOVE: *A Stauffer label from 1827, which reads: "Nach dem Modell"* (translated: *"After the design")/ "des Luigi Legnani 3347/von Johann Anton Stuffer & Co. in Wien." It carries Stauffer's red wax seal featuring the double-headed eagle of the House of Habsburg.*

Luigi Legnani (1790–1877) was a guitar virtuoso as well as an amateur violin and guitar maker who helped both Stauffer companies (those of Johann Georg and his son Johann Anton) to design and develop their guitars. This is perhaps the most long-standing of all player–maker relationships, and the collaboration between Legnani and the Stauffers was probably more than simply an endorsement on Legnani's part. In 1822, J. G. Stauffer and his compatriot the violin maker Johann Ertl (1776–1828) received a 'privilege' for five years, extended in 1828, to 'improve' guitars. This privilege was probably a patent filed through the strict guilds, which at that time in Vienna controlled not only the right to make instruments but also whom one trained and even the prices one could charge. Some of their improvements included the raised fingerboard, a screw mechanism for neck adjustment and a new metal alloy for longer-lasting frets. These features appear on the Legnani models, but were most certainly a feature on regular Stauffer guitars as well.

There are seven bridge pins.

19th-century guitars: American

This section features two guitars by the New York-based maker C. F. Martin, the most famous of all American flat-top makers, plus guitars by the less well-known James Ashborn and John Haynes. All three makers are equally important, though, when considering the development of the American guitar, along with Elias Howe, the Larson Brothers and Robert Maurer.

C. F. Martin: Stauffer model, *c.*1834

In 1833 Christian Frederick Martin (1796–1873) came to New York from Markneukirchen, Germany, establishing his store and guitar-making workshop. By 1834 he was making his first American guitars, and the example here is his earliest-known New York instrument. It is constructed very much in the Stauffer style – the head, the adjustable neck with floating fingerboard, and the bridge with downwards-pointing mustachios. However, the semi-circular abalone inlay and ivory cap to the bridge were Martin's own.

- **DATE** *c.*1834
- **ORIGIN** New York, USA
- **WOOD**
  Front/Back & Sides
  Spruce/bird's-eye maple
- **UNUSUAL FEATURE**
  Many Panormo-school guitars used small circular inlays around the circumference; here, Martin used a more elegant semi-circular design.

C. F. Martin: 2½-40, *c.*1850

This would have been one of Martin's most expensive models at the time, the size designation of 2½ being aimed at the women's market. The spruce used for the soundboard was taken from the Adirondack mountain range located in the north-eastern part of New York State. An unusual feature for Martin is that the back is not solid; instead, the Brazilian rosewood is lined on the inside with pine. This is an early example of Martin's x-bracing system, albeit still designed for gut strings.

- **DATE** *c.*1850
- **ORIGIN** Pennsylvania, USA
- **WOOD**
  Front/Back & Sides
  Spruce/rosewood
- **UNUSUAL FEATURE**
  The pine lining to the inside of the back is a feature more common in French-made guitars of this period.

The head is recognizably Stauffer-shaped.

The fingerboard is raised.

Note the ivory-bound fingerboard, reserved for Martin's finest models.

The semi-circular abalone inlays are possibly made of button blanks.

The bridge has downwards-pointing mustachios.

The amount of pearl decoration identifies this as model 40. The more decoration used, the higher the model.

Ivory is used for the bridge, saddle and bridge pins.

James Ashborn: Style 1, 1855

Probably a British engineer, James Ashborn (*c.*1810–?) is thought to have emigrated to the USA and started making guitars in Connecticut. He seems to have had some Spanish influence while producing guitars of a very individual nature. This is not immediately apparent until one looks more closely at the constructional features of his instruments, as many have parquet inlays and French-style veneered necks. They are very carefully and cleanly made, rivalling those of C. F. Martin in craftsmanship, although the materials and decorative elements are not of such high quality. Many of his guitars were distributed through the Hall and Firth companies.

John Haynes: Tilton model, 1870

William B. Tilton was a New York maker who licensed his designs to other manufacturers, and this instrument was made by John Haynes in Boston to a Tilton design. Tilton patented his improvement – reducing the mass of the neck and bottom blocks to give the soundboard more area to vibrate and adding a wooden dowel to compensate for the less-rigid structure – for this design in the 1850s. The patent included the addition of a tailpiece to relieve string tension, so allowing for lighter x-bracing.

- **DATE** 1870
- **ORIGIN** Massachusetts, USA
- **WOOD**
  Front/Back & Sides
  Spruce/rosewood
- **UNUSUAL FEATURE**
  The guitar has a tailpiece and wooden dowel stick.

The head shape is not very American, and is therefore presumed to be a replacement.

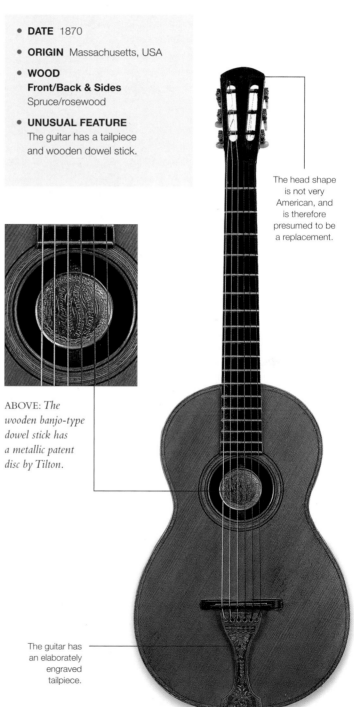

ABOVE: *The wooden banjo-type dowel stick has a metallic patent disc by Tilton.*

The squared-off head is a traditional American style.

These are unusually long string-relief ramps.

- **DATE** 1855
- **ORIGIN** Connecticut, USA
- **WOOD**
  Front/Back & Sides
  Spruce/rosewood
- **UNUSUAL FEATURE**
  The veneered neck is a rare feature on American-made guitars.

The plain rosette identifies it as a 'style 1'.

The instrument has a two-piece bridge.

The guitar has an elaborately engraved tailpiece.

19th-century guitars:
unusual varieties

There are very few innovations and designs in modern guitars that were not already tried and tested during the 19th century – including ways to make instruments louder, have a broader range, play more in tune, have a better tone, and be easier to play or transport. Some of these are still in use now, but the majority fall into the class of odd-ball fantasies that have had their time and been discarded.

Mauchant Frères archtop, c.1820

Many 19th-century French luthiers learnt their trade from violin makers and often produced both types of instruments. Little is known about the Mauchants, but clearly they designed this early archtop guitar with the cello in mind, as the internal bracing has a double cello-style bass bar running either side of the round soundhole. A guitar similar to this is pictured in Francisco Molino's famous *Grande Méthode Complète* of 1823.

- **DATE** *c.*1820
- **ORIGIN** Mirecourt, France
- **WOOD**
  Front/Back & Sides
  Spruce/maple
- **UNUSUAL FEATURE**
  This the earliest guitar with an arched top.

This two-dimensional scroll-shaped head is the reverse of the Stauffer head or today's Fender design.

This guitar has two cello-style c-holes, as well as the traditional round soundhole.

The bridge is floating rather than being fixed, as with instruments of the violin family.

It also has a traditional guitar-pin bridge.

C. F. Bauer double soundhole, c.1850

C. F. Bauer worked near Markneukirchen in Germany. Like Martin he had worked with Stauffer in Vienna, and some of his guitars show this influence. Inside, Bauer's name is stamped rather than using a label, something Martin continues today. The extended bass accounts for the extra soundhole and the off-kilter neck, which is mounted so as to centre the bridge on the body.

- **DATE** *c.*1850
- **ORIGIN** Klingenthal, Saxony, Germany
- **WOOD**
  Front/Back & Sides
  Maple
- **UNUSUAL FEATURE**
  This guitar has two soundholes, which allows the ten strings to resonate more.

There are four extra tuning machines to accommodate the sub-bass strings.

The neck is fixed at an angle to the body.

The two soundholes feature Stauffer-style rosettes.

The body is very large for a guitar of this period.

Unlabelled, probably Viennese: "Painted Scene", c.1850–60

Although it was fashionable for some French guitars to have painted scenes, usually to the back of the instrument, this guitar is certainly Germanic in origin. The decoration separating the Biedermeier scene from the many cherubs and two songbirds 'standing' on the bridge mustachios is executed with three-dimensional relief paintwork. Apart from the decoration, the guitar is an ordinary mid-19th-century Austrian guitar with a rosette that is quite typical of the instruments from the Stauffer workshop.

George Lewis Panormo (attributed): Bambina Guitar, 1874

G. L. Panormo (1815–77) – not to be confused with his father George Panormo or his uncle Louis Panormo – continued the family business, and towards the end of his career made these small instruments, an early form of travel guitar, for the Victorian guitarist and guitar teacher Madame Pratten and her students. Confusingly, they were labelled 'Bambina', which means 'child', and hence they are often thought to be a children's model. The Bambina measures just 536mm (21⅛in) total length with a string length of 336mm (13¼in) – this was around half the length of a regular guitar of the time.

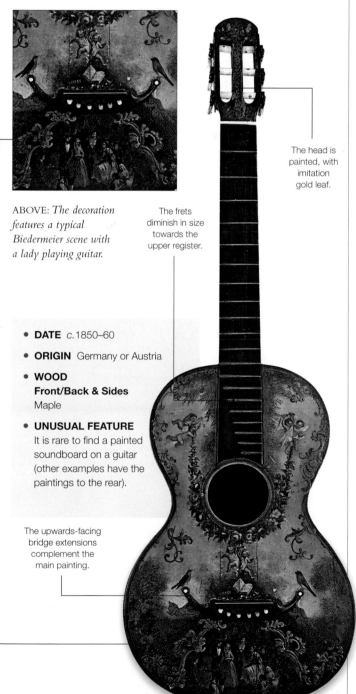

ABOVE: *The decoration features a typical Biedermeier scene with a lady playing guitar.*

The head is painted, with imitation gold leaf.

The frets diminish in size towards the upper register.

- **DATE** c.1850–60
- **ORIGIN** Germany or Austria
- **WOOD**
  Front/Back & Sides
  Maple
- **UNUSUAL FEATURE**
  It is rare to find a painted soundboard on a guitar (other examples have the paintings to the rear).

The upwards-facing bridge extensions complement the main painting.

- **DATE** 1874
- **ORIGIN** London, England
- **WOOD**
  Front/Back & Sides
  Spruce/coromandel
- **UNUSUAL FEATURE**
  Its diminutive size made this a 19th-century forerunner to today's travel instruments.

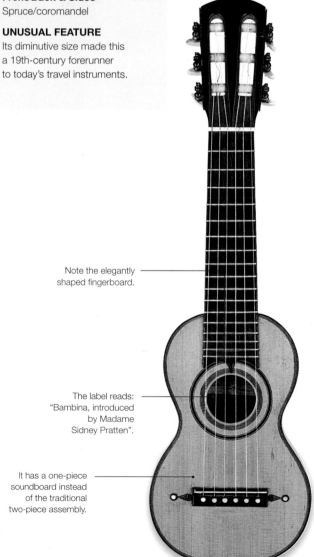

Note the elegantly shaped fingerboard.

The label reads: "Bambina, introduced by Madame Sidney Pratten".

It has a one-piece soundboard instead of the traditional two-piece assembly.

19th-century classical guitar makers: Antonio de Torres

Antonio de Torres (1817–92) is the father of the modern classical guitar, his instruments representing the summit of 19th-century design. His soundboard bracing and his synthesizing of what had gone before earned him this title, and no maker since has had such influence. He had two making periods; in between he ran a china shop. Of the 320 or so guitars he is thought to have made, around 100 are known today.

FE18, 1864

Guitars from Torres' 'first epoch' (FE) of guitar making are rare and have no serial numbers (meaning forgers often try to fake them). This guitar has been designated FE18 – the 18th FE guitar known and arranged, in approximate chronological order. Francisco Tárrega's guitar (FE17) uses wood cut from the same tree. Torres often locked little secret signs into his carpentry, such as the three incomplete sets of white inlays in the rosette.

- **DATE** 1864
- **ORIGIN** Seville, Spain
- **WOOD**
  Front/Back & Sides
  Spruce/maple
- **UNUSUAL FEATURE**
  There are deliberately built-in design defects.

As with the majority of surviving Torres guitars the tuning machines are not original.

The bone tie-block covering on the bridge is typical of many guitars of this period.

ABOVE: *Like Tárrega's guitar from the same year, there seem to be some intentional, possibly Masonic, signs locked into the carpentry by Torres' hand.*

SE39, 1882

This has the serial number SE39 ('second epoch' 39) and is one of the larger guitars for which Torres is famed – although only about a third of his guitars are of this type. It still has its original polish – useful for musicologists studying the playing wear to determine the techniques of previous owners. The bracing has 'open harmonic' bars, which increase the vibration area of the soundboard.

- **DATE** 1882
- **ORIGIN** Almería, Spain
- **WOOD**
  Front/Back & Sides
  Spruce/rosewood
- **UNUSUAL FEATURE**
  The soundboard is braced with open-harmonic bars.

Note the distinctive three-arched head.

This guitar has two extra paper labels, indicating various restoration work.

The 'book-matched' grain (where the lumber is split and unfolded like two pages of a book) used for the soundboard shows that the two halves are from the same tree.

SE127, 1889

This guitar belonged to the Spanish poet, novelist and literary editor Carlos Barral. Although the use of three pieces of wood to make up the back was common in Spanish lutherie, Torres also used three separate pieces – mahogany/walnut/mahogany – to make the sides of the body. The rosette is made up of 27 concentric circles of various inlaid woods. This guitar's scale length, which also determines where the metal frets are positioned, is 648mm (25½in), which is very close to today's standard of 650mm (25⅝in) string length.

This guitar has French tuning machines made by Eon et Fils.

- **DATE** 1889
- **ORIGIN** Almería, Spain
- **WOOD**
  Front/Back & Sides
  Pine or spruce/mahogany and walnut
- **UNUSUAL FEATURE**
  The sides, like the back, are made of three strips, two of mahogany and one of walnut.

The soundboard thickness ranges from 1.8mm (⅟₁₆in) to 2.3mm (⅛in).

Although this guitar sounds exceptional, the low quality of the materials used to construct it would not be used by luthiers today.

SE142, 1890

This is one of the last guitars that was made by Torres. Although the back and sides are constructed from cypress, which is now associated with the flamenco guitar, it is thought that in Torres' day there was no distinction. Instead, this guitar was probably built for the local amateur musician. Unfortunately, because Torres took the thinness of his soundboards down to absolute limits, many of his guitars have not survived intact. This one still maintains its original soundboard and thicknesses, albeit with some restorations.

This guitar originally had wooden tuning pegs but was later fitted with metal tuning machines.

- **DATE** 1890
- **ORIGIN** Almería, Spain
- **WOOD**
  Front/Back & Sides
  Spruce/cypress
- **UNUSUAL FEATURE**
  The soundboard is made of three pieces.

The soundboard is made of three pieces of spruce instead of the more traditional two pieces.

Even for a relatively modest Torres guitar, this one is highly prized by both players and collectors.

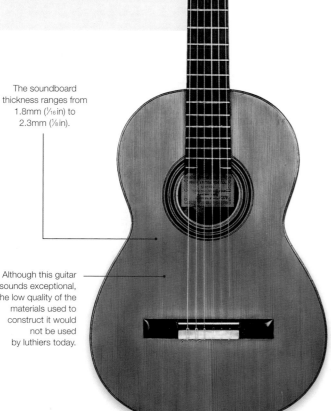

19th- and early 20th-century classical guitar makers

Early guitars by Vicente Arias (1833–1914) and Enrique Garcia (1868–1922) were much like those of Torres. Later, they developed their own styles, as did Manuel Ramírez and Francisco Simplicio, with guitars by all these makers tending to become more heavily constructed. Although Francisco Tárrega played guitars by Torres, there are photographs where he is clearly posing with guitars by Arias and Garcia.

Vicente Arias, 1889

Guitars by Arias were thought to be very rare. However, many owners are not aware of the significance of this maker, and thus there are probably many undiscovered examples. Arias is known for his beautiful rosettes, but this particular guitar was constructed in a simple Torres-like style, and at a time when Torres was ready to pass on the baton. As with a similar-sized Torres guitar, this has just five fanbraces supporting the soundboard.

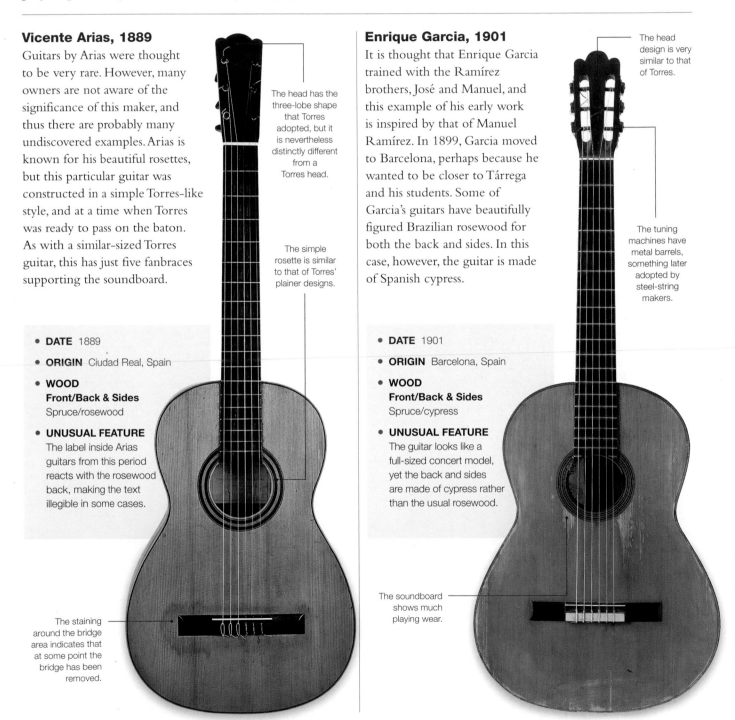

The head has the three-lobe shape that Torres adopted, but it is nevertheless distinctly different from a Torres head.

The simple rosette is similar to that of Torres' plainer designs.

- **DATE** 1889
- **ORIGIN** Ciudad Real, Spain
- **WOOD**
  Front/Back & Sides
  Spruce/rosewood
- **UNUSUAL FEATURE**
  The label inside Arias guitars from this period reacts with the rosewood back, making the text illegible in some cases.

The staining around the bridge area indicates that at some point the bridge has been removed.

Enrique Garcia, 1901

It is thought that Enrique Garcia trained with the Ramírez brothers, José and Manuel, and this example of his early work is inspired by that of Manuel Ramírez. In 1899, Garcia moved to Barcelona, perhaps because he wanted to be closer to Tárrega and his students. Some of Garcia's guitars have beautifully figured Brazilian rosewood for both the back and sides. In this case, however, the guitar is made of Spanish cypress.

The head design is very similar to that of Torres.

The tuning machines have metal barrels, something later adopted by steel-string makers.

- **DATE** 1901
- **ORIGIN** Barcelona, Spain
- **WOOD**
  Front/Back & Sides
  Spruce/cypress
- **UNUSUAL FEATURE**
  The guitar looks like a full-sized concert model, yet the back and sides are made of cypress rather than the usual rosewood.

The soundboard shows much playing wear.

Manuel Ramírez, 1911

The younger brother of José Ramírez I, Manuel Ramírez initially worked with his brother before they opened separate workshops. This guitar, with its wooden tuning pegs and ivoroid (fake ivory) tap-plate, has the appearance of a flamenco guitar. However, the back and sides are of rosewood, more commonly linked with classical instruments. This guitar was constructed just a year before Manuel Ramírez presented one to the youthful Andrés Segovia (1893–1987).

Many guitars from this period have had their wooden tuning pegs converted to tuning machines; this one retains its original pegs.

- **DATE** 1911
- **ORIGIN** Madrid, Spain
- **WOOD**
  Front/Back & Sides
  Spruce/rosewood
- **UNUSUAL FEATURE**
  Today, instruments featuring wooden tuning pegs, a tap-plate and with the back and sides of rosewood would be called *flamenca negra* guitars.

The pearl shapes used for the rosette were probably brought in by the maker.

The ivoroid tap-plate is used to protect the soft soundboard from nail wear.

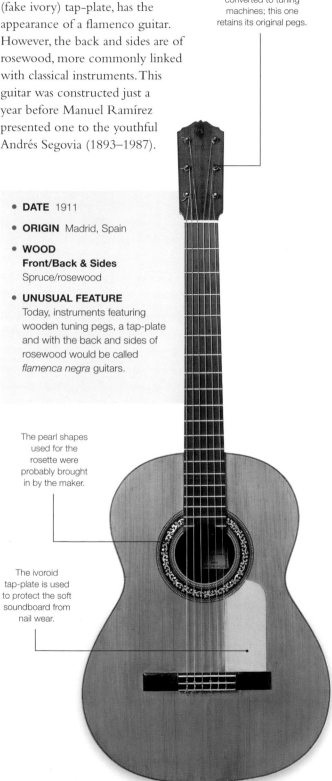

LEFT: *The beautifully carved rosewood head was reserved for their finest instruments. The tuning machines have solid mother-of-pearl buttons and the strings are attached by tying them around a small protruding knob.*

Francisco Simplicio, 1929

Enrique Garcia was Francisco Simplicio's teacher. This guitar has a metal *tornavoz* inside the soundhole, a device thought to have been first employed by Torres to help deepen the bass sound. The head is beautifully carved, a feature that became standard with many of the Argentinian makers, although it is also seen on some earlier German-made guitars. The bridge tie-block is enclosed by mother-of-pearl, which is also used for the tuning buttons.

- **DATE** 1929
- **ORIGIN** Barcelona, Spain
- **WOOD**
  Front/Back & Sides
  Spruce/rosewood
- **UNUSUAL FEATURE**
  This guitar has a bass-enhancing metal cylinder, a *tornavoz*, inside the soundhole.

The wooden marquetry of the rosette and the circumference of the body is exceptionally intricate.

The bridge has mother-of-pearl edging.

20th-century classical guitar makers: the Ramírez dynasty

From the time of José Ramírez I (1858–1923), founder of the Madrid school, the Ramírez family's business spans around 130 years. Their famous patrons have included Agustín Barrios, Narciso Yepes, George Harrison and Andrés Segovia. Only C. F. Martin & Co. has a longer history. The family also trained many luthiers who became established in their own right, including Paulino Bernabe and Felix Manzanero.

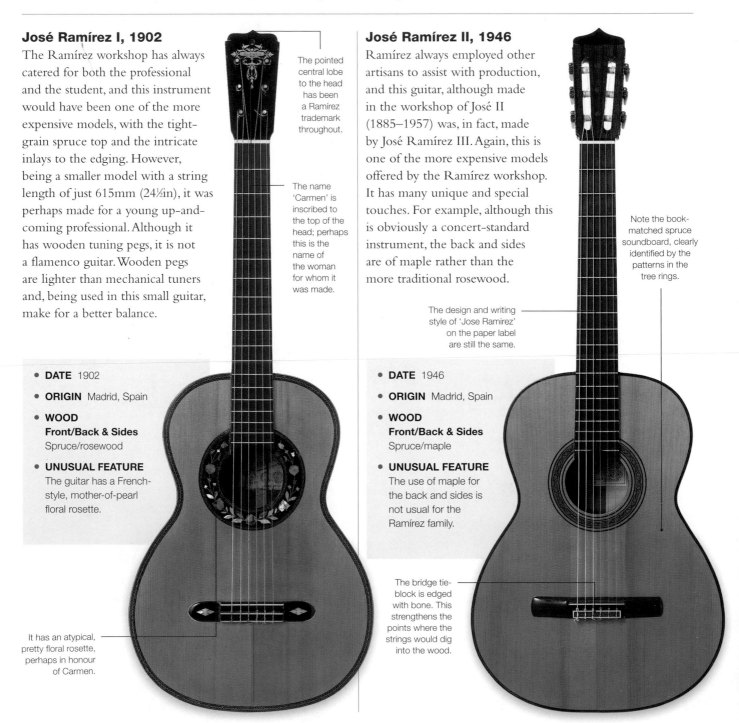

José Ramírez I, 1902

The Ramírez workshop has always catered for both the professional and the student, and this instrument would have been one of the more expensive models, with the tight-grain spruce top and the intricate inlays to the edging. However, being a smaller model with a string length of just 615mm (24⅛in), it was perhaps made for a young up-and-coming professional. Although it has wooden tuning pegs, it is not a flamenco guitar. Wooden pegs are lighter than mechanical tuners and, being used in this small guitar, make for a better balance.

The pointed central lobe to the head has been a Ramírez trademark throughout.

The name 'Carmen' is inscribed to the top of the head; perhaps this is the name of the woman for whom it was made.

- **DATE** 1902
- **ORIGIN** Madrid, Spain
- **WOOD**
  Front/Back & Sides
  Spruce/rosewood
- **UNUSUAL FEATURE**
  The guitar has a French-style, mother-of-pearl floral rosette.

It has an atypical, pretty floral rosette, perhaps in honour of Carmen.

José Ramírez II, 1946

Ramírez always employed other artisans to assist with production, and this guitar, although made in the workshop of José II (1885–1957) was, in fact, made by José Ramírez III. Again, this is one of the more expensive models offered by the Ramírez workshop. It has many unique and special touches. For example, although this is obviously a concert-standard instrument, the back and sides are of maple rather than the more traditional rosewood.

Note the book-matched spruce soundboard, clearly identified by the patterns in the tree rings.

The design and writing style of 'Jose Ramirez' on the paper label are still the same.

- **DATE** 1946
- **ORIGIN** Madrid, Spain
- **WOOD**
  Front/Back & Sides
  Spruce/maple
- **UNUSUAL FEATURE**
  The use of maple for the back and sides is not usual for the Ramírez family.

The bridge tie-block is edged with bone. This strengthens the points where the strings would dig into the wood.

José Ramírez III, 1960

This guitar was selected by Andrés Segovia to be one of his concert instruments. It bears the initials 'PB' inside, which indicates that in fact it was constructed by the Ramírez foreman Paulino Bernabé. José Ramírez III (1922–95) is famous for introducing the use of cedar as a soundboard material in the mid-1960s. This one was made just before that period and thus uses the more traditional spruce. Another innovation was the introduction of the longer string length of 664mm (26⅛in), perhaps to suit Segovia's large hands.

- **DATE** 1960

- **ORIGIN** Madrid, Spain

- **WOOD**
  Front/Back & Sides
  Spruce/rosewood

- **UNUSUAL FEATURE**
  This instrument has a long string length of 664mm (26⅛in).

Classical guitars were fitted with tuning machines as standard by 1960.

José Ramírez III chose to lacquer his guitars rather than French-polish them.

This was one of the last guitars Ramírez III made with a spruce soundboard, cedar becoming his preferred material.

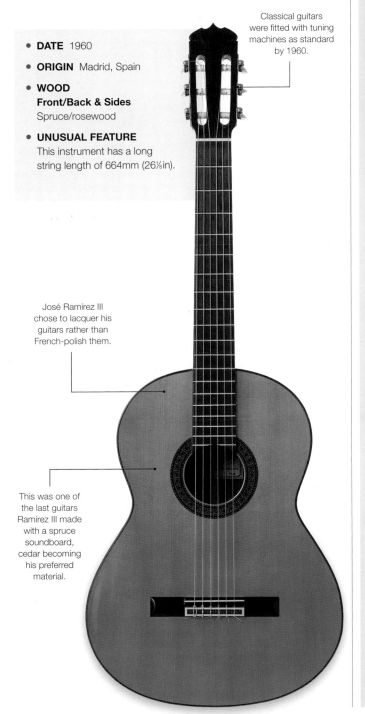

Amalia Ramírez

ABOVE: *Amalia Ramirez's hands-on approach in running the Ramirez guitar-making dynasty. Besides supervising the other artisans in her workshop and giving their guitars her final approval, she has also has designed some new and more affordable models.*

RIGHT: *This guitar was made by Amalia herself and, like Ramirez's time-honoured tradition of her predecessors, it meets the highest of standards. The back is of rosewood and the soundboard is made from spruce/rosewood. The paper label inside the soundhole is extended and carries the date of manufacture (1997), the serial and model number and Amalia's signature.*

The fingerboard is of ebony, the preferred hard-wearing material.

Note the trademark Ramírez head shape.

The central motif for the rosette is of red roses.

José Ramírez IV died at the young age of 47, leaving his sister Amalia (b. 1955) in charge of the business. Unlike many factory owners, she is actually hands-on, producing this beautifully handcrafted instrument herself. The classic José Ramírez head shape with its central peak is still observed, even after five changes of leadership. With many players struggling to manage the difficult left-hand stretches needed to play the Ramírez 664mm (26⅛in) string length, Amalia Ramírez has returned to the 650mm (25⅝in) option.

20th-century classical guitar makers: the Paris School

Classical guitar making in Paris began with the Spaniard Julian Gómez Ramírez (1879–c.1943), who was influenced by Torres and Manuel Ramírez. In turn, Robert Bouchet (1898–1986) learnt from J. G. Ramírez. Following on, Daniel Friederich (b. 1932) experimented more, while Dominique Field (b. 1954) keeps the tradition alive. These examples show how little body shape has changed over the four generations.

Julian Gómez Ramírez, 1939

In 1934, J. G. Ramírez repaired the Torres guitar SE39, which undoubtedly influenced his own making. He built guitars for many people – including the guitar maker Robert Bouchet, the maker and player Mauro Maccaferri and the husband-and-wife duo Ida Presti and Alexandre Lagoya – and he would write a dedication to them on a paper label. This guitar is undedicated and has the handwritten statement "Comme modèle" (literally translated 'Like other models').

- **DATE** 1939
- **ORIGIN** Paris, France
- **WOOD**
  Front/Back & Sides
  Spruce/rosewood
- **UNUSUAL FEATURE**
  The tuning machines are archaic in design, with butterfly-shaped buttons.

The tuning machines are 19th-century in style.

The rosette is a simple Torres-like design.

This is a Torres-style bone tie-block cap.

Robert Bouchet, 1962

This guitar belonged to the leading Austrian guitarist and musicologist Karl Scheit (1909–93). Robert Bouchet was an artist and art teacher in Paris and only a part-time guitar maker, yet he managed to make more than 150 guitars, including instruments for many prominent players, such as the British guitarist Julian Bream (b. 1933) who, until it was stolen, had an instrument from the same period as this one.

- **DATE** 1962
- **ORIGIN** Paris, France
- **WOOD**
  Front/Back & Sides
  Spruce/rosewood
- **UNUSUAL FEATURE**
  The tuning machines are in a typical 19th-century style.

The head shape is similar in style to some 19th-century French guitars.

The tuning machines are said to have been made or adapted by Bouchet.

Being an artist, Bouchet's paper labels were beautifully designed.

Daniel Friederich: Serial No. 184, 1967

This is an early example of one of Friederich's concert models. However, many of the characteristics of his later instruments are already present, including the relief carving on the rosewood head and an early version of his much-admired rosettes. These features make it distinguishable from the student models that he made around this time, as does the superb craftsmanship and choice of materials and the inclusion of a serial number on the label. Like most classical guitars from this period, it has a spruce soundboard, although Friederich later became known for using cedar soundboards on slightly heavier instruments.

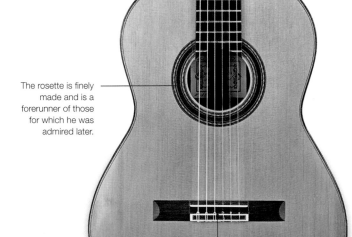

- **DATE** 1967
- **ORIGIN** Paris, France
- **WOOD**
  Front/Back & Sides
  Spruce/rosewood
- **UNUSUAL FEATURE**
  Friederich was not concerned with meeting the public demand of using figured Brazilian rosewood. In fact, he often used a different species of rosewood, coincidentally also from Brazil.

The head has a relief carving of a 'dart', which is a common feature on Friederich's guitars.

The rosette is finely made and is a forerunner of those for which he was admired later.

The tie-block uses the same central motif as the rosette decoration.

Dominique Field, 1998

Although he started out as a serious classical guitarist, Dominique Field became interested in making instruments in the 1970s, and he was lucky enough to be able to assist Robert Bouchet with the maintenance of several of Bouchet's guitars. He has subsequently had great success as a maker himself – to date he has made over 200 guitars and has a waiting list of around 15 years. This guitar is made of the finest woods, and the standard of his workmanship has helped earn Paris a world-class reputation as a centre for guitar makers.

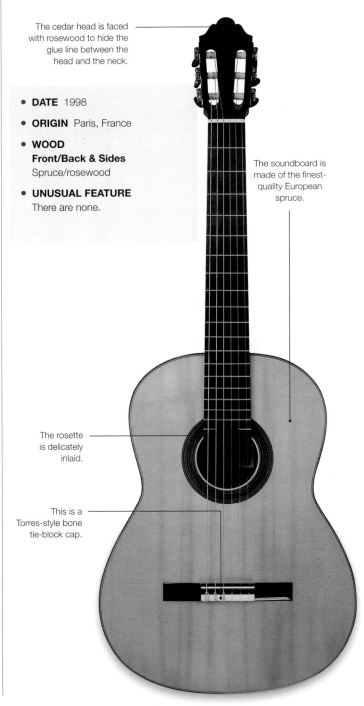

The cedar head is faced with rosewood to hide the glue line between the head and the neck.

- **DATE** 1998
- **ORIGIN** Paris, France
- **WOOD**
  Front/Back & Sides
  Spruce/rosewood
- **UNUSUAL FEATURE**
  There are none.

The soundboard is made of the finest-quality European spruce.

The rosette is delicately inlaid.

This is a Torres-style bone tie-block cap.

20th-century classical guitar makers: the Hauser family

The Hauser tradition of instrument building goes back to Josef Hauser (1854–1939), who started making instruments (mainly zithers) in the 1870s. However, it wasn't until the 1920s that his son Hermann Hauser I started building the guitars that we still recognize today as the 'modern' classical guitar. Three generations on, this tradition is continued by Hermann Hauser III and his daughter Katherin.

Hermann Hauser I: Viennese style, 1911

Hermann Hauser I (1882–1952) is indisputably the most famous 20th-century maker, and his Spanish-style guitars are in high demand with players and collectors. Before he started to make Spanish guitars, however, he made historic instruments in the Viennese style. This guitar has an adjustable neck, a rounded body shape and a very contoured side profile, a 19th-century Viennese style adopted by many German builders.

- **DATE** 1911
- **ORIGIN** Germany
- **WOOD**
  Front/Back & Sides
  Spruce/maple
- **UNUSUAL FEATURE**
  This design is very antiquated, particularly when it is compared with contemporary guitars such as those made in Madrid.

Hermann Hauser I: 'Segovia' model, 1937

After Hauser I met Andrés Segovia, he concentrated on making the more modern form of the Spanish guitar. Seeing some Torres guitars and closely inspecting Segovia's 1912 Manuel Ramírez, he produced what Segovia called the "greatest guitar of our epoch", the famous 1937 guitar now in the Metropolitan Museum, New York. Many modern makers still base their instruments on that one. The guitar here is from the same year.

- **DATE** 1937
- **ORIGIN** Germany
- **WOOD**
  Front/Back & Sides
  Spruce/rosewood
- **UNUSUAL FEATURE**
  Made over 70 years ago, this is still the most copied guitar design.

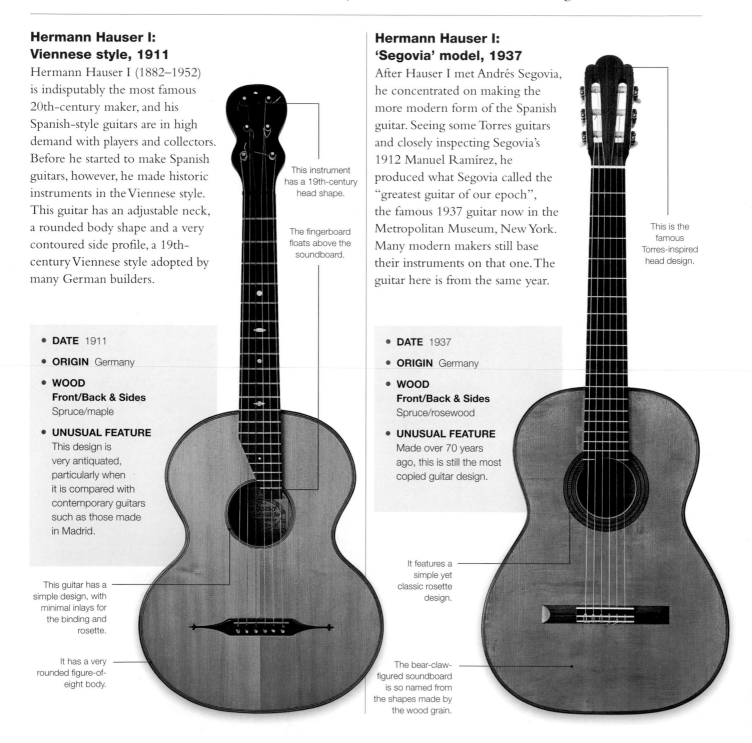

This instrument has a 19th-century head shape.

The fingerboard floats above the soundboard.

This is the famous Torres-inspired head design.

This guitar has a simple design, with minimal inlays for the binding and rosette.

It has a very rounded figure-of-eight body.

It features a simple yet classic rosette design.

The bear-claw-figured soundboard is so named from the shapes made by the wood grain.

Hermann Hauser II, 1958

In 1930, after a four-year apprenticeship in a Mittenwald violin-making school, Hermann Hauser II (1911–88) started working in his father's workshop, taking on the business after his father's death in 1952. He went on to make a further 500 guitars, which, rather than French-polishing them, he chose to lacquer. Over time, this results in the appearance of fine, checked lines (known as lacquer checking or crazing), a sure sign that the finish is original, and which is important to the sound. This guitar has a scale length of 646mm (25½in), which some players today prefer.

- **DATE** 1958
- **ORIGIN** Germany
- **WOOD**
  Front/Back & Sides
  Spruce/rosewood
- **UNUSUAL FEATURE**
  This guitar has a lacquer finish rather than the more typical French polish.

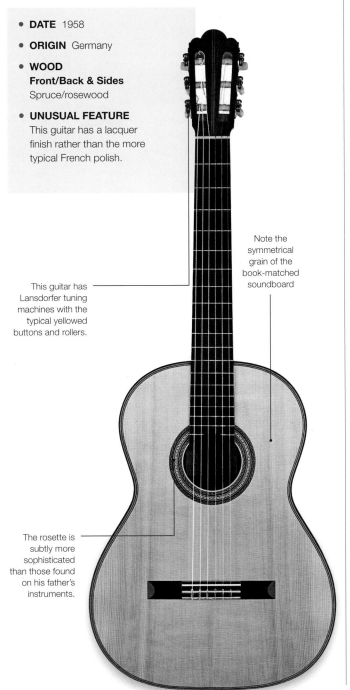

This guitar has Lansdorfer tuning machines with the typical yellowed buttons and rollers.

Note the symmetrical grain of the book-matched soundboard

The rosette is subtly more sophisticated than those found on his father's instruments.

Herman Hauser III, 1988

In 1974, Hermann Hauser III (b. 1958) started making his own guitars in the same workshop as his father. He makes his guitars in batches – and, like a farmer, certain processes are seasonal. His yearly output is usually up to 17 guitars. Besides making guitars in the style of his father and grandfather, Hauser III makes some that are based on those of Miguel Rodríguez, and also a model he dreamt up himself. Unlike his forebears, he also has the luxury of using cedar for his soundboards, as in this example.

- **DATE** 1988
- **ORIGIN** Germany
- **WOOD**
  Front/Back & Sides
  Cedar/rosewood
- **UNUSUAL FEATURE**
  This guitar has a cedar soundboard.

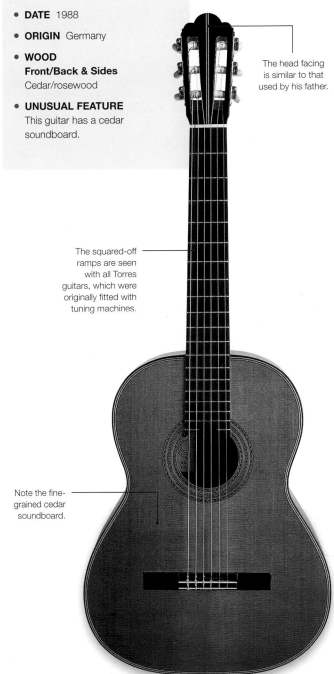

The head facing is similar to that used by his father.

The squared-off ramps are seen with all Torres guitars, which were originally fitted with tuning machines.

Note the fine-grained cedar soundboard.

Mid 20th-century classical guitars

These instruments capture the spirit of the modern Spanish guitar. Here, we see the schools of Madrid (Hernández y Aguado), Barcelona (Fleta) and, although José Romanillos worked in Britain, he now builds in the Andalucian style of Torres. During their careers, John Williams has played Fleta guitars, while Julian Bream favoured guitars by Romanillos, but they have both owned the same guitar by Hernández y Aguado.

Hernández y Aguado, 1963

In guitar making it is rare to find a partnership of two makers working together under the same label. Manuel Hernández (1895–1975) and Victoriano Aguado (1897–1982) met while working for a piano-making firm, Hernández constructing the bodies and Aguado working as a French polisher. However, Aguado was a keen guitarist, and they soon formed a partnership and began to make guitars. Their apprenticeships as piano makers means that their guitars have some unusual features, such as joining the two-piece backs without the usual dividing inlays.

- **DATE** 1963
- **ORIGIN** Madrid, Spain
- **WOOD**
  Front/Back & Sides
  Spruce/rosewood
- **UNUSUAL FEATURE**
  The back is of two halves joined without the usual central inlay.

Ignacio Fleta & Sons, 1974

Making smaller Torres-style guitars was how Ignacio Fleta (1897–1977) started his career. In the 1930s and 1940s he only made one guitar roughly every two years, because his skill in making orchestral and concert instruments was much in demand. He also made some archtop jazz guitars, which combined the traditional f-holes with a round soundhole. By the time this example was made, working with his sons Francisco and Gabriel, Fleta guitars had taken on a distinctive form, incorporating nine fanbraces under the soundboard.

- **DATE** 1974
- **ORIGIN** Barcelona, Spain
- **WOOD**
  Front/Back & Sides
  Cedar/rosewood
- **UNUSUAL FEATURE**
  The bridge has extra decorative bone inlays.

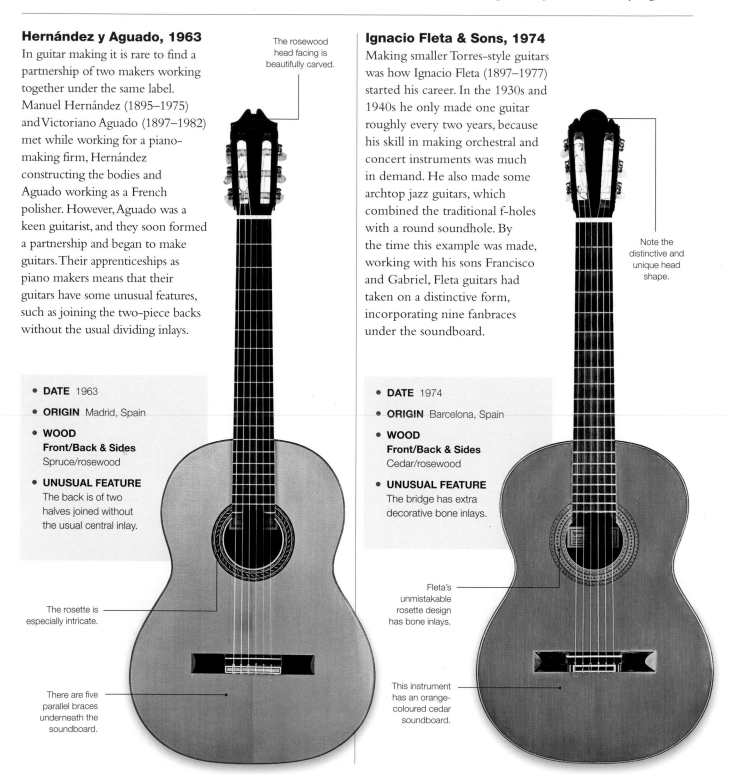

The rosewood head facing is beautifully carved.

Note the distinctive and unique head shape.

The rosette is especially intricate.

There are five parallel braces underneath the soundboard.

Fleta's unmistakable rosette design has bone inlays.

This instrument has an orange-coloured cedar soundboard.

José Romanillos, 1978

In 1967, José Romanillos (b. 1932) moved from Madrid to Britain. Julian Bream started playing his guitars, and they formed a close working relationship. On Romanillos' return to Spain, his son Liam, who had worked alongside his father since 1982, continued the business. Romanillos' legacy is not just his many truly finely crafted concert guitars but also the Spanish–guitar museum he established in Sigüenza, Spain, and the meticulously researched books on the history of musical instruments that he and his wife Marian Harris Winspear have written.

- **DATE** 1978
- **ORIGIN** Dorset, England
- **WOOD**
  Front/Back & Sides
  Spruce/rosewood
- **UNUSUAL FEATURE**
  Romanillos gave his guitars names. This one is called 'La Madreselva' (the Honeysuckle).

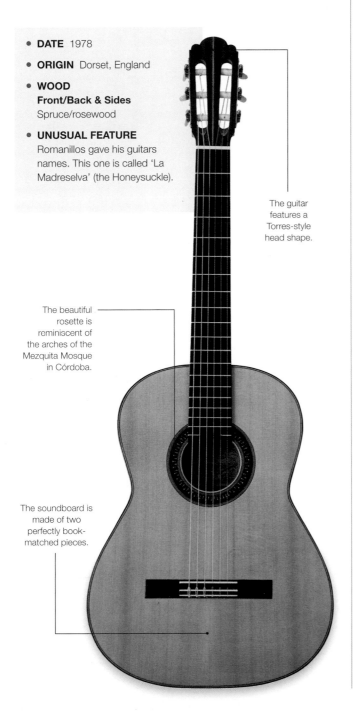

The guitar features a Torres-style head shape.

The beautiful rosette is reminiscent of the arches of the Mezquita Mosque in Córdoba.

The soundboard is made of two perfectly book-matched pieces.

Julian Bream

London-born Julian Bream, OBE (b. 1933) played on lutes and historic guitars as a youth, as well as a Maccaferri harp-guitar, and he made his professional debut at London's Wigmore Hall on a 19th-century Martin 0-28. Soon, however, he required instruments that could cope with the demands of the many compositions written for him by leading 20th-century composers, playing guitars by Edgar Mönch, Hauser, Bouchet, Hernández y Aguado, David Rubio, Romanillos and, later, Kenny Hill and Cohen and Southwell. Obtaining the 1940 Albert and Rose Augustine Hauser guitar rekindled much of his interest in body resonances, as the body resonance of the Hauer was extremely low at E♭, which produces a very profound base to the tone. For much of his later life he has been concerned with the acoustic harmony of what he calls the 'box'. This has resulted in him favouring an E♭ body resonance, even encouraging several guitar makers to construct guitars for him with this characteristic. These include guitar makers Kevin Aram, Brian Cohen and Gary Southwell.

ABOVE: *Julian Bream in concert in 1970, showing his perfect hand positions and posture. He is playing one of the first guitars made for him by José Romanillos — choosing to concertize and record on his guitars during much of the 1970s.*

Late 20th- and early 21st-century classical guitars: part one

It is notable that although Antonio de Torres 'standardized' guitar design over 150 years ago, today's makers still find ways to keep the market interesting, varied and buoyant. The guitars here show this well, offering a choice of woods, an array of soundboard struts allowing for different tones, a range of pitches, an alternative soundhole shape and even a smaller body size.

Masaru Kohno, 1974

Having been taught by Arcángel Fernández, himself a student of Marcelo Barbero, Masuro Kohno (1926–98) set up his company in Tokyo. In 1967 he won gold in the Concours National de Guitare in Belgium, where Ignacio Fleta and Robert Bouchet were on the jury. This guitar is the 'Model 15', a lower-priced Kohno model but still of exceptional quality. The scale length is a large 664mm (26⅛in) (many Japanese guitarists prefer a 645mm/25⅜in scale). The company is now called Sakurai Kohno, run by Kohno's nephew.

- **DATE** 1974
- **ORIGIN** Tokyo, Japan
- **WOOD**
  Front/Back & Sides
  Spruce/rosewood
- **UNUSUAL FEATURE**
  The 664mm (26⅛in)
  scale length is larger
  than usual.

Kenny Hill: FE18, 2009

As a master luthier, Kenny Hill's (b. 1948) 'Signature Series' guitars are of truly exceptional quality. However, he also operates under the name of the Hill Guitar Company, a small operation that produces the 'Performance' and 'Master' series, the latter of which comprises uncannily precise replicas of famous models. This 'Master Series' guitar is a close copy of the 1864 Torres FE18. Hill's version was initially aimed at the younger player, but, because of its tone and volume, many adults have taken it up.

- **DATE** 2009
- **ORIGIN** California, USA
- **WOOD**
  Front/Back & Sides
  Spruce/flamed maple
- **UNUSUAL FEATURE**
  This guitar for younger
  players compares well
  with many full-sized models.

The head outline is reminiscent of guitars by Ignacio Fleta.

The scale length of the strings is the same as the José Ramírez 'Segovia' guitars.

The isosceles-trapezium-shaped tie-block is distinctive.

The head is a classic Torres design.

The body measures just 438mm (17¼in) long.

The striking green inlays, reserved for Torres' finest models, are replicated in this instrument.

Note the diamond-shaped pearl-and-bone additions to the bridge.

David Whiteman: concert guitar, 2007

Having studied guitar making at the London College of Furniture, David Whiteman (b. 1965) built this instrument to mark his 20th year as a professional maker. The back, sides and headstock are of highly figured satinwood, which is a rare and highly prized tonewood. There are subtle mother-of-pearl embellishments in the rosette and bridge, and delicate hand-crafted purflings adorn the top and headstock. The tuners are hand-made by David Rodgers.

Rohan Lowe, 2008

Self-taught, Rohan Lowe (b. 1962) began guitar making in 1993. Coming from an artistic background, he likes to experiment with the design of the guitar, as this model testifies. To keep the air resonance down, and thus produce a good bass response, the top is well supported using two longitudinal bars, so allowing more of the sounding area than usual the opportunity to vibrate. This soundboard-bracing concept was partly inspired by the 19th-century Parisian maker Etienne Laprévotte.

The headstock is faced with satinwood.

- **DATE** 2007
- **ORIGIN** Sussex, England
- **WOOD**
  Front/Back & Sides
  Spruce/satinwood
- **UNUSUAL FEATURE**
  It is rare to see satinwood used by modern classical guitar makers.

The rosette and bridge have mother-of-pearl inlay.

The circular pearl dots on the bridge complement those in the rosette.

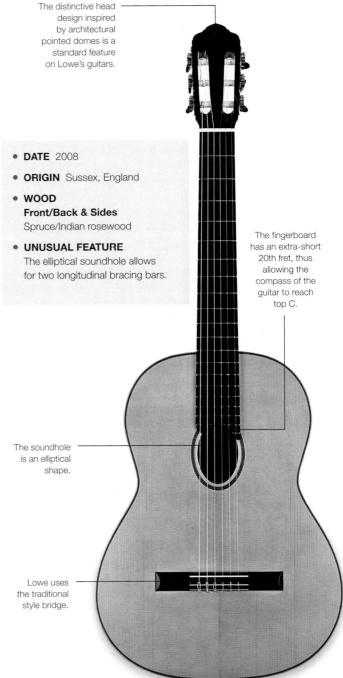

The distinctive head design inspired by architectural pointed domes is a standard feature on Lowe's guitars.

- **DATE** 2008
- **ORIGIN** Sussex, England
- **WOOD**
  Front/Back & Sides
  Spruce/Indian rosewood
- **UNUSUAL FEATURE**
  The elliptical soundhole allows for two longitudinal bracing bars.

The fingerboard has an extra-short 20th fret, thus allowing the compass of the guitar to reach top C.

The soundhole is an elliptical shape.

Lowe uses the traditional style bridge.

Late 20th- and early 21st-century classical guitars: part two

Many makers continue to strive to build the perfect guitar, often driven by the professional player. Sometimes these modifications replicate experiments tried out by earlier makers, but more often than not today's luthiers arrive at these conclusions independently. Here we see some modern guitars in the true sense of the word, including the use of new materials in their construction.

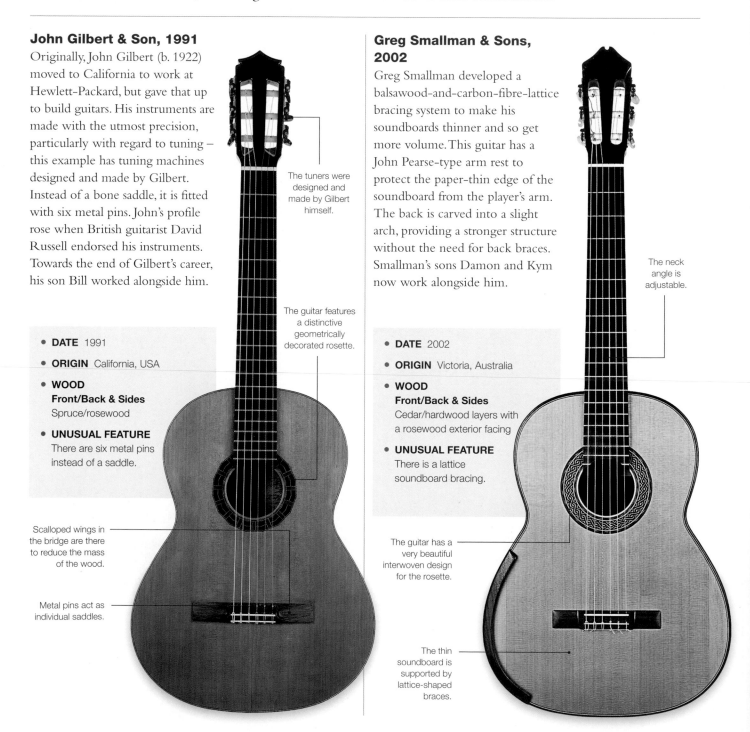

John Gilbert & Son, 1991

Originally, John Gilbert (b. 1922) moved to California to work at Hewlett-Packard, but gave that up to build guitars. His instruments are made with the utmost precision, particularly with regard to tuning – this example has tuning machines designed and made by Gilbert. Instead of a bone saddle, it is fitted with six metal pins. John's profile rose when British guitarist David Russell endorsed his instruments. Towards the end of Gilbert's career, his son Bill worked alongside him.

- **DATE** 1991
- **ORIGIN** California, USA
- **WOOD**
  Front/Back & Sides
  Spruce/rosewood
- **UNUSUAL FEATURE**
  There are six metal pins instead of a saddle.

The tuners were designed and made by Gilbert himself.

The guitar features a distinctive geometrically decorated rosette.

Scalloped wings in the bridge are there to reduce the mass of the wood.

Metal pins act as individual saddles.

Greg Smallman & Sons, 2002

Greg Smallman developed a balsawood-and-carbon-fibre-lattice bracing system to make his soundboards thinner and so get more volume. This guitar has a John Pearse-type arm rest to protect the paper-thin edge of the soundboard from the player's arm. The back is carved into a slight arch, providing a stronger structure without the need for back braces. Smallman's sons Damon and Kym now work alongside him.

- **DATE** 2002
- **ORIGIN** Victoria, Australia
- **WOOD**
  Front/Back & Sides
  Cedar/hardwood layers with a rosewood exterior facing
- **UNUSUAL FEATURE**
  There is a lattice soundboard bracing.

The neck angle is adjustable.

The guitar has a very beautiful interwoven design for the rosette.

The thin soundboard is supported by lattice-shaped braces.

Martin Woodhouse: 'Brahms' guitar, 2010

The first guitar Martin Woodhouse (b. 1981) made was under David Rubio, and one of Rubio's projects towards the end of his life was the so-called 'Brahms' guitar, which Woodhouse took on. The idea was to build an eight-string guitar – inspired by the 17th-century orpharion – to extend the range so that music by Brahms could be included in the guitarist's repertoire. This guitar has eight individual string lengths ranging between 615–650mm (24¼–25⅝in). The British guitarist Paul Galbraith is known for playing this instrument.

The head accommodates an extra two tuning pegs.

The nut, frets and saddle are all positioned at different angles.

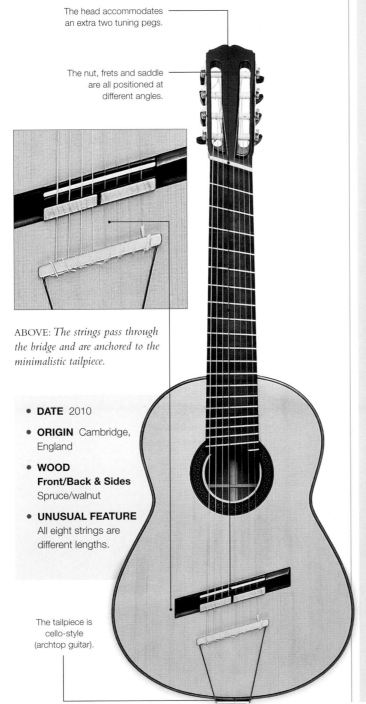

ABOVE: *The strings pass through the bridge and are anchored to the minimalistic tailpiece.*

- **DATE** 2010
- **ORIGIN** Cambridge, England
- **WOOD**
  Front/Back & Sides
  Spruce/walnut
- **UNUSUAL FEATURE**
  All eight strings are different lengths.

The tailpiece is cello-style (archtop guitar).

John Williams

The recording by John Williams (b. 1941) of "Cavatina", the haunting theme tune to *The Deer Hunter*, was a rare occasion when a classical guitarist entered the charts. Williams was first taught by his father Len, the founder of the Spanish Guitar Studios in London, but from the age of 11 he attended masterclasses with Andrés Segovia – Segovia called him 'the prince of the guitar'. He studied piano at the Royal College of Music because they had no guitar department at that time (the guitar was deemed not to be a serious instrument to study) – and by 17 he had made his first recording. Projects have included working with fellow guitarists Julian Bream and Paco Peña, and founding the 1970s classical-rock group Sky with Herbie Flowers. His Australian roots have led to a long friendship with and patronage of his fellow Australian, the guitar maker Greg Smallman. The Grammy award-winning guitarist boasts over 150 recordings credited with his name, and in 2007 he was presented with the Edison lifetime achievement award.

ABOVE: *John Williams in concert, demonstrating his perfect technique. In this photograph, taken during the 1960s, Williams is playing a more traditional-style guitar. In the early part of his career, he favoured guitars by Ignacio Fleta; he also had an instrument by Manuel Hernández and Victoriano Aguado that fellow guitarist Julian Bream had previously owned.*

20th-century flamenco guitars

Although Torres made some cypress models, it was in the 20th century that the light and low-strung flamenco guitar was really defined as a very different instrument from the classical. Some notable flamenco guitar makers were from such cities as Córdoba (Manuel Reyes) and Almería (Gerundino Fernández), but Madrid was the centre for master builders of the flamenco guitar, as seen in these examples.

Viuda de Manuel Ramírez (constructed by Santos Hernández), 1916

This guitar was built in the Manuel Ramírez workshop for his *viuda* (widow) by Santos Hernández (1874–1943) just three months after Ramírez died, and it is one of the earliest instruments that could truly be called a flamenco guitar. Segovia's famous 1912 'Manuel Ramírez' classical guitar, now on display in the Metropolitian Museum, New York, was also constructed by Hernández.

This guitar has a capo fitted, which is used to change the guitar's key to suit an individual singer's voice.

The 'Viuda de Manuel Ramírez' label has Santos Hernández's initials.

- **DATE** 1916
- **ORIGIN** Madrid, Spain
- **WOOD**
  Front/Back & Sides
  Spruce/cypress
- **UNUSUAL FEATURE**
  The *golpeador* protects the spruce soundboard from the player's nails.

This is the original ivory *golpeador*.

Domingo Esteso, 1934

Originally, Domingo Esteso (1882–1937) worked for Manuel Ramírez. After Ramírez's death he worked for Ramírez's widow until moving to his own workshop in 1919, which is still there today. Notice the Ramírez-shaped headstock and the similar use of colours in his rosette to that of the 1916 Viuda de Manuel Ramírez guitar. This guitar is very light, weighing just 1.1kg (2½lb), and Esteso kept the weight down further by using wooden tuning pegs as opposed to metal tuning machines.

Wooden tuning pegs are preferred by many traditional flamenco guitarists.

This is the original yellowed bone nut.

- **DATE** 1934
- **ORIGIN** Madrid, Spain
- **WOOD**
  Front/Back & Sides
  Spruce/cypress
- **UNUSUAL FEATURE**
  Unusually for a flamenco instrument, it lacks a protective *golpeador*.

The string-scale length, at 657mm (25⅞in), is a little larger than standard.

Marcelo Barbero, 1954

Before setting up his own workshop, Marcelo Barbero (1904–56) apprenticed under José Ramírez II. He also worked for a short while for Santos Hernández's widow. Barbero's early guitars have small white or black *golpeadores*, but this one, being a later model, has a double transparent one to protect the bass side of the soundboard from damage caused by the guitarist's thumbnail resting on the sixth string. On the evidence of known guitars, Barbero seems mainly to have made flamenco instruments and only a few classical ones.

Arcángel Fernández, 1958

Having learnt his craft from Marcelo Barbero, Arcángel Fernández (b. 1931) works in the Spanish tradition. Like Santos Hernández and Domingo Esteso, he worked for Barbero's widow after his master's death. In turn, Fernández taught Barbero's son, Marcelo Barbero II. This particular guitar is fitted with tuning machines and has a decorative pearl inlay to the tie-block. These are very subtle 'modern' elements that Fernández has added to the otherwise traditional instrument. This guitar has a 660mm (25⅞in) string-scale length.

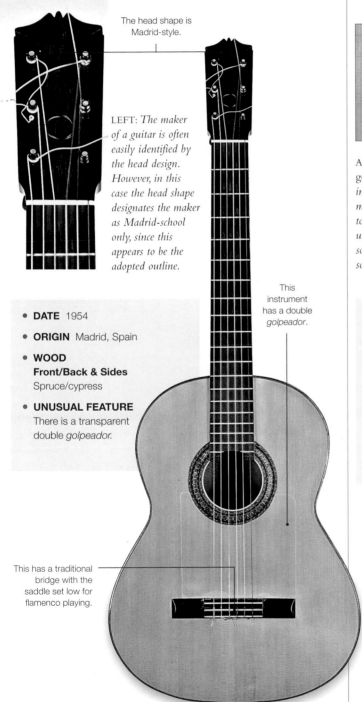

The head shape is Madrid-style.

LEFT: *The maker of a guitar is often easily identified by the head design. However, in this case the head shape designates the maker as Madrid-school only, since this appears to be the adopted outline.*

This instrument has a double *golpeador*.

- **DATE** 1954
- **ORIGIN** Madrid, Spain
- **WOOD**
  Front/Back & Sides
  Spruce/cypress
- **UNUSUAL FEATURE**
  There is a transparent double *golpeador*.

This has a traditional bridge with the saddle set low for flamenco playing.

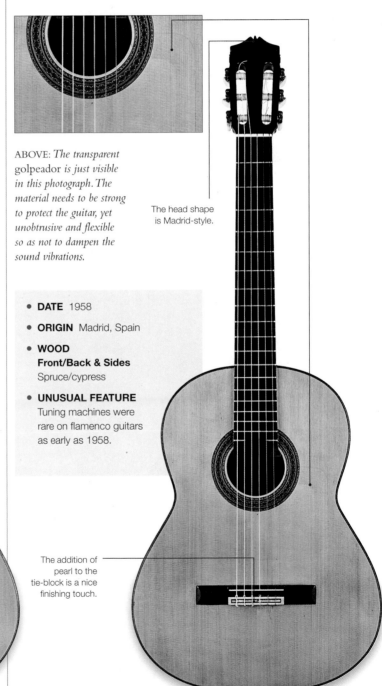

ABOVE: *The transparent golpeador is just visible in this photograph. The material needs to be strong to protect the guitar, yet unobtrusive and flexible so as not to dampen the sound vibrations.*

The head shape is Madrid-style.

- **DATE** 1958
- **ORIGIN** Madrid, Spain
- **WOOD**
  Front/Back & Sides
  Spruce/cypress
- **UNUSUAL FEATURE**
  Tuning machines were rare on flamenco guitars as early as 1958.

The addition of pearl to the tie-block is a nice finishing touch.

Late 20th- and early 21st-century flamenco guitars

Flamenco is a traditionalist art form, and what is required of the flamenco guitar has changed very little over time. Hence, guitar makers who like to add something of their own personality to the instrument usually do so in subtle ways – the unique head shapes of Manuel Reyes, Gerundino Fernández and the Conde Hermanos, for example, or Pablo Requena's pearl-inlaid rosettes.

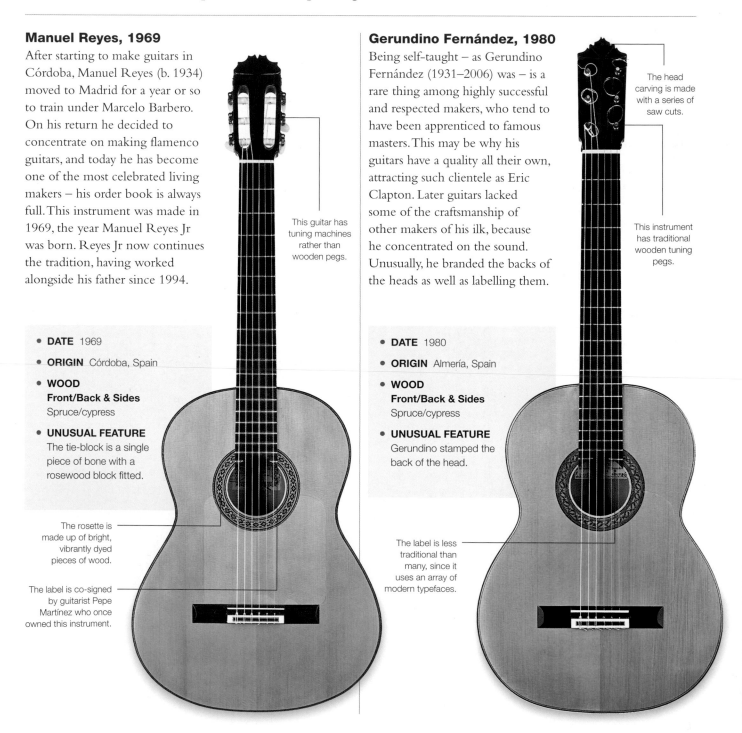

Manuel Reyes, 1969

After starting to make guitars in Córdoba, Manuel Reyes (b. 1934) moved to Madrid for a year or so to train under Marcelo Barbero. On his return he decided to concentrate on making flamenco guitars, and today he has become one of the most celebrated living makers – his order book is always full. This instrument was made in 1969, the year Manuel Reyes Jr was born. Reyes Jr now continues the tradition, having worked alongside his father since 1994.

This guitar has tuning machines rather than wooden pegs.

- **DATE** 1969
- **ORIGIN** Córdoba, Spain
- **WOOD**
  Front/Back & Sides
  Spruce/cypress
- **UNUSUAL FEATURE**
  The tie-block is a single piece of bone with a rosewood block fitted.

The rosette is made up of bright, vibrantly dyed pieces of wood.

The label is co-signed by guitarist Pepe Martínez who once owned this instrument.

Gerundino Fernández, 1980

Being self-taught – as Gerundino Fernández (1931–2006) was – is a rare thing among highly successful and respected makers, who tend to have been apprenticed to famous masters. This may be why his guitars have a quality all their own, attracting such clientele as Eric Clapton. Later guitars lacked some of the craftsmanship of other makers of his ilk, because he concentrated on the sound. Unusually, he branded the backs of the heads as well as labelling them.

The head carving is made with a series of saw cuts.

This instrument has traditional wooden tuning pegs.

- **DATE** 1980
- **ORIGIN** Almería, Spain
- **WOOD**
  Front/Back & Sides
  Spruce/cypress
- **UNUSUAL FEATURE**
  Gerundino stamped the back of the head.

The label is less traditional than many, since it uses an array of modern typefaces.

Conde Hermanos: A26, 2007

The Conde brothers were apprenticed to their uncle, Domingo Esteso, and after his death in 1937 worked for his widow under the label 'Viuda y sobrinos de Esteso' until her death in 1958. They then changed their label to 'Sobrinos de Domingo Esteso', later 'Hermanos Conde' and finally 'Conde Hermanos'. All this time they were operating from their uncle's workshop at Gravina, 7, Madrid. Today, guitars are still being sold from this address by Viuda de Faustino Conde. They are most famous for their flamenco guitars, including *negra* (rosewood) models, and they are instantly recognizable by the head shape and orange polish.

For years, this distinctive head shape has indicated that this guitar is their top model.

The orange polish makes this pale spruce soundboard look like cedar.

- **DATE** 2007
- **ORIGIN** Madrid, Spain
- **WOOD**
  Front/Back & Sides
  Spruce/cypress
- **UNUSUAL FEATURE**
  The colour of the polish is a bright orange.

The use of light and bright colours in the rosette makes them stand out.

Pablo Requena, 2004

A Spanish luthier based in England, Pablo Requena (b. 1968) builds guitars inspired by makers such as Santos Hernández and Marcelo Barbero. This example has a German spruce top and cypress back and sides – a combination of woods favoured for flamenco guitars – and is built in a traditional way, with very light bracing and timbers to produce a rich, percussive sound. Requena has made classical guitars with equal success, and players include Paul Gregory and John Mills – Island Records even ordered one of Requena's parlour guitars for singer Amy Winehouse.

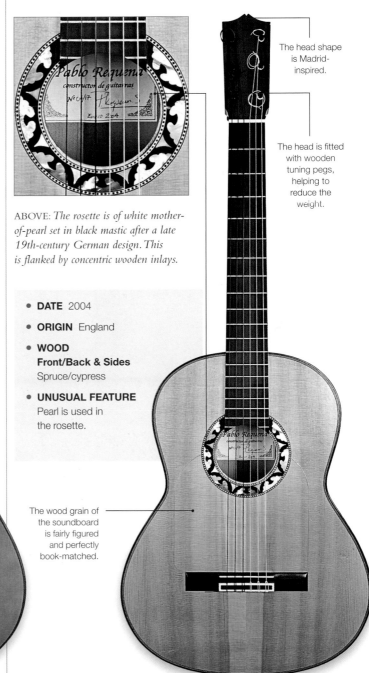

ABOVE: *The rosette is of white mother-of-pearl set in black mastic after a late 19th-century German design. This is flanked by concentric wooden inlays.*

The head shape is Madrid-inspired.

The head is fitted with wooden tuning pegs, helping to reduce the weight.

- **DATE** 2004
- **ORIGIN** England
- **WOOD**
  Front/Back & Sides
  Spruce/cypress
- **UNUSUAL FEATURE**
  Pearl is used in the rosette.

The wood grain of the soundboard is fairly figured and perfectly book-matched.

20th-century flat-top steel-string guitars: Gibson

Perhaps more famous for their superior archtop instruments, Gibson's flat-tops were not so highly regarded. However, their high-end pre-war flat-tops were very good indeed. The development of their body size can be seen in these rare examples, starting with Robert Johnson's small-bodied L-1, through the deeper-bodied 'Nick Lucas' to the larger Dreadnought type, concluding with the enormous Jumbos.

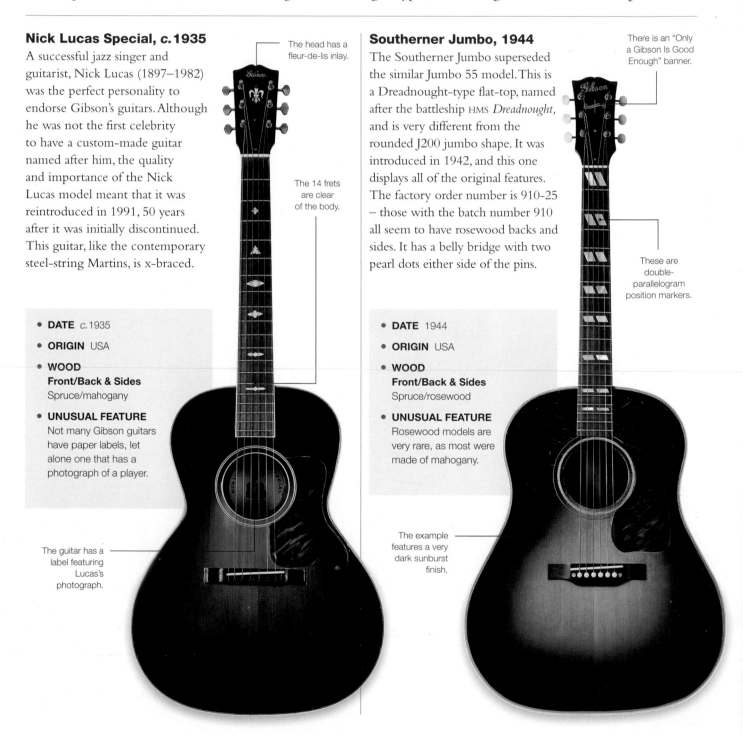

Nick Lucas Special, c. 1935

A successful jazz singer and guitarist, Nick Lucas (1897–1982) was the perfect personality to endorse Gibson's guitars. Although he was not the first celebrity to have a custom-made guitar named after him, the quality and importance of the Nick Lucas model meant that it was reintroduced in 1991, 50 years after it was initially discontinued. This guitar, like the contemporary steel-string Martins, is x-braced.

The head has a fleur-de-lis inlay.

The 14 frets are clear of the body.

- **DATE** *c.* 1935
- **ORIGIN** USA
- **WOOD**
  Front/Back & Sides
  Spruce/mahogany
- **UNUSUAL FEATURE**
  Not many Gibson guitars have paper labels, let alone one that has a photograph of a player.

The guitar has a label featuring Lucas's photograph.

Southerner Jumbo, 1944

The Southerner Jumbo superseded the similar Jumbo 55 model. This is a Dreadnought-type flat-top, named after the battleship HMS *Dreadnought,* and is very different from the rounded J200 jumbo shape. It was introduced in 1942, and this one displays all of the original features. The factory order number is 910-25 – those with the batch number 910 all seem to have rosewood backs and sides. It has a belly bridge with two pearl dots either side of the pins.

There is an "Only a Gibson Is Good Enough" banner.

These are double-parallelogram position markers.

- **DATE** 1944
- **ORIGIN** USA
- **WOOD**
  Front/Back & Sides
  Spruce/rosewood
- **UNUSUAL FEATURE**
  Rosewood models are very rare, as most were made of mahogany.

The example features a very dark sunburst finish.

J200, 1952

The SJ200 Super Jumbo – not to be confused with the very different Southerner Jumbo (SJ) released a few years later – was introduced late in 1937. Early models were of rosewood with a dark sunburst finish, but by the late 1940s it was a maple guitar, and this is a rare blonde-finish maple example. The J200 has a large rounded 'jumbo' body, which, with the unusual 'moustache' bridge, makes it a very distinctive guitar.

- **DATE** 1952
- **ORIGIN** USA
- **WOOD**
  Front/Back & Sides
  Spruce/maple
- **UNUSUAL FEATURE**
  Whether cows' horns or moustaches inspired the bridge design is unclear, but it is unusual either way.

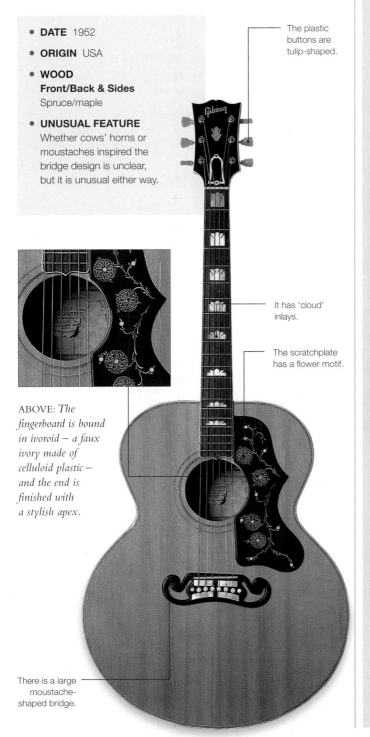

The plastic buttons are tulip-shaped.

It has 'cloud' inlays.

The scratchplate has a flower motif.

ABOVE: *The fingerboard is bound in ivoroid – a faux ivory made of celluloid plastic – and the end is finished with a stylish apex.*

There is a large moustache-shaped bridge.

Robert Johnson

The term 'legend' is over-used in many discussions of guitar players, but Robert Johnson (1911-38) is one of the figures who genuinely merits the term. The influence of his few recordings on generations of blues musicians can hardly be over-stated: Eric Clapton has called him 'the most important blues singer that ever lived'. Few real facts are known about Johnson's life beyond the most basic biographical details; his entire recorded output was captured in a total of just five days in the recording studio. He seems to have been active as a professional performer for roughly the last eight years of his short life; an unexplained sudden improvement in his guitar ability during this time may have contributed to the myth which subsequently became as powerful as his musical legacy: that he met the Devil at a crossroads at midnight and sold his soul in return for mastery of the guitar. Johnson may have knowingly encouraged the myth by writing songs such as 'Crossroad Blues' and 'Hellhound on my Trail'.

ABOVE: *Legendary American blues singer-songwriter and guitarist Robert Johnson (1911–38), left, with fellow blues musician Johnny Shines (1915–92), c.1935. This image is one of only three known photographs of Johnson which all show how long his 'guitar-playing' fingers were.*

20th-century flat-top steel-string guitars: C. F. Martin & Co., part one

Frank Henry Martin (1866–1948) was head of C. F. Martin & Co. guitar production when it really took off. During his tenure, the company made some of its finest x-braced guitars. The model numbers were in two parts: first by size, then by what Martin called the 'style'. As a general rule, the higher the number, the higher the style – but not always; for example, the 1-27 was more expensive than the 1-28.

00-42, 1902

In 1902, the 00-42 model was the most expensive guitar Martin offered and had the largest body, roughly the size of a standard classical guitar. Having abalone inlays to the soundboard, around the fingerboard and in the rosette, it was the forerunner of the famous 45, although the lack of any inlays to the back and sides marks it out from the 45. The body as well as the fingerboard binding, the bridge and the tuning pegs are all ivory. It was made as a gut-string instrument.

The tuning pegs are made of ivory.

It has 'Snowflake' abalone position markers.

- **DATE** 1902
- **ORIGIN** Pennsylvania, USA
- **WOOD**
  Front/Back & Sides
  Spruce/rosewood
- **UNUSUAL FEATURE**
  There is a lining of self-resinous lignum vitae wood inside the peg hole, which lubricates the action of the ivory friction tuning pegs.

The pyramid bridge is so called because of the shapes of the bridge extensions.

0-28, 1915

This is a classic fingerpicker's guitar. At this time, the 28 style used body trimmings of inlaid wood, imported from Germany, resembling a continuous herringbone design. All Martin guitars up to this point were made for gut strings. This guitar has a slotted headstock with mechanical tuning machines, and just a few years later they would become useful following the introduction of the steel-string Hawaiian models.

The slotted headstock has German-made tuning machines (earlier models often had French ones).

This guitar features ivory bindings, but just two years later Martin started to use celluloid.

- **DATE** 1915
- **ORIGIN** Pennsylvania, USA
- **WOOD**
  Front/Back & Sides
  Spruce/rosewood
- **UNUSUAL FEATURE**
  Martin traditionally did not use paper labels. Instead, the company chose to hot-iron-brand its guitars.

It has the famous Adirondack spruce soundboard.

OM-28, 1930

This guitar has the same style number as the 0-28, but it couldn't be more different: the neck joins the body at the 14th, not the 12th, fret like most gut-string guitars; it has an 'advanced' x-bracing capable of supporting the soundboard against the extra tension of steel strings; and it is fitted with banjo tuners. By the late 1920s, all non-Spanish-style Martin guitars were fitted with steel strings as standard. The size designation OM stood for 'Orchestra Model' and was specifically designed to compete in volume with the banjo orchestras that were popular in the 1930s.

D-18: 'Elvis guitar', 1942

The D-18 was one of Martin's cheaper models, although pre-war versions are much sought after for their volume and sustain. This example was bought second-hand by the young country-music-inspired Elvis Presley – you can still see 'ELVI' on the soundboard. By now Martin's steel-string guitars had mechanical tuning machines and a wider 'belly' bridge, which was less likely to split than the older-style pyramid ones. There is much wear to the top and back caused by Presley's chunky jewellery and belt buckles.

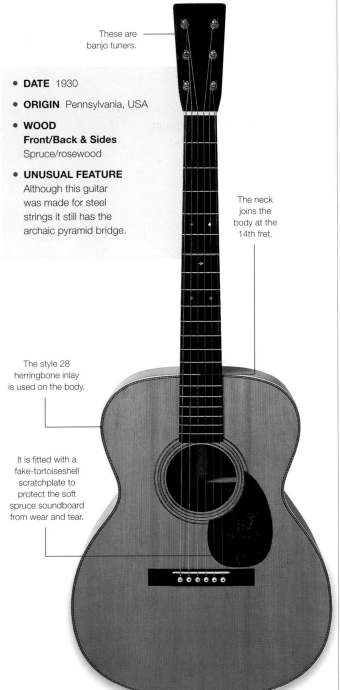

These are banjo tuners.

- **DATE** 1930
- **ORIGIN** Pennsylvania, USA
- **WOOD**
  Front/Back & Sides
  Spruce/rosewood
- **UNUSUAL FEATURE**
  Although this guitar was made for steel strings it still has the archaic pyramid bridge.

The neck joins the body at the 14th fret.

The style 28 herringbone inlay is used on the body.

It is fitted with a fake-tortoiseshell scratchplate to protect the soft spruce soundboard from wear and tear.

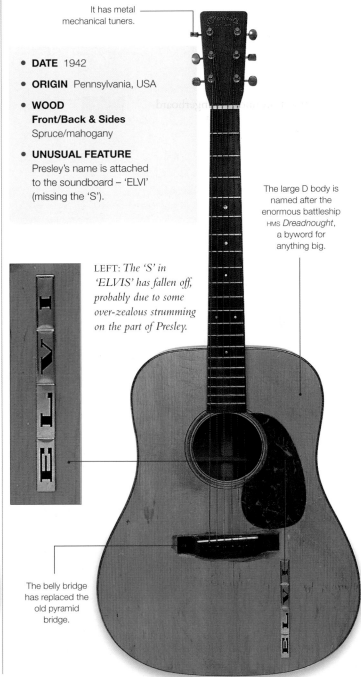

It has metal mechanical tuners.

- **DATE** 1942
- **ORIGIN** Pennsylvania, USA
- **WOOD**
  Front/Back & Sides
  Spruce/mahogany
- **UNUSUAL FEATURE**
  Presley's name is attached to the soundboard – 'ELVI' (missing the 'S').

The large D body is named after the enormous battleship HMS *Dreadnought*, a byword for anything big.

LEFT: *The 'S' in 'ELVIS' has fallen off, probably due to some over-zealous strumming on the part of Presley.*

The belly bridge has replaced the old pyramid bridge.

20th-century flat-top steel-string guitars: C. F. Martin & Co., part two

The Martin Guitar Company was never content with just producing best-sellers. As a successful business, it would have been so easy to sit back and just count the money. As with most artisans, the creative side often takes over, and the ultimate goal becomes to produce the perfect instrument. The examples here, however, were all produced to meet individual requirements.

'America', 1906

This guitar – basically an 0-28 with two bodies – designed by Daniel Schuyler and made by Martin, is one of only two known examples. The purpose of the second back seems to have been to stop the back vibrations being dampened by the player, thus giving the instrument more projection. This is similar in principle to the René Lacôte design for Dionisio Aguado from c.1830, which went one step further by putting a soundhole in the rear.

- **DATE** 1906
- **ORIGIN** Pennsylvania, USA
- **WOOD**
  Front/Back & Sides
  Spruce/rosewood
- **UNUSUAL FEATURE**
  This guitar has two bodies that are perfectly constructed.

N-20, 1968

This is the famous 'Willy Nelson' model. The N-20 was not actually made for Nelson, but he is associated with this guitar because he plays one – which is instantly identifiable because of the large hole worn through the soundboard and through which you can see one of the fanbraces. Since the advent of steel-string guitars, Martin has continued to make gut- and, later, nylon-string models but, apart from the N-20, these have been overshadowed by steel-string instruments.

- **DATE** 1968
- **ORIGIN** Pennsylvania, USA
- **WOOD**
  Front/Back & Sides
  Spruce/rosewood
- **UNUSUAL FEATURE**
  This is the most talked-about Spanish classical guitar Martin ever made.

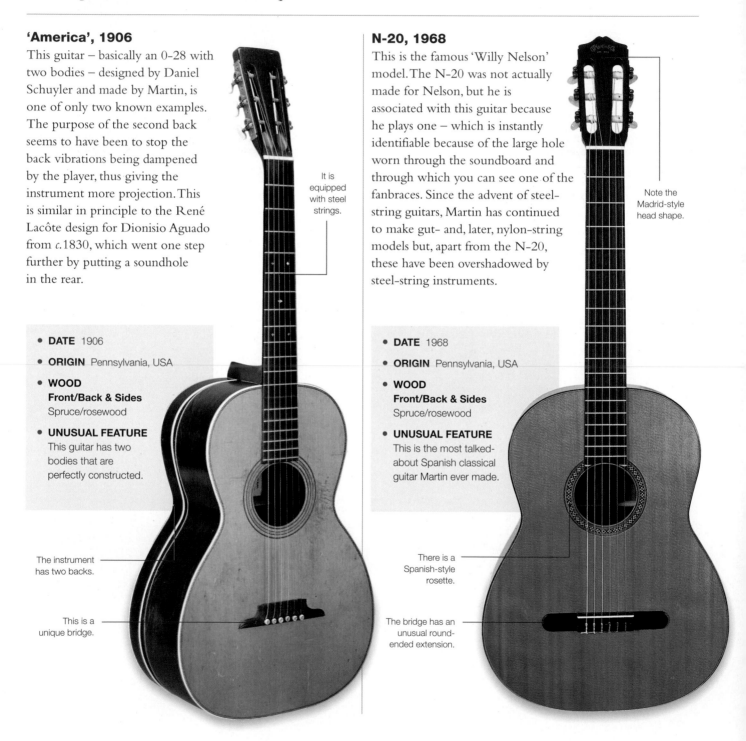

It is equipped with steel strings.

Note the Madrid-style head shape.

The instrument has two backs.

This is a unique bridge.

There is a Spanish-style rosette.

The bridge has an unusual round-ended extension.

One-millionth guitar, 2004

Martin made this to commemorate its one-millionth guitar. Although the company did not use serial numbers until 1898, it had kept order books from the beginning so could estimate the number of guitars made up to that point. So, starting at number 8,000, 106 years later it reached the million. This guitar is covered with inlays, including depictions of two cherubs 'crowning' one of the earliest Martin designs and an American eagle in flight. Not to waste any potential opportunity for decoration, even the soundhole is 'closed' in a lavish design.

ABOVE: *Detail of the inlays which shows the lute-like rose. The whole guitar is garnished with 141 gemstones, including 65 diamonds, emeralds, fossilized ivory, copper, silver, and yellow and white gold.*

- **DATE** 2004

- **ORIGIN** Pennsylvania, USA

- **WOOD**
  Front/Back & Sides
  Spruce/rosewood

- **UNUSUAL FEATURE**
  The rose is a lute-type and delicately carved.

An eagle, the symbol of America, is used as decoration.

Even the rosewood body is lavishly inlaid with abalone.

A backpacker in space, 1994

As we have seen, travel guitars are nothing new. However, Martin managed to bring simplicity to its natural conclusion with this little portable instrument. To reduce the weight, there is no heavy truss-rod installed, so it comes with either low-tension steel or nylon strings. Another consideration is low cost, which enabled Martin to also sell mandolin and ukulele versions that would otherwise have been superfluous, since standard versions of these instruments are already small. It did this by outsourcing production to Mexico and not adding any of the famous Martin trimmings. Although the guitar is perfectly audible, it comes with a bridge-fitted transducer, enabling it to be amplified. Its portability has meant that it has been seen in places where carrying extra luggage is an issue – such as on an expedition to the South Pole and a mission into space.

ABOVE: *Pierre Thuot playing a c.1994 Martin Backpacker on the space shuttle* Columbia. *In C. F. Martin I's time it would have taken more than 90 days to travel around the world. He could never have imagined that 150 years later one of his company's guitars would be transported on the same trip in just 90 minutes.*

Among other things, the scratchplate decoration features the soundboard of a Dreadnought guitar, showing the internal bracing and an array of guitar-making tools.

It has metal bridge pins.

20th-century flat-top steel-string guitars: North American

Giving the consumer a wide choice of guitars helps keep instrument makers in business, and here we see four very different acoustic guitars: one small, one with 12 strings, one with a cutaway and one fitted with pickups and played left-handed. Although the Washburn parlour guitar dates from the 1920s, it is so popular again today that many companies are reissuing the smaller old-style instruments.

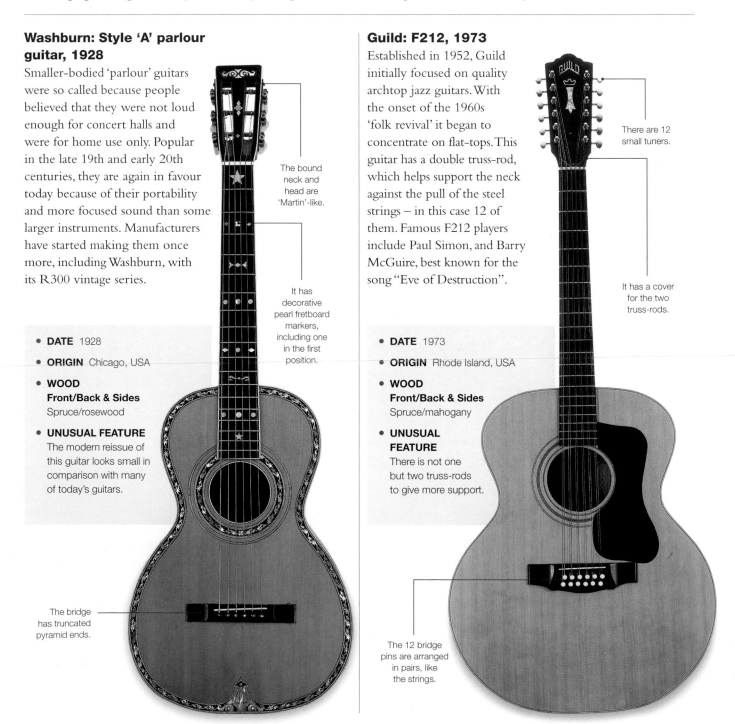

Washburn: Style 'A' parlour guitar, 1928

Smaller-bodied 'parlour' guitars were so called because people believed that they were not loud enough for concert halls and were for home use only. Popular in the late 19th and early 20th centuries, they are again in favour today because of their portability and more focused sound than some larger instruments. Manufacturers have started making them once more, including Washburn, with its R300 vintage series.

The bound neck and head are 'Martin'-like.

It has decorative pearl fretboard markers, including one in the first position.

- **DATE** 1928
- **ORIGIN** Chicago, USA
- **WOOD**
  Front/Back & Sides
  Spruce/rosewood
- **UNUSUAL FEATURE**
  The modern reissue of this guitar looks small in comparison with many of today's guitars.

The bridge has truncated pyramid ends.

Guild: F212, 1973

Established in 1952, Guild initially focused on quality archtop jazz guitars. With the onset of the 1960s 'folk revival' it began to concentrate on flat-tops. This guitar has a double truss-rod, which helps support the neck against the pull of the steel strings – in this case 12 of them. Famous F212 players include Paul Simon, and Barry McGuire, best known for the song "Eve of Destruction".

There are 12 small tuners.

It has a cover for the two truss-rods.

- **DATE** 1973
- **ORIGIN** Rhode Island, USA
- **WOOD**
  Front/Back & Sides
  Spruce/mahogany
- **UNUSUAL FEATURE**
  There is not one but two truss-rods to give more support.

The 12 bridge pins are arranged in pairs, like the strings.

Larrivée: C10, 1989

Canadian maker Jean Larrivée apprenticed under Edger Mönch, the luthier who made Julian Bream's first concert nylon-string instruments. The C10 is one of Larrivée's top models. Famous for their exquisite inlays, this one includes a seahorse to the headstock and a sequence of a bird in motion inlaid to the fingerboard. It has a Florentine cutaway, designed for easier access to the higher register, and is factory-fitted with a clear scratchplate.

- **DATE** 1989
- **ORIGIN** Vancouver, Canada
- **WOOD**
  Front/Back & Sides
  Spruce/rosewood
- **UNUSUAL FEATURE**
  The guitar has a pointed Florentine cutaway.

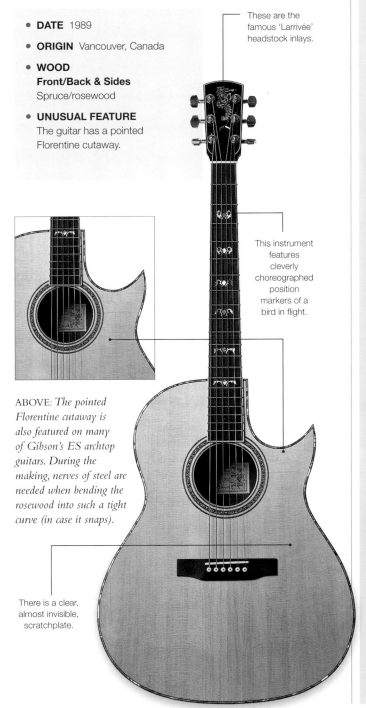

These are the famous 'Larrivée' headstock inlays.

This instrument features cleverly choreographed position markers of a bird in flight.

ABOVE: *The pointed Florentine cutaway is also featured on many of Gibson's ES archtop guitars. During the making, nerves of steel are needed when bending the rosewood into such a tight curve (in case it snaps).*

There is a clear, almost invisible, scratchplate.

Kurt Cobain

Best known as the lead singer and guitarist of the grunge band Nirvana, Kurt Cobain (1967–94) was a southpaw, but he ignored left-handed guitars and, like Jimi Hendrix, chose to play right-handed models upside down and reverse-strung – as here with this *c.*1958 Martin D-18E that he is playing on an *MTV Unplugged* show. The D-18 was the largest guitar Martin produced in the 1950s, designed to be loud. However, it was not loud enough to compete with electric instruments, so Martin released the D-18E, which came with two factory-fitted pickups. On this example, Cobain added a third pickup, bending the MTV's 'unplugged rules' by playing it through his Fender Twin Reverb amp. The guitar has three rotary controls and a pickup selector. As with all D-18 models it has a mahogany body with a spruce soundboard. The scratchplate on this guitar is an unusual shape in order to accommodate the large pickup surrounds.

ABOVE: *This photograph of Kurt Cobain is taken from Nirvana's appearance on the TV show* MTV Unplugged *which took place on 18 November 1993 in New York. A live album of material from this acoustic set was posthumously released following his suicide, which occurred just five months later. He is seen here playing a modified 'workhorse' Martin D-18E.*

20th- and 21st-century flat-top steel-string guitars: North American

Gibson, Fender and Martin are the undisputed leaders in the US acoustic-guitar business. However, Taylor, Santa Cruz, Ovation and Collings have all attracted big names, with the likes of Keith Richards, Pete Townshend, Eric Clapton, Emmylou Harris, Andy Summers, David Crosby, Joni Mitchell, Glen Campbell, Lou Reed, John Fogerty and Joan Baez all playing one of these brands at certain points in their careers.

Taylor: 614 CE, 1998

Westland Music Company was established in 1974, but because the name would not fit on the head of a guitar, it was renamed Taylor Guitars after co-founder Bob Taylor. At first the company produced affordable alternatives to Martins, but today they are a fierce competitor. The instruments have some unique qualities – the head and bridge shapes, for example. This Grand Auditorium Venetian CE (cutaway electric) has a honey-sunburst finish.

- **DATE** 1998
- **ORIGIN** California, USA
- **WOOD**
  Front/Back & Sides
  Sitka spruce/maple
- **UNUSUAL FEATURE**
  The leading edge of the bridge curves, which makes it difficult to position accurately during construction.

Santa Cruz: Tony Rice Model, 2000

Richard Hoover's company is based in Santa Cruz, CA, hence the name. Santa Cruz is a small outfit producing high-quality guitars, favoured by leading players such as Eric Clapton. Another guitarist associated with the maker is Tony Rice, and the model featured here is based on Rice's pre-war Martin D-28 and even features Martin's herringbone inlays, although the sound is very different. Unusually, the Santa Cruz logo is positioned on the fingerboard.

- **DATE** 2000
- **ORIGIN** California, USA
- **WOOD**
  Front/Back & Sides
  Sitka spruce/rosewood
- **UNUSUAL FEATURE**
  The Santa Cruz logo is positioned on the fingerboard.

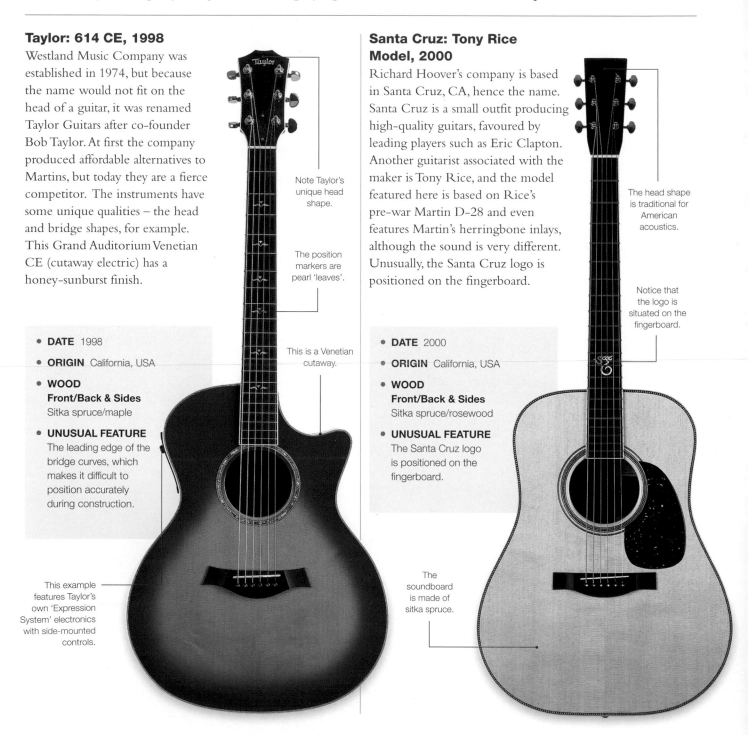

Note Taylor's unique head shape.

The position markers are pearl 'leaves'.

This is a Venetian cutaway.

This example features Taylor's own 'Expression System' electronics with side-mounted controls.

The head shape is traditional for American acoustics.

Notice that the logo is situated on the fingerboard.

The soundboard is made of sitka spruce.

Ovation: Custom Legend, 2006

Charles Kaman, the founder of Ovation guitars, trained as an aeronautical engineer, specializing in helicopter design. He applied his engineering background to guitars, and his first radical designs appeared in 1966. Even the materials were revolutionary – the use of fibreglass in the construction of the bowl-shaped back, for example. The Custom Legend is a high-end model, with its five-piece mahogany-and-maple neck, abalone inlays and gold-plated tuners.

Collings: D2H Koa/Koa, 2009

Bill Collings operates his guitar- and mandolin-making business in Austin, Texas. This Dreadnought model is not only designed for vocal accompaniment, but is also popular with bluegrass flatpickers who need to be heard alongside the louder banjos and fiddles. The D2H model has the decorative elements of the Martin D-28 and D-45 rolled into one, namely the herringbone trim and the abalone 'torch' inlays. This guitar has the added luxury of having not only the back and sides made of Hawaiian koa wood but also the front.

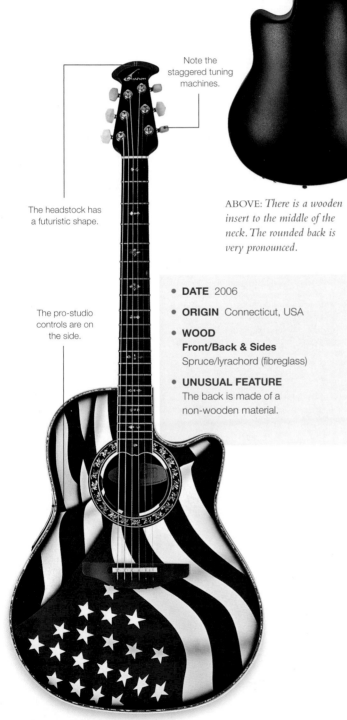

Note the staggered tuning machines.

The headstock has a futuristic shape.

The pro-studio controls are on the side.

ABOVE: *There is a wooden insert to the middle of the neck. The rounded back is very pronounced.*

- **DATE** 2006
- **ORIGIN** Connecticut, USA
- **WOOD**
  Front/Back & Sides
  Spruce/lyrachord (fibreglass)
- **UNUSUAL FEATURE**
  The back is made of a non-wooden material.

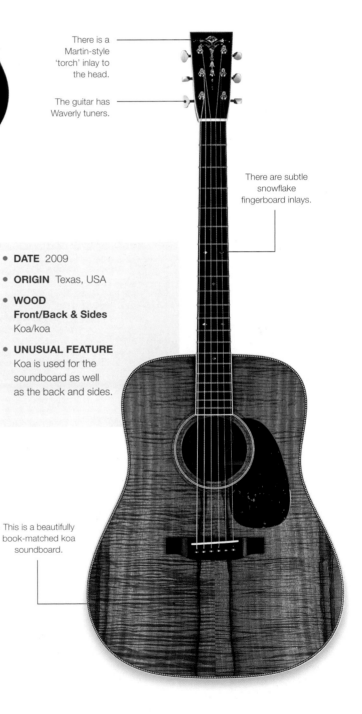

There is a Martin-style 'torch' inlay to the head.

The guitar has Waverly tuners.

There are subtle snowflake fingerboard inlays.

- **DATE** 2009
- **ORIGIN** Texas, USA
- **WOOD**
  Front/Back & Sides
  Koa/koa
- **UNUSUAL FEATURE**
  Koa is used for the soundboard as well as the back and sides.

This is a beautifully book-matched koa soundboard.

20th- and 21st-century flat-top steel-string guitars: European

Many European makers have had their share of what is often considered to be the American guitar market. Some of them have broken away from the much-copied 'jumbo' and Dreadnought designs, each developing their own bracing systems and giving their instruments their own unique sound. Often, smaller outfits will build guitars to a player's individual requirements.

Levin: Goliath, 1964

Herman Carlson Levin's (1864–1948) company existed for around 80 years – even being owned by C. F. Martin at one stage – and in that time produced over 500,000 instruments, making it the largest manufacturer in Scandinavia. The Goliath was so called because of its size and, according to the company's adverts, it was 'designed for accompanying'. There was also the Super Goliath, which was slightly more expensive because better-quality woods were used.

- **DATE** 1964
- **ORIGIN** Sweden
- **WOOD**
  Front/Back & Sides
  Spruce/maple
- **UNUSUAL FEATURE**
  Shaded tops seem
  to be a thing of
  the past.

The original gold Levin logo has faded.

There is a fancy metal truss-rod cover.

This guitar has a dark sunburst finish.

Andy Manson: Magpie Slide Slammer, 1987

Known chiefly for custom work, Andy Manson (b. 1949) also makes unusual instruments such as multi-necked guitars. This is an OM-sized guitar with a palm-operated B-string bender on the bridge, a device more commonly found on electrics. The headstock carries a device called Slide Slammer, which allows the nut to be raised for slide playing without disturbing the pitch. Manson designed and made both devices.

- **DATE** 1987
- **ORIGIN** UK
- **WOOD**
  Front/Back & Sides
  Spruce/rosewood
- **UNUSUAL FEATURE**
  This is equipped with
  two inventive devices:
  a B-string bender
  and raisable nut.

The Slide Slammer is fitted to the headstock.

Note that the label is to one side.

The B-string bender is attached to the bridge.

George Lowden: Richard Thompson Model, 2002

George Lowden (b. 1951) started making guitars professionally in 1973. Being self-taught, he did his own experimenting and came up with his famous A-frame bracing with 'dolphin'-shaped profiles. Based in Northern Ireland, his guitars have at times been mass-produced outside of the country, but are now made by a small team of people there. This guitar, one of Lowden's 'Signature Models', was designed with some input from Richard Thompson, after whom it was named. The woods chosen are beautifully figured, and the head is faced (front and back) with the same wood as the back and sides.

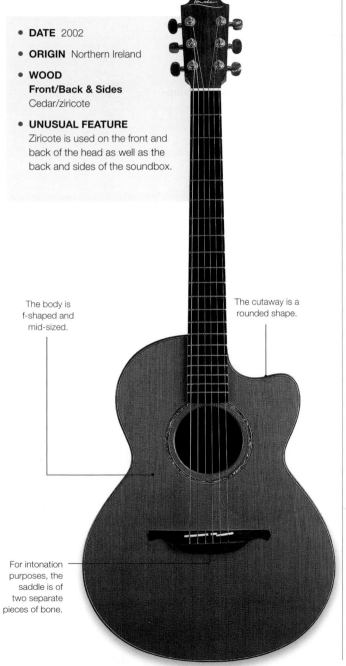

- **DATE** 2002
- **ORIGIN** Northern Ireland
- **WOOD**
  Front/Back & Sides
  Cedar/ziricote
- **UNUSUAL FEATURE**
  Ziricote is used on the front and back of the head as well as the back and sides of the soundbox.

The body is f-shaped and mid-sized.

The cutaway is a rounded shape.

For intonation purposes, the saddle is of two separate pieces of bone.

Fylde: Custom-built 'Harlequin', c.2003

In 1973, Fylde Guitars was founded by Roger Bucknall in Lancashire after he turned his hobby into his profession. His background in fine woodwork, music, engineering and acoustics led him to make instruments for many of the world's top musicians, including Gordon Giltrap and Davy Graham. He works mostly with hand tools, helped by a small team of assistants. He believes that the art of guitar making is a 'calling' and the maker's personality should be in every component part of the instrument.

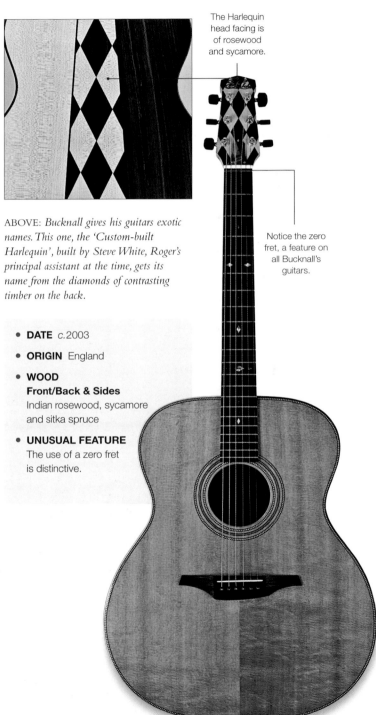

The Harlequin head facing is of rosewood and sycamore.

ABOVE: *Bucknall gives his guitars exotic names. This one, the 'Custom-built Harlequin', built by Steve White, Roger's principal assistant at the time, gets its name from the diamonds of contrasting timber on the back.*

Notice the zero fret, a feature on all Bucknall's guitars.

- **DATE** c.2003
- **ORIGIN** England
- **WOOD**
  Front/Back & Sides
  Indian rosewood, sycamore and sitka spruce
- **UNUSUAL FEATURE**
  The use of a zero fret is distinctive.

20th-century archtop guitars: American classics, part one

Here we see three of Gibson's classic archtop designs. Although the big-band era from which they come is long gone, Gibson's guitars from this period are still much in demand by players and collectors alike. Lloyd Loar was an acoustical engineer at Gibson. He had a profound influence on the company's designs in the 1920s, and all the instruments here were influenced by his innovations.

Gibson: Super 400, 1936

Launched in 1934, the Super 400 had a price tag of $400, hence the name. It was a top-of-the-range archtop and was made to impress, with its gold-plated metal parts, 457mm (18in) body, choice woods finished in 'Cremona Brown' (named after the violin-making school of Cremona), special pickguard, engraving on the tailpiece, and the open-back Grover tuners. The split-diamond headstock inlay was later used by Gibson on its Les Paul electric instruments.

- **DATE** 1936
- **ORIGIN** USA
- **WOOD**
  Front/Back & Sides
  Spruce/maple
- **UNUSUAL FEATURE**
  The pickguard has a brown, mottled-effect.

Gibson: L5, 1937

The L5 is one of the classic Gibsons and was the first Gibson guitar to feature f-holes. It went through many changes after its first appearance in 1922, originally having dot fingerboard markers, the famous snake-head shape, birch back and sides and a 406mm (16in) body. By the time this example was made 15 years later, it had block markers, a wider headstock, maple back and sides, and a 432mm (17in) body, as well as a number of other different designs.

- **DATE** 1937
- **ORIGIN** USA
- **WOOD**
  Front/Back & Sides
  Spruce/maple
- **UNUSUAL FEATURE**
  The 'Cremona Brown' sunburst is almost black.

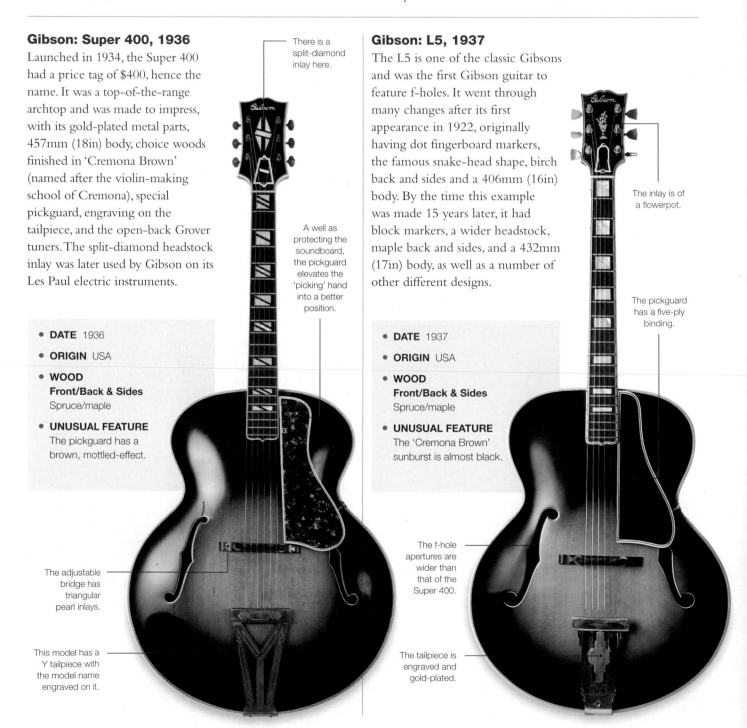

There is a split-diamond inlay here.

A well as protecting the soundboard, the pickguard elevates the 'picking' hand into a better position.

The inlay is of a flowerpot.

The pickguard has a five-ply binding.

The adjustable bridge has triangular pearl inlays.

This model has a Y tailpiece with the model name engraved on it.

The f-hole apertures are wider than that of the Super 400.

The tailpiece is engraved and gold-plated.

Gibson: L7C, 1963

The L7 is a cheaper version of the L5; the main differences are only cosmetic. Although the L5C was introduced in 1939, the L7 didn't appear with a cutaway 'C' option until 1948. The crown head inlay was used on many Gibson models, including the Hummingbird acoustic, the SG electric and the EB bass guitar. This example has a pickup added as a later modification, so it can be used either plugged or unplugged.

The crown head inlay was used on a number of different Gibson guitars – both electric and acoustic.

ABOVE: *Gibson's serial numbers overlapped in the 1960s, and this can lead to confusion when dating the guitars. In the absence of a firm date, the different styles of 'Gibson' logos can help date the instrument.*

- **DATE** 1963

- **ORIGIN** USA

- **WOOD**
  Front/Back & Sides
  Spruce/maple

- **UNUSUAL FEATURE**
  This guitar has a single humbucker pickup with top-mounted volume and tone controls.

The cutaway is in the Venetian style.

The three-raised-parallelogram tailpiece

Lloyd Loar

When Lloyd Loar's (1886–1943) name is mentioned in connection with Gibson instruments, collectors, dealers, musicians and historians all become rather excited. However, he was neither an instrument maker nor did he work for Gibson for very long – in fact, for less than five years. But during his short time at Gibson he had a huge influence on the design and future of both the guitar and mandolin, and it is this that makes him a very special figure. By the age of 20 he was a professional musician, and he played and promoted Gibson's mandolins and mandolas, among many other instruments. In 1919, after Orville Gibson had left the company that he had founded, Loar was hired as an acoustical engineer. He worked mainly on the 'Master Model' instruments, which included the L5 archtop guitar and the F5 mandolin, and many of these instruments were signed by him.

ABOVE: *The Fisher Shipp Concert Company included Lloyd Loar on mandolin and Miss Fisher Shipp, the company manager and vocalist who later became Loar's wife (left). Here, Loar is holding a Gibson ten-string mando-viola – compared with a regular mandolin, the lower registers would have sounded better with the relatively higher-voiced female singers.*

20th-century archtop guitars:
American classics, part two

There is a long tradition of immigrant workers in America becoming successful instrument makers – C. F. Martin from Germany, Adolph Rickenbacker from Switzerland and the Greek Epaminondas Stathopoulo (Epiphone), to name but a few. This applies no more so than to the elite archtop builders: the Italian-influenced makers D'Angelico, D'Aquisto and Benedetto, and the Swedish Stromberg.

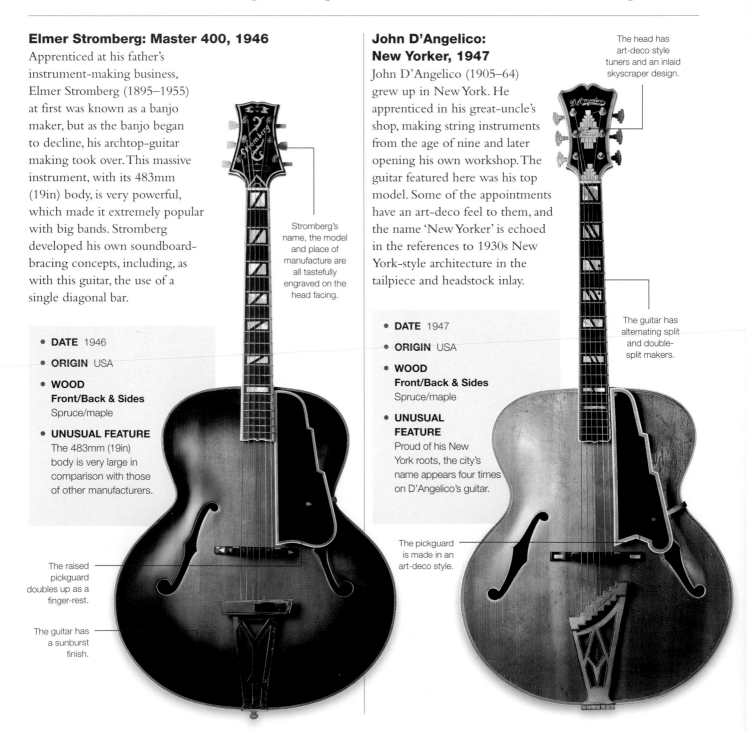

Elmer Stromberg: Master 400, 1946

Apprenticed at his father's instrument-making business, Elmer Stromberg (1895–1955) at first was known as a banjo maker, but as the banjo began to decline, his archtop-guitar making took over. This massive instrument, with its 483mm (19in) body, is very powerful, which made it extremely popular with big bands. Stromberg developed his own soundboard-bracing concepts, including, as with this guitar, the use of a single diagonal bar.

Stromberg's name, the model and place of manufacture are all tastefully engraved on the head facing.

- **DATE** 1946
- **ORIGIN** USA
- **WOOD**
  Front/Back & Sides
  Spruce/maple
- **UNUSUAL FEATURE**
  The 483mm (19in) body is very large in comparison with those of other manufacturers.

The raised pickguard doubles up as a finger-rest.

The guitar has a sunburst finish.

John D'Angelico: New Yorker, 1947

John D'Angelico (1905–64) grew up in New York. He apprenticed in his great-uncle's shop, making string instruments from the age of nine and later opening his own workshop. The guitar featured here was his top model. Some of the appointments have an art-deco feel to them, and the name 'New Yorker' is echoed in the references to 1930s New York-style architecture in the tailpiece and headstock inlay.

The head has art-deco style tuners and an inlaid skyscraper design.

- **DATE** 1947
- **ORIGIN** USA
- **WOOD**
  Front/Back & Sides
  Spruce/maple
- **UNUSUAL FEATURE**
  Proud of his New York roots, the city's name appears four times on D'Angelico's guitar.

The guitar has alternating split and double-split makers.

The pickguard is made in an art-deco style.

James D'Aquisto: Excel, 1970

Jimmy D'Aquisto (1935–95) was born in Brooklyn of second-generation immigrants from Palermo, Sicily. He was a serious guitarist and first met John D'Angelico as a client. Not long after this, he started working in D'Angelico's workshop. After the death of the master in the 1960s, he continued to work on guitars in various locations in the state of New York and eventually bought the business from the D'Angelico family. Many of his guitars were custom orders, and through this he stamped his own personality on the instruments by using features such as s-holes, wooden tailpieces and the metal-pip headstock finials.

Robert Benedetto: Cremona, 1994

In 1968, Robert Benedetto (b. 1946) started building guitars and making his own individual instruments. He has made over 800 instruments, of which more than half are archtop guitars. Benedetto is also an author, and one of his titles is the seminal *Making an Archtop Guitar*. The special custom-made guitar here was ordered by the violin maker Frank Passa. The back is made of 150-year-old curly European maple, which was probably supplied by Benedetto's customer. These instruments command a high price – in 1999, the recommended retail price of a standard Cremona was a staggering $60,000.

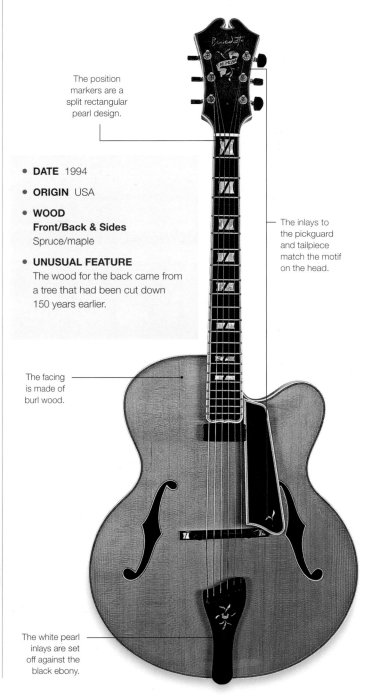

The head design is reminiscent of D'Angelico's.

- **DATE** 1970
- **ORIGIN** USA
- **WOOD**
  Front/Back & Sides
  Spruce/maple
- **UNUSUAL FEATURE**
  The guitar has D'Aquisto's trademark s-holes.

There is a Florentine cutaway.

This guitar has a dark, natural finish.

The position markers are a split rectangular pearl design.

- **DATE** 1994
- **ORIGIN** USA
- **WOOD**
  Front/Back & Sides
  Spruce/maple
- **UNUSUAL FEATURE**
  The wood for the back came from a tree that had been cut down 150 years earlier.

The inlays to the pickguard and tailpiece match the motif on the head.

The facing is made of burl wood.

The white pearl inlays are set off against the black ebony.

20th-century archtop guitars: other classics

Gibson had cornered the mainstream archtop-guitar market, while handmade ones by makers such as D'Angelico sold well to professional players and collectors. However, as these examples show, there were other companies that also had a degree of success in this field. While some are clearly Gibson-influenced instruments, others show some originality and unique features.

C. F. Martin: F-7, 1935

Martin had three ranges of archtop guitars: C, R and F. Both the F-7 and F-9 were short-lived, only being produced between 1935 and 1942. The F-9 cost $250, more than the similar-sized and similarly appointed Martin D-45 flat-top. These are very rare models, made even rarer because people have been converting them to flat-tops, in particular the F-9, being made into D-45-type instruments.

The Martin logo is vertically inlaid.

The hexagonal position markers are like those used on the D-45.

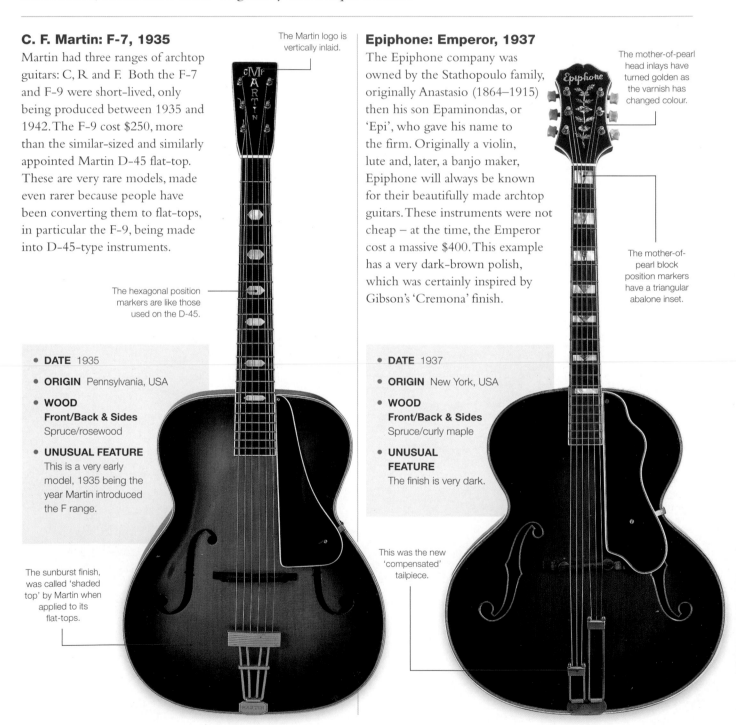

- **DATE** 1935
- **ORIGIN** Pennsylvania, USA
- **WOOD**
  Front/Back & Sides
  Spruce/rosewood
- **UNUSUAL FEATURE**
  This is a very early model, 1935 being the year Martin introduced the F range.

The sunburst finish, was called 'shaded top' by Martin when applied to its flat-tops.

Epiphone: Emperor, 1937

The Epiphone company was owned by the Stathopoulo family, originally Anastasio (1864–1915) then his son Epaminondas, or 'Epi', who gave his name to the firm. Originally a violin, lute and, later, a banjo maker, Epiphone will always be known for their beautifully made archtop guitars. These instruments were not cheap – at the time, the Emperor cost a massive $400. This example has a very dark-brown polish, which was certainly inspired by Gibson's 'Cremona' finish.

The mother-of-pearl head inlays have turned golden as the varnish has changed colour.

The mother-of-pearl block position markers have a triangular abalone inset.

- **DATE** 1937
- **ORIGIN** New York, USA
- **WOOD**
  Front/Back & Sides
  Spruce/curly maple
- **UNUSUAL FEATURE**
  The finish is very dark.

This was the new 'compensated' tailpiece.

Gretsch: Synchromatic, 1940s

Friedrich Gretsch (1856–95) formed the Gretsch Company in 1883 and at first made tambourines, soon moving into drums and guitars. When this guitar was made, Friedrich's son Fred had just about retired from being director of the company, and his grandson, also Fred, was now in charge. This Synchromatic was the company's first attempt at challenging Gibson's supremacy. The 'cat's-eye' soundholes, the stepped bridge and the harp-shaped tailpiece are all inspired by art deco.

- **DATE** 1940s
- **ORIGIN** New York, USA
- **WOOD**
  Front/Back & Sides
  Spruce/maple
- **UNUSUAL FEATURE**
  The whole design of this guitar is inspired by the styles of the art deco movement.

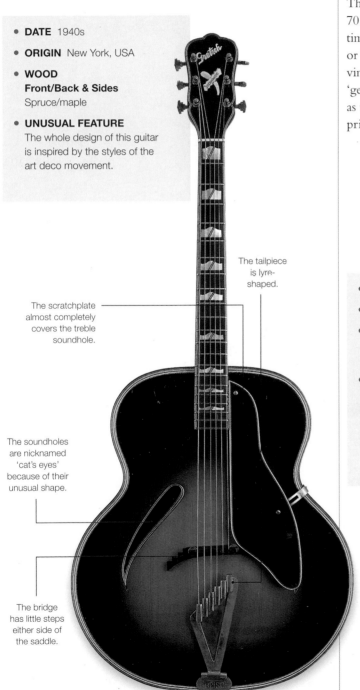

The scratchplate almost completely covers the treble soundhole.

The tailpiece is lyre-shaped.

The soundholes are nicknamed 'cat's eyes' because of their unusual shape.

The bridge has little steps either side of the saddle.

Höfner: Committee, 1957

Karl Höfner (?1864-1955) founded the Höfner company in 1887. His sons Josef and Walter joined in the 1920s. New factories, where this guitar was made, were built in 1950. Besides a rare model called the 'Golden Höfner' there were four archtops that the company offered in their catalogues. The cheapest was the Congress, then came the Senator, next was the President and the most expensive in this line was the Committee – so called because it was designed by a 'committee' of six of the UK's top guitarists. This 1957 electric version cost 70 guineas in Britain at the time, whether it had a 'Blonde' or 'Brunette' finish. The current vintage market dictates that 'gentlemen prefer blondes', as these command a higher price today.

As well as the name appearing on the head, it also occurs as a transfer on the body.

There are lavish inlays – even the truss-rod cover is inlaid with pearl.

This guitar is fitted with two pickups, and unlike the later thin-bodied versions, this model could be played either plugged in or acoustically.

- **DATE** 1957
- **ORIGIN** Bubenreuth, Germany
- **WOOD**
  Front/Back & Sides
  Spruce/veneered maple
- **UNUSUAL FEATURE**
  The scratchplate is made of clear celluloid, a nice feature since it is less obstructive to the eye.

20th-century gypsy guitars

Just like flamenco guitars, gypsy guitars are designed with one style of playing in mind – in this case, the jangly percussive sound made while vamping. Mario Maccaferri (1900–93) designed these guitars for the Parisian company Selmer. Selmer also offered four- and even seven-string versions, and those made for gut-strings. However, none is more prized than a six-string, metal-strung Selmer-Maccaferri instrument.

Selmer: Maccaferri D-hole, 1932

The Selmer-Maccaferri D-hole guitars were made only for a few years, c.1832–1934, but they have left a strong legacy. This model has a secondary soundbox with a sound reflector fitted inside, which may have been inspired by the many late 19th-century mandolins that were fitted with inner 'shelves'. Having no bone saddle or being adjustable, they came with a choice of bridges of different heights, the central part of the bridge not being fixed. This example has the full four-octave range.

- **DATE** 1932
- **ORIGIN** France
- **WOOD**
  Front/Back & Sides
  Spruce/laminated rosewood
- **UNUSUAL FEATURE**
  There are an internal sound chamber and reflector.

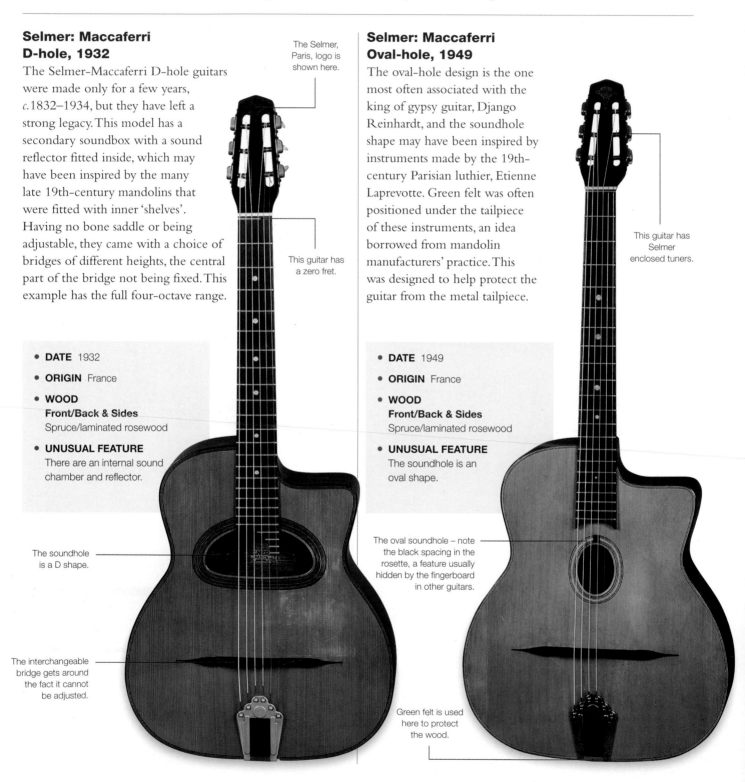

The Selmer, Paris, logo is shown here.

This guitar has a zero fret.

The soundhole is a D shape.

The interchangeable bridge gets around the fact it cannot be adjusted.

Selmer: Maccaferri Oval-hole, 1949

The oval-hole design is the one most often associated with the king of gypsy guitar, Django Reinhardt, and the soundhole shape may have been inspired by instruments made by the 19th-century Parisian luthier, Etienne Laprevotte. Green felt was often positioned under the tailpiece of these instruments, an idea borrowed from mandolin manufacturers' practice. This was designed to help protect the guitar from the metal tailpiece.

- **DATE** 1949
- **ORIGIN** France
- **WOOD**
  Front/Back & Sides
  Spruce/laminated rosewood
- **UNUSUAL FEATURE**
  The soundhole is an oval shape.

This guitar has Selmer enclosed tuners.

The oval soundhole – note the black spacing in the rosette, a feature usually hidden by the fingerboard in other guitars.

Green felt is used here to protect the wood.

Jacques Favino, 1975

Initially, Jacques Favino (b. 1920) worked for Bernabe Busato, later venturing out on his own. This guitar, like the original Selmers that Favino copies, features a zero fret, which helps keep the string action as low as possible above the frets and assists with the required tone. The leading edge of the bridge is hugely compensated, which is more crucial than with gut- or nylon-string guitars. These copies are close to the Selmer originals, with the main difference being a larger body size. Favino retired from building guitars in 1978, and today his son Jean-Pierre continues the business.

- **DATE** 1975

- **ORIGIN** France

- **WOOD**
  Front/Back & Sides
  Spruce/laminated rosewood

- **UNUSUAL FEATURE**
  The bridge is hugely compensated.

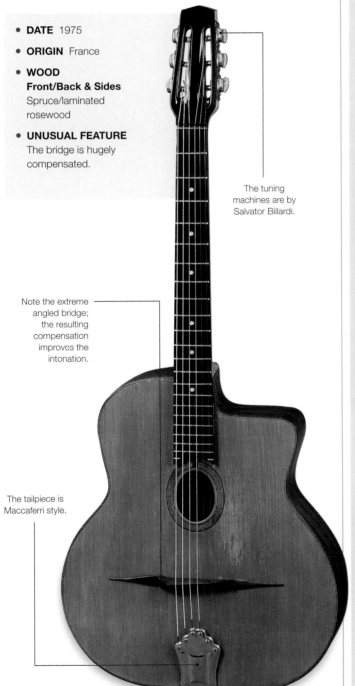

The tuning machines are by Salvator Billardi.

Note the extreme angled bridge; the resulting compensation improves the intonation.

The tailpiece is Maccaferri style.

Django Reinhardt

The name of Django Reinhardt (1910–53) is synonymous with gypsy jazz. He is undoubtedly one of the major figures in the whole of jazz – and indeed guitar – history. Although other musicians of his stature have had a direct, easily traceable influence on generations of players, Django's sound and style have not echoed down the years in the same way – with the exception of the large number of players who are devoted to sounding exactly like him. Reinhardt's musical vocabulary was strikingly different from that of even his closest musical collaborator, violinist Stéphane Grappelli. This difference was shaped by the well-known fact that he partly lost the use of his left hand at the age of 18 when he narrowly survived a fire in his caravan. Forced to adapt his technique to compensate for having only two usable fingers, Reinhardt nonetheless achieved an astonishing fluidity in his improvised playing. His injury may not have been immediately audible in the speed or the fluency of his playing, but it had a direct influence on his highly individual melodic choices.

ABOVE: *To add even more cool to the 1940s tweed suit and obligatory cigarette, Reinhardt is shown here playing an Epiphone Zephyr. This was the only electric jazz guitar he ever played, usually favouring his Selmer-Maccaferri instruments.*

19th- and 20th-century multi-string harp-guitars

Harp-guitars are very popular again today, especially in America, as they have been at various periods in the past – in Britain during the early 19th century, France in the mid-19th century and in America at the turn of the 19th century. There are many musicians associated with this resurgence in interest, but none more so than Gregg Miner, who has been a key figure in promoting the harp-guitar's recent popularity.

René Lacôte: Decacorde, 1826

There were many multi-stringed guitars made by René Lacôte (1785–c.1860), most with seven (heptacorde) or ten strings (decacorde). This one is slightly unusual in that it has five strings (not six) over the neck and five (not four) 'floating'. In the *Méthode Complète pour le Decacorde Nouvelle Guitare*, by Ferdinando Carulli, it states that the top five strings are tuned like a regular guitar (ADGBE), with the bass strings diatonically tuned GFEDC (descending).

In the past, the sounding length of the bass strings could be altered by moving some levers that are now missing.

The head accommodates ten wooden tuning pegs.

The frets are for only five of the strings, since the others are not intended to be stopped.

- **DATE** 1826
- **ORIGIN** Paris, France
- **WOOD**
  Front/Back & Sides
  Spruce/rosewood
- **UNUSUAL FEATURE**
  Note the unusual division of the strings (5+5 strings instead of the more usual 6+4).

Note how small the body is for such a large neck and head.

Luigi Mozzani: Nine-string Dual-arm Harp-guitar, 1910

As well as being a luthier, Luigi Mozzani (1869–1943) was a composer, teacher and concert guitarist, and he switched between concert tours and overseeing his workshops. He employed several young children, which shows in some of the workmanship, especially the hand-drawn decorations. Mozzani produced many forms of harp-guitars and regular guitars, which were inspired by earlier Viennese models, as well as violins and other instruments. This harp-guitar has two arms and a gingko-leaf pattern.

The regular tuning machines here are not very accessible.

The top two strings have a two-octave fingerboard.

The upper soundhole is part of the gingko-leaf pattern.

- **DATE** 1910
- **ORIGIN** Ferrara, Italy
- **WOOD**
  Front/Back & Sides
  Spruce/poplar
- **UNUSUAL FEATURE**
  The dual arms each have their own additional soundholes.

There are three separate saddles to the bridge.

Gibson: Style U, 1916

Unlike other harp-guitars, which are used for solo playing, the Style U was conceived as part of a family of instruments. For centuries, musical instruments had been made in different sizes for consort playing – the classic family being the violin, viola, cello and double-bass – and in photographs of mandolin orchestras from the early 20th century the Style U is often seen at the rear. The body of the large Gibson Super 400 archtop guitar measures 457mm (18in) at its widest point; the Style U, however, is a gigantic 533mm (21in). The guitar has a regular six-string neck with 12 sub-basses tuned chromatically, descending from the low E string.

John Sullivan/Jeffrey Elliot: 20-string Harp-guitar, 1986

The harp-guitarist John Doan commissioned celebrated maker Jeffrey Elliot to make him a harp-guitar. John Sullivan was called in to give his expertise on the project, and he contributed some significant elements to the basic design. At the time, Elliot had a seven-year waiting list, so they decided to let Sullivan do the making. Not wanting to create a clone of the famous Knutsen or Dyer harp-guitars, they set out to design something that was radically different. The finished result sports some 20 strings arranged with six on a standard neck, six sub-basses and eight zither-like super trebles.

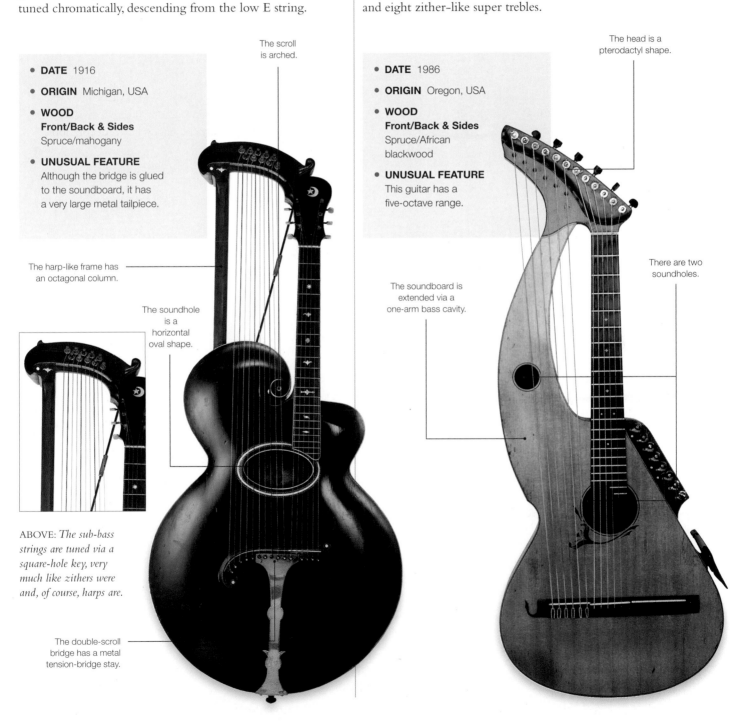

The scroll is arched.

- **DATE** 1916
- **ORIGIN** Michigan, USA
- **WOOD**
  Front/Back & Sides
  Spruce/mahogany
- **UNUSUAL FEATURE**
  Although the bridge is glued to the soundboard, it has a very large metal tailpiece.

The harp-like frame has an octagonal column.

The soundhole is a horizontal oval shape.

ABOVE: *The sub-bass strings are tuned via a square-hole key, very much like zithers were and, of course, harps are.*

The double-scroll bridge has a metal tension-bridge stay.

The head is a pterodactyl shape.

- **DATE** 1986
- **ORIGIN** Oregon, USA
- **WOOD**
  Front/Back & Sides
  Spruce/African blackwood
- **UNUSUAL FEATURE**
  This guitar has a five-octave range.

The soundboard is extended via a one-arm bass cavity.

There are two soundholes.

20th-century guitars: unusual varieties

Innovative instrument making continued into the 20th century, and German and Austrian luthiers built many of the most interesting guitars, as the following examples show. The instruments were evidently very popular in their day, but for the most part the makers' ideas were never developed or refined; they were probably considered to be impractical, or they simply fell out of fashion.

Ludwig Reisinger: *Wappen* form, 1910

Ludwig Reisinger (1863–?; stopped making in 1938) was one of the finest Viennese makers. He was a student of Ignaz Johann Bucher, who was in his turn a student of Johann Georg Stauffer. Like many Stauffer guitars, this guitar has a clock-key adjustable neck. Guitars in *Wappen* ('coat-of-arms') form were very popular and were so called because they were shield shaped.

- **DATE** 1910
- **ORIGIN** Vienna, Austria
- **WOOD**
  Front/Back & Sides
  Spruce/maple
- **UNUSUAL FEATURE**
  The body shape is nicknamed *Wappen*, which means 'coat of arms'.

The head has an aperture that is identical to the early Viennese guitars by Hermann Hauser I.

The body design has pointed cutaways.

Note the twin soundholes.

August Strohmer: Bass-lute, *c*.1920–30

Nuremberg maker August Strohmer was the grandfather of Max Strohmer, who still makes instruments there today. Lute-guitars were very popular in Germany in the early 20th century, and many makers made different varieties. This one has a regular six-string neck with four extra bass strings attached to another head via a decorative arm. The maple back is bowl-shaped like Renaissance and Baroque lutes.

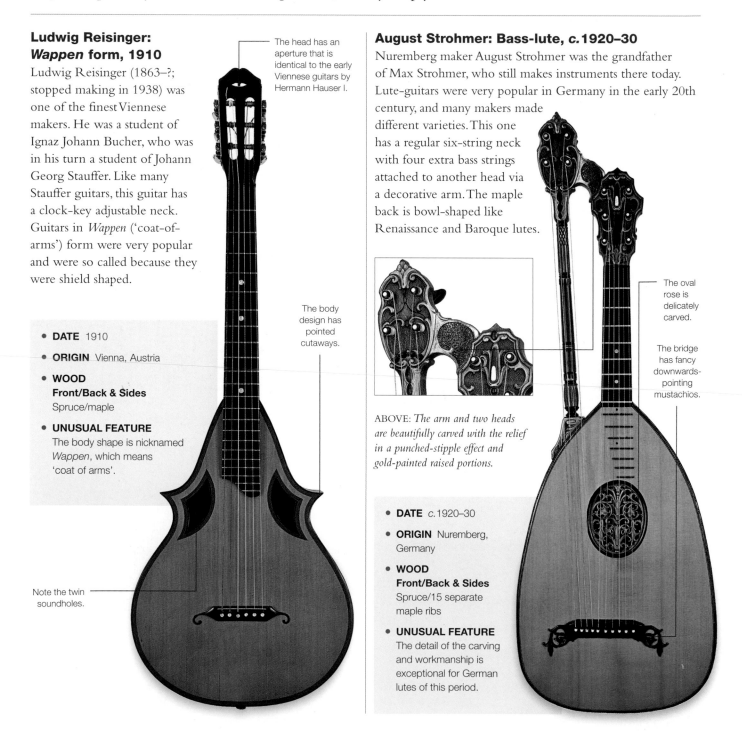

ABOVE: *The arm and two heads are beautifully carved with the relief in a punched-stipple effect and gold-painted raised portions.*

The oval rose is delicately carved.

The bridge has fancy downwards-pointing mustachios.

- **DATE** *c*.1920–30
- **ORIGIN** Nuremberg, Germany
- **WOOD**
  Front/Back & Sides
  Spruce/15 separate maple ribs
- **UNUSUAL FEATURE**
  The detail of the carving and workmanship is exceptional for German lutes of this period.

Alfred Schaufuß (attributed): Archtop guitar, c. 1940–50

Alfred Schaufuß (1904–80) made this extremely fancy archtop guitar in Adorf, near the instrument-making town of Markneukirchen. After working for other local makers, he started his own business in 1924. His instruments are very richly decorated, in part because his wife worked in a pearl factory, thus making it easy for him to obtain the necessary materials for the opulent decorations. Although it is very well made, it may not be surprising to learn that this guitar was once the property of a clown.

The white celluloid-and-pearl inlays extend to the head.

- **DATE** c. 1940–50
- **ORIGIN** Markneukirchen, Germany
- **WOOD**
  Front/Back & Sides
  Spruce/maple
- **UNUSUAL FEATURE**
  There is a Baroque-style sunken rose.

The neck is adjusted with a clock key.

This is a Baroque-style sunken rose.

The sunburst finish avoids covering the decorative border.

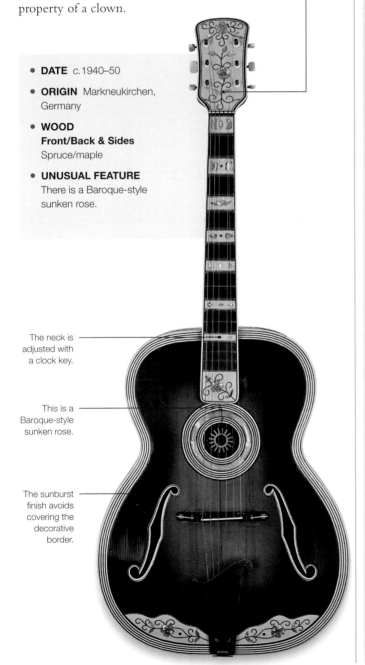

Hans Vogl slide guitar, 1914

This guitar has an inscription written on the inside of the back that translates as: "This instrument is an original invention. If it is successful, I'll never know." It has 51 metal strings, which hover over three 'scalloped' fretboards. Each set of strings is tuned differently. It is not clear whether the brass tube is a slide or a capo, or both.

RIGHT: *The brass tube is operated via the handle to the rear.*

BELOW: *The performer must have been an excellent musician to have been able to master playing 51 strings.*

This style of tuning peg is usually found on German zithers.

The ivory position markers contain the notes at that position.

The brass tube may have been a slide and/or a capo.

There are three lute-style carved roses.

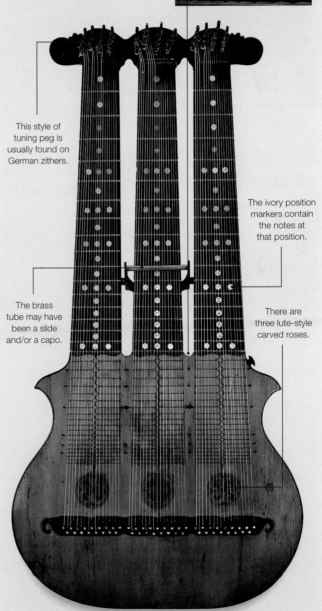

20th-century resonator guitars

Before the electric guitar, players were increasingly demanding more volume from makers. Until the 1920s, their solution was to make larger-bodied guitars, then George Beauchamp and John Dopyera had the idea of crossing a guitar with a phonograph. This, however, had already been patented by John Stroh of London, so Dopyera decided to rest the bridge on three aluminium cones, and the rest, as they say, is history.

Dobro: Style 66 Roundneck, 1929

John Dopyera and his four brothers started making instruments for the Dobro (DOpyera BROthers) company in 1928. This particular wooden-bodied resonator uses only a single cone. The body is made of magnolia, and the French-scroll pattern is achieved by sandblasting. There are two screen holes and three small open holes above the central-cone cover plate. The rectangular cutouts to the cover plate are shaped like four fans.

The Dobro transfer is visible on the head.

- **DATE** 1929
- **ORIGIN** USA
- **WOOD**
  Front/Back & Sides
  Magnolia veneer and three-ply unspecified wood
- **UNUSUAL FEATURE**
  The head is decorated in the same manner as the body.

There are five extra soundholes.

The 'resonator' plate conceals the resonator cone.

The guitar has a violin-like tailpiece.

National: Tricone Square-neck, 1930

John Dopyera registered the National String Instrument Corporation in 1926 (just two years before he started making instruments for his Dobro company). This is an all-metal-body tricone resonator. The lack of any engraving gives this guitar the Style-1 model designation. The Tricone, as the name suggests, has three cones, two on the bass side and one on the treble. Many square-neck resophonic guitars with wooden necks were converted to round-neck playing – probably by dealers to broaden their client base. However, this was not possible with the metal-neck ones.

There is a shield transfer.

- **DATE** 1930
- **ORIGIN** USA
- **WOOD**
  Front/Back & Sides
  All German silver metal
- **UNUSUAL FEATURE**
  Many square-neck models have their tuners reversed for lap playing, but this one still has its tuners in their original positions.

Two extra soundholes are used on this guitar.

The bridge cover and hand-rest form a T-shape.

Kerry Char: Resonator Guitar, 2000

If anyone knows what sound is required from a square-neck resophonic guitar, Hawaii-born Kerry Char (b. 1955) does. He now works in Oregon and has built a reputation for building and restoring unusual instruments. This guitar has a wooden body made completely from Hawaiian koa wood, and all the hardware is gold-plated. The square neck is specifically designed for slide and lap-steel playing.

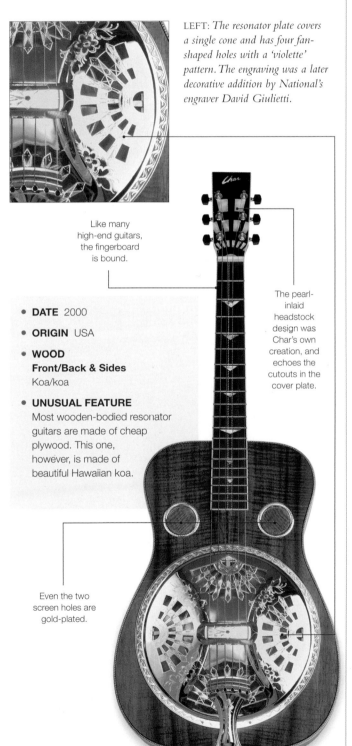

LEFT: *The resonator plate covers a single cone and has four fan-shaped holes with a 'violette' pattern. The engraving was a later decorative addition by National's engraver David Giulietti.*

Like many high-end guitars, the fingerboard is bound.

- **DATE** 2000
- **ORIGIN** USA
- **WOOD**
  Front/Back & Sides
  Koa/koa
- **UNUSUAL FEATURE**
  Most wooden-bodied resonator guitars are made of cheap plywood. This one, however, is made of beautiful Hawaiian koa.

The pearl-inlaid headstock design was Char's own creation, and echoes the cutouts in the cover plate.

Even the two screen holes are gold-plated.

Resonator mandolins

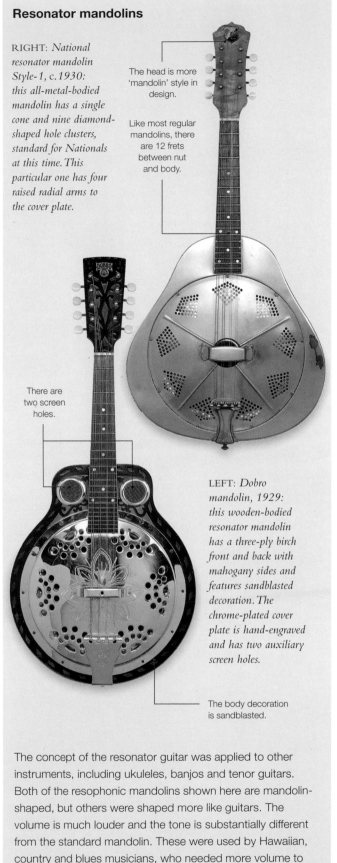

RIGHT: *National resonator mandolin Style-1, c.1930: this all-metal-bodied mandolin has a single cone and nine diamond-shaped hole clusters, standard for Nationals at this time. This particular one has four raised radial arms to the cover plate.*

The head is more 'mandolin' style in design.

Like most regular mandolins, there are 12 frets between nut and body.

There are two screen holes.

LEFT: *Dobro mandolin, 1929: this wooden-bodied resonator mandolin has a three-ply birch front and back with mahogany sides and features sandblasted decoration. The chrome-plated cover plate is hand-engraved and has two auxiliary screen holes.*

The body decoration is sandblasted.

The concept of the resonator guitar was applied to other instruments, including ukuleles, banjos and tenor guitars. Both of the resophonic mandolins shown here are mandolin-shaped, but others were shaped more like guitars. The volume is much louder and the tone is substantially different from the standard mandolin. These were used by Hawaiian, country and blues musicians, who needed more volume to compete with other band members.

20th-century acoustic bass guitars

Before the advent of the electric pickup, acoustic basses, by virtue of the slow-moving, low frequencies of the long, thick strings, had to be large in size. They were designed to be played in groups with other instruments spanning the whole possible acoustical range – in some cases these were 60-piece orchestras. Some were related to the mandolin and others to the guitar, and each was tuned accordingly.

Jean Rowies (attributed): Gelas Mando-bass, 1924–29

This mando-bass, attributed to Jean Rowies, is one of a quartet of Gelas-designed instruments. It is about 1.8m (6ft) tall and one of the most unusual designs imaginable: the bridge is fixed to the true, or inner, soundboard, which is cranked at approximately a 20-degree angle to the fingerboard. The upper soundboard is largely conventional, but the inner soundboard runs beneath it, so it has no need for any bracing.

Notice the metal rollers or barrels instead of ivory or bone used for gut-strung instruments.

- **DATE** 1924–29
- **ORIGIN** France
- **WOOD**
  Front/Back & Sides
  Spruce/maple
- **UNUSUAL FEATURE**
  It has two soundboards. The strings pass through a fixed bridge and are anchored to a tailpiece.

This is the true, or inner, soundboard.

This is the upper soundboard.

The bridge is glued to the soundboard.

The strings attach to the base of the instrument.

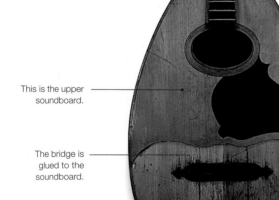

Gibson: Mando-bass, 1929

The Gibson mando-bass has a place in history all of its own. If the violin (which is tuned the same as a mandolin) could be a part of a wider family (viola, cello and double-bass), then why, asked Gibson, couldn't the mandolin? So the company created the mandola, mando-cello and the mando-bass, and mandolin orchestras swept the USA. Unlike the Neapolitan mandolin, however, the oval-shaped Gibson flat-backed mandolin family had an arched rather than a flat soundboard. This one is a 'black face', named after its black finish.

The Gibson logo is located here.

- **DATE** 1929
- **ORIGIN** USA
- **WOOD**
  Front/Back & Sides
  Spruce/maple
- **UNUSUAL FEATURE**
  This has a so-called 'black-face' finish, but many were made in red-mahogany sunburst, brown or plain orange.

Note the black finish.

The guitar has a carved archtop soundboard.

Prairie State Bass, *c.*1930

Made by the Larson Brothers under the name Prairie State, this whopping acoustic bass, although officially classed as a flat-top guitar, has a slight arch to the soundboard. It has a movable bridge and a cello-like spike at the bottom. To help support the large surface area and the pull of the hefty bass strings there is an internal supporting rod running from the lower to the upper block.

Mexican Six-string Bass, 1960

The mariachi band can include violins, guitars, trumpets and vihuelas (five-string), all of which are underpinned by the acoustic basses. The mariachi tradition goes back to the 19th century, but here we have an example of an instrument from the 1960s. The idea is thought to have been introduced by the Spanish, and this instrument is reminiscent of the 1759 Sanguino guitar (see '18th- and early 19th-century transitional guitars, part one') with its deep body and comparatively short neck.

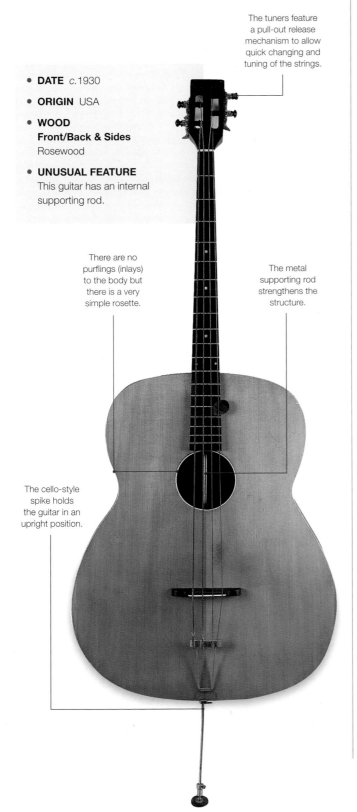

The tuners feature a pull-out release mechanism to allow quick changing and tuning of the strings.

- **DATE** *c.*1930
- **ORIGIN** USA
- **WOOD**
  Front/Back & Sides
  Rosewood
- **UNUSUAL FEATURE**
  This guitar has an internal supporting rod.

There are no purflings (inlays) to the body but there is a very simple rosette.

The metal supporting rod strengthens the structure.

The cello-style spike holds the guitar in an upright position.

- **DATE** 1960
- **ORIGIN** Mexico
- **WOOD**
  Front/Back & Sides
  Cedrela/mahogany
- **UNUSUAL FEATURE**
  Traditionally bass guitars have four strings. This one, however, has six.

The six tuning machines have paddle-shaped heads.

The neck here is tapered.

The unusual choice of woods make it even more exotic-looking.

ABOVE: *Many arched guitar backs are carved by skilled craftsmen. However, this guitar has a particularly pronounced bent back which, because of the severity of the arching, was probably done in a hot press.*

20th- and 21st-century acoustic bass guitars

With each passing decade, guitars were getting louder – then came a lull. Under the influence of TV programmes such as *MTV Unplugged*, as well as Neil Young's annual Bridge Benefit concerts, the idea of playing acoustically while retaining a band atmosphere became popular. Acoustic bass guitars often feature in these sessions, with a sound somewhere between an electric bass and a double bass.

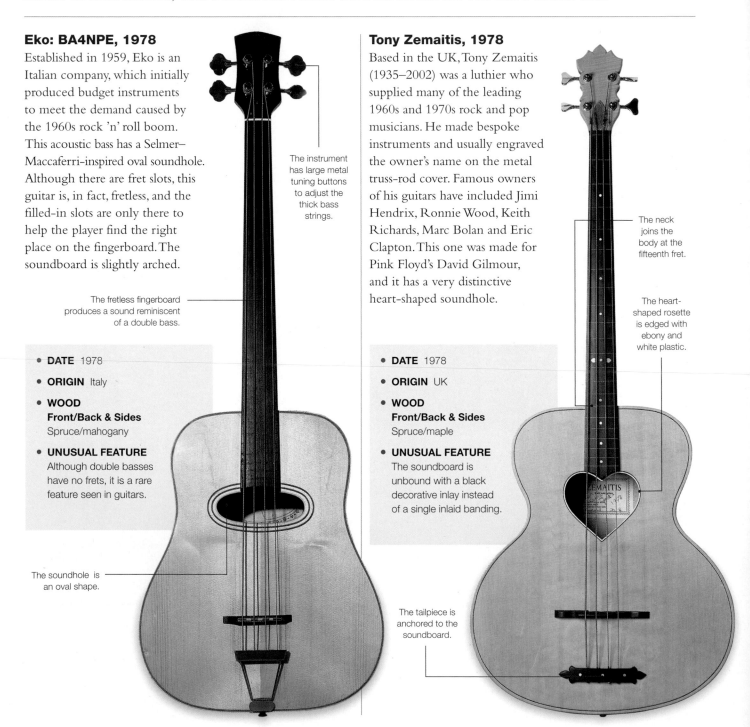

Eko: BA4NPE, 1978

Established in 1959, Eko is an Italian company, which initially produced budget instruments to meet the demand caused by the 1960s rock 'n' roll boom. This acoustic bass has a Selmer–Maccaferri-inspired oval soundhole. Although there are fret slots, this guitar is, in fact, fretless, and the filled-in slots are only there to help the player find the right place on the fingerboard. The soundboard is slightly arched.

The fretless fingerboard produces a sound reminiscent of a double bass.

- **DATE** 1978
- **ORIGIN** Italy
- **WOOD**
  Front/Back & Sides
  Spruce/mahogany
- **UNUSUAL FEATURE**
  Although double basses have no frets, it is a rare feature seen in guitars.

The soundhole is an oval shape.

The instrument has large metal tuning buttons to adjust the thick bass strings.

Tony Zemaitis, 1978

Based in the UK, Tony Zemaitis (1935–2002) was a luthier who supplied many of the leading 1960s and 1970s rock and pop musicians. He made bespoke instruments and usually engraved the owner's name on the metal truss-rod cover. Famous owners of his guitars have included Jimi Hendrix, Ronnie Wood, Keith Richards, Marc Bolan and Eric Clapton. This one was made for Pink Floyd's David Gilmour, and it has a very distinctive heart-shaped soundhole.

The neck joins the body at the fifteenth fret.

The heart-shaped rosette is edged with ebony and white plastic.

- **DATE** 1978
- **ORIGIN** UK
- **WOOD**
  Front/Back & Sides
  Spruce/maple
- **UNUSUAL FEATURE**
  The soundboard is unbound with a black decorative inlay instead of a single inlaid banding.

The tailpiece is anchored to the soundboard.

C. F. Martin: B-65, 1990

The B-65 was designed by Dick Boak, now Martin's archivist and the Director of their Artists Relations. This is essentially a Martin jumbo-sized acoustic bass guitar with a factory-fitted Fishman pickup with pre-amp. The volume and tone knobs are located on the bass-side of the upper bout, and it has an imitation tortoiseshell scratchplate. Four-string guitars are not a new thing for Martin, as the company has been making tenor guitars since the 1920s.

Fender: Kingman SCE, 2010

Leo Fender (1909–91) formed the Fender Electric Instrument Co. in 1946, mainly making electric lap-steels and amplifiers. However, in the 1950s he became famous for producing electric guitars, notably the Telecaster and the Stratocaster. This guitar has a classic Fender neck with a C-shaped (oval) profile and Gibson-style block position markers. It also has a Fishman pre-amp with a guitar tuner. It is of a Dreadnought size, but with a cutaway to the treble side.

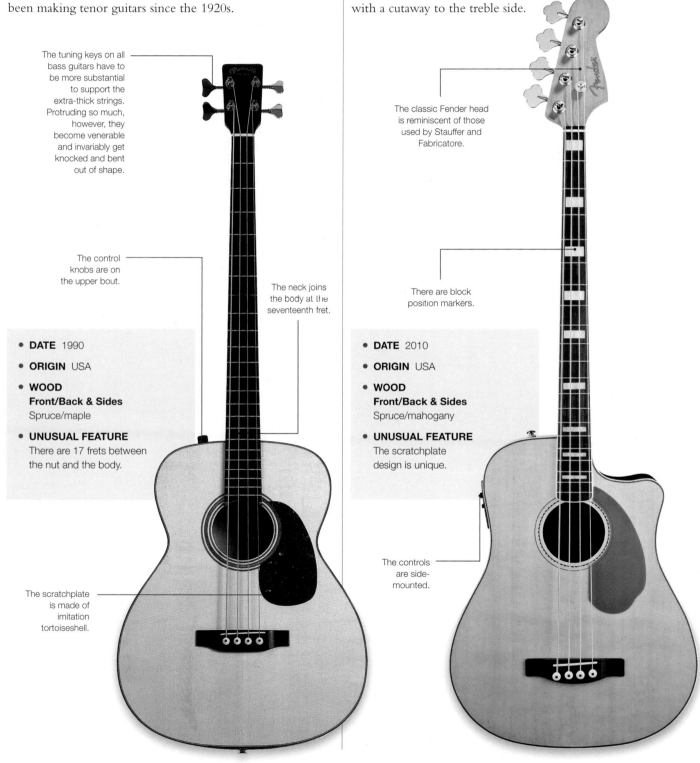

The tuning keys on all bass guitars have to be more substantial to support the extra-thick strings. Protruding so much, however, they become venerable and invariably get knocked and bent out of shape.

The control knobs are on the upper bout.

The neck joins the body at the seventeenth fret.

The scratchplate is made of imitation tortoiseshell.

The classic Fender head is reminiscent of those used by Stauffer and Fabricatore.

There are block position markers.

The controls are side-mounted.

- **DATE** 1990
- **ORIGIN** USA
- **WOOD**
  Front/Back & Sides
  Spruce/maple
- **UNUSUAL FEATURE**
  There are 17 frets between the nut and the body.

- **DATE** 2010
- **ORIGIN** USA
- **WOOD**
  Front/Back & Sides
  Spruce/mahogany
- **UNUSUAL FEATURE**
  The scratchplate design is unique.

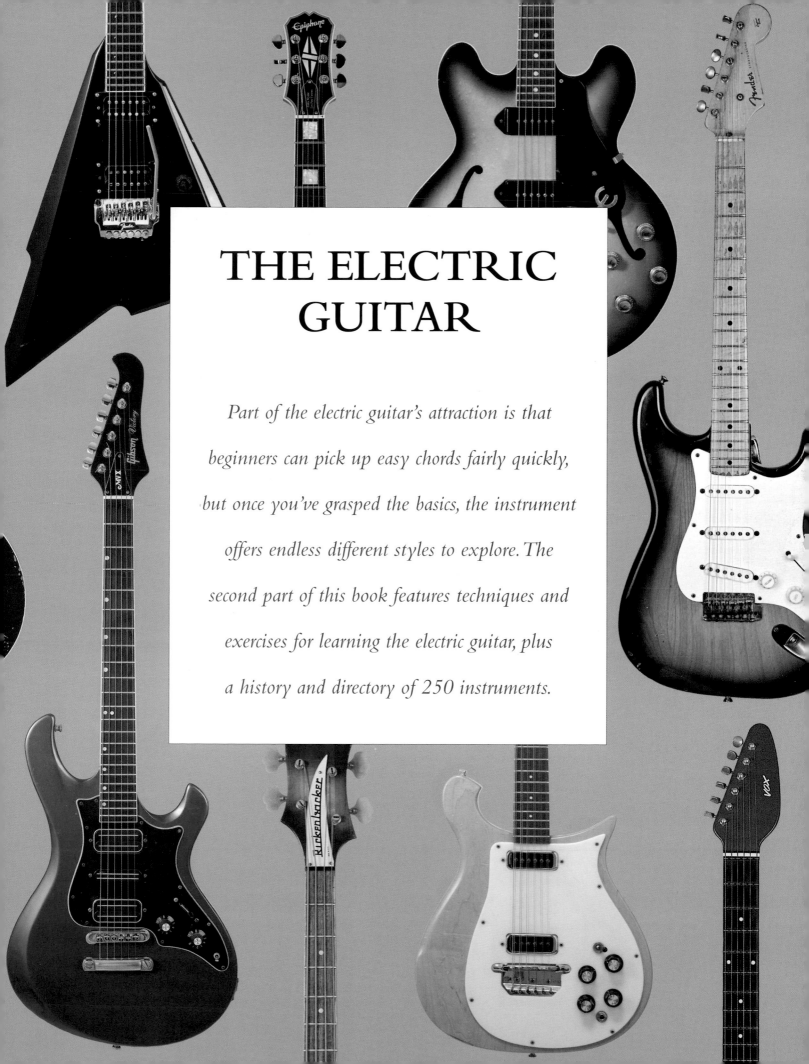

THE ELECTRIC GUITAR

Part of the electric guitar's attraction is that

beginners can pick up easy chords fairly quickly,

but once you've grasped the basics, the instrument

offers endless different styles to explore. The

second part of this book features techniques and

exercises for learning the electric guitar, plus

a history and directory of 250 instruments.

There is an enormous diversity to the sounds that an electric guitar can produce, making it a fantastically versatile and beginner-friendly instrument.

How to play electric guitar

Taking you through everything from basic set-ups to advanced scales and modes, and covering a wide range of musical styles, this chapter has all you need to know to get started on the electric guitar, and improve your playing quickly and easily.

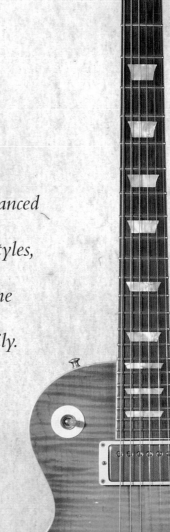

Buying an electric guitar

Electric guitars come in many different shapes and styles. The process of buying one involves a number of decisions; apart from price, the best way to narrow down the possibilities is to consider to which musical style(s) you feel most drawn. If you are a passionate music fan, it may of course be even simpler: who are your guitar 'heroes', and what instruments do they play?

What is an electric guitar?

An electric guitar is one which requires connection to an amplifier or other audio equipment in order to make a useful sound. Most electric guitars have a solid body with little or no ability to resonate acoustically, and therefore they make almost no sound when the strings are played unplugged. Some electric guitars have hollow (or semi-hollow) bodies, however. These are known as semi-acoustic guitars and should not be confused with electro-acoustic guitars. The former are essentially electric guitars that are partially hollow, while the latter are fully functioning acoustic guitars that may be connected to amplification.

Electric guitars can be acoustically almost silent because they incorporate magnetic pickups which, rather than capturing sound, produce an electric current in response to the movement of metal strings within a magnetic field. The two main types of electric guitar pickup are known as *single-coil* and *humbucker* pickups respectively. In very general terms, the former produce a clean, crisp sound, while the

LEFT: *A combo (combination amplifier) has all the electronics contained in one unit, plus one or more loudspeakers. The Fender Concert amps were designed in the 1960s, and underwent a revival in the 1980s.*

latter produce a thicker tone with a higher output level that will result in more distortion at any given overdriven amp setting (see 'Amplifiers and other equipment'). As the pickups produce the sound in the first place, and are generally the only significant electrical components in the guitar, the choice of pickup type will be a crucial factor in your final decision about which guitar you choose.

ABOVE: *A humbucker (dual-coil) pickup. As the latter name suggests, these are easy to spot because they are twice the width of a single coil.*

ABOVE: *The simplest form of magnetic pickup is made from a single coil of copper wire that is wound around a row of six pole-pieces (one per string).*

ABOVE: *These 'bare knuckle' humbucker pickups are even more easily identified because the absence of a pickup cover clearly reveals the two sets of pole pieces.*

The four basic guitar types

While there are thousands of guitar makers, most electric guitars are more or less closely based on the pioneering designs of just two companies – Fender and Gibson – and these guitars are usually the most expensive. Roughly eight out of ten electric guitars in any music shop will, in spite of individual styling differences, be identifiable at a glance as belonging to one of four basic types. It is therefore a good idea to have some familiarity with these types before narrowing down your choice any further.

The Gibson Les Paul

Although its eponymous inventor was mainly a jazz player, the Gibson Les Paul guitar has earned its place as *the* rock guitar, particularly at the heavier end of the musical spectrum. The classic design incorporates two humbucker pickups and a fixed bridge, with a solid mahogany body and neck. Often paired with a Marshall valve amp (see 'Amplifiers and other equipment'), the Les Paul can produce a wide repertoire of sounds ranging from full, warm and slightly jazzy to cutting rock distortion. The original Les Paul is famous for its light weight – a real consideration for anyone susceptible to back pain – but this does not necessarily apply to other guitars based on the design.

Famous players
- Jimmy Page
- Slash
- Joe Perry
- Pete Townshend

The Fender Stratocaster

Developed a few years after the Telecaster, the Stratocaster (often abbreviated to 'Strat') incorporated several new design features, the most important being the tremolo arm and the addition of a third pickup. The latter greatly expands the range of available sounds. Many of the sounds that have come to be associated with this instrument are produced using one of the five-way pickup selector's 'in-between' positions, where two pickups are connected in reverse polarity, creating a 'hollow' sound. The tremolo arm (also known as a whammy bar, or vibrato arm) was intended as a mechanism for producing vibrato (rapid, decorative fluctuations in pitch), but is more often used to execute melodic bends.

Famous players
- Jimi Hendrix
- David Gilmour
- Stevie Ray Vaughn
- Ritchie Blackmore

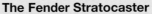

The Fender Telecaster

Fender's first electric guitar design was as starkly simple as it was revolutionary. It consisted of a solid wooden body, a bolt-on neck and two single-coil pickups (initially just one). Many of the sounds of which this guitar is capable are grouped together under the term 'twang'. The Telecaster is often associated with country music, but is also popular in blues and rock.

Famous players
- James Burton
- Keith Richards
- Roy Buchanan
- Jeff Buckley

The semi-acoustic guitar

Perennially popular with jazz players, semi-acoustic guitars come in a number of different flavours, and are suitable for almost any other musical style too. The hollow body imparts a warmth and fullness of tone, and this is usually reinforced by humbucker pickups. Unlike acoustic guitars, which have a round soundhole, semi-acoustics usually have f-holes on either side of the strings.

Famous players
- Larry Carlton
- Chuck Berry
- Paul Weller
- B.B. King

Amplifiers and other equipment

As the electric guitar makes almost no sound on its own, some form of amplification is essential; without it you will be unable to hear the results of your playing properly (and not even whether you are completely in tune), and will not develop full control of volume and tone. A few other items of equipment, such as multi-effect pedals, while not essential, can also be extremely versatile and useful.

Types of guitar amplifier

The guitar amplifier ('amp') can take many forms, from those designed to power headphones only to set-ups that will allow you to be heard in a vast stadium. While it is unlikely that you will need stadium-filling power just yet, you may well wish to invest in an amp loud enough to be heard in a band setting involving a drummer.

The simplest form of guitar amp is known as a combo, which is short for combination amplifier. This places all the necessary electronics in one unit, together with one or more loudspeakers.

The other common form of amplification is known as a stack. Here, the amplification circuitry is in a single unit, which is connected to one or more speaker cabinets. This makes it possible to create a far larger amp than could be feasibly carried in the form of a combo. For this reason stacks are not generally suitable for quiet practice at home!

There are several amplification solutions that are geared towards the home practice environment. Traditionally, the term 'practice amp' simply means a small, low-powered combo. For situations where even this would be too loud, some practice amps include a headphone output; dedicated headphone guitar amps dispense with speakers altogether.

Another option involves connecting your guitar to a computer using a dedicated interface. These are usually bundled with amp 'modelling' software, simulations of other hardware such as effects pedals (see below), and often a simple recording application is included.

This route is an easy way to try out a full palette of guitar sounds that would otherwise mean investing in many different amps and pedals. Of course, note that the output volume will only be as loud as your computer speakers (or headphones) can achieve.

LEFT: *A classic 1959 Marshall stack, which has a total of eight 12in speakers, when assembled.*

Valve versus transistor

In the formative years of electric guitar technology, all voltage-amplifying appliances were based on a component called the thermionic valve (also known as the vacuum tube). The advent of transistors (and, later, multiple miniaturized transistors on an integrated circuit or 'silicon chip') resulted in valves becoming redundant for most applications. However, many guitarists judged the transistor sound poor compared with valves, so many guitar amps still use valves, particularly at the professional end of the market. Valve amps are generally more expensive and require regular maintenance, however. Valves also generate a great deal of heat and are inherently fragile and sensitive to movement, particularly when hot.

For these reasons, a transistor amp is usually the most convenient option for the beginner, and in any case modern transistor amps usually sound pretty good. A third option is the modelling amp, which essentially contains computer

circuitry running modelling software as discussed above. This makes it possible to access emulations of many classic guitar amps (including valve amps) in one box.

LEFT: *The valve's size, fragility and heat production have meant that it has been almost totally replaced in the field of electronics by transistors and integrated circuits; guitar amplification is one of its last strongholds.*

Distortion and other effects

Amps were originally designed to amplify the guitar's sound without changing it. However, the technology available was generally less than perfect for this purpose, and guitarists began to notice that they liked the slight distortion that occurred if they pushed their amps to their upper volume limits. In response, designers began to investigate ways to increase the amount of distortion available, and also to achieve it at lower volumes. This gradually resulted in changes to the standard guitar amp design (so that distortion and overall volume could be controlled independently), and also in the development of external units designed to produce distortion or other sonic effects, which offer much greater flexibility and ease of use for live playing.

Pedal effects

Today, almost any sound that you might conceivably want to produce can be achieved using a combination of effects pedals. As the name suggests, these are small units that can be operated with the feet while playing. The following list includes some of the most important effects:

- Distortion/overdrive: allows access to different distortion sounds without changing amps.
- Delay/echo: adds one or more echoes to the source signal.
- Chorus: adds a sweeping, shimmering effect.
- Wah-wah: the name of this pedal describes perfectly the sound that is created.

ABOVE: *The wah-wah pedal alters the tone of a signal to create a distinctive effect that mimics the human voice.*

ABOVE: *A phaser pedal creates a slow, warm 'whoosh' sound which is a great effect if you want to create moody chords.*

ABOVE: *Chorus pedals are great for ballads and atmospherics.*

ABOVE: *A tremolo pedal creates rhythmic fluctuations in volume.*

ABOVE: *A digital delay pedal adds echoes at adjustable intervals.*

ABOVE: *The feedback loop creates the sound of on-stage feedback.*

ABOVE: *Compression pedals reduce dynamic range.*

ABOVE: *With digital distortion, extreme sonic effects can be made.*

ABOVE: *A genuine spring reverb unit, as found in vintage shops.*

ABOVE: *Multi-FX: Many types of effect are accessible here.*

ABOVE: *This type of pedal creates '60s psychedelic fuzz.*

ABOVE: *A type of basic fuzz found in classic '60s pedals.*

ABOVE: *A pedal that is popular in experimental electronic styles.*

ABOVE: *A bass distortion pedal can also be used with a guitar.*

Popular set-ups

If you have a guitar, an amplifier and various different accessories, these can be connected together in many different ways. Exactly how you connect your equipment depends on such factors as the musical style you want to adopt, the type of amplification chosen and whether you will be playing with a band or solo. The quality of the sound produced will also depend on a number of different factors.

The simplest set-up

The most basic guitar equipment set-up consists of a guitar and a combo amplifier connected by a cable (known as a jack cable, terminated by connectors called jack plugs). For many years, this was essentially all most players used; of course, the bigger the venue, the bigger the amp needed. Louder bands would tend to use stack amplifiers instead of combos, and many still do (see 'Amplifiers and other equipment').

In this case, the amp head and speaker cabinet are also usually connected with a jack cable. However, these two jack cables must not be mixed up, even though they may look the same from the outside. The cable between the guitar and amp (known generically as a signal cable or coaxial cable) is made from a central core that carries the signal with a braided outer copper shield to protect the core from radio interference. A speaker cable contains two thicker copper cores, much like a mains cable.

If you connect the guitar using speaker cable, it will work, but is likely to result in hum and other interference. Connecting the amp to the speaker using signal cable may also work, but the thinner copper may heat up under the higher power signal, and this could ultimately be a fire hazard.

If you plan to transport a stack to gigs or rehearsals, you may wish to label your speaker cable to avoid getting it confused with other jack cables.

ABOVE: *A basic guitar and amp set-up, which would allow you to get started.*

BELOW LEFT and RIGHT: *Signal cable (L) and speaker cable (R). Do not get these two mixed up.*

Between guitar and amp

A number of devices may be connected between the guitar and amp. The most obvious choice here, regardless of musical style, is a tuner in pedal form. This has no effect on the guitar signal when not in use, but when activated most models mute their output signal so that the guitar may be tuned silently using the visual display. This is of great benefit to the gigging guitarist, allowing discreet tuning between songs.

Other pedals can also be connected between the guitar and amp. Most effects will work here, including distortion (if your amp has none, or when you want to use other types of distortion), delay (echo) and chorus, which adds a silky, shimmering effect.

Some effects pedals do not always work well if they are connected between the guitar and amp. For example, the chorus effect will work provided a clean amp setting is used.

For chorus to work well with distortion, however, the distortion must occur before the signal reaches the chorus effect; the opposite sounds awful. This can of course be achieved by placing a distortion pedal before the chorus, but in order to use the amp's own distortion, a different solution is required.

Most guitar amplifiers have an *effects loop* (often labelled 'FX loop'): two sockets that enable external devices to be connected between the pre-amp (which produces the distortion) and the power amp (the part that does the actual 'heavy lifting', producing a signal powerful enough to drive a speaker). The FX loop output ('send') is connected to the input of the pedal; the pedal's output is connected to the FX loop input ('return'). Some pedals, including delay and wah-wah, may be placed either before the amp or in the loop, but with rather different results.

Pedalboards and multi-FX

If many effects pedals are to be used, these may be permanently connected together and fixed with Velcro to a rigid base known as a *pedalboard*. This may include a power supply – most pedals may be powered via a 9V DC supply instead of a battery. This has many advantages: the pedals are permanently connected together in a favoured configuration and there is no need to spend time changing batteries. However, pedalboard set-ups have their limitations: some songs may call for a different configuration and there is not usually time to make the necessary changes between songs.

A multi-FX unit, as its name suggests, incorporates many effects into one unit. In floorboard form, effects can to some extent be turned on and off using individual footswitches, but more importantly, programs can be created and accessed instantly, enabling the whole effects configuration to be changed instantly. Like individual effects pedals, multi-FX units may be placed either between the guitar and amp or in the FX loop, depending on the effects in use and whether the amp's own distortion is to be used.

Some of the more comprehensive multi-FX units, particularly those which include a pre-amp or distortion modelling, also have their own FX loops so that the most frequently used pedals may be switched in and out as required.

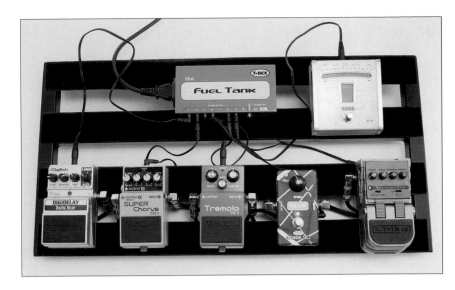

ABOVE: *When using several pedals, a pedalboard will help save time, batteries and frustration.*

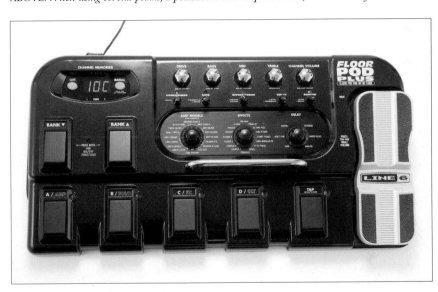

ABOVE: *A multi-FX unit allows many effects and functions to be accessed in pre-set configurations.*

Connection to a PA system

For large gigs, the electric guitar sound may need to be fed to the venue's own PA system. There are two principal ways to do this. The traditional method involves placing a microphone in front of the guitar amp. This guarantees that something close to the actual sound of the amp will be captured: guitar amps use speakers with a severely restricted frequency response – the opposite of hi-fi – which is a key part of the sound.

Some amps also feature speaker emulation: a circuit which emulates the response of a guitar speaker, allowing direct connection to a PA system. Without this, the output of a guitar amp will make an unpleasant sound when fed into PA speakers.

LEFT: *Although many sound engineers hang a microphone in front of the speaker, pointing down, a better sound is usually achieved by pointing the microphone towards the speaker.*

Anatomy of the electric guitar

All electric guitars share a great deal in common with the acoustic guitar, and also with one another, but different models also display considerable variations in design and inbuilt features. It is impossible to cover every feature that might be encountered on an electric guitar here; instead, let's take a close look at two of the most important archetypes to get a basic understanding of the anatomy of the electric guitar.

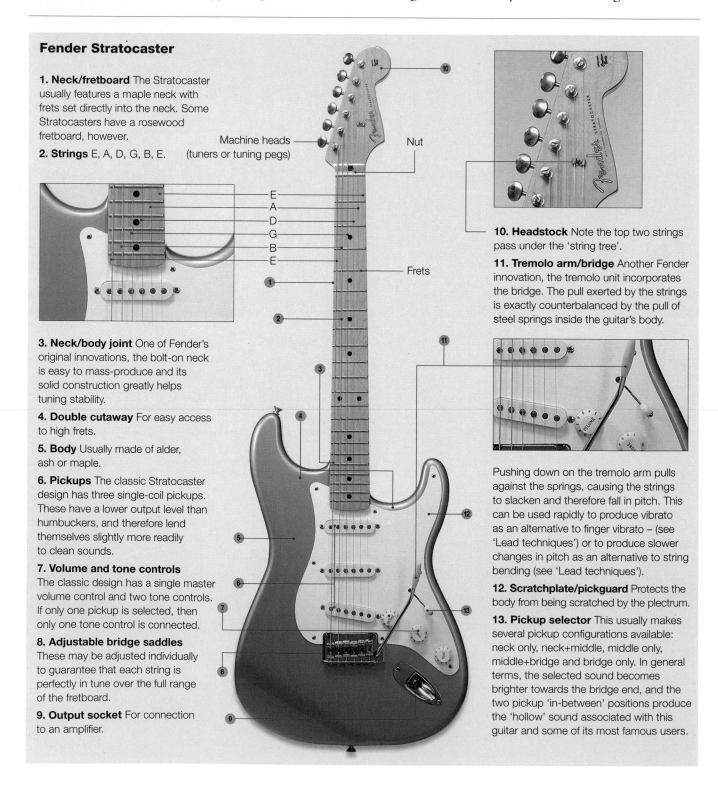

Fender Stratocaster

1. Neck/fretboard The Stratocaster usually features a maple neck with frets set directly into the neck. Some Stratocasters have a rosewood fretboard, however.

2. Strings E, A, D, G, B, E.

Machine heads (tuners or tuning pegs)

Nut

E
A
D
G
B
E

Frets

3. Neck/body joint One of Fender's original innovations, the bolt-on neck is easy to mass-produce and its solid construction greatly helps tuning stability.

4. Double cutaway For easy access to high frets.

5. Body Usually made of alder, ash or maple.

6. Pickups The classic Stratocaster design has three single-coil pickups. These have a lower output level than humbuckers, and therefore lend themselves slightly more readily to clean sounds.

7. Volume and tone controls The classic design has a single master volume control and two tone controls. If only one pickup is selected, then only one tone control is connected.

8. Adjustable bridge saddles These may be adjusted individually to guarantee that each string is perfectly in tune over the full range of the fretboard.

9. Output socket For connection to an amplifier.

10. Headstock Note the top two strings pass under the 'string tree'.

11. Tremolo arm/bridge Another Fender innovation, the tremolo unit incorporates the bridge. The pull exerted by the strings is exactly counterbalanced by the pull of steel springs inside the guitar's body.

Pushing down on the tremolo arm pulls against the springs, causing the strings to slacken and therefore fall in pitch. This can be used rapidly to produce vibrato as an alternative to finger vibrato – (see 'Lead techniques') or to produce slower changes in pitch as an alternative to string bending (see 'Lead techniques').

12. Scratchplate/pickguard Protects the body from being scratched by the plectrum.

13. Pickup selector This usually makes several pickup configurations available: neck only, neck+middle, middle only, middle+bridge and bridge only. In general terms, the selected sound becomes brighter towards the bridge end, and the two pickup 'in-between' positions produce the 'hollow' sound associated with this guitar and some of its most famous users.

Gibson Les Paul

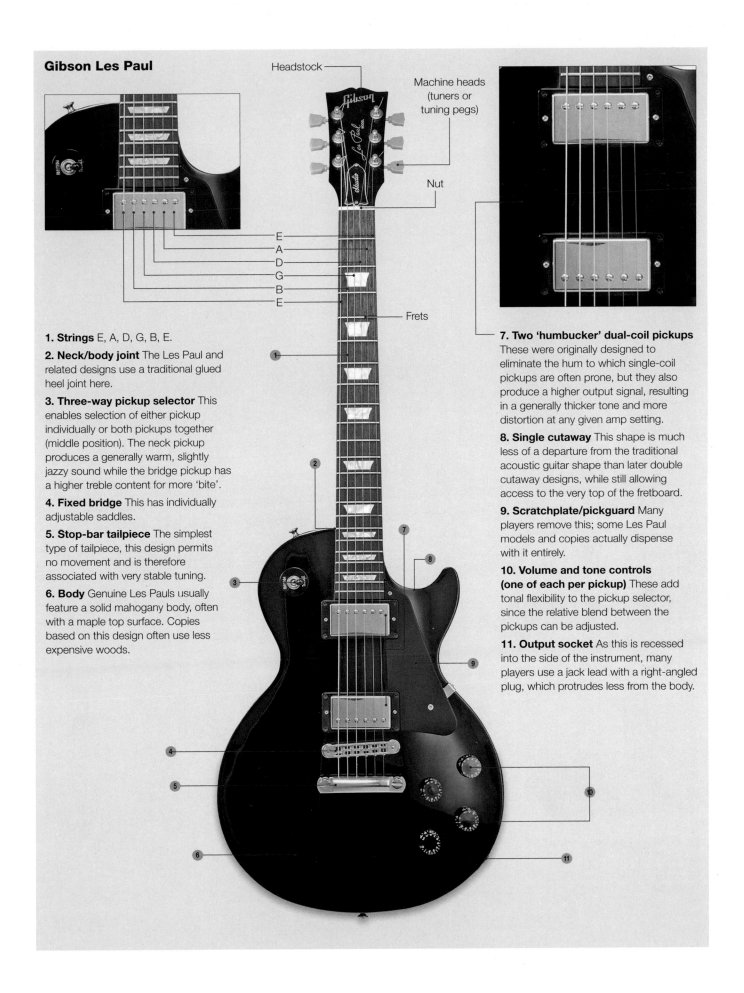

Headstock

Machine heads
(tuners or
tuning pegs)

Nut

E
A
D
G
B
E

Frets

1. Strings E, A, D, G, B, E.

2. Neck/body joint The Les Paul and related designs use a traditional glued heel joint here.

3. Three-way pickup selector This enables selection of either pickup individually or both pickups together (middle position). The neck pickup produces a generally warm, slightly jazzy sound while the bridge pickup has a higher treble content for more 'bite'.

4. Fixed bridge This has individually adjustable saddles.

5. Stop-bar tailpiece The simplest type of tailpiece, this design permits no movement and is therefore associated with very stable tuning.

6. Body Genuine Les Pauls usually feature a solid mahogany body, often with a maple top surface. Copies based on this design often use less expensive woods.

7. Two 'humbucker' dual-coil pickups These were originally designed to eliminate the hum to which single-coil pickups are often prone, but they also produce a higher output signal, resulting in a generally thicker tone and more distortion at any given amp setting.

8. Single cutaway This shape is much less of a departure from the traditional acoustic guitar shape than later double cutaway designs, while still allowing access to the very top of the fretboard.

9. Scratchplate/pickguard Many players remove this; some Les Paul models and copies actually dispense with it entirely.

10. Volume and tone controls (one of each per pickup) These add tonal flexibility to the pickup selector, since the relative blend between the pickups can be adjusted.

11. Output socket As this is recessed into the side of the instrument, many players use a jack lead with a right-angled plug, which protrudes less from the body.

From acoustic to electric

One of the great things about learning the electric guitar is that if you already play acoustic guitar to any level of proficiency, all of your skills can be transferred to the electric instrument. From the word go you will be making sounds that are not possible on an acoustic guitar. However, not all techniques can be transferred between instruments without an element of adaptation.

Similarities and differences

Like the acoustic guitar, the electric guitar has six strings, and the standard tuning is the same (E A D G B E). The fretboard is arranged in exactly the same way – one fret per semitone – so both chords and melodies can be transferred between instruments. There are various important differences, however. The electric guitar is usually equipped with much lighter strings, allowing techniques such as bends and vibrato (see 'Lead techniques') that are difficult, not to say impossible,

on an acoustic. The volume of sound that an electric guitar can produce ranges from silent to ear-splitting, depending on the amplifier and its volume setting. All this available volume means that the electric guitar can generally be played with a comparatively light touch: there is simply no need to play harder in order to be louder. Furthermore, as electronic amplification picks up on even the most minimal vibration in the strings, it allows for far greater sustain on notes that would soon become inaudible on an acoustic instrument.

Right-hand technique

Most fingerpicking techniques can be transferred to the electric guitar to some extent. However, the strings are usually set both closer together and closer to the body of the instrument, so plectrum technique tends to dominate. The electric guitar generally requires less physical exertion (due to amplification and because the strings are lighter), so wrist (not elbow) motion is used almost exclusively. To aid accuracy, the right hand may rest lightly on or around the bridge, but take care not to accidentally push down on the tremolo arm.

RIGHT: *The right hand may rest on or around the bridge for greater control, but it should not be anchored rigidly.*

The left hand

There is little difference in the basics of left-hand technique between acoustic and electric guitar. However, the lighter strings of the electric guitar not only permit techniques such as those mentioned above, but they are also easier to play in general terms. This means that barre chords, which often present difficulties for the novice acoustic player, are easier to hold down on the electric guitar.

Acoustic players rarely stray beyond the twelfth (sometimes fourteenth) fret, which is where the neck joins the body. Although there are higher frets, it is quite difficult to use them with any fluidity. The electric guitar fretboard, by contrast, is usually easily accessible right to the top of its range, enabling some very high notes to be played.

RIGHT: *On most electric guitars, the left hand may access the very top of the fretboard with comparative ease.*

Posture

Most electric guitars can be played while either sitting down or standing. A few body shapes (particularly futuristic shapes such as the Gibson Flying V and some of the even spikier designs popular with heavy metal players), however, tend to slide straight off the knee when the guitar is worn sitting. When standing, the strap should be adjusted so that the guitar is neither too high nor too low against the body. The best rule of thumb is this: when moving from a standing position to a seated position, the strap should not slacken noticeably, but nor should the guitar remain suspended far above the thigh.

It is often advisable to use a strap even when sitting. This will prevent a slippery guitar from sliding off your thigh (unconventional or spiky-shaped guitars are often impossible to play sitting down otherwise), and will also counteract any tendency to hunch forwards, which can be bad for your back.

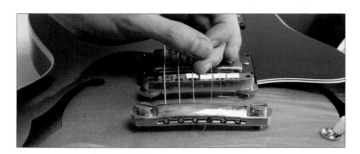

ABOVE: *A new string must be fed through the Gibson-style bridge from the far side.*

ABOVE: *With a 'strings-through-body' bridge design such as the Fender Telecaster's, new strings must be fed through the body first.*

Changing strings

At the headstock, the strings are fastened to machine heads that are very similar to those found on an acoustic guitar. The bridge end is slightly different, however, and not all electric guitars employ the same design. Broadly speaking, most Gibson guitars (and derivative designs) have a two-piece bridge/tailpiece; the strings are fastened at the tailpiece and then pass over the bridge. On most Fender-type guitars, the strings usually pass through the body and are held in place on the rear of the guitar, secured by recessed metal ferrules. In the case of Stratocaster-type guitars, the strings are held within the tremolo mechanism.

Protection

Changing strings is easiest with the guitar lying flat on a table. You may wish to place a soft cloth underneath, to avoid scratching the back of the instrument.

 Remove the old string.

2 Feed the new string through the bridge.

3 Leaving enough slack for the string to be wound around the machine head at least 3-4 times, feed the string through the machine head and make a kink in the string on the other side (the treble strings may be looped through again for greater friction and extra stability).

4 Turn the machine head, slowly at first, to wind the string on to the roller. Carefully trim the excess string with pliers.

Introducing lead guitar

The guitar can make a huge variety of sounds, either when accompanying the voice or when played as a solo instrument. It can move from quietly strummed chords to screaming distorted solos. The term *lead guitar* is usually associated with the electric instrument, and it means that, in contrast to the *rhythm guitar*, the guitar is in the foreground and playing single-note melodies.

Getting started

Melodies can of course be played on the acoustic guitar, but the electric guitar can more easily be thrust into the musical foreground by virtue both of the greater available volume and the range of sounds available.

The problem facing the aspiring lead guitarist may be: where do I start? Many lead guitar styles require mastery of a number of specific techniques, including string bending, vibrato, slides, right-hand tapping, manipulation of distortion and use of the tremolo arm. However, as with most other aspects of guitar playing, paying attention to some fundamentals will bring rewards later, so we shall concentrate on these first.

Alternate picking

Efficient use of the right hand is the key to progress from the simplest melodies to more advanced playing. The right hand usually employs a technique known as alternate picking. This involves the use of down- and up-strokes according to the basic rhythmic subdivisions of the material. For example, if the melody contains few or no notes shorter than quavers (half a beat in $\frac{4}{4}$), it makes sense to alternate between down- and up-strokes at the rate of once per quaver, in other words: down-strokes on the beat (every other quaver) and up-strokes on the offbeat (the quavers in between). As with syncopated strumming patterns, this rule should be preserved even when the melodic material does not simply consist of alternating quavers. For example, if two consecutive notes are offbeats, both should be played using up-strokes. This requires a 'phantom' down-stroke in between – the plectrum moves downwards but does not actually strike the string.

ABOVE: *Alternate picking involves continuous down- and up-strokes of the hand. An up-beat such as an even-numbered eighth note or, at faster tempos, sixteenth note, will always be played with an upward picking stroke, while the down-beats are always played with downward picking strokes.*

ABOVE RIGHT: *Using alternate picking will help you progress to higher levels of playing.*

EXERCISE 1

This exercise consists of a simple melody in G major in continuous quavers. Down-strokes and up-strokes should be alternated strictly: down-strokes on the beat, up-strokes on the offbeat.

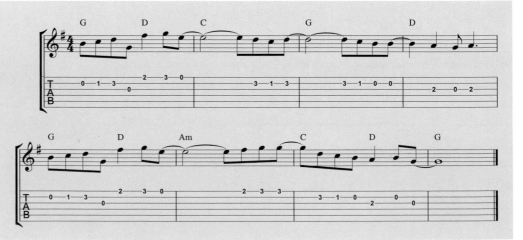

Choosing a sound

Using a guitar amplifier's clean channel or setting will result in an amplified sound somewhat similar to that of an acoustic guitar. However, this is only one possibility among a myriad of styles that are offered by electric guitar amplification. Many can be played using some distortion; some styles positively demand it in large amounts. Adding distortion (either by turning up the amplifier's gain control, switching to the distortion channel or connecting a distortion pedal) can make the guitar sound completely different. Try all of the exercises here first using a clean sound, and then try increasing the amounts of distortion.

Distortion does many things to the guitar sound. For one thing, the guitar becomes much more sensitive, so that the slightest unintended noise is often much more noticeable than it would be with a clean sound. Playing with distortion can therefore require smaller, more careful right-hand movements, and can also benefit from minimal use of

right-hand palm muting – in which the side of the right hand rests across the bridge, just touching the strings. This prevents open strings from ringing unintentionally. For more on the creative use of palm muting, see 'Rock rhythm guitar'.

ABOVE: *Careful use of palm muting can help to keep your sound under control when using distortion, but be careful not to choke off the sound altogether.*

Setting up a distortion sound and level matching with clean sound

1 Assuming you have a basic working sound on the clean channel which you are happy with, select the overdrive channel, either using a button on the front panel or with the footswitch.

2 Raise the gain control for the overdrive channel until you have the amount of overdrive/distortion desired. Don't worry if this also raises the volume to an alarming level – this will be corrected in the next step.

3 Now reduce the channel volume as necessary until the distortion volume matches the clean volume, and check this by flipping between channels.

EXERCISE 2

This exercise is another melody in G major. For any melodic exercise, the melody will be most effective if heard against the chord sequence – try recording yourself playing some chords, and then play the melody. If any chords here are unfamiliar to you, they can be found in 'Rock chord vocabulary'.

Lead techniques

The electric guitar has lighter (thinner) strings than the acoustic instrument, and therefore lends itself to certain playing techniques that are more difficult, or impossible, with heavier strings. The most important among these are string bends and vibrato; the latter is best approached having learnt the basics of string bending. It is a technique that requires some practice to be mastered properly.

Bends

The defining feature of the techniques we will consider here is that a guitar string may be stretched out of position while a note is sounding. Crucially, finger pressure must be maintained so that the string continues to vibrate. The string must therefore keep contact with the fret; the fretting finger pulls or pushes the string parallel with the fretboard. In this simple form, the technique is known as *string bending*.

Bending the string has the effect of raising its pitch to produce a higher note. The available range (how high the pitch may be raised) is limited by several factors: the gauge (thickness) of the string, the location of the fretted note on the fretboard and the player's finger strength. The most obvious point is that heavier (thicker) strings need to be stretched to a higher tension than lighter strings to produce a given pitch, and will therefore require greater finger strength to produce a bend. For this reason, string bending is much harder on the acoustic guitar than on the electric. Even on electric guitar, beginners often choose lighter strings in order to facilitate easier bending.

Although some players are renowned for their ability to produce much larger bends, the most common bends in use are known as whole-tone and semitone bends: the fretted note is bent upwards by either a whole tone or a semitone.

Because the pitch produced by string bending can be varied continuously, it is very easy to produce notes that are not in tune. In most styles, however, the aim is to reach a target pitch that is in tune – in other words the same pitch as a higher fretted note on the guitar. While perfecting this technique, you may wish to play the target note for reference first, so that you can hold this note in your head while producing the bend. For a whole-tone bend, the target note can be found

two frets above the note to be bent (on the same string). For a semitone bend, the target note is just one fret higher. In the step-by-step example opposite, the target note E can also be found on the open top E string.

On four of the guitar's six strings, bends can be produced by either physically pushing or pulling the string; most players use a combination of both techniques in different situations, so it is a good idea to practise both. The outer strings, however, can only be bent inwards (towards the centre of the fretboard). In practice, the A and B strings also tend to be bent inwards as there is no risk of coming off the fretboard.

Of course, regardless of the physical direction, the string's pitch will always be shifted upward.

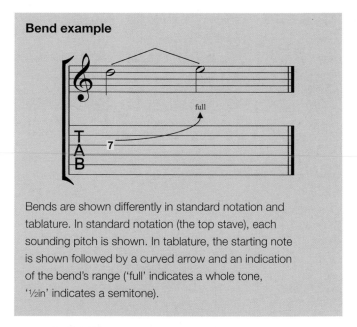

Bend example

Bends are shown differently in standard notation and tablature. In standard notation (the top stave), each sounding pitch is shown. In tablature, the starting note is shown followed by a curved arrow and an indication of the bend's range ('full' indicates a whole tone, '½in' indicates a semitone).

 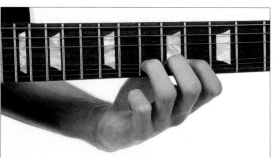

FAR LEFT and LEFT: *The middle D and G strings can be bent in either direction physically, but in both cases the fretted note is raised in pitch.*

Executing a whole-tone bend on the G string

1 Fret the note D on the G string, seventh fret, using the third finger. Add the first and second fingers for extra strength at the fifth and sixth frets respectively. Pick the G string to produce the note D.

2 Push the string vertically upwards, maintaining pressure. The pitch of the resulting note should rise gradually. In this example, the target pitch is reached when the string produces the note E.

3 To ensure you are correctly executing a whole-tone bend, play your target note and compare the pitch with your bent note. The two should sound the same.

Vibrato

This term describes an effect produced by rapid fluctuations in pitch. If you are unsure what this effect sounds like, the one place you are absolutely sure to find copious amounts of vibrato is in opera – the singer's characteristic 'warble' is an example of vibrato. Vibrato is also used liberally in many lead guitar styles, most obviously in heavy metal.

Most instruments capable of continuous pitch variation can produce vibrato; most classical string players rarely play a note without it. Vibrato on a fretless stringed instrument is relatively easy: the finger is simply moved rapidly up and down, in line with the string. On the guitar and other fretted instruments, note pitch is determined by the placement of the frets. Vibrato is therefore a little harder to produce, and effectively involves many string bends in rapid succession. The actual range of these bends is usually small – rapid whole-tone bends are difficult to produce and would in any case sound rather extreme.

Vibrato is shown in both standard notation and tablature by the use of a simple wavy horizontal line.

EXERCISE 1

This exercise involves a number of whole-tone and semitone bends on the G and B strings. To help keep each note in tune, this example involves playing a fretted target note first in each case. Keep this note in your head as you execute the bend.

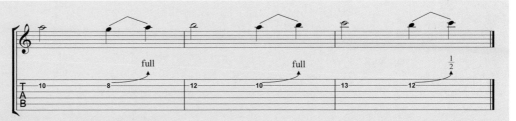

EXERCISE 2

This simple melodic exercise uses a combination of bends and vibrato.

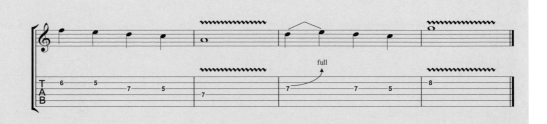

Electric blues guitar

Some styles of music are inextricably associated with a particular instrument, and vice versa. The blues and the guitar form one such close marriage. Although the roots of the blues lead back to the acoustic guitar, the electric guitar has dominated the blues for many years: it's a perfect fit. Furthermore, without the forerunner of electric-blues, there would be no rock 'n' roll.

Blues lead guitar

Whether accompanying the voice or another instrument, or taking centre stage and playing solo, the electric guitar is versatile enough to fulfl a number of roles. It also boasts the great virtue of easy portability. Combined with a modern guitar amplifier that can produce a range of sounds from clean to full distortion, the guitar's expressive possibilities within the blues are almost limitless. There are many possible starting points for learning to play the blues. One of these is the blues scale. This is actually just a handy simplification to describe a few different notes – many other notes are also used all the time by blues players – but nonetheless the scale provides a convenient set of notes that will work successfully in any blues context.

The commonest blues scale combines the most important notes of the key (steps one, four and five of the major scale) with the three characteristically 'blue' notes in the same key: the flattened third, the flattened fifth and the flattened seventh.

The blues bend

'Blue notes' are central to the blues. These notes produce an unresolved, yearning tension. However, analyzing the work of great blues players reveals that some blue notes belong neither to the major scale, nor to the blues scale, but actually somewhere in between. These notes are produced by bending the strings by an interval smaller than a semitone. This type of bend is known as either a blues bend or a quartertone bend.

This interval is an approximation, however – blues bends are produced by ear. The flattened third of the blues scale is often bent upwards by about a quartertone to produce a note somewhere between the flattened third and the major third. In the most popular position/shape for the blues scale (below), one of the flattened thirds is played by the index finger on the G string. Other fingers do not support it, but the blues bend is still easy to do as the interval is very small.

RIGHT: *The blues scale in C, covering two octaves. As the key of C major has no sharps or flats, the blue notes are easy to spot in this key: they are the notes preceded by accidentals (sharp or flat symbols). The shape shown here is often known as the basic blues scale shape, or 'position one'.*

The blues bend: notation

To show a blues bend in standard notation, a curved line is used rather than a specific target pitch. In tablature, '¼' indicates a quartertone bend, although this is usually an approximation.

RIGHT: *If asked to list names of the most important guitarists in the history of the blues, few contemporary players would omit the name of John Lee Hooker, whose 'talking blues' style fused the traditional Delta blues with a more free-form style of delivery where the twelve-bar structure was interpreted rather loosely.*

More bends

Standard whole-tone and semitone bends are used almost constantly in the electric blues. This enables fluid movement between steps of the blues scale. Notes occurring on the G and B strings are particularly suitable for this treatment: the fourth may be bent upwards by either a semitone to the flattened fifth or a whole tone to the fifth. The flattened seventh is frequently bent upwards by a whole tone to the tonic (key) note.

Although strictly speaking it is only possible to bend strings upwards, it is possible to produce the effect of a downward bend by bending the string *before* playing the note. The bend is then released as the note is played. This type of bend is known as a *pre-bend*. In another version, the fretted note is played first, but bent upwards very rapidly. The bent note may then be held, or released as with a pre-bend. This rapid bend is usually known as a *grace-note bend*.

Example of more bends

In the first bar of this example, the note B♭ is bent upwards by a whole tone to C before being released. In the second bar, a rapid grace-note bend is executed on the same note, which is then released. The tablature here gives a very useful graphical representation of these bends.

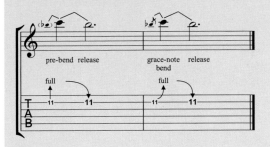

EXERCISE 1

This simple blues tune uses the blues scale in C in eighth position as shown left; a simple repetitive riff is flavoured with blues bends.

Playing tip

The blues bend does not arrive at a precisely defined pitch, and in fact repeated blues bends, as shown in this exercise, do not have to reach the same pitch. In particular, the second bend on each C7 may be bent higher than the first to musical effect.

EXERCISE 2

This blues tune uses pre-bends and grace-note bends to join up the notes of the blues scale.

Playing tip

To improve your melodic awareness, try playing this exercise without bends (using fretted notes to find the pitches reached by the bends here).

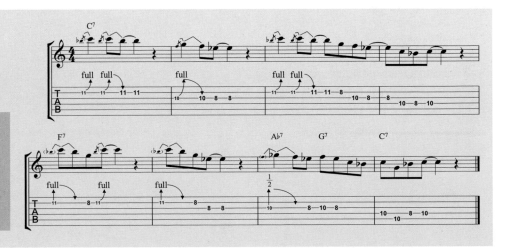

Rhythm guitar styles

The term 'rhythm guitar' refers to the guitar in a supportive role, when it is accompanying vocals or a melody instrument. This can take many different forms, from simple strumming to ringing arpeggios, and many points in between. When the sonic capabilities of amplification, such as distortion, are added, the electric guitar becomes a highly versatile instrument of accompaniment.

Strumming and chugging

Electric strumming works in much the same way as it does on the acoustic guitar, except that much smaller movements are usually involved – it is the amplifier that does the work of producing volume. Therefore the right hand usually pivots at the wrist rather than at the elbow.

If you explore the continuum of amplified sounds available, from completely clean to heavily distorted, you will notice that distortion does not generally lend itself to complex chords: the sound can easily become congested and the notes of the chord seem to be fighting one another. As a very general rule, therefore, the more distortion that is applied, the simpler the chords need to be. Using barre chords based on E and A shapes (see 'Rock chord vocabulary'), or the first position E and A chords themselves, the easiest way to simplify a chord so that it will work with heavy distortion is to play only the lower two or three strings. This way only the root and fifth of the chord are present, leaving out the major or minor third (it is this third note that causes congestion with heavy distortion). The resulting shapes are known as power chords (see 'Power chords' for more on these.)

Power chords (with or without distortion) are often played using a simple quaver rhythm (half a beat each). For consistency, this usually involves down-strokes only, and often some degree of palm muting. This technique is often known as *chugging*.

LEFT: *While the right hand often rests on the bridge or body of the guitar for picking work, a greater range of movement may be required for more energetic rhythm work.*

Pickup effects

For rhythm playing using full barre chords or power chords, try to listen to the different sonic effects that can be produced by alternative choices of pickup. As with so much else, experimentation is the best way forward in achieving the optimum possible sound.

EXERCISE 1

This exercise treats the same simple chord sequence in two contrasting ways. Firstly it uses strumming, alternating up- (∨) and down- (⊓) strokes. The second line applies the chugging rhythm style to the same sequence, using the lower two strings of each shape and down-strokes only. To play this as a continuous exercise, either a clean sound or very slight distortion ('crunch') will produce the best result.

Mark Knopfler

After a period dominated by synth-driven pop, the release of Dire Straits' album *Brothers In Arms* in 1985 brought Mark Knopfler's sensitive blend of blues, rockabilly, folk and jazz influences to an enormous audience: the album was the first million-seller on CD and still remains one of the best-selling albums of all time. Knopfler's signature sound is achieved using an alternating thumb/finger action; the album's quieter moments also showcased his slide playing abilities and the use of the distinctive Dobro sound). Then there was the overdrive sound used on the track "Money For Nothing", which was achieved purely by accident in the studio. Few players have even come close to replicating it, though not for want of trying.

ABOVE: *Dire Straits' best-selling album* Brothers in Arms *opened the collective eyes of a generation of budding guitarists to a world of possibilities beyond straightforward rock guitar and plectrum technique.*

Arpeggio patterns

Playing the notes of a chord in succession produces an *arpeggio*. This can take various forms; for rhythm guitar, each note is allowed to ring for as long as possible while the other notes of the chord are played. Chords played in this way are sometimes known as *broken chords*. While some electric players, along with most acoustic players, adopt the fingerstyle technique using the thumb and fingers separately, most electric players play all notes with the plectrum. It is important not to mute ringing notes accidentally with the flesh of the right hand.

As with lead playing and many strumming styles, broken chords are usually produced using alternate picking: down-strokes on the beat, up-strokes on the offbeat.

Chop!

When playing with a band, it is often necessary to leave some space for other instruments. Many musical styles employ short, sharp guitar 'chops' either on each beat, or more often on alternate beats.

These are produced using *left-hand muting*. Shortly after playing the chord, the left-hand finger pressure is released, which immediately silences the chord. This assumes that the notes of the chords are all fretted rather than being on open strings; for this reason, barre chords lend themselves particularly well to this technique. Sometimes the opposite effect can work better (avoid playing at all on beats 2 and 4, leaving a gap for the snare drum to 'punch through').

EXERCISE 2

In this exercise, a broken chord picking pattern is applied to the previous chord sequence. Remember to alternate down-/up-strokes throughout as shown in the first bar. Very slight distortion will work well here, as will modulation effects such as chorus (see 'Amplifiers and other equipment').

EXERCISE 3

Here, muted 'chops' are applied to the same chord sequence. However, the first position shapes used above will not work with left-hand muting, so barre chords are used. For simplicity, the E shape is barred at the fifth, tenth and twelfth frets, producing the chords A, D and E respectively.

Rock chord vocabulary

There are thousands of possible chords available, but rock and pop music often uses only a handful of well-loved chord shapes. It's worth making sure at this point that you are familiar with all the standard major and minor shapes in first position, as well as the basics of movable barre chord construction. These items of knowledge, taken together, will take you a very long way as a rock rhythm guitarist.

First position 'open' chords

Many classic rock songs and riffs are built around chords with open strings. These can deliver a chiming sound that works well with a clean, or moderately distorted (crunch), sound. There are ten basic first position major and minor chords. In constant use in their own right, they also form the basis for many other common chords on the fretboard, whether you move them up the neck as barre chords (see opposite) or against open strings for a variety of effects.

RIGHT: *A chord involves playing more than two notes at a time. Open chords are usually played using the first three frets of the guitar and involve at least one open string. Here are eight crucial shapes in first position.*

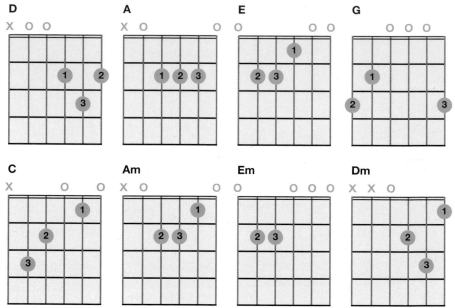

Thumb muting and thumb chords

When playing the electric or acoustic guitar, the left-hand thumb normally stays somewhere behind the neck; indeed classical-guitar teachers generally maintain that it should never move from this position.

Rock players often use the thumb in more creative ways, however. In many chords, for example D and A, one or more of the bass strings is not played (for example, the note E does not belong to the D chord; an 'X' is therefore placed over the bottom string to show that it is not played).

While it is certainly possible, at least with gentle strumming or fingerpicking styles, simply to avoid these strings using careful right-hand control, this becomes more difficult with more energetic playing styles, so many players use the left-hand thumb to mute the bottom strings when playing shapes where the bass note is not on the bottom E string, such as D, A or C.

RIGHT: *The left-hand thumb muting the bottom strings when playing the D major chord. The thumb should exert enough pressure to mute the strings but not so much that a note is produced.*

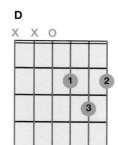

In certain situations, the thumb can also be used to form part of a chord shape. A favourite trick of many rock players involves using the thumb to fret the second fret of the bottom E string (rather than merely muting it). This note is an F♯, which, unlike the open E, is present in the D chord. The resulting chord is known as D/F♯ ('D over F sharp'). This type of chord is known as an inversion (meaning that a chord note other than the root is used as the bass note). Inversions have many uses, including 'joining up' other chords in a sequence. A favourite use of D/F♯ is between the chords G and Em, producing a descending bass line.

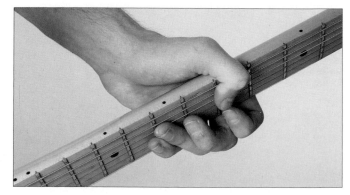

Barre chords

An important part of every rock guitarist's vocabulary, barre chords are essentially moveable versions of the first-position chords. The index finger is placed across all six strings at once at a given fret, effectively raising the pitch of the open strings correspondingly. The remaining fingers are then used to make a chord shape relative to the index finger. The chords E, A, Em and Am are the easiest shapes to turn into barre chords. For example, raising the pitch of the Em chord by one fret in this way results in the chord of Fm (one fret equals one semitone).

The A chord itself can be a little tricky to form, as three fingers have to be crammed into the same fret space on adjacent strings, and this gets even harder further up the neck where the frets are closer together.

Many players apply a different solution to produce an A-shape barre chord: the third finger can make a partial barre across the D, G and B strings. If you have exceptionally flexible fingers, you may be able to form this partial barre in such a way that the top E string is not touched. Most players simply leave out the top E string with this shape, however, or rather it is effectively muted.

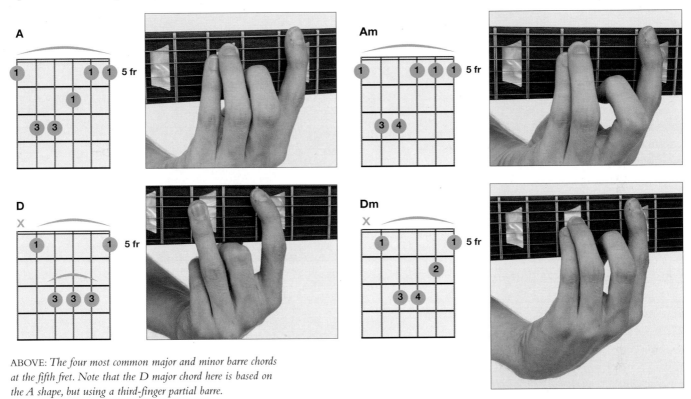

ABOVE: *The four most common major and minor barre chords at the fifth fret. Note that the D major chord here is based on the A shape, but using a third-finger partial barre.*

Slash

To many aficionados Slash emerged in the 1980s as the last great original rock guitarist. At the same time, his style is obviously steeped in the blues–rock tradition, and is particularly indebted to a handful of influences, including Jimmy Page and Aerosmith's Joe Perry. Guns N' Roses' *Appetite For Destruction* is the best-selling debut album of all time, and it produced a string of huge international hits, all powered by Slash's infectious guitar riffs and blistering solos. At a time when many of rock's 'dinosaurs' were moving in a heavily produced pop direction, Guns N' Roses insisted that rock 'n' roll should be faithful to its blues roots, and raw, loud and gutsy. Most of Slash's guitar sounds are produced using little more than a Gibson Les Paul and a Marshall amplifier; a few tracks used wah-wah more effectively than anyone since Jimi Hendrix.

ABOVE: *Continuing the tradition established by The Rolling Stones and Aerosmith, with songs such as "Satisfaction" and "Walk This Way", many of Guns N' Roses' most famous songs are powered by a simple but highly memorable riff or melodic guitar motif.*

Rock 'n' roll

In the 1950s, rock 'n' roll was the blues-based music that swept the world. It has had a direct effect on almost all popular music produced since that time, and it remains inextricably linked with the electric guitar. Rock 'n' roll idols such as Elvis Presley and Buddy Holly inspired a generation of teenagers to learn the guitar, among them future members of influential groups such as The Beatles and The Rolling Stones.

The birth of lead guitar

Rock 'n' roll established the standard lineup for a rock band that has endured to this day: drums, bass, rhythm guitar, lead guitar and vocals. While the rhythm guitarist provides a chordal accompaniment, the lead player plays melodic material in counterpoint to the vocals, as well as frequently taking centre stage for guitar solos and other instrumental passages, resulting in a sense of musical and sparring between the vocalist and lead guitarist (unless they are the same person).

A few guitar techniques crop up over and again in 1950s rock 'n' roll, in particular bends (see 'Lead techniques'), double stopping, hammer-ons and trills.

Double stopping

The technique of 'double stopping', often used on stringed instruments, could be more accurately termed 'double fretting' when applied to the guitar. The technique simply involves melodic playing using two notes simultaneously. On the electric guitar, each pair of notes usually appears on adjacent strings, as this is easier to play with a plectrum and allows easy access to harmonically effective intervals such as thirds and fourths.

LEFT: *A double-stopped fourth on the B and E strings at the fifth fret. Double stops at the same fret are usually played using one finger. Rather than a full barre, this involves using just the top section of the finger (from the tip to the first joint).*

Hammer-on, trill and blues content

As its name implies, this technique involves the use of left-hand fingers 'hammering' on to the strings to produce notes. The classic hammer-on involves first playing a note using the plectrum and then hammering on to the string at a higher fret to produce the next note. This is shown in the notation by using a curved line (slur) between the two notes.

A trill is a rapid alternation between two notes, usually adjacent notes within the key of the piece. On the guitar, trills are executed using alternating hammer-ons and pull-offs.

For a typical trill, the first note is fretted with the first finger and played using the plectrum. The second or third finger then hammers rapidly on and off the string.

A great many rock 'n' roll songs follow the twelve-bar blues structure; early rock 'n' roll was essentially a highly energized form of blues. Most guitar solos in this style are constructed using the blues scale, although the flattened third of the blues scale is often 'softened' by resolving up one semitone to the major third of the key. This occurs frequently in the exercise shown on the opposite page.

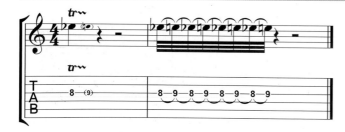

ABOVE: *A typical 'bluesy' trill on the G string. In the key of C, this is a trill between the flattened third of the blues scale (Eb) and the major third (E). The first bar here shows one form of trill notation; the second bar gives an approximation of the actual notes played (although many players find it difficult to get this many notes into one beat).*

Sound and the volume control

Rock 'n' roll evolved in the heyday of the valve amp. When cranked up loud, these produced slight, subtle distortion as a by-product of their design. Deliberate, full distortion only became popular in later years. This slight distortion is called *crunch*. Some amps have a dedicated crunch channel; some effects pedals also produce it. The guitar's volume control can be used to control distortion, as it affects the level of signal going *to* the amp. Reducing the guitar's volume will make any distortion sound cleaner before it affects overall volume.

Executing a simple double-stopped motif

Many double-stopped melodic ideas are constructed by harmonizing the major scale in thirds. While learning the whole scale like this is ultimately desirable, the first three steps, as shown here, provide a useful start.

1 This simple double-stopped figure is in the key of A major and uses the G and B strings. First, play the notes A and C# using the first finger at the second fret.

2 Now play the notes B and D using the third and second fingers respectively at the fourth and third frets.

3 Now you can slide this shape up two frets so that you can play the notes C# and E.

Chuck Berry

John Lennon said, "If you tried to give rock 'n' roll another name, you might call it 'Chuck Berry'." Many people have been held up as 'the inventor' of rock 'n' roll. In reality, there is no such single person, but of all the contenders Chuck Berry probably has had the greatest influence on the archetypal rock 'n' roll song form and orchestration, from the intro (lead guitar instrumental) to the rhythm pattern (the 'Chuck Berry Shuffle') and the guitar solo (occurring after the second chorus and usually echoing the intro figure). Chuck Berry's best-known songs ("Johnny B. Goode", "Roll Over Beethoven", "Sweet Little Sixteen" and many more) have become standards. They have been learned and performed by legions of aspiring rock guitarists and bands, from The Beatles and The Rolling Stones to Aerosmith and Van Halen.

RIGHT: *Chuck Berry is considered one of the pioneers of rock 'n' roll music, making the sound distinctive as well as developing the music and attitude associated with it.*

EXERCISE 1

Many rock 'n' roll intros move once through the twelve-bar structure. This is a typical example of an intro which uses both double stopping and hammer-ons. As a general rule, alternate picking should be used for this type of playing, although repeated double-stopped quavers may be played with down-strokes only to provide added energy.

Power chords

The term 'power chord' can mean slightly different things to different players. The central concept, however, is that complex chords often do not sound good when played with heavy distortion. In most rock music, the heavier the guitar sound in use, the more likely it is that guitar chords will contain a major or minor third, and more likely still that they will not contain other notes such as the seventh.

Root and fifth

Paring any chord down to two notes guarantees that the result will sound good even with heavy distortion (this is because distortion introduces additional harmonic content to the guitar sound which can easily clash with other chord notes). The resulting shape also falls very easily under the fingers and is very easy to move around the neck.

This type of power chord is usually built from a root note played by the first finger on the bottom E or A string.

The fifth is added using the third finger, two frets higher on the next string. For a thicker sound, the octave (the root note again, but one octave higher) may be added using the fourth finger. These chords are usually notated using a chord symbol comprising the root note and the number 5, for example 'G5'.

BELOW: *Root/fifth and root/fifth/octave power chords. Take care not to let the remaining strings sound: this will usually result in unmusical harmonic clashes. Many players mute unwanted strings with the side of the index finger.*

Root/Fifth A⁵

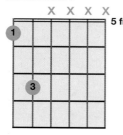
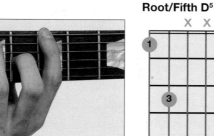

Root/Fifth D⁵

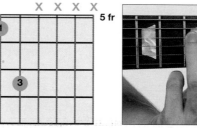

Root/Fifth Octave A⁵

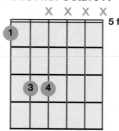

Root/Fifth Octave D⁵

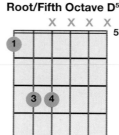

EXERCISE 1

This exercise uses simple root/fifth power chords to outline a common rock-chord sequence. Although the guitar chords themselves are neither major nor minor in this exercise, the internal relationships between them place the sequence in the key of G; G5, C5 and D5 here all imply major chords, while E5 implies Em.

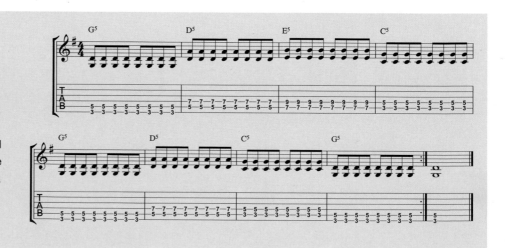

'Open' power chords

It is possible to find chords with only the root and fifth using one or more open strings. The basic fretted power-chord shapes (left) translate directly into simple E5 and A5 shapes when the root note is located on the open E or A strings. The root may also be located on the open D string: this D5 shape is essentially a standard D chord but without the top note (F#). The use of open strings also allows the construction of power chords containing several instances of both the root and fifth. These shapes sound uniquely 'ringy' and form an important part of the repertoire of many of the biggest names in rock guitar including Pete Townshend and Angus Young.

BELOW: *Open E, A and D power chords. Many rock classics have been written in keys that take advantage of these shapes.*

BELOW: *'Ringy-power' chord shapes. Note that the G5 shape here does not contain a fretted note on the A string. This string should instead be muted using the side of the index finger as it frets the bottom E string.*

Open E⁵

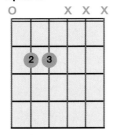

Open A⁵

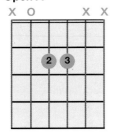

Open D⁵

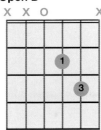

Ringy power G⁵

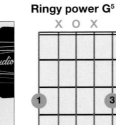

Ringy power E⁵

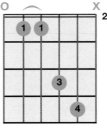

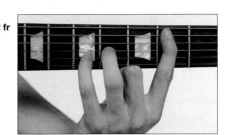

Ringy power A⁵

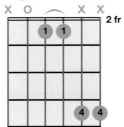

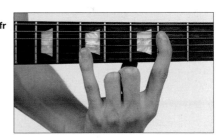

EXERCISE 2

This exercise uses a combination of both open and fretted power chords. For a varied texture, try using light palm muting for the lower strings of the 'open' power chords; release the palm muting to play the upper strings and let the chord ring.

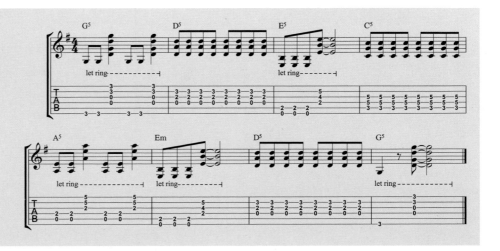

Rock rhythm guitar

The rhythm guitarist performs a crucial role in rock music. Unlike the lead player, who sometimes seems to have the luxury of playing when he likes, the rhythm player usually has to keep going consistently throughout a song. Rhythm guitar need not be boring, however: many great rock songs are built on a simple, distinctive rhythm guitar figure, from "Alright Now" to Paolo Nutini's "Jenny Don't Be Hasty".

Make it interesting

While the rhythm player may just strum simple chords, rock players often add just enough melodic interest to bring their part out of the shadows, but not so much as to dominate the arrangement. As we have seen, guitar-driven songs are often written in keys that make use of first-position 'open' chords and power chords. There are several reasons for this, one of which is that such chords can easily be 'joined up' using melodic ideas on the bass strings. For general-purpose rhythm guitar, however, the emphasis should generally be on the chords; if the melodic content takes over, the result is known as a riff (see 'Riffs').

Palm muting

One way to create a rhythm part which is rhythmically busy and yet does not distract too much from other instruments is to use palm muting. This involves resting the fleshy part of the right hand over the bridge to mute the strings slightly.

For effective palm muting, the side of the hand must cover the strings at the bridge very lightly and in exactly the right spot. The aim is to be able to play notes that decay very quickly and sound more percussive than ordinary picking, and yet which still have identifiable pitches. If too much pressure is applied, or the hand is placed too far along the vibrating length of the string, the note will be 'killed' altogether, causing a dull sound with no identifiable pitch. It is equally easy to create insufficient muting if the flesh of the hand works on the wrong side of the bridge. The range of sounds available via small changes in right-hand position can be used to great effect. In many muted rhythm-guitar parts (such as Exercise 2, right), strong accents may be produced by releasing the muting action to allow certain notes/chords to sound fully. Palm muting is usually shown with the indication 'P.M.' placed between the notation and tablature staves.

BELOW: *It is important to find the right hand position for palm muting. These photographs show the hand too far back; in the correct position; and too far forward. The only way to get to grips with this technique is to experiment and, above all, listen to the resulting sound.*

EXERCISE 1

The rhythm pattern here uses four power chords connected together using a simple stepwise movement on the bass strings. A rather subtle difference can be achieved by using either alternating down-/up-strokes or constant down-strokes – try both.

Angus Young

While other heavy rock bands have woven a range of new
influences into rock music, from Middle-Eastern tonality to
jazz harmony, by contrast the Australian rock band AC/DC
remained doggedly faithful to the original ingredients of
rock 'n' roll (which is indeed exactly how they prefer to describe
their music): blues-based, three-chord songs backed by
two guitars, bass and drums. The twin guitars of Angus and
Malcolm Young mesh together on record to create AC/DC's
signature sound: warm yet cutting, with the sense of width
and power achieved by two guitars playing nearly, but not
quite, identical parts. The AC/DC 'formula' generally includes
a high-octane bluesy guitar solo by Angus, which is then played
over a reiteration of the song's main riff or chord sequence by
Malcolm. Like Eddie Van Halen, Angus Young's stage act is
highly energetic and often very acrobatic, and it has probably
been just as big an influence on the continuing popularity
of AC/DC's distinctive guitar sound.

RIGHT: *Angus Young's influences include Little
Richard, Jimi Hendrix, Chuck Berry and John
Lee Hooker. His energetic guitar style has been
an inspiration to many young musicians.*

EXERCISE 2

This rhythm idea uses open-position
Am, Em, D5 and G5 chords (see
'Power chords'). Pay attention to the
'P.M.' indications – muting should be
applied to the notes covered by dotted
lines, but released elsewhere.
As some of these chords are full
minor chords rather than power
chords, care should be taken over
the amount of distortion used –
by all means add slight 'crunch',
but avoid heavy distortion here.

EXERCISE 3

This simple shuffle-rhythm pattern
is much easier than it may appear.
The A shape is played using a first-
finger barre; the D/A shape is created
by simply adding the second and third
fingers as shown in the tablature stave.
Be careful that the top E string is not
allowed to sound during the A chord.

More on lead guitar

One of the keys to successful lead-guitar playing is fluidity: a guitar solo or other lead line should usually sound as fluid and 'joined up' as that of a wind instrument or bowed stringed instrument. The guitar player is naturally disadvantaged here: the guitar sound has a comparatively fast decay and a greater range of left-hand movement is required. Guitarists use a number of techniques to get around these problems.

Slides and slurs

Rather than picking every single note with the right hand, which is not always very fluid, fretted notes can be 'joined up' in a number of ways. The simplest technique is the hammer-on (see 'Rock 'n' roll') and its near relative, the pull-off. The pitch range of these techniques is restricted by the physical size of your left hand, however. Another way to link notes involves sliding from one note to the next, often covering a much wider interval. Having played the first note, the fretting finger maintains pressure on the string while physically sliding up or down to the next note. The entire length of the string is accessible in this way; sliding may be used as an effect in its own right, but it is also a useful way to connect ideas in different positions on the fretboard. For example, a phrase may start in first position, incorporate a slide, and end up at the twelfth fret or higher.

Simple hammer-on and pull-off

1 To play a simple hammer-on, first play any fretted note with the first finger.

2 While this first note is sounding, 'hammer' one of the other fingers on to a higher fret on the same string. This should raise the pitch of the sounding note instantly without reducing its volume, if sufficient force and pressure is used.

3 The reverse of the hammer-on is the pull-off. Staying with these two notes, the higher finger can be pulled away rapidly to lower the sounding pitch.

David Gilmour

Pink Floyd remains one of the best-selling recording acts the world has ever seen. The band's enormously successful 1973 album *The Dark Side Of The Moon* has probably sold more copies than all other progressive rock albums combined. David Gilmour's guitar was a central component of the Pink Floyd sound and, along with Roger Waters' poetic lyrics, a key reason for its success. Pink Floyd successfully fused a gutsy, sometimes blues-tinged sound and feel with a poignant, very English melodic sense and harmonic sophistication. Pink Floyd managed not only to bridge the gap between popular music and 'serious' culture, but also to render the distinction meaningless.

ABOVE: *David Gilmour is best known for his lead guitar work, and as singer and songwriter with Pink Floyd. He has also worked as a solo artist and record producer for other artists.*

Vertical versus horizontal

Another approach involves taking a 'horizontal' view of the guitar fretboard. Scales and other musical building blocks are often learned 'vertically', or in a single fretboard position. With the addition of a little knowledge of simple music theory, however, musical ideas can to some extent be created horizontally, or up and down the fretboard on a single string. More importantly, this approach is very helpful in improving fretboard knowledge to the point where any scale/key can be used in any position.

The horizontal approach to the guitar fretboard requires a bit of basic knowledge… and then a whole lot of work. All the scales of Western music are constructed from a combination of tones and semitones (and, in the case of pentatonic and blues scales, the minor third, which is made up of one tone plus a semitone). On the guitar, two notes one fret apart create the interval of a semitone; two frets' separation gives us a tone.

This knowledge can now be combined with a basic understanding of scale construction. Starting with the tonic or 'key' note, the four most useful scales are constructed as follows (T=tone, S=semitone, m3=minor third):

Major:	T – T – S – T – T – T – S
Natural minor:	T – S – T – T – S – T – T
Minor pentatonic scale:	m3 – T – T – m3 – T
Blues scale:	m3 – T – S – S – m3 – T

To commit this knowledge to memory, start on any open string and use the patterns above to find the scale on that string. For example, if the first interval is 'T', the second note will be found at the second fret. Continue through the pattern; the result should sound familiar (very familiar in the case of the major scale), and you should reach the tonic note again, after the last interval in the pattern, at the twelfth fret. If you finish anywhere else, you've made a mistake on the way.

EXERCISE 1

This melodic exercise uses slides to join up three-note phrases in G major, all on the G string. Slides are shown using a diagonal line; the accompanying slur (curved line) indicates that the second note is not picked. Notes joined by slurs should only be played using hammer-ons and pull-offs (pick the first note only).

EXERCISE 2

This exercise uses slides to join up more extended phrases (spanning several strings each) in A major. To avoid tying your fingers in knots, pay attention to the left-hand fingering (shown between the staves).

Grunge

The grunge style is very much based on the punk ethos: that anyone can play the guitar and sing, and anyone can be in a band. The popularity of grunge was responsible for the near demise of the guitar solo in rock music. If there should be anything that approximates to a solo in a grunge song, it generally takes the form of a simple thematic statement, often doubled in octaves for added 'thickness'.

Simple materials

It is no surprise, then, that most of the grunge classics are built on simple musical ideas: power chords, barre chords and open string drones.

Open string drones form an important part of the grunge vocabulary, possibly because they allow the creation of some fairly dark harmonic ideas without requiring any actual knowledge of harmony. To experience the effect of this, try playing fretted notes on the A string while simultaneously picking the low E string. The resulting effect depends on the interval created: for example, the note E is found at the seventh fret on the A string, and playing this together with the open E results in a simple octave. Move the fretted note up just one fret, however, and the resulting interval (a minor ninth) will sound very dark indeed. Continue up the A string: the tenth fret (G) effectively outlines an E minor chord; the eleventh fret (G$\sharp$) produces a E major sound.

Playing like this on an adjacent pair of strings can generate some instantly viable grunge ideas. Of course, moving to another string pair, or another type of musical device entirely, can help add variety. This idea can also be extended by moving whole chord shapes around against open strings.

Power chords

Borrowing a device directly from punk, grunge guitar often uses power chords (see 'Power chords') in high-energy rhythmic guitar parts where many of the shapes used fall outside the strict confines of a major or minor key. The most famous example of this is Nirvana's "Smells Like Teen Spirit", where the repeated chord sequence F5–B$\flat$5–A$\flat$5–D$\flat$5 comprises the central musical idea. To come up with your own ideas in this vein, simply experiment with power chords moved around the neck until you hit upon a pleasing sequence. The key to this type of riff sound is to play loudly with plenty of energy and lots of distortion, but not so much that the odd harmonic effects are lost.

ABOVE: *F5 power chord (the root note F is on the E string, 1st fret).*

ABOVE: *B$\flat$5 power chord (the root note B$\flat$ is on the A string, 1st fret).*

ABOVE: *A$\flat$5 power chord (the root note A$\flat$ is on the E string, 4th fret).*

ABOVE: *D$\flat$5 power chord (the root note D$\flat$ is on the A string, 4th fret).*

Playing tip: Flat tuning

The practice known as flat tuning is common in grunge, and in some other heavy styles. Rather than retuning in order to change the pitch relationships between the strings, flat tuning simply shifts the entire instrument down by a given amount. Therefore anything playable in standard tuning is also playable in flat tuning. The most popular options are to tune down by a semitone (known as E$\flat$ tuning) or by a whole tone. Most grunge players using flat tuning do so because it can result in a better defined (more grungy) tone. Flat tuning is often used in connection with drop D tuning (see 'Metal guitar in drop D').

Recommended listening:

- Nirvana: *Nevermind*
- Pearl Jam: *Ten*
- Soundgarden: *Badmotorfinger*

EXERCISE 1

This exercise uses a drone on the bottom E string, against which fretted notes on the A string create a dark thematic idea. Slight palm muting works well here, and down-strokes should be used throughout. Some notes are marked with accents ⟩ – these should be played with a little more force than other notes in order to bring out the melody. This accent pattern should be maintained throughout.

EXERCISE 2

This exercise uses barre chords throughout (see 'Rock chord vocabulary'). Down-strokes should be used throughout. To play bars with the rhythm of the first bar, left-hand damping should be used: release pressure on the left hand immediately after playing the second of each pair of quavers. This creates a short, sharp effect that accentuates the rhythm. Don't worry too much about playing every single string of these chords; the desired sound is definitely 'bottom heavy'.

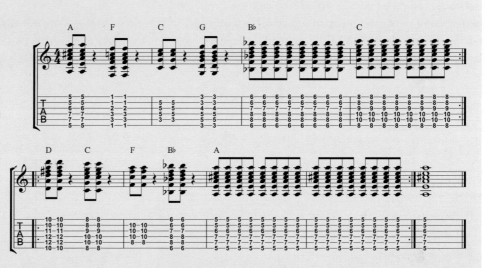

Stone Gossard

Emerging from the Seattle grunge scene as one of the most successful 'alternative' rock bands of the nineties, Pearl Jam was formed in 1990, by founding members Jeff Aments, Mike McCready, Eddie Vedder and Stone Gossard. Through his role – somewhere between rhythm and lead guitarist – Gossard has managed to reach a larger public than most guitarists are able to do. He wrote or co-wrote the majority of the songs on Pearl Jam's most commercially successful album *Ten*. His guitar style and apparent influences place him squarely in the mainstream rock canon, however, with inspiration from guitarists such as both Jimi Hendrix and Jimmy Page in particular. Repetitive funky riffs form an important part of Pearl Jam's stylistic repertoire, although the guitar tone is usually of the straight-ahead rock variety.

ABOVE: *Pearl Jam's Stone Gossard plays guitar on stage at a concert in Irvine, California in 1992, which formed part of the Lollapalooza music festival held annually at that time.*

Riffs

A riff is an instrumental musical idea that may be melodically or harmonically based, and which is always highly rhythmic. A riff acts as a kind of musical 'theme tune', and, in the case of the best riffs, often competes for attention with the vocals. Many classic rock and pop songs are built around a great guitar riff, which is often the first component of the song to be written.

The art of repetition

The first rule for constructing a great riff is: don't be afraid of repetition. Most riffs are only two or four bars long, but they are interesting enough to stand being played many times during the course of a song. This repetition may be exact and unchanging, or it may be transposed to follow a chord sequence.

The simplest type of riff consists of a melodic idea played on the bass strings; low notes are inherently more powerful. Guitar riffs are often doubled (played at the same pitch or an octave lower) on the bass guitar to provide maximum propulsive effect. The Beatles' "Day Tripper" is probably the most famous example.

Many songs driven by guitar riffs are written in keys taking advantage of the guitar's open strings, specifically E and A. This allows fretted notes slightly higher up the fretboard to be incorporated, while alternating with open-string notes that 'anchor' the riff firmly in the bass register. A riff may also incorporate a distinctive chord, even a fairly dissonant one, to punctuate a melodic riff.

Use of the blues scale

The blues scale provides an excellent vehicle for constructing simple guitar riffs. For an effective and driving riff, stick to the bottom three strings and experiment with the available notes to produce satisfying melodic ideas. A simple but distinctive repeated rhythm is often effective too, as heard in Aerosmith's classic "Walk This Way".

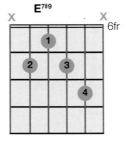

E7#9

6fr

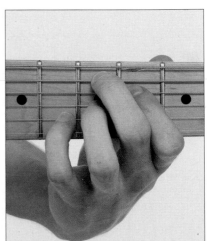

LEFT AND BELOW: *The E7#9 chord, as featured on Jimi Hendrix's "Purple Haze". The key of E allows the fretted chord to sound against the open low E string for a big sound that is full of impact.*

Recommended listening:

- The Beatles: "Day Tripper"
- David Bowie: "Rebel Rebel"
- T. Rex: "Twentieth Century Boy"

ABOVE: *The blues scale in E, first position. This key allows riffs to be built from the open E string, and to incorporate hammer-ons from open strings to fretted notes. E5 and A5 power chords also often feature heavily in bluesy riffs in E.*

EXERCISE 1

This riff uses the lower octave of the E blues scale shown above. The wavy line in the second bar indicates vibrato (see 'Lead techniques'); a quarter-note bend could also be effective here.

George Harrison

'The quiet one' in The Beatles may have been overshadowed by Lennon and McCartney as a singer and songwriter, but nonetheless he made a vital contribution to the group's sound. From the band's earliest days, Harrison made the effort to prove himself by learning his heroes' solos note for note and absorbing all the harmonic knowledge he could from books such as Bert Weedon's *Play In A Day*. Harrison was responsible for many of the milestones in the rapid evolution of The Beatles' sound (and, therefore, that of almost every pop group of the time), including the use of 12-string guitar, slide guitar and Indian instruments. Every time George Harrison found a new instrument of choice (from Gretsch semi-acoustics in the early years through Rickenbackers to Fenders later on), the favoured company's fortunes would take a steep upward turn.

RIGHT: *George Harrison was originally inspired to take up the guitar by listening to Lonnie Donegan. His lead guitar style with The Beatles mixed blues with rock and a strong melody.*

EXERCISE 2

This extended riff idea spans eight bars – a perfect length for an intro or ending (or both). All the single notes here should be played in second position: first finger at the second fret, second finger at the third fret, and so on. The full D, A and E chords provide a moment of contrast and therefore may be heavily accented.

EXERCISE 3

This riff uses the E7#9 'Hendrix' chord to classic effect. Chord-based bars alternate with single-line figures in first position using the E blues scale. You may want to try to move between these positions as quickly and quietly as possible; alternatively, you could try making a feature of the transition by sliding the second E7#9 chord down the fretboard.

Indie rock

It's hard to define exactly where rock music ends and Indie music begins. The Indie sound (its name derived from the abbreviation of 'independent') has its roots in Britain and often has an identifiably British character. It was directly influential in shaping the guitar-led 'Britpop' style. Although there are some similarities with punk, Indie music usually emphasizes interesting melody, harmony and song structure.

The art of repetition

Indie songs tend to be rooted firmly in the major/minor key system, rather than being blues-based. Indie guitar ideas often make extensive use of open strings. In particular, a 'chiming' sound is often achieved using moving fretted notes against an adjacent open string. This is very similar in principle to the drone effect encountered in grunge, but the use of higher strings creates a very different effect.

Having found a sequence of fretted notes that works well against one or more adjacent open strings, this idea can be executed in a number of ways. Notes may be arpeggiated (played rapidly one after the other), or all played together using continuous down-strokes for a more aggressive effect.

ABOVE: *Radiohead's harmonic language often lends a mysterious and slightly menacing flavour to their Indie rock music.*

EXERCISE 1

This idea uses moving fretted notes on the G string against the open B and top E strings. It is important to let all the notes ring for as long as possible and not to move too soon from one fretted note to the next (the shift should be made just before each fretted note). In this way, the notes on the G string join up to form a melodic strand.

EXERCISE 2

This exercise uses first position add9/sus2 chords and then movable 'lazy barre' shapes based on the E chord. Although the chords in the second line are written to ring, you could also experiment with some of the busier strumming styles here.

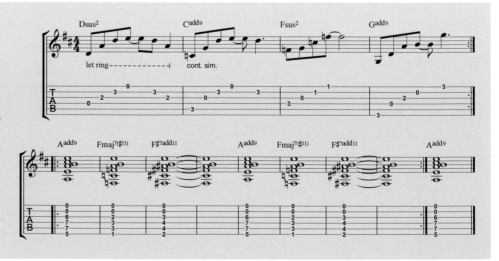

Chord vocabulary

Indie players love slightly mysterious chords. Instead of plain majors and minors, many chords are 'spiced up' using extra notes. Rather than adding a seventh, which would give a jazzy sound, many chords incorporate an added ninth (the note a whole tone above the root of the chord). For example, adding the note D to the chord of C major produces C$^{(add9)}$; adding E to D major produces D$^{(add9)}$. By convention, 'add9' is used if the third of the chord is also present; if the ninth replaces the third, the result is instead known as a 'sus^2' chord. These chords can also, depending on the context, give a folky, contemporary flavour to an otherwise standard chord sequence.

Movable 'lazy barre' shapes are also a very useful and versatile addition to your repertoire when playing or composing in this style of music. These are essentially chords that are based on barre-chord shapes, but with one or more open strings (usually the top strings). These shapes are moved up and down the fretboard much like regular barre chords, except that as the open-string notes do not change, tensions are created against the fretted notes. This can result in some fairly complex-sounding chords with bafflingly long names, but there is no need to get bogged down with the technical theory behind them – the important thing is the effect. If it sounds good, it is good.

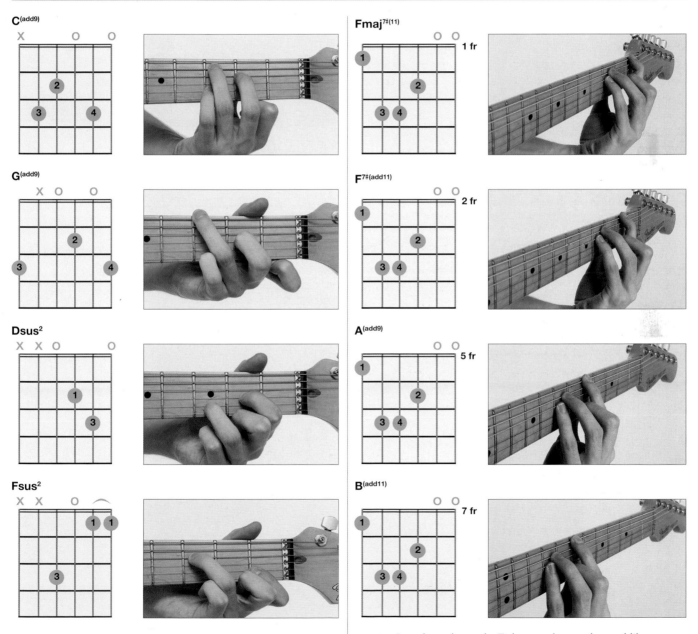

ABOVE: *Sus^2 chord: Add^9/sus^2 in first position. Although there is only one note that differentiate each of these chords from the standard major chords, the result that is achieved from this technique is immediately more harmonically sophisticated.*

ABOVE: *Lazy barre shapes: the E shape can be moved around like a barre chord but with open B and top E strings. The four shapes that are shown here are the most useful and are all widely used, even though they all incorporate some dissonance.*

Accompaniment with fills

Many guitar parts inhabit an area between the strictly defined territories of rhythm and lead guitar. Fills are short melodic nuggets that supply interest, often between vocal lines, while integrating into a part that functions as an unobtrusive rhythm accompaniment. Many different scales and techniques can be used to generate fills; we'll look at some of the most important ideas here.

A matter of style

The first thing to establish when playing an accompaniment with fills is: what is the musical style? Broadly speaking, modern guitar styles can be divided between those that are overtly blues-based and those that are not. This distinction will have a fundamental effect on your choice of notes. In a blues-based context, the blues scale (see 'Electric blues guitar') can be used throughout; for other chord sequences in major keys, ideas derived from the major scale are likely to sound better. The use of blues ideas over non-blues sequences is likely to sound dissonant.

In this type of playing, the gap between chords and melody is often bridged using melodic double stops (see 'Rock 'n' roll'), and single notes are often embellished using hammer-ons and pull-offs.

Building a vocabulary

One way to get started with this type of playing is to work up a vocabulary of 'licks' which you can execute confidently. Of course, the ultimate aim is to be more inventive than this – nobody wants to hear the same handful of licks in every song you play – but you have to start somewhere.

One popular way to 'dress up' a rhythm part, adding both rhythmic and melodic interest, is to use hammer-ons and pull-offs to move between chord notes and adjacent scale notes on nearby frets. Often a partial barre will be involved for this type of fill. Another popular device is the grace-note hammer-on: a very quick hammer-on using a 'crushed' rhythm (played as quickly as possible without affecting the timing of the main notes).

The pentatonic scale is also very useful for this type of playing. This is actually the same set of notes as the blues scale (see 'More on lead guitar'), except that the flattened fifth (the most bluesy/dissonant note) is omitted. Any given pentatonic scale can be considered as having two different key centres: the major and the minor, which are a minor third or three semitones apart. For example, the A minor pentatonic scale actually uses the same set of notes as the C major pentatonic. For simple chord sequences in the major key, the major pentatonic scale can be used to construct simple fills that will work over any part of the chord sequence.

LEFT: Two classic-sounding decorative hammer-on/pull-off fill ideas. Note the grace-note hammer-ons (small notes) in the second example. These should be played as quickly as possible so the main rhythm (large notes) is not affected.

Recommended listening:

- The Beatles: "Don't Let Me Down"
- Jimi Hendrix: "The Wind Cries Mary"
- Red Hot Chilli Peppers: "Under The Bridge"
- The Jacksons: "Blame It On The Boogie"

RIGHT: The C major pentatonic scale in fifth position. Note that this is the same set of notes as the A minor pentatonic scale.

Ray Phiri

As a working guitarist in a culturally isolated country in the early 1980s, Ray Phiri probably had little idea of the influence he was soon to exercise on popular music the world over. When Paul Simon decided to write and record in Johannesburg with South African musicians, Ray Phiri's group Stimela formed the backbone of the resulting album *Graceland*. Although other styles are woven through the album, the excitement felt by American and European audiences resulted from the dominance of the South African mbaqanga style (sometimes known as Township Jive), with its high, melodic guitar fills and propulsive bass work in constant counterpoint to the vocal line. *Graceland*'s enormous success played a large part in the emerging popularity of 'World Music' with Western audiences, and Ray Phiri's guitar style in particular continues to inspire imitation a quarter of a century later.

RIGHT: *South African musician Ray Phiri founded Stimela, who played with Paul Simon and Ladysmith Black Mambazo on the* Graceland *project.*

EXERCISE 1

This exercise integrates simple fills into a very common pop chord sequence (C–Am–F–G). All of the fills use the C major pentatonic scale. The chords themselves are played on beat 3 of each bar; beat 2 is left empty – in pop production this helps the snare drum to drive the rhythm without drowning the rest of the production.

EXERCISE 2

This exercise uses hammer-on/pull-off fills to decorate a sequence of just three chords: E, F#m (barre chord at the second fret) and A. In general, fills in this type of playing should be as 'ringy' as possible; if your amp or effects unit has a reverb effect, this is a perfect time to use it.

LEFT: *Reverb can help 'paper over' any rhythmic gaps in fill-based playing, and achieve a 'ringy' feel.*

Using wah-wah and other effects

For many players, the electric guitar itself is only one part of the enormous creative palette that guitar technology makes available to them. Obviously amplification is crucial, but many of the guitar sounds we know and love also depend on the use of effects. From Jimi Hendrix to U2 and Coldplay, effects including wah-wah, delay and chorus have often been essential elements in the electric guitarist's armoury.

Wah-wah

The sound of this effect is beautifully described by its name. It has a history older than the electric guitar (brass players use a special mute to produce a similar effect). Unlike most other pedals where the foot operates a simple on/off switch, the wah-wah effect is continuously variable; rocking the foot plate back and forth operates a circuit a little like the guitar's tone control. More specifically, the circuit boosts a range of frequencies; this range is 'swept' up and down by the foot. In 'heel down' position, lower frequencies are boosted, resulting in a warm, muffled sound. In 'toe down' position, the high frequencies are accented for a harsh, cutting tone. The pedal is turned on and off by pushing the toe down sharply.

The wah-wah pedal can sometimes be left activated in a static position, but is usually rocked back and forth in time with the pulse of the music. Whether playing chords or lead figures, the easiest and most intuitive way to use the wah-wah pedal is as follows: toe down on the beat, heel down on the offbeat (the 'and' between beats).

The exercises here (on the opposite page) will naturally be of most benefit if you have access to the type of effect intended, but they are also useful as a means of stylistic exploration in their own right. The wah-wah effect is largely intuitive, so feel free to explore the possibilities.

Wah-wah pedal

The pedal is usually rocked backward and forward: the 'heel down' position (on the offbeat) boosts lower frequencies, while the 'toe down' (on the beat) accents the high frequencies.

ABOVE: *Heel down position.*   ABOVE: *Toe down position.*

Delay

The delay effect produces an echo at a precisely timed interval after playing a note, rather like the effect of clapping your hands and hearing the sound echoing back from a nearby wall or building. This effect has many uses. A single, very short delay (known as 'slap back' delay) adds a sort of rhythmic 'snappiness' and also thickens the sound. This type of delay is essential to 1950s rock 'n' roll and rockabilly-related styles. The controls should be set to produce a single delay; the delay time should be long enough for the delayed note to be discernible, but also much shorter than even the fastest notes being played.

Operating delay pedals

Other more modern uses of the delay effect require a little more understanding of the parameters of the effect. The exact controls on a delay pedal vary, but the following are generally present, and this description serves as a guide to the principles in operation:
• Delay time: the basic time interval between the arrival of the input signal (playing a note) and the delayed signal.
• Delay level/mix: governs the balance between the input signal and the delayed signal. This is usually continuously adjustable all the way from all input (no delay) to all delay (no sound is heard until after the delay time). Creative uses of delay involve setting this somewhere between the two.

• Feedback: controls the amount of delayed signal that is fed back to the input. At the maximum setting, this will result in infinite repetition. Lower settings produce a series of delays of gradually decreasing volume. When this control is set at zero, only a single repeat is heard.
• Loop function: some delay pedals allow an entire musical phrase to be recorded and then played back repeatedly, or 'looped' in real time. The pedal switch is pushed once to start recording and again to stop, at which point anything played in between is repeated until playback is stopped. This can be used to set up an instant rhythmic idea, with a solo played on top. Rhythmic delays can be used for both rhythm and lead playing.

Setting up a pedalboard

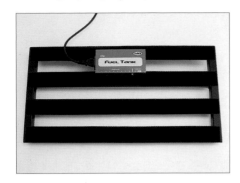

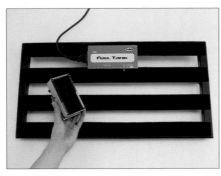

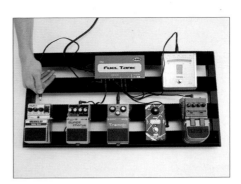

1 Place the power supply in a central position so that power cables may reach all points on the board.

2 Attach self-adhesive fabric tape strips to the underside of each pedal (some manufacturers do this for you).

3 Place the pedals at convenient positions on the board, making sure your foot can access them all easily, and connect a power cable from the power supply to each pedal.

4 Add patch cables to connect the pedals in series, making sure each connects the output of one with the input of another.

Recommended listening:
- Jimi Hendrix: "Voodoo Chile"
- Eric Clapton: "Bad Love"
- U2: "Pride (In The Name Of Love)"
- Van Halen: "Why Can't This Be Love?"

EXERCISE 1

Try this simple bluesy riff with wah-wah. The '+' symbol indicates the toe position while the 'o' symbol indicates the heel. Don't worry too much about getting this exactly as notated, however; musical wah-wah technique is largely intuitive.

EXERCISE 2

This simple motif can generate many different ideas depending on the delay time used. Try a delay time corresponding to any number of semiquavers (sixteenth notes), or even quaver (eighth-note) triplets. Delay times are usually best adjusted by ear, although if you need to conform to a precise tempo a calculator may be useful! Experiment and enjoy yourself.

Funk and disco

In most modern music, three important elements predominate: melody, harmony and rhythm. Many pop styles focus heavily on rhythm, and the range of styles known collectively as funk lie at the extreme end of this tendency. Although funk uses a similar harmonic and melodic vocabulary to other urban American music, it is rhythm that dominates. To get to grips with funk, it is essential to master a few rhythmic basics.

Continuous semiquavers (sixteenths)

Most classic funk-guitar parts are built on semiquavers, which are also known as sixteenth notes. Each of these lasts for one sixteenth of a bar in $\frac{4}{4}$ or a quarter of a beat. When playing a funk rhythm part in sixteenths, it is crucially important to maintain strict alternation between down- and up-strokes.

Exactly the same principle applies to most rock and pop rhythm playing, but in funk and disco the basic division is the sixteenth note (semiquaver) rather than the eighth note (quaver). In funk rhythm styles, the right hand maintains this basic motion continuously; on any given sixteenth, the right hand may either strike the strings or miss them. This idea may

be used to create very busy parts (most sixteenths sounding), very sparse parts (only a few notes sounding in each bar) or anything in between. In every case, the basic right-hand motion is the same (up/down continuously in sixteenths) so that it would be hard to distinguish visually between parts that sound quite different.

As an alternative to missing the strings altogether between fully sounding chords, the right hand may play muted timing strokes instead: left-hand finger pressure is released between sounding chords, so that only a percussive muted sound is heard. In this way, a very even right-hand pattern can be maintained, resulting in accurate timing throughout.

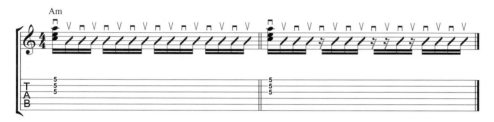

LEFT: *Two examples of continuous sixteenths motion showing down-strokes ⊓ and up-strokes ∨. In the first bar, every single sixteenth note sounds. In the second, some strokes are missed in order to create a more interesting rhythm.*

Funk chord vocabulary

One chord shape looms large in funk guitar: the dominant ninth, usually known simply as a ninth or '9' chord. There are many different possible voicings of ninths chords, but one shape is by far the most popular. This involves the use of the third finger to make a partial barre across the top three strings, as shown below.

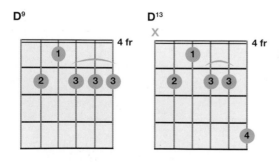

ABOVE: *Dominant ninth and thirteenth shapes in the classic funk voicing, shown here in D. The root note is on the A string (note D); for a slightly lighter sound, this note can be omitted when playing with a bass player. The thirteenth shape is formed by simply adding the little finger, which may be a bit of a stretch at first. Many funk and disco classics have been written around this idea.*

Recommended listening:
- James Brown: "Sex Machine"
- Prince: "Kiss"
- Tower of Power: "Soul with a Capital 'S'"
- Curtis Mayfield: "Soul Music"

ABOVE: *Curtis Mayfield's guitar playing became more experimental in the late 1960s, following the influence of players like Jimi Hendrix, with the inclusion of wah-wah effects on the Temptations' album Cloud Nine.*

The muted line

Although full chord-based accompaniment is an important tool for most funk players, there are many times when a sparser approach is required. Funk and disco players often play minimal repetitive melodic ideas too, usually in unison with the bass or keyboards. To keep these lines sounding snappy but unobtrusive, they are usually played using right-hand palm muting (see 'Rock rhythm guitar' for a full introduction to this technique). As with any other use of palm muting, the aim is to achieve a very high level of control over the effect: hand position and pressure both play a part in the technique.

RIGHT: *Hand position is very important in palm muting. Too little muting, and notes will ring fully and probably be too loud; too much, and the notes will be choked off altogether, resulting in a percussive sound but no identifiable sense of pitch.*

LEFT: *Approaching any chord by sliding up or down by one or more frets can add spice to funk rhythm parts.*

Using a slide

Funk chords are often approached using a slide. Typically, the whole shape is first fretted one fret lower than the target chord. This is played, and the slide is executed rhythmically (as one semiquaver note) before continuing with the pattern. It is important not to let the use of a slide interrupt the right hand's rhythmic flow: for example, if the slide replaces an up-stroke, the next stroke should still be a down-stroke.

EXERCISE 1

This exercise is a classic funk rhythm part using dominant ninths and thirteenths. The patterns here make use of sliding chords. Take care to execute the slide as rhythmically as possible – the effect should be just as rhythmically precise as if each chord were played with the right hand. For variety, this figure can be played equally well without the slide: just play D9 twice (down/up).

EXERCISE 2

This piece consists of a 'minimal' muted melodic line. As with chord-based funk rhythm work, it is important to maintain a continuous right-hand motion in semiquavers, even though the use of muting will mean that the range of motion will be very small, and not to allow the use of hammer-ons to interrupt the basic flow.

Melodic jazz guitar

The guitar has occupied an important place in jazz since it took over from the banjo early on in its history. Although early jazz musicians played acoustic guitar, the electric guitar has also been used since the 1940s. Like the piano, the guitar works both as an accompanying instrument and as a melody instrument. Most of the big names in the history of jazz guitar have been great soloists. We'll focus on its melodic role here.

Jazz basics

There's little point trying to make jazz guitar sound like it's something that can be mastered in an afternoon. It's the exact opposite: you need a lot of study to become a proficient jazz player. Improvisation is central to jazz, and fluid jazz improvisation requires a thorough knowledge of complex harmony, as well as an intuitive familiarity with the musical language of the style. Most aspiring jazz players begin by exploring the repertoire of jazz 'standards': a body of compositions and songs that every serious jazz musician should know. Jazz evolved out of various other styles, most importantly the blues, and knowing the blues scale all over the fretboard will stand you in good stead as a jazz player.

However, the blues scale is just the beginning. Advanced jazz players draw on many other harmonic and melodic resources, which there is not space to describe here. But there is one scale that no introduction to jazz would be complete without: the melodic minor scale. After the blues scale and the major scale, this is definitely the next one you need to learn.

Every major key is related to a minor key, which is found a minor third below the keynote of the major scale. For example, C major and A minor share the same key signature; the A natural minor scale consists of exactly the same set of notes as the C major scale, but with a different key centre. All other minor scales are derived from this, but with one or more notes modified. In a jazz context, the scale known as the melodic minor scale is constructed by raising the sixth and seventh steps of the scale by a semitone.

So, the A melodic minor scale contains an F♯ rather than an F, and a G♯ rather than a G. The melodic minor scale may also be viewed as a major scale with a flattened third (in A major, the third would be C♯, which becomes C natural in A minor).

RIGHT: *The A melodic/jazz minor scale. The easiest way to play this as written is to start in fifth position (first finger at the fifth fret) but shift to fourth position from the D string onwards. This is a very useful jazz-scale shape.*

Larry Carlton

Many budding guitarists have dreamt of achieving a career as a top-flight 'session man', living in Los Angeles, playing on one million-selling record after another for high multiples of the standard pay rate. In reality, only a very few players have ever inhabited this realm, but Larry Carlton is definitely one of them. During the 1970s and early '80s he completed over 3,000 studio sessions, yielding more than 100 gold-certified albums. Some of the most famous results of this remarkable period include much of the output of Joni Mitchell and Steely Dan, Michael Jackson's *Off The Wall* and a five-year stint with jazz-fusion group The Crusaders. Carlton has also made significant contributions to film and TV music (including his Grammy Award-winning theme for Hill Street Blues) and has pursued a recording career that would justify his position as one of the true guitar heroes in his own right; any putative list of the greatest guitar solos on record should include his work on Steely Dan's "Kid Charlemagne".

ABOVE: *During the 1970s and '80s Larry Carlton worked as a session musician in Los Angeles as well as with the jazz-rock group, the Crusaders, in the 1970s.*

Swing

Both of the exercises here, and indeed most mainstream jazz, is played using swing rhythm. This means that although a melody is written using quavers (half-beat notes), these are not actually played as an even flow of equal half-beats. Instead, the offbeats are played late, so that they fall closer to the next beat than to the previous beat. Exactly how late they should be played depends on factors such as the tempo of the piece.

Recommended listening:
- Charlie Christian: *The Genius Of The Electric Guitar*
- Wes Montgomery: *The Incredible Jazz Guitar Of Wes Montgomery*
- Pat Metheny: *Question & Answer*
- Jim Hall: *Circles*

RIGHT AND FAR RIGHT:
Melodic jazz playing often requires the execution of consecutive notes by using the same fret on adjacent strings (for example the G and B strings, as seen here). Instead of using two different fingers, or trying to shift one finger very rapidly, the most fluid result is usually achieved by 'rolling' the fingertip between strings. Reversing the order shown here is a little trickier, but ultimately any fluent player would be able to carry off this move in both directions.

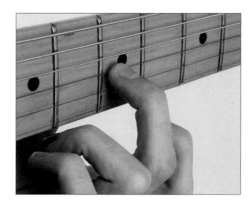

EXERCISE 1

This simple modern jazz tune is written entirely using the A jazz/melodic minor scale as shown above. Notice that the fourth and fifth notes of the first bar (E on the B string and C on the G string) are played at the same fret. These should be played by the same left-hand finger (the second finger), but rather than lifting it from the B string and pressing it back down on the G string, the fingertip should be 'rolled' between the two notes. This is a very common jazz 'move'.

EXERCISE 2

This exercise is a simple jazz blues in G. It is almost entirely written using the blues scale, but note also the use of the major third (B natural, played here on the G string, fourth fret). This use of both the major third and blues third is very common in bluesy jazz. In this example, all the major thirds are approached using a rapid hammer-on from the blues third one fret below. For extra flavour, you could turn this into a trill between the two notes.

Reggae

Guitarists, bass players and drummers all claim to play *the* most important instrument in reggae, and all of these claims hold some truth. In reggae, more than any other style, each instrument does a unique job without which the music as a whole would simply not work. To master reggae on the guitar, therefore, we also need to be aware of what the other instruments contribute to the style.

Where not to play

The foundations of the reggae sound are laid by the drums, and the kit is used in a very different way compared to other styles of music. In most pop and rock music, the snare drum plays a strong 'backbeat' on beats 2 and 4 of each bar; the bass drum works around this (playing on beats 1 and 3 is the simplest option). This creates a fairly uniform flow of sound over which it is possible to play guitar (and bass) parts that are fairly evenly accented throughout the bar. In reggae, however, the bass drum and snare drum are usually played simultaneously (known as playing 'drops') on beats 2 and 4, which manages to create a much more powerful accent here; only the hi-hat cymbal is played elsewhere. This powerful low-frequency accent is counterbalanced by the bass guitar, which accents beats 1 and 3 heavily.

To smooth over these powerful accents somewhat, the guitar usually plays 'chops' (see 'Rhythm guitar styles') on every offbeat (the 'AND' between beats). These should be short and sharp, co-existing but not overlapping with the distinct niches occupied by the other instruments.

Melodic fills

For variety, reggae players often depart from playing straight rhythm chops at certain points in the song's structure. While this occasionally sounds similar to the unison ideas found in funk and disco, more often the guitar plays short melodic interjections that leave space in the arrangement for the bass and drums. These may be played with light palm muting, or alternatively may sound more fully, often using effects (see exercises below and opposite).

RIGHT: *Bob Marley remains the world's best-known player of Jamaican music. He was lead singer and rhythm guitarist for the reggae band Bob Marley and the Wailers from 1963–81.*

EXERCISE 1

Reggae often uses simple major and minor chords rather than sevenths or anything more complicated. Relatively high voicings are usually used, leaving the bass frequencies to be occupied by the bass guitar. The shapes here use the top four strings only; it may help to view them as derived from familiar 'E'-shape major and minor chords, or even to fret these full shapes but to avoid playing the bottom strings.

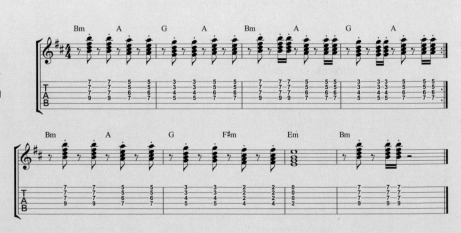

Popular effects

Classic reggae often has a somewhat 'swampy', warm, organic sound. Various factors contribute to this, among them the use of two favourite guitar effects: wah-wah and phasing. For straightforward reggae rhythm chops, a standard wah-wah pedal can be used to accent each chord.

To achieve a more uniform effect here, some players prefer to use an auto-wah effect. This essentially uses the same circuit as a standard wah-wah, but the 'foot movement' is created automatically, usually in response to the volume of the incoming signal.

A phaser effect sounds a little like chorus but generally has a more radical effect on the tone, which seems to 'sweep', usually slowly, from harsh to warm and back again. This can be great for adding interest to chords that are held for a long time, but is equally useful for standard reggae rhythm and lead work.

RIGHT: *The wah-wah pedal is great for accentuating reggae rhythm 'chops' — simply push the toe down in time with each right-hand down-stroke and bring it back in between them.*

EXERCISE 2

This exercise consists of melodic arpeggiated 'interjections', using the same chord sequence as Exercise 1. These exercises do not give the full reggae effect as solo parts: if you can, record a simple bass line based on the chords shown (see 'Constructing a bass line'); if you have a drum machine, find a reggae beat to play with. At the very least, tap your foot on beats 1 and 3, and more heavily on beats 2 and 4.

Country guitar techniques

One of the 'twin pillars' of American musical heritage (the other being the blues), country music has been dominated by the electric guitar since the instrument's invention. The Fender Telecaster, in particular, is almost ubiquitous in this genre. Most country guitar involves relatively simple rhythm work and lead ideas, but the style has also spawned more than its fair share of 'hot' virtuoso players.

The double bend

The name of this technique is rather confusing as it doesn't usually involve bending two notes. Rather, one note is bent while at least one other note sounds on another string. In country music, this is normally used to generate an implied chord, where the note being bent starts off as a 'neighbour' note (a note outside the chord) and is bent upwards, coming to rest on a chord note. This may work in a number of ways: the notes may be struck together, before executing the bend.

Alternatively, the bend may be executed first, and the target note allowed to ring on as the other notes in the chord are sounded. Double bends can of course be played using standard plectrum technique. But the use of *hybrid picking* is just as common. In this technique the plectrum is held between the thumb and index finger as usual, while the remaining three fingers are used for fingerpicking. For a simple two-note chord bend, the lower note is usually played by the plectrum while the higher note is played with the middle finger.

BELOW: *The classic country chord bend in two forms.*

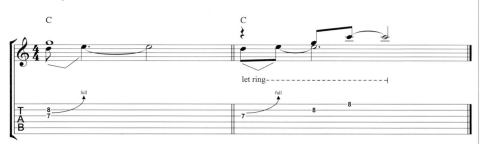

ABOVE: *The C major chord is implied by the target note (E) and the note G; this can also be used over other chords, including Em and Am7, or indeed in any situation where a pentatonic scale is in use (in this instance C major pentatonic or A minor pentatonic/blues scale).*

ABOVE: *The full C major chord bend. For both versions, the bend itself is executed by the third finger with the first and second fingers adding support if needed. The fourth finger frets the higher notes. In the first example here, the bend is executed while the higher note rings; in the second, ascending notes are added one at a time.*

Sound

Full distortion is rarely heard in mainstream country music. A very small amount of 'crunch' overdrive sometimes works well, but even this is quite unusual. Instead, a crisp, clean sound is generally preferred, although this is often adorned with effects. Slap-back delay works well in almost any country context (use a delay pedal or effects unit set to a delay period shorter than the fastest rhythmic subdivision in the music). Low riffs, such as appear in Exercise 2 opposite right, also work very well with a tremolo effect, which produces rhythmic fluctuations in volume. This is a built-in feature on some classic amplifier designs, but is also widely available both in individual pedal form and within multi-FX and modelling solutions.

The low twang

The word 'twang' is inextricably associated with country music and it describes perfectly the type of low guitar riff heard on many country records. For maximum effect, this type of riff – and country guitar in general – should usually be played on a guitar equipped with single-coil pickups, most typically a Fender Telecaster. However, the optimal range of notes for this sort of work is right down at the bottom of the guitar's low E string, or even below that. For this reason, many Nashville studio guitarists keep at least one instrument tuned below standard pitch, with the bottom string tuned as low as C or B. This generally works best with heavy-gauge strings.

EXERCISE 1

This exercise outlines a simple three-chord sequence using chord bends. Repeated instances of the same bend are shown here as pre-bends, i.e. the bend is held in position throughout the phrase. All the chord bends here occur either with the bend on the G string or with the bend on the B string. The accompanying note on the top E string is played with the fourth finger; the bend itself is executed by the third finger with the first and second fingers adding support if necessary.

EXERCISE 2

This simple tune is a typical 'twangy' low country riff incorporating repeated semitone bends on the bottom strings. For fun and added effect, if you have relatively heavy strings ('elevens' or higher), you may wish to try this with the guitar tuned down a major third (C–F–B♭–E♭–G–C) – it creates a very authentic 'growly' country sound.

Albert Lee

With a position in country music similar to that of Eric Clapton in the blues, Albert Lee is a British-born guitarist who is widely regarded as one of the very finest exponents of a quintessentially American style. Lee has been voted 'best country guitarist' innumerable times. He has worked with a number of bands since the late 1950s, playing country music, R&B and rock 'n' roll, but came to prominence in the early 1970s as a member of now-legendary British country-rock band Heads, Hands & Feet. After this he headed to America to play with some of country music's biggest names. He replaced James Burton in Emmylou Harris's Hot Band in 1976 and quickly became one the most sought-after session musicians of the day. Lee is perhaps the ultimate ' guitarist's guitarist' – any live appearance is a guarantee that a high percentage of both professional and amateur guitarists will be in the audience, many of whom can only gaze in wonder at 'Mr Telecaster' and his astonishingly fluid style.

ABOVE: *Albert Lee is a highly successful live performer. While not achieving huge commercial success for himself, songs such as "Country Boy" helped redefine the country guitar for a generation of players.*

Electric slide guitar

The slide guitar technique has an important place in both the blues and country music, and the many styles that have evolved from these two genres. To start playing slide guitar, all you need is a tube-shaped glass or metal slide, which is available from almost any music store. This represents easily the least expensive way to get a radically different sound from an ordinary electric guitar.

Basic slide technique

The slide is a metal or glass tube worn on one finger of the left hand, usually the fourth finger. In slide technique, the strings are not pushed down to make contact with the frets; instead, the slide rests lightly on the string without pressing it down. This means that the length of the string, and thus its pitch, is continuously variable.

If you rest the slide on the strings near the nut, then play a note and shift the slide up the neck as the note sounds, you will immediately be producing a basic slide-guitar sound. It involves a characteristic gradual fluid swoop that sounds very different from a series of precisely defined pitches produced by fretted notes.

Executing this simple slide will almost certainly illustrate some of the technical issues that accompany slide playing. On an ordinary electric guitar, it is difficult to avoid accidentally pressing the strings down, with the result that the slide collides with the frets, producing an unpleasant 'clunk'.

There are two solutions to this. Firstly, strings of a heavier gauge, having a higher tension, will offer more resistance to downward pressure. If you have several guitars, you could therefore try stringing one of them with heavy strings such as a set of twelves or thirteens (the number refers to the gauge of the top E string in thousandths of an inch).

Serious slide players, however, have their guitars specially set up for slide playing, which involves replacing the nut and adjusting the bridge height so that the strings are much further from the fretboard. It's important to note that this solution results in a guitar that is difficult or impossible to use for standard fretted playing, so you have to be very serious about developing your slide playing before having this work done to your guitar. If you want to play slide exclusively, this will probably mean investing in a dedicated instrument for slide.

LEFT: *The slide in use. Most players wear the slide on the fourth finger so that the other fingers may be used to dampen the strings behind the slide, thus preventing unwanted ringing string sounds.*

Ry Cooder

Although much of his music is quintessentially American, including the almost ubiquitous use of slide guitar, Cooder's output often straddles musical boundaries. This applies whether he's in Tex-Mex territory (a blend of Texan and Mexican styles) or working with Cuban musicians as he did for the groundbreaking Buena Vista Social Club album, which brought surprise international fame to a forgotten generation of Cuban musicians and also managed to rekindle interest in Latin-American music worldwide. As a guitarist, Cooder's rank among the great slide players is beyond doubt; as well as conventional song-based albums, much of Ry Cooder's success stems from critically acclaimed, highly atmospheric soundtracks to films such as *Paris, Texas* and *Crossroads*, which make heavy use of his plaintive slide work.

ABOVE: *Ry Cooder is one of the most quietly influential musicians of recent years, having spent several decades collaborating with artists from around the globe.*

Standard versus open tuning

The slide can produce a note anywhere along the length of the string; the resulting pitches follow those of fretted notes. Perfectly 'in tune' notes correspond with positions exactly above the frets themselves, rather than fretted finger positions between the frets. Any melodic idea that can be played using fretted notes can therefore be translated into a slide idea by applying this principle.

The main restriction imposed by the slide is that it can only be positioned over one fret at a time, so conventional full chord shapes cannot be accessed in standard tuning using the slide alone. Standard tuning is therefore usable for melodic slide playing, but most of the sounds associated with slide playing in its classic form are associated with open tunings. In an open tuning, the open strings are tuned to the notes of a chord. The whole chord (or parts of it) can then be transposed up the neck using the slide. For example, if the open strings are tuned to a G major chord, placing the slide at the fifth fret results in a C major chord and at the seventh fret produces D major. The G major chord can be found one octave higher at the twelfth fret. In principle, any type of chord may be used, and there are endless possibilities; in practice, the two firm favourites among slide players are usually open D and G major.

RIGHT: *The pitches of the open strings in open D and open G tunings. Note that not all strings need to be changed from standard tuning; those that do can generally be tuned in octaves against other strings. For example, to retune from standard tuning to open G, the first step is to drop the bottom string down from E to D so that it sounds perfectly in tune with the D (fourth) string.*

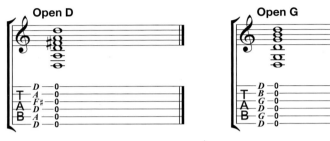

EXERCISE 1

This melodic slide exercise uses standard tuning. Care should be taken to keep the piece in tune by targeting positions exactly above the frets. Notes linked by a slur and a straight diagonal line should be joined together with a sliding motion in the rhythm indicated without re-picking the second note.

EXERCISE 2

This exercise is written in open G tuning and uses the three primary chords in G major: G, C and D. Arpeggiated notes within the same chord/fret position should be allowed to ring freely. Although physical slide movements are not indicated here, try experimenting firstly with long audible swoops between positions, then damping the strings so there is no sound during the movement. You will probably find that somewhere between these two extremes sounds best; where is a matter of taste. If the last two chords are not joined up with a slide motion, the D chord can be made staccato (short).

Buying a bass guitar

There's a strong case for calling the bass guitar the most important instrument in popular music. Rock and pop in general would be very different without this recent invention, and styles such as reggae, funk and disco would simply not exist without it.

The Fender bass

For many years, musicians often called the bass guitar the 'Fender bass'. Leo Fender identified the need for a portable bass instrument, and created a bass guitar that drew heavily on the design of the Fender Telecaster. These origins are of enormous benefit to guitarists: if you can play guitar, you can automatically play bass guitar to a basic level. The four strings of the bass guitar are tuned to the same pitches as the guitar's four lowest strings, but one octave lower. Unlike the double bass, the bass guitar's frets ensure that all notes are automatically in tune when fretted.

All bass guitars are more or less based on Leo Fender's original design. A few other basses have also achieved iconic status, and the following overview of some of these, along with classic Fender basses, will be of use to the prospective buyer.

Fender Precision bass

Leo Fender's original bass is a case study in simplicity. A one-piece neck, reinforced with a steel truss rod, is bolted to a solid, guitar-shaped body. All the hardware components are essentially large, chunky versions of those found on the Fender Telecaster; the sound is captured by a single 'split' pickup.

One-piece reinforced neck

Fender Jazz bass, 1963

Pickups

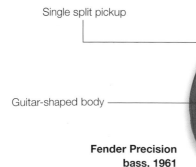

Single split pickup

Guitar-shaped body

Fender Precision bass, 1961

Fender Jazz bass

The Jazz bass is physically very similar to the Precision. The main difference lies in the pickup configuration and the range of sounds available. Rather than a single split pickup, the Jazz bass uses two pickups spanning all four strings; standard Jazz bass pickups have two pole-pieces per string. The sound tends to be brighter than the Precision, with slightly less emphasis on the fundamental bass note and more on the mid-range.

Höfner violin bass

The Höfner Model 500/1 bass is usually known as the violin bass or Beatle bass. Paul McCartney used the Höfner bass almost exclusively for approximately the first half of The Beatles' career. Like a semi-acoustic guitar, the Höfner bass is fundamentally an electric instrument, with magnetic pickups, but the hollow body contributes a rich, more complex tone a little like that of the double bass. Combined with a short-scale length, the hollow body results in a lightweight instrument that is both easy to play and to carry. Although other manufacturers have made direct copies of the violin bass design, its real impact has been felt through a number of other semi-acoustic basses that it has influenced. More importantly, it sent a message to a whole generation of young guitar players that they could easily play the bass too.

Rickenbacker bass

The Rickenbacker bass also benefited from Paul McCartney's patronage, although the instrument is also associated with other players, most notably Lemmy of Motorhead and other 1970s heavy rock players. The Rickenbacker sound is warm and full, with a clear high end and a long sustain in the low end.

Höfner violin bass, 1955

Magnetic pickups

20-fret fingerboard

Hollow body

Split pickup

Rickenbacker bass, 1961

Bass amplification

Essentially, bass amps are somewhat 'beefed-up' versions of guitar amp designs, with circuitry optimized for producing a clean, punchy tone (bass distortion is not desired in most pop and rock styles) and loudspeakers constructed to reproduce bass frequencies.

For initial practice purposes, it is possible to make do with an ordinary electric guitar amp. This solution is far from ideal, however: the output of the bass guitar should be physically felt as well as being heard. Speakers designed for electric guitars, while conveying the audible pitches of notes being played, are not generally able to provide the low-frequency energy or 'oomph' that is an important function of the bass guitar. If you are using a guitar amp, it is also advisable not to turn it up too loudly, as these bass frequencies can ultimately damage a standard guitar speaker. For both of these reasons, it is highly advisable to buy a bass amp along with your bass guitar.

Bass amps come in the same forms and designs as guitar amps: as combos and stacks, with valve- or transistor-based circuitry. They are available in many sizes and levels of power output, from practice amps to wardrobe-sized stacks.

Bass guitar: first steps

Although the bass guitar is based on the six-string electric guitar in many respects, the instrument makes different technical demands on both the left and right hands. If you intend to focus on the bass guitar across a range of styles, you will probably need to keep your right-hand fingernails short; the disadvantage is that this may compromise their suitability for fingerstyle guitar playing.

The right hand

There are several different right-hand techniques in common use by bass players. The easiest for the electric guitarist is simply to use a plectrum in the familiar fashion. Bass-guitar strings, being thicker and heavier, require more energy in order to be set in motion than electric or acoustic guitar strings, so thicker plectrums tend to be used. Also the bass guitar is seldom – if ever – strummed, so wrist (rather than elbow) motion is used exclusively.

Most serious bass players use a different technique, however. The first two fingers of the right hand are used in an alternating motion, a little like the rest-stroke technique used by classical guitarists. The main difference is that the fingertips are used rather than the nails, which also means that the fingers are generally kept straight rather than being curved. This helps to avoid accidental use of the nails, although if your nails are very long (as they may be if you are serious about fingerstyle or classical guitar), it may be difficult to keep them from coming into play. Unlike six-string guitars, the bass guitar does not usually respond well to the use of fingernails. Unfortunately, this is a fundamental conflict that cannot easily be reconciled: if your preferred guitar style requires fingernails, you may have to play the bass with a plectrum.

Left-hand finger motion can be controlled much more easily if the thumb is anchored to some point on the body of the bass. The exact position will depend on many things, including the design of the bass guitar, the size of the player's hands and the style of music being played. Most players anchor the thumb to one of the pickups or the very end of the fretboard. If your bass has two pickups, you will probably want to use the 'front' pickup (the one furthest from the bridge), although switching position to the bridge pickup may be useful from time to time for a more percussive sound.

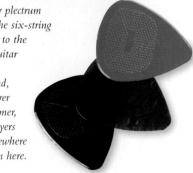

ABOVE: *Bass-guitar plectrum technique. As with the six-string guitar, playing closer to the bridge on the bass guitar produces a sharper, more percussive sound, whereas playing nearer the neck gives a warmer, softer tone. Most players stick to an area somewhere in between, as shown here.*

ABOVE: *Fingerstyle bass-guitar technique. On this bass guitar, the 'front' pickup provides a convenient anchor point for the thumb. The first and second fingers are generally used in alternation; although many players practise scales using strictly alternating fingers, this rule is usually relaxed a little in the real world.*

The bass clef

The standard bass guitar's four strings are tuned to the same pitches as the bottom four strings of the guitar, but one octave lower. This means that any note or musical phrase playable on the guitar can be found in the same place on the bass. Bass-guitar parts are usually written either in standard notation, with or without the addition of a tablature stave. The latter works in exactly the same way as guitar tablature. Bass parts in standard notation are usually written using the bass clef, which fixes the second line down on the stave as the note F.

Basic alternating fingers technique

1 Find a convenient resting place for the right-hand thumb, for example one of the pickups. Otherwise, resting on the end of the fretboard will generally give a warm, full sound.

2 Play the E string using the index finger. Be careful not to use too much force: if the string makes physical contact with the pickup, a sharp unpleasant 'clank' will be heard.

3 Now play the E string using the second finger; the index finger should simultaneously move back into position to play the string.

EXERCISE 1

This simple bass line uses just three notes: open E, G (third fret) and open A. The rests in this bass line are almost as important as the notes; in order to stop notes ringing through rests, one of two damping techniques may be used. Left-hand damping works by releasing left-hand finger pressure to stop a sounding note and is the most important technique for this purpose, but it cannot be used on open-string notes such as the open E and A here. To stop these notes, a right-hand finger must come to rest

lightly on the string to absorb its energy. This should generally be done with whichever finger has played the note, leaving the other finger free to play the next note, whether on the same string or another string.

EXERCISE 2

This exercise, consisting of an E natural minor scale and E minor arpeggio, should be practised using strictly alternating right-hand fingers, starting with the index finger (i). The ability to play like this lies at the core of good bass-guitar technique, even though many players also depart from this pattern for certain types of musical phrase.

Constructing a bass line

The role of the bass in pop and rock bands is to underpin the harmonic foundations of the music, and usually also to supply rhythmic interest and momentum. As a guitarist, you might have a clear idea of what to play in a given style over a given chord sequence, but how does this transfer to the bass? Of all the notes available under the fingers, which ones do you choose?

Root and fifth

Most bass lines can be categorized as harmonic or melodic, or a combination of the two. The ability to construct a harmonic bass line is arguably the most important basic skill for a bass player, and it requires a few simple pieces of knowledge in order to find appropriate notes in relation to the chord sequence. The easiest place to start is with the root and fifth of each chord.

To any guitarist familiar with power chords (or the bottom end of most barre chords), the tonal relationship of root and fifth will be both easy to find and musically useful (see 'Power chords'). The power-chord shape translates into the two most useful notes to play over (almost) any chord type, so you can

RIGHT: *The interval of a perfect fifth. This one will get you started on the bass and is the easiest to remember. Any two notes separated by one string and two frets, will be a perfect fifth apart and can be used over most chords including any major, minor or seventh chord.*

apply this pattern broadly when playing bass lines. There are of course many ways to construct a bass line and though it may not be the most captivating, this root-and-fifth approach will rarely sound wrong. The fact that it almost always works means that the root-and-fifth pattern is one of the most commonly used patterns used by bass players.

Having located the root and fifth of the chord, the next step is to find a rhythm in which to play them. This will largely be dictated by the style of music; if in doubt, listen to a song in the style of the one you are trying to emulate. One essential aspect of most bass lines will work in your favour here: repetition. If a given rhythmic combination of root and fifth works well over the first chord in the sequence, repeating the same rhythm for the next chord is usually a safe way to proceed, as it will help to build the level of rhythmic continuity that most popular music requires. Most bass-line rhythms are very simple, a case in point being illustrated by the steady stream of quavers found in many rock styles. In this instance, you may find that you don't even need the fifth but can instead get by with playing steady quavers on the root of each chord – the simplest possible bass line!

Further variation can be achieved by varying the number of times each note is played: rather than simply playing root, fifth, root, fifth: try root, root, fifth, fifth, and so on.

Adding the third

After the root and fifth, the next most important note in any chord is the third. Unlike the root and fifth, however, the third will be different depending on the basic quality of the chord (major or minor). The major and minor third can be found either on the same string as the root (four and three

frets higher, respectively) or on the next string up (one or two frets lower). Being able to find the third as well as the root and fifth of each chord enables the construction of bass lines that fully reflect the chord sequence: the root, third and fifth together constitute the simplest form of arpeggio (see 'Rhythm guitar styles').

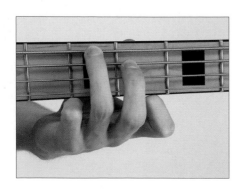

RIGHT: *The interval of a major third can be found anywhere on the bass between two adjacent strings; the third is located on the higher string, one fret lower than the root.*

RIGHT: *The minor third can also be found on adjacent strings anywhere on the bass; the third is located on the higher string but two frets lower.*

Melodic bass lines

While an interesting melodic bass line may be internally satisfying, anything too busy can of course distract from the vocal line, which is the focus in most pop music. In many songs known for busy bass lines, the action is in fact concentrated in the instrumental sections, with relatively simple accompaniment under the vocals.

LEFT: *The lower the bass is worn, no matter how cool it may look, the greater the risk of back pain and finger/wrist strain. It is inadvisable to wear the bass any lower than shown here.*

Recommended listening:

- The Beatles: "Fixing A Hole"
- Muse: "Time Is Running Out"
- Rush: "YYZ"

EXERCISE 1

This simple descending chord sequence works very well in many rock styles, using a simple quaver pattern of alternating roots and fifths. Try it with both plectrum and fingerstyle technique.

EXERCISE 2

The same descending chord sequence as in the exercise above, in a Latin-jazz style, positively demands the use of the root and fifth of each chord in a 'dotted' rhythm (the first note of each bar is a dotted crotchet and thus lasts for a beat and a half). At moderate tempos this pattern suggests the

Bossa Nova style, but the pattern works equally well when played at faster speeds, where the flair that this gives the exercise suggests a *samba* style.

EXERCISE 3

This exercise adds the third of each chord into the sequence previously encountered. Playing exactly the same arpeggio in exactly the same rhythm in each bar here would be a little *too* repetitive, so both the note order and the rhythm are varied while maintaining an overall sense of steady

repetition (bars one and three have the same structure, as do bars two and four). Note how the penultimate note (G#) seems to *want* to resolve upwards to A.

Melodic bass playing

Knowing where to find the root, third and fifth of any chord makes for a good start as a bass player. However, this is far from the whole story. The bass can also play melodically, acting as an independent strand working in parallel with other melodic elements such as the vocals and lead guitar. Of course, this only works if the bass line also makes harmonic sense.

Chords and keys

There is no instant formula for creating a melodic bass line. However, if knowing where to find the notes of any basic chord is a good starting point, the other obvious one is an understanding of the underlying harmony of the piece. A chord sequence is not usually a series of unrelated events; normally, the chords in a piece can be identified as belonging to a particular major or minor key. In looking for notes to use to join these chords up melodically, those belonging to the key will probably be more suitable than those falling outside it.

Let's take the key of C major as an example. This has no sharps or flats – every note is a 'natural', corresponding to the white notes of the piano keyboard. If a chord sequence contains the chords C, F and G major, the key is C major and so the scale of C major may be used freely. These chords

(and the secondary chords in the sequence: Am, Dm and Em) can give rise to a better bass line than just using the notes of the C major scale with the component notes of each chord.

The notes of the parent scale can in fact be used in two distinct ways: firstly to connect chord notes within a chord, and secondly to create melodic material to connect the chords of the sequence. Usually, the latter example will mean focusing on the root note of each chord and then finding notes in the scale to join them up.

BELOW: *The notes of the C major scale in the first five frets. For flexible fretting options and easily transferrable knowledge, it is advisable not to become too dependent on the open strings; therefore open-string notes (apart from the low E) are also shown as fretted notes at the fifth fret.*

Luizão Maia

Considered by many to be one of Brazil's greatest bass-guitar players, Luizão Oliveira da Costa Maia began his playing career when he was just 13 years of age. In spite of a lack of formal training, and although he never made a solo album, Maia played with seemingly every Brazilian musician of note, including Antonio Carlos Jobim, Ellis Regina, João Bosco, Djavan Caetano Viana and Chico Barque, and accompanied mainstream jazz artists, including George Benson and Lee Ritenour. Maia played on Jobim and Regina's landmark 1974 album *Ellis & Tom*; his deep sound, coupled with a restrained yet infectiously rhythmic approach to accompanying both singers and melody instruments essentially created a template followed to this day by bass players across the full range of modern Latin-American music styles.

RIGHT: *Luizão Maia is widely regarded as the father of modern Brazilian bass playing.*

Recommended listening
- The Beatles: "Penny Lane"
- The Knack: "My Sharona"
- The Zombies: "She's Not There"

LEFT: *The Knack was an American rock band that had a following in the LA clubs of the 1970s. Their music combined melodic sounds reminiscent of The Beatles along with New Wave influences. They instantly became famous in 1979 when they were signed up to record the hit "My Sharona". Prescott Niles (far left) was the bass player who produced the memorable baseline for this song. Their album* Get the Knack *took seven days to record and four days to mix.*

EXERCISE 1

This exercise applies one simple principle to an entire chord sequence in C major. Find the root, third and fifth of each chord. Next, find two passing notes from the C major scale for use with each chord (one between the root and the third, the other between the third and the fifth). For variety, use one available passing note alongside the chord notes for each chord in the sequence.

EXERCISE 2

This exercise uses passing notes both to join the notes within each chord, and to join the root notes of the chord sequence into a melodic line. If you can, record these sequences with a guitar or using auto accompaniment software and play along on the bass. This not only helps you play in time, but it can also help you to generate bass-line ideas of your own.

Slap bass

As we have seen, most rock and pop bass-playing styles use one of two techniques: either alternating the first two fingers, or employing guitar-style plectrum technique. Funk and disco styles also make use of a technique known as slap bass, in which the thumb and fingers are used in a very different way to produce a highly percussive range of sounds perfectly suited to the sound world of these styles.

Slap basics

The slap that gives this technique its name is produced by the side of the thumb. The thumb is held stiffly and a short, sharp flick is executed by rotating the entire right forearm so that the thumb strikes the string. The thumb must then immediately spring back from the string in order to leave it ringing; prolonged contact would quickly prevent the string from vibrating.

The slap is complemented by an equally important move: the pop. This is produced by the first or second finger, usually on one of the higher strings. To produce a pop, the first joint curls slightly under the string, in order to pull it away from the instrument and subsequently release it. The release produces a sharp popping sound.

Both slaps and pops may be used to produce pitched notes as described above. Another important component of the style is the use of these techniques to produce percussive sounds with no identifiable pitch – a technique variously described as damping or muting. In this case, the right-hand techniques are identical to the standard slap and pull, but the left hand rests lightly on the string in order to damp the sound and prevent any resulting pitched sound.

Because exactly the same motion is required for each slap or pop, fast ideas can be difficult to execute. Hammer-ons are often used to double the rate of motion in a slap line. So for each note that is slapped or popped, the next note is created on the same string using a hammer-on; this is exactly the same as standard guitar hammer-on technique. Beginners often find that the sound tends to disappear, or suffer a drop in volume. The solution to this is practice: the left-hand fingertips need to develop calluses hard enough to avoid damping the ringing string, and enough strength to be able to re-energize the string.

LEFT: *The four basic components of slap bass technique are shown in notation and tablature with specific symbols. From left to right: pitched slap, pitched pop, muted slap, muted pop.*

ABOVE: *Bootsy Collins, American funk bassist, combined humorous vocals with a driving bass guitar. He collaborated closely with James Brown in the late 1960s and with Parliament-Funkadelic in the 1970s.*

Tips for smooth slap technique

With so much physical energy going into this technique, together with the energy stored in a tense steel string, it is easy to produce a rather uneven sound when learning this technique. A few tips will help you to produce a smooth and refined slap sound. Firstly, be aware of the potential for physical contact with the pickup pole-pieces. If thumb slaps are executed above one of the pickups, the string may be pushed down on to the pickup at the point of contact, producing an unmusical 'clanking' sound. For this reason, many players avoid slapping near the pickups.

Many beginners also find that their slaps and pops sound *much* louder than ordinary fingerstyle work, making it difficult to integrate the two techniques into the same performance. Practice will improve this situation, and you should try to make a conscious effort not to use more force than is necessary to produce the characteristic slap/pop effect. Finally, a *compressor* circuit (included in some amps and also available in pedal format) can 'squeeze' the dynamic range of the signal, to smooth out extreme differences between loud and soft notes.

Fretting the F chord

1 The thumb slaps a low A on the E string (fifth fret).

2 The first or second finger executes a pop to play A one octave above this (D string, seventh fret).

3 The thumb slaps the E string again, but this time left-hand finger pressure is released in order to produce a muted percussive note.

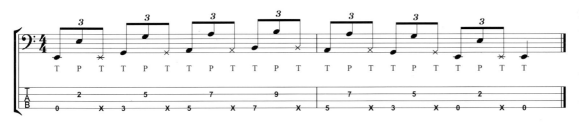

LEFT: The key to success here is in the distinction between pitched slaps (ordinary noteheads) and percussive slaps (crossed noteheads), which should be played using left-hand muting.

EXERCISE

This twelve-bar bass line is played entirely using slaps, muted slaps, pops and hammer-ons; the technique to be used for each note is shown between the staves (H = hammer-on). This line looks difficult, but is in fact very repetitive with only one basic pattern to master,

and it will work very well played as slowly as 70 beats per minute. Note also the use of paired octaves (such as the first two notes), where the lower note is slapped and the upper note popped. This stock-in-trade funk/disco idea is usually played with the first and third fingers of the left hand.

Recommended listening

- Level 42: "Heathrow"
- Victor Wooten: "Natives"
- Bootsy Collins: "Stretchin' Out"
- Stanley Clarke: "School Days"

Heavy rock techniques

Like any musical style, heavy rock has its own vocabulary of sounds and techniques. For both rhythm and lead work, heavy rock players tend to use a very distorted sound, although a clean tone may also be used for contrast, usually in introductions and opening verses. As we have seen, the use of heavy distortion tends to favour simple chords; it also makes some techniques particularly effective.

Pinch harmonics

The pinch harmonic, or squeal harmonic, is essentially an artificial harmonic which is executed with the side of the right-hand thumb. While playing a note with standard plectrum technique, the thumb 'digs in' to touch the string and produce a harmonic.

For an octave harmonic, the thumb's point of contact should correspond to exactly 12 frets above the fretted note. In practice, this technique is normally used with high distortion, making harmonics much easier to produce, and on high fretted notes (so that various harmonics are available within every portion of the picking area). Pinch harmonics often have something of an accidental quality, therefore.

When playing with a heavily distorted lead sound, if you generally dig in with the thumb as an inherent part of your right-hand technique, there is a good chance that many notes will be turned into squeals.

A well-judged squeal harmonic can also be combined with extreme whammy-bar technique – see below – to produce a sound reminiscent of a horse.

The whammy bar

The tremolo arm (see 'Anatomy of the electric guitar') is often known by the alternative term 'whammy bar' in a heavy rock context: 'whammy' describes the more extreme range of pitch popular in heavy rock. In Leo Fender's original design, the tremolo arm was intended to facilitate vibrato (rapid fluctuations in pitch – tremolo is in fact the same type of effect but with variation in volume, so the term 'tremolo arm' is actually a misnomer). The tremolo arm can be used to produce vibrato that sounds fundamentally different from finger vibrato, and with a greater degree of control over speed – from a fast shake to a slower periodic wobble. In the hands of rock players, however, the tremolo arm is often used for various types of more noticeable types of pitch bend.

While the original Fender tremolo was inherently able to bend downwards only, later designs such as the Floyd Rose tremolo are also able to bend upwards.

If you have a tremolo mechanism that will bend upwards, take care, because the theoretical range of the mechanism may be greater than that which would break a string. Bending downwards is always safe, however; the worst thing that can happen is that the guitar will return to less-than-perfect tuning. To bend downwards, simply play a note or chord and then push the bar downwards towards the guitar body. The bend can either be held (by keeping the arm depressed), released slowly (by gradually releasing pressure on the arm), or released almost instantly (by allowing the sprung action of the mechanism to return the arm quickly to its rest position).

ABOVE: *Some players only touch the tremolo arm occasionally to give the sound an extra dimension.*

ABOVE: *Others keep it permanently tucked under the fourth finger when playing lead guitar, and use it on almost every note.*

Three common techniques

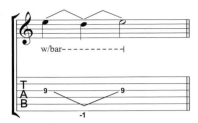

1 **Dive and return** – the pitch of the note is dropped to another specific pitch and then brought back again, in rhythm.

2 **Scoop** – in this popular technique, the bar is depressed before the note is played, and then allowed to return quickly.

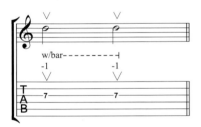

3 **Dip** – an already sounding note is bent rapidly to a specific pitch and back again.

The Floyd Rose floating tremolo

The mechanism here 'floats' on a sharp edge to minimize friction; coupled with the locking nut, this is designed to ensure that the guitar will return to perfect tuning.

ABOVE: *Locking nut.*

ABOVE: *Tremolo unit detail showing fine tuners.*

ABOVE: *Tremolo hanging down when not in use.*

ABOVE: *Floyd Rose tremolo in use.*

EXERCISE 1

This melodic piece uses some of the whammy-bar techniques detailed on this page. The final note should be slowly bent downwards to an indeterminate pitch; if your tremolo has sufficient range, the note will die off as the string becomes too slack to vibrate. The abbreviation 'P.H.' indicates a pinch harmonic which is performed using the side of the right-hand thumb.

Exploring rock and metal styles

Most rock and heavy rock is to some extent derived from the blues. There are other important strands, however, where the blues influence takes a back seat or is absent altogether. The most important of these, which appears in a number of different heavy rock styles, is often called *neo-classical* rock. This musical style consists of elements that can be found in both classical and heavy metal music.

Classical harmony and melody in rock

The classical influence in heavy rock manifests itself in both its melodic and harmonic content. Where blues-based rock often gets by with three chords and the blues scale, this style tends to use the major–minor key system in a manner that is much influenced by European classical music, particularly that of the Baroque era. Neo-classical metal musicians today, such as Yngwie J. Malmsteen and Joshua Perahia, were inspired by the elaborate nature of this music.

One aspect of this line of influence often puts beginners off these styles of music: there is an emphasis on virtuoso musicianship. However, in addition to genuine virtuosity, many tools and tricks are often used to give the *appearance* of a highly technical virtuoso performance, when in fact the underlying technique is deceptively easy. For example, right-hand tapping (see 'Right-hand tapping') makes possible fast arpeggiated motion that would be extremely difficult with a conventional picking technique. The use of open string pedal notes (as in Exercise 1, below) is also common.

Working towards the kind of speed and fluidity that is generally heard in this style of playing is definitely a long-term project. The best approach to mastering the sound is to opt for simple and short practice exercises (such as the exercise shown below) and build up speed gradually. The most important thing is to concentrate on your right-hand technique and the co-ordination between the hands, maintaining strict alternate picking (down/up) and aiming for consistent tone and volume.

Playing effectively with high levels of distortion takes some time to perfect, both in terms of choice of sound and the greater level of control that is required: pick glitches and ringing open strings can more deeply affect the fluidity of the end result than when using a clean sound.

Recommended listening

- Yngwie Malmsteen: *Odyssey*
- Muse: *Absolution*
- Deep Purple: "Highway Star"
- Vinnie Moore: "Tailspin"

EXERCISE 1

This exercise uses the open top E string as an inverted pedal; each group of four notes (semiquavers) consists of one fretted note followed by three occurrences of open E. Start by practising this very slowly and then gradually build up your speed, making absolutely sure that you maintain strict alternate picking throughout (this is an excellent practice exercise to develop your right-hand and left-/right-hand co-ordination). For economy of left-hand motion, try to use all four fingers rather than simply moving the first finger around. For example, the fretted notes in the first bar should be played by the first, third and fourth fingers, requiring no left-hand position shifts.

Playing tip

This type of single-string figure can of course translate to any one of the guitar's six strings, but it tends to work best if the repeated open string forms an important note in the harmony, such as the dominant (fifth note of the scale).

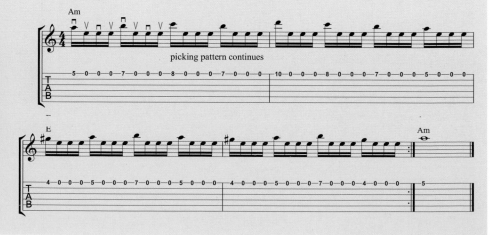

Scalloped fretboards

Many neo-classical players, and metal 'shredders' in general, favour the so-called scalloped fretboard design. Here, the spaces between frets are hollowed out in order to reduce friction between the fingers and fretboard. This may be applied to the entire fretboard range, but is more often seen only in the second octave (above the twelfth fret) as a compromise, enabling chords to be played lower down the fretboard.

RIGHT: *Ibanez JEM series guitars such as this one come with the last four frets scalloped as standard.*

EXERCISE 2

This exercise takes the form of a short classical 'étude' or speed study, using both scalic and arpeggio-based ideas. The whole exercise can be played in second position (i.e. first finger at the second fret). Ultimately, you will probably want to play this type of low riff using heavy distortion; slight palm muting is often used to keep the sound under control.

Yngwie Malmsteen

A strong contender for 'most technically accomplished guitarist of all time', Yngwie Malmsteen, from Sweden, can also claim to have largely invented the neo-classical heavy metal style. In the early 1980s, the full-scale fusion of heavy metal textures, rhythms and techniques with classical harmony and melody was a fairly radical proposition (although tentative moves in this direction had been made by Deep Purple, Iron Maiden and other heavy rock megastars). Yngwie Malmsteen brought the two together in spectacular fashion, drawing heavily on the influence of the Italian 19th-century violinist Niccolò Paganini for both compositional style and sheer technical bravura. Known for his supercharged solo style employing ultra-rapid alternate picking, sweep-picked arpeggios and right-hand tapping, Malmsteen has had many imitators since achieving prominence, but none has inhabited the neo-classical metal style as fully and as convincingly as him. In recent years, appreciation of the neo-classical metal style has been largely confined to enthusiasts away from the mainstream, although there has been some neo-classical influence shown from metal bands such as Children of Bodom and Protest the Hero.

ABOVE: *Yngwie Malmsteen is considered to be the original king of neo-classical rock of the mid-to-late 1980s, which were the 'golden age' of neo-classical music, with many acts signed to the Shrapnel label.*

Metal guitar in drop D

Players of metal guitar are not known for using open or altered tunings. Two alternatives to standard tunings are used very frequently, however – and often together. The first is down-tuning or flat tuning, which is standard tuning but at a lower absolute pitch (as explored in 'Grunge'). The other is drop D, in which the bottom E string is tuned to D, a whole tone lower than usual.

Instant metal

The lower guitar strings are usually tuned a perfect fourth apart. Dropping the bottom string to D changes the interval between this and the next string to a perfect fifth. This happens to be the interval between the two notes of a two-note power chord; the next highest string (D) is a perfect fourth above that, generating the third note in a three-note power chord. This relationship means that two- or three-note power chords can be played in drop D tuning using just one finger. For example, barring across the bottom three strings at the second fret produces the notes E–B–E, or an E5 power chord. At the fifth fret we get G–D–G, or G5. The ability to play single-finger power chords enables fast-moving riffs to be harmonized in fifths.

In order to move smoothly between these chords, it is necessary to use several fingers. Ideally you should be able to form the partial barre with any left-hand finger; in practice, the fourth finger is used less often than the others.

If you have trouble moving between these three-note shapes, just the bottom two strings will work equally well, producing a slightly less thick-sounding two-note power chord. If you have big fingers, you may not even need to form a barre to play these: many players simply use the tip of the finger on both strings simultaneously.

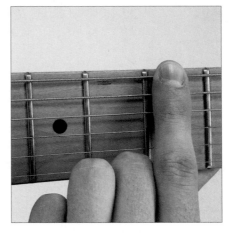

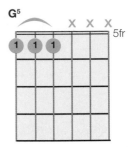

LEFT AND ABOVE:
The one-finger power chord in drop D tuning. At the fifth fret, this produces G5.

Drop D tuning is very easy to achieve in seconds, by plucking the bottom string and comparing the sound against the open D (fourth) string while retuning. As soon as the bottom string reaches D, the characteristic 'beating' effect, produced by two notes that are not quite in tune, will disappear completely. This will be particularly noticeable if you use distortion.

It is not a coincidence that many rock and metal songs using drop D tuning are in the key of D, where the tonic chord can be played using precisely no fingers at all!

Alexi Laiho

Finnish guitarist Alexi Laiho, of the band Children of Bodom, is one of the leading lights of the style known as melodic death metal (which takes both its sound and production style from death metal but combines this with the fast, melodic lead guitar style of contemporary British heavy metal). Frequently voted one of the greatest (and fastest) metal guitarists of all time, Laiho's guitar style lies somewhere between those of Iron Maiden and fellow Scandinavian Yngwie Malmsteen, drawing on elements of baroque harmony against the conventional fast-paced death metal backdrop. Laiho's success and popularity have resulted in guest appearances on recordings by many international metal acts, including Annilhilator and Megadeath.

RIGHT: *Alexi Laiho, whose nickname is 'Wildchild', is a Finnish singer, composer and heavy metal guitarist.*

Combining drop D and flat tuning

Metal players often use flat tunings for a thicker, 'grungier' tone (see 'Grunge'). This technique is often combined with drop D tuning. To achieve this, first drop the tuning of all the strings by a tone or semitone as required, and then drop the bottom string down by a further tone as described above. Alternatively, you may wish to retune all six strings from scratch using a tuner, in which case the tuning notes are C# – G# – C# – F# – A# – D# (one semitone down) or C – G – C – F – A – D (one tone down). Note also that C# and especially C are very low notes for a standard bottom string and may result in fret buzz using a standard gauge string; a heavier gauge (at least ½in) may be preferred.

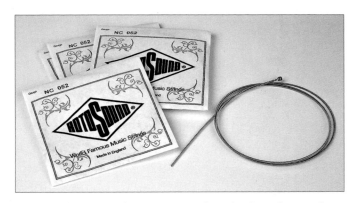

ABOVE: *A heavy-gauge bottom string may be preferred in order to reach low C or C#. Also, a guitar with a tremolo arm may need to be adjusted to balance the lower total string tension of flat tunings.*

EXERCISE 1

This slow riff acts as a useful exercise to help you to get started with drop D riffing. At a slow pace, you could get away with using only the index finger, but for greater long-term benefit at least the first, second and third fingers should be combined. For example, the first bar should be played with the first and third fingers.

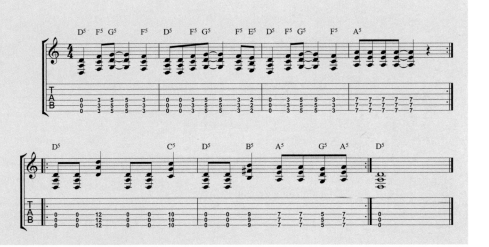

EXERCISE 2

This exercise consists of a typical metal riff harmonized using power chords in drop D. This type of riff is usually played at a tempo of between 60 and 70 beats per minute, so although there are a lot of semiquavers here, it's actually not very fast; you may need to practise it at an even slower tempo at first. For textural variety, you could try using light palm muting, particularly on the open D5 chord, and working with the contrast between muted and fully sounding chords.

Recommended listening
- Rage Against The Machine: "Killing In The Name"
- Opeth: "Blackwater Park"
- Nickelback: "Never Again"
- Mötley Crüe: "Doctor Feelgood"
- Shadows Fall: "Dead and Gone"

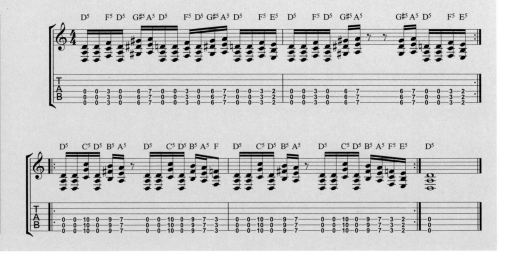

Musical resources: scales

For many players, the electric guitar was made to play solos. But when it's your turn to shine, exactly what do you pull out of your musical bag? What you choose to play may be affected by many things, including the style of music, the chord sequence and how you feel at the time, but knowing a little about some important building blocks will help. Here we look at scales, and on the next two pages, arpeggios.

The major scale

This scale is the set of notes that defines a major key. So a piece in G major will use the notes of the G major scale, at least mainly; there may of course also be notes that come from outside the scale, which are called chromatic notes. There are 12 different major scales; in addition each scale can be found in many different positions/shapes on the fretboard. Multiplying all these possibilities and describing them in detail would be enough to fill a small book on its own – without even considering the many types of scale that exist other than the major scales.

Fortunately, many other important scales can be defined by their relationship to the major scale, either in relative terms (the same set of notes but starting on a different one) or comparatively (starting with the same set of notes but modifying one or more of them).

There's no shortcut to instant familiarity with every possible scale all over the fretboard; you will derive the greatest long-term benefit from learning scales if you have to work out a few things as you go along. For this reason, the major scale is presented here in its most important shapes within the first five frets: if you can find a barre chord by finding its root note on the E or A string, you can also transpose any of these scales into any key.

Other scales are presented in one position/shape only, along with the important information: namely how each differs from or relates to the major scale. This will enable you to find any of these scales in other shapes too. As an exercise, try transposing some of the scales below into other keys by simply moving them up the fretboard. For instance, the F major scale here becomes G major if every note is moved up by a tone, or two frets (starting at the third fret).

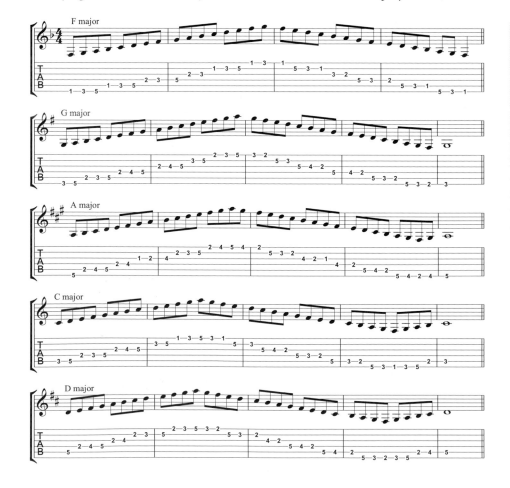

Practise with scales

Scales make great practice resources, but simply playing up and down is just the beginning. Once you are reasonably familiar with a given scale in a given position, try breaking it down into small patterns or melodic cells (for instance, play overlapping sets of three notes: 123, 234, 345, and so on).

LEFT: *F, G, A, C and D major scales within the first five frets. Transferring these shapes into other keys further up the neck will enable you to play in any key all over the fretboard.*

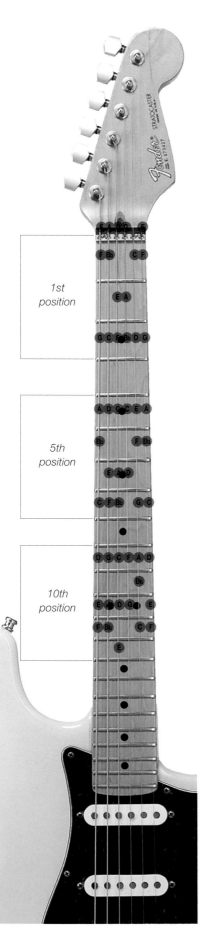

1st position

5th position

10th position

LEFT: *The F major scale in three different positions: 1st, 5th and 10th. These are three of the most useful and frequently encountered major scale shapes on the guitar.*

BELOW: *Three types of A minor scale. These are all based on the C major scale shape (left), but with some steps modified as indicated. These are the most important minor scales, and are worth learning as they are essential knowledge in many styles of music.*

Other scales

After the major scale, the next three important scales to learn are all minor scales. There are a number of different minor scales; one thing they all have in common is that they can be related or compared to a major scale. Relative to the tonic (first) note of the major scale, the tonic note of a minor scale is found a minor third (three semitones) below. For example, the key signature of C major (no sharps or flats) is shared by A minor, and various minor scales can be built from this set of notes starting on the note A.

For A *natural minor*, no notes are modified. For the *harmonic* minor scale, the seventh step is raised by a semitone, so in A harmonic minor every occurrence of the note G becomes G#. For the melodic/jazz minor scale, both the sixth and seventh steps are raised by a semitone. So for A melodic minor, the note F becomes F# and G becomes G#. This principle can be used to generate all three types of minor scale based on all five major-scale shapes shown above.

A natural minor - no notes modified from C major

A harmonic minor - seventh step raised (G becomes G#)

A melodic minor - sixth and seventh steps raised (F becomes F# and G becomes G#)

ABOVE AND ABOVE RIGHT: *A proper grasp of alternate picking is fundamental to most lead guitar styles, and essential to practising scales with any speed or fluency. For all of these scales written in quavers, always use down-strokes on the beat (L) and up-strokes on the offbeat (R).*

Musical resources: melodic arpeggios

Knowledge of scales is important to understanding the basics of music. Playing up and down scales also makes for excellent technical practice, but there is a great deal more you can do with the musical knowledge associated with scales. Practising arpeggios, as well as being good for both left- and right-hand technique, will help you begin to unlock the musical potential of the simple major scale.

Arpeggios for melodic use

The word 'arpeggio' is often used loosely to describe any occasion when the individual notes of a chord are played separately rather than all together, for example in connection with guitar accompaniment styles where the individual notes of a chord shape are played one after the other and allowed to ring on. For melodic playing and associated practice purposes, however, the term is defined differently and much more precisely. Just as a major scale represents the notes that define a major key, in ascending/descending order, so an arpeggio in this sense consists of the notes of a chord played in the same fashion. This type of arpeggio cannot be played by simply holding down a chord shape, but instead requires finger movement as each note of the chord has to be found throughout the arpeggio's range. The notes of the arpeggio should be played as a melodic line, and should therefore not be allowed to ring over each other. For practice purposes they are usually played first ascending and then descending, exactly like scales. Practise the notes until you can play the arpeggio smoothly and without thinking about it.

There are many ways to approach learning, practising and using arpeggios. One method involves learning fingering shapes for each individual chord type from any given root note (major, minor, dominant seventh, minor seventh and so on). Another approach to learning arpeggios involves breaking a given scale/key into its component arpeggios and playing them all within a single scale position. We'll take a look at both of these approaches.

Basic two-octave major and minor arpeggios

Any chord can be turned into an arpeggio by playing all of its notes separately and in sequence. As Western music is built primarily on major and minor chords, it makes sense to begin with major and minor arpeggios. These can be found all over the fretboard in many different shapes; many can be related to familiar chord shapes, which not only helps with memorizing them, but provides a starting point for using them in lead playing: if a chord sequence contains a certain chord, finding the related arpeggio will give you some notes to play that are guaranteed to work as part of a solo.

The arpeggios shown below should be practised exactly as written, using alternate picking throughout: down-strokes on the beat, up-strokes on the offbeat ('AND'). Left-hand fingerings are shown between the staves. Where consecutive notes occur at the same fret and are played by the same left-hand finger, you may be tempted to play them as a broken chord (that is to say, letting one note ring on over the next). While this device is of course used in many styles, particularly for accompaniment, it is counterproductive when learning arpeggios for melodic use, where each note should be heard distinctly and separately.

LEFT: *F major and minor arpeggios with the root on the E string, first fret. The lowest notes on each string belong to the familiar F and Fm barre chords found at the first fret.*

Four-note arpeggios

In one sense, the major and minor arpeggios could actually be described as incomplete. Literate musicians (and jazz musicians in particular) generally tend to be aware of the chords and arpeggios in the major key which are harmonized to include four notes.

In simple terms, a four-note chord uses every other note from the major scale. So in the key of G major (G A B C D E F# G), we get G B D F#, A C E G, B D F# A, and so on.

There are four resulting arpeggio or chord types: major 7th (on steps I and IV of the scale), minor 7th (II, III, VI), dominant 7th (V) and 'half diminished' (VII).

Jeff Beck

Although a member of seminal 1960s group The Yardbirds, through whose ranks Eric Clapton and Jimmy page also passed, Jeff Beck has never achieved the commercial success of many of his contemporaries, remaining instead something of a 'musician's musician'. In over four decades since leaving The Yardbirds, Beck's music has encompassed heavy rock, various fusions of rock and electronic music, and jazz-rock fusion. His own projects are often largely instrumental, but his abilities have seen him contributing to the work of dozens of top-flight artists, including Roger Waters, Kate Bush and Stevie Wonder.

RIGHT: *Beck's guitar style and sound are notoriously difficult to imitate. He plays mainly with his thumb rather than using a plectrum, and makes almost constant use of the tremolo arm, and frequent use of the guitar's volume control, to produce an effect which is rather reminiscent of slide guitar.*

Arpeggiating

Although the 'heart' of an arpeggio shape may use the same fingers as an associated chord shape, these should always be played as separate notes in sequence rather than as a broken chord, as shown below.

1 F (D string, 3rd fret, 3rd finger).

2 Release pressure from the F note as you play A (G string, 2nd fret, 2nd finger).

3 Release pressure from the A note as you play C (B string, 1st fret, 1st finger).

EXERCISE: HARMONIZED MAJOR SCALE

This exercise consists of the G major scale in second position, followed by the same scale broken into four-note harmonized arpeggios. To make this a fluid and worthwhile exercise, each arpeggio spans one octave, and alternating up/down motion is used. This results in the beginnings of musical material emerging from the simplest of sources, and provides an excellent means of memorizing both the sounds and the names of the important chords/arpeggios in the major key. This exercise can be played entirely in second position, which means the first finger always plays the second fret, the second finger plays the third fret, and so on.

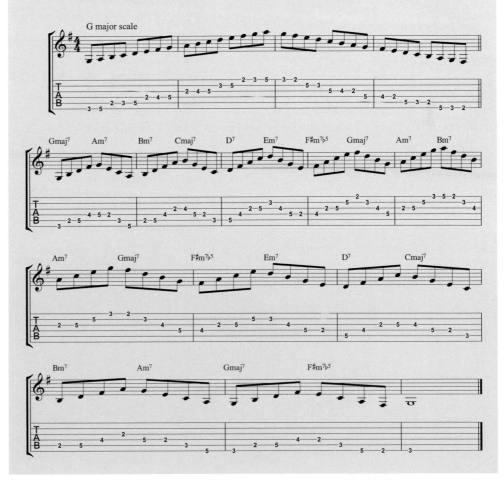

Advanced scales and modes

The major and minor scales represent the core of Western harmony, but there are many other scale resources which can be used in both composition and improvisation to provide added colour and expanded melodic possibilities. Many such scales are based on familiar major and minor scales. This section looks at some of the basic modes derived from major and minor scales.

Modes

Few topics cause quite as much mystification to beginner guitarists as the subject of modes. To put it as simply as possible: a mode is a scale that is derived from another scale; it uses the same set of notes but treats another note as the key centre. The natural minor scale that we have already encountered is in fact the sixth mode of the major scale; in musical parlance it is known as the Aeolian mode.

Although understanding the derivation of modes can help greatly with learning them, focusing too heavily on their relationship to the major scale would be to miss the point: each mode has a unique melodic and harmonic flavour, which is a product of its own internal structure. For example, the Dorian mode is the second mode of the major scale. Thus, the D Dorian mode consists of the same set of notes as the C major scale. But playing and listening to the Dorian mode makes it clear that it is in fact also a type of minor scale, which differs internally from the natural minor scale by having a raised sixth step (in D, this is the note B). This note gives it a particular folky flavour, and it is often described as sounding particularly English, although it is also a firm favourite in psychedelic and progressive rock.

Some important modes of the major scale

The major scale has seven steps or intervals; consequently there are seven modes (counting the major scale itself, sometimes known as the Ionian mode). Some of these are far more useful than others, however. After the Aeolian (natural minor), the next modes to consider are the Dorian (mode II), Lydian (mode IV) and Mixolydian (mode V).

Rather than present all of these in relation to a single major scale, they are all shown here starting from the same note/key centre: D. This helps to emphasize the completely different sound-world that each mode inhabits. Each mode shown below can be found within the first five frets, and is related to a known major scale.

To really get the flavour of each of these modes, try playing them against a static chord; if you can, it helps to record yourself playing a simple strumming pattern on one chord and then play the mode over this. Appropriate chord suggestions are shown above each mode. For example, try playing the D Dorian mode over a recorded background vamp using the Dm7 chord.

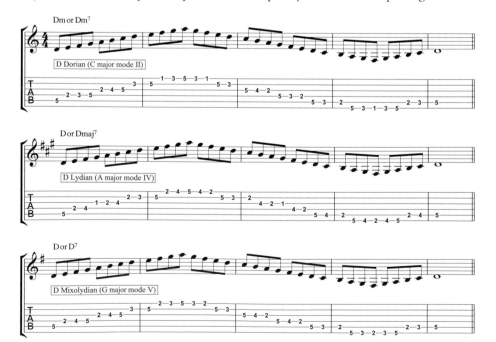

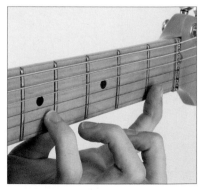

LEFT AND ABOVE: *The modes shown here are all defined as being in second position, that is to say the left-hand first finger is at the second fret in its 'home position'. However, these positions often require stretches, in which certain notes are played by either stretching the fourth finger up one fret, or by stretching the first finger down one fret.*

John McLaughlin

Widely regarded as a pioneer of the styles broadly termed 'jazz fusion', McLaughlin experimented with combining jazz with rock music, and also with elements of Indian classical music. McLaughlin came to prominence as a member of Miles Davis's band in the late 1960s, appearing on seminal albums such as *In A Silent Way* and *Bitches Brew*, with a stellar lineup including Herbie Hancock, Chick Corea and Dave Holland. Like Miles Davis himself, McLaughlin is a musician who has refused to rest on his laurels, bringing his virtuoso technique and love of exotic harmony to bear on a string of musical projects, from his fusion ensembles Mahavishnu Orchestra and Shakti, to collaborations with other guitarists including Al di Meola and Paco de Lucia, and bassists Jaco Pastorious and Stanley Clarke, to name just a few.

RIGHT: *British guitarist John McLaughlin played with bands in the 1960s before moving to the USA and collaborating with jazz musicians such as Miles Davis. His electric band, the Mahavishnu Orchestra, fused Indian influences with jazz.*

Minor scale modes

Just as modes can be derived from the major scale, so they can also be from any other scale. Both the harmonic and melodic minor scales have related modes that are important in jazz and heavy rock respectively. Mode V of the harmonic minor scale, also known as the Spanish Phrygian scale, is often encountered in a heavy rock/metal context, particularly where there is a neo-classical flavour. Modes IV and VII of the melodic minor are used constantly in jazz improvisation. For comparative purposes, these three modes are shown from the same root (D on the A string). Again, to get the best idea of their individual flavours, try playing these modes, and improvising with them, over the chords suggested.

Many jazz players lean heavily on the second and third modes here, both derived from the jazz melodic minor scale. In fact, their standard uses when improvising over dominant-seventh chords have nothing to do with minor tonality as such: they work for entirely different and more complicated reasons, but nonetheless the easiest way to learn them is as modes of the melodic minor scale.

Playing tip

These three modes can all be used when improvising over dominant seventh chords, but with very different results. The Spanish Phrygian Mode, as its name suggests, can impart a Spanish or even North African flavour, but also occurs frequently in styles including gypsy jazz and neo-classical heavy metal. The harmonic minor scale, like many other basic resources, turns out to be extremely versatile.

RIGHT: *Three useful modes for improvising over dominant seventh chords, all derived from conventional minor scales.*

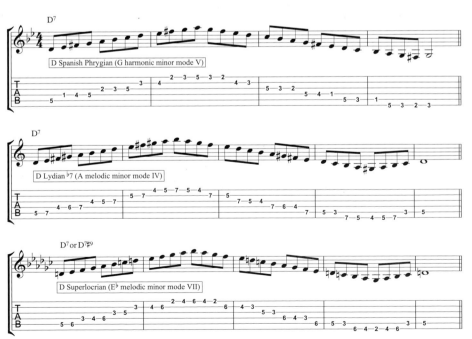

Right-hand tapping

This advanced technique, popular with rock and metal players, is actually simpler than it first appears. Left-hand hammer-ons and pull-offs are used to give increased fluidity in many playing styles; adding the right hand into the equation opens up the possibilities even more. Instead of the normal way of producing notes using the plectrum, the right hand plays notes by hammering on to the fretboard.

Adding pull-offs and hammer-ons

Having produced a note by hammering, the right-hand finger then executes a pull-off, either to an open string or (more often) to a lower note fretted by the left hand. In many patterns this note is also then pulled off to produce an even lower note. Reversing this idea using hammer-ons produces an ascending line; alternating between the two enables both fast scalic and arpeggiated patterns (see 'Musical resources: Scales' and 'Melodic arpeggios') to be played.

Fast tapping of this type is usually associated with a heavily distorted guitar sound, which helps to smooth out any unevenness in volume, but can also result in much unwanted noise if adjacent strings are allowed to sound randomly. These are usually damped using the left hand. When playing music using no open strings, a piece of soft cloth may also be placed under the strings around the first fret which will prevent open strings from sounding.

Right-hand tapping has also been used to great effect in a jazz context by players such as Stanley Jordan, who often uses several right-hand fingers to play melodically while the left hand taps chords on lower strings.

Recommended listening
- Eddie Van Halen: "Eruption"
- Eddie Van Halen: solo on Michael Jackson's "Beat It"
- Stanley Jordan: "Eleanor Rigby"
- Steve Vai: "Midnight"

Tapping technique

1 The first finger of the left hand is positioned on the 7th fret of the 1st string. The 1st finger of the right hand is placed near to the 11th fret to pull off the note.

2 With the note sustaining, the 3rd finger of the left hand hammers on the 9th fret of the 1st string.

3 Pull off the 11th fret by plucking the string alongside the fret and releasing the finger. Pull off with the other two fingers in a similar manner.

Tapping pattern

In this basic tapped pattern, the right hand taps the top E string at the twelfth fret, producing the note E (1). The left hand should already be in position with the index finger at the fifth fret and the little finger at the eighth fret. Pulling off the right-hand finger produces the note C (2); the subsequent pull-off from eighth fret to fifth fret produces the note A (3), resulting in an A minor arpeggio.

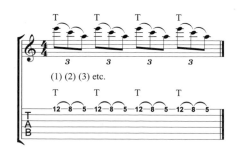

LEFT: *This tapped A minor arpeggio can easily be modified to reflect other chords: shifting the top note up to the 13th fret outlines F major; using the 14th effectively outlines D7.*

Integrated tapping

While prolonged excursions into right-hand tapping can sound out of place in some playing styles, integrating it into regular lead playing can yield some interesting effects.

Bend and tap

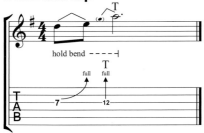

Here the right hand taps a single note on to a string which has already been bent up, in this case by a tone. Listen to Larry Carlton's solo on Steely Dan's "Kid Charlemagne" for a classic illustration of this technique.

Bend, tap and release

As above, but in this example, the bend is released while holding down the tapped finger.

Tapped trill

This is exactly like a regular trill, except that the right hand is responsible for the higher note. This enables the trill to span a much wider interval, for example an octave. Try moving either note around while executing this, for an unusual effect.

Tapping and the plectrum

Most playing situations involving tapping also demand regular rhythm and/or lead work using the plectrum. One easy way to achieve this is to use the middle finger for tapping, so the thumb and index finger can hold the plectrum throughout.

Another popular choice involves cupping the plectrum in the palm of the hand. However, both of these techniques are difficult, if not impossible, to combine with more advanced tapping styles using several right-hand fingers.

EXERCISE 1

Our first tapping piece uses the tapped A minor shape (opposite) and moves it around within the key of A minor for harmonic variety.

EXERCISE 2

This second tapping piece combines a few different tapping ideas. including left-hand taps and slides. For maximum fluency, practise this piece very slowly at first, gradually increasing speed while taking care to maintain rhythmic accuracy and an even volume throughout the piece.

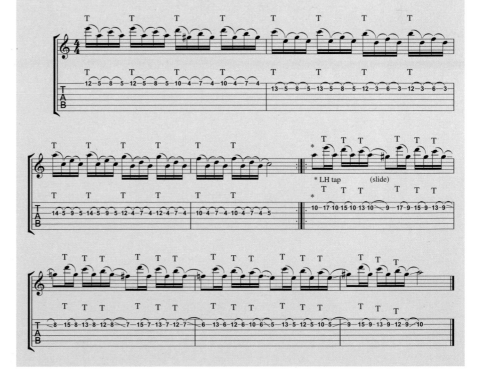

Jazz/rock fusion techniques

The musical territory that exists between the different styles of jazz and rock can be explored from a number of angles, and there is no more appropriate an instrument on which to do it than the guitar. From swing-based jazz with a warm, clean tone to avant-garde harmony with a rock sound – the electric guitar is uniquely suited to the whole spectrum of such music.

Combination of elements

The term 'fusion' is usually applied to music that is harmonically and melodically identifiable as jazz, while drawing heavily on the rhythmic feel and sonic palette of rock. As such, it encompasses an extremely broad range of styles and playing techniques. A few of them are often mentioned in the same breath, however, and they are described in more detail below.

Legato

As a general musical term, *legato* simply means smooth or fluid playing, and is generally used to mean the opposite of *staccato,* so the notes are connected. The term also has various more precise instrument-specific meanings. On the guitar, legato usually refers to the playing of melodic ideas without picking every individual note: each note on a new string is picked, but subsequent notes on the same string are produced using a combination of hammer-ons, pull-offs and slides. For melodic playing, this is most effective if it is accompanied by some rethinking of scale shapes so that more notes can be played on each string.

BELOW LEFT: *An ascending G major scale using legato technique. This covers four notes per string using a slide between the first two and then hammer-ons; other combinations are equally feasible. These use of four notes per string allows this scale to span almost the entire range of the guitar.*

Sweep picking

This technique is often used in conjunction with legato, as it can result in a similar level of fluidity. Essentially the opposite of alternate picking, rather than observing a strict rule whereby the basic subdivisions of the music dictate when up- and down-strokes are used (for example, in quavers: down-strokes on the beat, up-strokes on the offbeat), sweep picking involves maintaining picking direction as the plectrum crosses from one string to the next. This makes it possible to play fast, fluid arpeggios. In order for this approach to work, the usual rules for when to use down-/up-strokes have to be relaxed, so it is important to be able to use both techniques as necessary, without creating any difference in volume or accent.

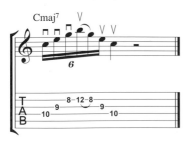

LEFT: *An example of a rapid arpeggio using sweep picking. A continuous down-stroke is used for the ascent and a continuous up-stroke for the descent. Note the use of a pull-off to aid fluidity: without it, there would be too many notes on the B string for sweep picking to work.*

LEFT: *The Gibson ES-335 guitar remains a firm favourite with fusion players; because it is essentially a semi-acoustic jazz archtop and a Les Paul rolled into one.*

LEFT: *Fusion players often tend to use a wider range of distortion sounds than rock players, from very slight crunch to full screaming feedback.*

Sound and rhythmic feel

While distortion has become an integral part of the electric guitarist's vocabulary, fusion players often use very slight distortion, but not normally so much as to eliminate dynamics. At high distortion settings, playing harder or softer makes little or no difference to the resulting tone and volume. At lower distortion settings, however, the guitar can really be made to 'speak' through the distortion sound: notes that are played harder are not only louder, but more distorted as the amplifier's pre-amp is driven harder. Equally, notes played with less attack will come out sounding cleaner.

EXERCISE 1

This exercise is a jazz ballad melody making liberal use of legato technique. Remember, slides are shown using a slur and a straight diagonal line; hammer-ons and pull-offs are shown using a slur only. Aim for a smooth, fluid tone throughout, and try to make sure each note lasts for its full written value.

Recommended listening
● Steely Dan: "Aja"
● Chick Corea/Elektric Band: "Inside Out"
● Allan Holdsworth: "Secrets"

Allan Holdsworth

There is a long list of guitar players who have acknowledged Allan Holdsworth as an influence, including Joe Satriani, Frank Zappa and Eddie Van Halen. The term 'fusion' usually describes a musical mixture of jazz and rock elements; Allan Holdsworth has been one of the few musicians to inhabit this territory while consistently pushing the boundaries of both. To non-guitarists, Holdsworth ranks as one of most original improvisers and composers since the 1960s, on any instrument, with a unique harmonic and melodic conception which harnesses advanced knowledge of scales and complex chord structures influencing many guitarists today. To guitarists, all of this is true, but they also revere his awe-inspiring technical proficiency based in part on the execution of extended legato phrases (where only the first note on each string is struck and the rest are produced by a combination of hammer-ons, pull-offs and slides).

ABOVE: *Allan Holdsworth has an innovative style of playing that combines elements of jazz and rock. In his solos he places an emphasis on extended legato, where he intends to make the sound between picked notes and legato notes indistinguishable.*

Unusual guitars and techniques

While the vast majority of players may be quite content with the standard, fretted, six-string electric guitar (or four-string bass guitar), there are in fact a great many other related instruments that hugely extend the range of sounds available to any electric guitarist with a bent to experiment further. There are also a few interesting ways to get unusual sounds out of ordinary guitars.

The fretless guitar

Although part of the reason for the invention of the bass guitar was to allow guitarists to play a bass instrument easily by using a familiar guitar fretboard, the fretless bass guitar first emerged in the 1960s and was popularized by the American jazz guitarist Jaco Pastorius in the 1970s.

As its name implies, this is a bass guitar with no frets. Its expressive possibilities have always made it popular with jazz players, for whom it constitutes a compromise between the sound of the double bass and the convenience of the bass guitar. In particular, it is possible to replicate the type of vibrato possible on a double bass and also to execute continuous slides (glissandi) between notes — although this technique can easily be overdone.

The fretless concept has also been carried across to the six-string guitar. Fretless guitars are often strung with nylon strings, as their greater thickness is friendlier to the fingers.

Fretless fingerboard

RIGHT: *Although the guitar and bass are primarily fretted instruments, as in this example, the Godin Multiac, fretless versions are available. Fretless six-string guitars are fairly rare since most players find it difficult if not impossible to play chords in tune.*

Beyond pick and fingers

Most guitar players are content to use either the plectrum, their fingers or a combination of the two. There are other ways to set the strings in motion, however. While some players such as Jimmy Page have experimented with the use of a 'cello bow, this is of limited practical use, as the flat arrangement of the guitar's strings makes it impossible to bow separate strings. The E-bow, which attempts to address this issue, is (as its name suggests) an 'electronic bow' in the form of a handheld device which uses a strong magnetic field to excite any string above which it is held. The resulting sound is reminiscent of a bowed instrument as there is no initial transient (the percussive sound produced by the pick or fingernail).

LEFT: *The E-bow can be used to create a variety of sounds that cannot usually be played on the electric guitar. It can also be used to fade in and out.*

LEFT: *The E-bow is a hand-held electronic device, which uses a magnetic field to vibrate the strings.*

Steve Howe

The 1970s group Yes is probably more closely identified with the loose-style term Progressive Rock (or simply prog) than any other band. Progressive rock emphasized musical complexity and instrumental virtuosity, often using unusual time signatures and long, technically challenging solos. Yes's Steve Howe inhabited this musical territory with ease, fusing rock rhythms and textures with classical harmony and form, and was noted for his enormous guitar collection, including many examples of that quintessential 1970s invention, the double-neck guitar. As well as his work with Yes, in latter years Steve Howe has been a prolific solo artist, releasing an album almost annually since 1991.

RIGHT: *Steve Howe was guitarist in the rock band Yes, one of the most influential bands from the 1970s. It has been said that he "elevated rock into an art form".*

Beyond six strings

Departures from the six-string norm take two main forms. The first is the electric 12-string guitar. Like the acoustic 12-string, this actually has six *pairs* of strings; each pair corresponds to a single string on the standard six-string guitar. Normally, the two highest pairs (E and B) are tuned in unison (both strings within each pair are tuned to the same pitch). The remaining four pairs are strung in octaves, with each pair consisting of one string at the standard six-string pitch, and one string tuned an octave higher. These octave pairs are chiefly responsible for producing the 12-string's characteristic rich, chiming sound.

In recent years, another alternative to six strings has become popular: the seven-string guitar. The additional string is usually tuned to a low B (a fourth below the bottom E string, for standard chord shapes) or A (a fifth below, for single-finger power chords corresponding to drop D tuning). Seven-strings are most popular with metal players (particularly those described as 'nu-metal') for whom they provide an alternative to flat tunings, giving simultaneous access to the latter's bass register and the higher range of standard tuning for solo work.

Another very different style of seven-string guitar, generally encountered in the form of semi-acoustic archtop designs, has found a niche among jazz players, where it provides a means to extend the instrument's bass range for 'all-in-one' arrangements incorporating bass, chords and melody.

The bass guitar's range can be extended in a similar way. The five-string bass has an additional low string, usually tuned to B. This extends the range of the instrument considerably, down to frequencies close to the threshold of human hearing, and it is useful for playing in keys whose tonic note lies just lower than the open E (such as E♭ or D). It also enables bass players to take a more 'vertical' approach to the neck, reducing the need for constant position shifts.

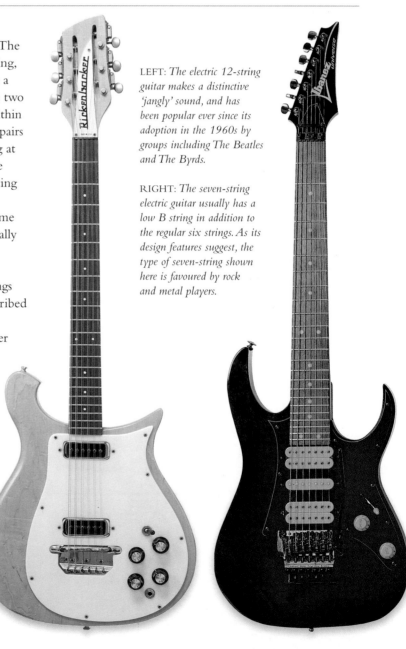

LEFT: *The electric 12-string guitar makes a distinctive 'jangly' sound, and has been popular ever since its adoption in the 1960s by groups including The Beatles and The Byrds.*

RIGHT: *The seven-string electric guitar usually has a low B string in addition to the regular six strings. As its design features suggest, the type of seven-string shown here is favoured by rock and metal players.*

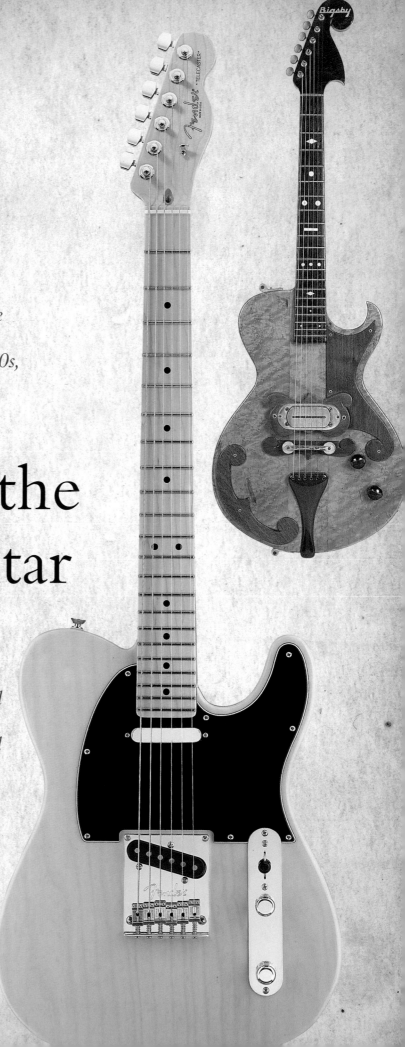

A thoroughly modern phenomenon, the electric guitar first appeared in the 1930s, but only really came of age in the '50s.

History of the electric guitar

Solidbody instruments – including Leo Fender's iconic Stratocaster – influenced the very nature of the music that would follow. Indeed, without the electric guitar, most of the popular music since the 1950s would simply not exist.

The principles of sound

We can only guess at the circumstances whereby ancient humans discovered the musical principles underlying all stringed instruments, but it is generally accepted by historians that the first instrument to use a string to create sound was the musical bow. Indeed, pictorial evidence of its existence has been found in cave paintings in France which date back at least 15,000 years.

String and bow

At its simplest, the musical bow was identical in construction to a hunting bow – it was a curved piece of wood with a string stretched tightly across that was tethered to each end. The string would have been made from animal intestines, usually those of a cow, sheep or goat. Although gut strings are also referred to as 'cat gut', there is no record of cats' intestines having ever been used for this purpose.

The basic principle by which the musical bow operates also applies to a guitar, or any other stringed instrument. The bow is played by plucking the string with one hand, or by striking it with a piece of wood or stone. If the other hand's fingers are placed at different points along the string – thus altering its length – different pitches can be achieved. Whenever any string is struck, the pitch of the note is determined by the frequency at which it vibrates. This is referred to as the note's fundamental. By shortening the length of the string, or by tightening it, hence increasing its tension, the frequency will be increased, so raising the pitch of the note. By lengthening the string, or by decreasing its tension, the frequency is reduced, thus lowering the pitch.

The soundbox

Any sound that you hear comes about as a result of the displacement of air. Since the string on a musical bow displaces only a tiny amount of air, the audible sound it creates is quite soft. What it lacks is a soundboard. When the string is connected to a soundboard, which has a larger surface area and thus displaces a greater volume of air, the sound produced is much louder. (You can hear this effect clearly by comparing the volume of a plucked elastic band when wrapped around two fingers with the sound it makes when one end is held on a wooden table.) The volume is further increased if the soundboard can be fixed on to a resonant cavity, such as the hollowbody soundbox of an acoustic guitar. The string sits atop the bridge on the soundboard – the top surface of the acoustic chamber – and when it is plucked, it causes the whole body to vibrate, disturbing the air inside the chamber.

ABOVE: *A stringed bow played by a San Bushman in the Kalahari, Botswana. The wooden bow is placed between his mouth and his foot. By pushing against it, the tension of the string is altered, creating notes at different pitches.*

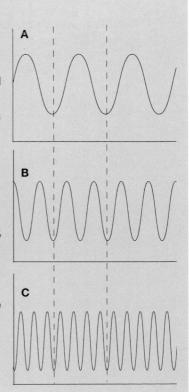

Soundwaves

The frequency at which a string vibrates creates its pitch. In the sine waves shown here, the horizontal axis represents the frequency a string vibrates each second, measured in Hertz (Hz), and the vertical axis represents its amplitude – the gentler a string is plucked, the lower its amplitude. Western concert pitch is defined by the note middle A having a value of 440 Hz. So, if diagram A is 440Hz, the soundwave of B has twice the number of peaks and troughs, raising the pitch by an octave. C is an octave higher again.

the sound. The vast majority of solidbody electric guitars built since 1950 have worked using either single or twin coils.

An alternative technology that is sometimes used in electric and electro-acoustic guitar construction is the piezoelectric pickup, which detects pressure variation caused by sound waves. Although these types of pickup have the benefit of not picking up any other magnetic fields, such as feedback or mains hum, they generate a very different sound to the more commonly used magnetic type.

Lloyd Loar and the first pickups

Although the principles of electromagnetism were well understood by the middle of the 19th century, it was not until the development of electrical amplification in the 1920s that the first experiments with pickups took place. A Gibson engineer and master luthier named Lloyd Loar is widely credited as the pioneer in this field, when he developed an electric pickup for a viola in 1924. In Loar's experiment, the strings passed vibrations through the bridge to the magnet and coil, which registered those vibrations and produced an electrical signal. These designs attempted to amplify the natural sound of the instrument, but produced a weak signal. It would be another seven years before the pivotal breakthrough in this field took place, with the invention of the 'Frying Pan' – the first true electric stringed instrument.

A solidbody electric guitar on the other hand has no resonant cavity and so the sound it generates acoustically comes mostly from the strings themselves. For it to be heard, it must be amplified electronically. While it would be possible to position a microphone connected to an amplifier and speaker close to the strings, the results would be unsatisfactory. The quality of an acoustic guitar's tone comes from the design and construction of the instrument's body, not from the strings themselves. Consequently, the sound would be thin, and the problem of feedback from the microphone might also degrade it further.

The magnetic pickup

A far more effective approach is to use a magnetic pickup that is fitted directly beneath the strings. A magnetic pickup consists of a permanent magnet (or series of magnets) wrapped with a coil made up of several thousand turns of fine copper wire. The two ends of the coil are connected to the output socket on the body of the guitar, usually via very basic volume and tone circuitry. The output socket of the guitar connects via a cable to an amplifier and loudspeaker.

When the strings on the guitar are plucked, the vibration modulates the magnetic flux linking the coil, thus creating a magnetic disturbance, and inducing an alternating current through the coil of wire. This signal is carried to the amplifier, and is then made audible by the loudspeaker.

There are many different approaches to pickup design. The two main ones are: single-coil designs; and twin-coil humbuckers which reduce the undesirable electronic background noise picked up by single-coil types, but alter the nature of

BELOW: *The vibrations of the guitar's strings are read by the pickups as electromagnetic disturbances that are passed along the cable to the amplifier. Here, the signal is boosted and made audible through the loudspeaker.*

The first electric guitars

Experiments into electrically amplifying the vibrations of stringed instruments date back to the early part of the 20th century. Indeed, patents exist showing how early telephone transmitters had been adapted to fit inside violins and other stringed instruments as far back as 1910. However, it was not until the early 1930s that the first true electric guitars began to appear.

The 'Frying Pan'

Lloyd Loar may have experimented with pickup design during the 1920s, but the first significant breakthrough in the amplification of the electric guitar came in 1931 when Adolph Rickenbacker, Paul Barth and George Beauchamp joined forces to form the Ro-Pat-In (from Electro-Patent-Instruments) company.

Beauchamp – himself a well-known musician – had already played a pioneering role in the development of the National Resonator acoustic guitar, and had worked with Barth in an attempt to create an electrical amplification system. Their experiments came to fruition in 1931 with a pair of lap-steel Hawaiian guitars – the A22 and A25 models.

Commonly known as the 'Frying Pan' because of their shape, these instruments were powered by a pair of large horseshoe magnets with individual pole-pieces positioned beneath each of the six strings. These instruments, although not true Spanish guitars, were nonetheless the first electric instruments to go into production. The prototype models featured a body and neck made from a single piece of maple, but by the time the instruments went on sale to the public, they were being constructed from cast aluminium.

The Hawaiian connection

It may seem strange to think that the electric guitar effectively evolved from the electric Hawaiian lap steel. The reason for this is quite simple: during the 1920s there was a major vogue in the United States for Hawaiian music, and at the time there was considerably more popular interest in the lap steel than in the Spanish guitar. The A-25 Frying Pan was immediately popular – its first documented public use was in Wichita in 1931 when it was played by Gage Brewer as part of a duet with George Beauchamp's guitar. A year later the first recordings using an electric instrument were made; although there is scant historical evidence, they are thought to have featured well-known Hawaiian musician Andy Iona.

In 1933, Ro-Pat-In was renamed the Electro String Company, and the brand name Rickenbacker was applied to the Frying Pan. Aluminium turned out to be a problematic choice of material, however, as it reacted to changes in humidity and temperature, causing tuning difficulties. Consequently, strong Bakelite plastic was used instead. These models would remain in production until well into the 1950s.

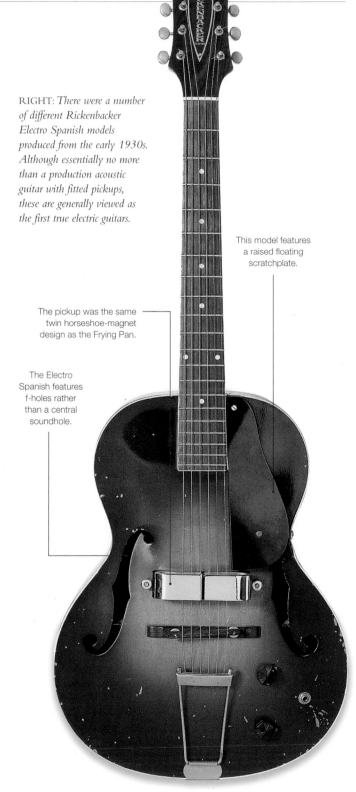

RIGHT: *There were a number of different Rickenbacker Electro Spanish models produced from the early 1930s. Although essentially no more than a production acoustic guitar with fitted pickups, these are generally viewed as the first true electric guitars.*

This model features a raised floating scratchplate.

The pickup was the same twin horseshoe-magnet design as the Frying Pan.

The Electro Spanish features f-holes rather than a central soundhole.

ABOVE: *Despite his brief professional life, Charlie Christian was the first influential electric guitarist.*

LEFT: *Allan Reuss, shown in 1938, playing with the Benny Goodman Orchestra: the magnetic pickup changed the role of the guitar in large ensembles forever.*

The electro Spanish

The specific time when the first true electric guitar emerged is, like many aspects of the instrument's history, a matter of conjecture. It seems that Ro-Pat-In included such an instrument in its 1932 catalogue, even if there is no evidence to support its existence at that time. We do know, however, that Rickenbacker himself had not been convinced that there was any commercial potential in electrifying the guitar. In 1935, however, the horseshoe circuitry from the Frying Pan was applied to a Spanish guitar shape. Within a year, a number of other well-established guitar manufacturers had applied magnetic pickups to acoustic guitars, among them the Gibson Guitar Corporation. Their first one, an electric Spanish-style model, the ES-150, was a substantially new instrument.

Because the ES-150 was not intended to be played as an acoustic instrument, Gibson's approach to its construction differed greatly from its usual way of making archtop guitars. The inside of the solid spruce top was not carved to follow the contours of the outside, which made it less well equipped to transfer the energy from the strings into the projection of sound, thus making it acoustically lower in volume. This also helped to reduce the problem of feedback (see 'Experimenting with solidbodies'). The electrics were simple: just a volume and tone control applied to a hexagon-shaped pickup.

The ES-150 became immediately popular among America's jazz orchestras. Although guitarist Eddie Durham is usually credited with making the first electric-guitar solo with the ES-150 (on Jimmie Lunceford's "Hittin' the Bottle"), in fact the player who would shape the immediate perception of the electric guitar was Charlie Christian, whose sublime playing, in an all-too-brief career (he died before his 26th birthday), alerted his contemporaries to the potential of this exciting new instrument.

The first amplifiers

Since the 1960s, players have debated the merits of various kinds of guitar amplification. When the first instruments appeared, however, no such choices existed. If you bought an electric guitar from a music store, it included everything you needed to make a sound: the Gibson ES-150 – so named because it was an electro-Spanish instrument with a retail price of $150 – came with an EH-150 amplifier and cable as part of the package. These first amplifiers were based largely on the circuitry found in a typical valve radio. They were small battery-operated units with a built-in loudspeaker, an output that was tiny by modern standards, and they had no means of altering either the volume or tone – any adjustment to the sound had to be made by using the controls on the guitar.

Leo Fender, selling only Hawaiian guitars and small amplifiers in 1946, created the first dedicated guitar amplifier to feature a volume control – the Fender Champion 600. A year later, Fender unveiled an upmarket model, the Dual Pro, which had two channels, each with its own volume control, and a single master tone control. It was not until 1952, with the Fender Bassman, that the kind of guitar amplifier with which we are now familiar came into being. As its name suggests, the amplifier was designed to work with Fender's new Precision bass guitar, the first mass-produced electric bass. However, its increased volume and sophisticated tone-shaping controls (separate treble, middle, bass and presence knobs) appealed to many guitar players, who chose it over other models designed specifically for their instrument.

RIGHT *First produced in 1958, the British-built Vox AC15 brought together a 15-watt amplifier with a single 305mm (12in) loudspeaker housed in a radio-style cabinet. This type of single-unit combination is still referred to as a 'combo'.*

Experimenting with solidbodies

During the 1940s, the amplified guitar slowly began to capture the imagination of jazz players in the United States. At this time, however, most of the early electric instruments were little more than standard acoustic models with a pickup fitted; it wasn't until the following decade that the electric guitar really evolved into an instrument in its own right.

Feedback

For most guitarists of the 1940s, the electrification of their instrument allowed them to be heard clearly. For the first time these musicians were able to compete as soloists with other loud acoustic instruments, such as horns. There was, however, an occupational hazard for the electric guitarist.

If the volume coming from the amplifier's speaker cabinet (or from the PA system) happened to be too loud, the guitar's acoustic chamber would resonate, causing the strings to vibrate of their own accord. This, in turn, created an unpleasant howling effect known as feedback. Some players had already begun to understand the nature of the problem; they noted that if they stuffed towelling or other material into the acoustic chamber through the soundhole(s) on the top of the body, the guitar was less likely to feed back. The key, it seemed, was to make the body of the guitar less prone to vibration by increasing its density.

Les Paul and the solidbody pioneers

Lester William Polsfuss (1915–2009), known professionally as Les Paul, was a country/jazz guitar player. An early convert to the electric guitar, he was all too aware of the feedback issue. Something of an inventor, Paul was determined to find a solution: if a vibrating body was the cause of the problem, then a redesign using materials less likely to vibrate was surely the answer. At this time, Paul was close friends with Epi Stathopoulo, the man behind the Epiphone guitar company, and during 1940 he was given access to his New York factory on Sundays when it was closed. Paul took a solid four-by-four piece of pine, attached a standard Gibson neck and a pair of his own home-built pickups, and (to make it look more conventional) he added the two halves of an Epiphone acoustic. The resulting instrument was dubbed 'The Log'. Les Paul thought that he would be able to interest other guitar makers in his invention, and he continued to refine his design. Guitar production in the United States was, however, severely disrupted during World War II, and it was not until 1946 that

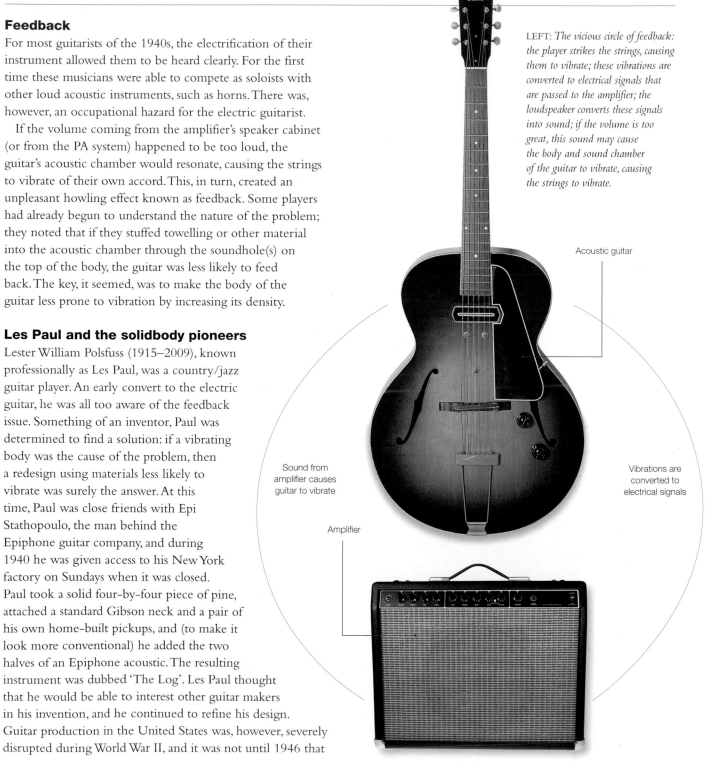

LEFT: *The vicious circle of feedback: the player strikes the strings, causing them to vibrate; these vibrations are converted to electrical signals that are passed to the amplifier; the loudspeaker converts these signals into sound; if the volume is too great, this sound may cause the body and sound chamber of the guitar to vibrate, causing the strings to vibrate.*

Acoustic guitar

Sound from amplifier causes guitar to vibrate

Vibrations are converted to electrical signals

Amplifier

ABOVE: *Les Paul pictured during the 1990s with his pioneering Log guitar, one of the precursors of the solidbody electric guitar.*

What affects the sound of an electric guitar?

Whenever you hear the sound of an electric guitar, a huge number of factors will have come together to create that specific tone – the materials, design, construction and electrics all contribute in unpredictable ways to make every guitar unique. It is also a subject of (often heated) debate among players and luthiers alike.

There is no doubt that different types of wood subtly affect the tone of an instrument. The specific choice is balanced against practical issues, such as weight and ease of working. Dense hardwoods, such as ash, alder, maple, mahogany, basswood and koa, have all been used widely for guitar bodies. Necks are most often made from maple, often with different woods used for the fingerboard.

One area of frequent disagreement concerns the way the neck is fitted to the body. On most electric guitars the neck is simply bolted on. In other cases, the neck is set in the form of a dovetail joint glued permanently into place. This is widely claimed to improve sustain, especially in the upper register. Less common is the neck-through-body approach, where the neck and central section of the body are carved from a single piece of wood. This is only usually found on prestige instruments, and is claimed to improve tone and sustain.

The most dramatic factor affecting the sound of an electric guitar, however, is the pickup itself. There are two basic types of pickup: single-coil and the twin-coil humbucker. Each creates a very different sound, even if fitted to the same guitar. There are numerous possible design variations that influence the sound, including the types of magnet and wire used and the number of windings. Furthermore, the position that a pickup is placed on the body, as well as the guitar's electrics – the tone and volume circuitry – will also have an effect on the guitar's overall sound.

Mahogany

Maple

Rosewood

Koa

ABOVE: *Tonewoods such as mahogany, maple and rosewood are all commonly used in the construction of guitars. Koa is a more exotic wood and, as a result, tends to be found on more exclusive instruments, often bass guitars.*

Paul demonstrated The Log to the heads of Gibson. As Paul would later recall, "They laughed at the guitar". By the end of the 1940s, Les Paul had become one of America's most successful musicians, releasing a string of hit records with his wife Mary Ford, and his invention frequently found use both on stage and in the studio. The Log's story was far from over.

Les Paul was not alone in his experiments. Similar research was known to have taken place at Rickenbacker and National, two Californian companies with a shared heritage. There is no documented evidence, however, of any specific instruments having emerged from this work. Also based in California, engineer/musician Paul Bigsby produced a solidbody electric guitar in collaboration with country picker Merle Travis. This instrument, built in 1948, is arguably the first *true* solidbody electric guitar. It didn't go into mass production, but very clearly had an impact on another Californian with an interest in the electric guitar – Leo Fender.

The great rivalry

During the early 1950s, a fierce new rivalry broke out in the guitar world. The story of Fender versus Gibson is a classic tale of old versus new, of a mighty corporation pitted against an upstart young competitor, and of craftsmanship pitted against the pragmatism of mass production. It was a rivalry that would remain in play for many generations.

Fender: production-line pioneers

In 1938, a young electronics enthusiast named Leo Fender set up a radio repair shop in his home town of Fullerton, California. By the end of World War II, having diversified and established a reputation for building PA systems for local musicians, he was quick to recognize the growing popularity of the amplified guitar. In 1949, Fender and one of his employees, George Fullerton, set out to create a solidbody electric guitar that could be mass-produced easily and cheaply, and so could be sold at a price that ordinary working musicians would find affordable.

His first prototype was a single-cutaway, single-pickup, solidbody instrument named the Esquire. Refining the design, a second pickup was added and, at the end of 1950, the first Fender Broadcasters came off the production line. These were the first mass-produced solidbody electric guitars. Fender salesmen reported that the new instrument was treated with a mixture of amusement and suspicion at trade shows. But musicians who tested the Broadcaster – mostly Western Swing players on the southern Californian music scene – responded favourably. The Fender Broadcaster, however, had a brief existence. Following a copyright infringement action initiated by the Gretsch Company in 1951, the Broadcaster was rechristened the Telecaster.

The return of 'the broomstick guy'

On the other side of the USA, a company named after its founder, Orville Gibson (1856–1918), had been responsible for many of the most important pre-war innovations affecting the guitar. These included the revolutionary acoustic body shapes, such as the arched tops, and the high-volume L-5, which had all but replaced the banjo in jazz bands. Then there was Lloyd Loar's pickup research and, of course, the ES-150 – undoubtedly the version that did the most to convince players that the electric guitar had a real future as a serious instrument.

Gibson had been caught on the hop by Fender's early success, but the company was nevertheless dismissive of an approach to making guitars that so contrasted with their own heritage of craftsmanship. Gibson's president Ted McCarty recalled that the attitude was "anyone with a band-saw and a router can make an electric guitar". Now the Fender factory at Fullerton was beginning to turn out large numbers of Telecasters. Furthermore, country player

LEFT: *Leo Fender's production-line approach to building guitars was viewed with scepticism by established luthiers such as Gibson.*

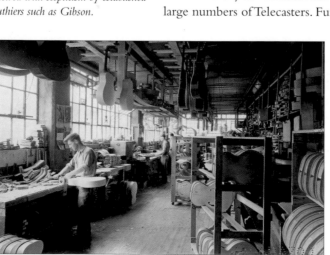

ABOVE: *The Snakehead Esquire: Fender and Fullerton's prototype of what would come to be known as the Telecaster was given a celebratory 60th-anniversary reissue in 2009 in a limited edition of 60, the body carved from 100-year-old pine.*

LEFT: *By the time Leo Fender started mass-producing electric guitars in 1950, the Gibson works, based at Kalamazoo, Michigan, had already been established for a half a century.*

The Les Paul reborn

The story of the Les Paul didn't end when production stopped. During the 1960s, a new generation of young blues-based rock guitarists discovered that the combination of a Les Paul and an overdriven valve amplifier produced a rich distortion ideally suited to this new music. As a result, original Les Paul models began to change hands for large sums of money – in particular those produced in the late 1950s, when the single-coil pickups had been replaced by Gibson-designed humbuckers. Noting this demand, Gibson once again began producing the Les Paul Standard model in 1968. It has remained in production ever since, and has established itself as one of the most important guitars of the past 60 years. It has since appeared in a huge array of popular variants.

These three classic instruments are without question the most famous electric guitars of all time. All three remain in production, and have been embraced by successive generations of musicians. Today the Fender and Gibson corporations remain the two giants of the US guitar world.

ABOVE: *Jimmy Page from Led Zeppelin is seen here performing live on stage at Earls Court in London in 1975, playing a Gibson Les Paul guitar with his typical flair and style.*

Jimmy Bryant, known as the "Fastest Guitar in the Country", was regularly seen brandishing a Tele on TV.

Gibson had spurned Les Paul when he showed them The Log in 1946. However, he was now one of America's best-known guitarists, and so he was recalled and invited to help with (and endorse) a new instrument. The result, the Gibson Les Paul, made its first appearance in 1952. A crafted instrument in the Gibson tradition built from mahogany and with a striking gold finish ("Rich means expensive" claimed Paul), the Les Paul nevertheless failed to capture the imagination of the public. By 1960 it had been withdrawn.

The iconic Stratocaster

Encouraged by the modest success of the Telecaster, Leo Fender sought to increase production with a new model. Aware that established competitors, such as Gibson and Gretsch, were producing more crafted instruments, he set about creating his own deluxe Fender. He cemented his early success by spending a lot of time listening to the views of his customers. Some Telecaster players were telling him that they wanted a more comfortably contoured body shape, better balance and wider tonal variety. Taking their views into account, in 1954 he unveiled the Fender Stratocaster. It was to become the most famous of all electric guitars.

The essential differences

Fender guitars have commonly used body woods such as ash and alder, and been fitted very simply with bolt-on necks; Gibson has tended to use mahogany bodies with the necks set and glued in place. With a number of notable exceptions, Fender guitars are usually fitted with single-coil pickups, creating a typically clean treble and bell-like tone capable of cutting through. Since the late 1950s, Gibson guitars have generally been fitted with twin-coil humbucking pickups, which reduce electromagnetic interference (mains hum, for example) and give a thick sound classically suited to rock.

ABOVE: *In production since 1954, the Fender Stratocaster is noted for its bright clean sounds and comfortable body shape; it remains widely used by rock, pop and blues musicians all over the world.*

ABOVE: *If you want to play rock, the Gibson ES355 1960 is a good choice, but it's also used for jazz and blues. This is an early version of the popular Gibson, which has a semi-hollow body, giving it a warm tone.*

The electric explosion

The electric guitar had established itself as a viable instrument in its own right during the 1940s, yet while it was commonly heard on popular recordings, it could never reasonably have been described as playing a central role in the music of that period. The decade that followed, however, saw the electric guitar enjoy a massive expansion in popularity, first in the United States and then across the globe.

Competitors emerge

Better known for its drums and percussion instruments, the Fred Gretsch Company of New York was one of the first major manufacturers to challenge the early success of the Fender Telecaster. The company had been sceptical about the simplicity of Fender's production-line approach to making guitars, but it changed course when the news broke that Gibson was bringing out the Les Paul model.

The Gretsch response was the twin-pickup Duo Jet, a partially solidbodied instrument that owed more than a little to the Les Paul design. Throughout the 1950s, Gretsch produced a succession of iconic instruments, such as the hollowbodied White Falcon, to give one example. More significant to the company at the time, however, were the Chet Atkins models. Designed in conjunction with country music's leading player, guitars such as the Country Gentleman were responsible for establishing Gretsch as a serious player in the guitar world.

Having created the first electric guitars in the early 1930s, the Rickenbacker name was already assured of its place in guitar history. The owner, however, had seen little commercial potential in electric guitars, and chose to concentrate on Hawaiian lap-steel instruments. Under new ownership from the early 1950s, Rickenbacker re-emerged with a number of important innovations, not least the straight-through neck.

In contrast to the other leading makers – Fender necks were simply bolted on and Gibsons were glued in place – the neck and central part of the body on Rickenbackers were cut from a single piece of wood, and the upper and lower wings were fixed on afterwards. This approach, although costly, was believed to be important with regard to the tone and sustain of the guitar. Rickenbacker became hugely successful in the 1960s following the patronage of John Lennon of The Beatles.

Europe and the Far East

The electric guitar was a wholly American development that gradually spread across the world with the advent of rock 'n' roll. Import tariffs in place at the time, however, made the US Gibsons, Fenders, Gretsches and Rickenbackers too expensive to export to foreign markets. In Europe, manufacturers such as Framus, Höfner and Hagström emerged to fill the void, but they mostly produced inferior models.

In the early 1960s, Burns in the UK arguably produced the first high-end rivals to the big American names, and the company's reputation was enhanced when its instruments were used by Britain's most popular pre-Beatles band, the Shadows.

Inevitably it was Japan that became master of cheap production-line electric guitars. During the early 1960s, a number of curious instruments were produced, strongly influenced by Mosrite, a lesser-known American brand. The reason for this was simple: while The Beatles were dominating the rest of the world, Japan's favourite band from the West was US surf-guitar instrumentalists The Ventures, who were, at that time, exclusive Mosrite users, and remain popular today.

BELOW: *Elvis Costello playing a Gretsch White Falcon, one of the most exotic – and expensive – production guitars of the 1950s.*

BELOW: *Keith Richards used a fuzz box in the introduction to that perenially enduring Rolling Stones' track "Satisfaction".*

ABOVE: *While the rest of the world was in thrall to The Beatles, Japanese teenagers favoured the twang of the US guitar-instrumental band The Ventures.*

One problem that many rock players found, however, was that they simply didn't sound the same as valves, especially when it came to achieving natural distortion. If you overdrive a valve amplifier, the sound is warm and sweet; if you overdrive transistors, the effect is abrasive and, for many, unpleasant. This dilemma led to a gradual movement back towards valve-based amplifiers – a rare example of new technology being rejected in favour of the old. While there are players who prefer the clinical sound of a solid-state amplifier – many jazz players, bass guitarists and keyboard players, for example – the general consensus is that valves play an important role in the classic electric-guitar sound. Transistorized guitar amplifiers do still exist, but they generally now appeal only to those on limited budgets.

Sound matters

Another important change took place during the 1960s. Many guitarists, especially those working in the rock and pop fields, began to place as much emphasis on the sound they produced as they did on their actual playing. The first electronically achieved effects had emerged by accident, for example by overdriving a valve amplifier to the point of distortion. However, from the middle of the 1960s, the technology surrounding the electric guitar took on an increasingly important role, opening up new ways for the guitarist to play, and creating new sounds that would otherwise have been impossible even to imagine.

Throughout the 1960s and the '70s, most of these developments took the form of stomp-box foot-pedal effects. These were small transistorized units that were inserted in the connection chain between the guitar and the amplifier. The first such device was a distorting transistor pre-amplifier known as a fuzz box. These were used to produce an alternative to valve overdrive, or to offer a more usable distortion to those with solid-state amps.

This effect can be heard on many classic rock tracks, one of the earliest being the Fuzz Tone FZ-1 used in 1965 by Keith Richards on the introduction to The Rolling Stones' "Satisfaction". Other effects that emerged over the decade included the wah-wah filter, phasing, flanging, echo, delay and octave-doubling. They all offered the guitarist a radically new sonic palate on which to draw, and had a huge impact on the music produced during the period.

Over time, the big Japanese factories began to concentrate on the production of copies of Telecasters, Stratocasters, Les Pauls and, occasionally, European brands such as Burns and Hagström. They were cheap, usually poorly made and difficult to play, and established a poor reputation for Far Eastern guitars that would take well into the 1980s to turn around.

Valves versus transistors

The 1960s saw a significant change in the sound technology relating to the guitar. At the start of the decade, the transistor, which had been invented in 1947 at AT&T's Bell Labs in the United States, had begun to make enormous inroads into everyday life. Thermionic valve technology, which had played a critical role in the evolution of radio broadcasting, television, radar, sound reproduction and telephone networks, was increasingly being rendered redundant by cheaper and more reliable solid-state transistor-based electronics.

Guitar amplification would succumb to the same pressures during the decade. On the surface, this was a wholly positive development. Valve amplifiers were bulky and heavy; valves behaved inconsistently and were delicate and hence prone to breakage or failure. Solid-state amplifiers were smaller, lighter, more reliable and a good deal cheaper to produce. Unsurprisingly, they were immediately popular. Indeed, throughout the 1970s the majority of guitar amplifiers produced were solid-state.

RIGHT: *The British-designed Vox wah-wah pedal first appeared in 1967. Rebranded by Vox's business partners in the USA as the Cry Baby, it was also famously used by Jimi Hendrix on many of his classic songs of the time.*

Altering the face of music

When the first electric guitars appeared in the 1930s, it is doubtful if even their pioneering inventors saw them as heralding a new era in music. They were, after all, a pragmatic response to a basic issue: despite alternative designs and the use of metal resonating units, acoustic guitars were simply not loud enough to be heard when played in a band with other instruments.

Early pioneers

Jazz, blues and country players were the first to embrace the new electric technology. Charlie Christian showed for the first time how important a role a soloing guitarist could take in a large ensemble. His work in the late 1930s redefined the role of the guitarist in jazz music, and set the benchmark from which other virtuoso players, such as Wes Montgomery, Jim Hall and Joe Pass, would develop.

Around the same time, Los Angeles-based musician T-Bone Walker became the first star of blues electric guitar. By the mid-1940s, Chicago was established as the home of electric blues, an emerging style that was perfected at the end of the decade by Muddy Waters. The contemporary blues scene was largely enjoyed by black audiences or white college students, and so it lacked widespread national recognition. Despite this, it was a fertile period in this genre. Star performers included Waters, B. B. King, John Lee Hooker, Buddy Guy and Albert King, and their music and style of playing would become an important influence on the rock bands of the 1960s. Indeed, players like Eric Clapton and Peter Green, and bands like The Rolling Stones, cut their teeth playing covers of blues classics recorded two decades earlier.

Influential players

When Leo Fender launched the first solidbody electric guitars in 1950, almost all of his early customers were country players from the southern Californian music scene. Indeed, it was TV appearances by Jimmy Bryant, the self-styled 'Fastest Guitar in the Country', on *Hometown Jamboree* that gave the Telecaster its first important exposure. As Fender recalled, "Everybody wanted a guitar like Jimmy Bryant."

The decade also saw the emergence of one particular electric country musician whose impact was almost as profound as Charlie Christian's in jazz. Chet Atkins was a technical master whose influence placed the electric guitar at the centre of the Nashville sound that dominated country music until well into the 1980s.

During the 1960s, as technology evolved, a wide array of new sonic options became available to the guitarist. The first and most enduring of these came about by accident. Early valve amplifiers were typically low in output, and when played at full volume were prone to distortion. Some players – especially those using the twin-coil humbucking pickups first developed by Seth Lover at Gibson in 1955 – realized that overdriving these valves could produce a very pleasing sound.

LEFT: *As rock musicians began playing in larger venues, the Marshall stack offered the necessary boost in volume. Eric Clapton is seen here with his guitar connected to two powerful valve amplifiers, or heads, controlling stacks of four cabinets that house a total of 16 speakers.*

The distorted guitar sound has remained at the heart of most forms of rock music ever since. Indeed, without the distorted electric guitar the very notion of rock music, and its manifold metal offshoots, could simply never have existed. The first deliberate use of distortion on record is a matter of dispute; Link Wray's 1958 instrumental "Rumble" is certainly a candidate. Widely credited as the first heavy-rock track, The Kinks' "You Really Got Me" in 1964 uses a heavily distorted power-chord sequence. Interestingly, both sets of sounds were achieved as much by cutting strips into the loudspeaker as by distorting the valves.

From this period onwards, the technology surrounding the electric guitar took on an increasingly important role. It opened up new ways for the guitarist to play, and created new sounds that previously were quite unimaginable. The technology available to the contemporary electric guitarist is largely unrecognizable from the pioneers of the 1930s. Modern amplification, digital modelling and multiple effects units provide even the beginner with sonic options that these players could not even dream of. Indeed, the art of the modern guitarist is as much about choosing and manipulating a palette of sound as it is about playing chords and notes.

The electric guitar in classical music

Although primarily used in the pop, rock, jazz and country fields, the electric guitar has also featured in the world of classical music. In the 1950s, it was mostly employed by experimental composers. The electric guitar had a small role in Karlheinz Stockhausen's 1957 composition *Gruppen*,

which featured three orchestras playing at the same time, each with its own conductor. In 1966, Morton Feldman composed *The Possibility of a New Work for Electric Guitar*, its unusual registers creating an effect that makes the instrument difficult to recognize. During the same period, Francis Thorne was one of the first composers to make regular use of the electric guitar; his jazz-tinged *Sonar Plexus* (1968) and *Liebesrock* (1969) are both notable works.

Towards the end of the 20th century, there was a greater acceptance of the electric guitar as a bona fide musical instrument, worthy of serious consideration. In 1987, Steve Reich was commissioned to compose *Electric Counterpoint*. It incorporated repetitive motifs typical of Reich's work for performance by jazz guitarist Pat Metheny. Another significant classical work to feature the electric guitar is Arvo Pärt's 1992 liturgical composition *Miserere*.

A generation of composers has emerged recently who have grown up playing the electric guitar in bands. They have used this experience, and some of the sounds, in new symphonic works. Perhaps the best-known exponent of this is American Glenn Branca, who has produced pieces for large ensembles of up to 100 electric guitars.

The rise and fall of guitar groups

Rock 'n' roll music was unquestionably born in the USA, and by the late 1950s the small ensemble format, with the electric guitar at its heart, was well established. But by 1962, the US pop charts were filled with clean-cut, lightweight balladeers, and the electric guitar stepped back out of the limelight. The next critical phase in the instrument's narrative came from across the ocean, where the electric guitar was far from passé.

The British influence

Across the Atlantic, a new impetus emerged. Britain loved the rock 'n' roll sound, and visiting American stars, who had fallen out of favour in their homeland (and so were more inclined to tour overseas), were still very enthusiastically received there. Even Bill Haley, the chubby middle-aged singer of "Rock Around the Clock", had caused fans to riot on his first visit to British shores.

During the late 1950s, a generation of British rockers had tried to compete but, with a few notable exceptions, they were pale imitations of their US counterparts. It was the second generation of Britain's rockers, and the widespread popularity of the beat group, that played such an important part in the evolution of guitar-based music. Teenage musicians began to form their own small-ensemble groups, influenced by classic rock 'n' roll and, significantly, electronic blues music, which had enjoyed little mainstream exposure in the US - it had been played mainly by black musicians for black audiences. This small-band format was also popular with promoters. Bands tended to be small and self-contained, providing their own instruments and amplification, so they could play in smaller venues. Gigs were plentiful.

Beatlemania

Spearheading this 'Beat Revolution' was Liverpool four-piece The Beatles, whose unprecedented popularity in Britain with teenage girls during 1963 was, in itself, enough to convince a significant proportion of their male counterparts to take up the electric guitar. Striving to match demand, Britain's musical instrument market was quickly saturated by cheap electric guitars from Japan and Germany.

Few imagined this so-called Beatlemania would be repeated outside the shores of the UK. However, during 1964, the band's popularity in the USA paved the way for an invasion of other popular British beat groups, such as Gerry and the Pacemakers, The Animals and the Dave Clark Five. Previously, it had been rare for a non-US artist to achieve popularity; now almost half of the US top-ten entries for 1964 were by British electric guitar-based groups. Of course, the impact of The Beatles encouraged a similar response from young American men in trying to emulate them, and a plethora of American guitar bands appeared.

The Beatles' success also impacted other musical genres. In August 1964, while visiting the USA, the band spent time in the company of acoustic protest singer Bob Dylan. His influence heralded a significant shift in the band's songwriting, particularly in the case of John Lennon, whose lyrics began to take on a more serious tone. Dylan, in turn, horrified passionate folk fans at the 1965 Newport Folk Festival by performing on electric guitar as part of a band, rarely returning to his acoustic troubadour roots. Both of these musical shifts could be said to presage symbolically much of the music created during the next two decades.

LEFT: *The Beatles cast a giant shadow over the 1960s, redefining not only music but popular culture in general. More than four decades after the band's 1970 breakup, they continue to influence successive generations of musicians of popular music.*

the thriving punk, noise and metal underground scenes still revolved around distorted guitar sounds. Furthermore, in the mid-1990s the phenomenon known as Britpop saw an explosion of guitar bands playing '60s-tinged pop music. Manchester's Oasis, in particular, briefly enjoyed album sales to rival The Beatles, the band on which their sound was all too clearly modelled.

Fuelled by universal access to high-speed online links, the past decade has seen the music industry struggle vainly to retain control of the market. As user-maintained social-networking websites wield ever more communal power, listeners have unprecedented access to most of the music ever made. Now that the market is so fragmented, it is increasingly difficult for a company to hold the necessary sway to influence major commercial shifts in musical fashion.

Indeed, the global nature of the Internet has enabled even the tiniest of niche musical cults to thrive, making room, quite literally, for every possible genre to coexist and thrive. Given that most of the popular music produced since the 1950s has revolved around the electric guitar, there is little to suggest that this is likely to change greatly in the future.

The importance of the soloist

From the middle of the 1960s, rock music began dividing into recognizable sub-genres – a process that continues to this day. The birth of heavy rock, exemplified by such bands as Cream and the Jimi Hendrix Experience, was accompanied by the first generation of electric-guitar virtuosi, players capable of wielding a technique that was equal to any classically trained player. Although his active life was brief – he died at the age of 27 – Jimi Hendrix is still viewed with awe more than four decades after his death. His musical prowess and subsequent canonization into guitar lore epitomizes the figure of the 'Guitar Hero'.

The electric guitar soloist would also be central to the metal sound that first emerged at the end of the 1960s. Initially a British phenomenon popularized by bands such as Black Sabbath and Deep Purple, by the 1980s it enjoyed global popularity with an ever-expanding list of niche sub-genres, such as death metal, drone metal, prog metal and grindcore to name but a few. Although often very different in tone, they are nonetheless united by combining heavily distorted electric guitar sounds with solos played at extremely high speed.

A new type of sound

During the 1980s, the electric guitar took less of a starring role in many areas of popular music, as the electro sound emerged in the wake of swiftly advancing keyboard and drum-machine technology. When the vogue for digital sampling took hold, and electronic dance music reached the peak of its popularity during the 1990s, the guitar was further relegated in importance. This is not to suggest that the electric guitar had had its day. Away from the public mainstream,

ABOVE LEFT: *During his brief career, Jimi Hendrix redefined the art of electric-guitar playing. Here he is playing the Olympic White Stratocaster he famously used at the Woodstock Festival in 1969.*

BELOW: *R.E.M. became one of the world's most popular alternative rock bands in the 1980s. Their unique sound was driven by the unusual lyrics of Michael Stipe and the nimble guitar work of Peter Buck (shown below).*

The modern era

Since the earliest days, guitarists with a bent for experimentation have taken standard models and customized them to their own individual needs. In the early 1980s, this vogue became so pronounced that it gave rise to new breed of guitar. This was a souped-up instrument known as the superstrat, and the production lines of companies such as Kramer, Jackon and Charvel were devoted to them almost entirely.

Genesis of the superstrat

The popularity of the various forms of metal music in the early 1980s led some players to seek out instruments that seemed better suited to the music they were making. Guitar heroes of the period, such as Ritchie Blackmore, did use standard Stratocasters, but they were heavily customized. Blackmore installed overwound pickups and non-standard tone circuitry. He scalloped his fingerboard, so that his fingers didn't come into contact with the fretboard.

It was Eddie Van Halen, a guitarist who routinely customized his instruments, who created the first well-known Superstrat. He liked the basic Stratocaster design but disliked almost everything else about it. He took a Strat body, added a thin Charvel neck, and teamed this with a Gibson PAF humbucker to create what he called 'the Frankenstrat'.

Another important development at this time was the Floyd Rose locking tremolo system. Metal players wanted a tremolo arm that could produce extreme pitch bends without putting their guitar out of tune. Floyd Rose came up with a double-locking floating bridge with a clamp behind the nut locking the strings in place. It was hugely successful and was used on virtually every high-performance guitar of the period.

Fender itself was in no position to respond. The marque had lost some of its lustre because it was generally believed that the quality of its instruments had diminishe significantly. As a result, some independent workshops that had been kept busy souping up standard models began to produce their own high-powered guitars. One name that became prominent during this time was Grover Jackson, whose Soloist, with its straight-through neck and 24-fret fingerboard, was the first Superstrat to be produced in quantity. Jackson would go on to produce other fine metal-geared instruments, such as the sharply angular Randy Rhoads model.

Fender eventually did manage to produce a series of high-performance rock guitars, models such as the Katana and Performer. Gibson even produced the US-1 – the company's first Strat-shaped instrument. None, however, achieved any great popularity.

During the mid-1990s metal fell out of fashion and most of the niche Superstrat makers went out of business, or were acquired by larger concerns. However, the desire for customized guitars clearly still remained, as Fender proved with its successful artist signature series, which has mainly consisted of heavily modified Stratocasters.

FAR LEFT: *Rock legend Randy Rhoads was killed in an air crash in 1982, aged just 25. His eponymous Jackson guitar, commissioned shortly before his death, remains extremely popular among metal players.*

LEFT: *Ritchie Blackmore was one of the founders of the English heavy-rock pioneers Deep Purple, and later formed his own band, Rainbow. He frequently customized his instruments, and was one of the first players to scallop his fingerboard, scooping out the wood between the frets, allowing for tonal variation and increasing the ease and range of string bends.*

Onboard technology

Over the past 50 years there have been attempts to marry guitars with every new technological innovation. Yet from the guitar-organs of the 1960s through the MIDI guitar synths of the 1990s, nothing of any *lasting* value came from this cross-breeding. This situation may have changed since the emergence of a new generation of computer-driven instrument in the 21st century. Perhaps the best example is the Gibson Robot series of guitars, launched in 2007, which feature an onboard computer capable of controlling the machine heads. Its use in practice is simple: you choose how you want your guitar tuned, press a button, and the machine heads turn until the strings are correctly tuned. Furthermore, it maintains the tuning while you play. It remains to be seen if this technology is destined to make a lasting impression – it *is* extremely expensive – but what it offers over earlier innovations is a basic functionality that every guitarist wants: that is the ability to stay in tune.

Different materials

If you flick through the pages of any guitar magazine nowadays, you could be forgiven for thinking that the majority of the instruments on sale are based on models that first appeared before 1960. Yet while much of the guitar market *is* decidedly retro, there have always been pioneers who want to push back the boundaries. One particular area of interest has been the use of materials other than wood. We may recall that the Rickenbacker Frying Pan was built from bakelite. In the 1970s, Kramer built a range of guitars with aluminium necks intended to improve sustain. These were popular among bass players, who often have a greater willingness to experiment. A decade later, Steinberger built a briefly popular series of instruments constructed entirely

ABOVE: *Matt Bellamy of Muse, a musician with a keen interest in innovative guitar technology, is seen here playing the Parker Fly, one of the most radical electric-guitar designs since the 1990s.*

RIGHT: *When it first appeared in 2011, the Gibson Firebird X was the most technologically advanced production guitar on the market. Not only did it feature automated on-the-fly tuning and an assortment of digital effects, but it also had modelling software to produce a variety of different amplifier sounds.*

from a proprietary mix of graphite and carbon fibre. Immediately recognizable for having no headstock, the Steinbergers were fine instruments that ultimately failed once their unusual appearance became unfashionable.

Arguably the most radical production guitar developed since the 1990s is the Parker Fly. Creator Ken Parker set out to build an instrument that was lower in mass than a regular guitar, but just as solid in strength. It consists of a wooden frame with an exoskeleton made from a powerful carbon fibre/epoxy composite; the neck also features a similar composite fingerboard. Also revolutionary, the Fly's electrics feature not only a pair of switchable humbuckers but also an internal battery-powered Fishman piezo pickup for an amplified acoustic sound.

First produced in 1993, the Fly has continued to evolve and is now an established high-end electric guitar, favoured by players such as Matt Bellamy of Muse, and Joe Walsh of the Eagles.

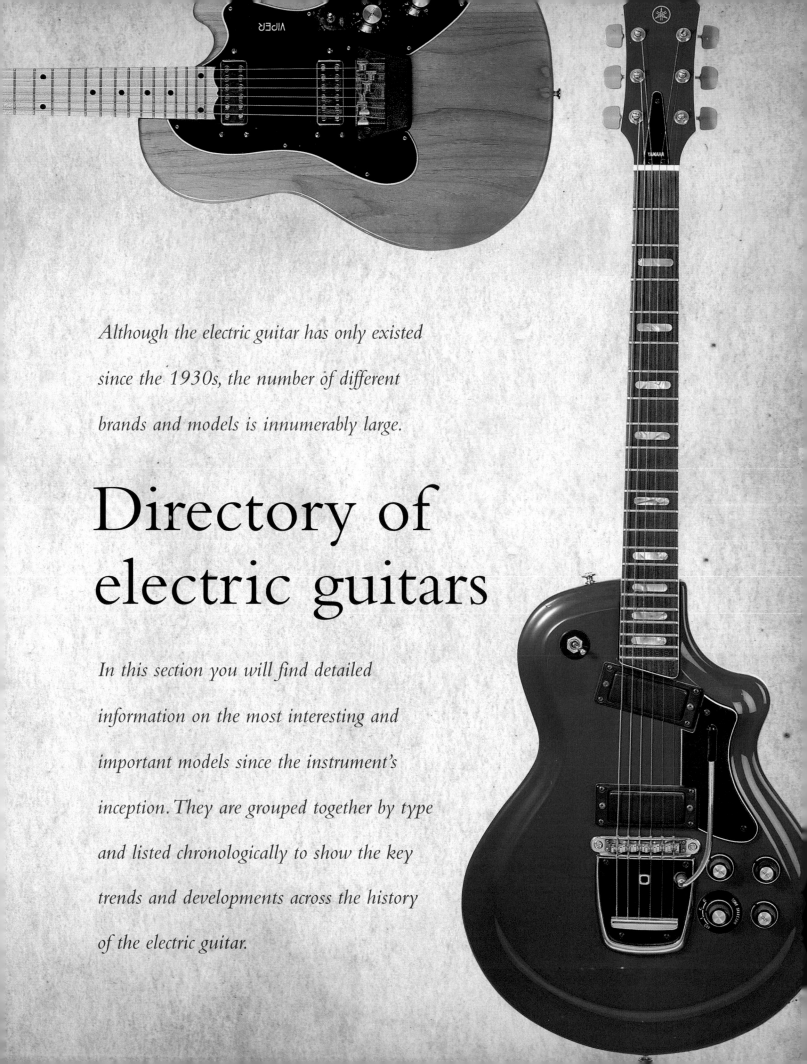

Although the electric guitar has only existed since the 1930s, the number of different brands and models is innumerably large.

Directory of electric guitars

In this section you will find detailed information on the most interesting and important models since the instrument's inception. They are grouped together by type and listed chronologically to show the key trends and developments across the history of the electric guitar.

Electric lap steels

By the start of the 1930s, the guitar was still to achieve mainstream popular recognition. Curiously, for an instrument that would have such an impact on the music and popular culture of the 20th century, the first electric guitars were modelled on the small Hawaiian lap-steel instruments rather than the more familiar figure-of-eight shapes associated with the traditional Spanish guitar.

Ro-Pat-In 'Frying Pan', 1931

The Ro-Pat-In electric lap-steel model, known as the 'Frying Pan' because of its body shape, was the first commercially marketed electric-stringed instrument. George Beauchamp's prototype was created from maple, but by the time it went into production had been redesigned from cast aluminium. The Frying Pan was plugged into an amplifier via connections to a pair of terminals on the body. Two models were built, the A-25 and the shorter-scaled A-22.

The cast aluminium construction was sturdy but heavy.

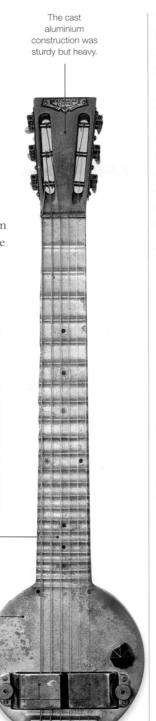

- ● **DATE** 1931
- ● **ORIGIN** Los Angeles, California, USA
- ● **WOOD**
  Prototype built from maple; cast aluminium used for production models.
- ● **UNUSUAL FEATURE**
  Pickup design featured a single coil of copper wire wrapped around a pair of horseshoe magnets.

The pitch on a lap-steel guitar is altered by moving a metal bar along the strings.

The first Frying Pans were built from aluminium; later they were made from Bakelite.

George Beauchamp's pickup was built from two 38mm (1½in) horseshoe magnets.

Rickenbacker Model B Lap Steel, 1935

By 1935 Ro-Pat-In had adopted the name of one of its founders, Adolph Rickenbacker. The Model B, although still a lap steel, saw the body shape of the Frying Pan taking on the familiar contours of the Spanish guitar. Construction also evolved as the cast aluminium – heavy and with intonation overly affected by temperature – was replaced by Bakelite, a robust plastic used on domestic electrical products of the period.

- ● **DATE** 1935
- ● **ORIGIN** Los Angeles, California, USA
- ● **WOOD**
  Hollow-cavity Bakelite body, bolt-on/detachable neck with frets moulded into the fingerboard
- ● **UNUSUAL FEATURE**
  Rickenbacker's Bakelite lap steels were produced until the company was sold in 1953.

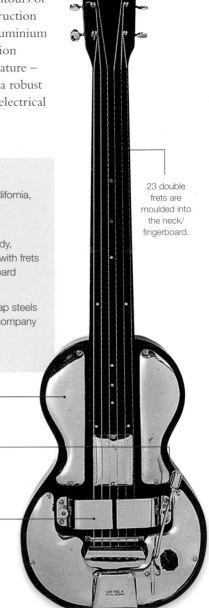

23 double frets are moulded into the neck/fingerboard.

The body cavities are covered by five chrome plates.

The Model B also featured a vibrato arm.

Single-coil horseshoe-magnet pickups were used on of the all early Rickenbackers.

Gibson EH-150 Lap Steel, 1936

Along with Martin and Epiphone, by the middle of the 1930s Gibson had become established as one of the USA's most important guitar manufacturers. Responding to the success of Rickenbacker, Gibson's first electric instrument was also a lap steel, the 1935 aluminium-bodied E-150. Less than 100 of these were built during its 18 months in production. This was followed a year later by the EH-150, in essence a small maple-topped guitar, which was available until 1943.

- **DATE** 1936

- **ORIGIN** Kalamazoo, Michigan, USA

- **WOOD**
  Hollowbody construction (solid mahogany body was introduced briefly in 1942) with maple top and screw-on back.

- **UNUSUAL FEATURE**
  There was one single-coil steel-magnet blade pickup with single volume and tone controls.

The rosewood fingerboard has pearl inlays.

Fret markers are positioned over more than two octaves.

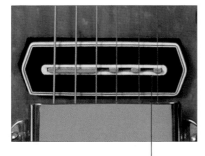

ABOVE: *The steel-magnet blade pickup is widely known as the Charlie Christian because of that guitar's close association with the pioneer of electric jazz guitar.*

Combined bridge and tailpiece is covered by a chrome plate.

Why Hawaii?

That the first commercially viable electric guitars were lap-steel instruments can be explained in part by the prevailing vogue in the USA during this period for Hawaiian music. The Panama Pacific Exhibition in San Francisco in 1915 is widely cited as having introduced Americans to the music of the island – indeed, so popular was the combination of ukulele and lap steel that within a year records of Hawaiian music had outsold all other genres. Not surprisingly, sales of ukuleles and lap-steel guitars gradually followed suit. The Spanish guitar at this time was something of a niche instrument, used mainly in folk and blues music, so it is hardly surprising that those experimenting with the first magnetic pickups would focus on instruments with the greatest sales potential. Additionally, construction of the lap-steel guitar was a simpler and cheaper process, requiring far less specialized skill than producing an acoustic instrument.

ABOVE: *Sol Hoopii (centre) and his trio were very important in the popularization of Hawaiian music in the USA. Seen here in the late 1920s playing a National Resonator, Hoopii took up the electric lap steel in 1935, quickly becoming one of the finest exponents of the instrument, even developing his own C# minor tuning system.*

The electrics on the EH-150 are identical to those used in Gibson's ES-150 – the first successful electric guitar.

Early archtops

With the Frying Pan, the principles of the magnetic pickup were proven as a means of amplifying volume, so Rickenbacker applied this invention to the Spanish guitar – and other makers quickly followed. These, however, were not designed as electric guitars but were regular steel-string acoustics with pickups fitted that were usually sold as part of a set that included a small amplifier.

Rickenbacker Electro Spanish, 1933

Arguably the first true electric guitar, Rickenbacker made use of his business connections to the National company, for whom his partner Beauchamp had designed the first resonator guitars. In truth, it was little more than a standard-issue National Trojan with horseshoe-magnet pickups fitted. As guitars, they were extremely basic, made with cheap plywood bodies. Rickenbacker himself had little faith in the idea of the electric guitar and thereafter concentrated on electric lap steels until he sold the company.

- **DATE** 1933
- **ORIGIN** Los Angeles, California, USA
- **WOOD**
  Plywood body with maple veneer, maple neck, rosewood fingerboard.
- **UNUSUAL FEATURE**
  Initial model had limited electrics; separate volume and tone controls were added on later instruments.

Gibson ES-150, 1936

A significant instrument, the ES-150 was the first commercially successful electric guitar. Some of its popularity can be attributed to its pioneering use as a solo instrument by jazz guitarist Charlie Christian – although equally important was that the ES-150 was a fine instrument, reflecting its Gibson pedigree. Electric guitars had been viewed with suspicion by many musicians, but hearing such an instrument played by a virtuoso all but established the electric guitar as a serious musical proposition.

- **DATE** 1936
- **ORIGIN** Kalamazoo, Michigan, USA
- **WOOD**
  Maple back and sides, spruce top, mahogany set neck, rosewood fingerboard.
- **UNUSUAL FEATURE**
  A single-coil steel-magnet blade pickup is in the neck position – replaced by P-90 in 1946.

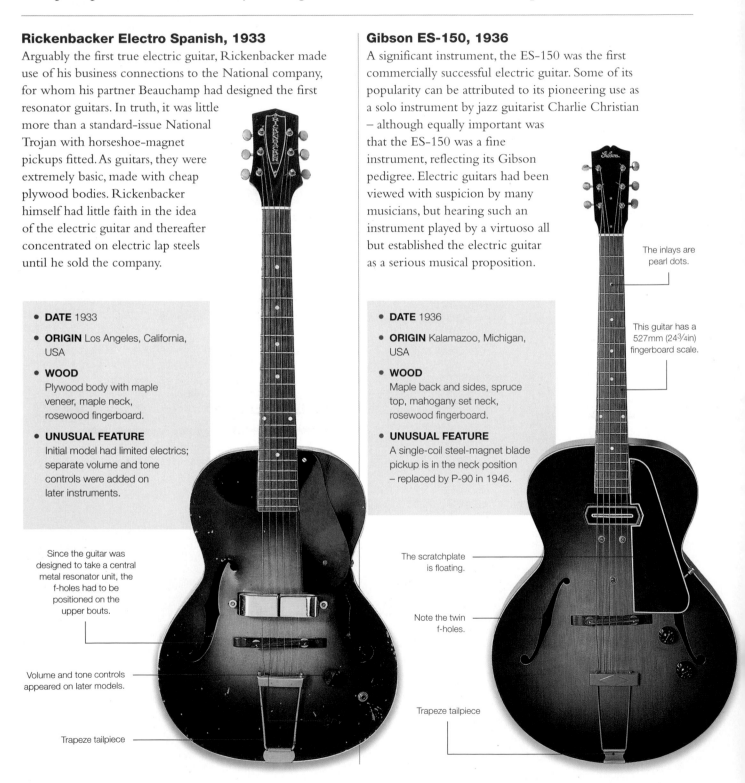

Since the guitar was designed to take a central metal resonator unit, the f-holes had to be positioned on the upper bouts.

Volume and tone controls appeared on later models.

Trapeze tailpiece

The inlays are pearl dots.

This guitar has a 527mm (24¾in) fingerboard scale.

The scratchplate is floating.

Note the twin f-holes.

Trapeze tailpiece

Gibson ES-125, 1938

With the ES-150 having established itself as the market leader among electric guitars, in 1938 Gibson introduced an entry-level electric, the ES-100. It was a basic, no-frills, small-bodied archtop with a single pickup and a sunburst finish, and it retailed for $49. In 1941 the ES-100 was renamed the ES-125. It featured an unbound rosewood fingerboard, a single-coil blade pickup in the neck position with a volume control and tone control. Production ended early in 1942, resuming after the end of World War II with a larger body and a P-90 pickup. It remained in production until 1970.

- **DATE** Launched in 1938 as ES-100; ES-125 from 1938

- **ORIGIN** Kalamazoo, Michigan, USA

- **WOOD**
  Maple top, mahogany sides, rosewood fingerboard.

- **UNUSUAL FEATURE**
  The Charlie Christian blade pickup was replaced by a P-90 in 1946.

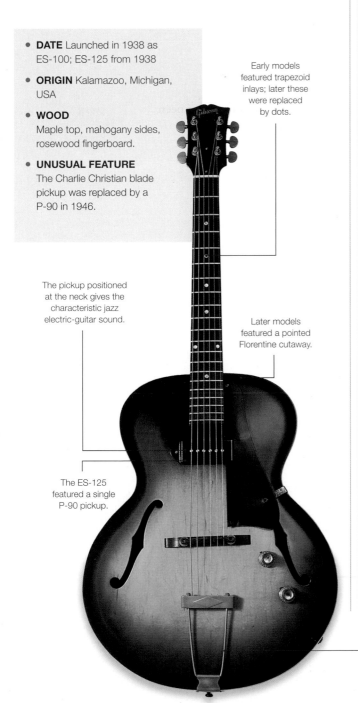

Early models featured trapezoid inlays; later these were replaced by dots.

The pickup positioned at the neck gives the characteristic jazz electric-guitar sound.

Later models featured a pointed Florentine cutaway.

The ES-125 featured a single P-90 pickup.

Trapeze tailpiece

Charlie Christian

A seminal figure in the history of jazz guitar, Charlie Christian (1916–42) enjoyed the briefest of careers before his sudden death at the age of 25. During the course of barely three years in the limelight, often with bandleader Benny Goodman, Christian combined his amplified Gibson ES-150 electric guitar with a virtuoso single-string technique that helped to bring the guitar out of the rhythm section and establish itself as an important solo instrument. In spite of a small body of recorded work, Christian was a major influence on the next generation of jazz players, including such famous names as Wes Montgomery, Barney Kessel, Herb Ellis and Jim Hall. His significance in paving the way for the modern electric guitar sound was also properly acknowledged in 1990 when he was inducted into the Rock and Roll Hall of Fame as an Early Influence.

ABOVE: *Charlie Christian playing his Gibson ES-150, in one of a small number of existing photographs of the first great electric soloist. Christian was to become an influence for successive generations of jazz guitarists.*

The luxury Gibsons

With the success of the ES-150, Gibson quickly became the brand of choice for the serious player. Throughout the 1940s, the company's only real competition came from Epiphone in New York. Indeed, during this time, the two companies enjoyed a rivalry only matched by that which later developed between Gibson and Fender during the 1950s.

Gibson Super 400P (Modified), 1939

The Super 400 archtop acoustic first appeared in 1934. With its grand auditorium body (457mm/18in), it was the largest guitar Gibson had ever built – and costing $400 at the height of the Great Depression, it also represented outrageous luxury. The model shown here is a modified Super 400P. In the early years of the electric guitar, some players, unhappy with stock electric models, had pickups fitted to superior acoustic instruments. Thus, the owner of this guitar is likely to have been a fairly wealthy, successful professional player.

- **DATE** 1939

- **ORIGIN** Kalamazoo, Michigan, USA

- **WOOD**
  Figured-maple back and sides, cross-braced top with twin f-holes and a single cutaway, mahogany set neck, ebony fingerboard.

- **UNUSUAL FEATURE**
  The bridge on this guitar is adjustable.

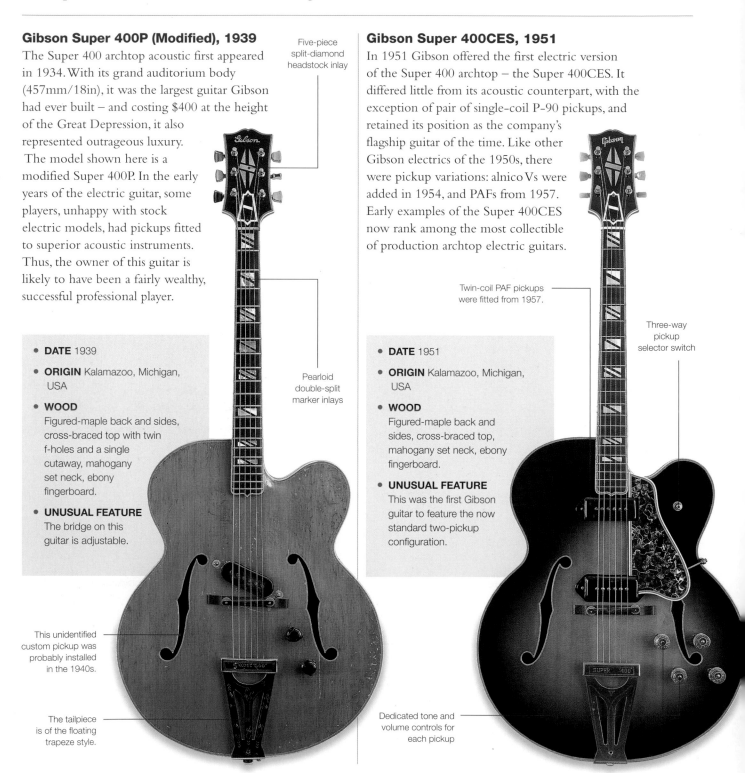

Five-piece split-diamond headstock inlay

Pearloid double-split marker inlays

This unidentified custom pickup was probably installed in the 1940s.

The tailpiece is of the floating trapeze style.

Gibson Super 400CES, 1951

In 1951 Gibson offered the first electric version of the Super 400 archtop – the Super 400CES. It differed little from its acoustic counterpart, with the exception of pair of single-coil P-90 pickups, and retained its position as the company's flagship guitar of the time. Like other Gibson electrics of the 1950s, there were pickup variations: alnico Vs were added in 1954, and PAFs from 1957. Early examples of the Super 400CES now rank among the most collectible of production archtop electric guitars.

- **DATE** 1951

- **ORIGIN** Kalamazoo, Michigan, USA

- **WOOD**
  Figured-maple back and sides, cross-braced top, mahogany set neck, ebony fingerboard.

- **UNUSUAL FEATURE**
  This was the first Gibson guitar to feature the now standard two-pickup configuration.

Twin-coil PAF pickups were fitted from 1957.

Three-way pickup selector switch

Dedicated tone and volume controls for each pickup

Gibson L5-CES, 1951

Radical in size and construction, the 1922 Gibson L-5 had been the premier rhythm guitar of the Big Band era. Later, European jazz pioneer Django Reinhardt garnered attention when, in 1946, he played an electrified L-5 that had been modified with a DeArmond pickup. In 1949 Gibson offered an L-5 variant, the ES-5, and in 1951 the L5-CES, 31 models of which came off Gibson's Kalamazoo assembly line. Only it was only ever produced in small quantities, it nonetheless has remained since then in the Gibson catalogue.

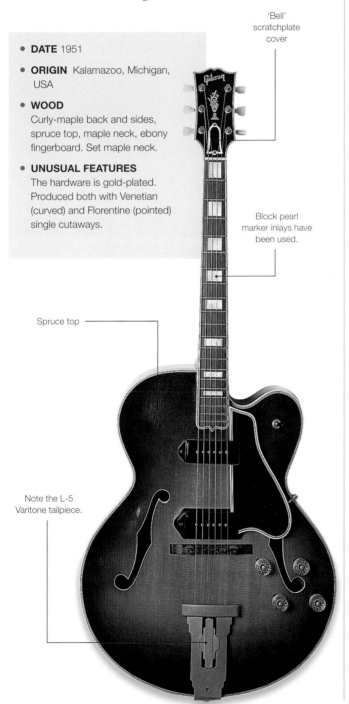

- **DATE** 1951

- **ORIGIN** Kalamazoo, Michigan, USA

- **WOOD**
  Curly-maple back and sides, spruce top, maple neck, ebony fingerboard. Set maple neck.

- **UNUSUAL FEATURES**
  The hardware is gold-plated. Produced both with Venetian (curved) and Florentine (pointed) single cutaways.

'Bell' scratchplate cover

Block pearl marker inlays have been used.

Spruce top

Note the L-5 Varitone tailpiece.

The electric transformation

Charlie Christian is widely credited for his role in the popularization of the electric guitar in the jazz world between 1939 and his death in 1942. He was by no means alone, though. There is no clear agreement about who made the first recordings featuring an electric guitar, but one strong candidate is George Barnes, who cut the sides "Sweetheart Land" and "It's a Low-Down Dirty Shame" in Chicago on March 1, 1938. Around the same time, the better-known Eddie Durham, with the Kansas City Five, cut the first recorded solo using Gibson's popular ES-150. It was Durham who would introduce the instrument to Charlie Christian. However, it was blues music that first adopted the electric guitar *en masse*. Chicago musicians, including T-Bone Walker, Muddy Waters, Big Bill Broonzy and Tampa Red, and country-blues players, such as Memphis Minnie, created a whole new genre in the early 1940s: electric blues.

ABOVE: *Memphis Minnie was part of the first generation of blues artists to use the electric guitar – and one the few women during that time to be treated seriously as an instrumentalist. She is best remembered for the 1929 song "When the Levee Breaks", which she co-composed with her husband Kansas Joe McCoy, and was famously covered in 1971 by Led Zeppelin.*

Gibson ES-175 family

In 1949, Gibson launched the single-pickup ES-175 archtop electric guitar. Retailing at $175 (Gibson's ES numbers were often named after their original shop price), it represented good value for an instrument bearing the Gibson marque and proved to be extremely popular, especially with a new generation of jazz musicians in the 1950s, which remains the same today.

Gibson ES-175, 1949

Launched as an electric counterpart to the mid-level F-4 acoustic archtop, the most striking feature of the ES-175 was the sharp Florentine cutaway – the first such design to feature on a Gibson guitar. This offered the player enhanced access to the upper register. The ES-175 was launched in 1949 with a single P-90 pickup. By the end of the 1950s, it had been upgraded to a pair of PAF humbuckers – a classic configuration that has undergone little change since then.

- **DATE** 1949
- **ORIGIN** Kalamazoo, Michigan, USA
- **WOOD**
  Maple back and sides, maple laminated top, mahogany set neck, rosewood fingerboard.
- **UNUSUAL FEATURE**
  P-90 pickups – Gibson PAF humbuckers were introduced in 1957.

Gibson ES-140, 1950

Following a year on after the launch of the ES-175 was the ES-140 – essentially a three-quarter-size jazz guitar aimed at students or smaller adults. Although these were budget instruments, they were nonetheless finished to Gibson's customary high production standards, and the pickups and circuitry were identical to the professional models. The ES-140 was replaced in 1957 with the ES-140T – an identical instrument but with a thinline body.

- **DATE** 1950
- **ORIGIN** Kalamazoo, Michigan, USA
- **WOOD**
  Maple-laminated body, one-piece mahogany set neck.
- **UNUSUAL FEATURES**
  There is a single P-90 neck pickup. Available in sunburst or natural finishes.

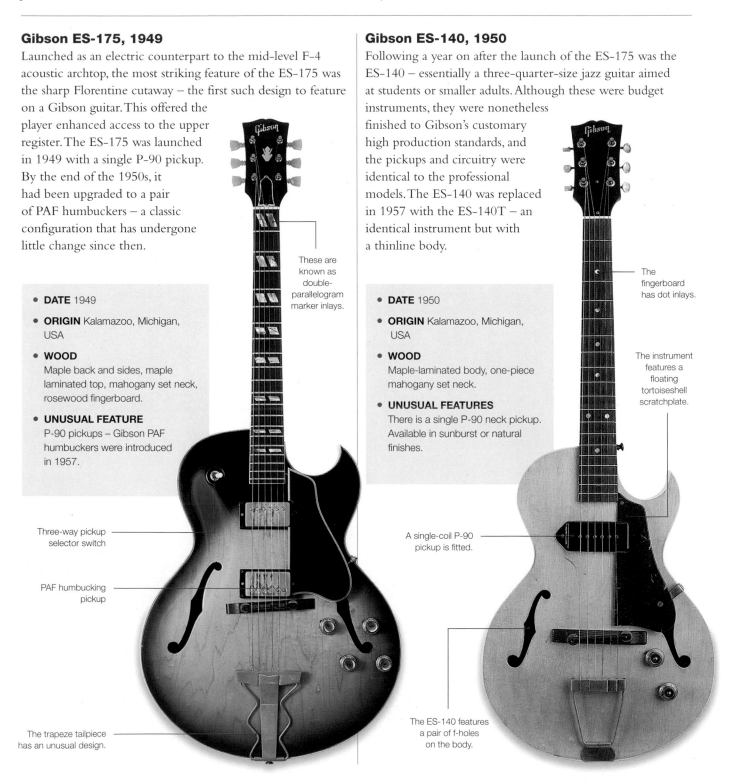

These are known as double-parallelogram marker inlays.

Three-way pickup selector switch

PAF humbucking pickup

The trapeze tailpiece has an unusual design.

The fingerboard has dot inlays.

The instrument features a floating tortoiseshell scratchplate.

A single-coil P-90 pickup is fitted.

The ES-140 features a pair of f-holes on the body.

Gibson ES-295, 1952

In 1952, Gibson decided to capitalize on the success of the rather modest ES-175, and offered an unusual upmarket alternative. Although retailing at over one hundred dollars more, the ES-295 was essentially just the same instrument. Cosmetically, however, it was a very different affair, presented in a shimmering, luxurious gold-paint finish with an ornate floral-patterned back-painted scratchplate. Very unpopular, it is now remembered principally as a hollowbody counterpart to the legendary Les Paul solidbody.

- **DATE** 1952

- **ORIGIN** Kalamazoo, Michigan, USA

- **WOOD**
  Maple back and sides, gold-finished laminated top, mahogany set neck, rosewood fingerboard.

- **UNUSUAL FEATURE**
  The Tune-o-matic bridge with trapeze tailpiece is used on this model.

Note the double-parallelogram marker inlays.

BELOW: *The ornate scratchplate of the ES-295 is decorated with a flower pattern painted on the reverse side of the clear plastic.*

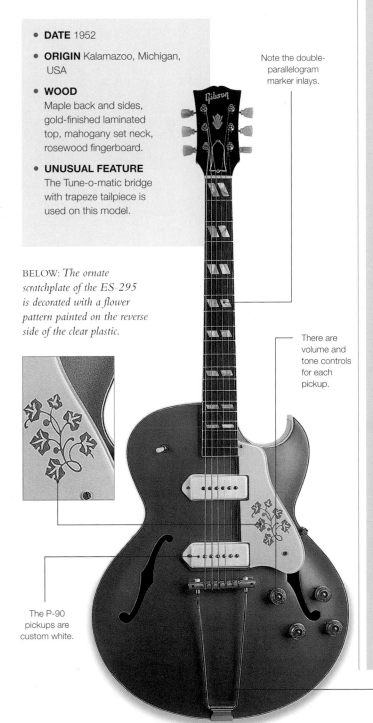

The P-90 pickups are custom white.

There are volume and tone controls for each pickup.

There is a long trapeze tailpiece.

The Gibson ES-175: the jazzer's choice

The ES-5 had been Gibson's flagship electric archtop, aimed squarely at the discerning jazz player. Yet it was the less expensive ES-175 that would ultimately establish itself as the most significant jazz guitar of them all. The first models featured one single-coil P-90 pickup in the neck position; a second alongside the bridge followed four years later. It was with the humbucker upgrade in 1957 that the smooth, warm tone, when played from the neck pickup, came to characterize perhaps the very essence of the classic jazz-guitar sound.

The list of ES-175 users reads like a who's who of jazz players, including Joe Pass, Pat Metheny, Kenny Burrell, Wes Montgomery, Pat Martino, Herb Ellis and Howard Roberts. Metheny achieves his own characteristic sound by using flatwound strings on his 1958 model, and playing off the neck pickup with the tone control rolled almost completely to the off position.

The ES-175 has also proved itself to be an unusually versatile instrument, its long association with Steve Howe of Yes being honoured by Gibson with his own signature model.

ABOVE: *Influenced by Django Reinhardt and saxophone legend Charlie Parker, Joe Pass was one of the finest exponents of solo jazz guitar. He played a Gibson ES-175 throughout most of his illustrious career.*

Early Epiphone electrics

The Epiphone company was founded in 1928 by Greek émigré Epaminondas 'Epi' Stathopoulos. Although we tend now to think of the brand as Gibson's 'affordable' line, before the 1950s Epiphone and Gibson were competing for largely the same market, and between them supplying high-end instruments to a significant number of professional musicians.

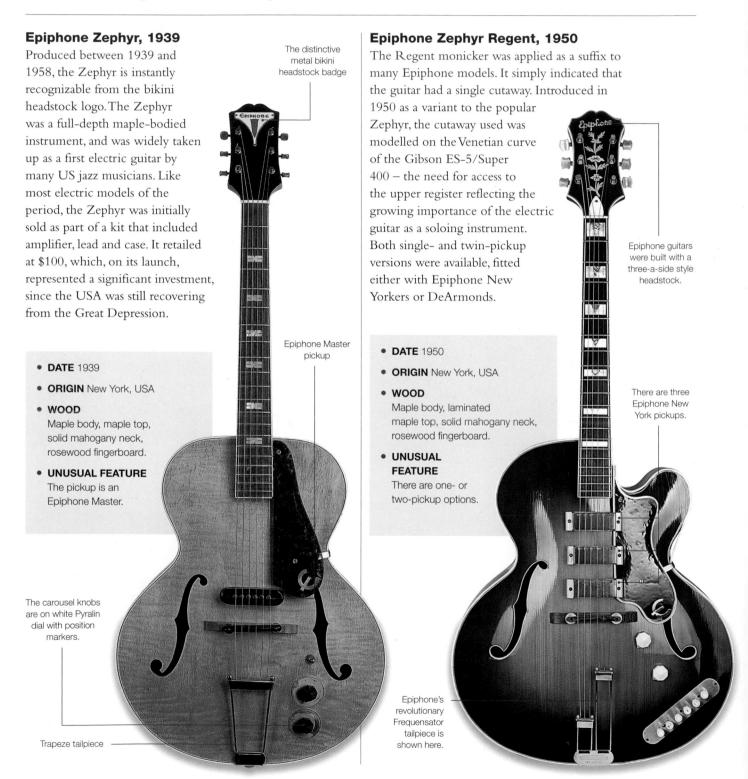

Epiphone Zephyr, 1939

Produced between 1939 and 1958, the Zephyr is instantly recognizable from the bikini headstock logo. The Zephyr was a full-depth maple-bodied instrument, and was widely taken up as a first electric guitar by many US jazz musicians. Like most electric models of the period, the Zephyr was initially sold as part of a kit that included amplifier, lead and case. It retailed at $100, which, on its launch, represented a significant investment, since the USA was still recovering from the Great Depression.

The distinctive metal bikini headstock badge

Epiphone Master pickup

- **DATE** 1939
- **ORIGIN** New York, USA
- **WOOD**
  Maple body, maple top, solid mahogany neck, rosewood fingerboard.
- **UNUSUAL FEATURE**
  The pickup is an Epiphone Master.

The carousel knobs are on white Pyralin dial with position markers.

Trapeze tailpiece

Epiphone Zephyr Regent, 1950

The Regent monicker was applied as a suffix to many Epiphone models. It simply indicated that the guitar had a single cutaway. Introduced in 1950 as a variant to the popular Zephyr, the cutaway used was modelled on the Venetian curve of the Gibson ES-5/Super 400 – the need for access to the upper register reflecting the growing importance of the electric guitar as a soloing instrument. Both single- and twin-pickup versions were available, fitted either with Epiphone New Yorkers or DeArmonds.

Epiphone guitars were built with a three-a-side style headstock.

There are three Epiphone New York pickups.

- **DATE** 1950
- **ORIGIN** New York, USA
- **WOOD**
  Maple body, laminated maple top, solid mahogany neck, rosewood fingerboard.
- **UNUSUAL FEATURE**
  There are one- or two-pickup options.

Epiphone's revolutionary Frequensator tailpiece is shown here.

Epiphone Sheraton E212T, 1958

When Gibson took over the ailing Epiphone company in 1957, the first batch of new instruments drew strongly on contemporary Gibson models. The Sheraton was a double-cutaway thinline semi-solid guitar, and modelled very closely on the parent company's newly issued ES-335. It was, however, able to retain some important Epiphone characteristics, such as the fascinating Frequensator tailpiece, an innovation that created different string lengths (from nut to tailpiece) between bass and treble strings: the shorter top strings have a lower tension and are thus easier to bend and play single-note parts in the upper register.

- **DATE** 1958

- **ORIGIN** New York, USA

- **WOOD**
  Solid maple centre block with maple wings, mahogany set neck, rosewood fingerboard.

- **UNUSUAL FEATURES**
  This model has New York pickups and a Frequensator tailpiece.

ABOVE: *One of the distinguishing features of the Epiphone Sheraton was the Frequensator tailpiece. It was used to lengthen the bass strings to obtain a better response. It was later replaced by a fixed stop bar.*

On later models, the tortoiseshell scratchplate featured the company's stylized E logo.

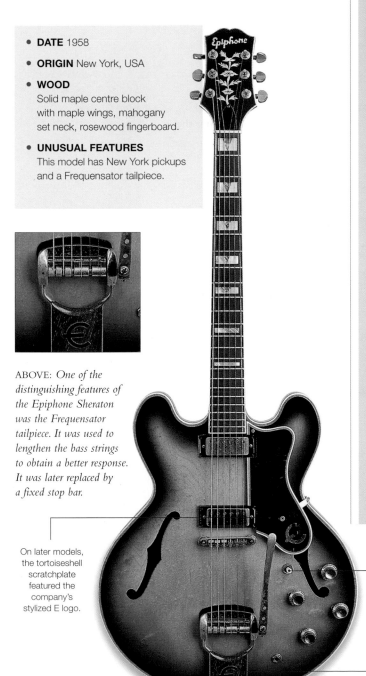

Epiphone and Gibson

ABOVE: *An Epiphone catalogue illustration from 1964. Epiphone remains one of the biggest-selling electric-guitar brands in the world. Its success, however, is now based on offering cut-price versions of classic Gibsons, rather than the high-end originals.*

The rivalry between Fender and Gibson is now legendary within the guitar world, drawing in both corporation and player alike. Yet before Fender's emergence on the scene in 1950, Gibson fought a similarly robust battle with Epiphone, both companies producing archtop guitars of the highest standard and competing for a share of the professional market.

The seeds of Epiphone's downfall were sown in 1944, when Epi Stathopoulos, the company's innovator and driving force, died from leukaemia. His brother Frixo took the reins, but the coming decade proved difficult, culminating in a crippling dispute with the workforce that resulted in closing the New York factory and moving to Pennsylvania.

In 1957, when Frixo Stathopoulos died, the company was unable to continue independently and was sold to its erstwhile rival Gibson. The Epiphone brand gradually evolved into Gibson's *de facto* diffusion name, offering cheaper, high-quality, Japanese-built versions of Gibson classics. Sales of the Epiphone brand now represent a critical part of Gibson's global business success.

Three-way pickup selector switch

Frequensator tailpiece

The solidbody pioneers

Nobody can say with any certainty who invented the solidbody electric guitar. What is clear, however, is that during the early 1940s there were a number of experimentally minded individuals seriously looking into the problems of electrified acoustic guitars – including issues of feedback and sustain – and independently they were reaching similar conclusions.

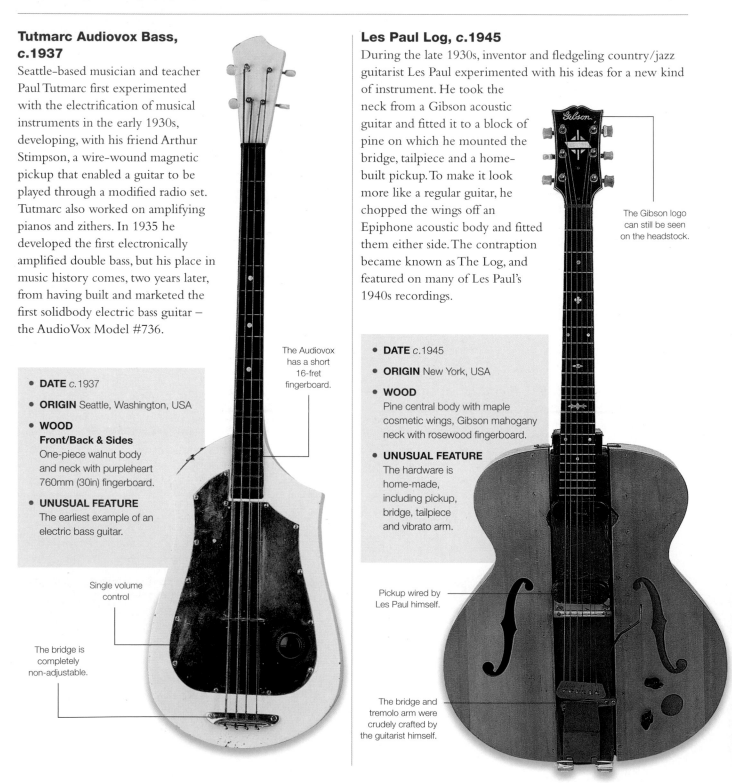

Tutmarc Audiovox Bass, c.1937

Seattle-based musician and teacher Paul Tutmarc first experimented with the electrification of musical instruments in the early 1930s, developing, with his friend Arthur Stimpson, a wire-wound magnetic pickup that enabled a guitar to be played through a modified radio set. Tutmarc also worked on amplifying pianos and zithers. In 1935 he developed the first electronically amplified double bass, but his place in music history comes, two years later, from having built and marketed the first solidbody electric bass guitar – the AudioVox Model #736.

The Audiovox has a short 16-fret fingerboard.

- **DATE** *c.*1937
- **ORIGIN** Seattle, Washington, USA
- **WOOD**
  Front/Back & Sides
  One-piece walnut body and neck with purpleheart 760mm (30in) fingerboard.
- **UNUSUAL FEATURE**
  The earliest example of an electric bass guitar.

Single volume control

The bridge is completely non-adjustable.

Les Paul Log, c.1945

During the late 1930s, inventor and fledgeling country/jazz guitarist Les Paul experimented with his ideas for a new kind of instrument. He took the neck from a Gibson acoustic guitar and fitted it to a block of pine on which he mounted the bridge, tailpiece and a home-built pickup. To make it look more like a regular guitar, he chopped the wings off an Epiphone acoustic body and fitted them either side. The contraption became known as The Log, and featured on many of Les Paul's 1940s recordings.

The Gibson logo can still be seen on the headstock.

- **DATE** *c.*1945
- **ORIGIN** New York, USA
- **WOOD**
  Pine central body with maple cosmetic wings, Gibson mahogany neck with rosewood fingerboard.
- **UNUSUAL FEATURE**
  The hardware is home-made, including pickup, bridge, tailpiece and vibrato arm.

Pickup wired by Les Paul himself.

The bridge and tremolo arm were crudely crafted by the guitarist himself.

Bigsby Merle Travis, 1947

It was a shared love of motorcycles that brought engineer Paul Bigsby and celebrated country guitarist Merle Travis together, and in 1946 Travis brought Bigsby a Gibson vibrato unit for him to repair. It was then that he came up with his own revolutionary – and still widely used – vibrato system. A year later, Travis showed Bigsby a sketch he had drawn of a new type of guitar and asked him if he could build it. The resulting instrument can lay claim to be the first solidbody guitar.

- **DATE** 1947

- **ORIGIN** Downey, California, USA

- **WOOD**
  Maple body, straight-through neck, rosewood fingerboard.

- **UNUSUAL FEATURES**
  The guitar has a home-built single-coil pickup, bass and treble tone controls, and filter switches.

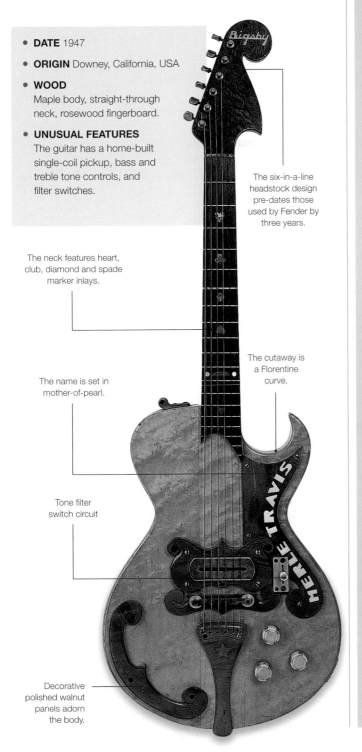

The neck features heart, club, diamond and spade marker inlays.

The name is set in mother-of-pearl.

Tone filter switch circuit

Decorative polished walnut panels adorn the body.

The six-in-a-line headstock design pre-dates those used by Fender by three years.

The cutaway is a Florentine curve.

Les Paul: musician, engineer and inventor

The name Les Paul is guaranteed immortality through the iconic Gibson electric guitar to which he gave his name – even if he played only a small part in its development. As a jobbing guitarist in the early 1940s, his dissatisfaction with the first wave of electro-Spanish guitars led him to experiment with alternative construction techniques – his Log was perhaps the first to show that by fixing neck, strings, bridge and pickup to a solid block of wood, feedback would be reduced and notes could be sustained for longer.

In 1946, Paul tried to sell his idea to Gibson, but the company was not interested at that time. Paul was also a pioneer of recording technology, one of the first to make successful use of sound-on-sound recording, a technique that enabled his famous recordings with his wife Mary Ford to feature multiple guitar and vocal parts.

ABOVE: *Les Paul was perhaps the first mainstream popular star of the electric guitar. His late1940s hits – recorded with his wife, the singer Mary Ford – invariably featured multiple layers of guitar that he claimed were created by an electronic invention he called the Les Paulverizer. He later revealed that this was achieved by multitrack recording – a little-known technology at that time.*

The Fender production line

Leo Fender had been successful building lap steels and amplifiers when, in 1948, he and employee George Fullerton drew up plans for producing an affordable production-line electric guitar. The first prototypes for an instrument called the Esquire were built in 1949, and a year later history was made when the first of Fender's new guitars – by now renamed the Broadcaster – came out of the factory.

Fender Broadcaster, 1950

Leo Fender's first production-line endeavour made an inauspicious debut. Within months, he received notification from the Fred Gretsch Company that one of its trademarks had been violated – there was already a line of Gretsch drum kits named Broadkaster. Rather than engage in legal action, Fender agreed to back down. It was salesman Don Randall who came up with the idea of namechecking America's favourite new medium of entertainment – the television. Thus was born the legendary Fender Telecaster.

- **DATE** 1950

- **ORIGIN** Fullerton, California, USA

- **WOOD**
  Ash body, maple bolt-on neck, maple fingerboard.

- **UNUSUAL FEATURES**
  There are single-line Kluson tuners and a fixed three-saddle bridge with through-body string fixings.

Fender Telecaster, 1951

The key to Leo Fender's success was in the way he simplified the construction process. Companies such as Gibson and Epiphone employed highly skilled traditional luthiers; the Telecaster was simply a slab of solid ash with a maple neck bolted on – indeed, one Gibson executive jibed that "anybody with a buzzsaw" could build a Fender. Nevertheless, aided by television appearances in the hands of Jimmy Bryant – the 'Fastest Guitar in the Country' – the Telecaster began to capture the imagination of Californian country players.

- **DATE** 1951

- **ORIGIN** Fullerton, California, USA

- **WOOD**
  Ash (alder and poplar also used), maple bolt-on neck, maple or rosewood fingerboard.

- **UNUSUAL FEATURE**
  This basic model has remained in production since the early 1950s.

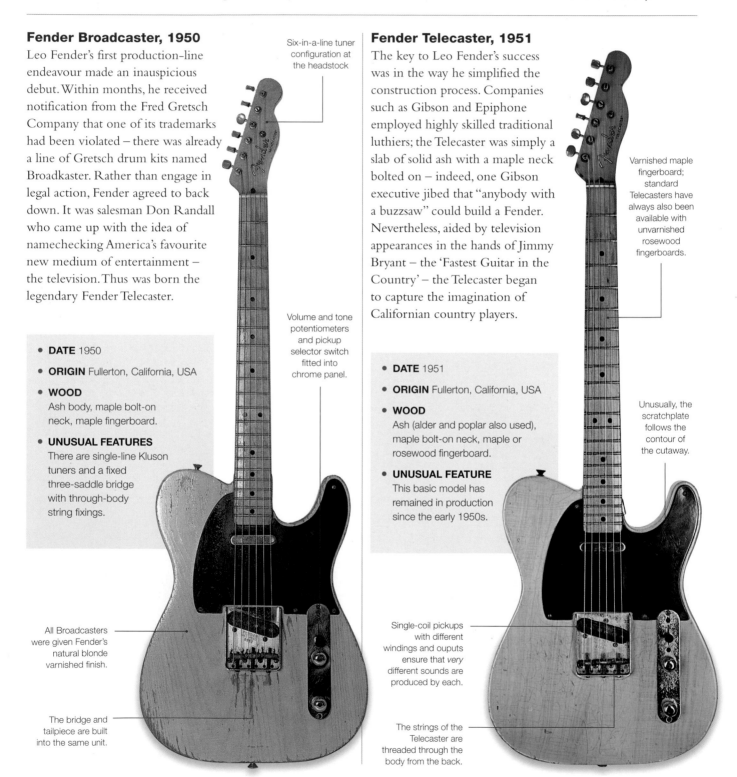

Six-in-a-line tuner configuration at the headstock

Volume and tone potentiometers and pickup selector switch fitted into chrome panel.

Varnished maple fingerboard; standard Telecasters have always also been available with unvarnished rosewood fingerboards.

Unusually, the scratchplate follows the contour of the cutaway.

All Broadcasters were given Fender's natural blonde varnished finish.

The bridge and tailpiece are built into the same unit.

Single-coil pickups with different windings and ouputs ensure that *very* different sounds are produced by each.

The strings of the Telecaster are threaded through the body from the back.

Fender Esquire, 1951

The Fender Esquire was a single-pickup instrument that evolved into the Broadcaster. Around 50 Esquires were built *before* the Broadcaster, but suffered from a number of design flaws – not least a lack of truss-rod support in the neck. The Esquire was made available as a production-line instrument in 1951. Even though it had just one pickup, the Esquire was built using the control plate from the Broadcaster, the pickup selector switch being wired to in-built tone-filter circuitry.

- **DATE** On the production line from 1951, but models bearing the name first produced in 1950
- **ORIGIN** Fullerton, California, USA
- **WOOD** Ash body (original prototypes built from pine), maple bolt-on neck, maple fingerboard.
- **UNUSUAL FEATURE** There is tone-filter switching.

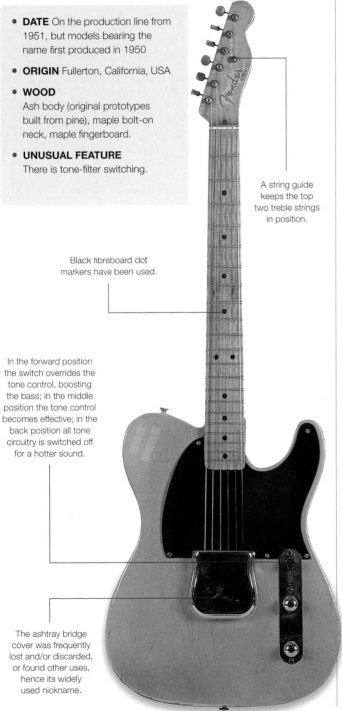

A string guide keeps the top two treble strings in position.

Black fibreboard dot markers have been used.

In the forward position the switch overrides the tone control, boosting the bass; in the middle position the tone control becomes effective; in the back position all tone circuitry is switched off for a hotter sound.

The ashtray bridge cover was frequently lost and/or discarded, or found other uses, hence its widely used nickname.

Fender Stratocaster, 1954

Although the Telecaster had taken off quickly, there was no denying that it was a very basic instrument, and Fender's feedback from players made it clear that some wanted a more sophisticated instrument. His response was the iconic Stratocaster – the most famous electric guitar ever made. Unlike its elder brother, the Strat's body was contoured for comfort, with a shape that worked just as well either standing or sitting. It also offered greater versatility in sound, with three pickups and a vibrato arm.

- **DATE** 1954
- **ORIGIN** Fullerton, California, USA
- **WOOD** Ash body (alder, poplar, basswood, mahogany and koa have also been used), maple bolt-on neck, maple or rosewood fingerboard.
- **UNUSUAL FEATURE** The bridge saddles are individually adjustable.

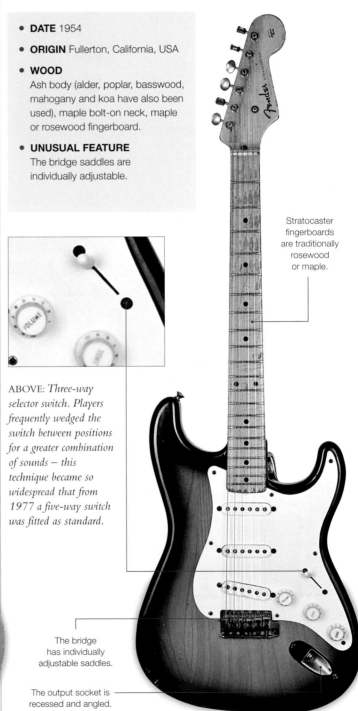

Stratocaster fingerboards are traditionally rosewood or maple.

ABOVE: *Three-way selector switch. Players frequently wedged the switch between positions for a greater combination of sounds – this technique became so widespread that from 1977 a five-way switch was fitted as standard.*

The bridge has individually adjustable saddles.

The output socket is recessed and angled.

Gibson Les Paul

In 1946, Les Paul had demonstrated his solidbody Log electric guitar to the management at Gibson. They had been unimpressed at the time, but five years later the success of Fender's solidbody electrics became a cause for concern. Les Paul – at the time a hugely popular celebrity musician – was offered the opportunity to put his name to Gibson's first solidbody electric instrument.

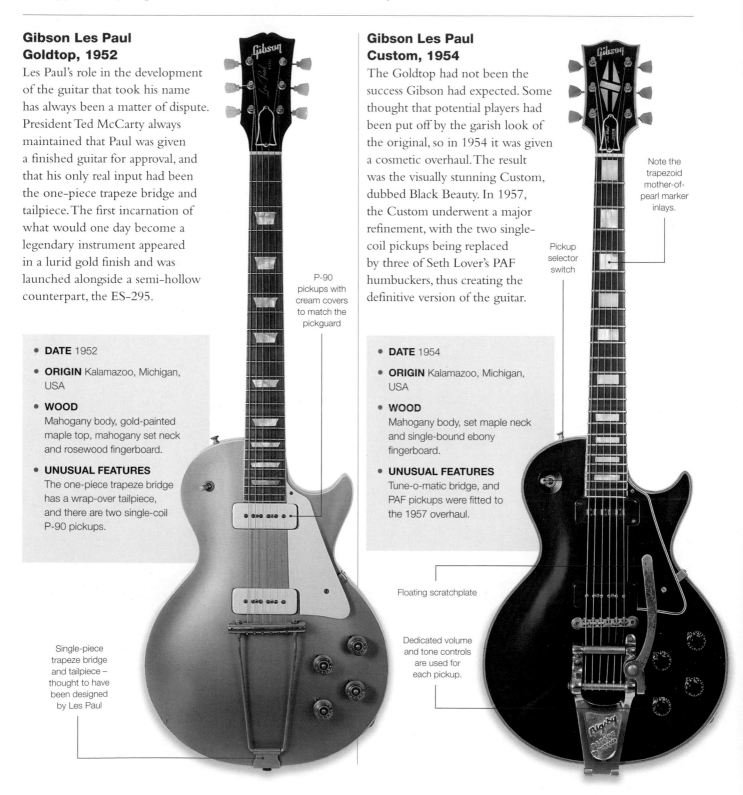

Gibson Les Paul Goldtop, 1952

Les Paul's role in the development of the guitar that took his name has always been a matter of dispute. President Ted McCarty always maintained that Paul was given a finished guitar for approval, and that his only real input had been the one-piece trapeze bridge and tailpiece. The first incarnation of what would one day become a legendary instrument appeared in a lurid gold finish and was launched alongside a semi-hollow counterpart, the ES-295.

- **DATE** 1952

- **ORIGIN** Kalamazoo, Michigan, USA

- **WOOD**
  Mahogany body, gold-painted maple top, mahogany set neck and rosewood fingerboard.

- **UNUSUAL FEATURES**
  The one-piece trapeze bridge has a wrap-over tailpiece, and there are two single-coil P-90 pickups.

P-90 pickups with cream covers to match the pickguard

Single-piece trapeze bridge and tailpiece – thought to have been designed by Les Paul

Gibson Les Paul Custom, 1954

The Goldtop had not been the success Gibson had expected. Some thought that potential players had been put off by the garish look of the original, so in 1954 it was given a cosmetic overhaul. The result was the visually stunning Custom, dubbed Black Beauty. In 1957, the Custom underwent a major refinement, with the two single-coil pickups being replaced by three of Seth Lover's PAF humbuckers, thus creating the definitive version of the guitar.

- **DATE** 1954

- **ORIGIN** Kalamazoo, Michigan, USA

- **WOOD**
  Mahogany body, set maple neck and single-bound ebony fingerboard.

- **UNUSUAL FEATURES**
  Tune-o-matic bridge, and PAF pickups were fitted to the 1957 overhaul.

Note the trapezoid mother-of-pearl marker inlays.

Pickup selector switch

Floating scratchplate

Dedicated volume and tone controls are used for each pickup.

Gibson Les Paul Junior, 1954

When Gibson launched the Les Paul Custom in 1954, it further extended the range with the Junior. As a basic instrument aimed at the beginner, it would prove to be a popular instrument, even among professionals. The earliest Junior was a single cutaway in the style of its elder brother, but in 1957 the body was given a dramatic overhaul. Paul Reed Smith would later use this new twin-cutaway shape as a template for his own hugely successful PRS brand.

- **DATE** 1954
- **ORIGIN** Kalamazoo, Michigan, USA
- **WOOD**
  Mahogany body, set mahogany neck, rosewood or ebony fingerboard.
- **UNUSUAL FEATURE**
  The body was significantly thinner than a standard Les Paul; body top was flat rather than arched.

ABOVE: *The Gibson P-90 single-coil pickup was introduced in 1946 as a replacement for the Charlie Christian. It was used on most Gibson electrics until the PAF humbucker appeared in the late 1950s.*

The twin-cutaway Les Paul Junior was the inspiration for Paul Reed Smith's PRS guitars.

The twin-cutaway body was introduced in 1957.

A Gibson stud bridge/tailpiece unit is used here.

Gibson Les Paul TV, 1955

The Les Paul Junior appeared primarily in white, sunburst or cherry red finishes. In 1955, Gibson launched the TV, a new version of the Junior with a natural butterscotch finish. The guitar was a response to Gibson's concerns that white guitars would glare too much on early black-and-white television broadcasts, hence a new finish was created that was aimed at preventing this effect. Two years later, the TV was given the same twin cutaway body update as the Junior.

- **DATE** 1955
- **ORIGIN** Kalamazoo, Michigan, USA
- **WOOD**
  Mahogany body, set mahogany neck, rosewood fingerboard.
- **UNUSUAL FEATURE**
  A single cutaway was used from 1955 to 1957; a twin cutaway from 1957 to 1963.

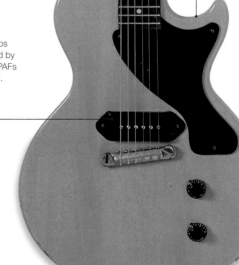

The original Les Paul TV, like the Junior, featured a single-cutaway body.

Acrylic dot markers

P-90 pickups were replaced by humbucking PAFs from 1957.

The electric bass

Leo Fender had already kicked off a revolution in 1950 with the creation of the Fender Broadcaster – the first production-line solidbody electric guitar. His second great innovation came a year later when he used the same construction principles to produce the first electric bass guitar. By the end of the decade, it was well on the way to rendering the upright acoustic bass redundant in most forms of popular music.

Fender Precision, 1951

A counterpart to the six-string Telecaster, the Precision bass shared many of its design features. Its appeal was clear: it was smaller and easier for the jobbing musician to take to gigs, and the fretted fingerboard required less skill than an acoustic bass to play accurately, which saw many guitarists able to double up on bass. Jazz player Monk Montgomery was the first professional player to adopt the Precision when touring with the Lionel Hampton Orchestra.

- **DATE** 1951

- **ORIGIN** Fullerton, California, USA

- **WOOD**
  Ash body, maple bolt-on neck and rosewood fingerboard.

- **UNUSUAL FEATURES**
  The Precision was given a redesign in 1953, and has remained in production ever since. It also has a single split-P pickup.

Gibson EB-2, 1958

Previously well established as America's leading guitar manufacturer, Gibson struggled with the pace of change forced by Fender during the 1950s, spending much of the decade chasing each new innovation. Gibson responded to the Fender Precision with the unusual EB-1 violin bass, and the later EB-2, a semi-hollowbody instrument, was launched as a bass counterpart to the ES-355 six-string. It was widely used by beat groups during the 1960s.

- **DATE** 1958

- **ORIGIN** Kalamazoo, Michigan, USA

- **WOOD**
  Maple top, maple back and sides, one-piece mahogany set neck.

- **UNUSUAL FEATURE**
  Single pickup; the twin pickup version – the EB-2D – was launched in 1968.

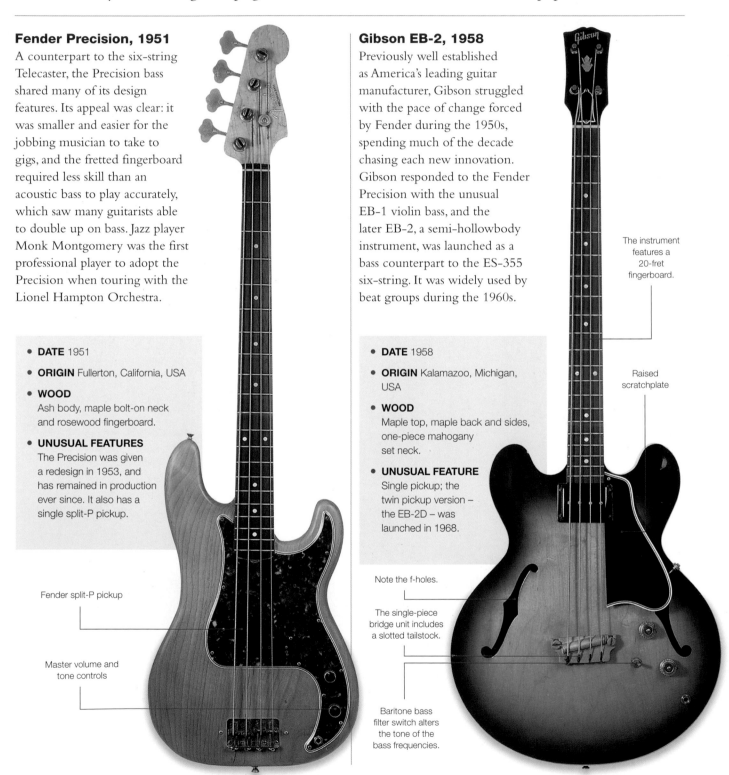

The instrument features a 20-fret fingerboard.

Raised scratchplate

Fender split-P pickup

Master volume and tone controls

Note the f-holes.

The single-piece bridge unit includes a slotted tailstock.

Baritone bass filter switch alters the tone of the bass frequencies.

Silvertone 1444, 1959

US retailing giant Sears, Roebuck and Company used the brand name Silvertone. From the middle of the 1950s, Silvertone budget electric guitars and amplification offered many young US musicians their first opportunity to own such equipment. Sears did not produce their own instruments, however – those supplied by established US names such as Danelectro, National, Harmony and Kay were simply rebranded. The model here, produced by Danelectro and based on its U Series, was one of the cheapest basses on the market – retailing on launch at $79.99 – and it sold in the 1960s in large quantities.

- **DATE** 1959
- **ORIGIN** Neptune, New Jersey, USA
- **WOOD**
  Pine frame, Masonite top and back, vinyl tape edging, bolt-on maple neck and rosewood fingerboard.
- **UNUSUAL FEATURE**
  The Silvertone 'dolphin-nose' headstock shape.

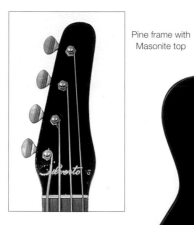

ABOVE: *Visually, the Silvertone models can be distinguished from their Danelectro counterparts by the headstock shape. Danelectros also have a characteristic contour like a Coke bottle.*

Vinyl tape edging

Pine frame with Masonite top

The Danelectro bridge unit is extremely basic. The string ends are secured in slots at the rear of a trapezoid metal block, and the saddle is simply a piece of rosewood. Overall height is governed by a screw on the metal block, and intonation is achieved by moving the saddle along the strings.

Who invented the bass guitar?

That Leo Fender was a great innovator is beyond all doubt. While he was responsible for the first mass-produced bass guitar, however, he certainly wasn't the first to come up with the idea. Indeed, Gibson's Lloyd Loar, who was known to have experimented with magnetic pickups during the 1920s, produced a prototype electric double bass. Perhaps the true father of the bass guitar, though, was Paul Tutmarc, a musician and inventor from Seattle, who began experimenting with a reduction in size of the double bass during the 1930s.

In 1935, he built an electronic upright bull fiddle, which he used primarily as a publicity device for his own Audiovox company. However, Tutmarc's place in history comes from the development of the Audiovox Model 736 Electronic Bass Fiddle. Launched in 1937, this solidbody fretted instrument, designed to be played in the horizontal position, was the first true electric bass guitar. That Tutmarc's invention was not a commercial success was probably related more to its unsuitability for the prevailing musical styles of the era rather than the quality of the instrument. Like the work of many other innovators, Tutmarc's invention was too far ahead of its time.

ABOVE: *Paul Tutmarc standing alongside his Audiovox Model 736, the first electric bass guitar.*

Gretsch solidbody electrics

The first electric guitar launched by Gretsch was the Electromatic Spanish, in 1939 – more than a half a century after German immigrant Friedrich Gretsch had settled in Brooklyn, New York, and created a successful music-retail business. During the 1950s, under the leadership of his son Fred Gretsch Jr, the company forged an international reputation for its drum kits and exquisitely designed electric guitars.

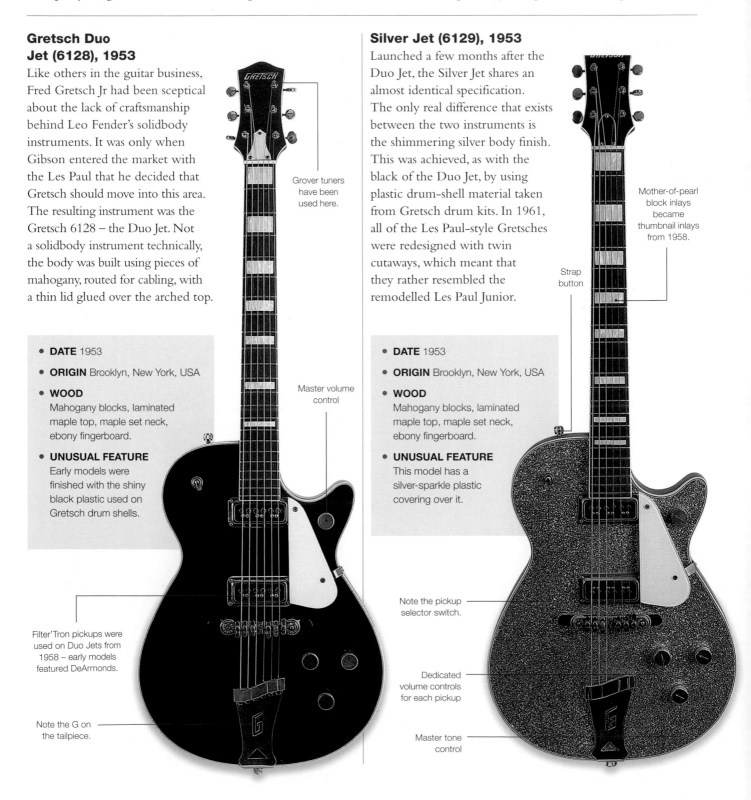

Gretsch Duo Jet (6128), 1953

Like others in the guitar business, Fred Gretsch Jr had been sceptical about the lack of craftsmanship behind Leo Fender's solidbody instruments. It was only when Gibson entered the market with the Les Paul that he decided that Gretsch should move into this area. The resulting instrument was the Gretsch 6128 – the Duo Jet. Not a solidbody instrument technically, the body was built using pieces of mahogany, routed for cabling, with a thin lid glued over the arched top.

- **DATE** 1953
- **ORIGIN** Brooklyn, New York, USA
- **WOOD**
  Mahogany blocks, laminated maple top, maple set neck, ebony fingerboard.
- **UNUSUAL FEATURE**
  Early models were finished with the shiny black plastic used on Gretsch drum shells.

Grover tuners have been used here.

Master volume control

Filter'Tron pickups were used on Duo Jets from 1958 – early models featured DeArmonds.

Note the G on the tailpiece.

Silver Jet (6129), 1953

Launched a few months after the Duo Jet, the Silver Jet shares an almost identical specification. The only real difference that exists between the two instruments is the shimmering silver body finish. This was achieved, as with the black of the Duo Jet, by using plastic drum-shell material taken from Gretsch drum kits. In 1961, all of the Les Paul-style Gretsches were redesigned with twin cutaways, which meant that they rather resembled the remodelled Les Paul Junior.

- **DATE** 1953
- **ORIGIN** Brooklyn, New York, USA
- **WOOD**
  Mahogany blocks, laminated maple top, maple set neck, ebony fingerboard.
- **UNUSUAL FEATURE**
  This model has a silver-sparkle plastic covering over it.

Mother-of-pearl block inlays became thumbnail inlays from 1958.

Strap button

Note the pickup selector switch.

Dedicated volume controls for each pickup

Master tone control

White Penguin (6134), 1955

The most desirable of Gretsch guitars, the White Penguin is the solidbody partner of the famous White Falcon. It is based broadly on the Duo Jet, but with a dramatic snow-white finish and opulent trimmings. The White Penguin's legendary status comes from the fact that nobody knows precisely how many of them were originally built – as few as 20, according to some experts – which explains why they can now reach $100,000 at auction.

Chet Atkins Solidbody (6121), 1955

The single most important figure in the popularization of Gretsch guitars was expert country-picker Chet Atkins. Long respected within the confines of the Nashville country-music scene, by the mid-1950s he was widely revered as one of the world's best guitarists. Gretsch put considerable efforts into courting Atkins before he finally agreed to put his name to two models: the 6121 Solidbody and the better-known 6120 Hollowbody.

ABOVE: *Long-term Gretsch employee Charles 'Duke' Kramer claimed the guitar was so named "because a penguin has a white front". The scratchplate also features a cartoon penguin.*

- **DATE** 1955
- **ORIGIN** Brooklyn, New York, USA
- **WOOD**
  Mahogany blocks, laminated maple top, maple set neck, ebony fingerboard.
- **UNUSUAL FEATURE**
  The gold-sparkle trim and gold-plated hardware.

A Melita Syncro-Sonic bridge has been used.

The arm-rest is gold-plated.

Gretsch G Cadillac tailpiece

Grover Imperial tuners have been fitted on the headstock.

- **DATE** 1955
- **ORIGIN** Brooklyn, New York, USA
- **WOOD**
  Mahogany body, maple top, maple set neck, ebony fingerboard.
- **UNUSUAL FEATURE**
  Early models had cowboy motifs, which Atkins disliked, so by 1958 these had been removed.

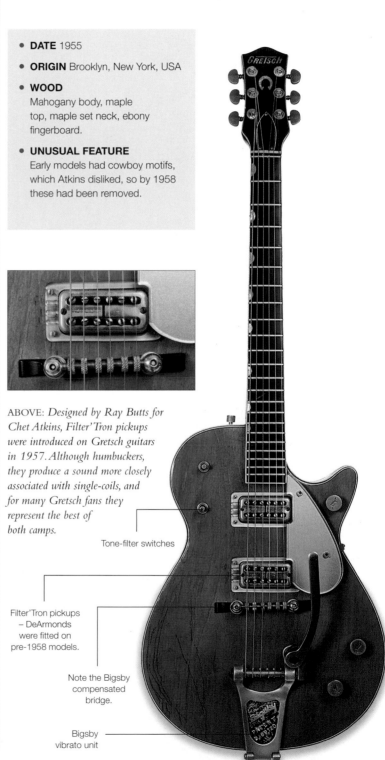

ABOVE: *Designed by Ray Butts for Chet Atkins, Filter'Tron pickups were introduced on Gretsch guitars in 1957. Although humbuckers, they produce a sound more closely associated with single-coils, and for many Gretsch fans they represent the best of both camps.*

Tone-filter switches

Filter'Tron pickups – DeArmonds were fitted on pre-1958 models.

Note the Bigsby compensated bridge.

Bigsby vibrato unit

Gretsch hollowbodies

The 1950s was a truly significant decade in the history of the guitar, most notably for the birth and rapid spread in popularity of solidbody electric instruments. Although the Gretsch company was quick to join this revolution, it is perhaps for its range of exquisite hollowbody models, launched during that same period, for which the brand is now most highly regarded.

Gretsch Country Club (6193), 1954

The Country Club was launched as Gretsch's flagship model, and it featured the characteristic curved single-cutaway body that would be seen on all of the company's hollowbody electric guitars during the 1950s. In addition to natural and sunburst finishes, the Country Club was also available in a striking Cadillac Green – the first of many unusual Gretsch paint finishes. It would remain in production for 27 years, making it the longest-lived model in the company's history.

- **DATE** 1954
- **ORIGIN** Brooklyn, New York, USA
- **WOOD**
  Maple body, mahogany set neck, rosewood fingerboard.
- **UNUSUAL FEATURE**
  There are volume controls for each pickup, master volume and tone controls.

Gretsch White Falcon (6136), 1954

One of the most distinctive-looking production guitars ever made, with its super-size body and sumptuous gold-plated hardware, the White Falcon was conceived by executive Jimmie Webster as "the Cadillac of guitars" – an instrument capable of outperforming anything else on the market. Advertised as "the finest guitar we know how to make", the White Falcon had a suitably high price tag – $600, equivalent to over $4,000 at today's prices.

- **DATE** 1954
- **ORIGIN** Brooklyn, New York, USA
- **WOOD**
  Mahogany body, laminated rock maple top, mahogany set neck, ebony fingerboard.
- **UNUSUAL FEATURE**
  It includes a pair of DynaSonic alnico magnet, single-coil pickups.

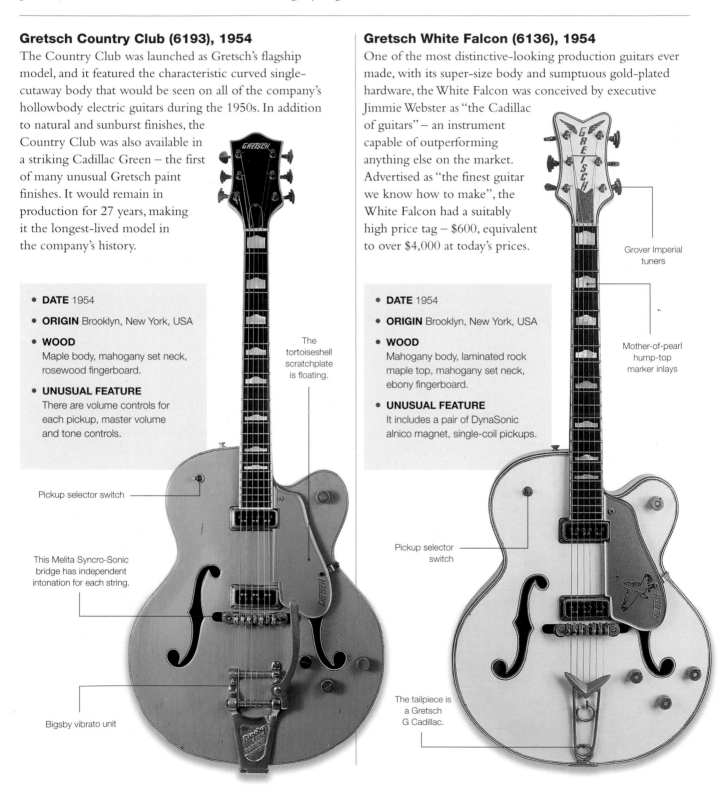

Pickup selector switch

This Melita Syncro-Sonic bridge has independent intonation for each string.

Bigsby vibrato unit

The tortoiseshell scratchplate is floating.

Grover Imperial tuners

Mother-of-pearl hump-top marker inlays

Pickup selector switch

The tailpiece is a Gretsch G Cadillac.

Chet Atkins Country Gentleman (7670), 1957

The ideal endorsee, Chet Atkins was rarely photographed without one of his signature Gretsch guitars at hand during the 1950s. Although both solidbody and hollowbody Chet Atkins models had been successful, Atkins himself had not been entirely happy with the sound of the pickups, nor the corny cactus-and-cattle motifs. In 1957, he was given the opportunity to address these concerns with a new signature model. Widely used in the USA by country and rockabilly players, the Country Gentleman was exposed to a wider audience in the 1960s when, for a period, it became George Harrison's preferred guitar while performing with The Beatles.

- **DATE** 1957
- **ORIGIN** Brooklyn, New York, USA
- **WOOD** Mahogany body, mahogany set neck, ebony fingerboard.
- **UNUSUAL FEATURES** Filter'Tron humbucking pickups and a Bigsby vibrato unit are used.

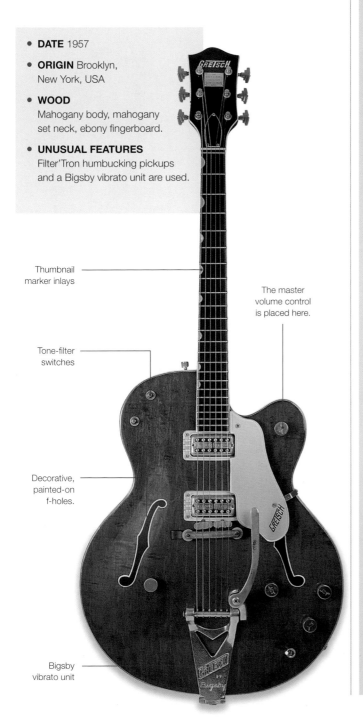

Thumbnail marker inlays

The master volume control is placed here.

Tone-filter switches

Decorative, painted-on f-holes.

Bigsby vibrato unit

Chet Atkins and Gretsch

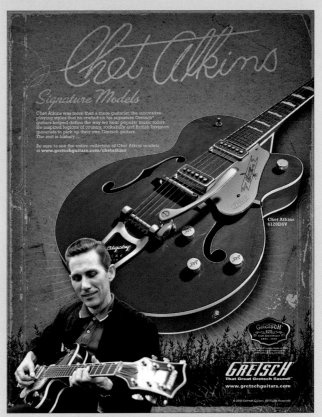

ABOVE: *Chet Atkins was widely known in Nashville as the Country Gentleman.*

Having taken the decision to compete directly with the new electric guitar market leaders, executive Jimmie Webster knew that what Gretsch needed was its own Les Paul-type endorsement. In Chet Atkins he found a young, respected Nashville session player on his way to a global reputation as one of the instrument's all-time masters. Although the guitarist would take considerable persuading, the first two Chet Atkins models emerged in 1955. These instruments would become massively successful – establishing Gretsch to be taken seriously as a guitar manufacturer for the first time – and yet the perfectionist Atkins was unhappy with the thin tone of the DeArmond pickup.

His solution was to commission sound expert Ray Butts to come up with a humbucking pickup that could nonetheless retain the characteristic single-coil treble bite. The result was the Filter'Tron, which would soon become standard on all Gretsch guitars, and contribute to the enduring success of the 1957 Chet Atkins' Country Gentleman. Without Chet Atkins' endorsement, Gretsch guitars would almost certainly not have enjoyed the same profile or enduring reputation. He certainly saw it that way: "If Jimmie Webster were alive, he'd tell you that the most important thing he ever did was sign me... because they started selling the hell out of guitars!"

American hollowbodies

While Gibson, Epiphone and Gretsch may have been the most notable commercial names in the production of hollowbody electrics, there were a number of other outstanding American manufacturers in the market. John D'Angelico made some of the finest pre-war acoustic archtops, and his apprentice James D'Aquisto would later be described by George Gruhn as a "modern-day Stradivarius".

Guild Stuart X500, 1953

The Guild brand was founded in 1952 in Manhattan, mainly to produce high-end archtop jazz guitars, although much of its commercial success came in the 1960s by producing flat-top acoustics for the New York folk scene. The Guild Stuart X-500 was designed to compete with premium competitors, such as the Gibson L-5CES and Epiphone Zephyr Emperor Regent. It features a 432mm (17in) Venetian cutaway body and gold-plated hardware throughout. Humbucking pickups were added in 1963.

- **DATE** 1953
- **ORIGIN** Manhattan, New York, USA
- **WOOD**
  Maple back and sides, spruce top, ebony fingerboard. Set mahogany neck.
- **UNUSUAL FEATURE**
  The scratchplate style is influenced by D'Angelico.

D'Angelico electric, 1955

New York luthier John D'Angelico had little interest in mass production, his output peaking in 1939 when 30 guitars came out of his workshop. D'Angelico's guitars were clearly styled after the Gibson L-5, but since they were all custom-built, there is huge variation in individual specifications. Although primarily a maker of archtop acoustics, he did produce a number of electrics, of which this left-handed model is one example.

- **DATE** 1955
- **ORIGIN** New York, USA
- **WOOD**
  European maple back and sides, hand-carved spruce top, set maple neck, ebony fingerboard.
- **UNUSUAL FEATURE**
  This model is a rare left-handed D'Angelico.

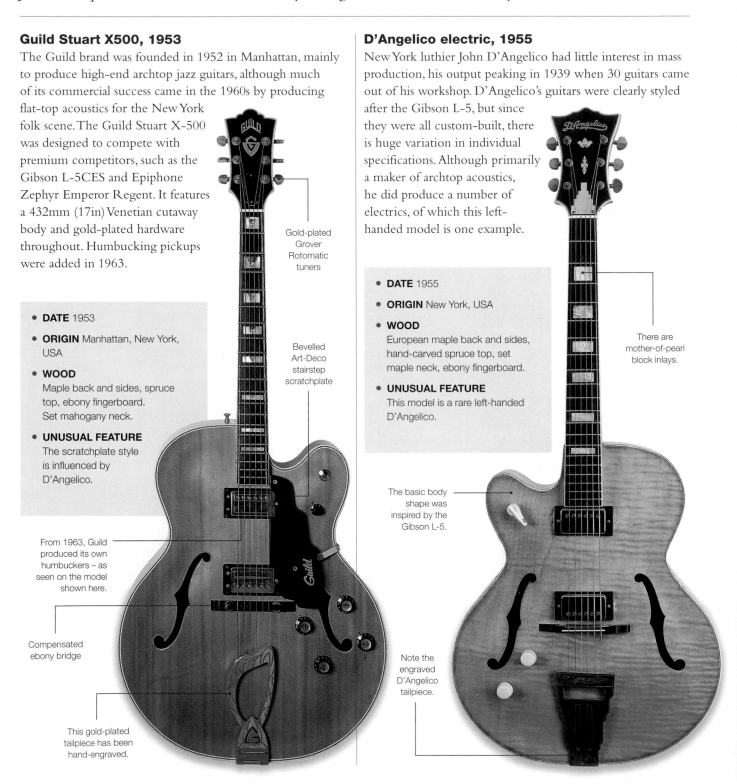

Gold-plated Grover Rotomatic tuners

Bevelled Art-Deco stairstep scratchplate

From 1963, Guild produced its own humbuckers – as seen on the model shown here.

Compensated ebony bridge

This gold-plated tailpiece has been hand-engraved.

There are mother-of-pearl block inlays.

The basic body shape was inspired by the Gibson L-5.

Note the engraved D'Angelico tailpiece.

Harmony H71 Meteor, 1958

While not in the same league as D'Angelico or D'Aquisto, Harmony was notable as one of the biggest producers of acoustic and electric archtops. The marque dates back to 1892, but only became a major player after it was acquired by Sears Roebuck in 1916. In the 30 years following the end of World War II, Harmony is estimated to have mass-produced more than 10 million guitars. The thin hollowbody Meteor range first appeared in 1958 and, although reasonably priced, was the very top end of the department-store guitar market.

- **DATE** Launched with the H70 model in 1958
- **ORIGIN** Chicago, Illinois, USA
- **WOOD**
  Laminated maple body, spruce top, rosewood fretboard.
- **UNUSUAL FEATURES**
  Single- and twin-pickup versions were available, and trapeze tailpiece or Bigsby vibrato options.

D'Aquisto electric, 1965

When John D'Angelico died in 1964, his former apprentice James D'Aquisto took over his workshop. Although his guitars show the clear influence of the D'Angelico tradition, D'Aquisto was soon established as one of America's most important luthiers, noted for his experimental approach to construction, bridge design and soundhole positioning. D'Aquisto died suddenly in 1995 – and his guitars can now fetch more than half a million dollars at auction.

- **DATE** 1965
- **ORIGIN** New York, USA
- **WOOD**
  European maple back and sides, maple top, set mahogany neck, ebony-covered headstock, ebony fingerboard.
- **UNUSUAL FEATURE**
  It has a pair of Guild gold-plated humbucking pickups.

The body is a blonde finish; the H70 was identical but with a sunburst finish.

The pickup selector switch is fitted to the cutaway horn.

Early models such as this featured Golden Tone pickups.

Each of the two pickups has dedicated volume and tone controls.

Mother-of-pearl block inlays

Two-piece carved ebony bridge

ABOVE: *Even on his early models, D'Aquisto added his own touches to D'Angelico's style, using smooth-edged f-holes, unlike the more pointed versions of his predecessor.*

The new Rickenbacker

Adolph Rickenbacker had been one of the pioneers of the electric guitar in the 1930s, but had chosen to concentrate on lap steels instead of Spanish designs. In 1953, with his market in decline, Rickenbacker sold his company to Francis C. Hall, who had seen the commercial potential of the electric guitar while working as a distributor for Leo Fender, and who successfully relaunched the brand.

Combo 600, 1954

The first of the new-era Rickenbacker solidbody instruments emerged in 1954. The Combo 600 was a 21-fret, single-pickup instrument. Positioned by the bridge, the large horseshoe-magnet pickup was essentially the same design as that created by George Beauchamp in the 1930s. The Combo 600 was the first Rickenbacker to feature the now-famous pointed swoosh logo on the truss-rod cover, a design created by Francis C. Hall's wife.

- **DATE** 1954
- **ORIGIN** Santa Ana, California, USA
- **WOOD**
  Maple body, set maple neck, rosewood fingerboard.
- **UNUSUAL FEATURE**
  Filter switch for altering the guitar's EQ.

Combo 800, 1954

Launched alongside the Combo 600, the Combo 800 was essentially the same instrument but with a different pickup arrangement. The 800 featured the unpatented Rickenbacker Multiple-Unit, which had twin coils. When used in combination, these coils were, in effect, humbuckers; when used separately, one coil accentuated treble and one bass. A switch beneath the tailpiece controlled this operation. The new Rickenbacker line was designed mainly by Paul Barth, who was one of the original founders of the company.

- **DATE** 1954
- **ORIGIN** Santa Ana, California, USA
- **WOOD**
  Maple body, set maple neck, rosewood fingerboard.
- **UNUSUAL FEATURE**
  The multiple-unit twin-coil pickup, coil switch and tone switch are notable.

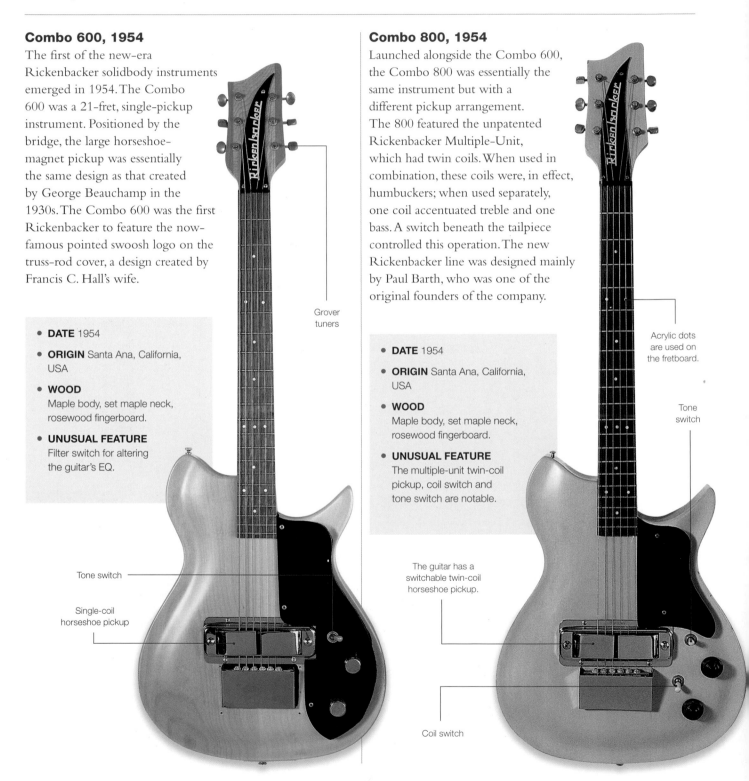

Grover tuners

Tone switch

Single-coil horseshoe pickup

Acrylic dots are used on the fretboard.

Tone switch

The guitar has a switchable twin-coil horseshoe pickup.

Coil switch

Combo 450, 1957

In 1956, Rickenbacker produced its first notable solidbody electric guitar, the single-pickup Combo 400, followed by the twin-pickup Combo 450. It was most significant, however, as the first Rickenbacker to use a straight-through neck construction, where the centre of the body and neck were cut from a single piece of wood, with treble and bass wings fixed on separately. Thought to improve tone and sustain, this technique became a standard feature of Rickenbackers thereafter.

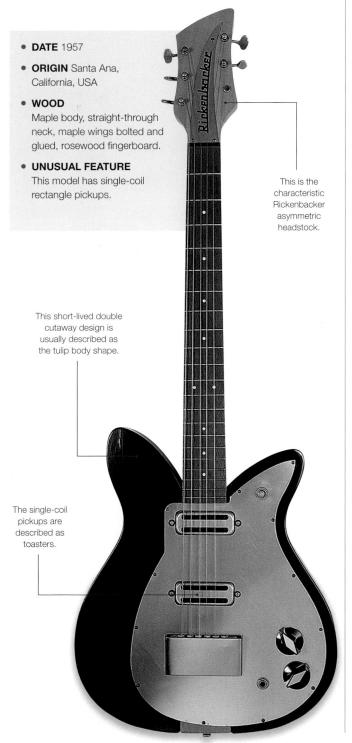

- **DATE** 1957
- **ORIGIN** Santa Ana, California, USA
- **WOOD** Maple body, straight-through neck, maple wings bolted and glued, rosewood fingerboard.
- **UNUSUAL FEATURE** This model has single-coil rectangle pickups.

This is the characteristic Rickenbacker asymmetric headstock.

This short-lived double cutaway design is usually described as the tulip body shape.

The single-coil pickups are described as toasters.

Model 1000, 1957

The double-cutaway tulip body shape enjoyed only a brief life, being replaced by the more famous cresting wave design in 1958. This range of instruments, however, saw the passing of the horseshoe pickup, in use in one form or another since the early 1930s. It was replaced by the smaller single-coil toaster design – so-called for its resemblance from above to a 1950s pop-up toaster. The Model 1000 was actually a three-quarter-size student model with an unusually short fingerboard of only 18 frets.

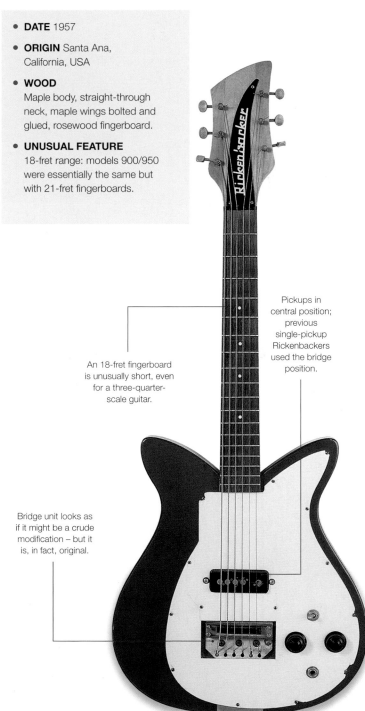

- **DATE** 1957
- **ORIGIN** Santa Ana, California, USA
- **WOOD** Maple body, straight-through neck, maple wings bolted and glued, rosewood fingerboard.
- **UNUSUAL FEATURE** 18-fret range: models 900/950 were essentially the same but with 21-fret fingerboards.

Pickups in central position; previous single-pickup Rickenbackers used the bridge position.

An 18-fret fingerboard is unusually short, even for a three-quarter-scale guitar.

Bridge unit looks as if it might be a crude modification – but it is, in fact, original.

Danelectro

Daniel Electrical Laboratories began life in 1947 in a New York loft. Founder Nathan Daniel was a talented engineer who established his company producing amplifiers for the Sears Roebuck retail catalogue. He built his first Danelectro guitars in 1954 with the aim of offering eye-catching designs, innovative construction techniques and, above all, an affordable price.

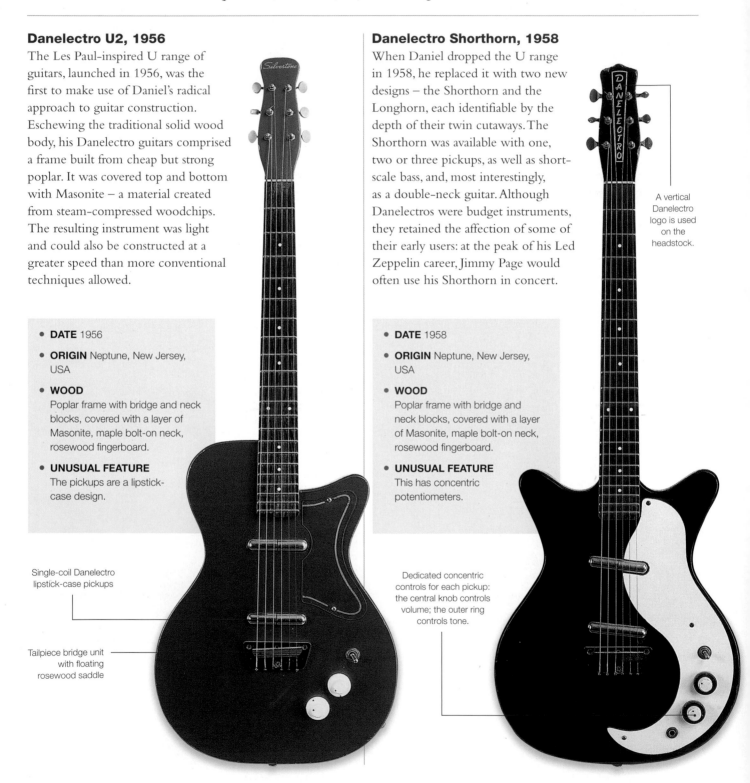

Danelectro U2, 1956

The Les Paul-inspired U range of guitars, launched in 1956, was the first to make use of Daniel's radical approach to guitar construction. Eschewing the traditional solid wood body, his Danelectro guitars comprised a frame built from cheap but strong poplar. It was covered top and bottom with Masonite – a material created from steam-compressed woodchips. The resulting instrument was light and could also be constructed at a greater speed than more conventional techniques allowed.

- **DATE** 1956
- **ORIGIN** Neptune, New Jersey, USA
- **WOOD** Poplar frame with bridge and neck blocks, covered with a layer of Masonite, maple bolt-on neck, rosewood fingerboard.
- **UNUSUAL FEATURE** The pickups are a lipstick-case design.

Single-coil Danelectro lipstick-case pickups

Tailpiece bridge unit with floating rosewood saddle

Danelectro Shorthorn, 1958

When Daniel dropped the U range in 1958, he replaced it with two new designs – the Shorthorn and the Longhorn, each identifiable by the depth of their twin cutaways. The Shorthorn was available with one, two or three pickups, as well as short-scale bass, and, most interestingly, as a double-neck guitar. Although Danelectros were budget instruments, they retained the affection of some of their early users: at the peak of his Led Zeppelin career, Jimmy Page would often use his Shorthorn in concert.

A vertical Danelectro logo is used on the headstock.

- **DATE** 1958
- **ORIGIN** Neptune, New Jersey, USA
- **WOOD** Poplar frame with bridge and neck blocks, covered with a layer of Masonite, maple bolt-on neck, rosewood fingerboard.
- **UNUSUAL FEATURE** This has concentric potentiometers.

Dedicated concentric controls for each pickup: the central knob controls volume; the outer ring controls tone.

Danelectro Longhorn Bass, 1958

For over five decades since its launch in 1958, the Danelectro Longhorn has polarized players with its extreme appearance. Originally available as a four-string or six-string bass and as the curious Guitarlin – a six-string guitar with the pitch range of a mandolin – it was frequently heard on twangy rock 'n' roll guitar instrumentals of the period. The four-string bass, with its distinctive low-end thud, remains popular today, even as a modern-day reissue.

- **DATE** 1958

- **ORIGIN** Neptune, New Jersey, USA

- **WOOD**
  Poplar frame with bridge and neck blocks, covered with 15mm (⅝in) Masonite, maple bolt-on neck, rosewood fingerboard.

- **UNUSUAL FEATURE**
  Unusually deep cutaways and elongated horns.

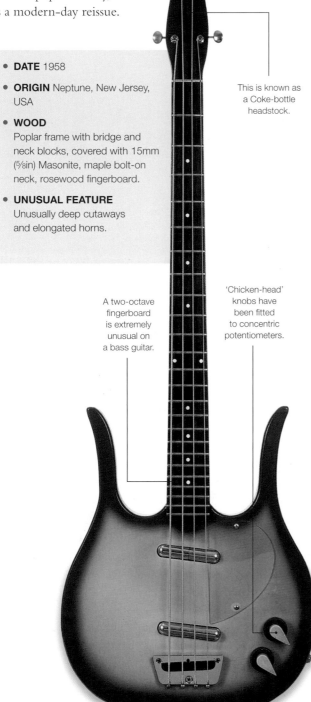

This is known as a Coke-bottle headstock.

A two-octave fingerboard is extremely unusual on a bass guitar.

'Chicken-head' knobs have been fitted to concentric potentiometers.

The Sears Roebuck effect

Silvertone has a special place in the affections of many American guitarists who, as teenagers, had a first taste of the electric guitar courtesy of the Sears Roebuck catalogue. These instruments were cheap, rudimentary and sold in massive quantities. Guitars and amplifiers were sourced by Sears from the likes of Danelectro, Harmony, Kay and National – and later from Japanese manufacturers such as Teisco. These guitars may have not have represented the last word in luthiery, but they were ideal for learning the basics. Age factors alone have now made some of these instruments quite desirable to collectors, or for young musicians seeking an authentic retro look.

ABOVE: *Beck Hansen is frequently seen in concert playing his vintage Silvertone 1448. Built by Danelectro in the early 1960s, it was sold by Sears Roebuck as part of the Amp-in-Case range. The package comprised a guitar, hard-shell case with small in-built amplifier and speaker, lead and how-to-play 7in record. It retailed for $67.95 – by contrast, during the same period, you could have expected to pay $450 for a brand new Gibson SG Custom.*

The Gibson Modernistic line

Although Gibson had produced some outstanding electric guitars, towards the end of the 1950s it looked increasingly as if it was Fender who had captured the imagination of the market. In an effort to redress the balance, Gibson President Ted McCarty set about personally designing a range of futuristic solidbody instruments aimed at shedding his company's conservative image.

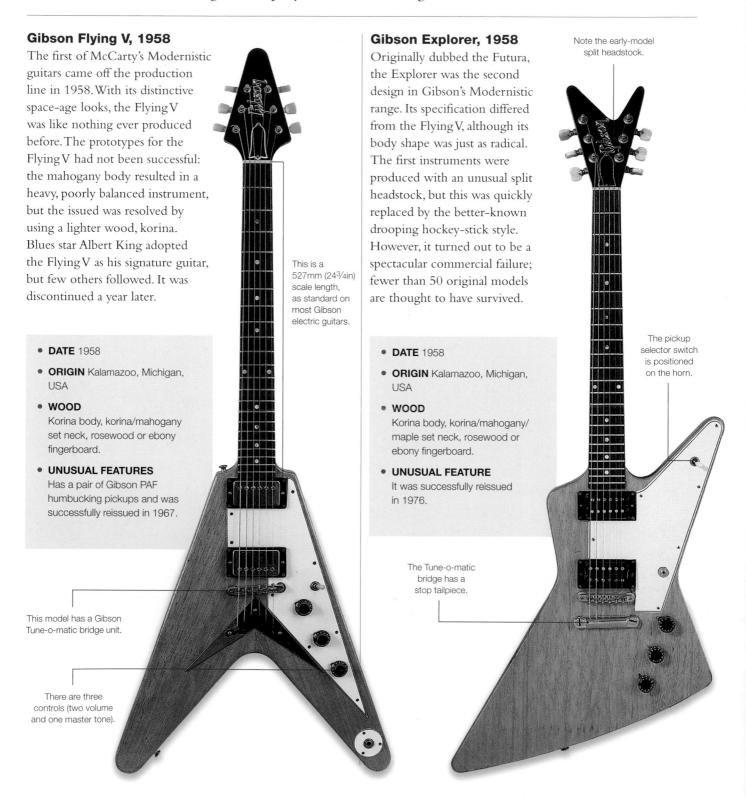

Gibson Flying V, 1958

The first of McCarty's Modernistic guitars came off the production line in 1958. With its distinctive space-age looks, the Flying V was like nothing ever produced before. The prototypes for the Flying V had not been successful: the mahogany body resulted in a heavy, poorly balanced instrument, but the issued was resolved by using a lighter wood, korina. Blues star Albert King adopted the Flying V as his signature guitar, but few others followed. It was discontinued a year later.

- **DATE** 1958
- **ORIGIN** Kalamazoo, Michigan, USA
- **WOOD**
  Korina body, korina/mahogany set neck, rosewood or ebony fingerboard.
- **UNUSUAL FEATURES**
  Has a pair of Gibson PAF humbucking pickups and was successfully reissued in 1967.

This is a 527mm (24¾in) scale length, as standard on most Gibson electric guitars.

This model has a Gibson Tune-o-matic bridge unit.

There are three controls (two volume and one master tone).

Gibson Explorer, 1958

Originally dubbed the Futura, the Explorer was the second design in Gibson's Modernistic range. Its specification differed from the Flying V, although its body shape was just as radical. The first instruments were produced with an unusual split headstock, but this was quickly replaced by the better-known drooping hockey-stick style. However, it turned out to be a spectacular commercial failure; fewer than 50 original models are thought to have survived.

- **DATE** 1958
- **ORIGIN** Kalamazoo, Michigan, USA
- **WOOD**
  Korina body, korina/mahogany/maple set neck, rosewood or ebony fingerboard.
- **UNUSUAL FEATURE**
  It was successfully reissued in 1976.

Note the early-model split headstock.

The pickup selector switch is positioned on the horn.

The Tune-o-matic bridge has a stop tailpiece.

Gibson Moderne, 1980

Ted McCarty's reinventions of the electric guitar concluded with the Moderne, which never actually made the production line in the 1950s. Possible prototypes have been described as the Holy Grail of collectible electric guitars, yet there is no proof that any instruments were ever built. Having successfully re-established the Flying V and Explorer years after their first, brief appearances, the Moderne finally debuted in 1980. It resembles a Flying V with a scooped-out treble bout and Gumby-style headstock, named after the animated character in a US television programme.

- **DATE** Designed in 1957 but first built in 1980.

- **ORIGIN** Kalamazoo, Michigan, USA

- **WOOD**
  Korina, mahogany or poplar body, mahogany set neck, rosewood or ebony fingerboard.

- **UNUSUAL FEATURE**
  Gibson models were built until 1983. Korean-built Epiphone Modernes were offered later.

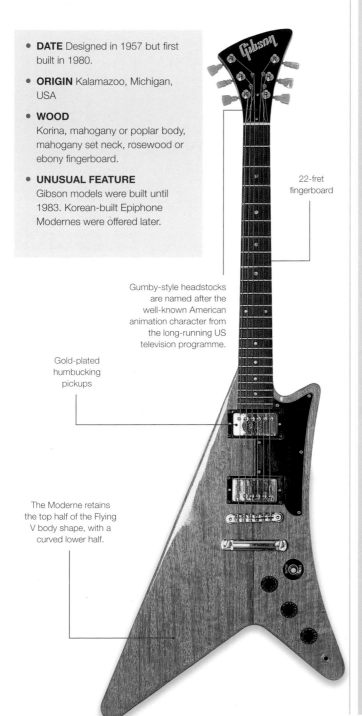

22-fret fingerboard

Gumby-style headstocks are named after the well-known American animation character from the long-running US television programme.

Gold-plated humbucking pickups

The Moderne retains the top half of the Flying V body shape, with a curved lower half.

The futuristic Gibsons

When asked in 2001 about the background to his Modernistic line, former Gibson president Ted McCarty gave a frank response: "Fender was talking about how Gibson was a bunch of old fuddie-duddies...I was a little peeved. So I said, 'Let's shake 'em up.' I wanted to come up with some guitar shapes that were different from anything else."

In 1957, US patents were granted for three new designs, and a year later the Flying V and Explorer models debuted at the annual NAMM trade show. Although they created a great deal of interest, they were dismal commercial failures. Mirroring the fate of the Les Paul, during the 1960s old Flying Vs began to increase rapidly in value until, in 1966, Gibson resumed production. Nowadays, however, vintage collectors regard these as among the most valuable of any Gibson production models.

ABOVE: *Albert King is considered to be one of the most influential electric blues guitarists of the 1950s. The only well-known musician to adopt a Flying V from the original launch, it became King's signature instrument throughout his career.*

Europe in the 1950s

The birth and evolution of the electric guitar was a wholly American phenomenon. In Europe, however, exacerbated by the limited availability of Fenders and Gibsons, it was still looked upon as something that was rare and exotic. Yet, as the hysteria surrounding Elvis, Buddy Holly and the early rock 'n' rollers began to cross the Atlantic, demand for electric guitars exploded.

Supersound Bass, 1958

The British Supersound company was known as a general retailer and manufacturer of musical, audio and cinema equipment. The impetus to produce electric guitars came with the involvement of a young ex-RAF engineer Jim Burns. The short-lived Supersound guitar brand was launched in 1958 with a pair of similar Telecaster-inspired models – one a six-string, the other a bass. These two Supersounds could lay reasonable claim to be the first mass-produced British electric guitars.

- **DATE** 1958
- **ORIGIN** Dartford, UK
- **WOOD**
  Maple body, set maple 'glued and screwed' neck, rosewood fingerboard.
- **UNUSUAL FEATURE**
  Single-cutaway Fender Telecaster styling, although the sharp pointing of the horn recalls the earlier Bigsby Merle Travis and presages some of Jim Burns' classic 1960s designs.

The marker inlays span the width of the fingerboard.

Electrics are mounted underneath the scratchplate.

Dallas Tuxedo, 1959

John E. Dallas and Sons was a well-established maker and importer of musical instruments when in 1959 it launched the Tuxedo, the first British-built electric guitar to sell in any volume. With its small, thin body, short scale length and appealing price tag, the Tuxedo made an ideal starter instrument. It was seen widely around the youth clubs and coffee bars of Britain into the early 1960s – and doubtless was found gathering dust in many an attic during the 1970s.

- **DATE** 1959
- **ORIGIN** London, UK
- **WOOD**
  Mahogany body and straight-through neck with rosewood fingerboard.
- **UNUSUAL FEATURE**
  Electrics were designed and built by Fenton-Weill. Single- and twin-pickup models were available.

Single-coil, Fenton-Weill neck pickup

Fender-style through-body string fittings

The Supersound bass featured a single pickup with tone and volume controls.

Rosetti Lucky Squire, 1960

At the budget end of the guitar market, it was common practice for retailers in the UK to import and rebrand instruments built by Continental and Japanese manufacturers. Founded in 1931, Dutch maker Egmond was among Europe's largest guitar producers by the end of the 1950s. The model shown here is an Egmond Princess semi-acoustic, which was relabelled and sold exclusively in the UK under the name Rosetti Lucky Squire.

- **DATE** 1960

- **ORIGIN** Best, Netherlands

- **WOOD**
  Plywood body, maple neck, rosewood fingerboard.

- **UNUSUAL FEATURE**
  The single pickup is in the neck position.

Three-a-side tuner configuration

ABOVE: *The Lucky Squire featured one single-coil pickup mounted at the neck, giving the guitar a tone that was mellow rather than biting. Paul McCartney reputedly restrung an Egmond-built Rosetti guitar with four piano strings to create his first bass.*

Floating bridge held in place by the pressure of the strings

Vibrato unit fitted to the base of the guitar

Trade restrictions

By the end of the 1950s, rock 'n' roll had successfully been exported from the USA to all corners of the globe. Yet, while the young teenage musicians of Europe became familiar with photographs and films of stars such as Buddy Holly playing a Fender Stratocaster and Eddie Cochran with his Gretsch Chet Atkins, until the early 1960s these instruments were extremely rare outside of the USA, largely for financial reasons.

The major US guitar brands – especially Gibson and Gretsch – were already expensive, and the cost of shipping across the Atlantic could increase the price by more than 20 per cent. At this time, punitive post-war trade controls were also still in place, limiting supply and making those that did get through even more expensive. Although US instruments slowly began to emerge in Liverpool, courtesy of the seamen working the Atlantic crossings, the first Stratocaster imported into the UK was bought by Cliff Richard as a gift for his guitarist Hank Marvin.

As a consequence, most British guitarists who came to the fore during the 1960s, and even into the 1970s, cut their musician teeth playing cheap Japanese imports, often of questionable quality.

ABOVE: *Singer Cliff Richard brought his guitarist Hank Marvin (left) the gift of a Fender Stratocaster from a trip to America in 1959. But, like many other young British players, Marvin learned to play on a cheap Antoria LG-50 – a stock model built by Guyatone in Japan and rebranded for sale in the UK.*

Fender: the second generation

The late 1950s saw Fender – a company that barely existed ten years earlier – now dominating the electric guitar market with its Telecaster and Stratocaster models, and its revolutionary Precision bass guitar was increasingly usurping the traditional territory of the upright acoustic bass. Yet Leo Fender was still able to identify areas in which he felt his range required further development.

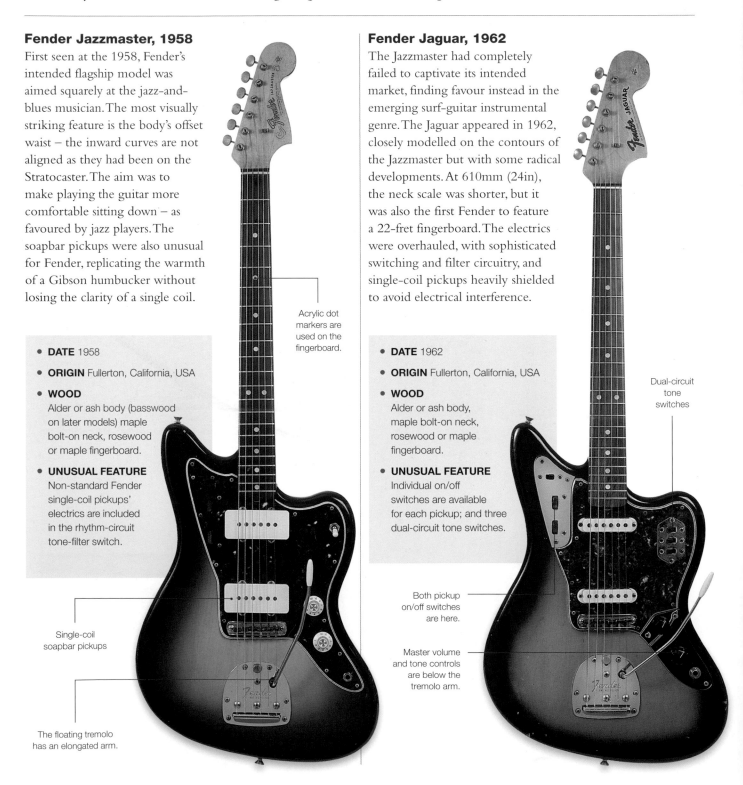

Fender Jazzmaster, 1958

First seen at the 1958, Fender's intended flagship model was aimed squarely at the jazz-and-blues musician. The most visually striking feature is the body's offset waist – the inward curves are not aligned as they had been on the Stratocaster. The aim was to make playing the guitar more comfortable sitting down – as favoured by jazz players. The soapbar pickups were also unusual for Fender, replicating the warmth of a Gibson humbucker without losing the clarity of a single coil.

- **DATE** 1958

- **ORIGIN** Fullerton, California, USA

- **WOOD**
  Alder or ash body (basswood on later models) maple bolt-on neck, rosewood or maple fingerboard.

- **UNUSUAL FEATURE**
  Non-standard Fender single-coil pickups' electrics are included in the rhythm-circuit tone-filter switch.

Acrylic dot markers are used on the fingerboard.

Single-coil soapbar pickups

The floating tremolo has an elongated arm.

Fender Jaguar, 1962

The Jazzmaster had completely failed to captivate its intended market, finding favour instead in the emerging surf-guitar instrumental genre. The Jaguar appeared in 1962, closely modelled on the contours of the Jazzmaster but with some radical developments. At 610mm (24in), the neck scale was shorter, but it was also the first Fender to feature a 22-fret fingerboard. The electrics were overhauled, with sophisticated switching and filter circuitry, and single-coil pickups heavily shielded to avoid electrical interference.

- **DATE** 1962

- **ORIGIN** Fullerton, California, USA

- **WOOD**
  Alder or ash body, maple bolt-on neck, rosewood or maple fingerboard.

- **UNUSUAL FEATURE**
  Individual on/off switches are available for each pickup; and three dual-circuit tone switches.

Dual-circuit tone switches

Both pickup on/off switches are here.

Master volume and tone controls are below the tremolo arm.

Fender Mustang, 1964

During the late 1950s, Fender had launched a number of basic models aimed at the novice player. With its small body, offset waist and three-quarter scale length, the new Mustang was ideal for small hands. Like Fender's other recent instruments, the Mustang also featured an unusual electronic arrangement for its time, notably in the way that each pickup can be switched on, off or out of phase. The Mustang achieved a degree of cult recognition during the 1990s through its use by such prominent alternative-rock bands as Sonic Youth.

- **DATE** 1964

- **ORIGIN** Fullerton, California, USA

- **WOOD**
  Poplar, alder, ash or basswood body, maplebolt-on neck, rosewood or maple fingerboard.

- **UNUSUAL FEATURE**
  The Dynamic Vibrato tailpiece was more sensitive than the existing standard Fender units.

Original Mustangs, like most Fender guitars, were available with rosewood or maple fingerboards.

ABOVE: *The highly regarded Dynamic Vibrato features an integral floating bridge. The strings are controlled by a tailpiece bar to which the tremolo arm is connected.*

Pickup on/off/ out-of-phase switch is featured here.

Surf sounds and guitar instrumentals

Originating in southern California at the start of the 1960s, the classic surf sound was pioneered by acts such as Dick Dale and Del-Tones. The music was usually instrumental and featured simple mid-tempo tunes played on an electric guitar with a reverb-drenched sound, often played with heavy use of a vibrato arm. The characteristic biting treble tone was typically derived from the single-coil pickups found on Fender guitars – the Stratocaster and Jaguar were particularly popular among surf musicians. There were many other guitar-instrumental bands during this time that produced a similar sound but were unconnected to Californian surf culture. The Ventures, for example, with their signature Mosrite guitars, proved to be curiously influential in Japan, where they were comparable in popularity with The Beatles throughout much of the decade. There was a strong resurgence of interest in this genre during the 1980s, and it has since remained a niche subculture with vibrant music scenes dotted around Europe and the USA.

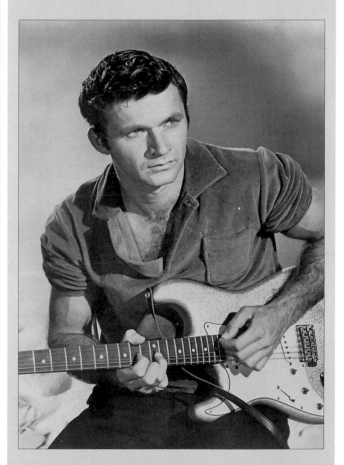

ABOVE: *Dick Dale was one of the pioneers of the surf-instrumental sound. His impressively high-speed alternating pick style can be heard on hits such as "Let's Go Trippin" and "Misirlou", with its influential use of the Hilaz Kar, or double harmonic scale. The latter would find a new audience in the 1990s through its use in Quentin Tarantino's cult film* Pulp Fiction.

Jim Burns

From the end of the 1950s right up to the end of his life in 1998, Jim Burns played a pivotal role in the evolution of the electric guitar in Europe. Burns was always more of an innovator than a businessman, but even though his commercial ventures would regularly fail, during the first half of the 1960s his company, Ormston Burns London Ltd, managed to produce many classic, enduring designs.

Burns Vibra Artist, 1960

Cutting his teeth in the late 1950s with the short-lived Burns-Weill brand, Jim Burns' first solo venture was introduced with a range of three instruments, the flagship of which was the Vibra Artist. With its curious twin-cutaway body, a pair of asymmetric horns gave access to the upper register of a two-octave fingerboard that was unusual for its time. Early Burns models exhibit marked variations between models, the bodies often carved from counter tops recycled from bar and restaurant renovations.

- **DATE** 1960
- **ORIGIN** London, UK
- **WOOD**
  Mahogany body (although different materials were frequently used at the whim of their creator), maple set neck, rosewood fingerboard.
- **UNUSUAL FEATURE**
  Many variations between models in terms of materials and design.

Burns Bison, 1961

The Bison could be described as the first luxury solidbody electric guitar to be produced outside of the USA. Striking in its black finish and heavily curved horns, Burns commissioned new pickups from Goldring, then one of Britain's top hi-fi companies; when combined with the unique Rez-o-Matik circuitry, the guitar could produce a startling range of sounds. Absurdly expensive to manufacture, the Bison retailed at £157 – at a time when the average Briton earned just £10 a week.

- **DATE** 1961
- **ORIGIN** London, UK
- **WOOD**
  Sycamore body, maple set neck, ebony fingerboard (although quickly replaced by a cheaper simplified version).
- **UNUSUAL FEATURE**
  This model has four single-coil Ultra-Sonic pickups.

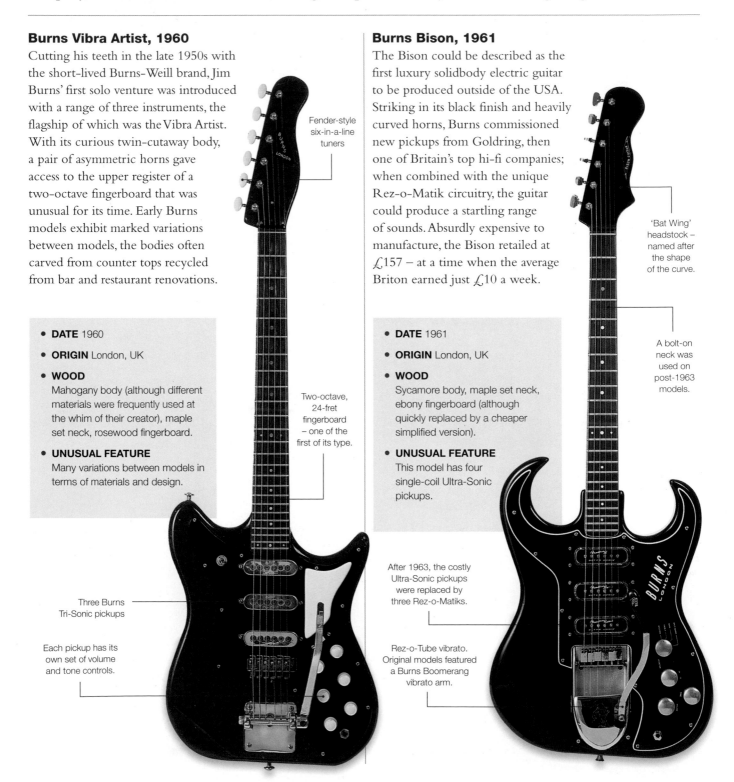

Fender-style six-in-a-line tuners

Two-octave, 24-fret fingerboard – one of the first of its type.

Three Burns Tri-Sonic pickups

Each pickup has its own set of volume and tone controls.

'Bat Wing' headstock – named after the shape of the curve.

A bolt-on neck was used on post-1963 models.

After 1963, the costly Ultra-Sonic pickups were replaced by three Rez-o-Matiks.

Rez-o-Tube vibrato. Original models featured a Burns Boomerang vibrato arm.

Burns Split Sonic, 1962

The Sonic had been the entry-level guitar of Burns' first range. It was a good basic instrument, affordable and popular among British lead guitarists. The Split Sonic first appeared in 1962 and was positioned in the range as an affordable alternative to the Bison. It only really differed from the original Sonic with the introduction of Burns' unique Split Sound pickup, which combined with on-board circuitry to enable the bass notes to be picked up at the neck pickup and the treble notes from the bridge.

- **DATE** 1962
- **ORIGIN** London, UK
- **WOOD**
  Mahogany body, maple bolt-on neck, rosewood fingerboard.
- **UNUSUAL FEATURE**
  A rotary pickup selector offered a choice of Treble (bridge pickup), Bass (neck pickup), Split Sound and Wild Dog – an out-of-phase effect with treble boost.

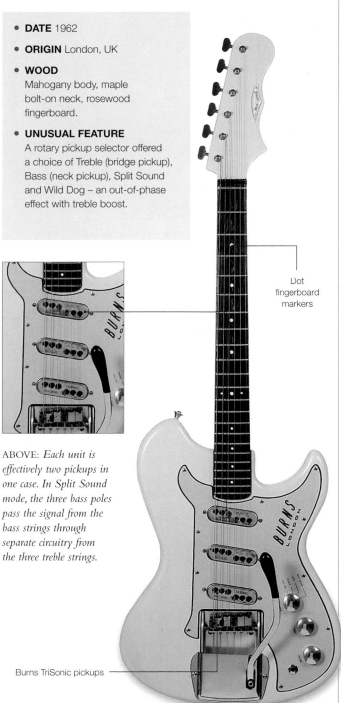

Dot fingerboard markers

ABOVE: *Each unit is effectively two pickups in one case. In Split Sound mode, the three bass poles pass the signal from the bass strings through separate circuitry from the three treble strings.*

Burns TriSonic pickups

Burns Hank Marvin, 1964

Britain's most popular band of the pre-Beatles era, the Shadows had carved out successful careers both backing pop singer Cliff Richard and creating instrumental guitar hits of their own. Famed for owning the first Fender Stratocaster in the UK, it was when guitarist Hank Marvin and colleague Bruce Welch began experiencing tuning problems with their Fender vibrato arms that they approached Jim Burns for a solution. His answer? The luxurious Burns Hank Marvin, one of the most collectible British guitars ever built.

- **DATE** 1964
- **ORIGIN** London, UK
- **WOOD**
  Honduras mahogany body, Canadian rock maple bolt-on neck, Indian rosewood fingerboard.
- **UNUSUAL FEATURE**
  The Rez-o-Tube vibrato unit was designed to avoid the tuning issues common on traditional systems.

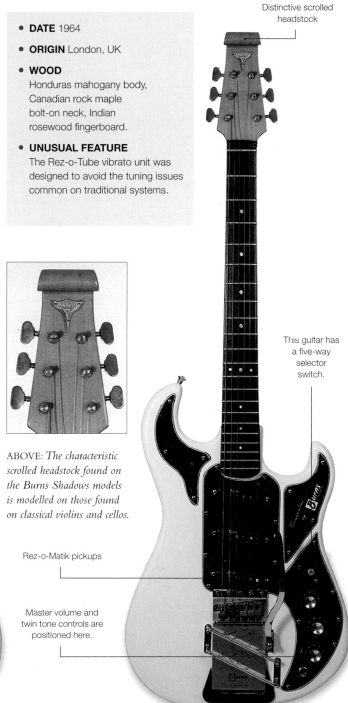

Distinctive scrolled headstock

This guitar has a five-way selector switch.

ABOVE: *The characteristic scrolled headstock found on the Burns Shadows models is modelled on those found on classical violins and cellos.*

Rez-o-Matik pickups

Master volume and twin tone controls are positioned here.

Britain in the 1960s

As the 1960s progressed, American guitars began to reach British shores in greater numbers. They were, however, very expensive. While Britain's first wave of electric guitar players were serviced by imports from Germany, Japan and the Netherlands, a number of local manufacturers began to emerge. Britain would never become a major force in the guitar world, but it produced some credible instruments nonetheless.

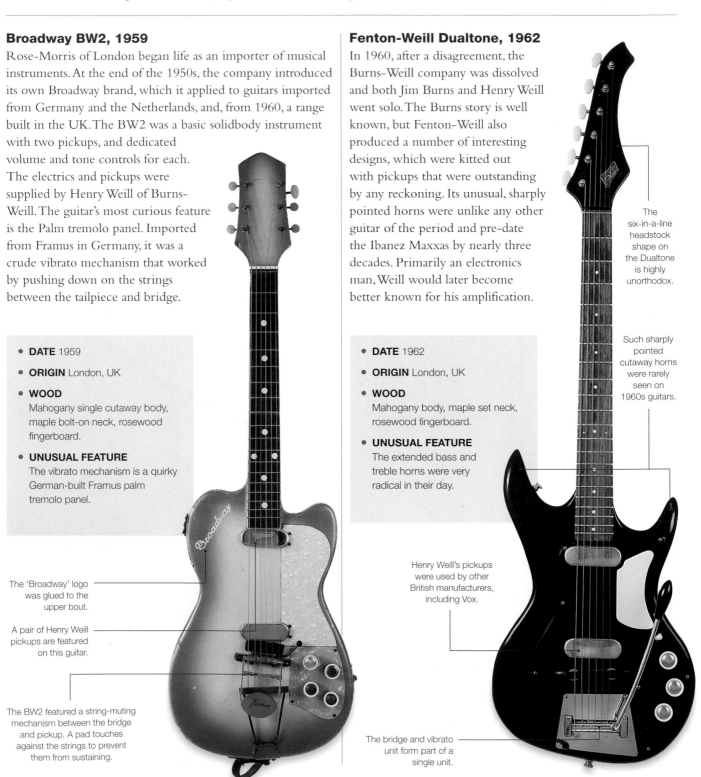

Broadway BW2, 1959

Rose-Morris of London began life as an importer of musical instruments. At the end of the 1950s, the company introduced its own Broadway brand, which it applied to guitars imported from Germany and the Netherlands, and, from 1960, a range built in the UK. The BW2 was a basic solidbody instrument with two pickups, and dedicated volume and tone controls for each. The electrics and pickups were supplied by Henry Weill of Burns-Weill. The guitar's most curious feature is the Palm tremolo panel. Imported from Framus in Germany, it was a crude vibrato mechanism that worked by pushing down on the strings between the tailpiece and bridge.

- **DATE** 1959
- **ORIGIN** London, UK
- **WOOD**
  Mahogany single cutaway body, maple bolt-on neck, rosewood fingerboard.
- **UNUSUAL FEATURE**
  The vibrato mechanism is a quirky German-built Framus palm tremolo panel.

The 'Broadway' logo was glued to the upper bout.

A pair of Henry Weill pickups are featured on this guitar.

The BW2 featured a string-muting mechanism between the bridge and pickup. A pad touches against the strings to prevent them from sustaining.

Fenton-Weill Dualtone, 1962

In 1960, after a disagreement, the Burns-Weill company was dissolved and both Jim Burns and Henry Weill went solo. The Burns story is well known, but Fenton-Weill also produced a number of interesting designs, which were kitted out with pickups that were outstanding by any reckoning. Its unusual, sharply pointed horns were unlike any other guitar of the period and pre-date the Ibanez Maxxas by nearly three decades. Primarily an electronics man, Weill would later become better known for his amplification.

- **DATE** 1962
- **ORIGIN** London, UK
- **WOOD**
  Mahogany body, maple set neck, rosewood fingerboard.
- **UNUSUAL FEATURE**
  The extended bass and treble horns were very radical in their day.

The six-in-a-line headstock shape on the Dualtone is highly unorthodox.

Such sharply pointed cutaway horns were rarely seen on 1960s guitars.

Henry Weill's pickups were used by other British manufacturers, including Vox.

The bridge and vibrato unit form part of a single unit.

Vox Apache, 1961

Alongside Burns, the Vox name is perhaps the best-known British music brand of the 1960s, even if it is remembered more for its famous AC15 and AC30 amplifiers than guitars. The first Vox guitars were outsourced models built by Guyatone in Japan. In 1961, owner Tom Jennings decided that his guitars needed a unique look, and he began building the iconic Phantom teardrop-shaped instruments. The Apache, which featured in the Vox catalogue from 1961 to 1966, is a rare relative of the Phantom, and sports an asymmetric teardrop body and an unusual hooked headstock.

- **DATE** 1961

- **ORIGIN** Dartford, UK

- **WOOD**
  Pine body, maple bolt-on neck, beech or rosewood fingerboard.

- **UNUSUAL FEATURES**
  Asymmetric body and a hooked headstock.

The headstock design features a six-in-a-line configuration of tuners.

The fingerboard features dot marker inlays.

The Apache has three single-coil pickups.

ABOVE: *The Vox Apache features a single volume control and two tone pots — one for treble, one for bass.*

The bridge unit also houses a vibrato system.

This take on the classic Vox 'teardrop' body shape features an unusual indentation at the bottom end.

The British scene

There have been relatively few major British guitar brands – at least those manufactured in the UK on any large scale. One name, of course, towers above all others: Jim Burns. Before making instruments bearing his own name, in the late 1950s he had been involved with the Supersound brand – arguably Britain's first production of electric guitars. His instruments gained an international reputation following his collaboration with Hank Marvin of the Shadows. He would continue to make guitars under his own brand or for Hayman, the predecessor or Shergold, which became Britain's last large-scale guitar maker in the late 1970s.

There was, however, a greater number of quasi-British manufacturers. Vox, for example, was an indisputably English company, building its own amplifiers and effects, but many of its best-known later models were actually built in Italy at the Eko and Crucianelli factories. Similarly, almost all of the cheap 'department store' models – such as Antoria, Jedson and Top Twenty – were in fact imported from the Teisco and Matsumoku factories in Japan, and then rebadged on arrival in the UK.

ABOVE: *Hank Marvin (right) takes delivery of the Burns guitar that bore his name. Jim Burns himself (left) points out the instrument's unusual scroll-top headstock. Original Burns Marvins are among the most collectible of British guitars.*

The birth of the SG

Throughout the 1950s, Gibson had persisted with the unpopular Les Paul range of solidbody electric guitars. Although its final incarnation, the Standard of 1958, is now recognized as one of the most desirable guitars of all, two years after this the company finally admitted defeat and ceased production, albeit temporarily. In its place, a new model was launched, the Solid Guitar – the Gibson SG.

Les Paul Standard, 1958

In 1958, the Les Paul was given its final makeover, the garish Goldtop replaced with a sober sunburst finish. Over the next two years, around 1,700 of these Standard models were produced before the introduction of the twin-cutaway SG. During the decade that followed, in the hands of young blues players such as Eric Clapton, the Standard gradually acquired its legendary status, and towards the end of the 1960s Gibson resumed production. The Les Paul has since remained one of the most popular electric guitars.

- **DATE** 1958
- **ORIGIN** Kalamazoo, Michigan, USA
- **WOOD** Mahogany body, maple top, mahogany set neck, rosewood fingerboard.
- **UNUSUAL FEATURE** Highly collectible, a Standard can fetch up to $250,000 at auction.

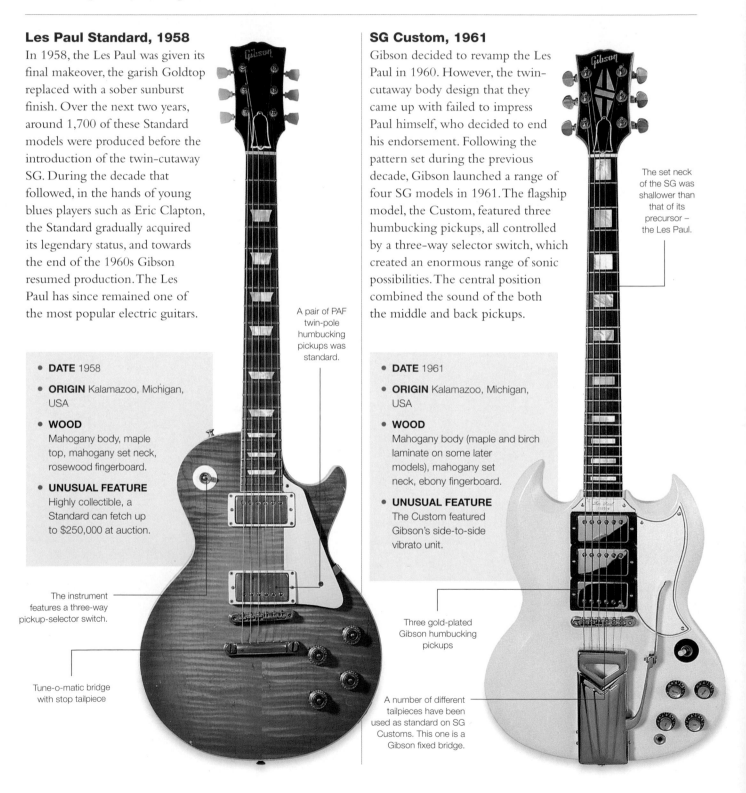

The instrument features a three-way pickup-selector switch.

Tune-o-matic bridge with stop tailpiece

A pair of PAF twin-pole humbucking pickups was standard.

SG Custom, 1961

Gibson decided to revamp the Les Paul in 1960. However, the twin-cutaway body design that they came up with failed to impress Paul himself, who decided to end his endorsement. Following the pattern set during the previous decade, Gibson launched a range of four SG models in 1961. The flagship model, the Custom, featured three humbucking pickups, all controlled by a three-way selector switch, which created an enormous range of sonic possibilities. The central position combined the sound of the both the middle and back pickups.

- **DATE** 1961
- **ORIGIN** Kalamazoo, Michigan, USA
- **WOOD** Mahogany body (maple and birch laminate on some later models), mahogany set neck, ebony fingerboard.
- **UNUSUAL FEATURE** The Custom featured Gibson's side-to-side vibrato unit.

The set neck of the SG was shallower than that of its precursor – the Les Paul.

Three gold-plated Gibson humbucking pickups

A number of different tailpieces have been used as standard on SG Customs. This one is a Gibson fixed bridge.

SG Special, 1961

Introduced at the same time as the Custom, the Special shared much of the same hardware as its luxury relative. The significant difference is in the pickups – the Special is fitted with a pair of high-output, single-coil P-90s. By this time most Gibsons were fitted with humbuckers, but the continued popularity of the single-coil Fenders, with their characteristic treble bite, suggested there was room for a Gibson counterpart. Rock luminaries such as Black Sabbath's Tony Iommi and The Who's Pete Townshend clearly agreed.

- **DATE** 1961
- **ORIGIN** Kalamazoo, Michigan, USA
- **WOOD** Mahogany body (maple and birch laminate on some later models), mahogany set neck, rosewood fingerboard.
- **UNUSUAL FEATURE** A wraparound stairstep tailpiece was fitted on early models.

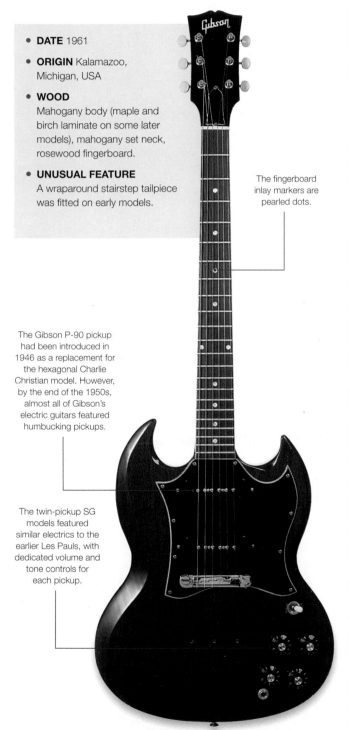

The fingerboard inlay markers are pearled dots.

The Gibson P-90 pickup had been introduced in 1946 as a replacement for the hexagonal Charlie Christian model. However, by the end of the 1950s, almost all of Gibson's electric guitars featured humbucking pickups.

The twin-pickup SG models featured similar electrics to the earlier Les Pauls, with dedicated volume and tone controls for each pickup.

SG Standard, 1961

Although superficially similar to the original Les Pauls, a significant difference lay in the curvature of the body. If you take a side-on look at a Les Paul you will see that the body has a straight edge; the SG – taking its cue from Fender's Stratocaster – had a scalloped contour, intended to make the instrument more comfortable, with no sharp corners pressed against the body. The Standard is the original SG. Very briefly replaced in 1971 with the Standard Deluxe, it remains Gibson's biggest-selling electric guitar.

- **DATE** 1961
- **ORIGIN** Kalamazoo, Michigan, USA
- **WOOD** Mahogany body (maple and birch laminate on some later models), mahogany set neck, rosewood fingerboard.
- **UNUSUAL FEATURES** The fingerboard has pearloid trapezoid inlays and the headstock has a crown inlay.

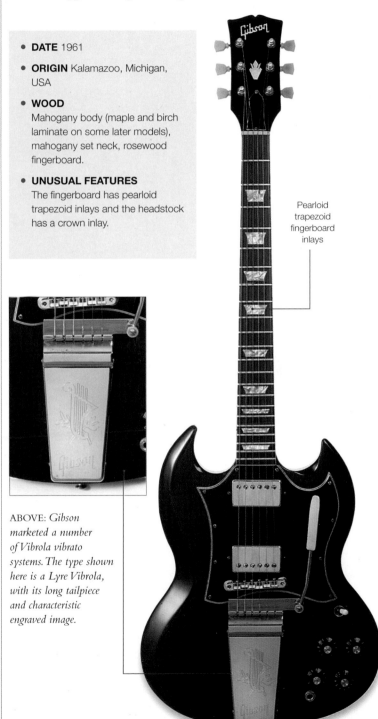

Pearloid trapezoid fingerboard inlays

ABOVE: *Gibson marketed a number of Vibrola vibrato systems. The type shown here is a Lyre Vibrola, with its long tailpiece and characteristic engraved image.*

Gibson ES thinlines

One of the factors that drove the development of the solidbody electric guitar was the elimination of feedback that often occurred in an electric instrument with an acoustic chamber. Some players, however, felt these solidbodies lacked the warmth and tone of their hollowbody counterparts. Launched in 1958, Gibson's thinline ES range sought to find a middle ground.

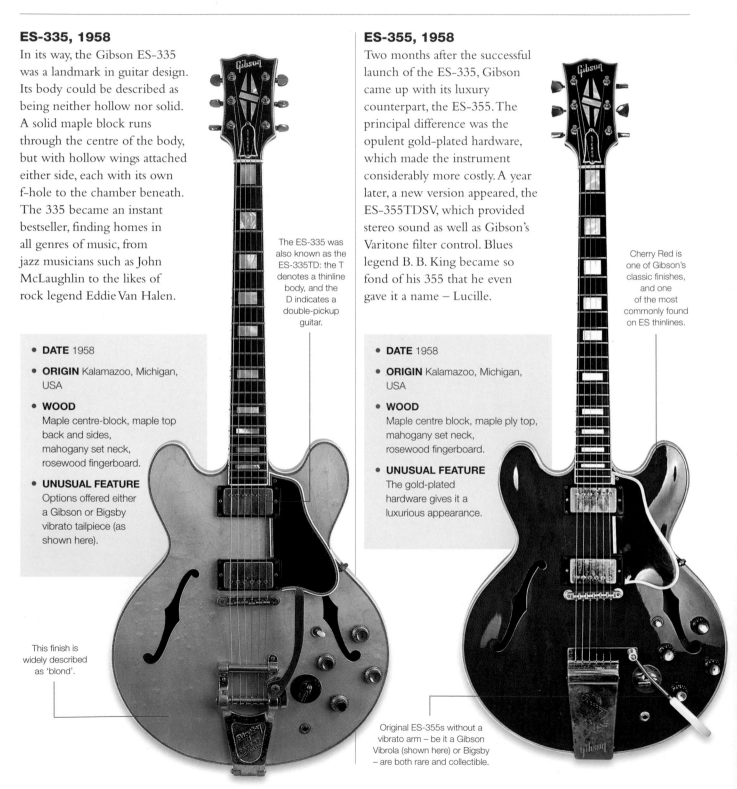

ES-335, 1958

In its way, the Gibson ES-335 was a landmark in guitar design. Its body could be described as being neither hollow nor solid. A solid maple block runs through the centre of the body, but with hollow wings attached either side, each with its own f-hole to the chamber beneath. The 335 became an instant bestseller, finding homes in all genres of music, from jazz musicians such as John McLaughlin to the likes of rock legend Eddie Van Halen.

The ES-335 was also known as the ES-335TD: the T denotes a thinline body, and the D indicates a double-pickup guitar.

- **DATE** 1958
- **ORIGIN** Kalamazoo, Michigan, USA
- **WOOD** Maple centre-block, maple top back and sides, mahogany set neck, rosewood fingerboard.
- **UNUSUAL FEATURE** Options offered either a Gibson or Bigsby vibrato tailpiece (as shown here).

This finish is widely described as 'blond'.

ES-355, 1958

Two months after the successful launch of the ES-335, Gibson came up with its luxury counterpart, the ES-355. The principal difference was the opulent gold-plated hardware, which made the instrument considerably more costly. A year later, a new version appeared, the ES-355TDSV, which provided stereo sound as well as Gibson's Varitone filter control. Blues legend B. B. King became so fond of his 355 that he even gave it a name – Lucille.

Cherry Red is one of Gibson's classic finishes, and one of the most commonly found on ES thinlines.

- **DATE** 1958
- **ORIGIN** Kalamazoo, Michigan, USA
- **WOOD** Maple centre block, maple ply top, mahogany set neck, rosewood fingerboard.
- **UNUSUAL FEATURE** The gold-plated hardware gives it a luxurious appearance.

Original ES-355s without a vibrato arm – be it a Gibson Vibrola (shown here) or Bigsby – are both rare and collectible.

ES-345, 1959

Gibson frequently offered its customers a range of options on its instruments. Launched in 1959, the ES-345 was a souped-up version of the 335. As a guitar, it was virtually identical, except for tiny cosmetic details such as the split-parallelogram fingerboard inlays (with no first-fret marker), and the small crown headstock design. The principal difference between the two was the introduction of stereo outputs and Gibson's six-way Varitone filter circuitry. The 345 remained a part of the Gibson production range until 1981.

- **DATE** 1959

- **ORIGIN** Kalamazoo, Michigan, USA

- **WOOD**
  Maple centre block, maple ply top, mahogany set neck, rosewood fingerboard.

- **UNUSUAL FEATURE**
  The ES-345 marked the first appearance of Gibson's Varitone filter control circuitry.

ABOVE: *The Varitone control is a six-way notched rotary potentiometer. From 1 up to 6, the higher the setting the greater the filtering out of low frequencies. B. B. King favoured setting 2 on his 355.*

Like all new Gibson electrics launched at the end of the 1950s, the ES-345 features PAF humbucking pickups.

B. B. King

Without doubt one of the most important blues guitarists of all time, B. B. King (b. 1925) established himself both as a player and singer from the late 1940s, with genre classics such as "Every Day I Have the Blues" and "Sweet Little Angel". His 1964 album *Live at the Regal* is rated by many critics as among the greatest-ever concert recordings.

King's extensive use of string bending, both as an interpretive playing technique and an alternative vibrato effect, has influenced successive generations of blues and rock guitarists, among them Jimi Hendrix, Eric Clapton, Buddy Guy and Robert Cray. Well into his ninth decade, and yet still an active performer at the time of writing, King is thought to have played over 15,000 concerts during his lifetime.

ABOVE: *Master bluesman B. B. King with his ever-present companion, Lucille – a black ES-355. King even named an album in 'her' honour in 1968. In 1982, Gibson launched the B. B. King Lucille models. At King's request, the f-holes were removed to reduce feedback. In the past, King had forced towels through the holes of his own 335s to achieve the same effect.*

The two pickups are controlled by dedicated volume and tone pots.

Gibson Firebirds

With the dismal failure of Gibson's Modernistic guitars in 1958, company president Ted McCarty tried a different approach, this time hiring car designer Ray Dietrich, who was noted for his work on Chryslers and Lincolns in the 1950s. The result was the Firebird, a luxury instrument with an unorthodox body shape that was quickly destined to undergo a drastic redesign.

Firebird I, 1963

Ray Dietrich's original design had remodelled Ted McCarty's failed Explorer, replacing the harsh points of the treble cutaway and body with gentler curves, reminiscent of the tailfin of a 1950s luxury car. The Firebird was notable as being the first Gibson model to be produced with a straight-through neck, a costly production technique that saw the neck and central block of the body cut from a single piece of wood. Proponents claim that it improved both tone and sustain.

- **DATE** 1963
- **ORIGIN** Kalamazoo, Michigan, USA
- **WOOD**
  Mahogany body, mahogany straight-through neck, rosewood fingerboard.
- **UNUSUAL FEATURE**
  Original Firebird variations were denoted by Roman numerals (I, III, V and VII), depending on hardware.

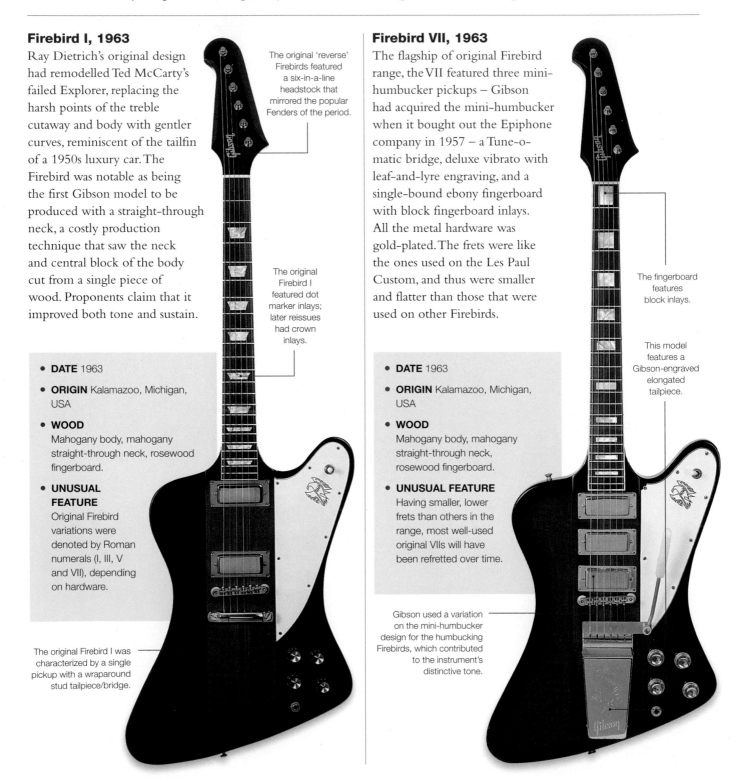

The original 'reverse' Firebirds featured a six-in-a-line headstock that mirrored the popular Fenders of the period.

The original Firebird I featured dot marker inlays; later reissues had crown inlays.

The original Firebird I was characterized by a single pickup with a wraparound stud tailpiece/bridge.

Firebird VII, 1963

The flagship of original Firebird range, the VII featured three mini-humbucker pickups – Gibson had acquired the mini-humbucker when it bought out the Epiphone company in 1957 – a Tune-o-matic bridge, deluxe vibrato with leaf-and-lyre engraving, and a single-bound ebony fingerboard with block fingerboard inlays. All the metal hardware was gold-plated. The frets were like the ones used on the Les Paul Custom, and thus were smaller and flatter than those that were used on other Firebirds.

- **DATE** 1963
- **ORIGIN** Kalamazoo, Michigan, USA
- **WOOD**
  Mahogany body, mahogany straight-through neck, rosewood fingerboard.
- **UNUSUAL FEATURE**
  Having smaller, lower frets than others in the range, most well-used original VIIs will have been refretted over time.

The fingerboard features block inlays.

This model features a Gibson-engraved elongated tailpiece.

Gibson used a variation on the mini-humbucker design for the humbucking Firebirds, which contributed to the instrument's distinctive tone.

Firebird I 'Non-reverse', 1965

Although fine instruments, the original Firebirds did not meet sales expectations. Also, some suggested that the body shape might have breached Fender's design patents on the Jazzmaster – if you compare the body shapes you can see that the Firebird mirrors the Fender guitar. So in 1965, Gibson remodelled the guitar on more conventional lines, with the bass horn extending further than the treble. By reversing the 'reversed' body shape of the original design, the new Firebirds became known as 'non-reverse' models.

Firebird III 'Non-reverse', 1965

Like their predecessors, the new Firebirds were available in a variety of configurations. However, an alternative numbering system was introduced: I and III models now respectively featured two and three single-pole P-90 pickups, while the V and VII models were kitted out with either two or three humbuckers. No 'non-reverse' single-pickup models were produced. Although popular with many blues and rock players, after several years of poor sales, the Firebird was finally discontinued in 1969.

- **DATE** 1965
- **ORIGIN** Kalamazoo, Michigan, USA
- **WOOD** Mahogany body, mahogany set neck, rosewood or ebony fingerboard.
- **UNUSUAL FEATURE** The instrument features a stud tailpiece with plastic-tipped vibrato arm.

- **DATE** 1965
- **ORIGIN** Kalamazoo, Michigan, USA
- **WOOD** Mahogany body, mahogany set neck, rosewood fingerboard.
- **UNUSUAL FEATURE** The unbound rosewood fingerboard with dot inlays distinguish the III from other models.

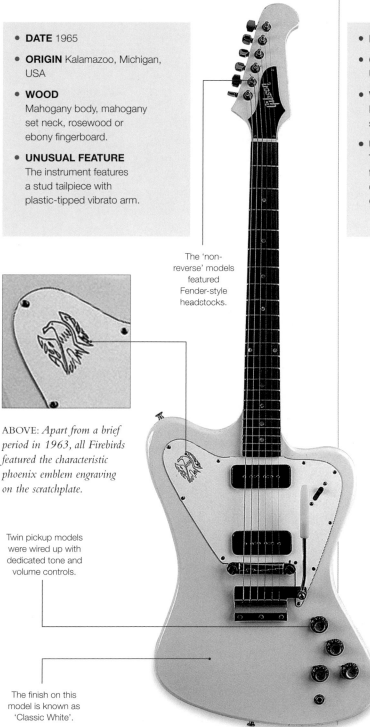

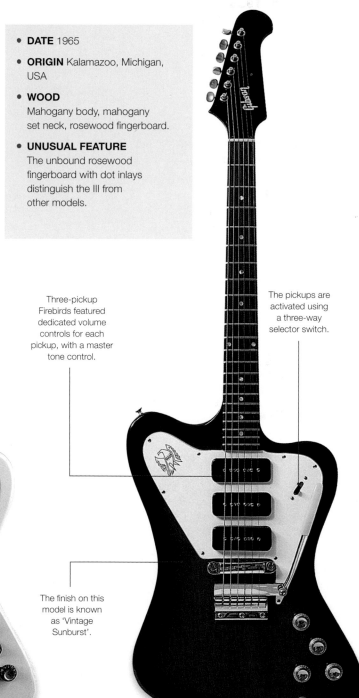

The 'non-reverse' models featured Fender-style headstocks.

ABOVE: *Apart from a brief period in 1963, all Firebirds featured the characteristic phoenix emblem engraving on the scratchplate.*

Three-pickup Firebirds featured dedicated volume controls for each pickup, with a master tone control.

The pickups are activated using a three-way selector switch.

Twin pickup models were wired up with dedicated tone and volume controls.

The finish on this model is known as 'Vintage Sunburst'.

The finish on this model is known as 'Classic White'.

Player-endorsed Gibson models

Celebrity-endorsed electric guitars are nowadays commonplace, with often seemingly limited-edition instruments marketed to music fans at a premium price. The artist-endorsed models Gibson produced from the 1950s were, however, often a collaborative effort between player and manufacturer, born more of a desire to produce a special instrument than to sell slight variants on existing models.

Byrdland, 1955

The large-bodied L-5 archtop acoustic of 1922 was a significant instrument in guitar history, as its size helped with issues of volume. In 1951, an electric cutaway version was launched – the L-5CES. Based on the suggestions of country-jazz players Hank Garland and Billy Byrd, who found it overly bulky, Gibson produced an exquisite thinline version, the Byrdland, with gold-plated hardware. The players also specified a short-scale neck, enabling the fingering of unusual stretched chord voicings.

- **DATE** 1955

- **ORIGIN** Kalamazoo, Michigan, USA

- **WOOD**
  Maple back and sides, spruce top, maple set neck, ebony fingerboard.

- **UNUSUAL FEATURE**
  The Byrdland has a 597mm (23½in) short-scale neck, 32mm (1¼in) shorter than the Gibson standard.

Johnny Smith, 1961

Well-respected and versatile as a player, Johnny Smith is now largely remembered for the instruments he endorsed. Having been approached by Gibson's Ted McCarty, Smith's specification was for a fully acoustic archtop guitar with a single rounded cutaway as well as a floating mini-humbucker positioned close to the neck. The instrument that emerged was an opulent L-5CES variant that retailed at a princely $795 on its 1961 launch – at the time, Gibson's most expensive guitar.

- **DATE** 1961

- **ORIGIN** Kalamazoo, Michigan, USA

- **WOOD**
  Maple back and sides, spruce top, set five-piece maple neck, ebony fingerboard.

- **UNUSUAL FEATURE**
  The electrics are built beneath the floating scratchplate on which the controls are mounted.

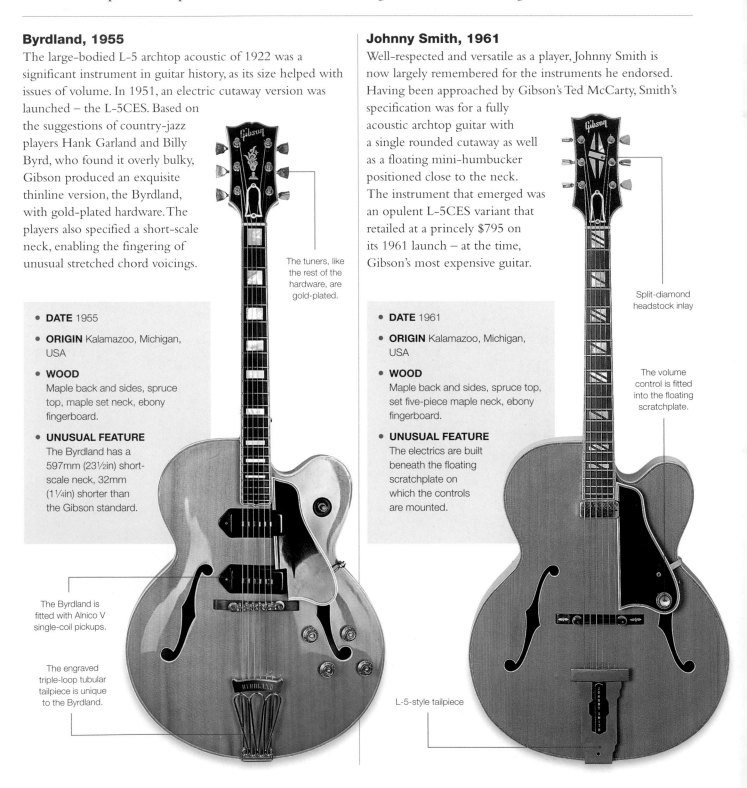

The tuners, like the rest of the hardware, are gold-plated.

Split-diamond headstock inlay

The volume control is fitted into the floating scratchplate.

The Byrdland is fitted with Alnico V single-coil pickups.

The engraved triple-loop tubular tailpiece is unique to the Byrdland.

L-5-style tailpiece

Barney Kessel, 1961

One of the most popular US jazz guitarists during the 1950s was Barney Kessel, and his signature model was launched alongside the Jimmy Smith. It resembles a thinline version of the ES-175, but with a double Florentine cutaway – although its body dimensions also reveal its L-5 connections. Two models were available: the Regular, which retailed at $399 and found some success in the jazz world, and the rarer and more luxurious Custom, which fared less well, most players preferring the similarly priced Byrdland.

- **DATE** 1961
- **ORIGIN** Kalamazoo, Michigan, USA
- **WOOD**
  Laminated maple back and sides, laminated spruce top, one-piece mahogany neck, rosewood fingerboard.
- **UNUSUAL FEATURE**
  The Kessel features two Florentine cutaways.

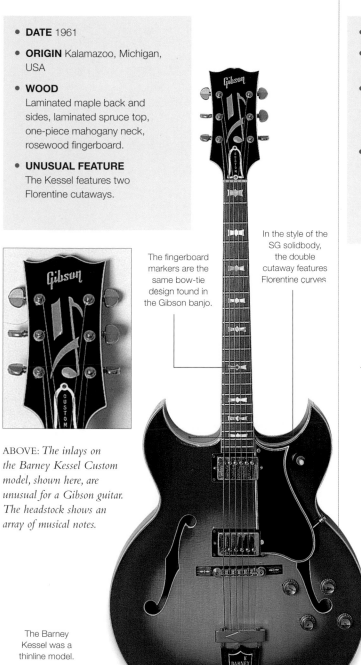

ABOVE: *The inlays on the Barney Kessel Custom model, shown here, are unusual for a Gibson guitar. The headstock shows an array of musical notes.*

The fingerboard markers are the same bow-tie design found in the Gibson banjo.

In the style of the SG solidbody, the double cutaway features Florentine curves

The Barney Kessel was a thinline model.

Trini Lopez, 1964

The first major Latino pop star, singer and guitarist Trini Lopez topped the charts across the world in 1963, with his version of the folk song "If I Had a Hammer". Gibson launched the Trini Lopez in 1964 to much hype, but, in truth, it was a cosmetically modified ES-335 with the f-holes replaced by unusual elongated diamond slits. The headstock also differed, the three-a-side design of the 335 replaced by the same six-in-a-row style that Gibson would use again a year later on the revamped Firebird.

- **DATE** 1964
- **ORIGIN** Kalamazoo, Michigan, USA
- **WOOD**
  Maple centre block, maple ply top, mahogany set neck, rosewood fingerboard.
- **UNUSUAL FEATURE**
  The use of the diamond-slit soundholes and the six-in-a-row machine-head configuration gives this guitar a unique look.

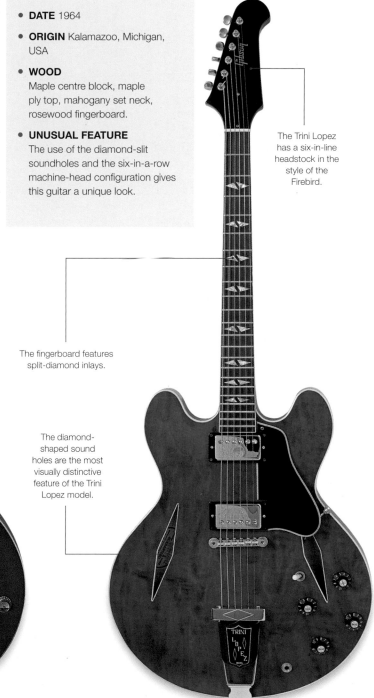

The Trini Lopez has a six-in-line headstock in the style of the Firebird.

The fingerboard features split-diamond inlays.

The diamond-shaped sound holes are the most visually distinctive feature of the Trini Lopez model.

Bass guitars in the 1960s

Apart from in the jazz world, by the time of the early 1960s beat boom, the acoustic upright double bass was all but dead in popular music. The Fender Precision, which had kick-started that revolution in 1951, was still the dominant bass instrument, but, as the decade moved on, other makers such as Gibson, Gretsch and, in particular, Rickenbacker, began to emerge as serious competitors.

Fender Jazz, 1960

Introduced in 1960, the offset-waisted Jazz was the bass counterpart to Fender's flagship guitar of the time, the Jazzmaster. As the name suggested, it was aimed squarely at acoustic-playing jazz bassists, suggesting they lay to rest their monsters and go electric. To this end, Fender offered a narrow neck width, ideal for the necessarily nimble-fingered jazzer, and twin single-coil pickups with two pole pieces per string, providing a cleaner treble sound at the bass end. The Jazz remains one of the most significant bass guitars ever built.

- **DATE** 1960
- **ORIGIN** Fullerton, California, USA
- **WOOD**
  Ash (sometimes alder) body, bolt-on maple neck, rosewood or maple fingerboard.
- **UNUSUAL FEATURE**
  The twin pole pieces on the pickups create a clean sound.

A circular string guide on the headstock keeps the D and G strings in place.

The twin-pickup Jazz had no selector switch built into the circuitry. The two larger knobs control the volume on each of the J pickups.

The Jazz is unusual in that there is no neck pickup – the second pickup is positioned at the centre of the body.

The smaller knob alongside the jack socket is a master tone control.

Gibson EB-3, 1961

Just as the 1958 semi-hollow EB-2 had been a bass counterpart to the ES-335, the EB-3 emerged in 1961 as part of the SG range. Gibson basses were, and have remained, rather unorthodox instruments. With its 762mm (30in) scale length, it was a full 102mm (4in) shorter than the Fenders, which in itself created a different sound in the lower register. It also featured a curious pickup configuration, with a large humbucker in the neck position and a mini-humbucker alongside the bridge.

- **DATE** 1961
- **ORIGIN** Kalamazoo, Michigan, USA
- **WOOD**
  Mahogany body, mahogany set neck, rosewood fingerboard.
- **UNUSUAL FEATURE**
  It has a basic bridge unit with limited adjustability.

Pearloid dot fingerboard inlay markers have been used.

The strings are held in place by positioning the ball-end in a slot; there are no individually adjustable saddles, although the one-piece saddle can be moved as a whole. Two large screws at either side enable the player to adjust the overall height of the bridge.

Rickenbacker 4001S, 1961

With its cresting-wave body shape and matching headstock, the 1957 Rickenbacker 4000 was a spectacular design that captured the imagination of players turning to the bass guitar. In 1961, in an effort to keep one step ahead of rival Fender – which had just introduced the Jazz – Rickenbacker created a deluxe model, the 4001. Equipped with two pickups – a large horseshoe for the bridge and toaster for the neck – the 4001 was also wired for the optional Rick-O-Sound twin-audio output. This would become a standard feature from 1971.

- **DATE** 1961
- **ORIGIN** Santa Ana, California, USA
- **WOOD**
  Maple body, straight-through neck, rosewood fingerboard.
- **UNUSUAL FEATURE**
  The Rick-O-Sound wiring allows a stereo cable to channel the sound from each pickup through its own input.

Unusually, the two-a-side tuners on the headstock are asymmetrically aligned.

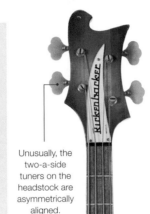

The 4001 has both horseshoe and toaster pickups.

ABOVE: *The Rickenbacker 4001 features an unusually well-engineered bridge. With a combination bridge and tailpiece, each saddle is fully adjustable for both intonation and height. The 4001 is one of the few bass guitars to have challenged the ubiquity of Fender's big two – the Telecaster and the Stratocaster.*

Gretsch 6073, 1967

In general, Gretsch is not celebrated for its basses, and the 6073 is probably its best-known model, primarily through its use by Peter Tork on the popular 1960s TV show *The Monkees* – indeed, it was widely marketed as the 'Monkees Bass'. A hollowbody, short-scale instrument (737mm/29in), the 6073 was modelled on the successful Chet Atkins Tennessean and equipped with a pair of Super'Tron humbuckers. Gretsch also produced the similar single-pickup 6071. Both remained in production until 1972.

- **DATE** 1967
- **ORIGIN** Brooklyn, New York, USA
- **WOOD**
  Single-cut mahogany body with comfort padding on the back, maple straight-through neck, rosewood fingerboard.
- **UNUSUAL FEATURE**
  The instrument has a muting mechanism that helps to replicate the thud of an acoustic bass.

The 6073 is noteworthy as one of a small number of Gretsch models with an in-a-line tuner configuration.

The fingerboard has dot marker inlays.

There are thumb and finger rests above and below the strings; few bass players have found them useful, and they are now rarely seen.

There is a master volume on the cutaway horn.

Epiphone: after the Gibson takeover

The 1960s was a transitional decade for the Epiphone brand. Having previously been one of the giants of the guitar world, it was now merely part of the Gibson empire – once its bitter rival. Although the instruments were still able to retain some their former character, there were clear indications of the brand's future – Gibson's eventual intention to treat Epiphone as a diffusion line.

Casino, 1958

One of the first new models to appear after the Gibson takeover, the Casino was essentially an Epiphone-branded version of the Gibson ES-330. A thinline, hollowbodied, twin-pickup, twin-cutaway instrument, the Casino was able to overshadow its high-end counterpart by virtue of one fact – its association with John Lennon and The Beatles. Indeed, all three guitar-playing members of the band owned Casinos. In 2010, a 1965 Elitist model appeared, an exact replica of Lennon's own guitar, with its scratchplate removed, as Lennon had done.

- **DATE** 1958
- **ORIGIN** Kalamazoo, Michigan, USA
- **WOOD** Solid maple centre block with maple wings, mahogany set neck, rosewood fingerboard.
- **UNUSUAL FEATURE** Modelled on the Gibson ES-330.

Single-coil P-90 pickups

The raised scratchplate features the characteristic Epiphone 'E' logo.

Trapeze tailpiece

Broadway, 1958

As an archtop acoustic guitar, Epiphone first introduced the Broadway in 1931, giving it a single cutaway two decades later. The electric archtop was launched in 1958. Like other models that spanned the Gibson takeover, the Broadway was initially built using existing stock from the Epiphone factory. Thus, the 1958 model shown here is equipped with a Frequensator tailpiece and New York pickups; from 1961, when old stocks were exhausted, Gibson mini-humbuckers and a Tune-o-matic bridge and end stop were installed.

- **DATE** 1958
- **ORIGIN** Kalamazoo, Michigan, USA
- **WOOD** Maple back and sides, spruce top, maple set neck, rosewood fingerboard.
- **UNUSUAL FEATURE** The unusual tailpiece was used when stocks ran out.

The New York pickups were replaced by Gibson mini-humbuckers from 1961.

The selector switch is found on the upper bout.

The tailpiece is an Epiphone Frequensator.

Coronet, 1958

The Epiphone Coronet was designed as cheaper entry-level alternative to the Les Paul Junior – although, with its thicker body, many rate it as a far better instrument. To put that into perspective, however, the Coronet retailed at around $120, which was still more than double the price of a starter model from the Sears catalogue. The first Coronets featured a single Epiphone New York pickup; from 1960, P-90s were fitted. They were built in the USA until 1970, after which time the production of all Epiphones moved to Japan.

Crestwood, 1958

The flagship of the Epiphone solidbody range, the Crestwood was pitched as a Les Paul alternative, but it was, in its own right, one of the finest models of the period – by the early 1960s, Crestwoods were being produced using the same woods and hardware as Gibson SGs. They were launched in 1958 with the characteristic symmetrical batwing cutaways, but a year later, renamed the Crestwood Custom, these were altered, with the treble horn made smaller. The Crestwood remained in production at Kalamazoo until 1970, resuming later in Japan.

- **DATE** 1958
- **ORIGIN** Kalamazoo, Michigan, USA
- **WOOD** Mahogany body, mahogany set neck, rosewood fingerboard.
- **UNUSUAL FEATURE** The cutaways meet the neck at a 90-degree angle, giving a straight line across the top of the body.

- **DATE** 1958
- **ORIGIN** Kalamazoo, Michigan, USA
- **WOOD** Mahogany body, mahogany set neck, rosewood fingerboard.
- **UNUSUAL FEATURE** The model shown here has characteristic white 'New York' volume and tone knobs.

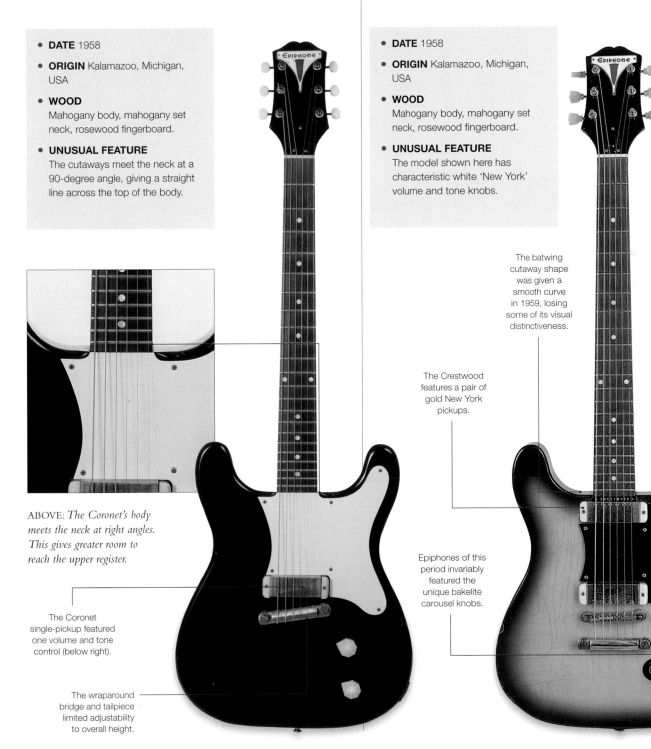

ABOVE: *The Coronet's body meets the neck at right angles. This gives greater room to reach the upper register.*

The Coronet single-pickup featured one volume and tone control (below right).

The wraparound bridge and tailpiece limited adjustability to overall height.

The batwing cutaway shape was given a smooth curve in 1959, losing some of its visual distinctiveness.

The Crestwood features a pair of gold New York pickups.

Epiphones of this period invariably featured the unique bakelite carousel knobs.

Rickenbacker in the 1960s

Throughout the 1950s, new owner Francis H. Hall skilfully managed the company's growth, establishing Rickenbacker as one of a handful of leading names in the American electric-guitar market. However, in 1964, the unexpected cultural tide that spread across the Atlantic from the UK – Beatlemania – suddenly made Rickenbacker guitars among the most immediately recognizable in the world.

325, 1958

Introduced as part of the 1958 Capri series, the Rickenbacker 325 was a semi-hollow, three-quarter scale-length model with three pickups. In 1960, while The Beatles were learning their trade in the clubs of Hamburg, John Lennon saw his first Rickenbacker. Clearly taken with the 325, he was rarely seen playing anything else during the Beatlemania period, and ended up owning four of them. Rickenbacker has since issued many limited-edition tribute models, such as the 325C58 Hamburg and the 325JL.

- **DATE** 1958
- **ORIGIN** Santa Ana, California, USA
- **WOOD** Maple semi-hollowbody, maple set neck, rosewood fingerboard.
- **UNUSUAL FEATURE** The short 527mm (20¾in) scale length is 102mm (4in) shorter than a standard Rickenbacker.

360, 1958

A part of the Rickenbacker 300 Series launched in 1958, the 360 is arguably the company's best-known instrument, both in its six- and twelve-string forms. It incorporates many standard Rickenbacker features, including a three-ply maple and walnut neck, shallow headstock and a thick rosewood fingerboard. The body features the characteristic crescent moon cutaway shape, rounded top edge, and the famous stylized R of the trapeze tailpiece.

- **DATE** 1958
- **ORIGIN** Santa Ana, California, USA
- **WOOD** Maple carved body, three-ply maple/walnut set neck, rosewood fingerboard.
- **UNUSUAL FEATURE** The pearloid-triangle fingerboard marker inlays.

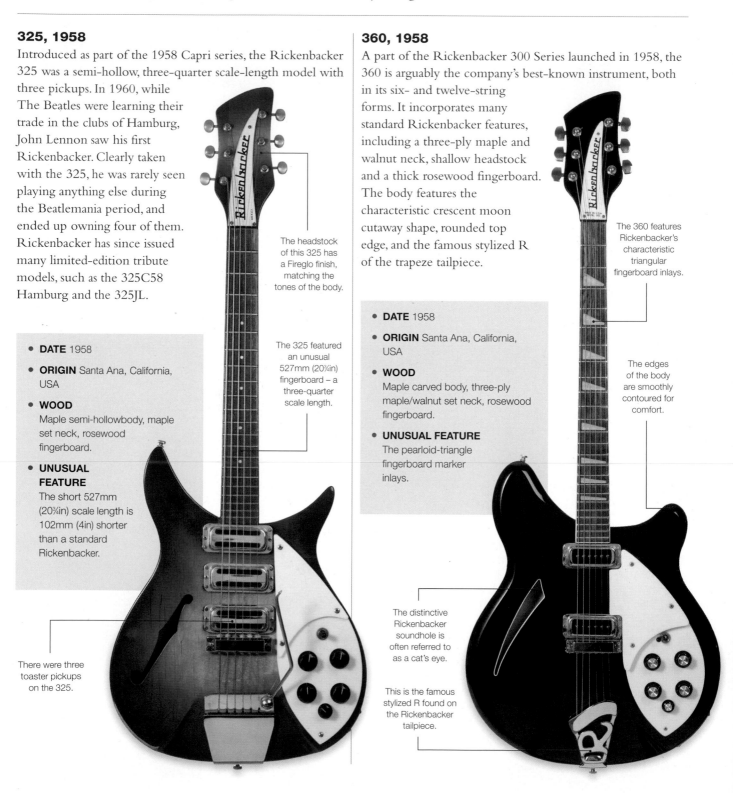

The headstock of this 325 has a Fireglo finish, matching the tones of the body.

The 325 featured an unusual 527mm (20¾in) fingerboard – a three-quarter scale length.

There were three toaster pickups on the 325.

The 360 features Rickenbacker's characteristic triangular fingerboard inlays.

The edges of the body are smoothly contoured for comfort.

The distinctive Rickenbacker soundhole is often referred to as a cat's eye.

This is the famous stylized R found on the Rickenbacker tailpiece.

460, 1961

The Rickenbacker range, while featuring a relatively small number of core models or body shapes, comprised many with minor variations. One such example, the cresting wave 460 introduced in 1961, is nothing more than a slightly more luxurious version of the earlier 450. The enhancements are few but nonetheless signify a deluxe instrument, with body binding and the simple dot inlays of the 450 replaced by pearloid triangle markers. The model shown here is from the first year of production; in 1962 the anodized metal scratchplate was replaced by plastic.

- **DATE** 1961

- **ORIGIN** Santa Ana, California, USA

- **WOOD**
  Maple body, maple straight-through neck, rosewood fingerboard.

- **UNUSUAL FEATURE**
  The anodized metal scratchplate on early models.

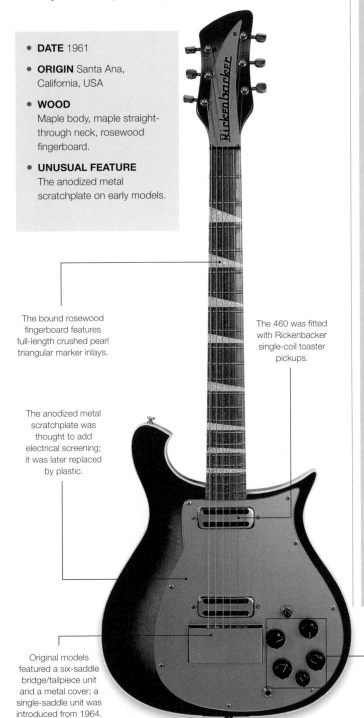

The bound rosewood fingerboard features full-length crushed pearl triangular marker inlays.

The anodized metal scratchplate was thought to add electrical screening; it was later replaced by plastic.

The 460 was fitted with Rickenbacker single-coil toaster pickups.

Original models featured a six-saddle bridge/tailpiece unit and a metal cover; a single-saddle unit was introduced from 1964.

The electrics comprise two pairs of volume and tone controls and one pickup balance.

Rickenbacker and The Beatles

In the UK, 1963 was the year of The Beatles, the first wave of what was to become known as Beatlemania. Although the band were largely unheard of in the USA at this time, European distributors began to send over press clippings of them, often featuring John Lennon and George Harrison playing Rickenbackers. Beatlemania repeated itself a year later in the USA, the band cementing its reputation with a celebrated performance on the *Johnny Carson Show*, with John Lennon singing at the front of the band and playing his Rickenbacker 325. After that evening, Rickenbacker was unable to produce enough guitars to satisfy demand, with the company's head office at Santa Ana receiving fan mail from all over the world.

The story continued in February 1964, when George Harrison was given one of the prototypes of Rickenbacker's new electric 12-string. He proceeded to use it heavily on the band's next album, *A Hard Day's Night*, including the famous opening chord chimes of the title track. The Beatles were, in the eyes of the public, a Rickenbacker band.

ABOVE: *The Beatles remain the most culturally significant pop group in history and, although they disbanded in 1970, their music continues to reach successive generations. Rickenbacker had previously been a well-respected name in the guitar world, but the marque's association with The Beatles suddenly made it one of the most desirable brands in the world.*

Japan in the 1960s

Having led the world in building cheap copies of American classics, Japan began to produce guitars with unique character as the 1960s progressed. They may have still been strongly inspired by Fenders, Gibsons and – perhaps surprisingly – models from Europe by makers such as Burns and Hagström, but this was the first generation of instruments from the Far East that hinted at future triumphs.

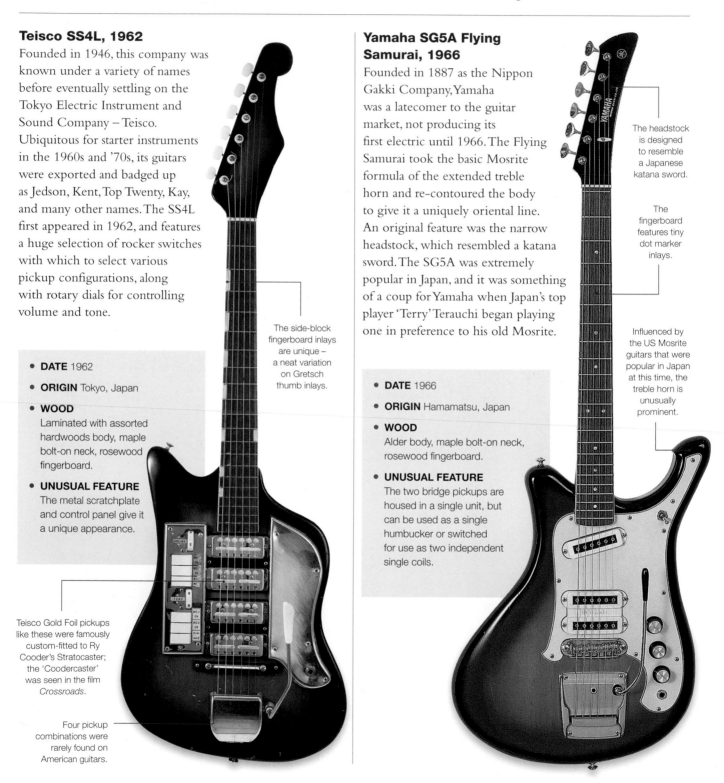

Teisco SS4L, 1962

Founded in 1946, this company was known under a variety of names before eventually settling on the Tokyo Electric Instrument and Sound Company – Teisco. Ubiquitous for starter instruments in the 1960s and '70s, its guitars were exported and badged up as Jedson, Kent, Top Twenty, Kay, and many other names. The SS4L first appeared in 1962, and features a huge selection of rocker switches with which to select various pickup configurations, along with rotary dials for controlling volume and tone.

- **DATE** 1962
- **ORIGIN** Tokyo, Japan
- **WOOD**
  Laminated with assorted hardwoods body, maple bolt-on neck, rosewood fingerboard.
- **UNUSUAL FEATURE**
  The metal scratchplate and control panel give it a unique appearance.

Teisco Gold Foil pickups like these were famously custom-fitted to Ry Cooder's Stratocaster; the 'Coodercaster' was seen in the film *Crossroads*.

Four pickup combinations were rarely found on American guitars.

The side-block fingerboard inlays are unique – a neat variation on Gretsch thumb inlays.

Yamaha SG5A Flying Samurai, 1966

Founded in 1887 as the Nippon Gakki Company, Yamaha was a latecomer to the guitar market, not producing its first electric until 1966. The Flying Samurai took the basic Mosrite formula of the extended treble horn and re-contoured the body to give it a uniquely oriental line. An original feature was the narrow headstock, which resembled a katana sword. The SG5A was extremely popular in Japan, and it was something of a coup for Yamaha when Japan's top player 'Terry' Terauchi began playing one in preference to his old Mosrite.

- **DATE** 1966
- **ORIGIN** Hamamatsu, Japan
- **WOOD**
  Alder body, maple bolt-on neck, rosewood fingerboard.
- **UNUSUAL FEATURE**
  The two bridge pickups are housed in a single unit, but can be used as a single humbucker or switched for use as two independent single coils.

The headstock is designed to resemble a Japanese katana sword.

The fingerboard features tiny dot marker inlays.

Influenced by the US Mosrite guitars that were popular in Japan at this time, the treble horn is unusually prominent.

Teisco Del Rey, *c*.1968

The name Jack Westheimer may not be widely known outside of the guitar industry, but he played a key role in fuelling the guitar boom by bringing affordable instruments into the USA. In 1964, he began importing good-quality Japanese guitars from the Teisco factory under the Teisco Del Rey brand. The Del Reys produced towards the end of the decade were generally more flamboyant in design, with colourful finishes and ornately decorated scratchplates. They continued to appear until around 1973, when the brand ceased production.

- **DATE** *c*.1968
- **ORIGIN** Tokyo, Japan
- **WOOD**
  Laminated with assorted hardwoods body, bolt-on neck, rosewood fingerboard.
- **UNUSUAL FEATURE**
  The highly decorative scratchplate is key to the overall look.

There is no selector switch, but each pickup has its own on-off control.

Like many Japanese models of the period, this Teisco is based around a classic Fender design.

Several Teisco models featured highly decorative scratchplates.

The volume and tone controls are built into a metal panel, in the style of the Fender Jaguar.

Heit Deluxe, *c*.1968

One of the more obscure American import brands, the Heit name was owned by G&H Imports of Lodi, New Jersey, which imported guitars largely from the Teisco factory, and later from Kawai. Many of the models it sold were inspired by the American Mosrite guitars that had made such an impact in Japan following the enormous success of surf band The Ventures. The Heit Deluxe shown here dates from around 1968, and displays a Stratocaster-style body with a rather elegant and distinctive rear cutaway.

- **DATE** *c*.1968
- **ORIGIN** Tokyo, Japan
- **WOOD**
  Laminated with assorted hardwoods body, maple bolt-on neck, rosewood fingerboard.
- **UNUSUAL FEATURE**
  The rear body cutaway gives it a distinctive and elegant look.

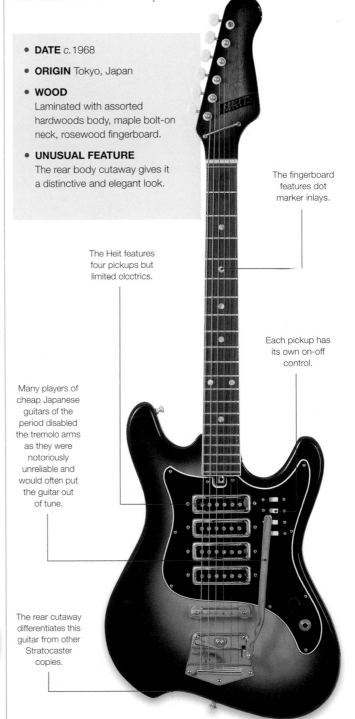

The fingerboard features dot marker inlays.

The Heit features four pickups but limited olcctrics.

Each pickup has its own on-off control.

Many players of cheap Japanese guitars of the period disabled the tremolo arms as they were notoriously unreliable and would often put the guitar out of tune.

The rear cutaway differentiates this guitar from other Stratocaster copies.

Northern Europe in the 1960s

As the 1960s progressed, so did electric guitar production outside of the USA. Jim Burns had shown in London that it was possible to produce viable, if often costly, alternatives to the Fenders, Gibsons, Gretsches and Rickenbackers that were by now being exported from across the Atlantic. Similarly, throughout other parts of Europe, guitar makers were slowly moving away from the world of cheap imitations of US models.

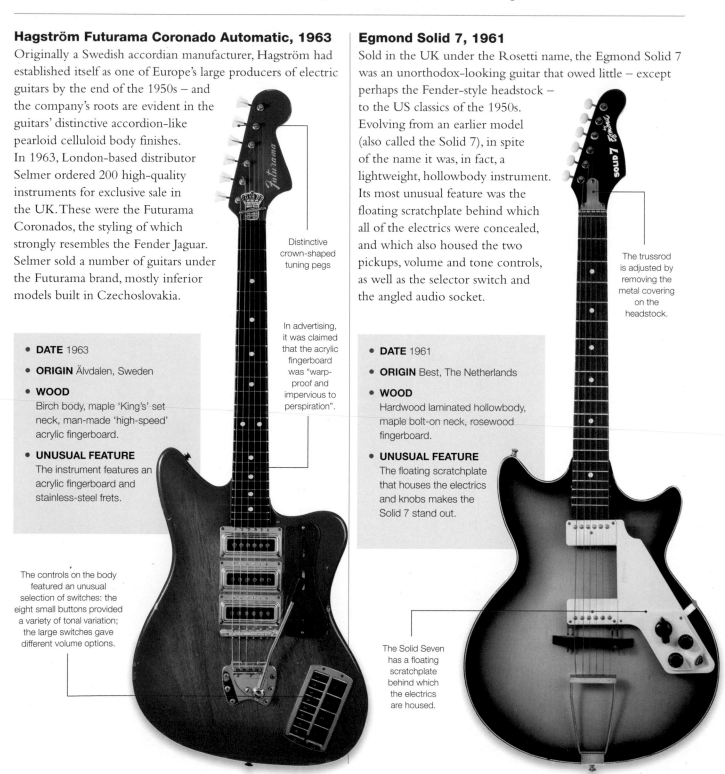

Hagström Futurama Coronado Automatic, 1963

Originally a Swedish accordian manufacturer, Hagström had established itself as one of Europe's large producers of electric guitars by the end of the 1950s – and the company's roots are evident in the guitars' distinctive accordion-like pearloid celluloid body finishes. In 1963, London-based distributor Selmer ordered 200 high-quality instruments for exclusive sale in the UK. These were the Futurama Coronados, the styling of which strongly resembles the Fender Jaguar. Selmer sold a number of guitars under the Futurama brand, mostly inferior models built in Czechoslovakia.

- **DATE** 1963
- **ORIGIN** Älvdalen, Sweden
- **WOOD**
  Birch body, maple 'King's' set neck, man-made 'high-speed' acrylic fingerboard.
- **UNUSUAL FEATURE**
  The instrument features an acrylic fingerboard and stainless-steel frets.

Distinctive crown-shaped tuning pegs

In advertising, it was claimed that the acrylic fingerboard was "warp-proof and impervious to perspiration".

The controls on the body featured an unusual selection of switches: the eight small buttons provided a variety of tonal variation; the large switches gave different volume options.

Egmond Solid 7, 1961

Sold in the UK under the Rosetti name, the Egmond Solid 7 was an unorthodox-looking guitar that owed little – except perhaps the Fender-style headstock – to the US classics of the 1950s. Evolving from an earlier model (also called the Solid 7), in spite of the name it was, in fact, a lightweight, hollowbody instrument. Its most unusual feature was the floating scratchplate behind which all of the electrics were concealed, and which also housed the two pickups, volume and tone controls, as well as the selector switch and the angled audio socket.

The trussrod is adjusted by removing the metal covering on the headstock.

- **DATE** 1961
- **ORIGIN** Best, The Netherlands
- **WOOD**
  Hardwood laminated hollowbody, maple bolt-on neck, rosewood fingerboard.
- **UNUSUAL FEATURE**
  The floating scratchplate that houses the electrics and knobs makes the Solid 7 stand out.

The Solid Seven has a floating scratchplate behind which the electrics are housed.

Framus Strato Deluxe, 1966

Fred Wilfler set up the Framus company in Bavaria after the end of World War II, when Germany was still an occupied nation. Initially producing violins, Framus noted the increasing demand for guitars during the 1950s, and soon became one of Europe's biggest producers. The Strato Deluxe was clearly inspired by Fender's flagship Jaguar, but also it incorporated additional circuitry to create an interesting organ–swell effect. It remains one the finest European instruments of the time.

- **DATE** 1966

- **ORIGIN** Bubenreuth, Germany

- **WOOD**
  Maple sandwich-cut body, maple bolt-on neck, rosewood fingerboard.

- **UNUSUAL FEATURE**
  The inbuilt Orgeleffekte – organ-effect – circuitry is a novel touch.

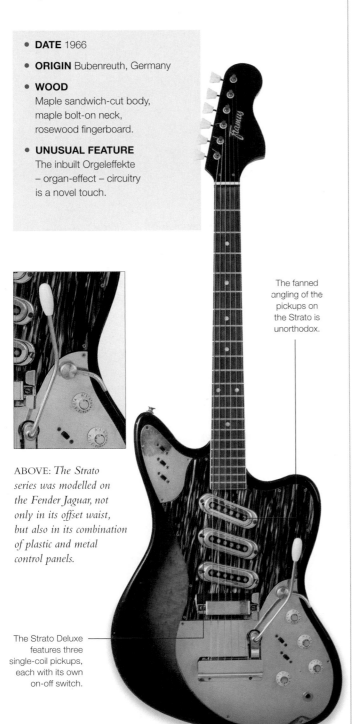

ABOVE: *The Strato series was modelled on the Fender Jaguar, not only in its offset waist, but also in its combination of plastic and metal control panels.*

The fanned angling of the pickups on the Strato is unorthodox.

The Strato Deluxe features three single-coil pickups, each with its own on-off switch.

The cult of Hagström

ABOVE: *Guitarist Pat Smear made his name in US punk band the Germs. He briefly toured with Nirvana prior to the death of Kurt Cobain, and then went on to form the Foo Fighters with Dave Grohl.*

In 1981, no longer able to compete with cheaper Japanese guitars, Karl-Erik Hagström ended production, and the company went into hibernation. The next two decades saw prices for used Hagström guitars on the rise, especially for the early models. Particularly prized was the P46, with its accordion-sparkle finish and reputation as the first production guitar fitted with four pickups – and the 2000s saw it heavily used on stage by the Scottish band Franz Ferdinand.

A key figure in more recent Hagström history is guitarist Pat Smear of US band Foo Fighters. Performing in one of the most popular rock groups in the world, Smear is rarely seen in concert without a Hagström guitar, creating huge interest in a brand largely unknown in America. Smear himself has one of the largest collections of original Hagström guitars in the world, and at one stage even approached Karl-Erik Hagström with plans to fund the revival of the brand.

In 2005, Hagström's son, Karl-Erik Jr, took over the business, and is once again producing some of the best-known models, this time built in China.

Double-neck guitars

It became clear from the earliest days of the electric guitar that there would be times when a performer would want to create different sounds from the same instrument within the same song, either in concert or in a recording studio. In an era that pre-dated multitrack recording and multiple-effect units, one solution was to create a guitar with more than one neck.

Stratosphere Twin, 1955

The classic double-neck guitar configuration was to combine six and twelve strings. The Stratosphere Twin was the first production guitar of this type. Curiously, the maker's recommended 12-string tunings were unorthodox, geared towards playing harmony lead lines rather than chords. Although country star Jimmy Bryant championed this pioneering guitar, even creating the instrumental "Stratosphere Boogie" for its use, it was generally viewed as a novelty instrument.

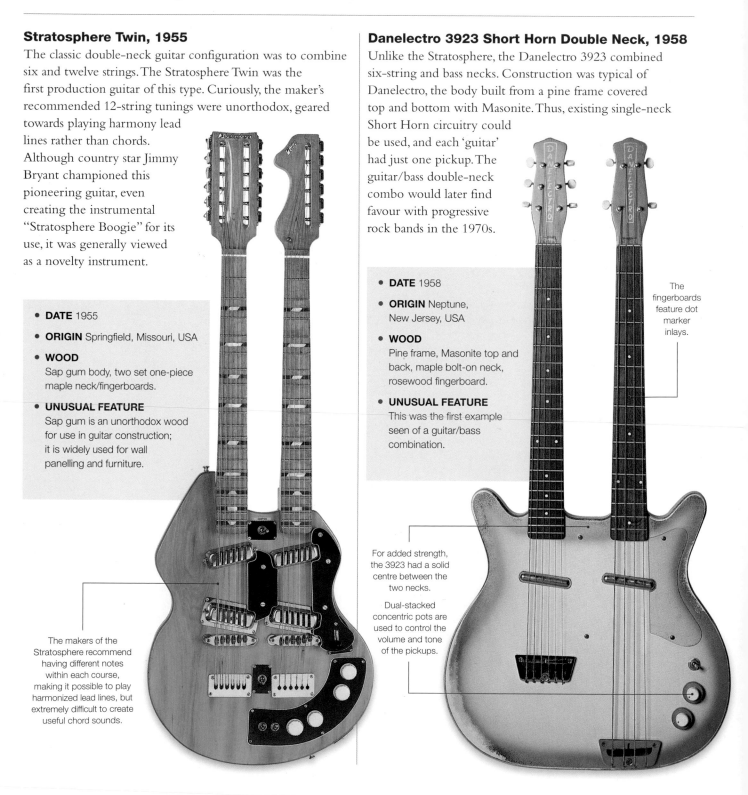

- **DATE** 1955

- **ORIGIN** Springfield, Missouri, USA

- **WOOD**
  Sap gum body, two set one-piece maple neck/fingerboards.

- **UNUSUAL FEATURE**
  Sap gum is an unorthodox wood for use in guitar construction; it is widely used for wall panelling and furniture.

The makers of the Stratosphere recommend having different notes within each course, making it possible to play harmonized lead lines, but extremely difficult to create useful chord sounds.

Danelectro 3923 Short Horn Double Neck, 1958

Unlike the Stratosphere, the Danelectro 3923 combined six-string and bass necks. Construction was typical of Danelectro, the body built from a pine frame covered top and bottom with Masonite. Thus, existing single-neck Short Horn circuitry could be used, and each 'guitar' had just one pickup. The guitar/bass double-neck combo would later find favour with progressive rock bands in the 1970s.

- **DATE** 1958

- **ORIGIN** Neptune, New Jersey, USA

- **WOOD**
  Pine frame, Masonite top and back, maple bolt-on neck, rosewood fingerboard.

- **UNUSUAL FEATURE**
  This was the first example seen of a guitar/bass combination.

The fingerboards feature dot marker inlays.

For added strength, the 3923 had a solid centre between the two necks.

Dual-stacked concentric pots are used to control the volume and tone of the pickups.

Gibson EDS-1275, 1963

Something of a niche among guitarists, double-necks are prized by some for their versatility, but many have also struggled with their bulk and top-heavy balance. Gibson had experimented with multi-necks in the late 1950s, notably with a mandolin/guitar, the EMS-1235. In 1963, Gibson produced what has since become the best-known example of its type – the SG-inspired EDS-1275. The instrument's continued popularity can largely be attributed to its use by Led Zeppelin's Jimmy Page during the first half of the 1970s.

- **DATE** 1963

- **ORIGIN** Kalamazoo, Michigan, USA

- **WOOD**
  Mahogany body, two mahogany set necks, rosewood fingerboards.

- **UNUSUAL FEATURE**
  The pearloid split-parallelogram fingerboard marker inlays are integral to the look.

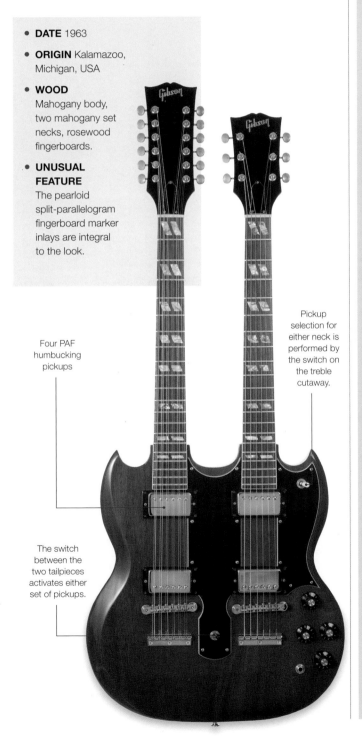

Four PAF humbucking pickups

Pickup selection for either neck is performed by the switch on the treble cutaway.

The switch between the two tailpieces activates either set of pickups.

Jimmy Page

From the early 1960s, Jimmy Page (b. 1944) had been one of the leading studio session guitarists on the London scene, used anonymously on recordings by diverse artists such as The Kinks, The Rolling Stones, Petula Clark, Johnny Halliday and Donovan. Unwilling for years to give up his lucrative career to join a band, after a brief stint with the Yardbirds (following Eric Clapton and Jeff Beck), he formed Led Zeppelin in 1968. Within three years, they were arguably the biggest band in the world, and Page was widely touted as the greatest rock guitarist of them all.

Page's choice of guitars was sometimes odd. Early film of Led Zeppelin live shows sees him coaxing the heaviest of the band's classic lead lines out of a Fender Telecaster. He would also sometimes use a cheap 1960s Danelectro in concert. He is, however, perhaps most famously associated with the Gibson EDS-125 double-neck.

ABOVE: *On stage, Jimmy Page frequently switched between six and twelve strings. In the 1976 concert film* The Song Remains the Same *we see the Gibson EDS-1275 being used on the band's anthem "Stairway to Heaven", as Page picks out the delicate opening on the lower, six-string neck, before flicking the selector switch to 12-string mode. The popularity of the double-neck guitar peaked in the 1970s, although, in recent years, it has begun to reappear with the resurgence of interest in progressive rock.*

Guitars from the Eastern Bloc

The Cold War between the West and the Soviet Union and other Communist Eastern European states saw limited cross-cultural contact between the two sides. Yet, even though rock 'n' roll music was actively discouraged by the authorities in the Eastern Bloc, the limited production of electric guitars did, nonetheless, take place, some results of which were exported to other parts of Europe.

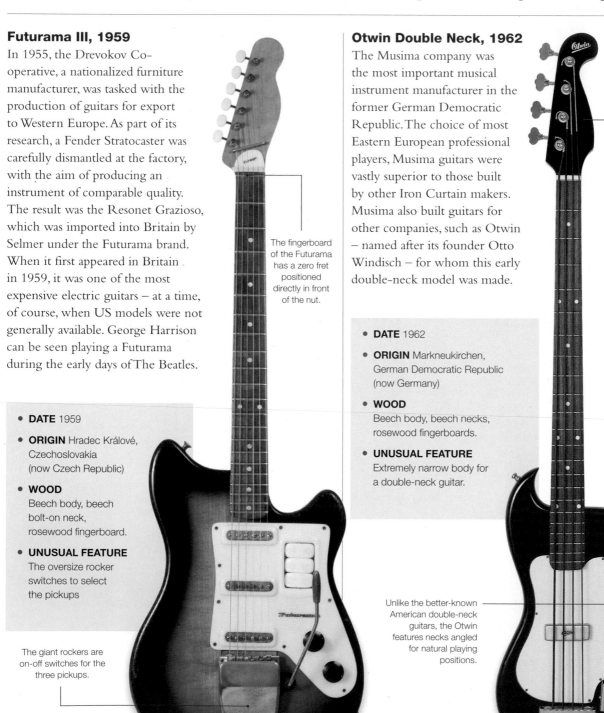

Futurama III, 1959

In 1955, the Drevokov Co-operative, a nationalized furniture manufacturer, was tasked with the production of guitars for export to Western Europe. As part of its research, a Fender Stratocaster was carefully dismantled at the factory, with the aim of producing an instrument of comparable quality. The result was the Resonet Grazioso, which was imported into Britain by Selmer under the Futurama brand. When it first appeared in Britain in 1959, it was one of the most expensive electric guitars – at a time, of course, when US models were not generally available. George Harrison can be seen playing a Futurama during the early days of The Beatles.

The fingerboard of the Futurama has a zero fret positioned directly in front of the nut.

- **DATE** 1959
- **ORIGIN** Hradec Králové, Czechoslovakia (now Czech Republic)
- **WOOD** Beech body, beech bolt-on neck, rosewood fingerboard.
- **UNUSUAL FEATURE** The oversize rocker switches to select the pickups

The giant rockers are on-off switches for the three pickups.

Otwin Double Neck, 1962

The Musima company was the most important musical instrument manufacturer in the former German Democratic Republic. The choice of most Eastern European professional players, Musima guitars were vastly superior to those built by other Iron Curtain makers. Musima also built guitars for other companies, such as Otwin – named after its founder Otto Windisch – for whom this early double-neck model was made.

The headstock is a hockey-stick design.

- **DATE** 1962
- **ORIGIN** Markneukirchen, German Democratic Republic (now Germany)
- **WOOD** Beech body, beech necks, rosewood fingerboards.
- **UNUSUAL FEATURE** Extremely narrow body for a double-neck guitar.

Unlike the better-known American double-neck guitars, the Otwin features necks angled for natural playing positions.

Aelita 1, 1978

More isolated from the West than the other states of Eastern Europe, the Soviet Union was the last among the Iron Curtain countries to mass-produce electric guitars. The Kavkaz factory in the city of Rostov-on-Don had formerly built furniture and balalaikas, but introduced a pair of electric guitars during the 1970s – the Aelita and the Bas. Although it was one of the better guitars produced during this period in the Soviet Union, by Western standards the primitive Aelita was a good 15 years out of date.

- **DATE** 1978
- **ORIGIN** Rostov-on-Don, USSR (now Russia)
- **WOOD**
  Front/Back & Sides
  Unspecified hardwood body, beech bolt-on neck, beech fingerboard.
- **UNUSUAL FEATURE**
  The Aelita uses a six-pin DIN output socket, not a jack plug.

The most distinctive design feature of the Aelita is the shape of the cutaways – slightly reminiscent of the Rickenbacker tulip of the 1950s or the Italian EKOs.

The finish on the scratchplate and the paddle headstock are matched.

ABOVE: *The Aelita 1 features a wide array of controls for its three single-coil pickups: three on-off switches sit above the pickups; three tone switches sit below the pickups; there are three individual volume controls; and, alongside the output socket, there is a master volume pot.*

Communism and the electric guitar

The arrival of rock 'n' roll was not at all welcomed in the Communist Eastern Bloc. Cold War sensibilities ensured there was distrust in all forms of popular culture that emanated from the West. Unsurprisingly, the Soviet Union took the strongest line, and with such a strong connection between rock music and the electric guitar, it was not until the 1970s that guitars were produced by state-owned factories. Rock music was not in itself against the law, but the legal framework was such that musicians had to be accepted by the State Concert Agency in order to gain professional status and earn money.

There was greater tolerance of Western culture in other Eastern European countries, and during the 1960s electric guitars were being produced in Hungary, Poland, Bulgaria, Czechoslovakia and East Germany (DDR). In some cases, these were exported across the Iron Curtain to help satisfy demand during the beat boom.

Although they were generally poorly made – not to mention unpleasant to play – Communist-era guitars are increasingly of interest to modern-day collectors.

ABOVE: *Stas Namin was the leader of the groundbreaking band Tvesty (which translates as Flowers). Often referred to as the 'Russian Beatles', they achieved enormous popularity throughout the Soviet Union during the 1970s; much of their following came about by the distribution of cassette tapes at their concerts. Namin himself is one of the most influential figures in the creation of an indigenous Russian rock-music scene.*

Rickenbacker 12-string electrics

It was during the 1920s that the 12-string guitar first achieved popularity. The twelve strings were grouped into six groups of pairs, each tuned either in unison or an octave apart, enabling one guitar to achieve the rich depth of two. It was with the early 1960s folk revival that a new generation of musicians became interested in the instrument, which itself led to the development of the first electric 12-string guitars.

360/12, 1964

By 1964, both Gibson and Danelectro had already dabbled with the idea of an electric 12-string guitar – with limited success. Rickenbacker's attempt took a standard hollowbody Model 360 and created a radical new headstock design that enabled all 12 machine heads to fit on to a regular-sized headstock. Rickenbacker owner Francis C. Hall presented a prototype to George Harrison, who used it on the opening chords of "A Hard Day's Night". The example here has rounded horns and no binding.

- **DATE** 1964
- **ORIGIN** Santa Ana, California, USA
- **WOOD**
  Carved maple body, three-ply maple set neck, rosewood fingerboard.
- **UNUSUAL FEATURE**
  The headstock design is a radical solution to the problem of accommodating 12 pegs.

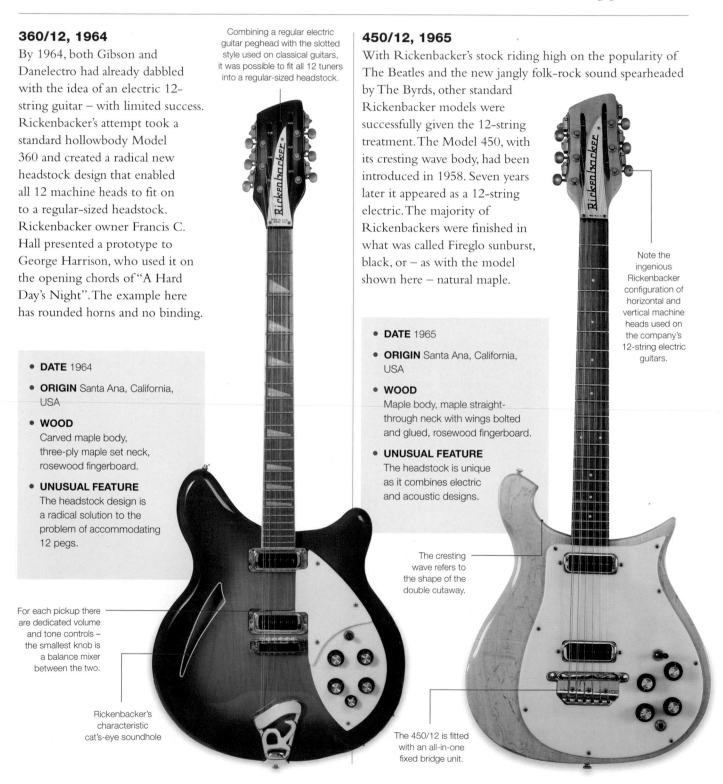

Combining a regular electric guitar peghead with the slotted style used on classical guitars, it was possible to fit all 12 tuners into a regular-sized headstock.

For each pickup there are dedicated volume and tone controls – the smallest knob is a balance mixer between the two.

Rickenbacker's characteristic cat's-eye soundhole

450/12, 1965

With Rickenbacker's stock riding high on the popularity of The Beatles and the new jangly folk-rock sound spearheaded by The Byrds, other standard Rickenbacker models were successfully given the 12-string treatment. The Model 450, with its cresting wave body, had been introduced in 1958. Seven years later it appeared as a 12-string electric. The majority of Rickenbackers were finished in what was called Fireglo sunburst, black, or – as with the model shown here – natural maple.

- **DATE** 1965
- **ORIGIN** Santa Ana, California, USA
- **WOOD**
  Maple body, maple straight-through neck with wings bolted and glued, rosewood fingerboard.
- **UNUSUAL FEATURE**
  The headstock is unique as it combines electric and acoustic designs.

Note the ingenious Rickenbacker configuration of horizontal and vertical machine heads used on the company's 12-string electric guitars.

The cresting wave refers to the shape of the double cutaway.

The 450/12 is fitted with an all-in-one fixed bridge unit.

336/12, 1966

In production for ten years after it first appeared in 1966, the 336/12 is identical to the pointed-horn version of the 360/12, with one very curious exception: it was fitted with a metal contraption referred to as the 12/6 converter unit. Patented by James Gross, the device was fixed alongside the neck pickup, and when engaged by the lever would push one of the strings from each pair down against the fingerboard. This enabled the player to switch quickly between six and twelve strings. It was of limited use, however, since it made string bending and other playing techniques extremely difficult to execute.

- **DATE** 1966
- **ORIGIN** Santa Ana, California, USA
- **WOOD** Carved maple body, three-ply maple set neck, rosewood fingerboard.
- **UNUSUAL FEATURE** The 12/6 converter unit – widely known as the comb – was used to turn it into a six-string.

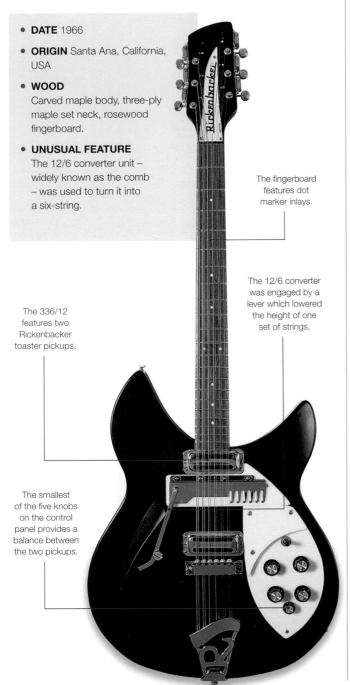

The fingerboard features dot marker inlays.

The 12/6 converter was engaged by a lever which lowered the height of one set of strings.

The 336/12 features two Rickenbacker toaster pickups.

The smallest of the five knobs on the control panel provides a balance between the two pickups.

370/12 RME1, 1988

Much of the enduring popularity of Rickenbacker 12-string electrics was down to the similarly timeless appeal of the pioneering folk-rock band The Byrds. Their 1965 worldwide hit single "Hey Mr Tambourine Man" and their subsequent recordings largely revolved around the Rickenbacker 12-string sound. In 1988, Roger McGuinn of The Byrds was honoured by Rickenbacker with his own limited-edition signature version of the three-pickup 370/12, the guitar with which he was most strongly identified.

- **DATE** 1988
- **ORIGIN** Santa Ana, California, USA
- **WOOD** Carved maple body, three-ply maple set neck, rosewood fingerboard.
- **UNUSUAL FEATURE** The scratchplate carries Roger McGuinn's signature.

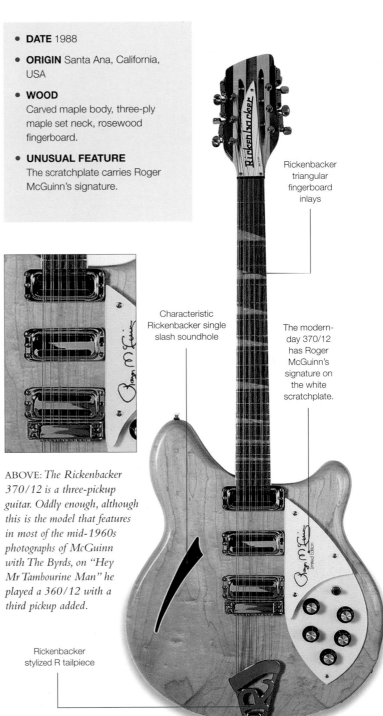

Rickenbacker triangular fingerboard inlays

Characteristic Rickenbacker single slash soundhole

The modern-day 370/12 has Roger McGuinn's signature on the white scratchplate.

ABOVE: *The Rickenbacker 370/12 is a three-pickup guitar. Oddly enough, although this is the model that features in most of the mid-1960s photographs of McGuinn with The Byrds, on "Hey Mr Tambourine Man" he played a 360/12 with a third pickup added.*

Rickenbacker stylized R tailpiece

Other 12-string electrics

In retrospect, Rickenbacker successfully seemed to have cornered the professional end of the 12-string electric market during the 1960s, but it was by no means the only company producing such guitars. Indeed, when the most successful pop group on the planet, The Beatles, started using Rickenbacker 12-string electrics, every manufacturer felt they had to join in.

Baldwin Double Six, 1964

Burns issued its first electric 12-string guitar, the Double Six, in 1964. Styled similarly to the Marvin and Shadows models, the crisp sound from its three Tri-sonic pickups were heard on numerous British recordings of the mid-1960s – famously the Searchers' "Needles and Pins". In 1965, near financial collapse forced Jim Burns to sell up, and the buyer, US piano company Baldwin, rebadged existing models. Newly manufactured instruments, however, deteriorated in quality, and in 1970 Baldwin ceased production.

- **DATE** 1964 (Baldwin from 1965)
- **ORIGIN** Romford, UK
- **WOOD**
  Hardwood body, maple bolt-on neck, rosewood fingerboard.
- **UNUSUAL FEATURE**
  The guitar features a multi-part plastic scratchplate.

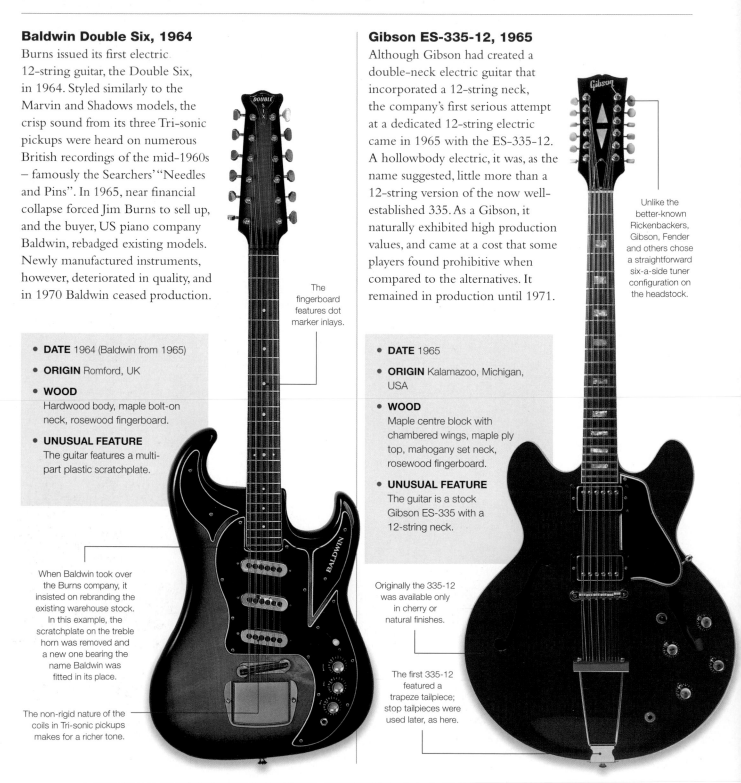

The fingerboard features dot marker inlays.

When Baldwin took over the Burns company, it insisted on rebranding the existing warehouse stock. In this example, the scratchplate on the treble horn was removed and a new one bearing the name Baldwin was fitted in its place.

The non-rigid nature of the coils in Tri-sonic pickups makes for a richer tone.

Gibson ES-335-12, 1965

Although Gibson had created a double-neck electric guitar that incorporated a 12-string neck, the company's first serious attempt at a dedicated 12-string electric came in 1965 with the ES-335-12. A hollowbody electric, it was, as the name suggested, little more than a 12-string version of the now well-established 335. As a Gibson, it naturally exhibited high production values, and came at a cost that some players found prohibitive when compared to the alternatives. It remained in production until 1971.

- **DATE** 1965
- **ORIGIN** Kalamazoo, Michigan, USA
- **WOOD**
  Maple centre block with chambered wings, maple ply top, mahogany set neck, rosewood fingerboard.
- **UNUSUAL FEATURE**
  The guitar is a stock Gibson ES-335 with a 12-string neck.

Unlike the better-known Rickenbackers, Gibson, Fender and others chose a straightforward six-a-side tuner configuration on the headstock.

Originally the 335-12 was available only in cherry or natural finishes.

The first 335-12 featured a trapeze tailpiece; stop tailpieces were used later, as here.

Fender Electric XII, 1965

Although the Electric XII was a commercial response to a sudden change in musical fashion, rather than following the lead suggested by Rickenbacker and Gibson – by altering the headstock and adding a set of tuners and a new bridge – Leo Fender decided to develop something purpose-built. It featured a bridge comprising individually adjustable saddles for each string, and split pickups. The Electric XII is also remembered for its 'hockey stick' headstock.

- **DATE** 1965
- **ORIGIN** Fullerton, California, USA
- **WOOD**
  Alder body, maple bolt-on neck, rosewood fingerboard.
- **UNUSUAL FEATURE**
  The headstock – widely referred to as the 'hockey stick' – is a distinctive feature of this model.

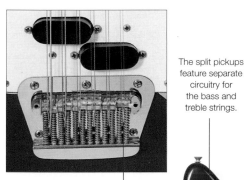

ABOVE: *The bridge unit of the Electric XII is unusual for a 12-string in that it comprises individual saddles for each string, making very precise intonation possible. The strings are threaded through the body Telecaster-style, to aid sustain.*

The split pickups feature separate circuitry for the bass and treble strings.

The body and overall styling is based on the Fender Jaguar.

Aria Diamond ADSG-12T, 1967

Founded in 1953 by Shiro Arai, Aria at first imported classical guitars to Japan and then began manufacturing them for export. Unusual among Japanese makers of the time, Arai was more concerned with quality than cost. Arai's first electric guitars were launched in 1966, and were among the best Japan had produced up to that time. In 1975, Arai adopted the Aria Pro II brand and, along with Yamaha and Ibanez, overhauled Japan's reputation for producing cheap 'knock-offs'.

- **DATE** 1967
- **ORIGIN** Nagoya, Japan
- **WOOD**
  Laminated hardwood body, three-piece maple bolt-on neck, rosewood fingerboard.
- **UNUSUAL FEATURE**
  The V-shaped split headstock marks out the instrument.

The fingerboard features dot marker inlays, but unusually they are placed on the side of the fingerboard, rather than centrally.

Like the better Japanese guitars of the period, the Aria may have been modelled on US instruments, but introduced oriental style flourishes in the shaping of the body and the headstock.

This guitar has a pair of single-coil pickups, with master volume and tone controls.

The Aria featured an all-in-one bridge, tailpiece and vibrato unit.

Fender in the 1960s

By the 1960s, Fender was a well-established leader in the electric guitar market. Leo Fender, however, soon found himself facing a new problem – his health. The gradual worsening of a long-standing sinus problem led him to believe – wrongly as it happened – that he was seriously ill, and in 1965 he decided to sell his company. The buyer was Columbia Broadcasting Systems (CBS), which paid Fender $13 million.

Stratocaster, pre-1965

There has been a great deal of debate about the impact of the CBS buyout on Fender guitars. When the new management took over, cost-cutting measures were implemented. Rather than adversely affecting the quality of the guitars overnight, there seems to have been a very slow deterioration, which becomes much more noticeable in models produced in the 1970s. As a consequence, what are now known as pre-CBS Fenders – such as the example shown here – are highly collectible instruments.

This model has a rosewood fingerboard; maple is also commonly found on Stratocasters.

- **DATE** Pre-dating CBS takeover in 1965
- **ORIGIN** Fullerton, California, USA
- **WOOD**
  Ash body, maple bolt-on neck, rosewood or maple fingerboard.
- **UNUSUAL FEATURE**
  Pre-CBS Stratocasters have solid steel inertia blocks at the bridge.

The finish shown here is classic Fender 'Sunburst'.

Coronado II, 1966

Designed by legendary luthier Roger Rossmeisl, the Coronado was a thinline, hollowbody guitar with two rounded cutaways. Rossmeisl had created many of Rickenbacker's classic designs and had been engaged by Fender to capitalize on the mid-1960s vogue for semi-acoustic guitars. Unlike the Gibson ES-335, which it superficially resembled, the Coronado was a genuine hollowbody instrument with a gently arched top – something of a departure for Fender.

Unusually for Fender, the Coronado features block inlays rather than the familiar dot markers.

- **DATE** 1966
- **ORIGIN** Fullerton, California, USA
- **WOOD**
  Beechwood back and sides, maple top, maple bolt-on neck, rosewood fingerboard.
- **UNUSUAL FEATURE**
  Available in Wildwood finish, made by injecting dye into the tree.

The pair of f-holes are a feature of this guitar.

The trapeze tailpiece features a Rickenbacker-style Fender F logo.

Telecaster, 1968

In December 1968, a custom-built Fender Telecaster with a solid rosewood body was flown across the Atlantic and delivered by hand to George Harrison of The Beatles. It would be used extensively throughout the band's *Let It Be* sessions and at their final live performance – filmed on the roof of their Apple HQ. In 1969, Harrison gave the guitar to his friend Delaney Bramlett, who treasured the guitar until 2003 when he sold it at auction for $434,750. The buyer was later revealed to be Olivia Harrison, George's widow. This model went into general production in 1969.

- **DATE** 1968

- **ORIGIN** Fullerton, California, USA

- **WOOD**
  Maple and rosewood body, rosewood bolt-on neck, separate rosewood fingerboard.

- **UNUSUAL FEATURE**
  Rosewood is very rarely used for solid guitar bodies.

The body of this instrument is built from two pieces of rosewood sandwiching a thin piece of maple. The guitar went into general production between 1969 and 1972.

ABOVE: *The original Telecaster bridge mechanism contained three saddles, two strings resting on each; they were fully height-adjustable, but intonation could only be altered in pairs.*

Jimi Hendrix

ABOVE: *Jimi Hendrix played a variety of different guitars, but he was most readily associated with the Fender Stratocaster. Although he was a left-handed player, Hendrix preferred to play on a restrung right-handed guitar.*

In a career that lasted barely four years in the limelight, Jimi Hendrix (1942–1970) took the electric guitar into new territory, setting new standards for blues and rock improvisation.

Hendrix first picked up the guitar at the age of 12, and learnt by listening to the great electric blues players of the period, such as Muddy Waters and Elmore James. After a brief period in the US Army, Hendrix found work as a back-up musician for touring R&B artists, among them the Isley Brothers, Ike and Tina Turner and Little Richard. Spotted in a New York blues club, he was brought over to the UK, where he formed the Jimi Hendrix Experience. Together, this incredible rock trio produced landmark albums such as *Axis: Bold as Love* and *Are You Experienced?* and gave concert performances of startling virtuoso musicianship. Although he died in 1970, Hendrix's playing has continued to influence successive generations of young rock musicians.

Other 1960s US solidbodies

It is easy to form the view that the likes of Fender, Gibson, Gretsch, Epiphone and Rickenbacker *were* the American guitar industry. In fact, there were numerous less auspicious brands available. Some, like the Harmony brand, sold huge numbers of cheaper instruments, but the 1960s also saw the early days of the independent boutique guitar brands that would begin to flourish a decade later.

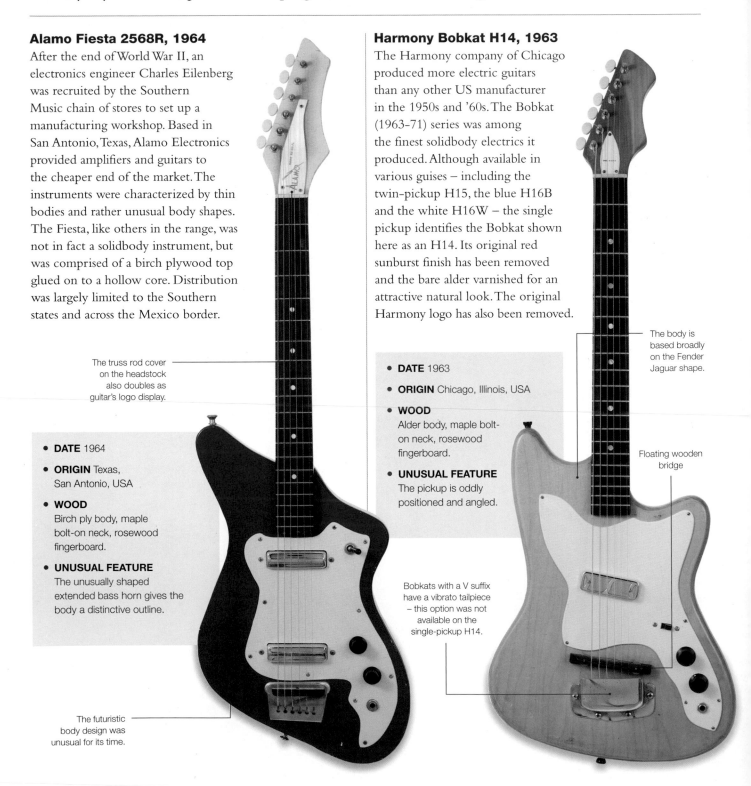

Alamo Fiesta 2568R, 1964

After the end of World War II, an electronics engineer Charles Eilenberg was recruited by the Southern Music chain of stores to set up a manufacturing workshop. Based in San Antonio, Texas, Alamo Electronics provided amplifiers and guitars to the cheaper end of the market. The instruments were characterized by thin bodies and rather unusual body shapes. The Fiesta, like others in the range, was not in fact a solidbody instrument, but was comprised of a birch plywood top glued on to a hollow core. Distribution was largely limited to the Southern states and across the Mexico border.

The truss rod cover on the headstock also doubles as guitar's logo display.

- **DATE** 1964
- **ORIGIN** Texas, San Antonio, USA
- **WOOD**
  Birch ply body, maple bolt-on neck, rosewood fingerboard.
- **UNUSUAL FEATURE**
  The unusually shaped extended bass horn gives the body a distinctive outline.

The futuristic body design was unusual for its time.

Harmony Bobkat H14, 1963

The Harmony company of Chicago produced more electric guitars than any other US manufacturer in the 1950s and '60s. The Bobkat (1963-71) series was among the finest solidbody electrics it produced. Although available in various guises – including the twin-pickup H15, the blue H16B and the white H16W – the single pickup identifies the Bobkat shown here as an H14. Its original red sunburst finish has been removed and the bare alder varnished for an attractive natural look. The original Harmony logo has also been removed.

The body is based broadly on the Fender Jaguar shape.

- **DATE** 1963
- **ORIGIN** Chicago, Illinois, USA
- **WOOD**
  Alder body, maple bolt-on neck, rosewood fingerboard.
- **UNUSUAL FEATURE**
  The pickup is oddly positioned and angled.

Floating wooden bridge

Bobkats with a V suffix have a vibrato tailpiece – this option was not available on the single-pickup H14.

Silvertone 1477, 1963

Produced by Harmony for Sears, Roebuck, the Silvertone 1477 is based on Harmony's own Bobkat H15. It featured a slimline three-quarter-scale-length neck, meaning that it was probably targeting the youth end of the market. The electronics were a notch up from other budget models, the pair of DeArmond Goldtone pickups being capable of producing a classic 1960s-style single-coil bite. With the ordinary guitar collector now priced out of the high end of the market, there is growing interest in models like this today.

- **DATE** 1963

- **ORIGIN** Chicago, Illinois, USA

- **WOOD**
  Alder or maple body, maple bolt-on neck, rosewood fingerboard.

- **UNUSUAL FEATURE**
  The use of upmarket DeArmond Goltone pickups on a budget instrument was unusual.

ABOVE: *The 1966 Harmony catalogue describes the Bobkat H15 / Silvertone 1477 as having "Torque Lok adjustable dual reinforcing rods". This refers to the adjustable twin truss rods that support the neck, and which are accessed via the truss-rod cover on the headstock.*

Differentiating it from the Harmony Bobkat, the 1477 features block fingerboard inlays.

Guitar making in the 1960s

The 1960s was a boom period for the electric guitar in the USA. While every fledgeling guitarist wanted a Fender, Gibson, Gretsch or Rickenbacker, these instruments were not aimed at the masses. For most, the alternative was provided by the Sears, Roebuck catalogue, which advertised and sold enormous volumes of Silvertone guitars – the most expensive of which cost barely 15 per cent of the price of a new Gibson.

These basic, mass-produced instruments were, of course, hardly comparable to the craftsmanship of the luthiers of Kalamazoo, Michigan, but they did provide an essential grounding in the electric guitar for just about every young American during the 1960s and '70s.

A significant proportion of the Silvertone-branded instruments were produced by the Chicago-based Harmony company and, as the examples here illustrate, were usually slightly modified versions of existing models. Harmony was the undisputed king of the production line, and, at its mid-1960s peak, it was building more electric guitars than all of America's other manufacturers put together.

ABOVE: *The Sears, Roebuck catalogue was the source for many a high-school band during the 1960s. At this time, a serviceable Silvertone electric guitar could be bought for around $60, while a Gibson SG Custom would have retailed at around $450.*

Italian electrics

Much of Italy's electric guitar manufacturing took place around Castelfidardo on the country's Adriatic coast. The area had been well known for producing accordions of global renown but had struggled in the aftermath of Italy's wartime defeat, and there was a corresponding decline in the popularity of the instrument. Some workshops saw the emerging popularity of the electric guitar as the way forward.

Wandré Rock Oval, c.1960

Luthier, anti-Fascist partisan fighter and conceptual artist, Antonio Pioli produced some extremely unorthodox guitar designs from the late 1950s to the start of the 1970s. Not only did he employ surreal body shapes – the Rock Oval is based on a Salvador Dalí painting – he also experimented with unorthodox materials; for example, using aluminium necks. The Rock Oval was usually labelled Wandré, Framez or Davoli (named after Pioli's collaborator Athos Davoli).

- **DATE** *c.*1960
- **ORIGIN** Italy
- **MATERIALS**
  Assorted hardwoods or fibreglass body, aluminium bolt-on neck.
- **UNUSUAL FEATURE**
  The body shape is like no other instrument.

The three-a-side, asymmetrically aligned tuners are positioned on a particularly wide headstock; with no string guides, this places greater stress on the nut.

This was perhaps the most extreme example of a cutaway ever seen in a guitar.

The Rock Oval's body shape is one of the strangest ever made. It seemed a futuristic design by the standards of 1960 when it was first produced, although it was inspired by Salvador Dalí's 1931 painting *The Persistence of Memory*. Despite its striking design, it was not entirely practical – it was almost impossible to play in the sitting position.

Eko 700/4V, 1961

Oliviero Pigini was among the first of Italy's accordion makers to turn to the electric guitar. Taking over his uncle's workshop in 1959, he brought a team of experienced luthiers to the region to make guitars under the Eko brand. In 1961, Pigini launched the 700 range. With its unique triple-cutaway body design and, on many models, the characteristic accordion-maker's sparkly plastic covering, it was an eye-catching instrument, and one that bore little resemblance to the popular classic US designs.

- **DATE** 1961
- **ORIGIN** Castelfidardo, Italy
- **WOOD**
  Mahogany body (other hardwoods were also used), maple set neck, rosewood fingerboard.
- **UNUSUAL FEATURE**
  The 700 featured a curious rear cutaway.

The third cutaway on the rear of the guitar remains an extremely unusual design feature.

The Eko 700/4V features an unusual array of electrics, including four pickups arranged in pairs. The multiple switches are wired for a range of pickup combinations.

Élite 40-V, 1962

The Crucianelli company had been building accordions in Castelfidardo since 1888. During the first half of the 1960s, its Élite range was Pigini's main competitor. Although the body shape of the 40-V is clearly Fender-inspired, the 'Italian' characteristics – the plastic sparkle covering used on accordions and the quirky pickup configuration – remain in place. Both the Crucianelli and Eko factories would later on produce some of the more distinctive models for the British-based Vox company.

- **DATE** 1962

- **ORIGIN** Castelfidardo, Italy

- **WOOD**
  Assorted woods, often basswood, used for the body, set neck.

- **UNUSUAL FEATURE**
  As with other Italian guitars, the Élite has a plastic sparkle finish similar to that used on accordions.

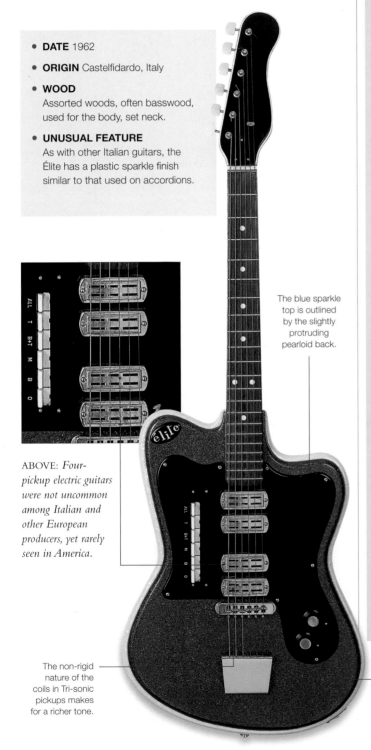

ABOVE: *Four-pickup electric guitars were not uncommon among Italian and other European producers, yet rarely seen in America.*

The blue sparkle top is outlined by the slightly protruding pearloid back.

The non-rigid nature of the coils in Tri-sonic pickups makes for a richer tone.

The Italian cult

The electric-guitar market in Italy thrived during the early 1960s. Like the rest of Europe, the popular US models were largely unobtainable, so a new industry emerged around the coastal town of Castelfidardo – formerly home to the country's celebrated accordion industry. Oliviero Pigini's Eko brand led the way – the Eko 700 range, with its unique rear cutaway, is perhaps the most celebrated Italian-built guitar of all time.

Almost all of the Castelfidardo guitar manufacturers evolved from accordion makers, which led to a number of curious similarities that set their instruments apart from those produced elsewhere, notably the strong tendency to take their decorative cues from the accordion: plain colours or natural finishes were largely eschewed in favour of sparkling plastic coverings. In the case of the Eko brand, Pigini developed a thick plastic protective coating, ensuring that the bodywork on many surviving examples of 50-year-old instruments remains in remarkably good condition. The electrics of these guitars were also unusual compared with models built elsewhere, favouring multiple pickups controlled by panels of large rocker switches.

Italian guitars of the 1960s are now highly collectible. While not in the same league as their famous US counterparts in terms of quality, their frequently eye-catching appearance has huge retro appeal.

ABOVE: *When demand for accordions began to dip, in 1956, 34-year-old Oliviero Pigini began successfully to import cheap guitars produced by the state musical instrument factory in neighbouring communist Yugoslavia. Talking a lead from Swedish accordion maker Hagström, Pigini set up his own manufacturing facilities in 1959, to produce EKO electric guitars.*

The body shape of the V-40 is curiously reminiscent of the 'non-reverse' Gibson Firebirds – even though it actually appeared three years earlier.

Is it a guitar or a bass?

There is a breed of instrument that occupies a kind of borderland between the bass and the guitar. These are six-string instruments designed with a scale length of between 660 and 762mm (26 and 30in), making them longer than a guitar but shorter than standard bass. This group includes baritone guitars and six-string basses, and although they are tuned differently, there is a good deal of crossover between the two.

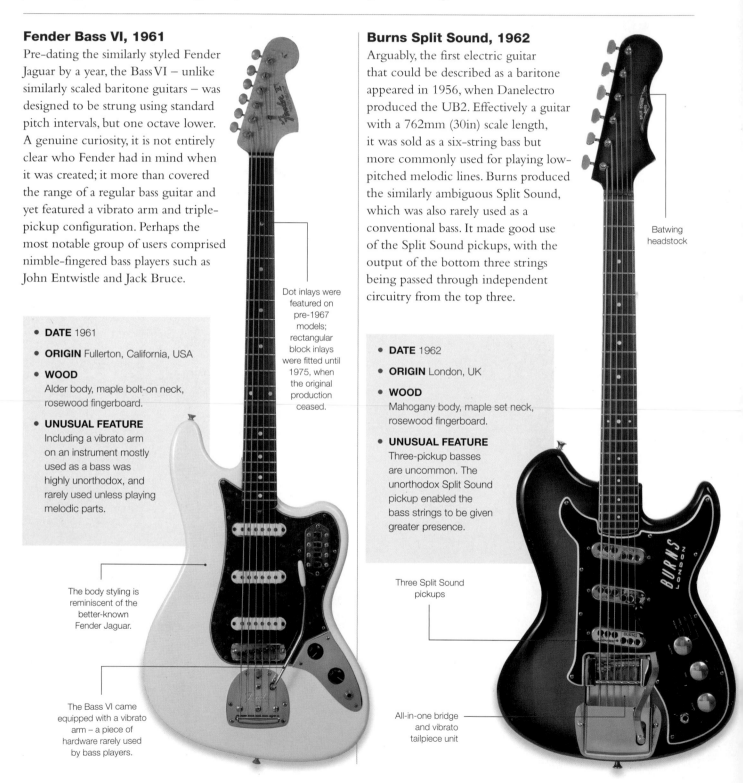

Fender Bass VI, 1961

Pre-dating the similarly styled Fender Jaguar by a year, the Bass VI – unlike similarly scaled baritone guitars – was designed to be strung using standard pitch intervals, but one octave lower. A genuine curiosity, it is not entirely clear who Fender had in mind when it was created; it more than covered the range of a regular bass guitar and yet featured a vibrato arm and triple-pickup configuration. Perhaps the most notable group of users comprised nimble-fingered bass players such as John Entwistle and Jack Bruce.

- **DATE** 1961
- **ORIGIN** Fullerton, California, USA
- **WOOD**
  Alder body, maple bolt-on neck, rosewood fingerboard.
- **UNUSUAL FEATURE**
  Including a vibrato arm on an instrument mostly used as a bass was highly unorthodox, and rarely used unless playing melodic parts.

Dot inlays were featured on pre-1967 models; rectangular block inlays were fitted until 1975, when the original production ceased.

The body styling is reminiscent of the better-known Fender Jaguar.

The Bass VI came equipped with a vibrato arm – a piece of hardware rarely used by bass players.

Burns Split Sound, 1962

Arguably, the first electric guitar that could be described as a baritone appeared in 1956, when Danelectro produced the UB2. Effectively a guitar with a 762mm (30in) scale length, it was sold as a six-string bass but more commonly used for playing low-pitched melodic lines. Burns produced the similarly ambiguous Split Sound, which was also rarely used as a conventional bass. It made good use of the Split Sound pickups, with the output of the bottom three strings being passed through independent circuitry from the top three.

Batwing headstock

- **DATE** 1962
- **ORIGIN** London, UK
- **WOOD**
  Mahogany body, maple set neck, rosewood fingerboard.
- **UNUSUAL FEATURE**
  Three-pickup basses are uncommon. The unorthodox Split Sound pickup enabled the bass strings to be given greater presence.

Three Split Sound pickups

All-in-one bridge and vibrato tailpiece unit

Teisco VN-4, 1965

One of Japan's biggest guitar makers of the time, Teisco had been one the most prolific early offenders in the cheap-copy market, but by the mid-1960s had begun to produce guitars with a unique character. The VN-4 was marketed as a baritone guitar, although with a scale length of 673mm (26⅓in) – only 25.4mm (1in) longer than a standard Fender – it is certainly among the shorter baritones. Often rebranded prior to export, the VN-4 can also be found with the Ayer, Demian and Silvertone labels.

- **DATE** 1965
- **ORIGIN** Tokyo, Japan
- **WOOD**
  Plywood body, maple bolt-on neck, rosewood fingerboard.
- **UNUSUAL FEATURE**
  The controls (pickup rocker switches and roll-on volume and tone controls) are quirky.

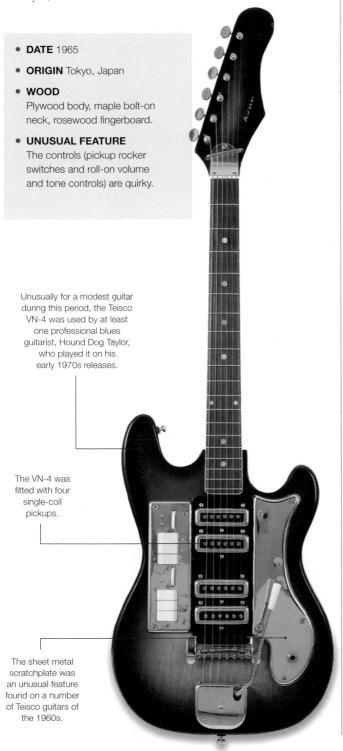

Unusually for a modest guitar during this period, the Teisco VN-4 was used by at least one professional blues guitarist, Hound Dog Taylor, who played it on his early 1970s releases.

The VN-4 was fitted with four single-coil pickups.

The sheet metal scratchplate was an unusual feature found on a number of Teisco guitars of the 1960s.

Baritone tuning

ABOVE: *A standard Gibson Les Paul with a 629mm (24¾in) scale length (left), shown alongside a baritone Les Paul with a 686mm (27in) scale length (right).*

There is no definitive fixed scale length in the world of the guitar or bass. Fenders, for example, are built with a 648mm (25½in) scale length, whereas Gibsons are typically 629mm (24¾in). The same is true with basses, which range from 762–914mm (30–36in). It is therefore difficult to define a baritone guitar by measuring the distance from the bridge to the nut.

The principal difference between a baritone guitar and a six-string bass is largely a matter of string type and tuning. Specialized string sets are generally required. Six-string basses, such as the Fender VI, are typically tuned to E-A-D-G-B-E – standard guitar tuning only one octave lower. It is possible to play them as regular bass guitars with the top two strings offering an extended register. Chords can also be played, although open chords may sound murky.

When using a set of baritone strings, standard tuning intervals are normally used, but taken down in pitch by a perfect fifth (A-D-G-C-E-A) or – more popularly among afficionados – a perfect fourth (B-E-A-D-F#-B).

Curious shapes

The vast majority of guitars ever produced have followed the traditional figure-of-eight Spanish style, later evolving towards single- or double-cutaway styles. However, there were guitar makers ready to look in different directions for inspiration, coming up with new basic shapes or creating personalized detailing. This thinking flourished in the 1980s, when metal guitarists began searching for ever-stranger shapes.

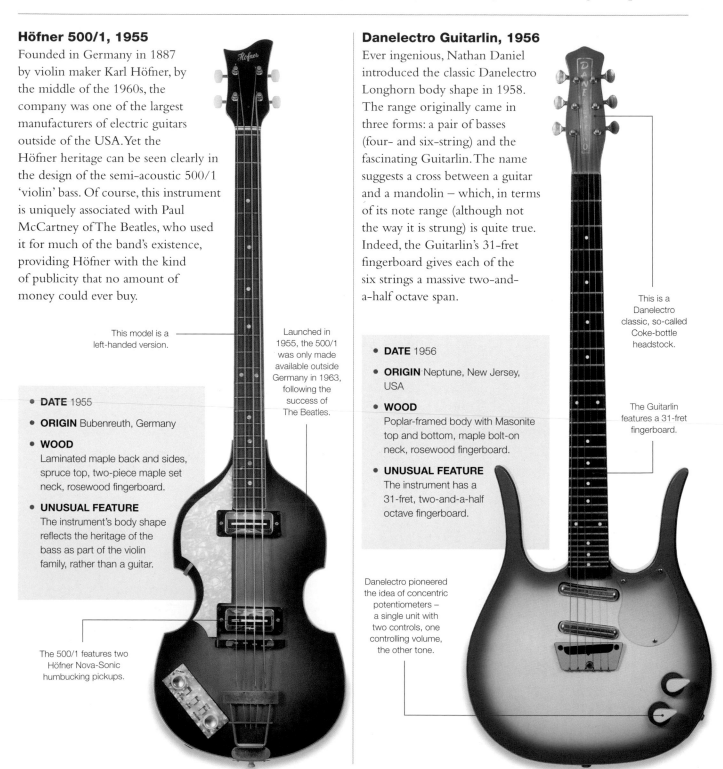

Höfner 500/1, 1955

Founded in Germany in 1887 by violin maker Karl Höfner, by the middle of the 1960s, the company was one of the largest manufacturers of electric guitars outside of the USA. Yet the Höfner heritage can be seen clearly in the design of the semi-acoustic 500/1 'violin' bass. Of course, this instrument is uniquely associated with Paul McCartney of The Beatles, who used it for much of the band's existence, providing Höfner with the kind of publicity that no amount of money could ever buy.

This model is a left-handed version.

Launched in 1955, the 500/1 was only made available outside Germany in 1963, following the success of The Beatles.

- **DATE** 1955
- **ORIGIN** Bubenreuth, Germany
- **WOOD**
  Laminated maple back and sides, spruce top, two-piece maple set neck, rosewood fingerboard.
- **UNUSUAL FEATURE**
  The instrument's body shape reflects the heritage of the bass as part of the violin family, rather than a guitar.

The 500/1 features two Höfner Nova-Sonic humbucking pickups.

Danelectro Guitarlin, 1956

Ever ingenious, Nathan Daniel introduced the classic Danelectro Longhorn body shape in 1958. The range originally came in three forms: a pair of basses (four- and six-string) and the fascinating Guitarlin. The name suggests a cross between a guitar and a mandolin – which, in terms of its note range (although not the way it is strung) is quite true. Indeed, the Guitarlin's 31-fret fingerboard gives each of the six strings a massive two-and-a-half octave span.

This is a Danelectro classic, so-called Coke-bottle headstock.

- **DATE** 1956
- **ORIGIN** Neptune, New Jersey, USA
- **WOOD**
  Poplar-framed body with Masonite top and bottom, maple bolt-on neck, rosewood fingerboard.
- **UNUSUAL FEATURE**
  The instrument has a 31-fret, two-and-a-half octave fingerboard.

The Guitarlin features a 31-fret fingerboard.

Danelectro pioneered the idea of concentric potentiometers – a single unit with two controls, one controlling volume, the other tone.

Harvey Thomas Custom Hollowbody, *c.*1962

Based in Kent, Washington, USA, Harvey Thomas was evidently a very unusual fellow, often seen performing locally during the 1960s with his own triple-neck guitar and an early electronic rhythm and effects device he called the Infernal Music Machine. His guitars were all handbuilt and appeared in a variety of unusual shapes – like the famous Maltese Surfer. The model shown here is particularly unusual in that the archtop body is in fact hollowed out of just a single piece of wood.

Mosrite Strawberry Alarm Clock, 1967

Semie Moseley had an excellent pedigree as a luthier – having trained under both Paul Bigsby and Rickenbacker's Roger Rossmeisl – and had established his Mosrite brand with the models he created for The Ventures. By 1967, however, surf instrumental bands were out of vogue, which led Moseley to look elsewhere – to America's most popular psychedelic pop group, the Strawberry Alarm Clock. The result was a brightly hand-painted instrument with its bizarre 'exoskeleton' that now looks like a rather curious period piece.

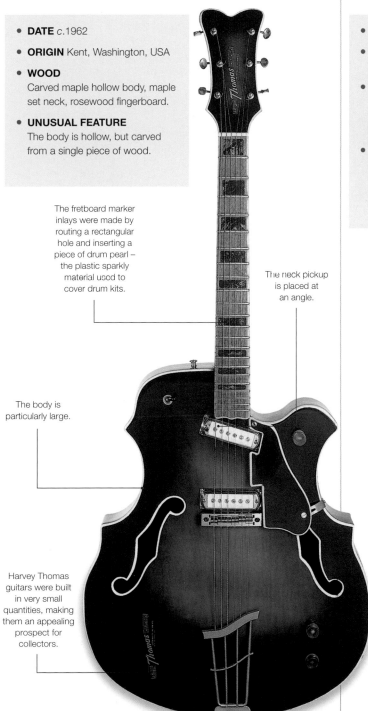

- **DATE** *c.*1962
- **ORIGIN** Kent, Washington, USA
- **WOOD**
  Carved maple hollow body, maple set neck, rosewood fingerboard.
- **UNUSUAL FEATURE**
  The body is hollow, but carved from a single piece of wood.

The fretboard marker inlays were made by routing a rectangular hole and inserting a piece of drum pearl – the plastic sparkly material used to cover drum kits.

The neck pickup is placed at an angle.

The body is particularly large.

Harvey Thomas guitars were built in very small quantities, making them an appealing prospect for collectors.

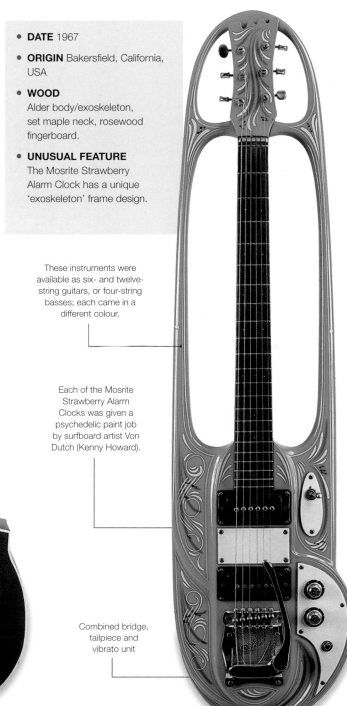

- **DATE** 1967
- **ORIGIN** Bakersfield, California, USA
- **WOOD**
  Alder body/exoskeleton, set maple neck, rosewood fingerboard.
- **UNUSUAL FEATURE**
  The Mosrite Strawberry Alarm Clock has a unique 'exoskeleton' frame design.

These instruments were available as six- and twelve-string guitars, or four-string basses; each came in a different colour.

Each of the Mosrite Strawberry Alarm Clocks was given a psychedelic paint job by surfboard artist Von Dutch (Kenny Howard).

Combined bridge, tailpiece and vibrato unit

Near misses

The process of invention is a mysterious one. Some 'Eureka!' moments may change the course of history; others may leave the world baffled. When an unnamed person at Rickenbacker asked, "Hey, wouldn't it be cool to have a guitar with coloured lights that flashed in time with what you were playing?", the surprising response was evidently, "OK, let's do it!" The rest of us can only guess what they had in mind.

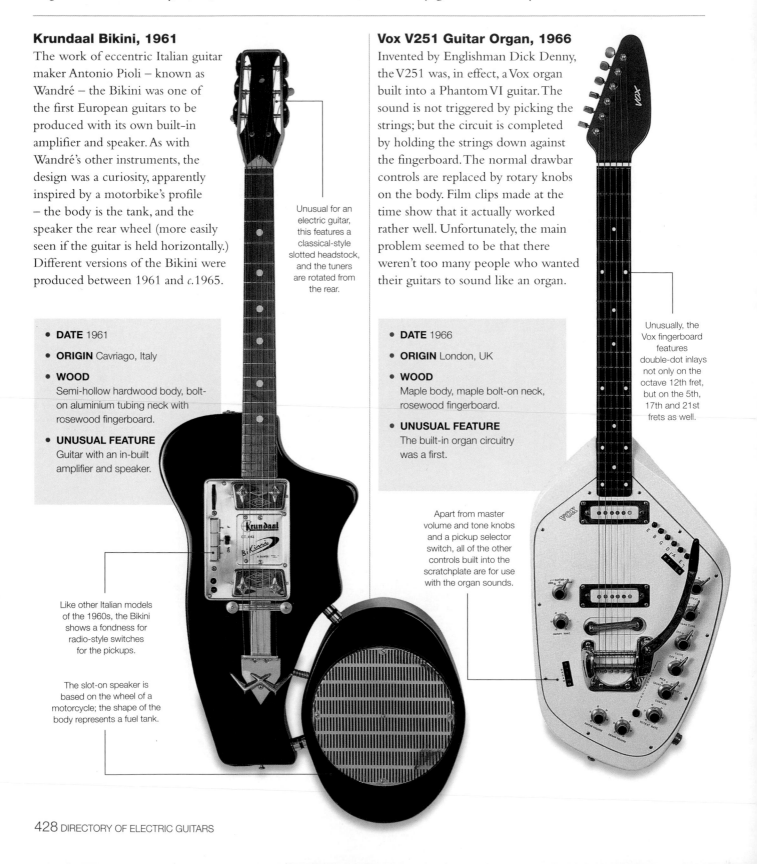

Krundaal Bikini, 1961

The work of eccentric Italian guitar maker Antonio Pioli – known as Wandré – the Bikini was one of the first European guitars to be produced with its own built-in amplifier and speaker. As with Wandré's other instruments, the design was a curiosity, apparently inspired by a motorbike's profile – the body is the tank, and the speaker the rear wheel (more easily seen if the guitar is held horizontally.) Different versions of the Bikini were produced between 1961 and *c*.1965.

Unusual for an electric guitar, this features a classical-style slotted headstock, and the tuners are rotated from the rear.

- **DATE** 1961
- **ORIGIN** Cavriago, Italy
- **WOOD**
  Semi-hollow hardwood body, bolt-on aluminium tubing neck with rosewood fingerboard.
- **UNUSUAL FEATURE**
  Guitar with an in-built amplifier and speaker.

Like other Italian models of the 1960s, the Bikini shows a fondness for radio-style switches for the pickups.

The slot-on speaker is based on the wheel of a motorcycle; the shape of the body represents a fuel tank.

Vox V251 Guitar Organ, 1966

Invented by Englishman Dick Denny, the V251 was, in effect, a Vox organ built into a Phantom VI guitar. The sound is not triggered by picking the strings; but the circuit is completed by holding the strings down against the fingerboard. The normal drawbar controls are replaced by rotary knobs on the body. Film clips made at the time show that it actually worked rather well. Unfortunately, the main problem seemed to be that there weren't too many people who wanted their guitars to sound like an organ.

Unusually, the Vox fingerboard features double-dot inlays not only on the octave 12th fret, but on the 5th, 17th and 21st frets as well.

- **DATE** 1966
- **ORIGIN** London, UK
- **WOOD**
  Maple body, maple bolt-on neck, rosewood fingerboard.
- **UNUSUAL FEATURE**
  The built-in organ circuitry was a first.

Apart from master volume and tone knobs and a pickup selector switch, all of the other controls built into the scratchplate are for use with the organ sounds.

La Baye 2X4, 1967

Hailing from Green Bay, Wisconsin, Dan Helland was responsible for the La Baye 2X4. In fact, the guitar is really not much more than neck bolted on to a block of 'two-by-four' wood. Helland was able to build his guitars using parts from a failing local guitar plant, Holman, and during 1967 he built 45 six- and twelve-string guitars and four basses. Helland took them to that year's NAMM trade show, created some interest, but generated no orders at all. He became a professional photographer shortly afterwards.

- **DATE** 1967
- **ORIGIN** Neodesha, Kansas, USA
- **WOOD**
  Unspecified hardwood, maple bolt-on neck, rosewood fingerboard.
- **UNUSUAL FEATURE**
  Its minimalist style sets it apart from more regular instruments.

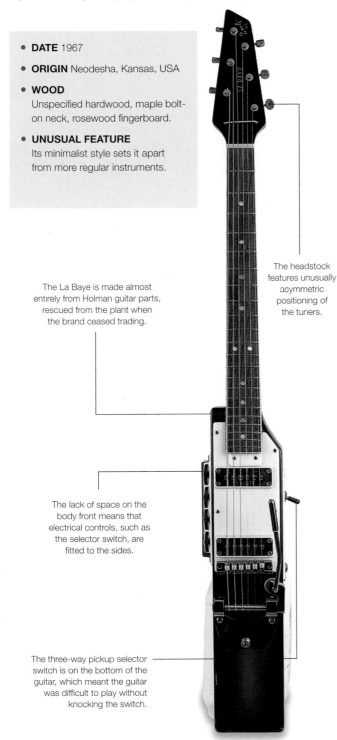

The La Baye is made almost entirely from Holman guitar parts, rescued from the plant when the brand ceased trading.

The headstock features unusually asymmetric positioning of the tuners.

The lack of space on the body front means that electrical controls, such as the selector switch, are fitted to the sides.

The three-way pickup selector switch is on the bottom of the guitar, which meant the guitar was difficult to play without knocking the switch.

Rickenbacker 331 Light Show Guitar, 1971

The model 331 was standard Rickenbacker with a clear plastic top under which a series of coloured lights were concealed. Responding to the audio frequencies being played, low pitches lit up the blue lamps, mid-range sounds switched on yellow, and the high pitches responded in red. In fact, Rickenbacker was not first to come up with this idea. Two centuries earlier, a monk named Castel built a keyboard that revealed different panes of coloured glass according to which notes were being pressed.

- **DATE** 1971
- **ORIGIN** Santa Ana, California, USA
- **WOOD**
  Maple body, maple straight-through neck, rosewood fingerboard.
- **UNUSUAL FEATURE**
  This is a basic 330 with added lights. Its relative rarity makes the guitar quite collectible.

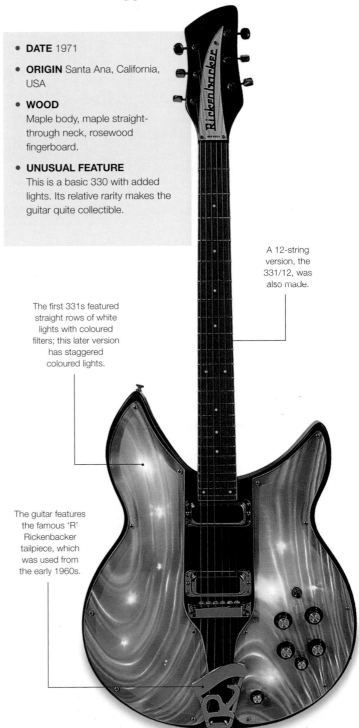

A 12-string version, the 331/12, was also made.

The first 331s featured straight rows of white lights with coloured filters; this later version has staggered coloured lights.

The guitar features the famous 'R' Rickenbacker tailpiece, which was used from the early 1960s.

The new Gibson Les Pauls

The Les Paul was produced throughout the 1950s, but when it became apparent that it was unable to stem the growing success of Fender – a company that had barely existed a decade earlier – Gibson decided to replace the line. However, when the popularity of second-hand Les Paul Standards began to bloom during the 1960s, Gibson decided to relaunch the model – and even brought some additions to the range.

Les Paul Deluxe, 1968

Among the first of the new 1968 Les Pauls, the Deluxe featured Gibson New York mini-humbuckers – leftover stock from when Gibson began switching Epiphone production to Japan. In its first incarnation, the Deluxe featured a one-piece body and slim three-piece neck; a year later this was replaced by the so-called pancake body – a thin layer of maple covering two layers of Honduran mahogany. The Les Paul Deluxe did not prove to be anything like as popular as the Standard, but continued until 1985.

The fingerboard features pearled trapezoid marker inlays.

- **DATE** 1968
- **ORIGIN** Kalamazoo, Michigan, USA
- **WOOD**
  Mahogany body (with maple pancake top from 1969), mahogany set neck, rosewood fingerboard.
- **UNUSUAL FEATURE**
  The New York mini-humbuckers set it apart from most other Les Pauls.

The New York mini-humbuckers were fitted to a standard P-90 cavity using an adaptor ring.

Les Paul Recording, 1971

The Les Paul Recording was part of the same controversial range that introduced the low-impedance Les Paul Personal and Professional models. Central to the idea was that these pickups would be suitable for direct input into a mixing board, and capable of a cleaner sound with a wider frequency response and reduction in hum. Unlike the other two models, there was an impedance switch as well on the control panel, which in Hi mode would still make the guitar capable of overdriving an amplifier.

Instead of the usual tone control, the Recording featured tone filter switches and separate bass and treble pots.

- **DATE** 1971
- **ORIGIN** Kalamazoo, Michigan, USA
- **WOOD**
  Clear Honduras mahogany with centre band, three-piece mahogany set neck, rosewood fingerboard.
- **UNUSUAL FEATURE**
  The low-impedance pickups and extensive on-board filter circuitry.

The Decade Control is an 11-position switch that tunes or alters the treble harmonics.

Long travel bridge

Les Paul Studio, 1983

Introduced in 1983, the Les Paul Studio, as the name suggests, was designed with the studio musician in mind. Unlike the early 1970s low-impedance models, however, the Studio features regular Les Paul electrics. The intention was to produce a lower-priced Les Paul stripped of the expensive cosmetics, such as body and neck binding and ornate inlays, but standard in most other ways. The Studio has, nonetheless, been seen frequently on stage – its slightly thinner body, lower weight and frugal appearance is attractive to many modern professional players.

- **DATE** 1983

- **ORIGIN** Kalamazoo, Michigan, USA

- **WOOD**
  Mahogany body, maple top, mahogany set neck, rosewood fingerboard (ebony on later models).

- **UNUSUAL FEATURE**
  The stripped-down look requires no binding on the body or neck.

The Studio is identifiable from the legend on the truss rod cover on the headstock.

Unbound neck

ABOVE: *The Tune-o-matic bridge was designed by Gibson president Ted McCarty, and first appeared in 1954 on the Les Paul Custom. Offering the possibility of altering the intonation for each string, it became standard on all of the company's fixed-bridge guitars.*

The body of the Studio is around 6mm (¹/₄in) thinner than a standard Les Paul.

Frank Zappa

Composer, singer, record producer, film director and dazzlingly brilliant guitarist, Frank Zappa (1940–93) released more than 60 albums over a period of 30 years, either as a solo artist or with his band The Mothers of Invention.

Freak Out!, the debut album by the Mothers, set the tone for his career, combining conventional pop and rock songs – often humorously digging at society, politics and religion – with free jazz improvisations and *musique concrète*-style studio-generated sound collages.

By 1969, although moderately successful, Zappa struggled to finance the nine-piece Mothers of Invention, and the group folded. Throughout the 1970s, he toured and recorded with a succession of small and highly disciplined ensembles, his music becoming increasingly jazz-rock oriented.

From the mid-1980s, Zappa became excited by the compositional possibilities of early digital sampling technology, and his attention switched away from the guitar. Indeed, apart from a brief guitar solo, his Grammy-winning 1986 album *Jazz from Hell* was produced entirely on a Synclavier sampler.

Zappa continued recording until shortly before his death in 1993 from prostate cancer.

ABOVE: *Throughout most of the 1970s, Frank Zappa was most often seen in concert playing a Gibson SG. The following decade he switched to a Les Paul Custom or Fender Stratocaster, both of which he retrofitted with DiMarzio pickups.*

The last Gibson originals

The 1970s and '80s proved to be a trying time for Fender and Gibson alike, their reputations both on the wane. The problem was a perceived fall in quality resulting from corporate takeovers, as well as competition from small independent manufacturers – some of which were producing instruments that made the American classic designs that had emerged in the 1950s seem increasingly dated.

S-1, 1976

Seth Lover had designed the first humbucking pickup in 1955, and from the end of the decade it was fitted to almost all Gibson electrics. Yet, into the 1970s, Gibson still made the occasional foray into traditional Fender single-coil territory. The 1975 S-1 was noted for its electrics, with the three 'see-thru' single-coil pickups designed by Bill Lawrence and backed by some of the most elaborate circuitry seen in a non-active guitar. A very versatile instrument, it remained in production for only four years, in spite of endorsements from Carlos Santana and The Rolling Stones.

- **DATE** 1976
- **ORIGIN** Kalamazoo, Michigan, USA
- **WOOD**
  Alder body, maple bolt-on neck, rosewood fingerboard.
- **UNUSUAL FEATURE**
  Single-coil pickups and a bolt-on neck were unusual on post-1960s Gibsons.

The headstock is modelled on that of the Flying V.

The complex wiring of the S-1 comes together on the four-position chicken-head phase switch. This, combined with other on-board switching, makes it possible to produce a wide range of single- and twin-coil sounds.

The S-1 features an adjustable bridge with a stop tailpiece.

RD Artist, 1977

Launched in 1977, the RD series of maple-bodied instruments were designed to create a brighter sound than existing Gibson models. They feature active electronics designed by synth pioneer Dr Robert Moog. In a further nod towards Fender, the RD guitars were built with a 648mm (25⅛in) scale length – 19mm (¾in) longer than Gibson's long-established standard. The flagship model, the RD Artist, features an electronic circuitboard that runs the full length of the body, and is powered by a 9-volt battery that is accessible from the back cover.

- **DATE** 1977
- **ORIGIN** Kalamazoo, Michigan, USA
- **WOOD**
  Maple body, laminated maple set neck, ebony fingerboard.
- **UNUSUAL FEATURE**
  The Fender-proportioned scale length on early models was new for Gibson, and the circuitry designed by Bob Moog was unique.

The tuners, like the rest of the hardware, are gold-plated.

The RD Artist has a pair of gold-plated Series VI humbucking pickups.

The body shape is based broadly on the 'reverse' Firebirds of the early 1960s.

Victory MVX, 1981

Launched in 1981, the two models in Gibson's Victory MV (multi-voice) range were created as direct competitors to Fender's big two. While the twin-pickup MVII was marketed towards Telecaster-toting country players, the MVX, with its "myriad of separate and distinct electric guitar tonalities" (according to the marketing literature), was pitched against the Stratocaster. The MVX was kitted with two newly designed magnet/iron-loaded humbuckers in the neck and bridge positions, and a Super Stack humbucker in the centre.

- **DATE** 1981
- **ORIGIN** Kalamazoo, Michigan, USA
- **WOOD**
  Maple body, three-piece bolt-on maple neck, rosewood fingerboard.
- **UNUSUAL FEATURE**
  Bolt-on necks are unusual on Gibson guitars.

ABOVE: *The Gibson Victory MV range was more than a little Fender-like in its appearance – both in body shape and six-in-a-line tuners on the headstock.*

Uniquely for Gibson, the dot markers are positioned along the side of the fingerboard.

The Victory MVX shown here has been modified, its original Gibson pickups having been replaced.

Corvus III, 1982

The 1980s saw the ascendency of a new breed of American guitar maker. Brands such as Kramer, B. C. Rich and Jackson began to capture the imagination of a new generation of rock guitarists, with their futuristic, angular body shapes and high-end hardware. Gibson's response to this trend was the curiously retro-looking Corvus series, its body widely known as 'the can opener'. The three Corvus models, kitted out with different pickup configurations, probably represent Gibson's last attempt at creating an original design.

- **DATE** 1982
- **ORIGIN** Kalamazoo, Michigan, USA
- **WOOD**
  American alder, maple bolt-on neck, rosewood fingerboard.
- **UNUSUAL FEATURE**
  Its body shape turned heads, with many describing it as 'the can opener'.

The Corvus III shown here has three single-coil pickups with a five-way selector switch; the Corvus I is equipped with a single high-output Alnico V humbucker; while the Corvus II has an Alnico V at the bridge and a regular Gibson humbucker at the neck.

Although an attempt at a 1980s reinvention, the Corvus rather recalls early 1970s guitars, such as the Ovation solidbodies – even down to the selection of colour finishes.

The rear cutaway gives the Corvus its 'can opener' soubriquet.

Yamaha

Appearing relatively late on the scene, Yamaha's first electric guitars did not emerge until 1966. In contrast to other Japanese guitar makers of the period, these were well-built instruments, which often exhibited interesting design features. It is perhaps unsurprising that, a decade later, Yamaha would be in the vanguard of the first wave of high-end Japanese guitar production.

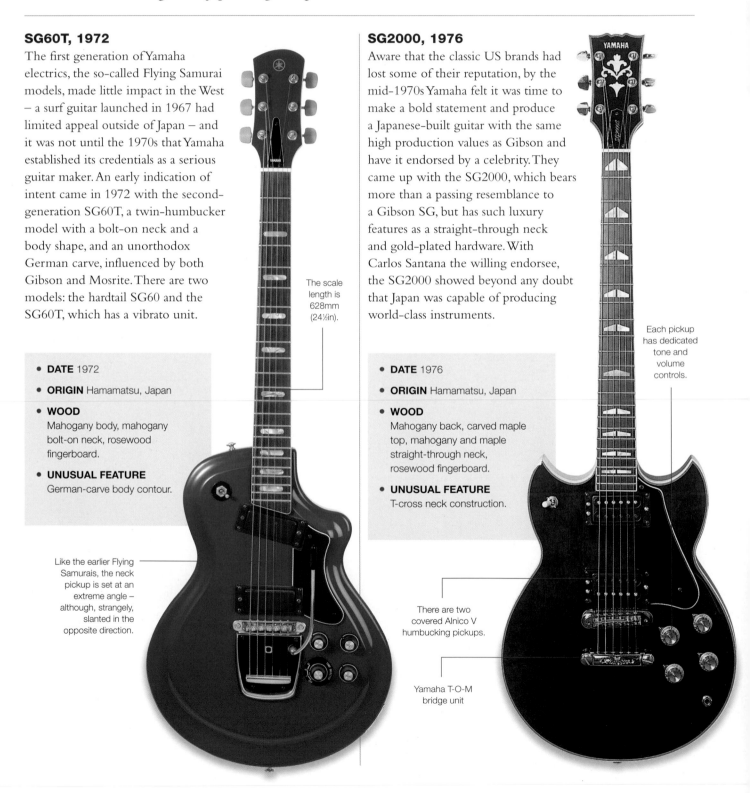

SG60T, 1972

The first generation of Yamaha electrics, the so-called Flying Samurai models, made little impact in the West – a surf guitar launched in 1967 had limited appeal outside of Japan – and it was not until the 1970s that Yamaha established its credentials as a serious guitar maker. An early indication of intent came in 1972 with the second-generation SG60T, a twin-humbucker model with a bolt-on neck and a body shape, and an unorthodox German carve, influenced by both Gibson and Mosrite. There are two models: the hardtail SG60 and the SG60T, which has a vibrato unit.

- **DATE** 1972
- **ORIGIN** Hamamatsu, Japan
- **WOOD**
  Mahogany body, mahogany bolt-on neck, rosewood fingerboard.
- **UNUSUAL FEATURE**
  German-carve body contour.

The scale length is 628mm (24½in).

Like the earlier Flying Samurais, the neck pickup is set at an extreme angle – although, strangely, slanted in the opposite direction.

SG2000, 1976

Aware that the classic US brands had lost some of their reputation, by the mid-1970s Yamaha felt it was time to make a bold statement and produce a Japanese-built guitar with the same high production values as Gibson and have it endorsed by a celebrity. They came up with the SG2000, which bears more than a passing resemblance to a Gibson SG, but has such luxury features as a straight-through neck and gold-plated hardware. With Carlos Santana the willing endorsee, the SG2000 showed beyond any doubt that Japan was capable of producing world-class instruments.

- **DATE** 1976
- **ORIGIN** Hamamatsu, Japan
- **WOOD**
  Mahogany back, carved maple top, mahogany and maple straight-through neck, rosewood fingerboard.
- **UNUSUAL FEATURE**
  T-cross neck construction.

Each pickup has dedicated tone and volume controls.

There are two covered Alnico V humbucking pickups.

Yamaha T-O-M bridge unit

Pacifica, 1989

The Yamaha Pacifica range is one the company's most enduring lines, having remained in production for over two decades. Designed as a test project at Yamaha's California custom shop, they went into production in Japan, the entry-level models proving to be particularly successful. The Pacifica range was clearly Fender-influenced, the double-cutaway – shown here – appearing as an elongated Stratocaster. There is also a Telecaster-type single-cutaway model. The budget models are all bolt-on neck constructions; however, early Pacificas, such as the PAC1412 models, had set necks and and other high-end features that ultimately proved too costly for Yamaha's market.

- **DATE** 1989

- **ORIGIN** Hamamatsu, Japan

- **WOOD**
  Alder body, maple neck (set or bolt-on depending on model), rosewood or maple fingerboard.

- **UNUSUAL FEATURE**
  The model here is a rare three-pickup model with a humbucker/single/single configuration.

The headstock features Yamaha's characteristic triple-tuning-fork logo.

This model has a rosewood fingerboard and dot marker inlays.

The electrics are exceptionally simple: a five-way selector switch and master volume and tone controls.

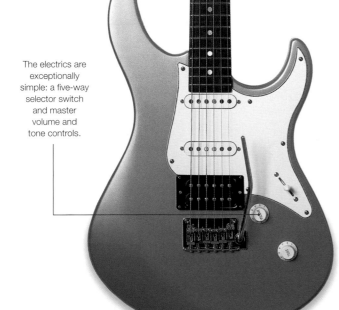

The new wave of Japanese manufacturers

The Yamaha guitars produced from the early 1970s brought about a change in the perception of instruments built in Japan. They were quickly joined by Ibanez, who, after Gibson's legal threats, began to produce a range of respectable originals such as the Iceman and the Axstar, through to the Steve Vai-developed Jem superstrats. Into the 1980s, Aria Pro II and the Westone brand (built at the Matsumoku factory) also made a mark with innovative and interesting instruments, and copies produced by Tokai were suddenly seen as serious rivals to the originals.

Such a rise in production values naturally meant higher manufacturing costs. As a consequence, low-end models or diffusion ranges were gradually brought in from countries with a cheaper labour force, such as South Korea, Mexico, Indonesia and more recently China. This has resulted in an upsurge of interest in Japanese-built instruments from the 1970s and '80s. For example, although they still don't enjoy the same brand cachet, the first Squier Stratocasters, produced from 1982 by Fender Japan, are now generally viewed as at least comparable to the more expensive 'real' Strats being built at the same time in the USA.

ABOVE: *Carlos Santana was the first major Western artist to endorse a Japanese-built guitar. He's seen here with a Yamaha SG2000, which he played a major role in popularizing. During the 1980s, he switched allegiance to the US Paul Reed Smith brand, and was an important figure in its early successes.*

1970s American solidbodies

From the end of the 1960s, a number of small American companies emerged to challenge the major names in guitar manufacture. Some, such as Ovation and Travis Bean, appeared on the scene with radical new ideas in construction and design; others, including Alembic and Peavey, came to guitar production from a successful background in electronics design.

Alembic Series 1, c.1971

Emerging from the late 1960s Californian music scene, Alembic initially supplied exclusive high-end sound equipment to top West Coast bands Jefferson Airplane and the Grateful Dead. They moved towards instrument manufacture, having pioneered a system of active on-board circuitry that gave their pickups a much wider audio bandwidth than traditional passive units. Although Alembic has produced six-string models, the company's reputation is based on having producing some of the finest basses ever.

The technology behind the early Alembics made them among the most advanced guitars on the market at that time.

- **DATE** *c.*1971
- **ORIGIN** Santa Rosa, California, USA
- **WOOD**
  Assorted woods, commonly maple/purpleheart straight-through neck with mahogany body 'wings' and ebony fretboard.
- **UNUSUAL FEATURE**
  The protrusion at the bottom of the body is a signature feature, as is the active circuitry.

Low-impedance pickups boosted by active circuitry gave the Alembic a wider dynamic range than passive pickups.

The pointed protrusion at the bottom was said to have been to encourage players to use a guitar stand.

Ovation Viper, 1973

With its reputation forged on groundbreaking electro-acoustic guitars, Ovation fared less well in the solidbody market. Its first attempt, 1971's Breadwinner, was simply too odd-looking for its time (and is now something of a cult instrument). Two years later, a more conventional model appeared, the Viper, which clearly resembles a scaled-down Ovation acoustic with a single cutaway. An outstanding guitar with biting high-output pickups, the Viper remained in production until the early 1980s.

The alder body followed the contours of a standard Ovation acoustic guitar; a single cutaway would later become commonplace on Ovation acoustics.

- **DATE** 1973
- **ORIGIN** New Hartford, Connecticut, USA
- **WOOD**
  Alder body, one-piece maple bolt-on neck and fingerboard.
- **UNUSUAL FEATURE**
  The high-output pickups, which were a selling point of the instrument.

Ovation advertising literature of the time claimed that the Viper's single-coil pickups had 30 per cent more windings than other similar models, resulting in a 6dB boost in output.

Kramer 450T, 1976

Gary Kramer set up his Neptune, New Jersey, factory in 1976 with the sole intention of making aluminium-necked guitars, an idea that he and his former business partner Travis Bean had pioneered earlier in search of greater sustain. The Travis Bean-branded models had used a straight-through neck design, which created an excellent sound, but they were extremely heavy and could react badly to temperature change. Kramer adapted the neck principle by using a T-shaped aluminium block filled with a walnut inlay on either side, reducing it to a more manageable weight.

- **DATE** 1976
- **ORIGIN** Neptune, New Jersey, USA
- **MATERIALS** Black burl walnut and birdseye maple body, aluminium straight-through neck with walnut inserts, ebanol fingerboard.
- **UNUSUAL FEATURE** The tuning-fork-shaped headstock topping off the aluminium neck is very distinctive.

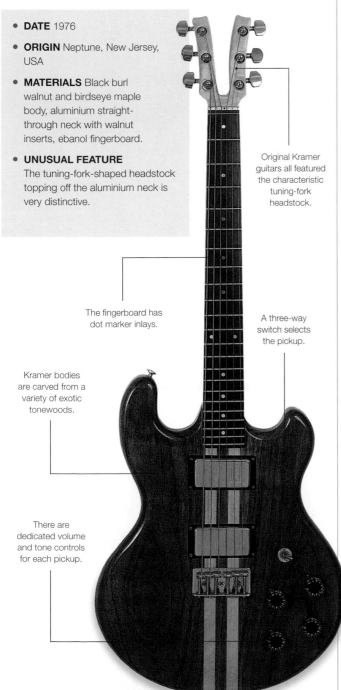

Original Kramer guitars all featured the characteristic tuning-fork headstock.

The fingerboard has dot marker inlays.

A three-way switch selects the pickup.

Kramer bodies are carved from a variety of exotic tonewoods.

There are dedicated volume and tone controls for each pickup.

Peavey T-60, 1978

Having designed and built his first guitar amplifier while still in high school, Hartley Peavey set up a small company in the basement of his home in 1965. Within a decade, Peavey was one of the biggest names in the world of music electronics. The first Peavey electric guitar, the T-60, launched in 1978, found an immediate place in guitar history as the first production model to be built using computer-controlled carving machines. The T-60 and its bass counterpart, the T-40, were both well regarded mid-market guitars in their day.

- **DATE** 1978
- **ORIGIN** Meridian, Mississippi, USA
- **WOOD** Ash body, rock maple set neck, rosewood fingerboard.
- **UNUSUAL FEATURE** The T-60 has a coil-switching function in the tone potentiometer.

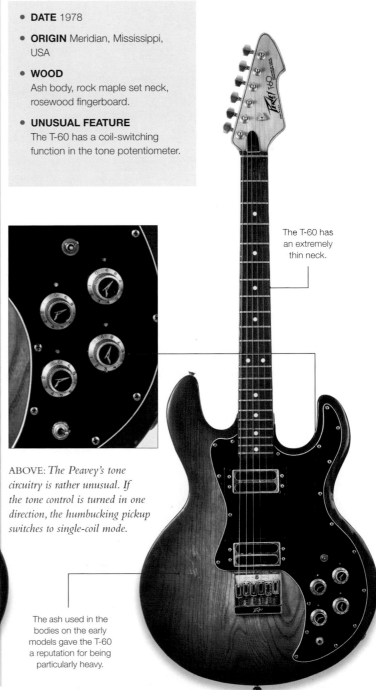

The T-60 has an extremely thin neck.

ABOVE: *The Peavey's tone circuitry is rather unusual. If the tone control is turned in one direction, the humbucking pickup switches to single-coil mode.*

The ash used in the bodies on the early models gave the T-60 a reputation for being particularly heavy.

Britain in the 1970s

The last decade in which British electric guitars were built in any great quantity, the 1970s saw the brief emergence of Shergold, which evolved from the Hayman brand, a key figure in which had been none other than Jim Burns, the 'British Leo Fender'. The second half of the decade saw Burns embark on two final ill-fated business projects, Burns UK and Jim Burns Actualizers.

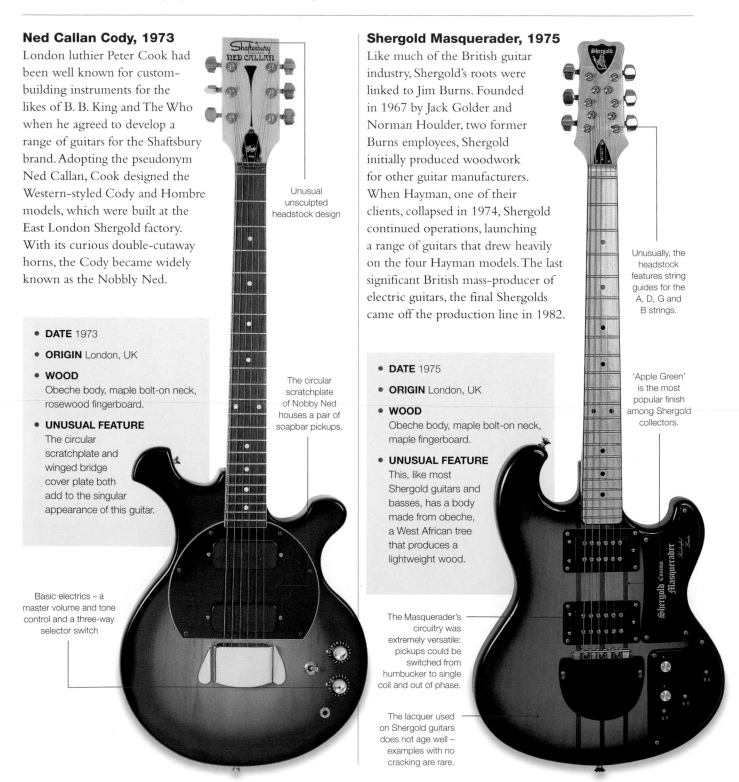

Ned Callan Cody, 1973

London luthier Peter Cook had been well known for custom-building instruments for the likes of B. B. King and The Who when he agreed to develop a range of guitars for the Shaftsbury brand. Adopting the pseudonym Ned Callan, Cook designed the Western-styled Cody and Hombre models, which were built at the East London Shergold factory. With its curious double-cutaway horns, the Cody became widely known as the Nobbly Ned.

- **DATE** 1973
- **ORIGIN** London, UK
- **WOOD**
  Obeche body, maple bolt-on neck, rosewood fingerboard.
- **UNUSUAL FEATURE**
  The circular scratchplate and winged bridge cover plate both add to the singular appearance of this guitar.

Unusual unsculpted headstock design

The circular scratchplate of Nobby Ned houses a pair of soapbar pickups.

Basic electrics – a master volume and tone control and a three-way selector switch

Shergold Masquerader, 1975

Like much of the British guitar industry, Shergold's roots were linked to Jim Burns. Founded in 1967 by Jack Golder and Norman Houlder, two former Burns employees, Shergold initially produced woodwork for other guitar manufacturers. When Hayman, one of their clients, collapsed in 1974, Shergold continued operations, launching a range of guitars that drew heavily on the four Hayman models. The last significant British mass-producer of electric guitars, the final Shergolds came off the production line in 1982.

- **DATE** 1975
- **ORIGIN** London, UK
- **WOOD**
  Obeche body, maple bolt-on neck, maple fingerboard.
- **UNUSUAL FEATURE**
  This, like most Shergold guitars and basses, has a body made from obeche, a West African tree that produces a lightweight wood.

Unusually, the headstock features string guides for the A, D, G and B strings.

'Apple Green' is the most popular finish among Shergold collectors.

The Masquerader's circuitry was extremely versatile: pickups could be switched from humbucker to single coil and out of phase.

The lacquer used on Shergold guitars does not age well – examples with no cracking are rare.

Burns UK Mirage, 1976

Jim Burns had always been more of an innovator than a businessman. Having been forced to sell the original Burns brand in 1965, he had been engaged by Dallas Arbiter to work on designs for the short-lived Hayman range. In 1974, he reappeared with the Burns UK brand and a small range of curious-looking instruments. These included the Flyte – a model based on the shape of the Concorde supersonic jet – and its close relative, the more obscure Mirage, described in the company literature as a "colourful swinging axe".

- **DATE** 1976

- **ORIGIN** Newcastle upon Tyne, UK

- **WOOD**
  Selected hardwood body, Canadian rock maple bolt-on neck, maple fingerboard.

- **UNUSUAL FEATURE**
  Both the body shape and the curiously positioned tuners are unique to this instrument.

ABOVE: *The positioning of the tuners on the headstock is quite extraordinary – they are both asymmetrically and inconsistently spaced.*

The pickups are the unusually shaped Burns Mach One Humbusters, featuring Alcomax four-bar magnets.

The scratchplate follows the contour of the body and secures the electrics.

Gordon-Smith Gypsy 60 SS, 1980

The largest guitar maker in Britain today, Lancashire-based Gordon-Smith is very well known for producing quality instruments based on classic US designs. The Gypsy range comprises both solid and semi-solid (SS) models, with single and twin cutaways, and resembles the Gibson Les Paul Junior. The Gypsy 60 SS is an attractive mahogany-bodied semi-solid with distinctively large twin f-holes.

- **DATE** 1980

- **ORIGIN** Partington, UK

- **WOOD**
  Mahogany body, mahogany set neck, rosewood fingerboard.

- **UNUSUAL FEATURE**
  The oversize f-holes are a feature of this instrument.

The headstock shape, like the body, echoes the lines of the original Gibson Les Paul.

The model shown here has two single-coil pickups – humbucking models are also available. The company make its own pickups, and was the first to offer coil-tapped humbuckers.

Distinctive dolphin soundholes

Far Eastern copies

At the dawn of the 1970s, many Japanese manufacturers started to scale back the mass production of electric guitars that they had undertaken during the previous decade. However, while there was a gradual shift towards the production of higher-quality instruments, some large factories, including Teisco, continued to turn out copies of the most popular Gibson and Fender models.

Jedson 'Telecaster' Bass, c.1971

Dallas Arbiter was a big name in British musical instruments in the early 1970s. Its Jedson brand – often passable models based broadly on Fenders and Gibsons and built at the Teisco factory in Japan – was ubiquitous among Britain's teenagers during the decade. Strangely, perhaps, it was the Telecaster copy that appeared in the widest number of variations – a 'true' copy, a shortscale bass, and single- and double-pickup versions with or without the largely unusable vibrato arm.

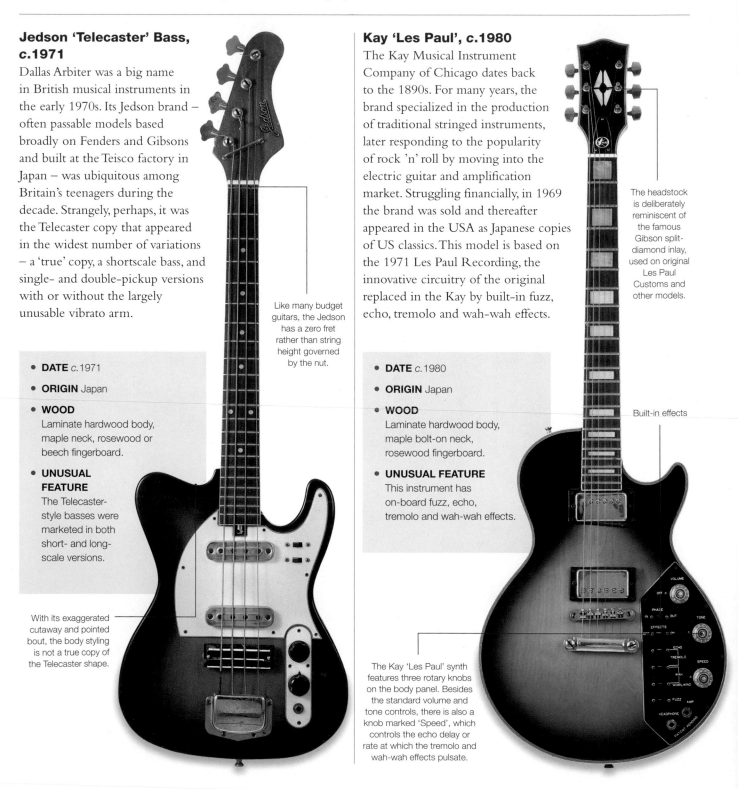

Like many budget guitars, the Jedson has a zero fret rather than string height governed by the nut.

- **DATE** *c.*1971

- **ORIGIN** Japan

- **WOOD**
  Laminate hardwood body, maple neck, rosewood or beech fingerboard.

- **UNUSUAL FEATURE**
  The Telecaster-style basses were marketed in both short- and long-scale versions.

With its exaggerated cutaway and pointed bout, the body styling is not a true copy of the Telecaster shape.

Kay 'Les Paul', c.1980

The Kay Musical Instrument Company of Chicago dates back to the 1890s. For many years, the brand specialized in the production of traditional stringed instruments, later responding to the popularity of rock 'n' roll by moving into the electric guitar and amplification market. Struggling financially, in 1969 the brand was sold and thereafter appeared in the USA as Japanese copies of US classics. This model is based on the 1971 Les Paul Recording, the innovative circuitry of the original replaced in the Kay by built-in fuzz, echo, tremolo and wah-wah effects.

The headstock is deliberately reminiscent of the famous Gibson split-diamond inlay, used on original Les Paul Customs and other models.

Built-in effects

- **DATE** *c.*1980

- **ORIGIN** Japan

- **WOOD**
  Laminate hardwood body, maple bolt-on neck, rosewood fingerboard.

- **UNUSUAL FEATURE**
  This instrument has on-board fuzz, echo, tremolo and wah-wah effects.

The Kay 'Les Paul' synth features three rotary knobs on the body panel. Besides the standard volume and tone controls, there is also a knob marked 'Speed', which controls the echo delay or rate at which the tremolo and wah-wah effects pulsate.

Tokai TST 50, 1982

By the beginning of the 1980s, the quality gap between Japanese copies and the US-built originals had narrowed to an unprecedented degree. It could be argued that the benchmark model was the 1982 launch of the Tokai TST range. So blatant were these imitations that Tokai even went as far as mimicking Fender's stylized headstock logo. These instruments sounded and played every bit as well as the Fenders coming out of the Fullerton factory – and sold for around half the price.

- **DATE** 1982

- **ORIGIN** Hamamatsu, Japan

- **WOOD**
  Alder body, maple bolt-on neck, rosewood or maple fingerboard.

- **UNUSUAL FEATURE**
  The stylized Tokai brand name on the headstock is a deliberate imitation of the Fender logo.

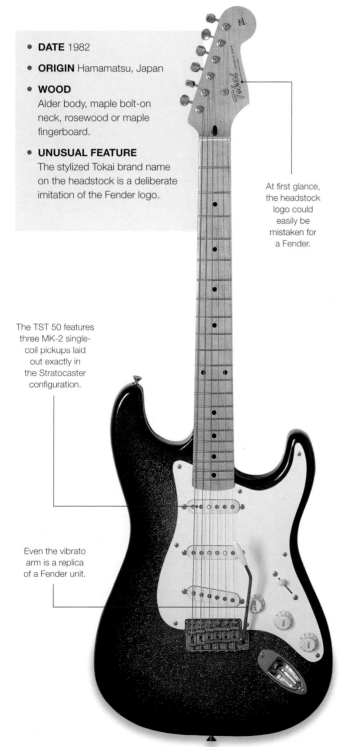

At first glance, the headstock logo could easily be mistaken for a Fender.

The TST 50 features three MK-2 single-coil pickups laid out exactly in the Stratocaster configuration.

Even the vibrato arm is a replica of a Fender unit.

How the copyists were stopped

The Japanese copy industry had always plagued the major guitar manufacturers, but it wasn't until 1977 that Gibson took decisive action, threatening Ibanez for – curiously enough – infringement of headstock designs. Ibanez, as a result, backed down and curtailed its imitative activities – and has since then produced extremely popular and innovative instruments of its own.

Fender took an entirely different approach: it started to make its own copies. In 1982, Fender Japan was established to take advantage of the cheaper production costs offered in the Far East. One of Fender's Japanese partners also owned the Greco brand name – one of the major copy competitors. Thus, a deal was struck that enabled it to build officially sanctioned guitars under the Fender Squier brand, and, at the same time, Greco 'Fenders' were removed from the market at a stroke.

Fender was quick to see the commercial advantages of a tiered approach to global production, and soon began producing genuine Fenders in different parts of the world. The flagship products are still made at the Corona factory in California, USA, but cheaper Fender-branded models have been produced in Japan, South Korea and Mexico.

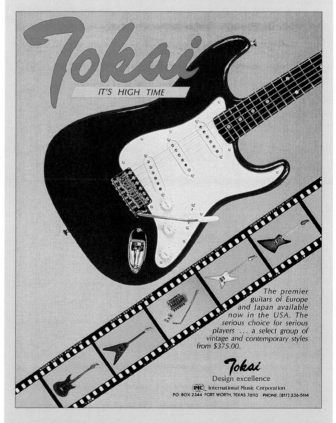

ABOVE: *A Tokai catalogue from the early 1980s prominently displays the company's logo. Its similarity to Fender – the company whose instruments it relentlessly copied – shows how close to the wind some of the Japanese manufacturers were prepared to sail.*

The new Fender classics

Fender was never a company to tinker too much with a winning formula. Amendments over the years to the already iconic Stratocaster and Telecaster models had thus far been subtle. In the 1970s, however, Fender decided to introduce a new range of three Telecasters: the hollowbody Thinline, and two models armed with Fender's state-of-the-art range of humbucking pickups.

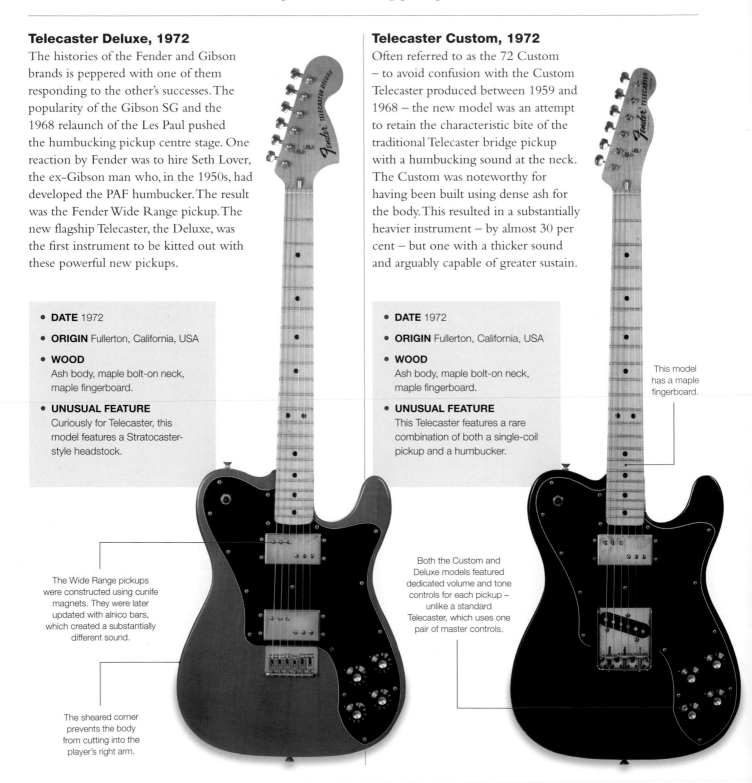

Telecaster Deluxe, 1972

The histories of the Fender and Gibson brands is peppered with one of them responding to the other's successes. The popularity of the Gibson SG and the 1968 relaunch of the Les Paul pushed the humbucking pickup centre stage. One reaction by Fender was to hire Seth Lover, the ex-Gibson man who, in the 1950s, had developed the PAF humbucker. The result was the Fender Wide Range pickup. The new flagship Telecaster, the Deluxe, was the first instrument to be kitted out with these powerful new pickups.

- **DATE** 1972

- **ORIGIN** Fullerton, California, USA

- **WOOD**
  Ash body, maple bolt-on neck, maple fingerboard.

- **UNUSUAL FEATURE**
  Curiously for Telecaster, this model features a Stratocaster-style headstock.

The Wide Range pickups were constructed using cunife magnets. They were later updated with alnico bars, which created a substantially different sound.

The sheared corner prevents the body from cutting into the player's right arm.

Telecaster Custom, 1972

Often referred to as the 72 Custom – to avoid confusion with the Custom Telecaster produced between 1959 and 1968 – the new model was an attempt to retain the characteristic bite of the traditional Telecaster bridge pickup with a humbucking sound at the neck. The Custom was noteworthy for having been built using dense ash for the body. This resulted in a substantially heavier instrument – by almost 30 per cent – but one with a thicker sound and arguably capable of greater sustain.

- **DATE** 1972

- **ORIGIN** Fullerton, California, USA

- **WOOD**
  Ash body, maple bolt-on neck, maple fingerboard.

- **UNUSUAL FEATURE**
  This Telecaster features a rare combination of both a single-coil pickup and a humbucker.

This model has a maple fingerboard.

Both the Custom and Deluxe models featured dedicated volume and tone controls for each pickup – unlike a standard Telecaster, which uses one pair of master controls.

Stratocaster, 1965

By the middle of the 1970s, the Stratocaster was still the most popular solidbody electric guitar in the world. However, there was a wide perception that production standards had dropped, and a growing market for used pre-CBS Stratocasters – those made before the CBS takeover in 1965. The basic Stratocaster has altered little since then: the most significant change took place in 1977 with the introduction of the five-way selector switch. This eradicated the age-old Stratocaster players' technique of wedging the original three-way switches to produce a greater variety of tones.

- **DATE** From 1965

- **ORIGIN** Fullerton, California, USA

- **WOOD**
  Ash body (variations have included alder, poplar, basswood, mahogany and koa), maple bolt-on neck, maple or rosewood fingerboard.

- **UNUSUAL FEATURE**
  Early Strats had a three-way selector switch, but since 1977, a five-way switch has been used.

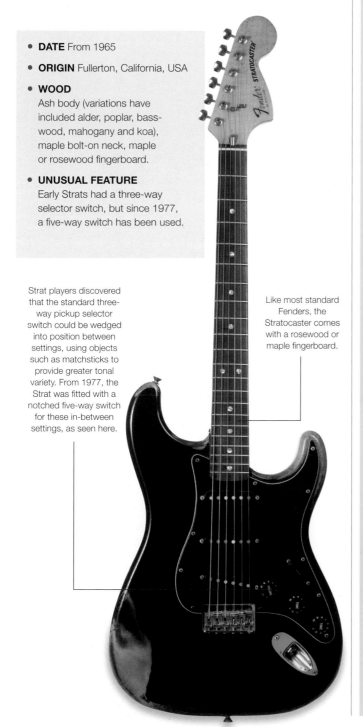

Strat players discovered that the standard three-way pickup selector switch could be wedged into position between settings, using objects such as matchsticks to provide greater tonal variety. From 1977, the Strat was fitted with a notched five-way switch for these in-between settings, as seen here.

Like most standard Fenders, the Stratocaster comes with a rosewood or maple fingerboard.

Eric Clapton

One of Britain's most noted guitarists, Eric Clapton (b. 1945) first came to attention as an 18-year-old member of the Yardbirds, an R&B band that played on the same club circuit as the young Rolling Stones. Leaving the band in 1965, when its sound shifted towards pop, Clapton joined John Mayall's Bluesbreakers, where he quickly established himself as one of the country's most gifted electric players.

In 1966, Clapton, with bassist Jack Bruce and drummer Ginger Baker, formed Cream, generally thought to be the first rock/blues power trio. Hugely popular on both sides of the Atlantic, Cream provided a template for much of the heavy-riffing rock that followed, particularly during the 1970s.

When Cream broke up, Clapton engaged in projects of varying note, among them Derek and the Dominoes, which recorded "Layla", one of rock's all-time great anthems.

Throughout the 1980s, he established a niche for easy-listening rock, which saw his guitar skills taking a back seat. He has since taken on the role of elder statesman of blues, famously performing unplugged.

ABOVE: *Eric Clapton playing Blackie, a composite Stratocaster he built in 1970 using parts taken from three 1956–57 models. He used it extensively live and in the studio until the early 1990s. In 2004, Blackie was sold at auction for $959,500 to raise funds for the Crossroads Centre, a drug-rehabilitation centre that Clapton himself had founded.*

Alternative materials

The early days of guitar electrification saw Rickenbacker experimenting with aluminium and Bakelite, and Dobro/National with metal bodies. Yet, as the electric guitar gained popularity, it was clear that guitarists were more interested in guitars built traditionally – using wood. This has not, however, prevented a number of maverick luthiers from experimenting successfully with other materials.

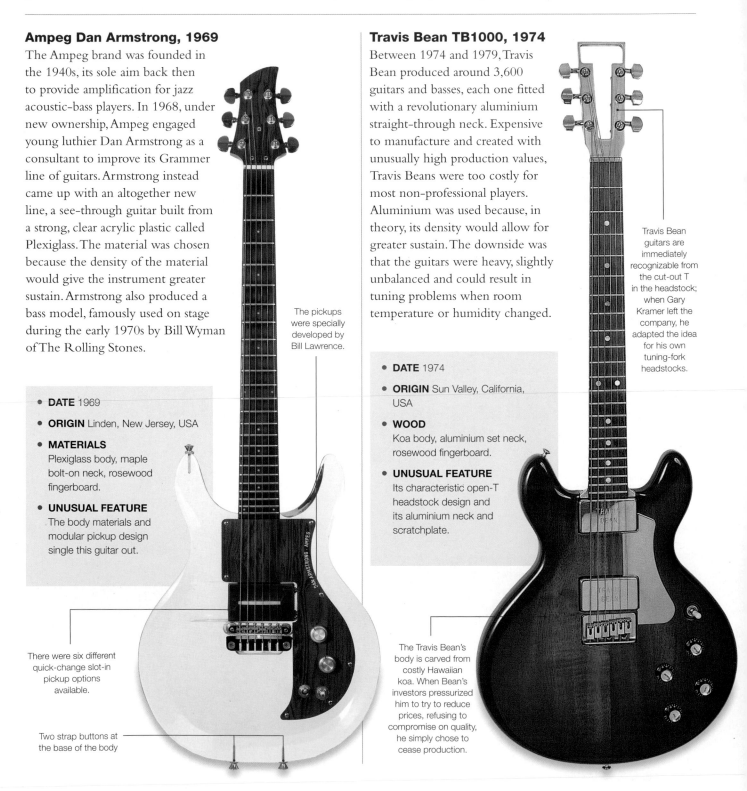

Ampeg Dan Armstrong, 1969

The Ampeg brand was founded in the 1940s, its sole aim back then to provide amplification for jazz acoustic-bass players. In 1968, under new ownership, Ampeg engaged young luthier Dan Armstrong as a consultant to improve its Grammer line of guitars. Armstrong instead came up with an altogether new line, a see-through guitar built from a strong, clear acrylic plastic called Plexiglass. The material was chosen because the density of the material would give the instrument greater sustain. Armstrong also produced a bass model, famously used on stage during the early 1970s by Bill Wyman of The Rolling Stones.

The pickups were specially developed by Bill Lawrence.

- **DATE** 1969

- **ORIGIN** Linden, New Jersey, USA

- **MATERIALS**
  Plexiglass body, maple bolt-on neck, rosewood fingerboard.

- **UNUSUAL FEATURE**
  The body materials and modular pickup design single this guitar out.

There were six different quick-change slot-in pickup options available.

Two strap buttons at the base of the body

Travis Bean TB1000, 1974

Between 1974 and 1979, Travis Bean produced around 3,600 guitars and basses, each one fitted with a revolutionary aluminium straight-through neck. Expensive to manufacture and created with unusually high production values, Travis Beans were too costly for most non-professional players. Aluminium was used because, in theory, its density would allow for greater sustain. The downside was that the guitars were heavy, slightly unbalanced and could result in tuning problems when room temperature or humidity changed.

Travis Bean guitars are immediately recognizable from the cut-out T in the headstock; when Gary Kramer left the company, he adapted the idea for his own tuning-fork headstocks.

- **DATE** 1974

- **ORIGIN** Sun Valley, California, USA

- **WOOD**
  Koa body, aluminium set neck, rosewood fingerboard.

- **UNUSUAL FEATURE**
  Its characteristic open-T headstock design and its aluminium neck and scratchplate.

The Travis Bean's body is carved from costly Hawaiian koa. When Bean's investors pressurized him to try to reduce prices, refusing to compromise on quality, he simply chose to cease production.

Ovation Adamas, 1977

Aeronautical engineer Charles Kaman enjoyed a successful career designing helicopters and aviation components. He was also a keen guitarist who, during the 1960s, used the cutting-edge technological capabilities of the Kaman Corporation to produce a new type of guitar. Accepting the orthodox view that the key to the quality of an acoustic guitar was in the design and tonewoods used in the soundboard, Kaman turned his attention to the back and sides. For this he created a bowled shape made from Lyrachord, a type of fibreglass which combined light weight with great strength, meaning that internal bracing – which interfered with the natural flow of the soundwaves – was no longer needed.

- **DATE** 1977

- **ORIGIN** New Hartford, Connecticut, USA

- **WOOD**
  Spruce top, Lyrachord bowled back and sides, set maple neck, rosewood fingerboard.

- **UNUSUAL FEATURE** The body shape and material, the decoration around multiple soundholes and piezo bridge transducer pickup all distinguish this instrument.

Multiple soundholes in the upper bout of the body

ABOVE: *The Kaman Corporation also developed a revolutionary piezo pickup housed inside the bridge and mounted on the underside of the soundboard. This went some way to solving the problem of amplifying an acoustic guitar in concert without using a microphone, while still maintaining the natural sound of the acoustic instrument.*

The pre-amp and controls are fitted to top side of the guitar.

Why wood?

ABOVE: *Aerosmith is one of the biggest-selling rock bands of all time, with global sales of over 150 million albums. Lead guitarsist Joe Perry was one of the most prominent users of the Dan Armstrong Plexiglass model.*

There is no question that the materials used to make an acoustic guitar have an enormous impact on its sound – different types of wood produce different tonal qualities. The same is true for an electric guitar, except that the design of the magnetic pickup is perhaps the biggest single factor affecting the way it sounds. This has led some to question as to whether wood is necessarily the best material to use. Alternative body materials, such as different types of plastic, have been shown to have little negative impact on sound. The most successful experiments have tended to concentrate on the area of scale length – from the fingerboard to the bridge. Materials that rival or surpass hardwoods in density, such as aluminium – or the graphite and carbon-fibre blend used successfully on Steinberger guitars in the 1980s – can often provide greater levels of sustain. It is notable that experiments in this area have been more readily taken on board in the four-string field, since bass guitarists seem more prepared to experiment than their six-string cousins are.

Curiosities

Over the years, guitars have appeared in all shapes and sizes. Some have been built to reflect the eccentricities of their makers, others – such as the Framus Super Yob – were built at the whim of wealthy and successful pop stars. Some have existed simply to market a band or its music. These curious designs, however, serve to illustrate the rich variety that exists in the electric guitar world.

Zemaitis, 1971

Tony Zemaitis produced guitars for the top end of the market, famously The Rolling Stones. During the 1960s, his London-based workshop had a clientele that included George Harrison, Jimi Hendrix and Eric Clapton. In 1970, attempting to combat feedback, he experimented with placing a metal shield over the body; the metalwork was then intricately hand-engraved. Since his death in 2002, his highly collectible guitars – all of which he personally handbuilt – have been fetching values as much as $30,000 at auction.

- **DATE** 1971
- **ORIGIN** Chatham, UK
- **WOOD**
  Mahogany body with hand-etched duralumin top, mahogany set neck, ebony fingerboard.
- **UNUSUAL FEATURE**
  The guitar has a hand-etched metal shield.

Engraved decorative metal panels matching the bodywork are found on the headstock.

The diamond and dot fingerboard inlays are carved from abalone.

Each Zemaitis engraving is unique.

Although outstanding instruments in their own right, the guitars produced by Tony Zemaitis after 1971 are prized as much for their ornate visual appearance. The duralumin shield on the front of each guitar was hand-etched by Danny O'Brien, a celebrated gun engraver.

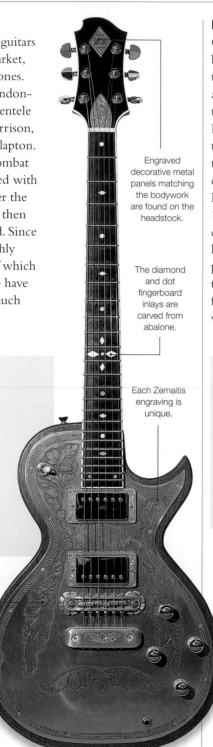

Framus Super Yob, 1974

One of the most popular British bands of the 1970s, Slade topped the charts with raucous terrace anthems such as "Cum On Feel the Noize" and "Skweeze Me, Pleeze Me". Guitarist Dave Hill, the only member of the band truly to embrace the glam-rock ethos, commissioned British luthier John Birch to produce a guitar styled as a 1950s sci-fi ray gun. Hill loved the design but disliked the guitar, and had German manufacturer Framus produce a new version. Christened the Super Yob, the guitar was frequently seen in concert as well as on British TV.

- **DATE** 1974
- **ORIGIN** Bubenreuth, Germany
- **WOOD**
  Alder body, maple set neck, maple fingerboard.
- **UNUSUAL FEATURE**
  The body shape is like no other instrument ever made.

The finish mimics the famous Rickenbacker Fireglo effect.

The gun shape necessitates positioning the bridge close to the centre of the body, causing the instrument to be neck-heavy.

The Super Yob moniker was a remnant from Slade's early days, when the members of the band presented themselves as aggressive skinheads.

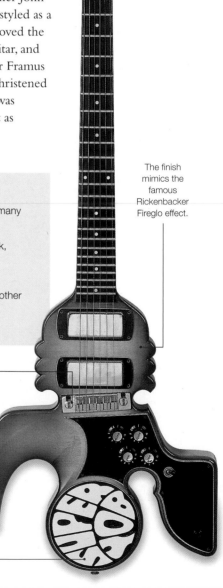

Rob Armstrong Cornflake, 1978

Custom-guitar builder Rob Armstrong came up with this unique design for Simon Nicol, a guitarist with the British folk-rock band Fairport Convention. Although built around a Kellogg's packet, it bears more than a passing resemblance to a South African oil-can guitar. Hardly intended as a serious instrument, this whimsical design was built using parts from a low-quality Japanese Columbus Les Paul copy, and it features two humbucking pickups with dedicated volume and tone controls mounted on the top side of the body.

- **DATE** 1978
- **ORIGIN** Coventry, UK
- **WOOD**
  Unidentified wooden body covered with cardboard box, maple neck, rosewood fingerboard.
- **UNUSUAL FEATURE**
  The Bo Diddly-style rectangular body shape is cut to fit a breakfast cereal packet.

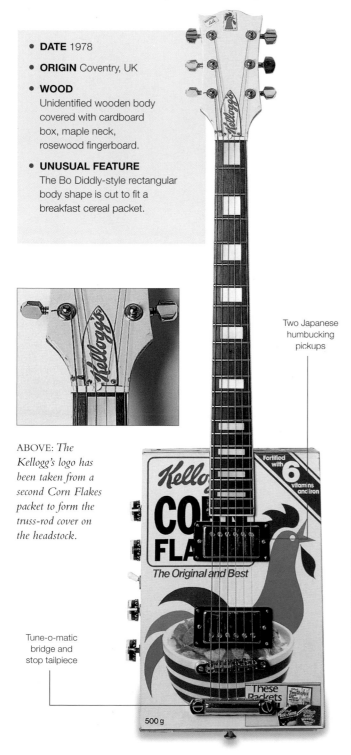

ABOVE: *The Kellogg's logo has been taken from a second Corn Flakes packet to form the truss-rod cover on the headstock.*

Two Japanese humbucking pickups

Tune-o-matic bridge and stop tailpiece

Eastwood Blue Moon, 1980

Creating a bespoke guitar to publicize a single might seem like an extreme measure, but that's just what British rock 'n' roll 'revival' band Showaddywaddy did in 1980 for their cover of the song "Blue Moon". Luthier Brian Eastwood was approached, and he quickly came up with this novelty instrument that sees the man in the moon emerging from behind a fluffy white cloud. The guitar was featured on the band's TV promotional events, and the single became a Top 40 hit. More recently, Eastwood has built an acoustic version.

- **DATE** 1980
- **ORIGIN** Rochdale, UK
- **WOOD**
  Laminated hardwood body and neck.
- **UNUSUAL FEATURE**
  The Blue Moon has a totally unique body shape, like several of Brian Eastwood's creations.

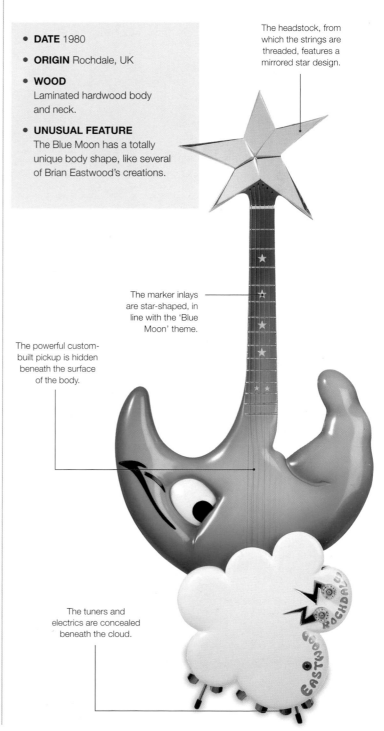

The headstock, from which the strings are threaded, features a mirrored star design.

The marker inlays are star-shaped, in line with the 'Blue Moon' theme.

The powerful custom-built pickup is hidden beneath the surface of the body.

The tuners and electrics are concealed beneath the cloud.

B. C. Rich

For a brand name that instantly conjures up images of the 1980s metal scene, B. C. Rich came from what would seem to be the unlikeliest of sources. Bernardo Chavez Rico was a highly accomplished acoustic player who, in 1966, began building flamenco guitars from his base in Los Angeles, California. Six years later, the first of B. C. Rich's visually distinctive electric models emerged.

Mockingbird, 1975

Rico's first electric guitars were surprisingly conservative by his later standards, designed clearly on the lines of Gibson Les Paul and EB-3 bass models, but in 1975, the Mockingbird appeared. The first B. C. Rich to achieve widespread recognition, it was based on a drawing by Johnny 'Go Go' Kallas and built by Neal Moser, one of Rico's talented luthiers. An enduring design, as late as 2010, *Guitar World* magazine ranked it as "the coolest guitar of all time".

- **DATE** 1975
- **ORIGIN** Los Angeles, California, USA
- **WOOD** Mahogany body, maple straight-through neck, rosewood body.
- **UNUSUAL FEATURE** Its radical body design was like nothing ever seen at the time of its launch.

The stylized R appears on the headstock of early B. C. Rich guitars.

Early US-built B. C. Rich models feature straight-through neck designs, as shown here. These 1970s models are now increasingly collectible.

With its built-in pre-amp and switching options, the Mockingbird was capable of a wide variety of tones.

Bich, 1977

Neal Moser was also responsible for the Bich, B. C. Rich's most radical instrument, the prototype of which was built – much to his annoyance – while Rico was on a visit to Japan. The revolutionary concept here was in the doubling up of the top four strings but leaving the two bass strings single, so there was a total of ten strings. Known widely as the 'Rich Bich', a more conventional six-string version (as shown here) was added, which proved to be extremely popular with metal bands.

- **DATE** 1977
- **ORIGIN** Los Angeles, California, USA
- **WOOD** Mahogany body, maple straight-through neck, rosewood body.
- **UNUSUAL FEATURE** The original concept has ten strings (six-string version shown here).

The 'Rich Bich' was one of the first models to feature the pointed headstocks that would soon characterize metal guitars.

The Bich shown here features the cloud fingerboard inlays used on early B.C. Rich models.

The cutaway beneath the bridge is a practical design feature of this guitar.

Warlock, 1981

Emerging in 1981, the Warlock is often thought of as the final one of B. C. Rich's classic five shapes, its claw-like design proving highly popular among metal players – both guitar and bass. By this time the brand had become so well known that high-end Japanese brands such as Aria began to produce imitations. Taking Fender's lead, Rico set up a Japanese operation, B. C. Rich NJ ('Nagoya, Japan', where the guitars were built). The vogue for unorthodox body shapes endured throughout the 1980s – and still has a niche following in the metal world – many of which could be traced back to B. C. Rich originals.

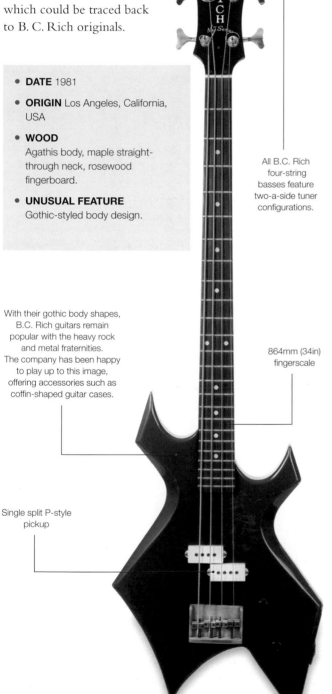

- **DATE** 1981

- **ORIGIN** Los Angeles, California, USA

- **WOOD**
  Agathis body, maple straight-through neck, rosewood fingerboard.

- **UNUSUAL FEATURE**
  Gothic-styled body design.

All B.C. Rich four-string basses feature two-a-side tuner configurations.

With their gothic body shapes, B.C. Rich guitars remain popular with the heavy rock and metal fraternities. The company has been happy to play up to this image, offering accessories such as coffin-shaped guitar cases.

864mm (34in) fingerscale

Single split P-style pickup

Changing shape of the guitar

The guitar is a practical instrument that has evolved slowly over the centuries. The narrow-waisted figure-of-eight body shape of an acoustic guitar came about because the instrument needed to sit comfortably on the lap of the seated player. The vogue for playing the guitar standing up is a relatively recent one, only becoming the predominant mode since the early 1950s. The electrification of the guitar played a fundamental role in this evolution: on stage, for example, the player need not stay in one position, close to a microphone, but by using a long cable or wireless transmitter, is free to roam the stage. Theoretically, then, these practical considerations are no longer so important.

Since the first electric guitars were little more than acoustic guitars with a pickup fitted, the slow evolution of electric body shape is perhaps not so surprising. Gibson attempted to challenge the figure-of-eight orthodoxy in the late 1950s with its Modernistic series, which included the famous Flying V, but customer reaction was negative, and they were withdrawn. During the 1960s, others emerged with unusual designs, such as the teardrop-shaped Vox Mark III, but these were generally viewed as niche instruments.

It was only in the 1980s that strange and exotic shapes, often inspired by late-1970s B.C. Rich designs, were more commonly seen, often in the hands of dark-metal players. However, the continued popularity of the early Fender and Gibson models, or modern-day derivatives such as those produced by Paul Reed Smith, would seem to provide strong evidence that guitarists are a pretty conservative bunch.

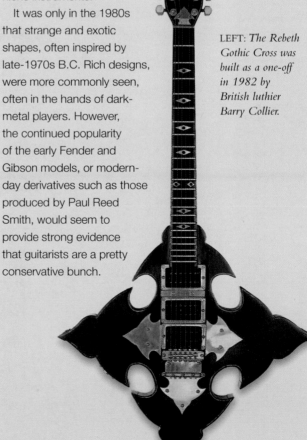

LEFT: *The Rebeth Gothic Cross was built as a one-off in 1982 by British luthier Barry Collier.*

Fenders from the 1980s

The major US guitar manufacturers have realized that when it comes to guitar design, the consumer is rarely interested in embracing innovation. The 1980s was the last decade that saw both the Fender and Gibson companies attempting to come up with original designs, before concentrating on turning their classic models into the high-end heritage brands they are today.

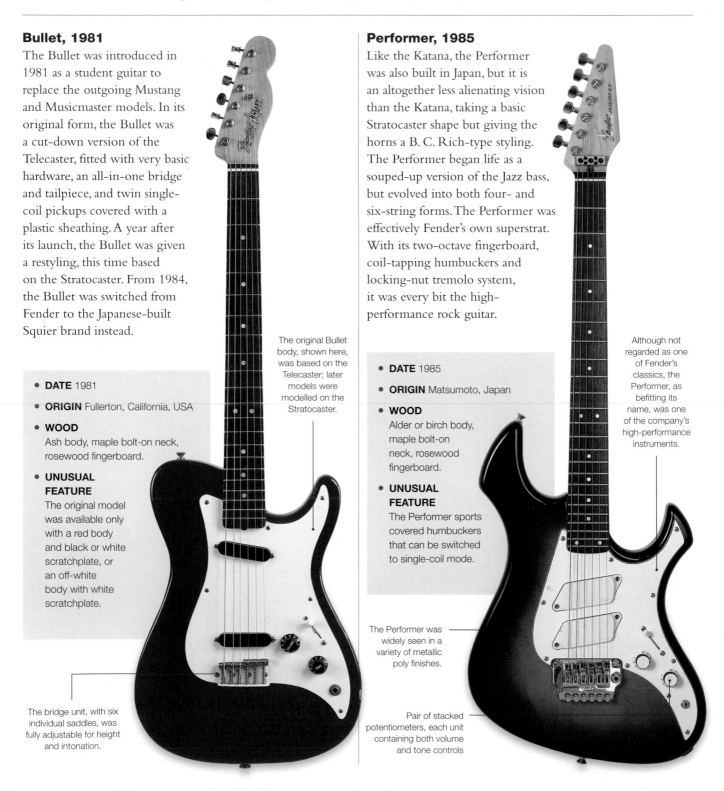

Bullet, 1981

The Bullet was introduced in 1981 as a student guitar to replace the outgoing Mustang and Musicmaster models. In its original form, the Bullet was a cut-down version of the Telecaster, fitted with very basic hardware, an all-in-one bridge and tailpiece, and twin single-coil pickups covered with a plastic sheathing. A year after its launch, the Bullet was given a restyling, this time based on the Stratocaster. From 1984, the Bullet was switched from Fender to the Japanese-built Squier brand instead.

- **DATE** 1981
- **ORIGIN** Fullerton, California, USA
- **WOOD**
  Ash body, maple bolt-on neck, rosewood fingerboard.
- **UNUSUAL FEATURE**
  The original model was available only with a red body and black or white scratchplate, or an off-white body with white scratchplate.

The original Bullet body, shown here, was based on the Telecaster; later models were modelled on the Stratocaster.

The bridge unit, with six individual saddles, was fully adjustable for height and intonation.

Performer, 1985

Like the Katana, the Performer was also built in Japan, but it is an altogether less alienating vision than the Katana, taking a basic Stratocaster shape but giving the horns a B. C. Rich-type styling. The Performer began life as a souped-up version of the Jazz bass, but evolved into both four- and six-string forms. The Performer was effectively Fender's own superstrat. With its two-octave fingerboard, coil-tapping humbuckers and locking-nut tremolo system, it was every bit the high-performance rock guitar.

- **DATE** 1985
- **ORIGIN** Matsumoto, Japan
- **WOOD**
  Alder or birch body, maple bolt-on neck, rosewood fingerboard.
- **UNUSUAL FEATURE**
  The Performer sports covered humbuckers that can be switched to single-coil mode.

Although not regarded as one of Fender's classics, the Performer, as befitting its name, was one of the company's high-performance instruments.

The Performer was widely seen in a variety of metallic poly finishes.

Pair of stacked potentiometers, each unit containing both volume and tone controls

Katana, 1986

The year 1985 was a strange one for Fender. An employee buyout saw the formation of the Fender Musical Instrument Corporation, and during the inevitable period of transition that followed, a number of curious models emerged, and none more so than the Katana, by some distance the oddest-looking Fender ever. The impetus to come up with a radical new shape came from Fender dealers, who had seen their market gradually eroded by contemporary designs from new companies like Jackson. So the Katana was born out of duress, designed by a marketing man fiddling with an art program on a Macintosh, built in Japan and halfheartedly launched by a company that disliked the product. It was dropped within a year.

- **DATE** 1986
- **ORIGIN** Matsumoto, Japan
- **WOOD**
  Ash body, maple glued-in neck, rosewood fingerboard.
- **UNUSUAL FEATURE**
  The Katana featured the Fender System 1 locking vibrato unit.

Note the tiny offset triangle inlays on the fingerboard.

The body is an unusual wedge shape with a bevelled edge.

Unlike traditional Fenders, the Katana had a glued-in neck.

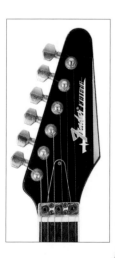

ABOVE: *The Katana was named after a Japanese broadsword – the design of the logo makes this relationship quite evident.*

A return to the classics

The Katana and Performer were the last genuinely unusual guitars to bear the Fender name. It was all too clear to Fender that the vast majority of their customer base wanted the classics – the Strats, Teles, Jaguars and Jazzmasters – and if they wanted odd-shaped superstrats, then they probably didn't want one produced by Fender. Since the beginning of the 1990s, Fender has concentrated on producing variations on original designs at every possible price point. So, beautifully crafted exact replicas of early Stratocasters are available – at a premium – from Fender in the USA; cheaper, workmanlike Fender Strats are built in Mexico or Japan; and quality starter Strats produced in Korea or China are labelled with Fender's Squier brand.

This does not give a complete picture, however. Now one of the biggest musical-instrument corporations in the world, since the early 1990s Fender has bought out, among others, the Jackson, Charvel and Hamer brands, so non-standard-shaped metal-style guitars *are* being produced by Fender, just under different names.

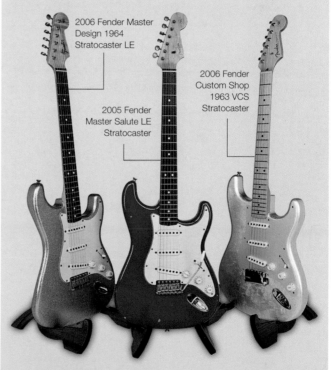

2006 Fender Master Design 1964 Stratocaster LE

2006 Fender Custom Shop 1963 VCS Stratocaster

2005 Fender Master Salute LE Stratocaster

ABOVE: *By the end of the 1980s, Fender had all but ceased producing new designs, concentrating instead on selling its illustrious history, producing heritage versions of its classics, original examples of which were increasingly being sought by wealthy collectors. Many of these were limited-edition models that were produced by the Fender Custom Shop in California.*

The Katana was designed to compete with metal guitars, such as the Jackson Randy Rhoads model.

Gibsons from the 1980s

Like Fender, Gibson's popularity was at a low by the mid-1980s, with a perception, rightly or wrongly, that quality had slipped. At the time, the vogue for high-performance guitars saw some leading players looking elsewhere, to the superstrats produced by Charvel, Jackson and Ibanez, or to the craftsmanship of Paul Reed Smith, whose Maryland factory produced guitars that combined the best of Gibson *and* Fender.

Nighthawk, 1993

While the short-lived Nighthawk superficially resembles a Les Paul, some elements of its design and sound are more reminiscent of Fenders. Not only does it feature a 648mm (25½in) scale length (like a Fender), but it also uses a slanted bridge pickup like a Telecaster. Although this was a humbucker, its low output gave it a cleaner, brighter tone more redolent of a Tele. Similarly, the Gibson mini-humbucker at the neck had a warm, mellow tone closer in character to a Stratocaster than a regular Gibson PAF. The Nighthawk could be considered a response to the versatility of the Paul Reed Smith models produced during the late 1980s.

- **DATE** 1993

- **ORIGIN** Kalamazoo, Michigan, USA

- **WOOD**
  Maple body with mahogany top, mahogany set neck, rosewood fingerboard.

- **UNUSUAL FEATURE**
  The Nighthawk's pickups are switchable between single-coil and humbucker.

The Nighthawk was made available in a number of variations: the model shown here features an NSX single-coil centre pickup.

The electrics feature a push/pull tone control: when pulled up, the humbuckers function as single-coil pickups. Using the selector switch, this gives the guitar ten different tonal possibilities.

Alpha Q-3000, 1985

By 1984, Eddie Van Halen was well established as rock god *du jour*. His eponymous band was one of the most popular in the USA, and he'd reached a global mainstream audience with his astonishing tapped solo on Michael Jackson's "Beat It". He was also the first major player associated with the superstrat – his influential self-built Charvel 'Frankenstein'. Gibson struggled to compete with these new instruments, producing a Q range of its own with a Strat-style body and a mix of single and humbucking pickups. Although excellent rock guitars, they failed to capture their intended market.

- **DATE** 1985

- **ORIGIN** Kalamazoo, Michigan, USA

- **WOOD**
  Mahogany body straight-through neck, ebonite fingerboard.

- **UNUSUAL FEATURE**
  'Fender'-style Gibson; ebonite fingerboard.

Explorer-style headstock, which had originally influenced the Charvel superstrat designs

The fingerboard is made from ebonite, a material created from vulcanizing rubber and commonly used to make bowling balls.

The Q series features a Kahler locking vibrato system.

Spirit II XPL, 1985

Modelled after the Les Paul Junior, Gibson's diverse Spirit range was introduced in 1982. While models differ greatly, all are characterized by a flat, slimline body. The XPL appeared three years later and was an attempt to combine the classic Gibson heritage with features more readily identified with the superstrats, such as a locking vibrato unit and an S/S/H pickup configuration. Some Spirits were also sold as Epiphones, but these did not sell well, and the remainder were rebranded – the original headstock logo can sometimes be seen faintly beneath the Gibson logo.

- **DATE** 1985
- **ORIGIN** Kalamazoo, Michigan, USA (some Spirits were built at Gibson's plant in Nashville, Tennessee)
- **WOOD** Mahogany body, mahogany set neck, rosewood fingerboard.
- **UNUSUAL FEATURE** A locking vibrato system, unusual on Gibson guitars.

Simple dot marker inlays

ABOVE: *Like the classic 1980s superstrats, the XPL is fitted with a locking vibrato system – the model shown here features a Kahler Flyer. These units enabled the guitarist to perform dive-bomb pitch bends and return to perfect tuning.*

Master volume and tone controls, and a variety of coil tap/series-parallel switching options

US-1, 1986

In 1986, with the company struggling, Gibson was bought by three investors looking for opportunities. One of the first instruments under the new ownership was the US-1, Gibson's first out-and-out superstrat. The most unorthodox aspect of the US-1 was its body construction, with a lightweight balsa core surrounded by curly maple. Poor sales once again illustrated that buyers wanted traditional instruments, as one of the owners later admitted, "Every time we strayed from what customers thought we should be we failed. What they wanted were the classic, good guitars."

- **DATE** 1986
- **ORIGIN** Kalamazoo, Michigan, USA
- **WOOD** **Front/Back & Sides** Balsa core surrounded by curly maple, set mahogany neck, rosewood fingerboard.
- **UNUSUAL FEATURE** The use of balsa wood in the body construction.

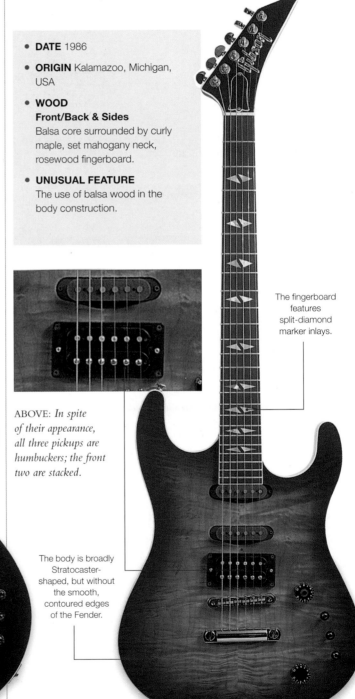

The fingerboard features split-diamond marker inlays.

ABOVE: *In spite of their appearance, all three pickups are humbuckers; the front two are stacked.*

The body is broadly Stratocaster-shaped, but without the smooth, contoured edges of the Fender.

Music Man and G&L

In 1971, two disillusioned Fender employees, Forest White and Tom Walker, formed a new company with Leo Fender as a silent partner, Music Man. In 1975, Fender was voted president by the board, and a year later the first Music Man guitars appeared. However, in 1979, disagreements surrounding business arrangements led to Fender forming a new company, G&L, with former colleague, George Fullerton.

Music Man StingRay Bass, 1976

In 1976, having first concentrated on a new hybrid valve/solid-state amplifier, Music Man produced its first range of instruments, the StingRay 1 and the StingRay bass. More than a little reminiscent of a Fender Precision, the bass featured a soapbar humbucker and a built-in active pre-amp – the first production guitars to use active circuitry to boost frequencies. The circuitboard inside the body was coated with epoxy to prevent it being reverse-engineered and copied.

- **DATE** 1976

- **ORIGIN** Fullerton, California, USA

- **WOOD**
  Ash body (alder used on some models), maple bolt-on neck, rosewood, maple or pau ferro fingerboard.

- **UNUSUAL FEATURE**
  The ovaloid scratchplate gives the instrument a distinctive look.

G&L Cavalier, 1983

In 1979, Leo Fender formed a new alliance with another name from his distant past, George Fullerton, with whom Fender had designed the Telecaster. G&L ('George and Leo') was formed with an agenda to build classic Fender-style guitars to the same high standard as those on which their reputation had originally been built – and which, throughout the 1970s, had diminished. Although Leo Fender and George Fullerton have both since passed on, G&L continues to produce instruments in the tradition of its founders.

- **DATE** 1983

- **ORIGIN** Fullerton, California, USA

- **WOOD**
  Ash body, rock maple bolt-on neck, rosewood or maple fingerboard.

- **UNUSUAL FEATURE**
  Unusual variation on the Stratocaster headstock design.

Unusual three-and-one configuration of tuners – with the G string on the treble side of the headstock

This sculpted headstock shape was introduced in 1982, and has been used on various G&L models since.

Pair of slanted MFD humbuckers

The StingRay was available as a single- or twin-pickup model, with an optional piezo pickup built into the bridge.

The Cavalier was a clear attempt by Fender and Fullerton to update the classic Stratocaster design they had come up with 30 years earlier.

Ernie Ball Music Man Axis Supersport, 1995

In 1984, five years after Leo Fender acrimoniously parted company from Music Man, the company was sold to Ernie Ball, the leading string manufacturer, who resumed guitar and bass production. In 1990, the company achieved an impressive coup, creating the Music Man EVH – a signature instrument for Eddie Van Halen. With its sumptuous quilted maple body and birdseye maple neck, the EVH was one of the instruments of the decade. When Van Halen's endorsement deal was over in 1995, the EVH was modified, rechristened the Axis and given a range of its own.

- **DATE** 1995
- **ORIGIN** San Luis Obispo, California, USA
- **WOOD**
  Basswood body with figured maple top, birdseye maple bolt-on neck, birdseye maple fingerboard.
- **UNUSUAL FEATURE**
  The Axis evolved from the EVH signature model built for rock guitarist Eddie Van Halen.

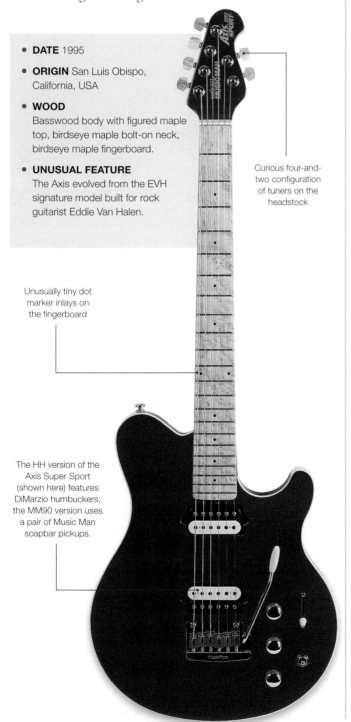

Curious four-and-two configuration of tuners on the headstock

Unusually tiny dot marker inlays on the fingerboard

The HH version of the Axis Super Sport (shown here) features DiMarzio humbuckers; the MM90 version uses a pair of Music Man soapbar pickups.

Leo Fender: the late years

When Leo Fender sold the company he founded in 1965, he was 56 years old and believed he didn't have long to live. So important was his name in the world of the electric guitar that CBS forced him into a non-competition deal that meant he was not allowed to set up a new guitar company for ten years after the sale date.

In 1975, he became president of Music Man. Its business structure, however, was complex. Former Fender employee Forest White owned Music Man, while Fender owned his own business, CLF Research, which produced the guitars for Music Man. In 1979, a bitter rift emerged between the two parties over financial arrangements, and CLF refused to build any more Music Man guitars. White brought in a young luthier named Grover Jackson in an attempt to keep Music Man going, but ultimately he was forced to sell the company. Fender, meanwhile, at the age of 70, set up a successful new company – G&L – producing classic Fender-style instruments.

Although a wealthy man, Leo Fender led a famously frugal life, bringing his own egg-salad sandwiches into work each day. He died on March 21, 1991, in Fullerton, California, a result of complications caused by Parkinson's disease. He is remembered globally as one of the most important figures in the story of the electric guitar.

ABOVE: *Well into his eighth decade, Leo Fender continued to play an active role in the development of new products with G&L, the company he co-founded.*

Ibanez

After the Gibson 1977 lawsuit, taken out in an attempt to curb the Far Eastern copy industry, Ibanez began to concentrate on the production of original models, which featured modern design elements such as slim necks and radical body shapes. The 1980s saw the company produce a number of notable 'pointed' metal guitars, later producing high-end superstrats in conjunction with guitar wizard Steve Vai.

Axstar AX45, 1984

With body styling that resembles an American B. C. Rich model, the Ibanez Axstar series was in many ways a typical mid-1980s rock guitar. It was initially available in three different models (AX40, 45 and 48), each with different pickup configurations. The AX45 here has a humbucking bridge pickup and two single coils, whereas the AX40 has two humbuckers and the AX48 two humbuckers and a single-coil. In 1986, the neck design of the Axstar was overhauled, and a series of Steinberger-styled headless models was introduced.

Rosewood fingerboard with small dot marker inlays

- **DATE** 1984
- **ORIGIN** Matsumoto, Japan
- **WOOD**
  American basswood body, maple bolt-on neck, rosewood fingerboard.
- **UNUSUAL FEATURE**
  The Axstar has a distinctly B. C. Rich-style body.

The original Axstars featured passive pickups; the 1986 models incorporated active circuitry.

Jem 77 BFP, 1987

In 1986, Steve Vai, one of the most technical of rock guitarists, took up an offer to design his own production instrument for Ibanez. The resulting guitar was the Jem, perhaps the ultimate superstrat, designed for the most versatile range of rock sounds and high-speed single-note soloing. It was available in a series of garish colours and patterns. The pickups are by DiMarzio: front and back are PAF Pro Humbuckers with a single-coil centre. The wiring is also interesting, featuring a five-way selector switch that combines the middle pickup with a humbucker coil in positions 2 and 4.

Floyd Rose-style locking tremolo system

- **DATE** 1987
- **ORIGIN** Matsumoto, Japan
- **WOOD**
  American basswood body, maple bolt-on neck, maple fingerboard.
- **UNUSUAL FEATURE**
  The decoration is elaborate, with intricate tree-of-life fingerboard inlays.

A unique feature of the Jem series is the monkey-grip carrying handle.

The blue floral pattern (BFP) from which this Jem takes its name was printed on cloth that was attached to the body and given a heavy nitrocellulose finish.

RG550, 1987

The briefest glimpse of the RG550's profile shows a clear link to the Jem series from which it was derived. The RG series, including its high-end Prestige option, was introduced in 1987 and features a characteristic slimline neck and high-output pickups that add up to make it an ideal rock guitar. A common problem with these original models, however, was severe neck warping that was caused by its thin profile. In 2007, Ibanez launched the RG550XX 20th Anniversary model, which addressed this issue.

- **DATE** 1987

- **ORIGIN** Matsumoto, Japan

- **WOOD**
  Basswood body, maple bolt-on neck, maple fingerboard.

- **UNUSUAL FEATURE**
  The slim neck made stability an issue on early RG550s. The neck design on later models made it a powerful rock tool.

To improve stability on the 2007 20th Anniversary model, the neck was built as a five-piece laminate, with three strips of hard rock maple and two thin strips of walnut, each layer having the grain arranged at a perpendicular angle.

The neck is supported by twin titanium rods on either side of the truss rod.

The RG saw the first appearance of the characteristic Ibanez pointed cutaway horns.

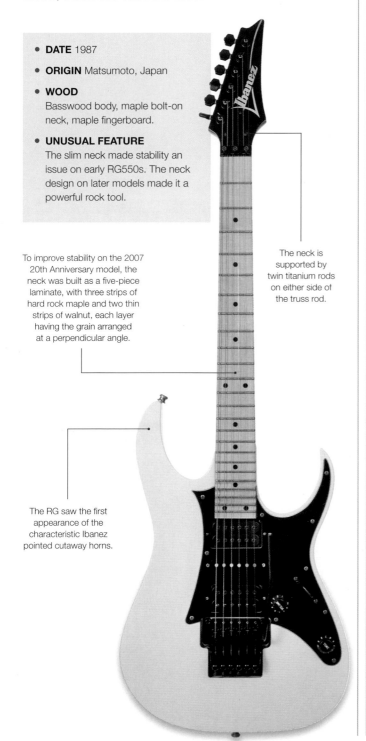

The evolution of Ibanez

ABOVE: *The Ibanez Iceman is broadly based on a Gibson Firebird, but with unique oriental styling. In 1977, Paul Stanley of Kiss was able to develop his own signature Iceman – the PS10.*

The first Ibanez electric guitars were built in 1957, and throughout the 1960s they were a mix of curious oriental styles and copies of established American and European classics – among them imitations of Burns and Hagströms. Towards the end of that decade, the demand for cheap, low-end electric guitars began to wane, and many Japanese manufacturers decided to move their businesses into other areas. Those that remained, however, began to concentrate more on producing quality instruments.

During the 1970s, Ibanez continued to produce copies, in particular high-quality versions of Gibson originals. In 1977, this resulted, perhaps bizarrely, in legal action by Gibson against Ibanez for copying headstock designs. An out-of-court settlement was agreed, and Ibanez thereafter concentrated on original designs.

In the 1980s, Ibanez raised its profile with a number of hi-spec ranges aimed at the rock market that were endorsed by celebrity players. The company now has one of the broadest ranges of production guitars of any manufacturer.

Beyond six strings

The guitar has not always been a six-string instrument. Those that pre-dated the modern classical guitar, emerging during the Renaissance and Baroque periods, were fitted with varying numbers of courses (pairs of strings, and sometimes three or more), and it wasn't until the end of the 18th century that six became the norm. However, there are still those for whom six strings just isn't enough.

Chapman Stick, 1974

Not a conventional guitar as such, the Stick is not even played in the same way. Developed in the late 1960s by US jazz guitarist Emmett Chapman, the Stick is a tapping instrument: sounds are produced by pressing the strings down against the frets rather than plucking them with a pick or fingers. The instrument is held in a near-vertical position, the right hand tapping the top five strings, and the left hand tapping the five bass strings. The skilled player can conjure up complex combinations of bass, rhythm and lead lines.

- **DATE** 1974
- **ORIGIN** Los Angeles, California, USA
- **WOOD**
  Ironwood (later models have used ebony, maple, wenge, padauk, bamboo and synthetic resins).
- **UNUSUAL FEATURE**
  Playing the Stick requires a completely different technique from a standard guitar.

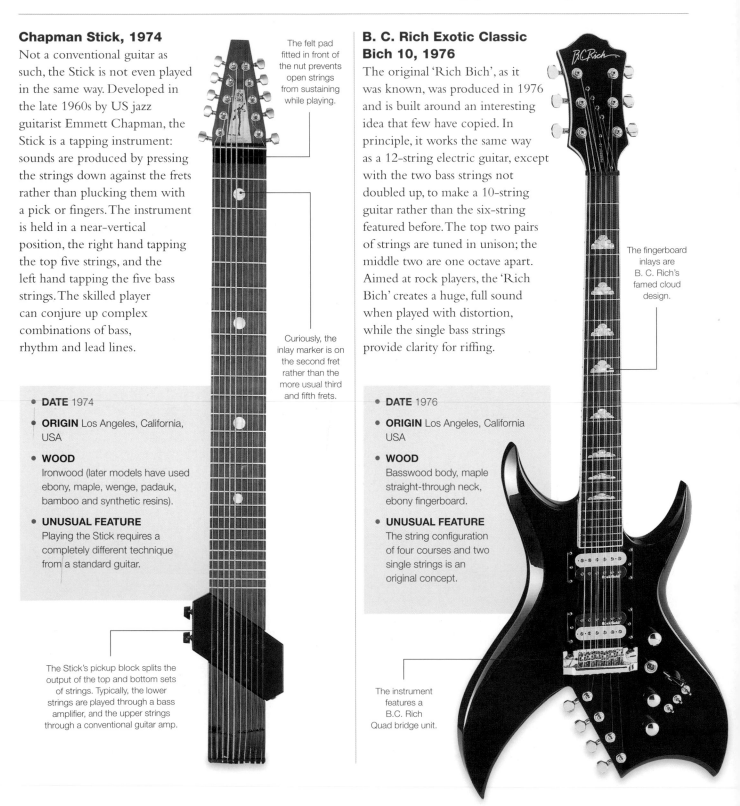

The felt pad fitted in front of the nut prevents open strings from sustaining while playing.

Curiously, the inlay marker is on the second fret rather than the more usual third and fifth frets.

The Stick's pickup block splits the output of the top and bottom sets of strings. Typically, the lower strings are played through a bass amplifier, and the upper strings through a conventional guitar amp.

B. C. Rich Exotic Classic Bich 10, 1976

The original 'Rich Bich', as it was known, was produced in 1976 and is built around an interesting idea that few have copied. In principle, it works the same way as a 12-string electric guitar, except with the two bass strings not doubled up, to make a 10-string guitar rather than the six-string featured before. The top two pairs of strings are tuned in unison; the middle two are one octave apart. Aimed at rock players, the 'Rich Bich' creates a huge, full sound when played with distortion, while the single bass strings provide clarity for riffing.

- **DATE** 1976
- **ORIGIN** Los Angeles, California USA
- **WOOD**
  Basswood body, maple straight-through neck, ebony fingerboard.
- **UNUSUAL FEATURE**
  The string configuration of four courses and two single strings is an original concept.

The fingerboard inlays are B. C. Rich's famed cloud design.

The instrument features a B.C. Rich Quad bridge unit.

Ibanez Universe, 1990

In 1987, rock virtuoso Steve Vai's collaboration with Ibanez produced the Jem superstrat. Three years later, driven by Vai's interest in evolving the electric guitar, Ibanez launched a seven-string version, the Universe. The seventh string, as is common on such guitars, is generally tuned a perfect fourth lower than bottom E – to a B – taking it into the sonic realm of baritone guitar. This kind of seven-string instrument has found a very definite niche among the more progressively minded speed-metal player.

- **DATE** 1990
- **ORIGIN** Matsumoto, Japan
- **WOOD**
  American basswood body, maple bolt-on neck, maple fingerboard.
- **UNUSUAL FEATURE**
  The first seven-string superstrat.

Apart from the additional string and lack of grip hole, the Universe is identical in specification to the six-string Ibanez Jem.

With its two-octave fingerboard, the seven-string Universe, when tuned conventionally (B, E, A, D, G, B, E) has an extraordinary note range of four octaves and five semitones.

DiMarzio Blaze II pickups are fitted.

The bridge unit is an Ibanez Lo-Pro Edge 7.

Steve Vai

From a technical perspective, there are few rock guitarists in the same league as Steve Vai (b. 1960). Born in Long Island, New York, Vai began playing guitar at the age of 13. Famously subjecting himself to lengthy and disciplined practice routines, he later studied at the Berklee College of Music. At the age of 19, he sent a transcription of Frank Zappa's fiendish "The Black Page" to the composer along with a tape of his playing, and within a year he was playing in Zappa's band. During the 1980s, Vai sought more rock-oriented engagements, joining Alcatrazz and ex-Van Halen David Lee Roth's solo outfit.

It was his award-winning 1990 solo album *Passion and Warfare* that established Vai's reputation for seemingly impossible pyrotechnics, in particular the track "For the Love of God". The six-minute instrumental is a tour de force, combining every contemporary rock technique, including vibrato effects, double-handed tapping, harmonics and volume swells. In 2008, readers of *Guitar World* magazine voted it among the top 30 guitar solos of all time.

ABOVE: *While regarded by many modern players as the ultimate rock guitar virtuoso, Steve Vai has also been criticized by some who see his complex playing as over-indulgent showboating. In 2004, he published his 30-Hour Path to Virtuoso Enlightenment, a brutal regimen conceived to be worked through over the course of three ten-hour sessions.*

Diffusion ranges

During the 1960s, the production of Japanese imitations made little difference to the likes of Gibson and Fender – they were of such poor quality that they posed no real threat. Furthermore, most teenage beginners couldn't afford the real thing, so playing a copy was the only real option – and, indeed, made the real thing all the more desirable – until, that is, the copies started matching the originals in quality.

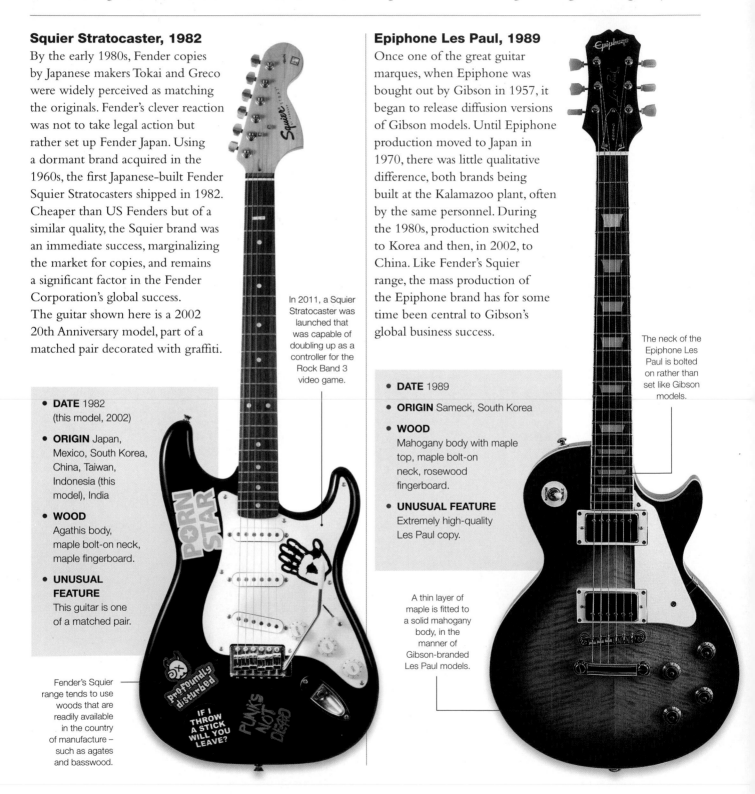

Squier Stratocaster, 1982

By the early 1980s, Fender copies by Japanese makers Tokai and Greco were widely perceived as matching the originals. Fender's clever reaction was not to take legal action but rather set up Fender Japan. Using a dormant brand acquired in the 1960s, the first Japanese-built Fender Squier Stratocasters shipped in 1982. Cheaper than US Fenders but of a similar quality, the Squier brand was an immediate success, marginalizing the market for copies, and remains a significant factor in the Fender Corporation's global success.

The guitar shown here is a 2002 20th Anniversary model, part of a matched pair decorated with graffiti.

In 2011, a Squier Stratocaster was launched that was capable of doubling up as a controller for the Rock Band 3 video game.

- **DATE** 1982 (this model, 2002)
- **ORIGIN** Japan, Mexico, South Korea, China, Taiwan, Indonesia (this model), India
- **WOOD** Agathis body, maple bolt-on neck, maple fingerboard.
- **UNUSUAL FEATURE** This guitar is one of a matched pair.

Fender's Squier range tends to use woods that are readily available in the country of manufacture – such as agates and basswood.

Epiphone Les Paul, 1989

Once one of the great guitar marques, when Epiphone was bought out by Gibson in 1957, it began to release diffusion versions of Gibson models. Until Epiphone production moved to Japan in 1970, there was little qualitative difference, both brands being built at the Kalamazoo plant, often by the same personnel. During the 1980s, production switched to Korea and then, in 2002, to China. Like Fender's Squier range, the mass production of the Epiphone brand has for some time been central to Gibson's global business success.

The neck of the Epiphone Les Paul is bolted on rather than set like Gibson models.

- **DATE** 1989
- **ORIGIN** Sameck, South Korea
- **WOOD** Mahogany body with maple top, maple bolt-on neck, rosewood fingerboard.
- **UNUSUAL FEATURE** Extremely high-quality Les Paul copy.

A thin layer of maple is fitted to a solid mahogany body, in the manner of Gibson-branded Les Paul models.

Epiphone G-310 Emily the Strange, 2009

A popular counterculture cartoon figure, Emily the Strange is a dark-haired teenage girl with a gothic outlook on life. She first appeared advertising a brand of skateboard and surfwear, later spawning a series of comic books and a feature film. The G-310 is a basic Epiphone SG, graffitied with one of Emily's catchphrases. In truth, this a more-than-reasonable instrument that isn't appreciably inferior to its Gibson counterpart, and it is available at less than a third of the price.

- **DATE** 2009

- **ORIGIN** Qingdao, China

- **WOOD**
  Basswood body,
  maple bolt-on neck,
  rosewood neck.

- **UNUSUAL FEATURE**
  The Emily cartoon decoration aims the model squarely at the young-adult market.

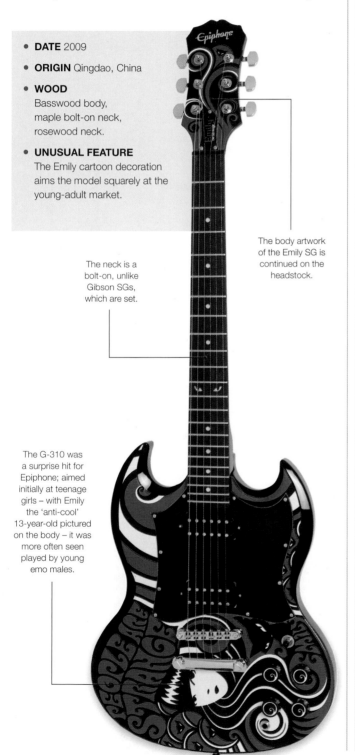

The neck is a bolt-on, unlike Gibson SGs, which are set.

The body artwork of the Emily SG is continued on the headstock.

The G-310 was a surprise hit for Epiphone; aimed initially at teenage girls – with Emily the 'anti-cool' 13-year-old pictured on the body – it was more often seen played by young emo males.

Guitar production tiers

The tiered production system championed so successfully by Gibson and Fender is a strange phenomenon, and one that is, in part, predicated on snobbery.

When Fender Japan first appeared in the early 1980s, it was to provide classic Fender designs at a lower price than the US-built models, steering customers away from the copies being produced in the region. By contracting some of those factories that had been manufacturing inferior imitations, Fender also managed to stem some of the supply. The high quality of these early Japanese Fenders resulted in a consensus at the time that there was little difference in practice between the Squiers and the original US models. This factor in itself helped to make the Squier brand become such an enormous success.

As manufacturing costs rose in Japan, further cut-price tiers of production were added: Mexico, South Korea, Indonesia and, more recently, China. In the modern era, Fender's specialized high-end guitars are produced at the Corona plant in California, whereas the majority of the company's standard models are built at Ensenada, Mexico, and the Squiers are built in Asia. The story is similarly true with the Gibson and Epiphone brands. In truth, all of the guitars produced are fine, serviceable instruments, but – rightly or wrongly – those produced in Mexico and Asia lack the cachet of those built in the USA.

ABOVE: *The 1990s 'riot grrrl' scene saw the first widespread uptake of the electric guitar among teenage females. As a consequence, new companies such as Daisy Rock emerged to produce instruments specifically for this market. In 2006, Fender joined forces with the Japanese Sanrio Corporation to produce a Squier model named after the Hello Kitty cartoon character.*

Europe in the 1980s

The 1980s saw the mass production of European instruments gradually dwindling, caught between the big names in the USA and the low labour costs in the Far East. Names such as Höfner have continued with success – and other famous brands such as Framus, Burns and Hagström have since re-emerged, third parties producing reissues of classic designs – although manufacture is usually in the Far East.

Musima Deluxe 25, c.1972

Guitars by Musima were produced in the former German Democratic Republic, now East Germany. The Deluxe 25 was clearly based around the Fender Jazzmaster/ Jaguar design, and it remained in production into the 1980s. Higher in quality than other Eastern European guitars of the period, the Musima is of a similar standard and build to a cheap Japanese copy, with a plywood body, plastic neck binding and a thin single-coil sound that may appeal to those with retro tastes.

The fingerboard features plastic block marker inlays.

- **DATE** c.1972
- **ORIGIN** Markneukirchen, Germany (former German Democratic Republic)
- **WOOD**
  Plywood body, beech set neck, beech fingerboard (stained to look like rosewood).
- **UNUSUAL FEATURE**
  The four-position tone switch.

The instrument has a separate bridge and tailpiece – the Deluxe 25V also sports a vibrato unit.

Stratocaster-style output jack socket.

Defil Jola 2, c.1977

During the Cold War era, Poland was one of the more Westernized of the Iron Curtain states, and rock music and other cultural imports from the West were broadly tolerated. By the early 1980s, there was a thriving punk and metal scene, to some extent a response to the imposition of martial law, and sales of cheap electric guitars soared. The Defil factory was among the country's major manufacturers of the time. While instruments such as the Defil Jola 2 had a look that was contemporary for the mid-1970s, these were nonetheless primitive guitars that were, out of necessity, widely customized.

The headstock of the Defil Jola 2 features three-a-side tuners – unlike the Fender-style six-in-a-line used on its predecessor.

Unusual full-width fingerboard markers

- **DATE** c.1977
- **ORIGIN** Lubin, Poland
- **WOOD**
  Hardwood body, maple bolt-on neck, rosewood fingerboard.
- **UNUSUAL FEATURE**
  The Jola has sliding volume and tone controls instead of the usual rotary potentiometers.

The Jola 2 is, surprisingly, one of the few production guitars to use fader controls.

Höfner Pro Sound Graphic S5E, 1982

One of the most interesting European production guitars of the period, the S5E is notable for its electrics, the standard tone adjustment being replaced by a graphic equalizer – instead of a single rotary control, tone is adjusted by a series of five faders, each controlling a specific band of audio frequency. The guitar features three single-coil pickups which can be selected in combinations by using the five-positional indents on the rotary control.

- **DATE** 1982
- **ORIGIN** Bubenreuth, Germany
- **WOOD**
  Double-lined maple body, maple neck, rosewood fingerboard.
- **UNUSUAL FEATURE**
  The graphic-equalizer tone control allows for precise tonal choice.

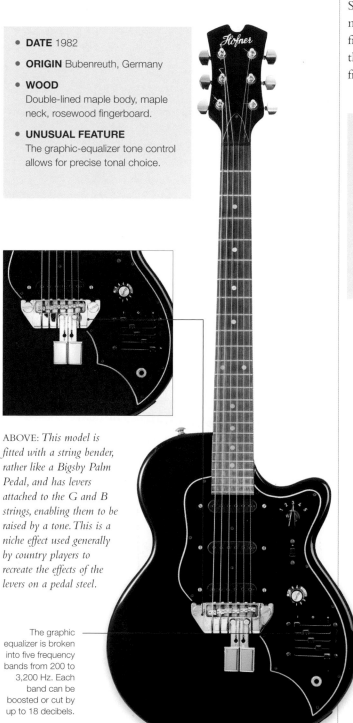

ABOVE: *This model is fitted with a string bender, rather like a Bigsby Palm Pedal, and has levers attached to the G and B strings, enabling them to be raised by a tone. This is a niche effect used generally by country players to recreate the effects of the levers on a pedal steel.*

The graphic equalizer is broken into five frequency bands from 200 to 3,200 Hz. Each band can be boosted or cut by up to 18 decibels.

Hohner Shark's Fin, 1987

The Hohner company was founded in 1857 in Trussingen, Germany, producing accordions and its world-famous harmonicas. Like many other musical instrument manufacturers, during the 1950s Hohner also started to produce electric guitars and basses. The 1980s saw the company's profile as a guitar producer peak, although by this time manufacture had shifted to Japan. The SE603 Shark Fin appeared in 1987 as part of Hohner's Arbor Series, and was a late arrival in an increasingly niche metal-guitar market. Taking its cues directly from the 'spiky' models produced by Jackson, the SE603 quite clearly takes its name from the six-in-line headstock.

- **DATE** 1987
- **ORIGIN** Japan
- **WOOD**
  Laminate hardwood body, bolt-on maple neck, rosewood fingerboard.
- **UNUSUAL FEATURE**
  The shark's-fin headstock shape is highly distinctive.

The fingerboard features dot marker inlays.

The body shape is stylistically similar to metal guitars made by superstrat-producing companies such as Jackson and Ibanez.

This model features two humbucking pickups.

The combined bridge and tailpiece also includes a non-locking vibrato unit.

Signature Stratocasters

The idea of a Fender signature model had been discussed in the early 1980s, both James Burton and Jeff Beck having been approached. However, it was the phenomenal success of the Eric Clapton signature Stratocaster released in 1988 that created a vogue for limited-edition models created with personalized variations specified by some of the world's greatest players.

Eric Clapton, 1988

Approached by Fender in 1985, Eric Clapton's response was to request an exact replica of his own long-term instrument, Blackie – the composite Stratocaster he had famously constructed using parts from three different mid-1950s models. Clapton also specified a neck in the style of his favourite Martin guitar and what he described as a 'compressed' pickup sound, which Fender achieved by using Gold Lace Sensor pickups and active circuitry with a mid-range boost.

- **DATE** 1988
- **ORIGIN** Corona, California, USA
- **WOOD**
  Alder body, maple bolt-on neck, maple fingerboard.
- **UNUSUAL FEATURE**
  To create the sound Clapton wanted, Fender fitted Gold Lace Sensor pickups and active circuitry.

Jeff Beck, 1991

Admired perhaps more by other musicians than the general public, Jeff Beck has operated in many styles – from his early blues and R&B work with the Yardbirds to his complex jazz-rock during the 1970s. The Jeff Beck signature model, issued in 1991, was a souped-up Strat Plus featuring a double bridge pickup, Schaller locking machine heads and an LSR roller nut. It also featured a narrow C-profiled neck with a rosewood fingerboard.

- **DATE** 1991
- **ORIGIN** Corona, California, USA
- **WOOD**
  Alder body, maple bolt-on neck, rosewood fingerboard.
- **UNUSUAL FEATURE**
  Before this model, humbucking pickups had rarely been seen on Stratocasters; one of the coils can be switched out to revert to a standard Strat bridge pickup sound.

The guitarist's signature appears at the top of the headstock.

The Clapton model has a maple fingerboard.

From 2001, Fender Vintage Noiseless single-coil pickups were adopted.

The Dually pickup is effectively two linked single-coils, one of which can be switched out using the push button between the two tone controls.

The Beck model does not use a standard Stratocaster bridge.

Richie Sambora, 1991

Bon Jovi was one of the biggest US bands of the 1980s, its classic rock sound based around the vocals of Jon Bon Jovi and the fretboard heroics of Richie Sambora. The guitarist had established his reputation using Jackson, Kramer and Charvel superstrats – a loose genre of high-performance, Stratocaster-inspired rock guitars. In 1991, Sambora was honoured with his own signtaure Strat, which featured a humbucking pickup on the bridge and a Floyd Rose locking tremolo unit.

- **DATE** 1991

- **ORIGIN** Corona, California, USA

- **WOOD**
  Alder body with ash veneer, maple bolt-on neck, maple fingerboard.

- **UNUSUAL FEATURE**
  The model has a mix of pickups: a DiMarzio PAF Pro bridge humbucker and a pair of Fender Texas Special single-coils.

The fingerboard features dot marker inlays.

The bridge pickup is a DiMarzio PAF Pro, a component commonly used on superstrats such as the Ibanez Jem, or for hot-rodding standard models.

The Sambora model is fitted with a Floyd Rose locking tremolo – many players have found that traditional Stratocaster vibrato units detune the guitar if overused.

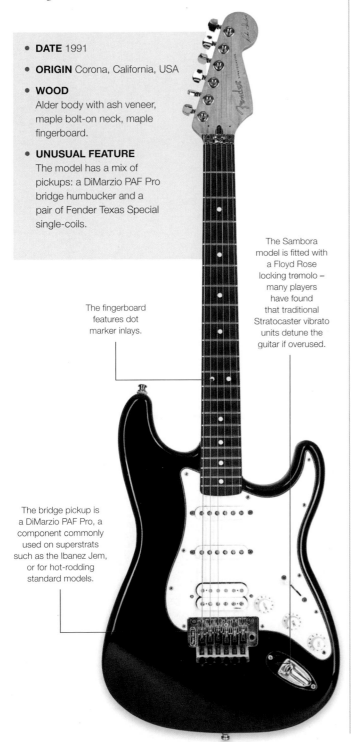

Stevie Ray Vaughan

ABOVE: *Stevie Ray Vaughan in concert, playing his customized Stratocaster, which he gave the name Number One.*

Born in Texas in 1954 – by coincidence, the same year as the guitar with which he would find fame first came off the production line – Stevie Ray Vaughan was inspired to take up the guitar by his elder brother, Jimmy, who later founded the Fabulous Thunderbirds. After most of the 1970s playing on the electric-blues scene in Austin, Texas, Vaughan achieved wider acclaim during the 1980s with his own band Double Trouble.

Vaughan came to public attention, however, as a rock session player, most notably on David Bowie's globally successful *Let's Dance* album. He was able to capitalize on this high-profile success, and during the second half of the 1980s, Stevie Ray Vaughan and Double Trouble were arguably the most popular live blues band in the world.

An exclusive Stratocaster user, his main instrument – which he called Number One – was a battered hybrid of a pair of 1962–63 models. Vaughan's unique customization was the addition of a left-handed vibrato unit, fitted initially so that he could imitate his hero Jimi Hendrix, who played a right-handed guitar left handed.

Having overcome sometimes debilitating alcohol and drug issues, Vaughan looked set for mainstream success, and he and Fender briefly discussed the idea of a signature model when, in 1990, he was killed in a helicopter crash. Two years later, he was paid the ultimate posthumous tribute, with an exact replica of Number One.

Travel guitars

The guitar has always been a travel instrument, many early musicians earning their living as wandering minstrels. Over the years, there have been many attempts to make guitars more portable. Some have been developed to be dismantled or folded at the neck, but a more common approach has been to alter standard dimensions – for example, reducing the scale length, or the size of the body and headstock.

Erlewine Chiquita, 1979

Texas-based luthier Mark Erlewine and his friend Billy Gibbons of the band ZZ Top designed the Chiquita travel guitar in 1979. Unlike other travel electric guitars, many of which are little more than toys, the Chiquita is a well-specified instrument built to a high standard. Following its being played by Michael J. Fox in the film *Back to the Future*, Erlewine licensed production to the Hondo brand during the early 1980s.

- **DATE** 1979
- **ORIGIN** South Korea
- **WOOD**
  Mahogany bound body, mahogany set neck, rosewood fingerboard.
- **UNUSUAL FEATURE**
  At 483mm (19in), the guitar has a short scale length and an extraordinarily small body.

The electrics on the Chiquita are somewhat frugal – the single humbucker passes through a single volume control.

The Chiquita is fitted with a Schaller bridge.

Kay K-45, 1981

Branded in the USA as the Austin Hatchet, the Kay K-45 travel guitar bears more than a passing resemblance to a rifle – especially when packed away in its own purpose-made brown leather case. A laminated through-neck construction, the K-45 features a nut, bridge and, unusually, fingerboard dot inlays all made of brass. In another quirky feature, when the guitar is packed in its case, the strap pokes out of the top, to be used as a carrying strap.

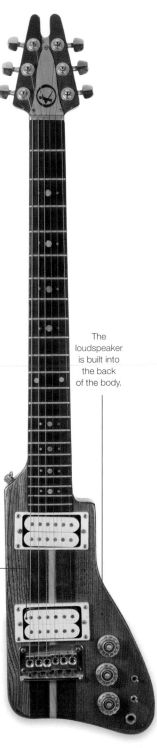

- **DATE** 1981
- **ORIGIN** South Korea
- **WOOD**
  Mahogany/maple/mahogany laminate through-neck design, rosewood fingerboard.
- **UNUSUAL FEATURE**
  The brass fittings, including fingerboard dot inlays, are very distinctive.

The loudspeaker is built into the back of the body.

ABOVE: *The K-45 features DiMarzio Super Distortion-style pickups. Each one has its own coil-tap mini-switch beneath the volume and tone controls.*

Synsonic Terminator, c.1989

A South Korean, short-scale, Strat-style instrument with a clunky oversize vibrato unit, the Synsonic Terminator features its own tiny in-built amplifier powered by a 9-volt battery, complete with speaker and headphone socket. In truth, while this enjoyed some popularity as a travel guitar, this is so only by virtue of its three-quarter scale length and electronics – in fact, it was intended simply as first guitar for a young beginner who didn't possess an amplifier.

- ● **DATE** *c.*1989
- ● **ORIGIN** South Korea
- ● **WOOD**
  Laminated hardwood body and bolt-on neck, rosewood fingerboard.
- ● **UNUSUAL FEATURE**
  The guitar features a built-in amplifier and speaker.

ABOVE: *A small loudspeaker is cut into the body of the guitar, and a low-output battery-powered amplifier is built into a recess at the back of the body.*

Two output sockets: one for a conventional output, the other a headphone socket from the built-in amplifier

Hohner G3T, 1993

Like the Terminator, this was not designed as a travel guitar, but is popularly used for that purpose by virtue of its size. In fact, it is a full-size guitar, with the same 648mm (25½in) scale length as a Stratocaster. However, the Steinberger-style lack of headstock, not to mention the tiniest of bodies, make the G3T more portable than many true travel guitars. It is also capable of a very wide range of sounds, courtesy of the twin single-coil/single humbucker pickup configuration.

- ● **DATE** 1993
- ● **ORIGIN** South Korea
- ● **WOOD**
  Maple body, maple straight-through neck, rosewood fingerboard.
- ● **UNUSUAL FEATURE**
  The headless stringing system helps to keep the overall size much shorter than for a conventional instrument.

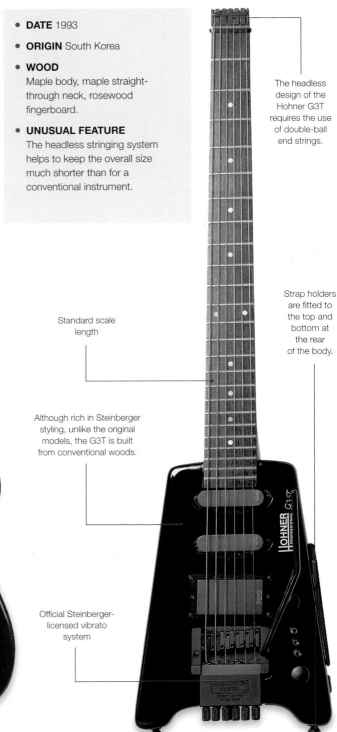

The headless design of the Hohner G3T requires the use of double-ball end strings.

Strap holders are fitted to the top and bottom at the rear of the body.

Standard scale length

Although rich in Steinberger styling, unlike the original models, the G3T is built from conventional woods.

Official Steinberger-licensed vibrato system

The birth of the superstrat

During the mid-1970s, specialist guitar workshops emerged in response to a demand for hot-rodding production-line electric guitars – frequently Fender Stratocasters. Some of this may have been down to the common perception that Fender's standards had slipped; another reason was the growing availability of third-party hardware alternatives. These souped-up instruments would soon become known as 'superstrats'.

Van Halen 'Frankenstrat', 1980

During the early 1970s, luthier Wayne Charvel opened a successful guitar-repair store in Asuza, California. In 1979, he sold the Charvel brand to one of his employees, Grover Jackson. The Charvel profile was already on the rise when a young guitarist named Eddie Van Halen burst on to the scene. Van Halen's 1978 debut album became an immediate rock classic, and the guitarist was depicted on the sleeve playing a custom-built Charvel, complete with his now-famous personalized striped decoration. Shown here is a commercially available exact replica of Eddie Van Halen's original 'Frankenstrat'.

- **DATE** 1980 (original model)

- **ORIGIN** Asuza, California, USA

- **WOOD**
  Ash body, maple bolt-on neck, maple fingerboard.

- **UNUSUAL FEATURE**
  This guitar was customized by Eddie Van Halen himself from a Charvel instrument.

This modern replica even incorporates Eddie Van Halen's unique rolled masking-tape pick holder.

The original pickup was a Gibson PAF humbucker removed from an ES-335. It was later replaced by a Seymour Duncan.

Jackson Randy Rhoads, 1981

In 1981, with Charvel's stock riding high, Randy Rhoads, the highly rated young guitarist with Ozzy Osbourne's band, approached the company to build his own instruments. One of the results was a Flying V shape with the upper half of the body extended to resemble a shark's fin. Grover Jackson was sufficiently impressed to contemplate putting the guitar into production, but believing the shape to be too outrageous for a Charvel, he rebranded it Jackson. When Rhoads was tragically killed in a plane crash, Jackson decided to name the guitar in tribute to him.

- **DATE** 1981

- **ORIGIN** Glendora, California, USA

- **WOOD**
  Maple body, maple straight-through neck, ebony fingerboard.

- **UNUSUAL FEATURE**
  The guitar takes the Gibson Flying V shape and alters it by having the upper fin elongated and lower fin shortened.

The design is a modern classic, still in production and widely used by metal players, among whom Rhoads' playing is still revered.

The Randy Rhoads design evolved from the guitarist's initial commission to produce a polka-dot Flying V-shaped instrument.

This version features a gold-plated scratchplate.

Jackson Soloist, 1984

Although only launched as a production model in 1984, custom versions of a Stratocaster-style body with a pointed Gibson Explorer-style headstock had been made at the Charvel workshop since the late 1970s. The Jackson Soloist became *the* basic superstrat template, with its body styling, Floyd Rose locking tremolo system – which enabled guitarists to perform dive-bomb pitch bends without putting the guitar out of tune – and the combination of single-coil and humbucking pickups.

- **DATE** 1984

- **ORIGIN** Glendora, California, USA

- **WOOD**
  Alder body with maple top, maple straight-through neck, ebony fingerboard. (Many different options were available.)

- **UNUSUAL FEATURE**
  This is unquestionably the most influential superstrat.

The headstock is Jackson's characteristic drop-nose style.

Unlike regular production Fender Stratocasters, the Soloist has a straight-through neck.

The Soloist features a Floyd Rose locking vibrato unit, a radical reinvention of the traditional whammy bar.

Eddie Van Halen

Born in the Netherlands in 1955, Eddie Van Halen's family emigrated to California when he was seven. A teenage guitar-obsessive, Van Halen admits to having spent hours on end copying solos by Eric Clapton and Jimmy Page – the two players he considers his major influences – note-for-note.

In 1976, Gene Simmons of Kiss saw Van Halen and his band live, and offered to record a demo tape. This resulted in a contract with Warner Bros. Released in 1978, Van Halen's eponymous first album was an enormous hit and is now recognized as one of the all-time-classic rock debuts.

The band's sixth album, *1984*, was a top-three hit and yielded the chart-topping single "Jump". During the same period, Van Halen's attention-grabbing, finger-tapping style led to a recording session invitation from producer Quincy Jones: the result was his sublime high-speed solo on Michael Jackson's global chart topper, "Beat It".

Since the turn of the millennium, the guitarist's ill health – including hip surgery to correct problems widely thought to have been caused by his stage acrobatics – placed the band on hold, and Van Halen dropped out of the public eye. In recent years, however, he has started touring again.

ABOVE: *Eddie Van Halen in 1978, with the first of his custom-built instruments – this one using parts procured from Wayne Charvel. Van Halen's characteristic decorative style has featured on all of his instruments.*

The growth of the superstrat

As far as the electric guitar was concerned, the 1980s really was the era of the superstrat. It was a time when no self-respecting rock guitarist would be seen playing a production instrument. When Fender, Gibson and other leading brands attempted to integrate some of the high-performance features found on their new competitors, it was usually with limited success.

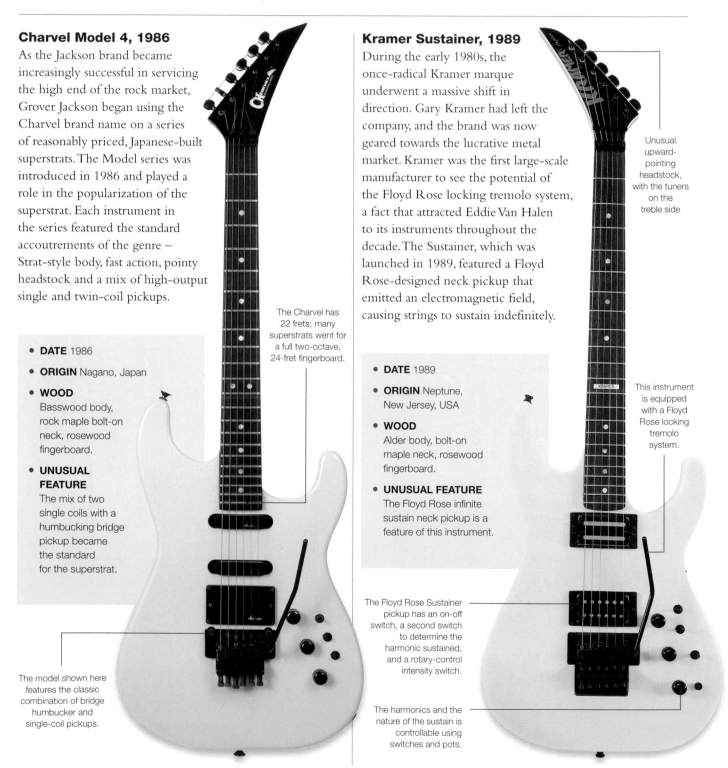

Charvel Model 4, 1986

As the Jackson brand became increasingly successful in servicing the high end of the rock market, Grover Jackson began using the Charvel brand name on a series of reasonably priced, Japanese-built superstrats. The Model series was introduced in 1986 and played a role in the popularization of the superstrat. Each instrument in the series featured the standard accoutrements of the genre – Strat-style body, fast action, pointy headstock and a mix of high-output single and twin-coil pickups.

- **DATE** 1986
- **ORIGIN** Nagano, Japan
- **WOOD**
  Basswood body, rock maple bolt-on neck, rosewood fingerboard.
- **UNUSUAL FEATURE**
  The mix of two single coils with a humbucking bridge pickup became the standard for the superstrat.

The Charvel has 22 frets; many superstrats went for a full two-octave, 24-fret fingerboard.

The model shown here features the classic combination of bridge humbucker and single-coil pickups.

Kramer Sustainer, 1989

During the early 1980s, the once-radical Kramer marque underwent a massive shift in direction. Gary Kramer had left the company, and the brand was now geared towards the lucrative metal market. Kramer was the first large-scale manufacturer to see the potential of the Floyd Rose locking tremolo system, a fact that attracted Eddie Van Halen to its instruments throughout the decade. The Sustainer, which was launched in 1989, featured a Floyd Rose-designed neck pickup that emitted an electromagnetic field, causing strings to sustain indefinitely.

Unusual upward-pointing headstock, with the tuners on the treble side

- **DATE** 1989
- **ORIGIN** Neptune, New Jersey, USA
- **WOOD**
  Alder body, bolt-on maple neck, rosewood fingerboard.
- **UNUSUAL FEATURE**
  The Floyd Rose infinite sustain neck pickup is a feature of this instrument.

This instrument is equipped with a Floyd Rose locking tremolo system.

The Floyd Rose Sustainer pickup has an on-off switch, a second switch to determine the harmonic sustained, and a rotary-control intensity switch.

The harmonics and the nature of the sustain is controllable using switches and pots.

Jackson Warrior Pro, 1990

Introduced in 1990, the Jackson Warrior Pro is one of the more dramatic of the shredder guitars. The body styling shows the influence of the Gibson Explorer, although with exaggerated pointed cutaways at both the neck and the rear. The Warrior features a straight-through maple neck with poplar wings and a two-octave, bound ebony fingerboard. The inlays are Jackson's characteristic pearl sharkfin design. At the time of its launch, it was the company's most expensive production model.

- **DATE** 1990

- **ORIGIN** Glendora, California, USA

- **WOOD**
  Poplar body, straight-through maple neck, ebony fingerboard.

- **UNUSUAL FEATURE**
  The body shape, with its multiple cutaways, is very distinctive.

The fingerboard features Jackson's Rickenbacker-influenced shark's tooth inlays.

The strap button is on the inside of the bass horn.

Unusually pronounced treble horn

The pickups are angled in the reverse way to Fender bridge pickups; this design produces a smoother treble sound and a tighter bass.

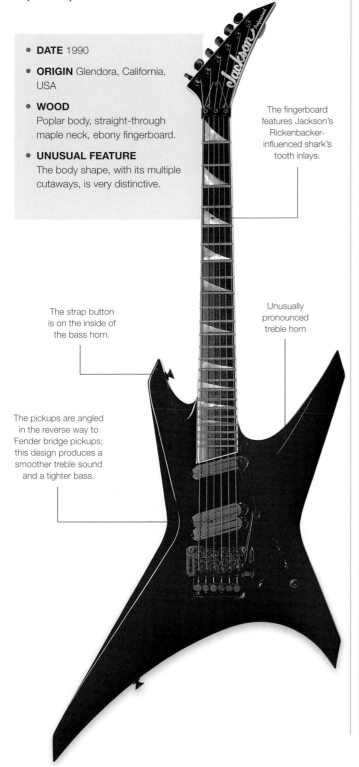

Response to the superstrat

The emergence of the superstrat changed the electric-guitar market during the 1980s, and has had a lasting impact. The move towards these new instruments started in the 1970s, when players realized that they could, with relative ease, hot-rod their existing production models, commonly altering pickups and electrics for a wider variety of sounds, or opting for wholesale replacement of necks and bodies. Fender and Gibson, both of which were in something of a slump during the 1980s, responded with their own takes on the style, but enjoyed little success.

By the mid-1990s, the shredding superstrats had fallen out of vogue, and classic retro styles were back in. What remained, however, was a greater understanding of the potential options for any electric guitar. Fender subsequently issued Stratocasters – often signature models – that combined the instrument's iconic features with superstrat-style combinations of single and switchable humbucking pickups, locking vibrato units and scalloped fingerboards.

LEFT: *The 1991 M-III was Gibson's final attempt at producing a guitar capable of matching the tonal versatility of the superstrat. It featured three humbucking pickups, all of which could be switched into single-coil mode.*

Guitar synthesizers

From the early days of the electric guitar, inventors have sought to incorporate technological innovation into their instruments. In the early 1960s, one of the boldest attempts was to build a Vox Continental organ into a guitar; others took the simpler step of adding analogue effects. With the popularity of the affordable synthesizer in the 1970s came the inevitable hybrid: the guitar synth.

Roland GS-500, 1977

Founded in 1972, Roland quickly established itself as one of Japan's leading music-technology companies. The first Roland guitar synthesizer, the GS-500, appeared in 1977. It was an Ibanez Les Paul-style guitar that connected to an external synthesizer unit, a GR-500. A divided pickup tracks the actions on each individual string and transmits control voltages to the synth unit via a 24-way cable. The guitar also features a humbucker, allowing it to be used as a regular instrument.

- **DATE** 1977
- **ORIGIN** Osaka, Japan
- **WOOD**
  Mahogany body with two-piece maple top, mahogany set neck, rosewood fingerboard.
- **UNUSUAL FEATURE**
  This is a conventional guitar with an external synthesizer unit.

Synthaxe, 1986

It was former BBC Radiophonic Workshop composer Bill Aitken who came up with the idea of the Synthaxe. As ingenious as Roland's first guitar synthesizer hybrids had been, tracking of the notes – the accuracy with which the note played on the guitar was translated electronically – was still a problem. The Synthaxe addresses this by using two separate sets of strings, one for plucking and another for holding down the notes. Pitch data are generated electronically, the frets themselves forming part of the circuitry when they are pressed down.

- **DATE** 1986
- **ORIGIN** Whitney, UK
- **MATERIALS**
  Fibreglass covering metal chassis and neck.
- **UNUSUAL FEATURE**
  This instrument is a controller rather than a guitar in its own right.

The socket on the side of the GS-500 connects to the synthesizer unit, which is equipped with its own stand for on-stage accessibility.

As the fingerboard is used to generate MIDI pitch data, the frets are spaced equally, making it feel unnatural to play for some guitarists.

The control panel features a combination of standard guitar controls and external controls for the GR-500 unit.

The Synthaxe has no sound of its own; rather it sends data to an external, MIDI-equipped unit. It can thus be used to control synthesizers or other instruments, such as electronic drums.

The splitting of the two sets of strings makes the Synthaxe a curious playing experience for many guitarists.

Starr Labs Ztar Z6S-XPA, 2010

The guitar synthesizer never really achieved widespread popularity and is now something of a niche product. Roland has continued to develop the technology in a low-key fashion, leaving new companies such as Starr Labs to innovate. The Ztar comprises strings for plucking notes, but the fingerboard replaces strings and frets with pressure-sensitive switches. The flagship model, the Z6S-XPA, like other MIDI controllers, has no internal sounds of its own but is designed to work with Ableton Live, the popular computer audio recording and looping software.

- **DATE** 2010
- **ORIGIN** San Diego, California, USA
- **WOOD** Composite body, unspecified wooden neck with plastic switches.
- **UNUSUAL FEATURE** The fingerboard and frets have been replaced by 144 switches.

The Ztar Z6S-XPA is configured for use with Ableton Live, the popular computer software.

Controllers for an assortment of software parameters.

Like the Synthaxe, the Ztar makes no sound in its own right; it simply alters parameters for the device it connects to, be it an external sound module or a computer.

MIDI (Musical Instrument Digital Interface)

ABOVE: *Jazz guitarist Pat Metheny was an early user of guitar synthesizer technology. His favoured set-up was a Roland GR-303 linked via MIDI (Musical Instrument Digital Interface) to a Synclavier, an early digital sampling system.*

Developed in 1982, MIDI (Musical Instrument Digital Interface) is a standardized communications protocol that enables suitably equipped instruments – keyboard synthesizers, electronic drums, digital samplers or computers running certain kinds of software – to send data to one another.

For guitarists with MIDI-equipped instruments, this means that whenever a note is played, it is converted into MIDI note data, so it has a pitch value, a dynamic value and an instruction to switch the note on and off. The signal itself has no musical value – the same data could generate any number of different sounds, depending on how the sound modules at the end of the chain have been programmed.

Rather than buying a specific instrument or controller, some guitarists prefer to attach a MIDI pickup to a standard guitar. With the possibility of setting up a separate MIDI channel for each string, one guitar playing live can be used to trigger six separate sound modules.

The modern bass

Since the launch of the first solidbody bass guitar in 1951, as a breed, bass players have since shown themselves to be more open-minded and prepared to experiment than their guitar-toting cousins. New designs and construction materials have become widely accepted, and over the past two decades, use of five- and six-string basses has become increasingly common.

Wal Pro Fretless Bass, 1978

Founded in 1974 by Ian 'Wal' Waller and Pete Stevens, the British-made Wal bass became something of a professional's choice during the late 1970s. Initially custom made, instruments were built from exotic tonewoods and crafted to extremely high standards. Using active circuitry, Wal basses were known for their exceptional sound and playability. In 1978, Wal launched the Pro series, which had fretless five- and six-string models in the range. The unexpected death of founder Waller in 1988 dealt the brand a huge blow, but the company continued operating until 2007.

- **DATE** 1978

- **ORIGIN** High Wycombe, UK

- **WOOD**
  Ash body, laminate ash bolt-on neck, rosewood fingerboard.

- **UNUSUAL FEATURE**
  The Pro series came with four options:
  I – one passive pickup;
  II –two passive pickups;
  IE – one active pickup;
  Pro IIE – two active pickups.

Early Wal Pro necks were a ten-piece laminate construction. The centre was formed from hornbeam with two strips of mukalungu and maple alternating towards the edge of the neck.

The model here is a Pro II, and is equipped with a pair of passive pickups.

Steinberger L Series Bass, 1979

New York luthier Ned Steinberger produced one of the most striking and innovative bass guitars of the past four decades, the L Series. First built in 1979, they are noteworthy both in terms of appearance and construction. The most startling factor is the complete lack of a headstock; the strings are threaded from behind the nut and then tuned from behind the bridge. The Steinberger is built not from wood, but from a proprietary mix of graphite and carbon-fibre, which creates a punchy attack, an even tone and an impressive sustain.

- **DATE** 1979

- **ORIGIN** Newburgh, New York, USA

- **MATERIALS**
  Steinberger Blend, a graphite and carbon-fibre mixture, cast in two pieces.

- **UNUSUAL FEATURE**
  The lack of headstock was radical in its day.

The strings are threaded behind the nut.

Unusual among bass guitars, the Steinberger has a two-octave, 24-fret fingerboard.

The unique body shape enables unimpeded access to the entire fingerboard.

In spite of its small body size, the Steinberger headless bass is well known for producing an even, powerful sound.

Special strings are required, with the balls at both ends. The tuners are concealed behind the bridge.

Fodera Victor Wooten Monarch, 1983

Founded in Brooklyn, New York, the Fodera workshop produces high-specification handmade instruments for the professional end of the market – some of its guitars retail at more than $20,000 with no shortage of takers. The Monarch was Fodera's first model, built from 1983. A very early convert from that year was Victor Wooten, who purchased instrument number 037, which has remained his main instrument throughout his extraordinary career. This signature model is an exact replica of Wooten's favourite bass guitar.

- **DATE** 1983

- **ORIGIN** Brooklyn, New York, USA

- **WOOD**
  Mahogany body with flame maple top, three-piece maple set neck, Indian rosewood fingerboard.

- **UNUSUAL FEATURE**
  Instruments are built to order, so numerous personalized variations are possible.

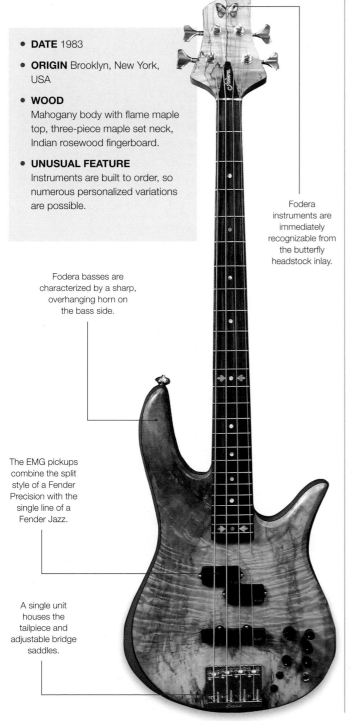

Fodera basses are characterized by a sharp, overhanging horn on the bass side.

The EMG pickups combine the split style of a Fender Precision with the single line of a Fender Jazz.

A single unit houses the tailpiece and adjustable bridge saddles.

Fodera instruments are immediately recognizable from the butterfly headstock inlay.

Warwick Corvette, 2008

Formed in 1982 in Markneukirchen, Germany, Warwick was originally a premium brand that produced a small range of models using the straight-through neck construction often found on high-end models. First built in 1995, the Corvette Standard is one of the company's best-known basses. It features MEC Dynamic Correction pickups – passive units with a powered pre-amp – that act as a kind of compressor, trimming the high frequencies and boosting the low. Corvette production has subsequently been moved to Korea.

- **DATE** 2008

- **ORIGIN** Markneukirchen, Germany (later models were built in Korea)

- **WOOD**
  Bubinga or swamp-ash body (custom models have been built using a wide variety of tonewoods), mahogany set neck, rosewood fingerboard.

- **UNUSUAL FEATURE**
  The MEC Dynamic Correction pickups help to boost the bass sounds.

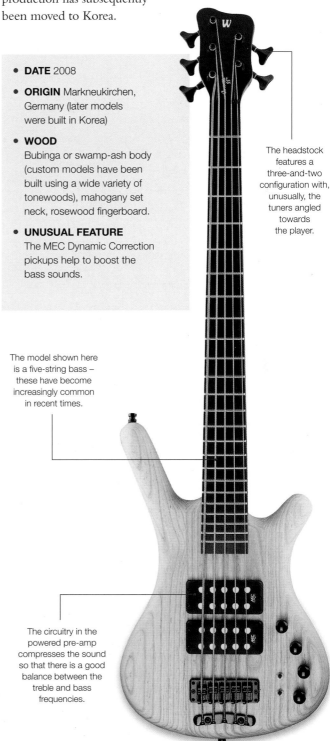

The headstock features a three-and-two configuration with, unusually, the tuners angled towards the player.

The model shown here is a five-string bass – these have become increasingly common in recent times.

The circuitry in the powered pre-amp compresses the sound so that there is a good balance between the treble and bass frequencies.

Curious Strats

During its 60 uninterrupted years of production, the Fender Stratocaster has appeared in numerous variations: different colour options and decorative finishes, and hardware and pickup configurations that are capable of dramatically altering the basic Stratocaster sound. Here is a selection of some of the more unusual offers that have been produced from the Fender Custom Shop.

Twin Neck Custom, 1989

During the first half of the 1970s, when the double-neck guitar was at the peak of its popularity, Fender was really not interested. The company didn't even produce a double-neck guitar until 1987, and the very first serial number produced by the Custom Shop (0001) was for a twin-six-string double-neck, one Stratocaster and one Telecaster. Two years later, the Custom Shop produced this more conventional model, with a Strat on the lower neck and an Electric XII, complete with hockey-stick headstock at the top.

- **DATE** 1989
- **ORIGIN** Fullerton, California, USA
- **WOOD**
  Ash body, maple bolt-on neck, rosewood fingerboards.
- **UNUSUAL FEATURE**
  This was the first Fender 12/6 double-neck.

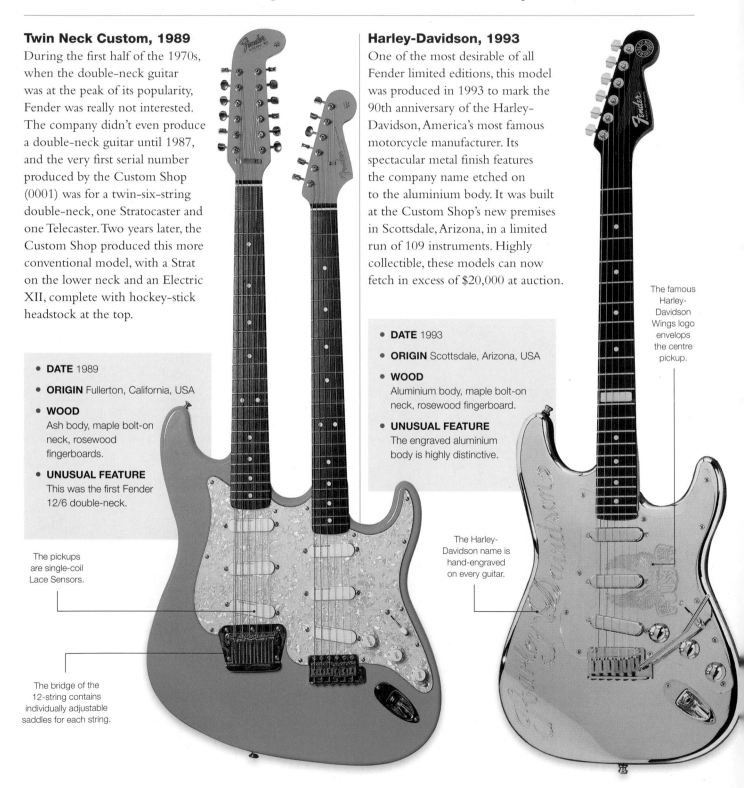

The pickups are single-coil Lace Sensors.

The bridge of the 12-string contains individually adjustable saddles for each string.

Harley-Davidson, 1993

One of the most desirable of all Fender limited editions, this model was produced in 1993 to mark the 90th anniversary of the Harley-Davidson, America's most famous motorcycle manufacturer. Its spectacular metal finish features the company name etched on to the aluminium body. It was built at the Custom Shop's new premises in Scottsdale, Arizona, in a limited run of 109 instruments. Highly collectible, these models can now fetch in excess of $20,000 at auction.

- **DATE** 1993
- **ORIGIN** Scottsdale, Arizona, USA
- **WOOD**
  Aluminium body, maple bolt-on neck, rosewood fingerboard.
- **UNUSUAL FEATURE**
  The engraved aluminium body is highly distinctive.

The famous Harley-Davidson Wings logo envelops the centre pickup.

The Harley-Davidson name is hand-engraved on every guitar.

Hendrix Monterey Pop Fesitval, 1997

On June 18, 1967, Jimi Hendrix reached the climax of his legendary Hendrix Monterey Pop Festival appearance by 'sacrificing' his hand-painted Fiesta Red Stratocaster – first by setting it alight and then smashing it against the floor. In 1997, Pamelina Hovnatanian – known professionally as guitar artist Pamelina H (who had attended the show as a child) – produced a hand-painted artwork that "evoked rather than reproduced" the original Hendrix design.

- **DATE** 1997
- **ORIGIN** Scottsdale, Arizona, USA
- **WOOD**
  Ash body with airbrushed finish, maple bolt-on neck, rosewood fingerboard.
- **UNUSUAL FEATURE**
  This is an authentic re-creation of a1965 Stratocaster.

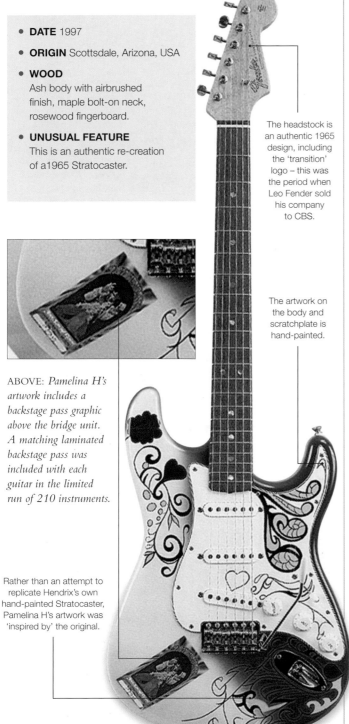

The headstock is an authentic 1965 design, including the 'transition' logo – this was the period when Leo Fender sold his company to CBS.

The artwork on the body and scratchplate is hand-painted.

ABOVE: *Pamelina H's artwork includes a backstage pass graphic above the bridge unit. A matching laminated backstage pass was included with each guitar in the limited run of 210 instruments.*

Rather than an attempt to replicate Hendrix's own hand-painted Stratocaster, Pamelina H's artwork was 'inspired by' the original.

Catalina Island Blues Festival, 1999

The Fender Custom shop has become well known for producing one-off designs. Pamelina H, arguably the leading figure in the world of guitar art, produced this instrument for the 1999 Catalina Island Blues Festival. Taking a body intricately carved by George Amicay, Pamelina H created the spectacular mermaid artwork by using airbrushing techniques. The festival ran from 1997 to 2001, a different design being produced for each year.

- **DATE** 1999
- **ORIGIN** Corona, California, USA
- **WOOD**
  Ash body, maple bolt-on neck, rosewood fingerboard.
- **UNUSUAL FEATURE**
  George Amicay's carving and Pamelina H's airbrushed artwork are incredibly intricate.

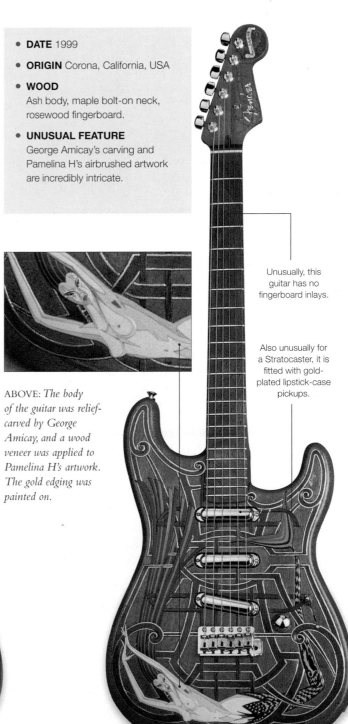

Unusually, this guitar has no fingerboard inlays.

Also unusually for a Stratocaster, it is fitted with gold-plated lipstick-case pickups.

ABOVE: *The body of the guitar was relief-carved by George Amicay, and a wood veneer was applied to Pamelina H's artwork. The gold edging was painted on.*

Fender in the 1990s

During the 1990s, while Fender concentrated its business on classic designs from the 1950s, it did also launch a number of new models. There was nothing as outré as the Katana or Performer from the previous decade, however, as, even though these were new designs, they were firmly rooted in the Fender tradition, with an emphasis on Stratocaster and Jaguar shapes.

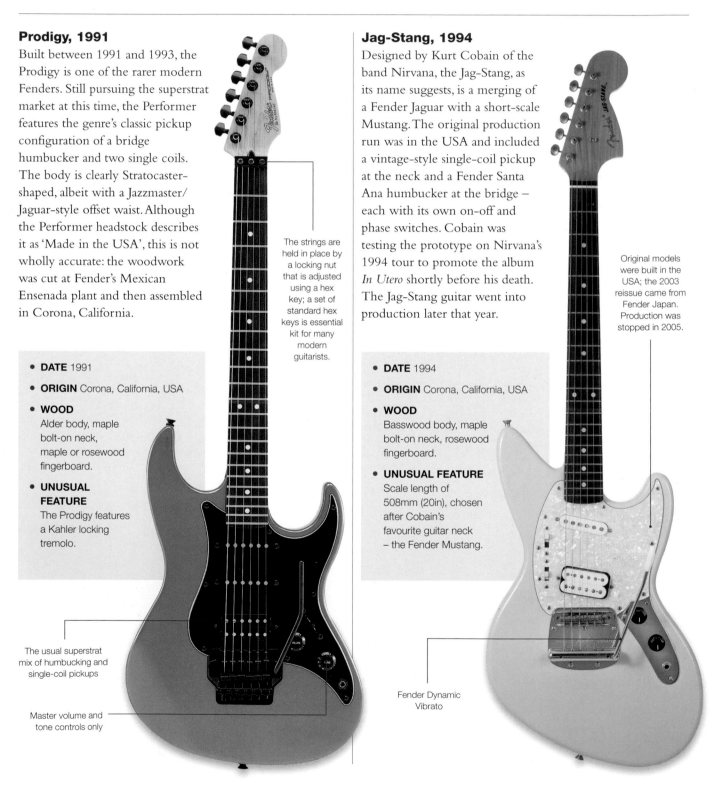

Prodigy, 1991

Built between 1991 and 1993, the Prodigy is one of the rarer modern Fenders. Still pursuing the superstrat market at this time, the Performer features the genre's classic pickup configuration of a bridge humbucker and two single coils. The body is clearly Stratocaster-shaped, albeit with a Jazzmaster/Jaguar-style offset waist. Although the Performer headstock describes it as 'Made in the USA', this is not wholly accurate: the woodwork was cut at Fender's Mexican Ensenada plant and then assembled in Corona, California.

- **DATE** 1991
- **ORIGIN** Corona, California, USA
- **WOOD** Alder body, maple bolt-on neck, maple or rosewood fingerboard.
- **UNUSUAL FEATURE** The Prodigy features a Kahler locking tremolo.

The strings are held in place by a locking nut that is adjusted using a hex key; a set of standard hex keys is essential kit for many modern guitarists.

The usual superstrat mix of humbucking and single-coil pickups

Master volume and tone controls only

Jag-Stang, 1994

Designed by Kurt Cobain of the band Nirvana, the Jag-Stang, as its name suggests, is a merging of a Fender Jaguar with a short-scale Mustang. The original production run was in the USA and included a vintage-style single-coil pickup at the neck and a Fender Santa Ana humbucker at the bridge – each with its own on-off and phase switches. Cobain was testing the prototype on Nirvana's 1994 tour to promote the album *In Utero* shortly before his death. The Jag-Stang guitar went into production later that year.

- **DATE** 1994
- **ORIGIN** Corona, California, USA
- **WOOD** Basswood body, maple bolt-on neck, rosewood fingerboard.
- **UNUSUAL FEATURE** Scale length of 508mm (20in), chosen after Cobain's favourite guitar neck – the Fender Mustang.

Original models were built in the USA; the 2003 reissue came from Fender Japan. Production was stopped in 2005.

Fender Dynamic Vibrato

Cyclone, 1997

Introduced in 1997, the Cyclone was styled on the Mustang student guitar of the 1960s, but with a significantly different specification. The body of the Cyclone is built from poplar, and is thicker than the body of a Mustang, which in recent guises had been built from basswood. Five years later, a number of cosmetic changes were introduced to the Cyclone II, including racing stripes. The new model also offered a wide variety of pickup options. The entire Cyclone range was discontinued by Fender in 2007.

Toronado, 1998

Part of Fender's Deluxe series of Mexican-built instruments, like the Cyclone, the Toronado also has a 629mm (24¾ in) scale length – which is the same standard length as Gibson guitars and 19mm (¾ in) shorter than most other Fenders. The Toronado body is styled on the lines of the Jaguar and Jazzmaster, and is fitted with a pair of Fender Atomic humbucking pickups. In 2004, a Korean version – known as the Toronado HH – was introduced, featuring metallic colours as well as racing stripes.

- • **DATE** 1997
- • **ORIGIN** Ensenada, Mexico (a US-built version was offered briefly in 2002)
- • **WOOD** Poplar body, maple bolt-on neck, rosewood fingerboard.
- • **UNUSUAL FEATURE** The humbucker/single/single pickup configuration is rare on a Fender.

- • **DATE** 1998
- • **ORIGIN** Ensenada, Mexico
- • **WOOD** Alder body, maple bolt-on neck, rosewood fingerboard.
- • **UNUSUAL FEATURE** The instrument has a 629mm (24¾in) scale length – shorter than a normal Fender.

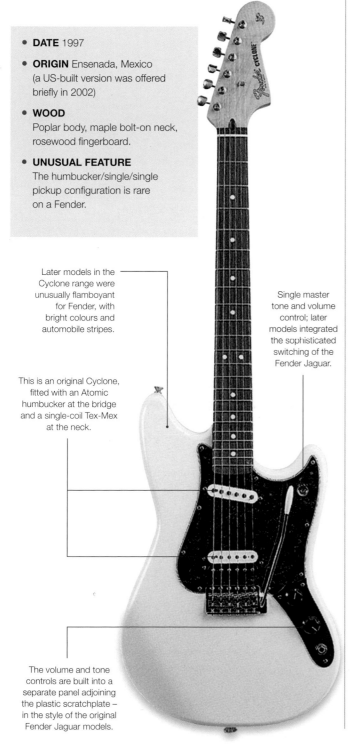

Later models in the Cyclone range were unusually flamboyant for Fender, with bright colours and automobile stripes.

Single master tone and volume control; later models integrated the sophisticated switching of the Fender Jaguar.

This is an original Cyclone, fitted with an Atomic humbucker at the bridge and a single-coil Tex-Mex at the neck.

The volume and tone controls are built into a separate panel adjoining the plastic scratchplate – in the style of the original Fender Jaguar models.

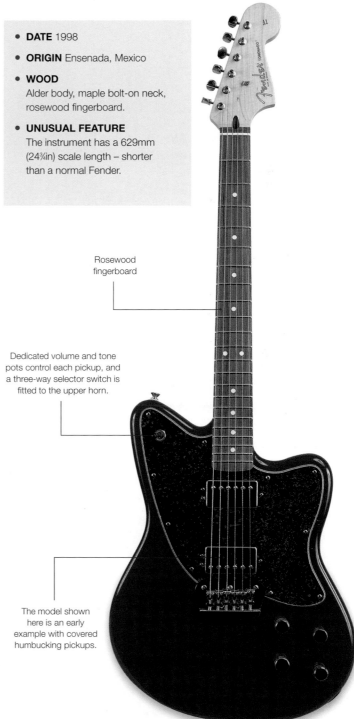

Rosewood fingerboard

Dedicated volume and tone pots control each pickup, and a three-way selector switch is fitted to the upper horn.

The model shown here is an early example with covered humbucking pickups.

The reissue vogue

By the 1990s, the vintage-guitar market was enjoying a period of rapid growth, with second-hand prices for vintage Fender and Gibson models – even those barely 20 years old – well beyond the pockets of most ordinary musicians. Taking advantage of this developing trend, both Fender and Gibson began programmes of reissuing authentic replicas of popular classics.

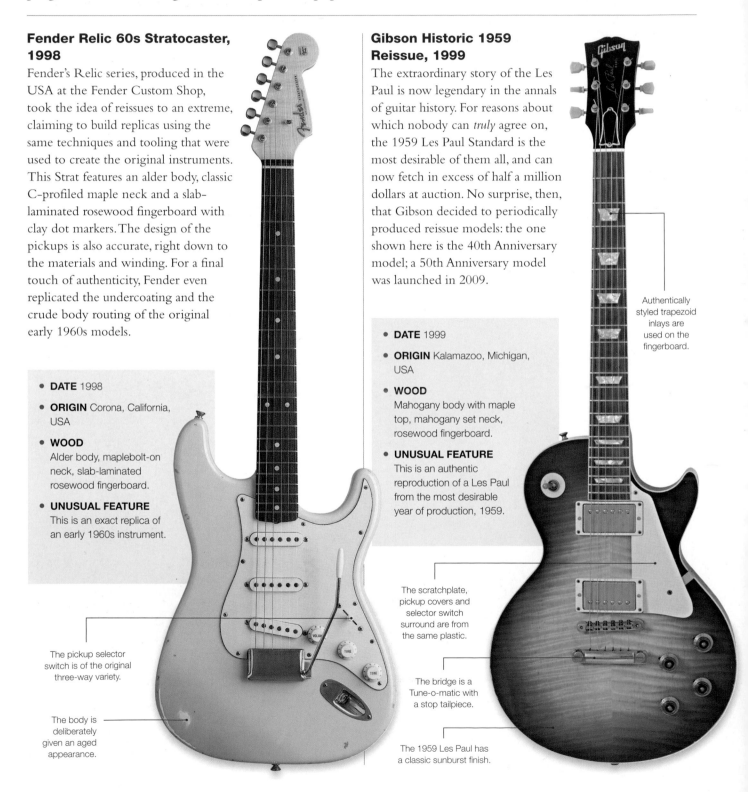

Fender Relic 60s Stratocaster, 1998

Fender's Relic series, produced in the USA at the Fender Custom Shop, took the idea of reissues to an extreme, claiming to build replicas using the same techniques and tooling that were used to create the original instruments. This Strat features an alder body, classic C-profiled maple neck and a slab-laminated rosewood fingerboard with clay dot markers. The design of the pickups is also accurate, right down to the materials and winding. For a final touch of authenticity, Fender even replicated the undercoating and the crude body routing of the original early 1960s models.

- **DATE** 1998
- **ORIGIN** Corona, California, USA
- **WOOD**
  Alder body, maplebolt-on neck, slab-laminated rosewood fingerboard.
- **UNUSUAL FEATURE**
  This is an exact replica of an early 1960s instrument.

The pickup selector switch is of the original three-way variety.

The body is deliberately given an aged appearance.

Gibson Historic 1959 Reissue, 1999

The extraordinary story of the Les Paul is now legendary in the annals of guitar history. For reasons about which nobody can *truly* agree on, the 1959 Les Paul Standard is the most desirable of them all, and can now fetch in excess of half a million dollars at auction. No surprise, then, that Gibson decided to periodically produced reissue models: the one shown here is the 40th Anniversary model; a 50th Anniversary model was launched in 2009.

- **DATE** 1999
- **ORIGIN** Kalamazoo, Michigan, USA
- **WOOD**
  Mahogany body with maple top, mahogany set neck, rosewood fingerboard.
- **UNUSUAL FEATURE**
  This is an authentic reproduction of a Les Paul from the most desirable year of production, 1959.

Authentically styled trapezoid inlays are used on the fingerboard.

The scratchplate, pickup covers and selector switch surround are from the same plastic.

The bridge is a Tune-o-matic with a stop tailpiece.

The 1959 Les Paul has a classic sunburst finish.

Fender Classic '72 Custom, 2004

The year 1972 was a key one for the Fender Telecaster, as three new models – the Thinline, Custom and Deluxe – were all introduced. In 2004, Fender launched the Classic '72 series, replicas of these three by now long-discontinued Telecaster models. The original Custom was produced until 1981, but it had retained a cult following in the years after its production ceased. The Classic reissue was at first built by Fender Japan, but production was later moved to the Ensenada plant in Mexico.

- **DATE** 2004
- **ORIGIN** Hamamatso, Japan and Ensenada, Mexico
- **WOOD** Alder body, maple bolt-on neck, maple or rosewood fingerboard.
- **UNUSUAL FEATURE** The pickups fitted to Japanese models create a different sound from the Mexican-built models.

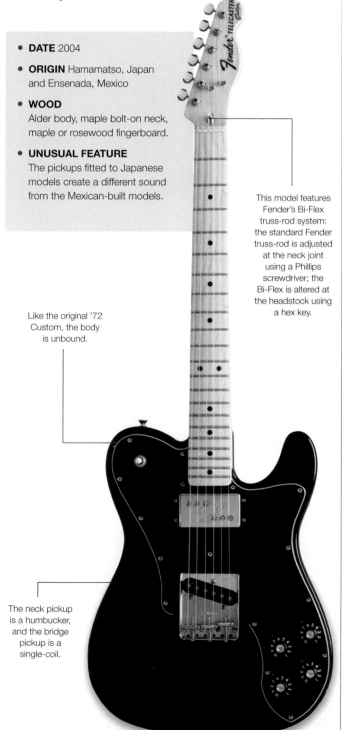

This model features Fender's Bi-Flex truss-rod system: the standard Fender truss-rod is adjusted at the neck joint using a Phillips screwdriver; the Bi-Flex is altered at the headstock using a hex key.

Like the original '72 Custom, the body is unbound.

The neck pickup is a humbucker, and the bridge pickup is a single-coil.

Gibson Les Paul 1958 Aged Reissue, 2008

The popularity (and rarity) of the 1958 and 1959 Les Paul models among young electric blues-rock players led Gibson to revive the design in 1968. Original models from 1958–59 are now so desirable that they pass hands for six-figure sums, and are rarely seen. In 2008, Gibson exhibited a new level of fetishism with an instantly collectible 200-run 50th Anniversary model that matched as closely possible the technical specifications of an original 1958, and was artificially aged to appear as if it had taken half a century of heavy use.

- **DATE** 2008
- **ORIGIN** Kalamazoo, Michigan, USA
- **WOOD** Mahogany body with maple top, mahogany set neck, rosewood fingerboard.
- **UNUSUAL FEATURE** The artificial ageing by Gibson luthier Tom Murphy helped to make this an instant classic for collectors.

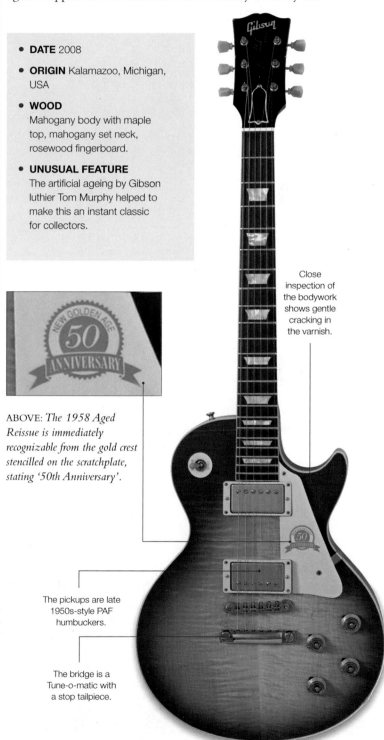

ABOVE: *The 1958 Aged Reissue is immediately recognizable from the gold crest stencilled on the scratchplate, stating '50th Anniversary'.*

Close inspection of the bodywork shows gentle cracking in the varnish.

The pickups are late 1950s-style PAF humbuckers.

The bridge is a Tune-o-matic with a stop tailpiece.

Washburn and Parker

Here we'll take a look at two small but nonetheless significant US guitar manufacturers. The Washburn brand name goes back to Chicago in the 1880s and makes much of its links to the early blues players, but the company as we know it today has only existed since 1974. Parker is an even newer name, noted especially for producing the Fly, one of the most important new guitars since the early 1990s.

Parker Fly Artist, 1993

The extraordinary Parker Fly is arguably the most radical production guitar of the past two decades to find itself with a degree of popular acceptance. Developed in 1993 by Ken Parker and Larry Fishman, their aim was relatively simple: to produce a guitar that was significantly lighter than others on the market, but that was just as solid in strength. They achieved this by creating a wooden frame with a shell built from a powerful carbon and fibreglass epoxy; the fingerboard is constructed from the same material.

- **DATE** 1993
- **ORIGIN** Wilmington, Massachusetts, USA
- **WOOD** Spruce frame with carbon and fibreglass shell, poplar set neck, carbon and fibreglass fingerboard.
- **UNUSUAL FEATURE** The construction and materials used are radical.

Washburn Bettencourt N8 Double Neck, 1995

Portuguese-born guitarist Nuno Bettencourt established his reputation for guitar heroics during the 1980s with the Boston band Extreme. In 1990, Washburn issued the first of a series of Bettencourt-designed signature guitars. The N8 is an exotic-looking double-neck, the twelve-string part of which features a standard headstock with the second string of each course tuned from behind the bridge.

- **DATE** 1995
- **ORIGIN** Chicago, Illinois, USA
- **WOOD** Swamp ash body, maple body, maple set necks, ebony fingerboards.
- **UNUSUAL FEATURE** The manner in which the second course of strings on the 12-string neck are secured and tuned behind the bridge.

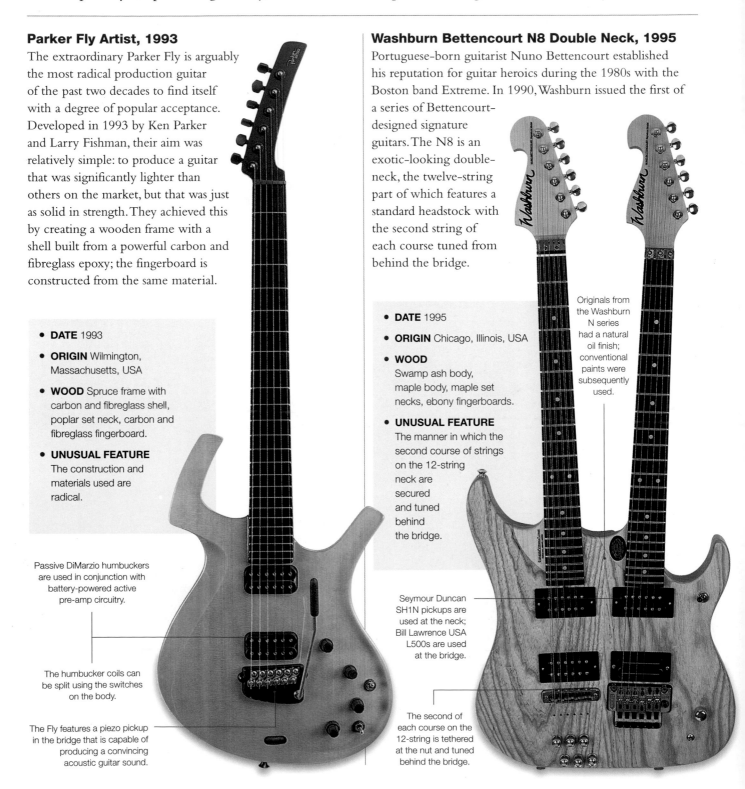

Passive DiMarzio humbuckers are used in conjunction with battery-powered active pre-amp circuitry.

The humbucker coils can be split using the switches on the body.

The Fly features a piezo pickup in the bridge that is capable of producing a convincing acoustic guitar sound.

Originals from the Washburn N series had a natural oil finish; conventional paints were subsequently used.

Seymour Duncan SH1N pickups are used at the neck; Bill Lawrence USA L500s are used at the bridge.

The second of each course on the 12-string is tethered at the nut and tuned behind the bridge.

Parker MIDIFly, 1998

Widely viewed as the best guitar MIDI controller around, the Parker MIDIFly has all the features of a standard Fly, although, unlike the early models, it was built with a solid mahogany body, as most standard Flys were by this time. The MIDIFly has both MIDI in and out sockets, connection to which is made via the MIDIAxe junction box, which then connects to an external sound module or suitably equipped computer for recording. There is also accompanying computer software for editing and configuring the MIDI interface.

- **DATE** 1998
- **ORIGIN** Wilmington, Massachusetts, USA
- **WOOD** Mahogany body, mahogany, carbon and fibreglass set neck, carbon-fibre fingerboard.
- **UNUSUAL FEATURE** Contains MIDI sockets alongside audio sockets.

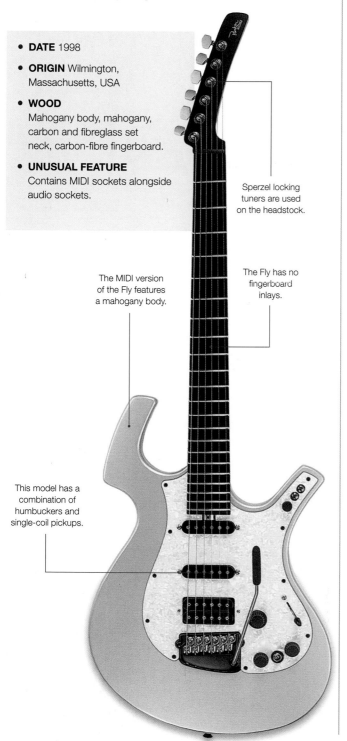

Sperzel locking tuners are used on the headstock.

The MIDI version of the Fly features a mahogany body.

The Fly has no fingerboard inlays.

This model has a combination of humbuckers and single-coil pickups.

Washburn Dimebag Darrell Stealth, 2000

When Washburn teamed up with 'Dimebag Darrell' Abbott in 2000, he was one of the most popular shredders of his time, having established his reputation with Pantera, one of America's top-selling metal bands. The Washburn Stealth was based on the Dean ML that Dimebag had popularized earlier in his career. The shape is Gibson-inspired – a Flying V crossed with the upper half of a Gibson Explorer, with all the extremities exaggerated. The Dimebag story ended in tragedy in 2004 when he was gunned down on stage by a paranoid schizophrenic who had become convinced that the guitarist was 'stealing' his thoughts.

- **DATE** 2000
- **ORIGIN** Chicago, Illinois, USA (budget models built in Korea)
- **WOOD** Mahogany body, mahogany set neck (Korean models bolt-on), ebony fingerboard.
- **UNUSUAL FEATURE** The V headstock is distinctive.

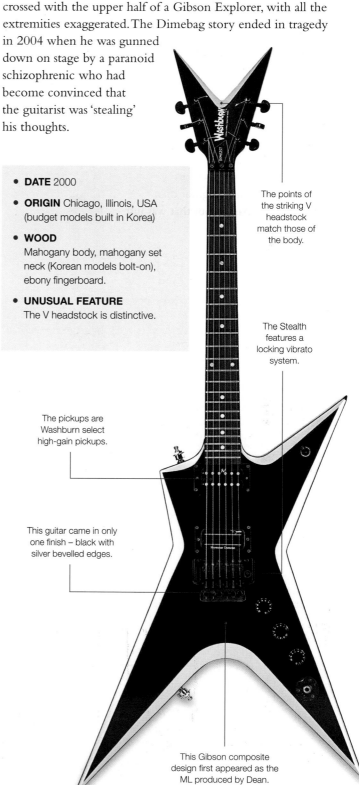

The points of the striking V headstock match those of the body.

The Stealth features a locking vibrato system.

The pickups are Washburn select high-gain pickups.

This guitar came in only one finish – black with silver bevelled edges.

This Gibson composite design first appeared as the ML produced by Dean.

Les Paul special models

Like most of the long-established guitar brands, a good deal of Gibson's business comes from limited-edition reissues of classic models. Sometimes these are attempts to replicate a popular original model from a specific period; on other occasions they are linked to a specific musician or a related brand. Here is a small selection of modern Les Paul special editions.

Gibson Les Paul 60 Corvette, 1995

"The Chevrolet Corvette and the Gibson Les Paul exemplify the innovative vision of two great American companies in the early 1950s" – so ran the press release for an intriguing pair of guitars. The 60 Corvette is, as the name suggests, a Les Paul Standard styled in the manner of a 1960 Corvette. Available in a variety of authentic Chevy paint jobs, the curved white panel follows the same contour as that found on the sides of the car, and includes the three chrome fins. The Corvette logo appears on the fingerboard as an inlay. Later that year, the Gibson Custom Shop produced a similar tribute – this time, 1963 Corvette Stingray styling was applied to an SG.

- **DATE** 1995
- **ORIGIN** Kalamazoo, Michigan, USA
- **WOOD** Mahogany body with maple top, maple set neck, rosewood fingerboard.
- **UNUSUAL FEATURE** The guitar was issued with authentic 1960s Corvette colours and styling features.

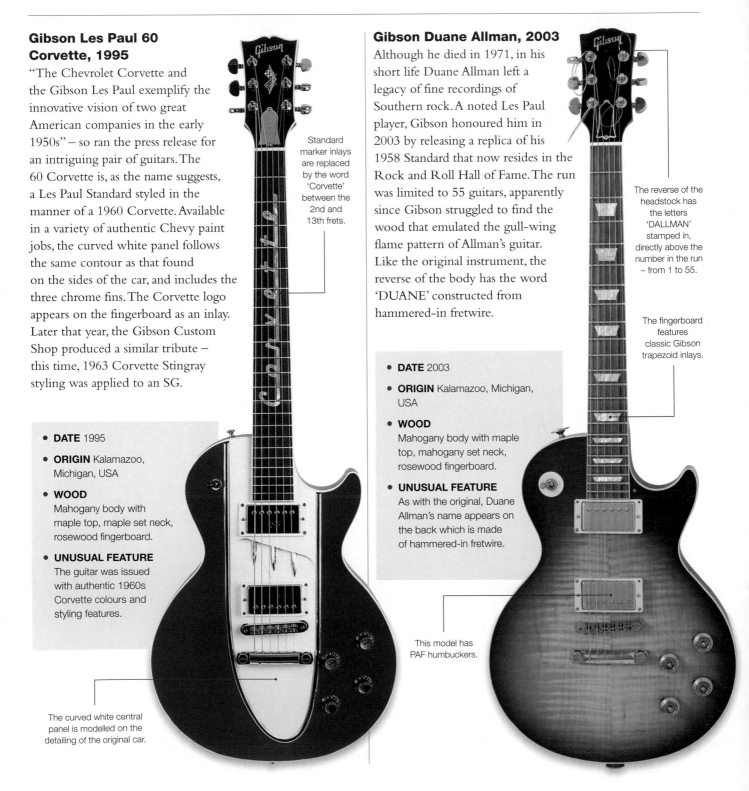

Standard marker inlays are replaced by the word 'Corvette' between the 2nd and 13th frets.

The curved white central panel is modelled on the detailing of the original car.

Gibson Duane Allman, 2003

Although he died in 1971, in his short life Duane Allman left a legacy of fine recordings of Southern rock. A noted Les Paul player, Gibson honoured him in 2003 by releasing a replica of his 1958 Standard that now resides in the Rock and Roll Hall of Fame. The run was limited to 55 guitars, apparently since Gibson struggled to find the wood that emulated the gull-wing flame pattern of Allman's guitar. Like the original instrument, the reverse of the body has the word 'DUANE' constructed from hammered-in fretwire.

- **DATE** 2003
- **ORIGIN** Kalamazoo, Michigan, USA
- **WOOD** Mahogany body with maple top, mahogany set neck, rosewood fingerboard.
- **UNUSUAL FEATURE** As with the original, Duane Allman's name appears on the back which is made of hammered-in fretwire.

The reverse of the headstock has the letters 'DALLMAN' stamped in, directly above the number in the run – from 1 to 55.

The fingerboard features classic Gibson trapezoid inlays.

This model has PAF humbuckers.

Epiphone Zakk Wylde Les Paul Custom Buzzsaw, 2004

Metal guitarist Zakk Wylde has been honoured with a number of Epiphone and Gibson signature guitars. He is particularly well known for two of his decorative patterns: the black-and-white Bullseye and the orange-and-black Buzzsaw shown here. The Buzzsaw is a Les Paul variation built in the Far East, kitted out with heavy-duty EMG humbuckers. Wylde's signature Epiphones are very popular with fledgeling rock players.

- **DATE** 2004

- **ORIGIN** Qingdao, China

- **WOOD**
  Mahogany body, maple set neck, rosewood fingerboard.

- **UNUSUAL FEATURE**
  The orange-and-black Buzzsaw pattern is a Zakk Wylde signature design.

The fingerboard has block marker inlays.

Unusual even for a modern Les Paul, the Zakk Wylde Epiphone is fitted with EMG active humbucking pickups powered by a 9-volt battery.

Both black-and-white Bullseye and orange-and-black Buzzsaw variations are immediately recognizable as Zakk Wylde signature models.

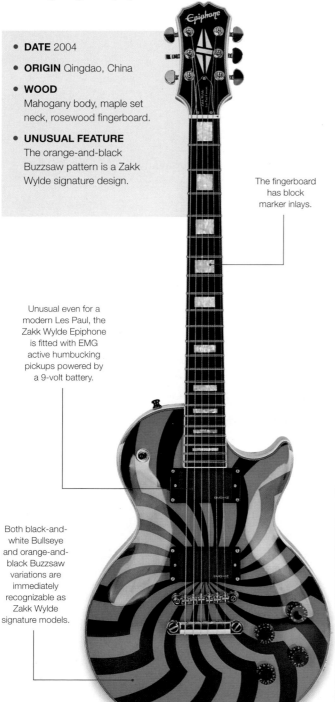

Zakk Wylde

ABOVE: *Zakk Wylde in action with Black Label Society during the band's 2011 UK tour. As always, Wylde is seen playing his signature black-and-white Bullseye Gibson Les Paul.*

Born in Bayonne, New Jersey in 1967, Zakk Wylde came to prominence in the late 1980s. Having sent a tape to Ozzy Osbourne, he joined the former Black Sabbath singer's band in 1989, and has been Osbourne's principal sideman for much of the time since. (Randy Rhoads, Osbourne's former guitarist, who had been tragically killed in a plane crash in 1982, remains Wylde's most significant influence, both as a player and performer.)

Wylde also tours and records with his own band, Black Label Society. With varying line-ups, it has been a staple of the global rock-festival circuit, and Wylde is now established as one of the finest classic-rock players of the modern era – a fact acknowledged in 2006 by his induction into the Hollywood Rock Walk of Fame.

Wylde is also well known for his endorsement of a variety of signature Gibson and Epiphone Les Paul models, all of which feature his characteristic black-and-white/black-and-orange Bullseye and Buzzsaw designs.

Perverse guitars

Occasionally a guitar designer emerges with an idea that rips up the original template and contemplates a radical redesign of the guitar. Both Allan Gittler in the 1970s and Ulrich Teuffel more recently went back to the most basic of questions: what does each element do, and is it really needed? Gittler suggested that a fingerboard was not required; Teuffel largely dispensed with the body.

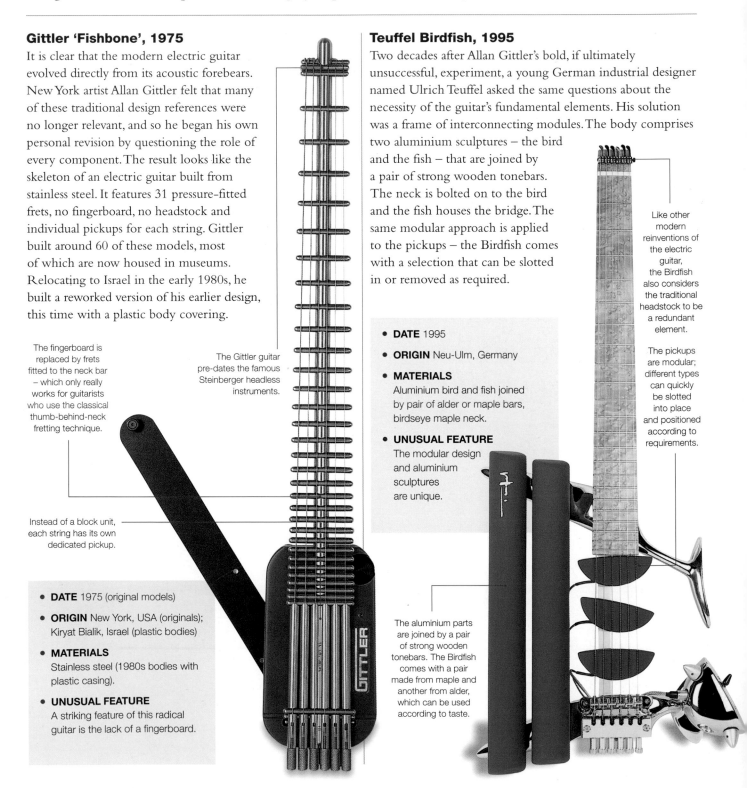

Gittler 'Fishbone', 1975

It is clear that the modern electric guitar evolved directly from its acoustic forebears. New York artist Allan Gittler felt that many of these traditional design references were no longer relevant, and so he began his own personal revision by questioning the role of every component. The result looks like the skeleton of an electric guitar built from stainless steel. It features 31 pressure-fitted frets, no fingerboard, no headstock and individual pickups for each string. Gittler built around 60 of these models, most of which are now housed in museums. Relocating to Israel in the early 1980s, he built a reworked version of his earlier design, this time with a plastic body covering.

The fingerboard is replaced by frets fitted to the neck bar – which only really works for guitarists who use the classical thumb-behind-neck fretting technique.

The Gittler guitar pre-dates the famous Steinberger headless instruments.

Instead of a block unit, each string has its own dedicated pickup.

- **DATE** 1975 (original models)
- **ORIGIN** New York, USA (originals); Kiryat Bialik, Israel (plastic bodies)
- **MATERIALS** Stainless steel (1980s bodies with plastic casing).
- **UNUSUAL FEATURE** A striking feature of this radical guitar is the lack of a fingerboard.

Teuffel Birdfish, 1995

Two decades after Allan Gittler's bold, if ultimately unsuccessful, experiment, a young German industrial designer named Ulrich Teuffel asked the same questions about the necessity of the guitar's fundamental elements. His solution was a frame of interconnecting modules. The body comprises two aluminium sculptures – the bird and the fish – that are joined by a pair of strong wooden tonebars. The neck is bolted on to the bird and the fish houses the bridge. The same modular approach is applied to the pickups – the Birdfish comes with a selection that can be slotted in or removed as required.

- **DATE** 1995
- **ORIGIN** Neu-Ulm, Germany
- **MATERIALS** Aluminium bird and fish joined by pair of alder or maple bars, birdseye maple neck.
- **UNUSUAL FEATURE** The modular design and aluminium sculptures are unique.

Like other modern reinventions of the electric guitar, the Birdfish also considers the traditional headstock to be a redundant element.

The pickups are modular; different types can quickly be slotted into place and positioned according to requirements.

The aluminium parts are joined by a pair of strong wooden tonebars. The Birdfish comes with a pair made from maple and another from alder, which can be used according to taste.

Hutchins Beast, 2008

Now into the realm of the slightly silly! One of the most striking reinventions of the guitar imaginable, the Hutchins Beast has six necks and covers pretty well all territories: it consists of one twelve-string, two six-strings, one seven-string, one four-string bass and one five-string bass. Hutchins is a young boutique company which is located in Lancing, Sussex, UK. Founder Gary Hutchins has already begun to carve a reputation for building high-quality guitars, many of which are also exquisite in appearance. As a promotional device, the Beast has been a great success, appearing in numerous magazines and books, as well as having been displayed in the 'Power of Making' exhibition held at London's Victoria and Albert Museum in 2011. It has also been used on stage at the Royal Albert Hall in London by popular British comedian and musician Bill Bailey.

All of the necks feature rosewood fingerboards.

- **DATE** 2008
- **ORIGIN** Lancing, UK
- **MATERIALS** Alder body, maple bolt-on necks, rosewood fingerboards.
- **UNUSUAL FEATURE** No other guitar is quite like this.

Although purely a promotional instrument, the Hutchins can only really be played by resting the body on the floor.

Boutique brands

What exactly is a boutique guitar? Typically, it is an instrument produced in very small numbers to an extremely high standard and sold to the kind of musician for whom retail price is a far lower priority than quality. Characteristically, such guitar manufacturers are also likely to offer a wide range of options, enabling the player to own a high-end, personalized instrument.

Campbell American Transitone, 2006

Founded in New England in 2002, Campbell American is one of the leaders in a growing US boutique market. Taking on a number of workers from the Guild factory in nearby Rhode Island when it was closed, Campbell American produces a small range of highly original custom instruments. Its most popular model is the curiously shaped single-cutaway Transitone. The appeal of a company such as this is the degree of personalization possible – the Transitone is available in a wide variety of materials and with options for at least four different brands of pickup to be fitted.

The Transitone is available with a variety of pickup options, including Seymour Duncan JB or Jazz, DiMarzio Bluesbucker, Lollar and TV Jones. This model features Seymour Duncan Charlie Christian Repro pickups.

- **DATE** 2006
- **ORIGIN** Westwood, Massachusetts, USA
- **WOOD** American linden body (maple, ash, mahogany or sapele can also be specified), maple neck, rosewood fingerboard (other options available).
- **UNUSUAL FEATURE** Retro body style.

Duesenberg Mike Campbell, 2008

Any small guitar company seeking endorsement by a name player will be forced to investigate less publicly celebrated figures: the German Duesenberg brand linked up with Mike Campbell, well respected for his work as Tom Petty's long-standing sideman. Duesenberg guitars are not wholly German-built, but parts are built to order in Korea and Germany and assembled at the company's workshop in Hanover. Campbell's signature model is a hollowbody archtop with a Duesenberg Grand Vintage humbucker at the bridge and Domino single-coil at the neck.

Rosewood fingerboard with dot marker inlays.

- **DATE** 2008
- **ORIGIN** Hanover, Germany
- **WOOD** Maple back and sides, hand-carved spruce top, maple set neck, rosewood fingerboard.
- **UNUSUAL FEATURE** German silver scratchplate.

The bodywork of the Duesenberg is finished to look like a Shelby Ford Mustang, complete with racing stripes.

Rob Williams Deluxe, 2008

British luthier Rob Williams builds instruments, as he says, "the old-fashioned way, by hand, by one bloke". His background has taken in repair work in the USA for Fender and Gibson, and later for Patrick Eggle guitars in the UK. At the top of Williams' CD range, the Set Neck Deluxe, befitting its moniker, is crafted from a variety of exotic woods – the model shown here is topped with flamed koa – and features two handwound humbucking pickups. For a final touch of extraordinary luxury, the embedded output-socket surround is carved from rosewood.

- **DATE** 2008

- **ORIGIN** Newtown, UK

- **WOOD**
  Swamp-ash body with flamed koa top, rock maple set neck, ebony fingerboard.

- **UNUSUAL FEATURE**
  The rosewood surround of the output-socket unit is a touch of luxury.

The ebony fingerboard features abalone dot inlays.

The pickups are handwound.

The five-way selector switch also acts as a coil splitter.

Grosh HollowTron, 2009

Don Grosh trained as a carpenter and cut his teeth as a luthier building guitars at Valley Arts (now Gibson-owned) for California's top session players. In 1993, Grosh set up his own custom shop producing a small number of designs, generally based on 1950s instruments. The Gretsch-inspired HollowTron is a hollowbody set-necked instrument with cat's-eye f-holes, Bigsby vibrato unit and a pair of TV Jones Classic Filter'Tron pickups.

- **DATE** 2009

- **ORIGIN** Broomfield, Colorado, USA

- **WOOD**
  Mahogany body with flamed maple top, mahogany set neck with ebony headstock, rosewood fingerboard.

- **UNUSUAL FEATURE**
  The ebony headstock gives it a luxurious feel.

The tuners are locking Gotoh 510s.

Abalone or pearl bullseye-dot fret-marker inlays

Thomas 'TV' Jones established his reputation hot-rodding classic Gretsch pickups, eventually producing his own range. His Filter'Trons are used on this Grosh.

The soundholes bring to mind the classic Rickenbacker cat's eye.

The exotic flame maple top is typical of the modern-day upmarket electric-guitar finish.

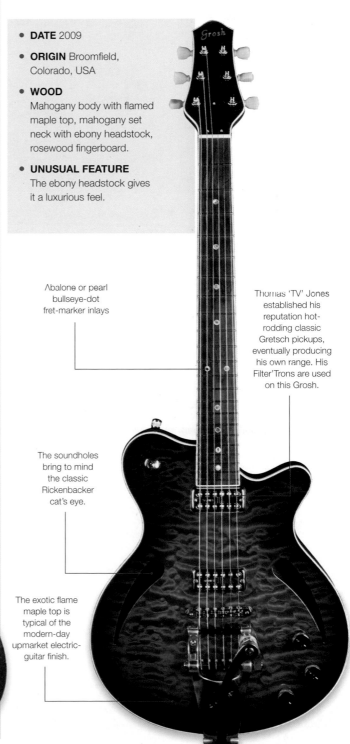

Paul Reed Smith

Arguably the most important new large-scale guitar manufacturer since the early 1980s, Paul Reed Smith's guitars were born of a desire to bring together the best aspects of the Gibson and Fender traditions. While they are expensive guitars, their attractive appearance and tonal versatility has made them massively popular among professional players in every musical genre.

Paul Reed Smith First Guitar, 1975

Uniquely for such a successful luthier, all of Paul Reed Smith's early one-off guitars – some built when he was a teenager – have been well documented. The model shown here is based on a single-cutaway Les Paul Junior and was built while he was a student at St Mary's College of Maryland. The guitar, which now stands proudly in the entrance hall of the PRS factory, earned its owner – who was a mathematics major – four college credits for completing an instrument "of professional quality".

- **DATE** 1975
- **ORIGIN** St Mary's City, Maryland, USA
- **WOOD**
  Mahogany body, mahogany set neck, rosewood fingerboard.
- **UNUSUAL FEATURE**
  This instrument has a Gibson Les Paul Junior single-cutaway-style body.

Smith settled early on the Gibson Les Paul Junior as his basic template; the classic PRS design would be based on the twin-cutaway version.

This first Paul Reed Smith has two single-coil P-90-style pickups.

Paul Reed Smith First 'Dragon', 1979

By 1979, Smith was establishing himself as a custom luthier of note, having sold guitars to the likes of Peter Frampton and Roy Buchanan. His model was still the Gibson Les Paul Junior, but now in its twin-cutaway form – and this has remained Smith's default body shape. This 1979 model is notable for the first appearance of the dragon motif. As a 16-year-old, Smith had dreamt of a guitar with intricate dragon inlays. Two decades later, this would form the basis for one of the most collectible modern guitar series.

- **DATE** 1979
- **ORIGIN** Annapolis, Maryland, USA
- **WOOD**
  Mahogany body, mahogany set neck, rosewood fingerboard.
- **UNUSUAL FEATURE**
  This guitar features ornate dragon inlays on the bodywork – a taster for the later PRS Dragon series.

The Americana inlays on the fingerboard show a bald eagle in different states of flight.

Smith took the Les Paul Junior shape and introduced a German carve – where the carving on the body dips below the height of the edge before rising towards the middle.

The control panel of this guitar is very simple, featuring one rotary potentiometer and two mini-switches controlling the humbucker on the bridge.

Paul Reed Smith Carlos Santana, 1980

As a young guitarist, one of Smith's heroes was Carlos Santana, and as a young luthier, his ambition was to build a guitar for his idol. In 1980, Smith met Santana before a show and showed him his new model. The guitarist was sufficiently impressed to use it at that night's concert. Afterwards they discussed alterations, and Smith left with a commission for a new instrument that would become Santana's preferred instrument for most of the 1980s.

- **DATE** 1980
- **ORIGIN** Annapolis, Maryland, USA
- **WOOD**
  Mahogany body with figured maple top, mahogany set neck, rosewood fingerboard.
- **UNUSUAL FEATURE**
  The guitar has a vibrato arm designed especially for this instrument.

ABOVE: *Santana had not liked the pickups on the guitar Smith had shown him. A pair of humbuckers were designed to order from Seymour Duncan.*

The bass horn is less pronounced than on later models.

Smith retained the single pot/double switch controls of his Dragon. When the Santana model went into production 15 years later, a more conventional master volume and tone control was incorporated, as shown here.

PRS Custom 22, 1985

1985 was the year when Paul Reed Smith 'Fine Handcrafted Guitars' moved to a factory facility and became PRS. The first models to come off the production line were the Custom range. Constructed on the lines of the Les Paul Junior, like Smith's earlier guitars, the Custom features a one-piece mahogany body capped with a distinctive maple top and bound at the edges. The pickups are humbuckers, but through the use of a five-way rotary switch they can also create Fender-style single-coil tones.

- **DATE** 1985
- **ORIGIN** Annapolis, Maryland, USA
- **WOOD**
  Mahogany body with carved figured maple top, mahogany set neck, rosewood fingerboard.
- **UNUSUAL FEATURE**
  This Custom features the intricate fingerboard inlays that characterize PRS guitars.

By this time, the now-familiar asymmetric PRS headstock design, with Paul Reed Smith's signature, had become standard.

The Custom 22 is named after its 22-fret fingerboard; PRS also made a two-octave, 24-fret model.

Over the years, PRS has continued to refine the Custom's electrics – the five-way switching system and pickup options, in particular.

The growth of PRS

In 1985, Paul Reed Smith made the transition from custom luthier to guitar producer. At first, overambitious and innovative ideas such as PRS amplifiers and a range of acoustic and bass guitars were quickly abandoned. It soon became clear that, while PRS guitars were very expensive, there was a definite market for such a versatile high-end instrument.

PRS Artist, 1991

By 1990, PRS was producing around 400 guitars each month, and that year the company grossed over $4 million. However, there were many traditional Gibson players who loved PRS guitars but bemoaned the lack of the 'fat' Les Paul sound. Smith began working with different construction techniques and making modifications to the dimensions to produce a better-quality acoustic sound. The results of these experiments were first seen in the flagship Artist range.

- **DATE** 1991
- **ORIGIN** Annapolis, Maryland, USA
- **WOOD**
  Mahogany body with carved figured maple top, mahogany set neck, rosewood fingerboard.
- **UNUSUAL FEATURE**
  The wood quality is exceptionally fine.

Inlay and purfling include an abalone-inlaid signature headstock logo.

The woods used in the upmarket Artist series were chosen from stock, and were deemed to be too good for standard production PRS guitars.

PRS McCarty, 1994

During the 1980s, Paul Reed Smith had befriended Ted McCarty, the man who had presided over Gibson in the 1950s. Smith acknowledged that he had learnt a lot from the man who had introduced the original Les Pauls. In 1992, Smith was approached by session guitarist Dave Grissom to produce a guitar that sounded like the original Les Paul used by Duane Allman. Based broadly on the Dragon design, with a thinner neck and PAF-style pickups, Smith named the resulting instrument the McCarty.

- **DATE** 1994
- **ORIGIN** Annapolis, Maryland, USA
- **WOOD**
  Mahogany body with East Coast maple top, mahogany set neck, rosewood fingerboard.
- **UNUSUAL FEATURE**
  The McCarty has a pair of brass-covered humbuckers styled on the Gibson PAF.

The McCarty model included some features that PRS players might have considered retro, such as non-locking tuners and the three-way toggle selector.

The body uses Michigan maple – the same wood used for the tops of 1950s Gibson Les Pauls.

Unusual stoptail bridge unit

PRS Dragon, 2002

One of the hallmarks of the PRS brand has been the number of limited-edition models produced, the most noted of which is the Dragon series. Inspired by Smith's teenage dream of a guitar with a dragon inlaid down the neck, the first PRS Dragon appeared in 1992. Each one in a run of 50 guitars featured a beautiful dragon mosaic made from 201 pieces of abalone, turquoise and mother-of-pearl. These first models have been known to fetch in excess of $40,000 at auction. The Dragon 2002 was the first single-cutaway guitar in the series. Announced at the 2002 NAMM trade show and offered for $30,000, orders for all 100 of the limited run had been taken by the end of the day.

- **DATE** 2002

- **ORIGIN** Annapolis, Maryland, USA

- **WOOD**
  Mahogany body, flame maple top, set Brazilian rosewood neck and fingerboard.

- **UNUSUAL FEATURE**
  It is one of the earliest PRS models with a single cutaway.

Until 2000, all PRS guitars had been built around the same basic body shape; the single cutaway design so strongly resembles a Gibson Les Paul that it was the subject of legal action by Gibson.

The design by Jeff Easley was created using over 300 pieces of shell and stone.

The bridge is a single-unit PRS stoptail.

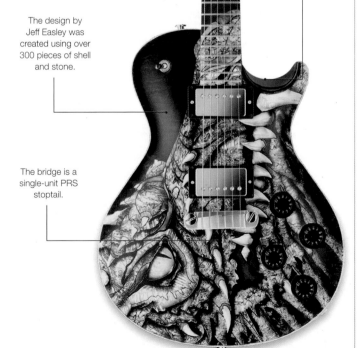

Carlos Santana

Born in Mexico in 1947, as a teenager Carlos Santana moved with his family to San Francisco. The Santana Blues Band was formed in 1967 and soon gained a reputation for its Latin-infused rhythms and Santana's searing, feedback-driven lead playing. In 1969, the band, by then known just as Santana, was one of the surprise hits of the legendary Woodstock Festival. This success led to the band's eponymous debut album hitting the top five.

The band's 1970 follow-up, *Abraxas*, was a global success from which such hit singles as "Black Magic Woman" and the sublime guitar instrumental "Samba Pa Ti" were taken. By now, Carlos Santana was one of the most influential guitarists in the rock world.

By the 1990s, however, Carlos Santana found himself struggling. His music was out of fashion, and he was without a record deal. His fortunes changed spectacularly with the 1999 *Supernatural* album, which saw the guitarist paired with a series of younger vocalists. The track "Smooth", with its irresistible cha-cha rhythm and Santana's neat fills, became a global hit, and the album went on to sell 15 million copies in the USA alone – by some distance Santana's biggest commercial success in his whole career.

Do-it-yourself guitars

With such a wide variety of production electric guitars available, it may be surprising to find some musicians still unsatisfied with what's on offer. Of course, there have always been a certain players with very specific requirements, or others who simply want to create something personal or innovative, or an instrument that sets them apart from everybody else.

Brian May Red Special, 1963

Perhaps the most famous of homebuilt guitars, the Red Special was made in 1963 by 16-year-old Brian May and his aviation-engineer father, Harold. A highly unorthodox instrument, it was built using wood from a reclaimed 18th-century mantel, and the body was chambered and covered with mahogany to give a solidbody appearance. The pickups were customized Burns Tri-Sonics, but were, rather unusually, wired in series rather than parallel. Abandoning his postgraduate studies – a PhD in astrophysics – May formed Queen and would use the Red Special on all of the band's biggest hits.

Versions of the Red Special were issued by Burns and Guild, but they are now produced by May's own company.

- **DATE** 1963
- **ORIGIN** London, UK
- **WOOD**
  Oak and blockboard body, covered front and back with mahogany, oak straight-through neck, painted oak fingerboard.
- **UNUSUAL FEATURE**
  The woods used are uncommon in guitar making.

Each of the three pickups has two control switches. One is a simple on-off switch, while the other controls phase polarity.

The body was finished with wood stain and Rustin's plastic coating – a varnish popular with British furniture makers.

Township Oil Can Guitar, 2000

Out of necessity – either through lack of availability or affordability – some musicians have built their own guitars. The oil can guitar is thought to be based on the four-string ramkiekie, an instrument said to have been developed by the Khoi people of South Africa after they came into contact with early European settlers. Township Guitars, based in Cape Town, exports high-quality oil can guitars across the globe. The distinctive metallic tone is vaguely reminiscent of a metal-bodied resonator, but when combined with the single-coil pickup creates a sound unlike any production-line instrument.

- **DATE** 2000
- **ORIGIN** Cape Town, South Africa
- **WOOD**
  Reclaimed Castrol oil can body, maple bolt-on neck and support, rosewood.
- **UNUSUAL FEATURE**
  The reclaimed materials used in the construction of this instrument give it a unique look and sound.

Soundholes are punched into the surface of the oil can.

This guitar features the original type of oil can body, but Township Guitars has also produced instruments from reclaimed olive oil cans.

John Entwistle Fender 'Frankenstein', 1967

In 2003, a year after his death, 350 personal items belonging to The Who's John Entwistle were auctioned at Sotheby's. On offer was Entwistle's 'Frankenstein' – a Fender he built himself from the remains of five smashed basses, and which he used exclusively from 1967 on some of the band's benchmark albums, including *Tommy* and *Quadrophenia*. As Entwistle himself admitted, demanding craftsmanship was not required: "Two hours with a Phillips screwdriver and a soldering iron, and I was ranting around my hotel room screaming, 'It's alive, it's alive!'" The 'Frankenstein' had been expected to raise around $7,000 at the auction; bidding ended at $100,000!

- **DATE** 1967

- **ORIGIN** Fullerton, California, USA

- **WOOD**
  Ash body, maple bolt-on neck, maple fingerboard.

- **UNUSUAL FEATURE**
  The guitar is a composite of four Fender Precisions and one Fender Jazz.

String guides are fitted to the headstock on the D and A strings.

Although built from five smashed basses, Entwistle's 'Frankenstein' appears to be a regular Fender Precision.

Entwistle fitted the finger rest to the scratchplate; many players in the past have taken these off.

The pickup is a standard Fender split-P.

Standard Precision adjustable bridge unit.

The do-it-yourself tradition

The electric luthier combines traditional, centuries-old craftsmanship with a touch of the experimental scientist. Despite this, the electric guitar is a relatively simple piece of technology that anyone who has rudimentary carpentry abilities and an understanding of basic electronics could easily make for themselves.

In the West, the unskilled, home-made tradition goes back to the diddley bow, which was taken over to the southern states of the USA by enslaved West Africans during the 18th century. This instrument was little more than a wire screwed at either end to a board, and was played by plucking with one hand and altering the pitch by sliding a bottle up and down. Later, during the American Civil War, cigar-box guitars became popular among troops away from home.

Numerous websites exist with detailed instructions on how to build instruments such as these, which, with care, can produce extremely usable results. Making an instrument from scratch can also provide the guitarist with a greater understanding of the factors that make their instruments work – indeed, many successful luthiers have been inspired by experimenting in this way.

ABOVE: *Blues artist Steven Wold – better known as Seasick Steve – was well into his 60s before he made his mark as a musician. Much of his work sees him backing himself with a home-built guitar and a stomp box. He is shown here playing a cigar-box electric guitar.*

Gibson Robots

Throughout this directory we've seen a great number of attempts to enhance the functionality of the guitar, from organ guitars in the 1960s, guitar synthesizers in the 1970s and, since then, a variety of approaches to MIDI control. The first decade of the new millennium saw Gibson come up with perhaps the most radical development in guitar technology – the Robot guitar.

Les Paul Robot, 2007

Gibson's first Robot guitar addresses an area of concern for every string player – tuning. German guitarist Chris Adams spent a decade developing his own Powertune system. With a small computer built into the underside of the stop bar, the system automatically checks the intonation for each string and sends messages to each of the six tuners, adjusting them where necessary. In 2007, Adams licensed the Powertune system, enabling Gibson to install it into the Les Paul Robot model.

- **DATE** 2007
- **ORIGIN** Kalamazoo, Michigan, USA
- **WOOD** Mahogany body with maple top, mahogany set neck, ebony fingerboard.
- **UNUSUAL FEATURE** The automated computerized tuning system was a first.

ABOVE: *The Powertune system not only enables guitarists to stay in tune, but also to change tuning by rotating the Master Control Knob.*

Dark Fire, 2008

A year after the first appearance of the Robot, Gibson came up with a new Les Paul, the Dark Fire. Not only did it feature Powertune, but it was also integrated with Chameleon Tone Technology – a system of on-board modelling electronics that provides eight different guitar tones, from acoustic to metal. These can be reprogrammed using computer editing software. The Dark Fire comes with the Robot Interface Pack (RIP), which enables the guitar to be plugged directly into a computer.

- **DATE** 2008
- **ORIGIN** Kalamazoo, Michigan, USA
- **WOOD** Mahogany body with maple top, mahogany set neck, ebony fingerboard.
- **UNUSUAL FEATURE** In addition to the Powertune automated-tuning system, the Dark Fire features Chameleon Tone Technology.

The neck pickup is a P-90H soapbar, a modern version of the classic single-coil P-90, reworked to reduce the notorious problem of 60-cycle hum.

The Master Control Knob (MCK) is the means by which the Dark Fire's on-board robot features are manipulated.

Firebird X, 2011

The Robot series seems to have polarized the opinion of hardcore Gibson fans: some traditionalists certainly seem to view them as an aberration. Gibson has carried on undeterred, however, and in 2011 produced the Firebird X, the most heavily armed of the series. The three additional toggle pots on the body mark it out as a very unusual beast, enabling software effects such as compression, distortion and echo to be switched in. There is also a piezo switch that produces a convincing acoustic sound.

- **DATE** 2011

- **ORIGIN** Kalamazoo, Michigan, USA

- **WOOD**
  Mahogany with maple top, mahogany set neck, ebony fngerboard.

- **UNUSUAL FEATURE**
  On-board features include the Pure-Analog updatable audio-engine circuitry.

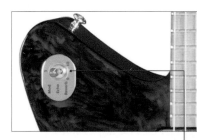

ABOVE: *The Firebird X features some of the most extraordinary technology ever seen on a guitar. Among the controls are a pair of toggle pots, which appear to be standard pickup-selector-type switches, but have a rotatable toggle shaft that enables sounds and effects to be morphed rather than crudely switched in.*

The coils in the three mini-humbuckers can be switched on or off, to reverse polarity, or switched between series and parallel wiring.

The bridge piezo pickup includes hex outputs so that each string can provide a separate output for computer or live-performance set-ups.

Computerized guitars

ABOVE: *Steve Stevens is best known for his work with Michael Jackson and Billy Idol. Having pioneered the use of Roland guitar synthesizers in the 1980s, he is shown here in 2008 with a Gibson Dark Fire.*

As far as guitars with in-built computing power go, the Firebird X is currently the final word. While a retail price of around $5,000 may seem high, there are surely plenty of limited-edition Gibson classics that cost more. Like any computer system, however, such instruments will stand or fall by the quality of upgrades to their operating systems, software and processing power. Where does this lead? As digital sampling becomes ever more subtle and sophisticated, will we see guitars with terabytes of in-built data that, at the flick of a switch, can produce convincing violin or cello tones? Since the mid-1980s, MIDI-equipped guitars have been able to control other devices to the same end, but the appeal would be in its self-containment. After all, the Firebird X isn't doing too much that can't be done through external figural processing.

For some, however, robot guitars are controversial instruments, striking at the heart of the very simplicity that gives the electric guitar much of its appeal. It remains to be seen whether 50 years from now these instruments will be viewed as having ushered in a new breed of 21st-century musical instrument, or whether they will appear as a brief blip, viewed much as we look on, say, the Vox organ guitar of the early 1960s, the makers of which doubtless sincerely believed at the time that they were writing the script for the future of the electric guitar.

Glossary

acoustic
A musical instrument the sound of which is not electrically enhanced or modified.

alfabeto system
An early development of guitar tablature notation.

altered tension chords
Dominant-seventh chords with extensions (extra notes) drawn from outside the parent major scale.

altered tuning
Ways of tuning the guitar other than 'standard tuning'.

alternate picking
A plectrum technique that alternates upward and downward strokes.

anodized
Metal coated with a layer of oxide.

archtop
A guitar with a curved top.

arpeggio
A chord that is played as a sequence of individual notes.

artificial harmonic
A harmonic formed on a shortened string that is fretted by the left hand.

bambino
A small guitar that was popular in the 19th century.

barre chord
A chord shape in which one finger, usually but not always the index finger, is pressed across the fretboard to fret several strings at the same time. By moving the hand up and down the neck, chords may be played in any key.

bass line
A low-pitched instrumental part that is played by a rhythm section instrument such as the bass guitar, double bass or synthesizer.

beat
A music genre fusing rock 'n' roll and R&B that evolved in the United Kingdom in the early 1960s; The Beatles are the most famous example.

bend
A change of pitch which is achieved by moving (pushing or releasing) a vibrating string sideways. A 'pre-bend' involves pulling the string first before picking the note, and then releasing it into position on the fingerboard.

Bigsby
Paul Bigsby (1899–1968) was an engineer who built an early solidbody guitar. He is best remembered for the vibrato arm that takes his name, the 'Bigsby vibrato tailpiece' (*see also* **tremolo arm/bridge**).

binding
An inlay fitted to the edges of acoustic guitars to protect the wood from impact and moisture damage; fingerboards are also sometimes 'bound', usually by a plastic strip running the length of the neck on each side.

blues scale
A scale including 'blue notes': notes that give the characteristic blues feel to the music. There isn't one definitive form of blues scale, but it will typically include the minor third from the root, the flattened fifth (as well as the perfect fifth) and the minor seventh.

bolt-on neck
Construction technique that sees the neck screwed on to the body of the guitar, usually with three or four bolts.

book-matched
Wood that has been sliced open with the grain arranged symmetrically.

bossa nova
A Brazilian style that was very popular in the 1960s, drawn from samba and with a strong jazz flavour.

bridge
The bridge is attached to the top (soundboard) of the guitar, and carries the saddle and the bridge-pins or tie-block that secure the strings at that end.

bridge saddle
Part of the bridge that comes into direct contact with the string.

Britpop
A music genre of the early 1990s characterized by English guitar-oriented bands influenced by 1960s pop music.

broken chord
See **arpeggio**

cant
When the soundboard is bent at the bridge, it is 'cant'.

capo (Cejilla)
A device which is fixed across the strings to raise the pitch.

catgut strings
Gut (from animals but not from cats; the origin of the term 'catgut' is uncertain) preceded nylon as the material for classical guitar strings, and is still preferred by some players.

chitarra battente
A particular type of Italian, wire-strung Baroque guitar.

chops
A musician's ability to play his or her instrument.

chord
Two or more notes sounded together or in quick succession.

chordophone
The technical term used to describe any stringed instrument.

chorus pedal
An electronic effect simulating the sound of two guitars playing at the same time.

chromatic scale
A succession of notes formed entirely of semitone steps.

chugging
A persistent rhythm characterized by playing a chord, often muted, on every half beat.

cistre, cittern or English guitar
A wire-stringed instrument that was popular in the late 18th century.

clean channel
An input channel on a guitar amplifier that adds no distortion or other effect.

cleats
Small pieces of added wood (usually to assist a repair).

clef
A symbol placed at the beginning of a musical staff that defines the pitch of the notes. A treble clef defines the notes on the lines as E, G, B, D, F; a bass clef defines them as G, B, D, F, A.

country picking
A style used especially in country music, typically with root and fifth alternating on the bottom strings and busy fingerwork on the top strings.

course
A pair of strings set close together and treated as one note.

cutaway
This term describes the shape of guitar body that gives the left hand the ability to access the highest frets on the fingerboard.

DADGAD
An alternative guitar tuning popular in folk and folk-rock.

damping
Touching a string shortly after playing it, to stop it from vibrating. Also referred to as 'choking'.

delay
Usually, a digital effect that repeats the sound of a signal. Extremely short delays are used with modulation to create phasing, flanging and chorus effects; longer delays can create echo and looping effects.

diatonic
Involving only notes proper to the prevailing key without chromatic alteration.

diminished chord
A chord containing the root note, minor third and diminished fifth.

dissonance
A combination of two or more notes that 'clash', i.e. that do not harmonize together comfortably.

distortion
The boosting (or overdriving) of a signal in the pre-amp stage of a guitar amplifier that creates the characteristic 'fuzz' sound used in rock music. It may also be created by an external footpedal.

dominant seventh
A chord formed from a major triad plus the minor seventh from the root, tending to resolve to a triad with the root a perfect fourth higher. In the major-minor key system, the dominant seventh chord is constructed from the fifth step of the scale (the dominant) and resolves to the tonic chord (which is constructed on the first step of the scale).

Dorian mode
A scale formed by playing the white notes of the piano from D to D (or starting from the second step of any other major scale).

double bend
The simultaneous bending of two strings.

double neck
A guitar with two necks; usually a six- and twelve-string, or six-string and bass.

double stopping
Playing two notes at the same time, either with one finger fretting both strings or two separate fingers.

drop D
A type of altered tuning that involves retuning the bottom E string down to D.

effects loop
The insertion of an effect into an electric guitar amplifier's signal path – usually between the pre-amp and power amp stages.

electro-acoustic
An otherwise standard acoustic guitar fitted with a magnetic pickup for the purposes of amplification.

extended chord
General term for ninth, 11th or 13th chords – chords that build on seventh chords by adding further thirds on top.

falsetas
Instrumental (guitar) phrases in flamenco music.

fan bracing
A typical pattern formed by the reinforcing wooden strips on the inside of a guitar body.

fifth (⅕) comma meantone temperament
The technical term for a type of tuning, different from 'equal temperament' (in which there are 12 equal semitones

in each octave). In meantone tuning, fifths are tuned slightly narrow, in order to achieve a better tuning of thirds. The 'comma' is a mathematical proportion, fractions of which define different varieties of meantone tuning.

fill
A short musical passage, riff or lick.

filter switch
An on-off control that channels the signal through additional tone circuitry. 'Treble boost', for example, increases treble frequencies while dropping those at the bass end.

fingerboard
Another name for the fretboard.

fingerstyle technique
Using the individual right-hand fingers to play different strings, as opposed to strumming across several strings.

fingertapping
Tapping on the fretboard to produce various notes, especially by using the right hand.

finial
A decorative terminal feature, usually an extension of the head.

fixed bridge
Bridge unit fixed in place on the body of the guitar.

flat tuning
Lowering standard guitar tuning in pitch by half a tone. Often used by metal bands.

floating bridge
A bridge that is not attached to the soundboard but which the strings pass over; it is attached towards the base of the guitar.

floating fretboard
A fretboard that is not attached to the soundboard.

floating tremolo
Style of vibrato unit that was first designed by Fender in 1958 for the Jazzmaster model.

fret dressing
Repairing the wear and tear on frets.

fretboard
The top section of neck containing the frets; also known as the fingerboard.

frets
A series of metal strips inserted into the fingerboard to create specifically pitched notes when they come into contact with the string. The left hand presses just behind a fret to shorten the vibrating length of the string and thereby alter (raise) the pitch.

fusion
A music genre that combines rock music with jazz, and which was briefly popular during the 1970s.

gauge
The thickness of a guitar string, designated in thousandths of an inch. Lighter gauges are easier to play.

German-carve
A body styling found on some guitars that is characterized by a gentle curve around the edges.

golpeador
The Spanish word for a scratchplate, applied especially in flamenco.

guide finger
Keeping a finger in contact with a string to help locate the next playing position for the left hand.

hammer-on
Sounding a new note, not by plucking it with the right hand but by changing the pitch of an already-sounding string with a hammer-like motion.

hardtail
A bridge unit that also incorporates the means of anchoring the strings in position.

hardware
In the context of a guitar, this largely refers to the 'non-wooden' parts, such as the bridge, machine heads or electrics.

harmonic
A note sounded not by fully pressing the string on to the fretboard but by lightly touching it at a 'node', a point that allows it to vibrate around the touching finger. Harmonics have a distinctive, pure sound.

headstock
Positioned at the end of the guitar neck, the headstock holds the strings and their tuning mechanism.

hollowbody
An electric guitar that has a non-solid body.

horn(s)
The body protrusion(s) at the upper bout.

humbucker
A twin-coil magnetic pickup developed in the mid-1950s by Seth Lover at Gibson, designed to reduce electrical hum.

inlay
Decorative material set into the wood; commonly used to indicate fret positions on the fingerboard.

interval
The distance from one note to another.

inversion
A chord where the tonic note is not the lowest-pitched note.

jack (jack plate)
The socket into which a cable is inserted for connection to an amplifier.

key
The tonic of a scale.

lap steel
A small guitar played horizontally on the lap, often referred to as a 'Hawaiian' guitar.

lead guitar
A guitar part which includes melody lines, instrumental fill passages, guitar solos and riffs within a song structure.

left-hand muting
A technique for deadening vibrating strings effected by releasing the tension of the fretting fingers.

legato
Notes played without perceptible breaks.

lick
A characteristic phrase, usually melodic. For instance, a blues lick is a typical blues figure.

locking nut
A nut which is secured after tuning using an Allen key; usually a part of a locking vibrato system.

luthier
A stringed instrument maker.

machine head
Mechanism fitted to the headstock for altering the tension – hence tuning – of strings; sometimes known as tuners.

major scale
A succession of seven notes with the following sequence of intervals: tone, tone, semitone, tone, tone, tone, semitone.

This sequence is formed when playing the white notes on a piano from C to C. It is one of the most commonly used scales in Western music.

minor scale
There are several forms of minor scale, but all crucially vary from the major in that the third of the scale is flattened, so that a C minor scale starts: C D E♭ F G.

mode
A series of diatonic notes within an octave. From the Latin *modus* meaning 'measure, it is a type of scale that dates back to the Middle Ages.

montuno
A type of repeating bass pattern much used in salsa and other Latin styles.

movable chord
A left-hand chord shape that can be moved up or down the fretboard.

mustachios
Decorative extensions to the bridge.

natural tension chords
Extended dominant chords (ninth, 11th and 13th chords); broadly speaking, these are the ones that keep to the notes of the parent major scale, as opposed to those with chromatic alterations.

neck
Part of the guitar to which the fingerboard, nut and machine heads are fitted.

neck plate
On a bolt-on guitar, this is the small piece of metal at the back of the body through which the screws are placed to secure the neck in place.

nut
The ridge that forms the junction between the neck and the headstock, over which the strings pass, and which defines their sounding length at that end.

octave
An interval of a perfect eighth from one note to the next note (up or down) with the same letter name. Octave relationships are useful when tuning a guitar.

on-board technology
Computer electronics that are found on some modern guitars.

open chords
Basic chords played without the need for an index-finger barre.

open tuning
System whereby the strings are tuned to the notes of a chord. 'Open G' and 'Open D' are among the most common.

output socket
See **jack (jack plate)**

PA system
Public Address System; configuration of amplifiers and loudspeakers used in music concerts.

PAF
Patent Applied For; name applied to the first Gibson humbucking pickup that was introduced in 1955 but for which a patent was not issued until 1959.

palm muting
A right-hand technique allowing the palm (or the edge of the palm, from below the little finger to the heel of the palm) to rest lightly on the strings just beside the bridge, damping the strings slightly. Often used in rock music to create a 'chugging' effect.

passing notes
Notes in a melody that do not belong to the underlying chords, which enable the linking of different chord notes to create melodic phrases.

pearloid
A type of plastic that is used for inlays intended to resemble the more costly mother of pearl.

pedal
In music theory, this term refers to a note that is held while the harmonies go through several changes. Most pedal notes are in the bass. It also refers to an external electronic device plugged between the guitar and amplifier to alter the sound.

pedal board
A platform on which multiple effect pedals can be fixed and wired up in a neat and convenient way.

peg box
The part of the headstock that houses the tuning pegs. Applies to classical instruments/slotted headstock only.

pentatonic scale
A five-note scale. One common pentatonic scale has a pattern of major seconds (tones) and minor thirds such as G A C D E (G), but other pentatonic scales are also possible. The 'Minor Pentatonic' is at the heart of much R&B and blues-based rock music.

Phrygian mode
A scale that is formed by playing the white notes of the piano from E to E (or starting from the second step of any other major scale).

pickguard
See **scratchplate**

pickups (magnetic pickups)
A unit comprising a set of magnets with copper wire winding necessary for an electric guitar to be amplified. Pickups capture vibrations from the strings and convert them into electrical signals.

pickup bar
When a piece starts on an upbeat (or anacrusis), this is notated as an incomplete bar or 'pickup bar' before bar 1.

piezo switch
An electrical rather than mechanical switch.

pin bridge
A type of bridge in which the strings are fixed with the aid of a pin.

pinch harmonics/squeal harmonics
A guitar technique in which the player's thumb or index finger catches the string after it is picked, cancelling the fundamental of the string; this lets an overtone dominate, and creates a high-pitched squeal.

pitch
How high or low a note sounds (as we perceive it), which is determined by its fundamental frequency.

plantilla
From the Spanish word meaning 'template', this refers to the outline of the body of a guitar,

plectrum
A small plastic disc held in the right hand, usually between thumb and forefinger, to pluck or strum the strings. Also called a 'pick'.

position markers
Symbols – usually dots – positioned on the fingerboard to indicate the fret number; usually placed on frets 3, 5, 7 and 9 with a double-dot on the 12th fret (the octave). The markers continue in the same intervals as these above the octave.

power chord
A chord containing only the root and fifth (plus any octave doublings). This is a key part of rock music, commonly played on electric guitars with distortion.

progression
The change from one chord to another.

pull-off
Sounding a new note not by plucking it with the right hand but by using a left-hand finger that was previously fretting a note, pulling the string and releasing it to make a lower note than it was previously sounding. It is the opposite of a hammer-on.

purflings
Decorative inlaid strips that are added on the edges of a guitar.

quaver
A note with a time value of a half a beat in a bar of $\frac{4}{4}$ time; a semiquaver has half the time value of a quaver.

re-entrant tuning
Any tuning in which the strings are not ordered from the lowest pitch to the highest.

relative tuning
The method of tuning the strings by successively tuning pairs of strings against each other. Typically, this will start by tuning the open A string against the low E string fretted at the fifth fret.

repertoire
A general term meaning a collection or list of pieces. The term is often used to define the list of pieces played by a performer.

rest stroke
A right-hand technique in which the finger presses the string downwards and, after releasing, then rests on the next string. On the last string, however, the player controls the finger rather than resting it.

rhythm
Regular or irregular pulses in music.

rhythm guitar
Guitar playing that concentrates on chord work rather than soloing.

riff
A repeated harmonic and/or melodic pattern forming the basis of a song. Often used in popular music and jazz.

right-hand tapping
A hammering technique using fingers of the picking hand, popularized by Eddie Van Halen in the 1980s.

roller holes
The holes in the side of the headstock in which the machine heads are fitted.

root and fifth
See **power chord**

root note
In a scale or chord, the root is the defining 'home' note.

rose
A two- or three-dimensional decoration covering the soundhole.

rosette
The decorative inlay that surrounds the soundhole.

saddle
The resting point on the bridge, from which the string length starts.

scale
A series of musical notes, ascending or descending, defined by unique sets of intervals between tonic and octave.

scratchplate
A thin plastic plate or other laminated material attached to the top face of the guitar just below the strings, to protect the guitar's finish from being scratched by fingernails or the plectrum. Also known as a 'pickguard'.

selector
A switch that introduces a pickup (or group of pickups) into the signal path.

semitone
On a guitar, this refers to the smallest interval between adjacent notes in Western harmony; on any given string, it is the interval from one fret to the next.

set neck
A guitar-building technique by which the neck of the guitar is glued to the body.

seventh chord
A four-note chord formed by taking a triad (formed of root, third, fifth) and adding a seventh.

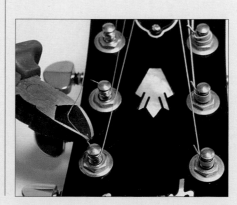

shuffle
A swung rhythm with a comfortable, easy feel and a repeated pattern such as the 'sixth shuffle'.

single coil
A pickup constructed by wrapping one coil of copper wire around a series of magnets; the type of pickup most associated with Fender guitars.

slap/slap bass
A bass guitar sound commonly used in funk that entails striking the string with the side of the bony joint in the middle of the thumb, and intentionally allowing the vibrating string to come into contact with the metal frets.

slide
Moving smoothly from one pitch to another by sliding the fretting finger up or down the string. Also refers to the metal or glass device used to create a particular sound.

slotted (bar) frets
Rectangular-shaped strips (*see also* **frets**).

slur
In notation, a curved line drawn from one note to a different note, indicating that the second should be played without separately enunciating it, for instance (in guitar music) by using a left-hand hammer-on or pull-off.

solidbody
A guitar without a hollow sound chamber.

sound box
The hollow body of an acoustic guitar. Also called the 'sounding box'.

soundboard
On an acoustic guitar, the resonating top part of the body.

soundport
A hole in the side of the guitar, designed to enhance the sound, especially for the player's benefit.

spread chord
A chord where the notes are not sounded simultaneously but one after another, and then allowed to ring so that the whole chord is heard.

square neck
A guitar neck that has been left square (not rounded) at the back.

staccato
A note with a very short duration; indicated in written music with a dot above the note.

standard tuning
A guitar tuned to E, A, D, G, B, E.

stave
The five lines that are used for conventional music notation.

stop-bar tailpiece
A unit, independent of the bridge, where the strings are anchored.

string bending
A glissando technique in which a string is pushed up or down to raise its pitch.

strumming
Playing all the strings of a guitar in a sweeping motion.

sunburst
A paint effect commonly used on guitars, characterized by a light colour in the centre of the body, darkening towards the edges.

superstrat
A genre of guitars influenced by the Fender Stratocaster, but with customized features.

suspended chord
A chord including a suspended note: one that 'wants' to resolve downwards or upwards to form a triad.

sustain
The duration of a note ringing before it naturally decays.

sweep picking
A technique whereby the sweeping motion of the pick is combined with matching fretting movements to produce sequences of notes that are fast and fluid.

swing rhythm
A lilting rhythm pattern often used in jazz-influenced music.

sympathetic strings
Strings that resonate independently of the main ones.

syncopation
A rhythm that cuts across the beat. It is fundamental in musical styles such as jazz, funk, reggae, progressive rock, heavy metal, samba and salsa.

synthesizer
An instrument (usually a keyboard) that is capable of producing a wide variety of electronic sounds. Synthesizers were first used in pop music in the 1960s.

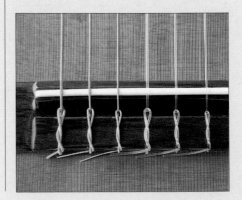

T-frets
T-shaped strips that are inserted into the fretboard, providing single points of contact for the strings (*see also* **frets**).

tablature
Guitar notation in which horizontal lines represent the strings, and numbers indicate the fret to be played.

tailpiece
The mechanism for anchoring the strings to the body of the guitar, at the opposite end from the headstock.

Terz guitar
A six-string guitar with a smaller string length (commonly 543–563mm, 21⅜–22¼in) tuned a minor third higher than a standard guitar.

theorbo
A long-necked lute with extra bass strings, used mainly in Baroque music.

thinline
A thin-bodied guitar.

three-chord trick
Chords I, IV and V: the chords most commonly used in any key, and sufficient for many songs, including the basic form of 12-bar blues.

through-neck
Construction method in which the guitar neck and central block of the body are cut from the same piece of wood.

thumb chord
A chord in which the left-hand thumb reaches around the fretboard to fret the lowest string, or occasionally even the lowest two strings.

thumb muting
Muting the sound by resting the thumb of the picking hand against the string.

tie-block
The component of the bridge just behind the saddle, to which the strings are tied.

timbre
The character or quality of a musical sound, sometimes described as the 'tone colour'. It is what makes one particular musical sound different from another, even if they may have the same pitch and loudness.

time signature
The underlying metre of the music. In notation, the time signature appears as a pair of numbers on the stave at the beginning of the piece: the upper number indicates how many beats in each bar, and the lower number indicates what note value each beat has.

tonebar
Bracing on the inside of an acoustic guitar, intended to add strength and improve tone.

tonewood
A type of wood suitable for use in the construction of a guitar.

tonic chord
If a piece of music is 'in C major', C is the tonic note and C major is the tonic chord. The tonic is the home note, or keynote.

transverse brace
A wooden bar that is used to support the soundboard, running from one rib to another.

tremolo arm/bridge (also whammy bar or vibrato arm)
A controlling lever that rapidly alters the tension in a guitar's strings, creating a vibrato effect.

triad
A three-note chord. In Western harmony, this is usually constructed using the root note, and notes a third and a fifth above this.

trill
Rapid alternation between two adjacent notes – usually a tone or semitone apart.

truss-rod
An adjustable steel rod within the neck of a guitar, designed to control the angle of the neck against the tension of the strings, and the pull that they exert on the neck.

Tune-o-matic bridge
A fixed bridge designed by Gibson's Ted McCarty in 1954, allowing the scale length of individual strings to be adjusted.

tuning pegs
These are housed in the headstock and are turned in order to tune the strings to the desired pitches.

vibrato
A musical effect consisting of a regular, pulsating change of pitch.

voicings
The way the notes of a chord are arranged. A chord may be voiced in different ways, by using combinations of different strings or frets.

volute
A strengthening enlargement to the neck where it joins the headstock.

wah-wah
A guitar effects pedal that uses changes in the player's foot movements to alter the tone of the signal.

x-bracing
A pattern of bracing used for the tops of many classical and acoustic guitars.

Index

A

Abbott, 'Dimebag Darrell' 483
Aelita 1 413
Aeolian mode 326
Aerosmith 445
Aguado, Dionisio 167, 168, 195
Aitken, Bill 472
Alamo Fiesta 2568R 420
Albéniz, Isaac 170
Alembic Series 1 436
Allman, Duane 484
alternate picking 268
alternating fingers bass technique 309
Altimíra, Agustin: six-string
  guitar 195
Am-based barre shapes 102
Ampeg Dan Armstrong 444
amplifiers 260–1, 307, 339, 345
anatomy of guitars 18–19, 264–5
Arcas, Julián 170
archtop guitars 202, 236–41, 247
Aria Diamond ADSG-12T 417
Arias, Vicente: classical guitar 206
Armstrong, Dan 444
Armstrong, Rob: Cornflake 447
arpeggios 42–3, 275, 324–5
artificial harmonics 110
Ashborn, James: Style 1 guitar 201
Atkins, Chet 79, 346, 373, 375

B

B. C. Rich 448
  Bich 448
  Exotic Classic Bich 10 458
  Mockingbird 448
  Warlock 449
Baldwin Double Six 416
Ball, Ernie: Music Man Axis
  Supersport 455
Bambina guitars 203
Barbero, Marcelo: guitar 221
baritone tuning 425
Barnes, George 359
Baroque guitar, the 163, 164–5, 172,
  186–7, 188
Barral, Carlos 205
barre chords 62–5, 85
Barth, Paul 338, 378
bass amps 307
bass distortion pedal 261

bass guitars 250–3, 306–7
  techniques 308–15
bass-lute 246
bass/strum style 40–1
Bauer, C. F.: double soundhole
  guitar 202
Bean, Travis 437, 444
  TB1000 444
Beatles, The 288, 289, 307, 344, 348,
  375, 402, 404–5, 412, 416
  see also Harrison, George; Lennon,
  John; McCartney, Paul
Beauchamp, George 338
Beck, Jeff 325, 464
"Beginner's Blues" 55
Bellamy, Matt 351
bends 270–1, 272–3, 302
Benedetto, Robert: Cremona 239
Berry, Chuck 279
Bettencourt, Nuno 482
Bigsby, Paul 341
  Merle Travis 365
Birch, John 446
Blackmore, Richie 350
blues techniques
  blues scale 54, 55, 272, 288, 298
  building a solo 58–9
  sixth shuffle 56–7
  12-bar blues 54, 278–9
  using notes with chords 60–1
Boak, Dick 253
Bohmann, Joseph 175
Bossa Nova 120, 121
Bouchet, Robert 210, 211
boutique guitars 488
Branca, Glenn 347
Brazilian rosewood 177
Bream, Julian 210, 215, 219
Brewer, Gage 338
Brickell, Edie 103
Broadway BW2 390
broken chords see arpeggios
Broonzy, Big Bill 359
Bryant, Jimmy 343, 346, 366, 410
Bucknall, Roger 235
Burns, Jim 344, 384, 388, 391, 462
  Bison 388
  Hank Marvin 389
  Split Sonic 389
  Split Sound 424
  UK Mirage 439
  Vibra Artist 388
Butts, Ray 375
Byrd, Billy 398
Byrds, The 332, 333, 414–15

C

Calace, Raffaele: mando-lyre 185
"Camptown Races" 51
Campbell American Transitone 488
Campbell, Mike 488

capo techniques 46–7
Carcassi, Matteo 190
  Allegro (excerpt) 117
Carlos II, King of Spain 164
Carlton, Larry 298
Carrassi, Matteo 195
Carulli, Ferdinando 168, 190
cases 24
Cash, Johnny 40
cejilla 173
Chapman Stick 458
Char, Kerry: guitar 249
Charvel, Wayne 468
  Model 4 470
chitarra battente 188, 189
choosing a guitar 16–17
chord boxes/diagrams 29, 128
  A 34, 131
  A barre 277
  A open 276
  A♭ 131
  A⁵ open power 281
  A⁵ ringy power 281
  A⁵ root/fifth 280
  A⁵ root/fifth octave 280
  A⁷ 36, 135, 145
  A♭⁷ 135, 145
  A⁷sus⁴ 151
  A♭maj⁷ 139, 149
  A♭sus⁴ 151
  A⁽ᵃᵈᵈ ⁹⁾ 153, 291
  Adim⁷ 141
  Am 32, 133
  Am barre 277
  Am open 276
  Am⁷ 137, 147
  Am⁷♭⁵ 143
  Am⁹ 153
  Amaj⁷ 139, 149
  A♯m⁷♭⁵ 143
  Asus⁴ 151
  B 131
  B♭ 131
  B⁷ 76, 135, 145
  B♭⁷ 135, 145
  B⁽ᵃᵈᵈ ¹¹⁾ 153, 291
  Bdim⁷ 141
  B♭dim⁷ 141
  Bm 78, 133
  B♭m 133
  Bm⁷ 137, 147
  B♭m⁷ 137, 147
  Bm⁷♭⁵ 143
  Bm¹¹ 153
  Bmaj⁷ 139, 149
  B♭maj⁷ 139, 149
  Bsus⁴ 151
  B♭sus⁴ 151
  B⁷sus⁴ 151
  C 30, 130
  C open 276

C⁷ 69, 92, 134, 144
C⁷♯⁹ 94
C⁷♭⁹ 94
C⁹ 94
C⁽ᵃᵈᵈ ⁹⁾ 291
C triad 68
Cdim⁷ 140
C♯dim⁷ 140
Cm 132
C♯m 132
Cm⁷ 69, 92, 136, 146
C♯m⁷ 136, 146
C♯m⁷♭⁵ 142
Cm⁷♭⁵ 142
Cm triad 68
Cmaj⁷ 69, 92, 138, 148, 152
C♯maj⁷ 152
Cm⁽ᵐᵃʲ⁷⁾ 69
Csus⁴ 150
D 29, 130
D barre 277
D open 276
D thumb chord 276
D♭ 130
D⁵ open power 281
D⁵ root/fifth 280
D⁵ root/fifth octave 280
D⁷ 36, 134, 144
D♭⁷ 134, 144
D⁹ 120, 296
D⁶ᐟ⁹ 152
D⁽ᵃᵈᵈ ⁹ᐟ¹¹⁾ 152
D¹³ 296
Ddim⁷ 140
Dm 132
Dm barre 277
Dm open 276
Dm⁷ 136, 146
D♯m⁷♭⁵ 142
Dm⁷♭⁵ 142
Dm⁹ 120
Dm⁶ᐟ⁹ 152
Dm⁽ᵃᵈᵈ ⁹⁾ 152
Dmaj⁷ 138, 148
D♭maj⁷ 138, 148
Dmaj⁹ 120, 152
Dsus² 291
Dsus⁴ 150
D♭sus⁴ 150
D⁷sus⁴ 150
E 34, 130

E open 276
E♭ 130
E⁵ open power 281
E⁵ ringy power 281
E⁷ 36, 78, 134, 144
E⁷#9 288
E♭⁷ 134, 144
Edim⁷ 140
E♭dim⁷ 140
Em 32, 132
Em open 276
E♭m 132
Em⁷ 136, 137, 146, 153
E♭m⁷ 136, 146
Em⁷♭5 142
Emaj⁷ 138, 148
E♭maj⁷ 138, 148
Esus⁴ 150
E♭sus⁴ 150
E⁷sus⁴ 150
F 130
F♯ 131
F⁷ 135, 145
F⁷#(add11) 291
F#⁷ 135, 145
F#(add11) 153
Fdim⁷ 140
F#dim⁷ 140, 141
Fm 132
F#m 132, 133
Fm⁷ 137, 147
F#m⁷ 137, 147, 153
F#m⁷♭5 143
Fm⁷♭5 143
F#m¹¹ 153
Fmaj⁷ 138, 149
F#maj⁷ 139, 149
Fmaj⁷#11 153, 291
Fsus² 291
Fsus⁴ 150
F#sus⁴ 151
G 30, 131
G open 276
G⁵ ringy power 281
G⁶ 153
G⁷ 36, 92, 135, 145
G⁷♭5 94
G¹³ 94
G⁷♭13 (G⁷#5) 94
G(add 9) 291
Gdim⁷ 141
G#dim⁷ 141
Gm 133
G#m 133
Gm⁷ 92, 137, 147
G#m⁷ 147
G#m⁷♭5 143
Gm⁷♭5 143
G#m⁷(13) 153
Gmaj⁷ 92, 139, 149
Gsus⁴ 151

in DADGAD
A 159
A(add 11) 159
Am 159
Bm⁷ 159
C 158
C(add 9) 158
D 158
D⁵ 158
D⁷ 158
Dm 158
Dm⁷ 158
Dsus⁴ 158
Em¹¹ 158
F⁶ 159
G 159
G/B 159
G(add 9) 159
Gm 159
Gmaj⁹ 159
Gsus²/B 159
A⁷sus4 159
in open D
A 157
Am 157
Am⁷ 157
Bm 157
Bm⁷ 157
C(add 9) 156
C#m 156
C#m⁷ 156
D 156
D⁵ 156
Dm 156
Dsus⁴ 156
Em 156
Em⁷ 156
F 157
G 157
Gm 157
in open G
A 155
A(add 9/11) 155
Am⁷ 155
B 155
Bm 155
C 154
C/G 154
C(add 9)/G 154
D 154
D⁷ 154
Dm 154
E 154
E⁷ 154
Em 154
Em⁷ 155
G 155
Gm 155
chord slashes 63
chord styles
funk 296

grunge 286
Indie rock 291
rock 276–7
chords 29
barre chords 62–5, 85
construction of 68–9
finding the root 65
half-open chords 102–3
seventh chords 36–7, 56, 57, 69
thumb chords 111
see also chord boxes/diagrams
chorus pedal 261
Christian, Charlie 339, 346, 357, 359
chromatic scale 53
chugging 274
CITES Act 177
citterns 182–3
Clapton, Eric 232, 346, 392, 395, 443, 446, 464
classical
compositions 347
guitars 16, 18, 206–19
techniques 114–17
Claus, Christian 183
cleaning 25
clefs 38
Cobain, Kurt 231, 478
Collings: D2H Koa/Koa 233
Collins, Bootsy 314
combo amps 260
Communism 413
compression pedals 261
computerized guitars 351, 496
computers, connecting guitars to 260
Conde Hermanos: guitar 223
continuous sixteenths 296
Cooder, Ray 304
Cook, Peter: Ned Callan Cody 438
Corbetta, Francesco 164
Coste, Napoleon 195
Costello, Elvis 344
country techniques 76–9, 302–3
Cousineau, George: guitar 192
crotchets 38
Crucianelli company 423

D
DADGAD tuning 90–1
essential chords in 158–9
Dale, Dick 387
Dallas Tuxedo 384
Danelectro 371
3923 Short Horn Double
Neck 410
Guitarlin 381, 426
Longhorn Bass 381
Shorthorn 380
U2 380
D'Angelico electric 376
D'Angelico, John: New Yorker 238
D'Aquisto electric 377

D'Aquisto, Jimmy: Excel 239
Davoli, Athos 422
Defil Jola 462
Deleplanque, Gerard: cittern 182
delay effects 294, 346
Denny, Dick 428
Dias, Belchior: Baroque guitar
(attrib.) 188
digital delay pedal 261
diminished sevenths 140–1
distortion 261, 269, 274, 331, 346–7
dital-harp 196
Doan, John 245
Dobro: Style 66 Roundneck 248
dominant seventh jazz voicings
144–5
Dopyera, John 248
Dorian mode 326
double-neck guitars 410–11
double-stopping 100–1, 278–9
Dowland, John 181
Drevokov Co-operative:
Futurama III 412
drone techniques 286–7
drop D tuning 320–1
drops 300
Duesenberg Mike Campbell 488
Durham, Eddie 339, 359
Dylan, Bob 31

E
EADGAE tuning 82, 83
EADGBD# tuning 82, 83
EADGBE tuning 20
Eastwood, Brian: Blue Moon 447
E-bows 332
effects loop 262
Egmond Solid 7 408
Eko 423
BA4NPE 252
700/4V 422
electro-acoustic guitars 17, 258
Electro String Company 338
Élite 40-V 423
Elliot, Jeffrey: harp-guitar 245
Embergher, Luigi: mandolin 185
English guitar 165, 166
Epiphone 362–3
Broadway 402
Casino 402

Coronet 403
Crestwood 403
Emperor 240
G-310 Emily the Strange 461
Les Paul 460
Sheraton E212T 363
Zakk Wylde Les Paul Custom
    Buzzsaw 485
Zephyr 362
Zephyr Regent 362
Erlewine Chiquita 466
Ertl, Johann 199
Esteso, Domingo: guitar 220

F

Fabricatore, Gennaro: six-string
    guitar 194
Fabricatore, Giovanni Battista 168,
    169, 193
    six-string guitar 194
Falla, Manuel de 172
Favino, Jacques: gypsy guitar: 243
feedback 340
feedback loop 261
Feldman, Morton 347
Fender 342–3, 441, 451, 461
    amps 339
    Bass VI 424
    Broadcaster 342, 366
    Bullet 450
    Classic 72 Custom 481
    Coronado II 418
    Custom Shop: 1963 VCS
        Stratocaster 451; Catalina Island
        Blues Festival 477; Harley
        Davidson 476; Hendrix
        Monterey Pop Festival 477;
        Twin Neck Custom 476
    Cyclone 479
    Electric XII 417
    Esquire 342, 367
    Jag-Stang 478
    Jaguar 386–7
    Jazz 400
    Jazz Bass 306
    Jazzmaster 386
    John Entwistle 'Frankenstein' 495
    Katana 451
    Kingman SCE 253
    Mustang 387

Performer 450
Precision 370
Precision Bass 306
Prodigy 478
Stratocaster 259, 264, 343, 350,
    367, 385, 387, 418; 1965 model
    443; Custom Shop 1963 VCS
    451; Eric Clapton 464; Jeff Beck
    464; Master Design 1964 LE
    451; Master Salute LE 451; Relic
    60s 480; Richie Sambora 465
Telecaster 10, 259, 342–3, 366,
    419; Custom 442; Deluxe 442
Toronado 479
Fender, Leo 339, 341, 342, 346, 366,
    371, 418, 454–5
Fenton-Weill Dualtone 390
Ferandiere, Fernando 167
Fernández, Arcángel: guitar 221
Fernández, Gerundino: guitar 222
fidicula 162
Field, Dominique: classical guitar 211
fills 292–3
finger independence 116
fingernails 28, 114
fingerpicks 40
fingers, labelling system 42
first position 50
five-string bass 333
five-string guitars 193
flamenco guitars 9, 172–3, 220–3
flamenco techniques 222–3
flat keys 67
flat-top steel-string guitars 174–5,
    224–35
flat tuning 286
    and drop D 321
Fleta, Ignacio 171
    classical guitar 214
Flowers, Herbie 219
Fodera Victor Wooten Monarch 475
four-course guitars 187
Framus 344, 462
    Strato Deluxe 409
    Super Yob 446
fret buzz 25
fretless guitars 332
Friederich, Daniel: Serial
    No. 184 211
Fullerton, George 342, 366, 454
funk 296–7
fuzz boxes/effects 261, 345
FX loop 262
Fylde: custom-built 'Harlequin' 235

G

G&L Cavalier 454
Garcia, Enrique: classical guitar 206
Garland, Hank 398
Gibbons, Billy 466

Gibson 174, 175, 342–3, 385, 441
    Alpha Q-3000 452
    Barney Kessel 399
    Byrdland 398
    Corvus III 433
    Dark Fire 496
    Duane Allman 484
    EB-2 370
    EB-3 400
    EDS-1275 411
    EH-150 Lap Steel 355
    ES-125 357
    ES-140 360
    ES-150 339, 342, 356, 357
    ES-175 360–1
    ES-295 361
    ES-335 330, 394
    ES-335-12 416
    ES-345 395
    ES-355 394
    Explorer 382–3
    Firebird I 396
    Firebird I 'Non-Reverse' 397
    Firebird III 'Non-Reverse' 397
    Firebird VII 396
    Firebird X 351, 496
    Flying V 382–3
    Gibson 00, 175
    Gibson Grand Auditorium (000)
        models 175
    J200 225
    Johnny Smith 398
    L5 236, 342
    L5-CES 359
    L7C 237
    Les Paul 10, 259, 265, 343; 60
        Corvette 484; 1959 Aged
        Reissue 481; Deluxe 430;
        Goldtop 368; Historic 1959
        Standard Reissue 480; Junior
        369; Les Paul Custom 368;
        Recording 430; Robot 496;
        Standard 343, 392; Studio 431;
        TV 369
    M-III 471
    mando-bass 250
    Moderne 383
    Nick Lucas Special 224
    Nighthawk 452
    RD Artist 432
    Robot series 351, 496
    S-1 432
    SG Custom 392
    SG Special 393
    SG Standard 393
    Southerner Jumbo 224
    Spirit II XPL 453
    Style U 245
    Super 400 236
    Super 400CES 358
    Super 400P (Modified) 358

Trini Lopez 399
US-1 453
Victory MVX 433
Gibson, Orville 342
Gilbert, John: classical guitar 218
Gilberto, João 120
Gilmour, David 284
Giron, Claude: guitar 192
Gittler 'Fishbone' 486
Gläsel, Mortz: guitar 198
glissando 107
golpeador 122, 173
Gordon-Smith Gypsy 439
Gossard, Stone 287
grace-note
    bends 273
    hammer-ons 292
Graham, Davey 66
Grappelli, Stéphane 118
Gray, David 39
"Greensleeves" 81
Gregory, Paul 223
Gretsch 344, 372, 385
    6073 401
    Chet Atkins Country
        Gentleman 344, 374
    Chet Atkins Solidbody 373
    Country Club 374
    Duo Jet 344, 372
    Silver Jet 372
    Synchromatic 241
    White Falcon 344, 374
    White Penguin 373
Grissom, Dave 492
Grosh HollowTron 489
Gross, James 415
grunge techniques 286–7
Guild
    F212 230
    Stuart X500 376
guitar heroes 11, 349
guitar synthesizers 472–3
Guitarlin 381, 426
guitarra latina 162
guitarra moresca 162
Guns N' Roses 277
Guy, Buddy 346, 395
gypsy guitars 242–3
gypsy-jazz style 118–19

H

H, Pamelina 477
Hagström 345, 409, 462
    Futurama Coronado Automatic 408
Haley, Bill 348
half-open chords 102–3
    chord diagrams 152–3
Hall, Francis C. 378, 404
Hall, Jim 346, 357
hammer-ons 74, 278, 284, 292
hand positions 27

Hansen, Beck 381
harmonic minor scale 118, 119
harmonics 106
Harmony 371, 421
  Bobkat H14 420
  H71 Meteor 377
harp-guitars 244–5
harp-lutes 196
Harrison, George 289, 375, 405,
  419, 446
Hauser, Hermann I 171
  Segovia model 212
  Viennese style guitar 212
Hauser, Hermann II: classical
  guitar 213
Hauser, Hermann III: classical
  guitar 213
Hawaiian music 338, 355
Haynes, John: Tilton model
  guitar 201
heavy rock 316–17
Heit Deluxe 407
Helland, Dan 429
Hendrix, Jimi 343, 345, 349, 395,
  419, 446, 477
Hernández, Santos 171, 172
  guitar 220
Hernández y Aguado: classical
  guitar 8, 214
Hill, Kenny: FE18 216
Höfner 344, 462
  500/1 426
  Committee 241
  Model 500/1 (violin bass/
    Beatle bass) 307, 477
  Pro Sound Graphic S5E 463
Hohner
  G3T 467
  Shark's Fin 463
holding a guitar 26–7
Holdsworth, Allan 331
Hooker, John Lee 272, 346
Hoopii, Sol 355
Hopkins, Lightnin' 61
'horizontal' fretboard technique 285
Hot Club Quintet 118
Howe, Steve 333, 361
humbucker pickups 258, 341, 346
Humphrey, Thomas 176
Hutchins Beast 487

I
Ibanez 435, 441, 452, 456–7
  Axstar AX45 456
  Iceman 457
  Jem 77 BFP 456
  RG550 457
  Universe 459
improvisation 104–5
Indie rock 290
Iommi, Tony 393
Iona, Andy 338
Ionian mode 326

J
jack cables/plugs 262
Jackson
  Soloist 469
  Warrior Pro 471
Jackson, Grover 350, 455
  Randy Rhoads 350, 468
  Soloist 350
Jansch, Bert 103
Japan 344–5, 406, 434, 440–1
jazz 298–9, 327
  chords 92–5
  classic licks 98–9
  dominant seventh voicings 144–5
  major seventh voicings 148–9
  minor seventh voicings 146–7
  12-bar blues in 96–7
jazz/rock fusion 327, 330–1
Jedson 'Telecaster' Bass 440
Jobim, Antonio Carlos 120
Johnson, Robert 225

K
Kallas, Johnny 'Go Go' 448
Kaman, Charles 233, 445
Kay 371
  K-45 466
  'Les Paul' 440
Keaggy, Phil 88
Kessel, Barney 357, 399
keys 66–7
King, Albert 346, 382–3
King, B. B. 346, 395
Kinks, The 347, 411
Knack, The 313
Knopfler, Mark 275
Kohno, Masaru: classical guitar 216
Kramer 351
  450T 437
  Sustainer 470
Krundaal Bikini 428

L
La Baye 2X4 429
Lacôte, René 168
  Decacorde 244
  six-string guitar 195
Lagoya, Alexandre 210

Laiho, Alexi 320
Lang, Eddie 104
Laprévotte, Etienne 217
Larrivée: C10 231
Larson Brothers 251
Latin jazz 120–1
Lawrence, Bill 432
lazy barres 102, 291
lead guitar 268–71, 284–5
Leadbelly 125
least movement principle 37
Led Zeppelin 411
Lee, Albert 303
left-hand
  basic technique 28–9
  first position 50
  muting 275
legato 330
Legnani, Luigi 169, 198, 199
Lennon, John 279, 344, 348, 402, 404
Levin: Goliath 234
Light, Edward: dital-harp 196
Llobet, Miguel 170
Loar, Lloyd 174, 237, 337, 371
Lopez, Trini 399
Lorca, Antonio de 168
Lover, Seth 346, 442
Lowden, George: Richard
  Thompson Model 235
Lowe, Rohan: classical guitar 217
Lucas, Nick 224
Lucia, Paco de 173
lutes 162, 181
Lydian mode 326
Lyon and Healy 175
Lyrachord 445
lyre-guitar 190

M
m$^{7\flat5}$ chords 142–3
Maccaferri, Mauro 210
McCartney, Paul 47, 307, 426
McCarty, Ted 342, 382, 492
McGhee, Brownie 58
McLaughlin, John 327, 394
Maia, Luizão 312
major chords: chord diagrams 130–1
major seventh chords: chord
  diagrams 138–9
major seventh jazz voicings 148–9
Malmsteen, Yngwie J. 318–19
mando-basses 250
mando-lyre 185
mandolins 184, 185
  resonator mandolins 249
Manson, Andy: Magpie Slide
  Slammer 234
Marley, Bob 300
Martin, C. F. & Co. 169, 174, 197
  0-28 226
  00-42 226

  2½-40 200
  "America" 228
  B-65 253
  Backpacker 229
  D-18 "Elvis guitar" 227
  Dreadnought 174, 176
  F-7 240
  N-20 228
  OM-28 227
  one-millionth guitar 229
  Stauffer model 200
Martín, Juan 173
Marvin, Hank 385, 389, 391
Mauchant Frères: archtop guitar 202
May, Brian: Red Special 494
Mayfield, Curtis 296
melodic minor scale 298–9
melodies, integrating 80–1
Memphis Minnie 359
Metheny, Pat 48, 347, 361, 473
MIDI (Musical Instrument Digital
  Interface) 473
Mills, John 223
minims 38
minor chords: chord diagrams 132–3
minor seventh chords: chord
  diagrams 136–7
minor seventh jazz voicings 146–7
minor thirds 285
Mitchell, Joni 82
Mixolydian mode 326
modelling amps 260
modes 326–7
Molino, Ferdinando 190
Montgomery, Monk 370
Montgomery, Wes 346, 357, 361
Montoya, Carlos 173
Montoya, Ramón 173
montuno 121
Moog, Dr Robert 432
Moretti, Federico 163, 167, 190
Morlaye, Guillaume 163
  Le Premier Livre 187
Moser, Neal 448
Mosrite 344
  Strawberry Alarm Clock 427
Mozzani, Luigi: harp-guitar 244
Mudarra, Alonso: *Tres Libros de
  Música en Cifra para Vihuela* 187
multi-FX units 261, 263

Music Man 454–5
    Stingray Bass 454
Musima
    Deluxe 462
    Otwin Double Neck 412
muting strings 90, 93

N
Namin, Stas 413
National guitars 341, 371
National: Tricone Square-neck 248
Ned Callan Cody 438
neo-classical rock 318–19
Nicol, Simon 447
notation
    chord boxes/diagrams 29, 128
    chord slashes 63
    dots 51
    standard notation 38, 129
    tablature (tab) 39, 129
    ties 51
notes, finding 38, 70–1

O
Oasis 349
octave relationships 70
"Ode to Joy" 49
offbeats 33
open D, essential chords in 156–7
open G, essential chords in 154–5
open-string drones 286–7
open tunings 86–9
Osbourne, Ozzy 468, 485
Otwin Double Neck 412
ouds 162, 180
Ovation
    Adamas 445
    Custom Legend 233
    Viper 436

P
PA systems, connecting to 263
Page, Jimmy 332, 380, 411
Pagés, Joséf 167, 168
    six-course guitar 191
Pagés, Juan: six-course guitar 191
palm muting 282, 297
pandura 162
Panormo, George Lewis:
    Bambina guitar (attrib.) 203

Panormo, Louis: guitars 168,
    169, 197
Parker Fly 351
    Fly Artist 482
    MIDIFly 483
Pärt, Arvo 347
Pass, Joe 346, 361
passing notes 44
Paul, Les 340–1, 343, 365
    The Log 340–1, 364–5
    see also Epiphone: Les Paul;
        Gibson: Les Paul
Peavey T-60 437
pedal effects 261
pedalboards 263
    setting up 295
Peña, Paco 173, 219
pentatonic scale 292
phaser pedal 261, 301, 345
Phiri, Ray 293
pickups 51, 258, 337, 341
Pigini, Oliviero 422–3
pinch harmonic 316
Pink Floyd 284
Pioli, Antonio 422, 428
plectrum techniques
    bass 308
    tapping 329
plectrums 27
Plexiglass 444
pops 314
position playing 48
posture 267
practice 52
practice amps 260
Prairie State Bass 251
Pratten, Madame Sidney 197, 203
pre-bends 273
Presti, Ida 210
Preston, John: cittern 183
PRS
    Artist 492
    Custom 22 491
    Dragon 493
    McCarty 492
Pujol, Emilio 170
pull-offs 75, 284

Q
quavers 38

R
Ramírez, Amalia 209
Ramírez, José I 172
    classical guitar 208
Ramírez, José II: classical
    guitar 208
Ramírez, José III: classical
    guitar 209
Ramírez, Julian Gómez: classical
    guitar 210

Ramírez, Manuel 171, 172
    classical guitar 207
Randall, Don 366
rasgueado technique 122, 123
Rautta, Petrus: cittern 182
Rebeth Gothic Cross 449
Recio, José 168
Red, Tampa 359
reggae 300–1
Reich, Steve 347
Reinhardt, Django 118, 242, 243
Reisinger, Ludwig: *Wappen* form
    guitar 246
R.E.M. 349
relative minors 67
Renaissance guitars 187
Renbourn, John 103
Requena, Pablo: guitar 223
resonator guitars 248–9
resonator mandolins 249
'rest stroke' technique 122–3
Reuss, Allan 339
Reyes, Manuel: guitar 222
Rhoads, Randy 468
rhythm guitar techniques 274–5,
    282–3
Ricardo, Niño 173
Rice, Tony 232
Rich, B. C. *see* B. C. Rich
Richards, Keith 344, 345
Rickenbacker 341, 344
    325 404
    331 Light Show Guitar 429
    336/12 415
    360 404
    360/12 414
    370/12 RME1 415
    450/12 414
    460 405
    4001S 401
    bass 307
    Combo 450 379
    Combo 600 378
    Combo 800 378
    Electro Spanish 356
    Model 1000 379
    Model B Lap Steel 354
Rickenbacker, Adolph 338–9,
    344, 378
Rico, Bernardo Chavez 448
riffs 288–9
right-hand tapping 328–9
rock 'n' roll techniques 278–9,
    282–3
Romanillos, José: classical guitar 215
Roland GS-500 472
Rolling Stones, The 277, 278–9,
    344, 345, 346, 411, 432, 443,
    444, 446
roots and fifths 44–5
roots of chords, finding 65

Ro-Pat-In 338–9
    'Frying Pan' 337, 354
Rose, Floyd 350
Rose-Morris 390
Rosetti Lucky Squire 385
Roudhloff, Dominic and
    Arnould 176
    guitar 197
Rowies, Jean: mando-bass
    (attrib.) 250
Ruck, Robert 176
Russell, David 218

S
Sabicas 173
Sambora, Richie 465
Sanguino, Francisco: seven-course
    guitar 190
Santa Cruz: Tony Rice Model
    232
Santana, Carlos 432, 434, 435,
    491, 493
Sanz, Gaspar 164, 172
scales 52–3
    blues scale 54, 55, 272, 288, 298
    C major 50, 53, 108
    chromatic scale 53
    D major 53, 108
    G major 53, 108, 109
    harmonic minor 118, 119
    major 322
    minor 299, 323
    pentatonic 292
    practice patterns 108–9
    Spanish Phrygian 327
scalloped fretboards 319
Schaufuß, Alfred: archtop guitar 247
Scheit, Karl 210
Schuyler, Daniel 228
Sears Roebuck 371, 377,
    380–1, 421
Seasick Steve 98, 495
Segovia, Andrés 171, 207,
    212, 219
Sellas, Matteo: guitar (attrib.) 186
Selmer-Maccaferri
    D-hole 242
    Oval-hole 242
semi-acoustic guitars 258–9
semiquavers 296

semitones 46, 285
setups 262–3
seven-course guitars 190
seven-string guitars 333
seventh chords 36–7, 56, 57, 69, 134–5
shapes of guitars 449
sharps 67
Shergold Masquerader 438
Showaddywaddy 447
shuffle feel 57
Silvertone 381, 421
   1444 371
   1477 421
Simon, Paul 103, 230
Simplicio, Francisco: classical guitar 207
single-coil pickups 258, 341
six-course guitar 191
six-string guitars 194–5
sixth shuffle 56–7
Slade 446
slap-back delay 294, 302
slap bass 314–15
Slash 277
slide guitar 112 13, 304–5
slides 107, 284, 297
slurring 74–5, 284
Smallman, Greg 176, 219
   classical guitar 218
Smear, Pat 409
Smith, Johnny 398
Smith, Paul Reed 449, 452
   Carlos Santana 491
   First 'Dragon' 490
   First Guitar 490
   see also PRS
solidbody guitars 340–1, 342
Sor, Fernando 168, 195
   Op. 35 115
sound
   factors affecting 341
   principles of 336–7
soundboards 336
soundwaves 336
Spanish Phrygian scale 327
Spanish-style models 339
spring reverb unit 261
squeal harmonic 316
Squier
   Hello Kitty Stratocaster 461
   Stratocaster 460
stacks 260
stands 25
Starr Labs Ztar Z6S-XPA 473
Stathopoulos, Epi 340, 362–3
Stathopoulos, Frixo 363
Stauffer, Johann Anton 169
   Legnani Terz guitar 198
Stauffer, Johann Georg 169
staves 38

steel-string acoustic guitars 16, 19, 174–5
Steinberger 351
   L Series Bass 474
Stevens, Steve 497
Stockhausen, Karlheinz 347
Stradivari, Antonio 165
   Baroque guitar 187
   choral mandolino 184
Stratosphere Twin 410
string winders 22
strings, changing 22–3, 267
Strohmer, August: bass-lute 246
Stromberg, Elmer: Master 400 238
strumming 274
   basic technique 27
   upwards 33
Sullivan, John: harp-guitar 245
Supersound Bass 384
superstrats 468–71
surf sound 387
suspended fourths: chord diagrams 150–1
sweep picking 330
swing feel 57, 299
syncopation 34–5
Synsonic Terminator 467
Synthaxe 472

T

tablature (TAB) 39, 129
tapping 328–9
   right-hand tapping 111
   tapped harmonics 110
Tárrega, Francisco 9, 170–1
Taylor Guitars: 614 CE 232
Taylor, James 37
Teisco
   Del Rey 407
   SS4L 406
   VN-4 425
Teuffel Birdfish 486
theorbo 180
thirds 69
Thomas, Harvey: Custom Hollowbody 427
Thompson, Richard 235
Thorne, Francis 347
three-chord trick 30–1
thumb muting/chords 111, 276
thumb, using in fingerpicking 44–5
Tielke, Joachim 181
ties 51
Tilton, William B. 201
Tokai TST 50 441
Torres, Antonio de 9, 170, 171, 204–5
   FE18 204
   SE39 204
   SE127 205
   SE142 205

Townshend, Pete 281, 393
Township Oil Can Guitar 494
transistor amps 260
transposition 72–3
   with a capo 46–7
travel guitars 466–7
Travis, Merle 77, 341, 365
tremolando 116–17
tremolo
   arm 316–17
   pedal 261
trills 278
   tapped trill 329
tunes, playing 48–9
tuning
   baritone 425
   capo, with a 47
   DADGAD 90–1
   drop D 84–5, 320–1
   EADGAE 82, 83
   EADGBD♯ 82, 83
   EADGBE 20
   flat 286, 321
   keyboard, to a 21
   open tunings 86–9
   relative tuning 20–1
   using a tuner 21
Tutmarc, Paul 371
   Audiovox Bass 364
twang riffs 302–3
12-bar blues 54, 278–9
   in jazz 96–7
12-string guitars 124–5, 333, 414–17

V

Vai, Steve 459
valve amps 260, 345
Van Halen, Eddie 394, 452, 455, 469
   'Frankenstrat' 350, 468
Vaughan, Stevie Ray 465
Vega, Suzanne 103
Venere, Wendelio 180
Ventures, The 344, 345, 387, 407, 427
vibrato 271
vihuela 8, 162, 189
Villaume, Alexis: guitar 192
Vinaccia, Antonio: mandolin 184
Vinaccia, Gaetano 168
Visée, Robert de 164
Voboam, Alexandre: Baroque guitar 186
Vogl, Hans: slide guitar 247
voice leading 92
Vox
   AC15 339
   Apache 391
   Mark III 449
   V251 Guitar Organ 428

W

wah-wah 261, 294–5, 345
   auto-wah 301
Wal Pro Fretless Bass 474
Walker, T-Bone 346, 359
Walker, Tom 454
Wandré 428
   Rock Oval 422
Wappen guitars 246
Warwick Corvette 475
Washburn
   Bettencourt N8 Double Neck 482
   Dimebag Darrell Stealth 483
   Style "A" parlour guitar 230
Waters, Muddy 346, 359
Webster, Jimmie 374–5
Westheimer, Jack 407
whammy bar 316–17
"When the Saints Go Marching In" 49
White, Forest 454–5
Whiteman, David: concert guitar 217
Wilfler, Fred 409
Williams, John 219
Williams, Rob: Deluxe 489
Winehouse, Amy 223
wood, types of 341, 445
Woodhouse, Martin: "Brahms" guitar 219
Wooten, Victor 475
Wray, Link 347
Wylde, Zakk 485

Y

Yamaha
   Pacifica 435
   SG5A Flying Samurai 406
   SG60T 434
   SG2000 434
Young, Angus 281, 283

Z

Zappa, Frank 431
Zemaitis, Tony
   acoustic bass guitar 252
   electric guitar 446

Acknowledgements

The publisher would like to thank the following for their kind permission to reproduce photographs in this book. Abbreviations: T = top; C = centre; B = bottom; L = left; R = right. All photography by Laurie Evans except the following:

Adrián Rius 9TR, 170TR.
akg-images 187R; Album / Oronoz 8BL.
Alamy The Art Archive 162BL, 163TL; B. O'Kane 293TR; Chesh 337BR; Images of Africa Photobank 336BL; Pictorial Press Ltd 151BR, 383TR.
Amalia Ramirez 206R, 207L, 208L, 208R, 209L, 209R, 209TC, 210L.
The Art Archive Tate Gallery London / Eileen Tweedy 165BL.
Bcrich.com 458R.
Bibleoteca de Catalunya, Barcelona 161TL, 164BL.
Bridgeman Images British Library, London, UK / British Library Board 181TR; Christie's Images 9TL, 169TR; Cincinnati Art Museum, Ohio, USA / Bequest of Mary M. Emery 166BL; Isabella Stewart Gardner Museum, Boston, MA, USA 172TR; Prado, Madrid, Spain / Index 166BR; Russell-Cotes Art Gallery and Museum, Bournemouth, UK 167C.
Bruce Banister / fineandrareguitars.com 210R, 212R, 215L.
Burns London Ltd 391TR.
C. F. Martin Archives 174TC, 175TL, 177BR, 226L, 226R, 229L, 229R.
Chris Andrada 228L.
Clarence L. Miller Family Local History Room, Kalamazoo Public Library, Michigan 342BC.
Collection Musée de la Musique / Jean-Marc Anglès 189R.

David E. Nelson 176BL, 219L.
Duesenberg Guitars 488R.
Ebow Makers 332BC.
Eko Music Group 423R.
E.L.V.H. Inc 256L, 468L.
EMP Museum, Seattle, WA 364L.
Eugene Earle Collection, Southern Folklife Collection, Louis Round Wilson Special Collections Library, University of North Carolina, Chapel Hill 355CR.
Fender Ltd 10T, 335C, 342BL, 342CR, 376R.
Fender Musical Instruments Corporation 252R.
Fodera.com 475L.
Fotolia NickR 263BL; Philippe Devanne 21CR.
François Charle 242L, 242R, 243L.
Getty Images 10BL, 54BR, 98BR, 101TR, 172BL, 174BL, 215R, 225R, 289TR, 290TR, 303BR, 325TR, 327TR, 341TL, 348BL, 349TL, 350BL, 357CR, 381R, 411R, 469R, 493R, 455R; AFP 37TR, 347CR; Archive Photos 339TC; Buyenlarge 161TL; Cover 80BR; FilmMagic 39TL, 459R, 496R; Frank Driggs 104BR; Hulton Archive 103BR, 125CR, 231R; Michael Ochs Archives 120BL, 141BR, 157BR, 296BR, 344BC, 345T, 359R, 365R, 387R, 419R; Michael Ochs Archives / Stringer 31BR, 58BR, 61CR, 77TR, 79TR; Redferns 47TR, 61TL, 66BR, 82BR, 139BR, 155BR, 171TL, 219R, 243R, 118BR, 275TR, 277BR, 281TR, 284BR, 298BR, 300CR, 304BR, 313, 319BR, 320BR, 333TR, 334TC, 334MC, 334BC, 339TL, 339TR, 343TL, 344BL, 346BL, 347, 349BR, 350BC, 351TR, 361R, 385R, 395R, 405R, 431R, 443R, 445R, 465R, 485R, 472R, 495R; Rolls Press / Popperfoto 40BR; Stockbyte 163BR; Time & Life Pictures 413R; Tom Copi 120BR; Visuals Unlimited 341 (panel); WireImage 48BL, 272BR, 283TR, 287BR, 314CR, 331BR, 409R, 435R, 457R.
Gibson Guitar Corp 425C, 497L, 497C, 351B.
Grosh Guitars 489R.
Guild of American Luthiers, www.luth.org 202L.
Guitar Salon International 211R.

Heritage Auctions 230R, 237L, 241L.
Hill Guitar Company Larry Darnell 216R.
Horniman Museum 188R.
iStock grynold 2, 126L; Özgür Donmaz 262TR, tunart 268CR, petrmaylshev 308B, rrvachov 311, TZfoto 340BR.
Jeff Babicz 161BL, 177TL.
John Doan 245R.
Lebrecht Music and Arts 170BL, 173TL.
London Guitar Studio 223L.
Malcolm Maxwell 39TR, 165TR, 169TL, 171CR, 173BR, 190R, 191TL, 191BL, 191R, 192L, 192C, 194R, 195L, 196L, 197L, 197C, 197R, 198L, 198R, 199TR, 202R, 203L, 203R, 204L, 204R, 205L, 205R, 206L, 207L, 207T, 212L, 217L, 220L, 223R, 239R, 244L, 246L, 246R, 247L, 247R, 321TR, 352L, 431L, 465L, 483R, 485L, 487.
Marshall Amps 260TC.
Museu de la Música de Barcelona 190L.
NASA Archives 229R.
Outline Press Ltd 127BR, 188L, 201L, 201R, 213R, 216L, 220R, 225L, 227L, 227R, 228R, 230L, 231L, 232L, 232R, 234L, 234R, 235L, 240L, 240R, 241L, 251L, 252L, 252R, 253L, 332CR, 333BR, 334L, 335TR, 338R, 340CR, 354R, 356L, 356R, 357L, 358L, 358R, 359L, 360R, 363L, 363L, 363C, 363R, 364L, 365L, 366L, 367L, 369R, 372L, 372R, 373L, 375R, 376L, 376R, 377L, 377C, 378L, 378R, 379L, 379R, 380L, 380R, 382L, 382R, 383L, 391L, 392R, 394L, 397L, 397R, 398R, 399R, 403R, 405L, 406R, 410L, 410R, 412R, 413L, 415L, 415C, 416L, 416R, 422L, 423R, 427L, 427R, 428L, 428R, 429L, 429R, 430L, 430R, 432L, 432R, 433R, 434R, 445C, 436L, 437L, 438L, 438R, 439L, 441L, 441R, 444R, 446L, 446R, 447L, 448L, 448R, 449R, 450L, 450R, 452L, 452R, 453CL, 453CR, 454R, 455L, 459L, 460R, 461L, 462R, 464L, 467R, 468L, 469L, 471L, 471R, 472R, 474L, 474R, 475R, 476L, 476R, 477L, 477R, 478L, 479L, 479R, 480L, 480R, 481L, 481C, 482L, 482R, 483L, 484L, 484R, 486L, 486R, 490L, 490R, 491L, 491R, 492L, 492R, 493L.

Philkeaggy.com 88BR.
Redpath Chautauqua Collection, University of Iowa Libraries, Iowa City 337TL.
Rudi Bults The Fellowship of Acoustics 185R.
Sotheby's 495L.
Starlabs.com 472L.
Terry Burrows 414R, 456R, 458L, 466L, 470R, 488L.
Topfoto Topham / Fotomas 168TC.
Township Guitars 494R.
Ulrich Wedemeier 180R, 183L.
University of Iowa Redpath Chautauqua Collection, University of Iowa Libraries, Iowa City 237R.
Victoria and Albert Museum 193L; Manuel Terrero 195C, 195R.
Vintaxe.com 421R.

With very special thanks to the following for allowing us to photograph their guitars: Esteban Antonio; David Crozier at Guitar Junction Ltd and Old School Guitars Ltd; Jim Forderer; Harris Hire, Beckenham; Hutchins Guitars, Lancing; Rainer Krause; Rohan Lowe; Guy Mackenzie; Gregg Miner; National Music Museum, South Dakota, USA; Pablo Requena; Miles Roberts at Kent Guitar Classics; Stefan Schwenteck; Michael Shellim; Taro Takeuchi; Juan Teijerio at London Guitar Studio; Chris Trigg of Vintage and Rare LTD, 6 Denmark Street, London WC2H 8CX; Malcolm Weller; James Westbrook; and Wunjo Guitars, Denmark Street, London.

FENDER®, STRATOCASTER®, STRAT®, TELECASTER® and P BASS®, and the distinctive headstock designs commonly found on these guitars are registered trademarks of Fender Musical Instruments Corporation, and are used herein with express written permission. All rights reserved.